September 8-11, 2015
Lausanne, Switzerland

I0038166

Association for Computing Machinery

Advancing Computing as a Science & Profession

DocEng'15

Proceedings of the 2015 ACM Symposium on
Document Engineering

Sponsored by:
ACM SIGWEB

Supported by:
Adobe, FX PAL, HP, OPPIDOC and EPFL

**Association for
Computing Machinery**

Advancing Computing as a Science & Profession

The Association for Computing Machinery
2 Penn Plaza, Suite 701
New York, New York 10121-0701

ISBN: 978-1-4503-3307-8 (Digital)

ISBN: 978-1-4503-4028-1 (Print)

Additional copies may be ordered prepaid from:

ACM Order Department
PO Box 30777
New York, NY 10087-0777, USA

Phone: 1-800-342-6626 (USA and Canada)
+1-212-626-0500 (Global)
Fax: +1-212-944-1318
E-mail: acmhelp@acm.org
Hours of Operation: 8:30 am – 4:30 pm ET

Printed in the USA

Welcome from the Symposium and PC Chairs

It is our great pleasure to welcome you to the *2015 ACM Symposium on Document Engineering – DocEng'15*. This year's symposium both continues and innovates in its tradition of being the premier forum for presentation of research results and experience reports on leading edge issues of document engineering. The mission of the symposium is to share significant results, to evaluate novel approaches and models, and to identify promising directions for future research and development. DocEng gives researchers and practitioners a unique opportunity to share their perspectives with others interested in the various aspects of document engineering. Document engineering is a rapidly developing field that encompasses both traditional topics and also new ideas and challenges related to new technologies and to changes in the ways in which information is created, managed, and disseminated.

This year we issued a new call for papers centered on new hot topics around the notion of document that has evolved to encompass a broader vision of the field. We therefore took pains to include new program committee members to supplement the overall expertise around these topics. Our call for papers attracted submissions from 25 countries (Algeria, Australia, Austria, Belgium, Brazil, Canada, China, Denmark, Ecuador, Ethiopia, France, Germany, India, Italy, Japan, Netherlands, Portugal, Qatar, Russian Federation, Singapore, Spain, Switzerland, Tunisia, United Kingdom of Great Britain and Northern Ireland, United States of America). All papers were carefully reviewed by a minimum of three program committee members. The program committee accepted 11 of 31 reviewed full paper submissions (35%) and 18 of 51 reviewed short paper submissions (35%) for oral presentations, for a combined acceptance rate of 35%. A further 10 short paper submissions were accepted for poster presentations. This year's program includes two poster sessions during which attendees will be given the opportunity to interact with authors of short papers accepted for poster presentation. The most covered topics this year are analysis, layout, authoring, querying, transformation, validation, management and semantics of documents, as well as related algorithms. We are happy to feature two keynote talks:

- *Documents as Data, Data as Documents: what we learned about Semi-Structured Information for our Open World of Cloud & Devices*, Jean Paoli (who is currently President at Microsoft Open Technologies, Inc.)

- *The Venice Time Machine*, Frédéric Kaplan (who is currently professor at EPFL)

Putting together *DocEng'15* was a team effort. We first thank the authors for providing the content of the program. We are grateful to the program committee members, who worked very hard in reviewing full and short papers and providing feedback for authors. We also thank Sonja Maier for organizing the first day with 3 tutorials and 1 workshop, Cerstin Mahlow for her efforts with ProDoc, Charles Nicholas in charge of the Birds of a Feather sessions, and Tamir Hassan for the publicity. We also thank the steering committee and in particular Steven Simske for his support. Finally, we thank the hosting university EPFL, our sponsor, ACM SIGWEB, and our generous corporate supporters: HP Labs, Fuji-Xerox Palo Alto Laboratory (FXPAL), Adobe, and Oppidoc.

We hope that you find this program interesting and thought-provoking and that this symposium provides you with a valuable opportunity to share ideas with other researchers and practitioners from leading institutions around the world.

<table>
<tr><td>**Pierre Genevès**</td><td>**Christine Vanoirbeek**</td></tr>
<tr><td>*DocEng'15 Program Chair*</td><td>*DocEng'15 Symposium Chair*</td></tr>
<tr><td>*CNRS*</td><td>*EPFL*</td></tr>
</table>

Table of Contents

DocEng 2015 Symposium Organization ix

DocEng 2015 Sponsor and Supporters xi

Keynote Talk I
Session Chair: Pierre Genevès *(CNRS)*

- **Documents as Data, Data as Documents - What We Learned about Semi-Structured Information for Our Open World of Cloud & Devices** 1
  Jean Paoli *(Microsoft)*

Layouts Improved
Session Chair: Dick Bulterman *(FXPAL)*

- **The Browser as a Document Composition Engine** 3
  Tamir Hassan, Niranjan Damera Venkata *(Hewlett-Packard Labs)*

- **Document Layout Optimization with Automated Paraphrasing** 13
  Yusuke Kido *(The University of Tokyo)*,
  Hikaru Yokono, Goran Topic, Akiko Aizawa *(National Institute of Informatics)*

- **Knuth-Plass Revisited: Flexible Line-Breaking for Automatic Document Layout** 17
  Tamir Hassan, Andrew Hunter *(Hewlett-Packard Labs)*

- **Hiding Information in Multiple Level-line Moirés** 21
  Thomas Walger, Roger David Hersch *(Ecole Polytechnique Fédérale de Lausanne)*

Knowledge Extraction
Session Chair: Steven Simske *(Hewlett-Packard Labs)*

- **TEXUS: A Task-based Approach for Table Extraction and Understanding** 25
  Roya Rastan, Hye-Young Paik, John Shepherd *(University of New South Wales)*

- **Multi-oriented Text Extraction from Information Graphics** 35
  Falk Böschen *(Kiel University)*, Ansgar Scherp *(Leibniz Information Centre for Economics - ZBW)*

- **Interlinking English and Chinese RDF Data Using BabelNet** 39
  Tatiana Lesnikova, Jérôme David *(University Grenoble Alpes and INRIA)*,
  Jérôme Euzenat *(INRIA and University Grenoble Alpes)*

- **Efficient Computation of Co-occurrence Based Word Relatedness** 43
  Jie Mei, Xinxin Kou, Zhimin Yao, Andrew Rau-Chaplin, Aminul Islam, Abidalrahman Moh'd,
  Evangelos E. Milios *(Dalhousie University)*

- **Automatic Extraction of Figures From Scholarly Documents** 47
  Sagnik Ray Choudhury, Prasenjit Mitra, Clyde Lee Giles *(The Pennsylvania State University)*

Information Summarized
Session Chair: David F. Brailsford *(University of Nottingham)*

- **Generating Abstractive Summaries from Meeting Transcripts** 51
  Siddhartha Banerjee *(The Pennsylvania State University)*,
  Prasenjit Mitra *(Qatar Computing Research Institute)*,
  Kazunari Sugiyama *(National University of Singapore)*

- **Enhancing Exploration with a Faceted Browser Through Summarization** 61
  Grzegorz Drzadzewski, Frank Wm. Tompa *(University of Waterloo)*

- **A Quantitative and Qualitative Assessment of Automatic Text Summarization Systems** 65
  Jamilson Batista, Rodolfo Ferreira, Hilário Tomaz, Rafael Ferreira,
  Rafael Dueire Lins *(Federal University of Pernambuco)*, Steven J. Simske *(Hewlett-Packard Labs)*,
  Gabriel Silva *(Federal Rural University of Pernambuco)*, Marcelo Riss *(HP Brazil R&D)*

- **Automatic Document Classification Using Summarization Strategies** 69
  Rafael Ferreira, Rafael Dueire Lins, Luciano Cabral, Fred Freitas *(Federal University of Pernambuco)*,
  Steven J. Simske *(HP Labs)*, Marcelo Riss *(HP Brazil R&D)*

Keynote Talk II
Session Chair: Steven J. Simske *(Hewlett-Packard Labs)*

- **The Venice Time Machine** 73
  Frédéric Kaplan *(Ecole Polytechnique Fédérale de Lausanne)*

Documents Made Accessible
Session Chair: Matthew Hardy *(Adobe)*

- **Towards Mobile OCR: How to Take A Good Picture of a Document without Sight** 75
  Michael P. Cutter, Roberto Manduchi *(University of California, Santa Cruz)*

- **MSoS: A Multi-Screen-Oriented Web Page Segmentation Approach** 85
  Mira Sarkis, Cyril Concolato, Jean-Claude Dufourd *(Telecom ParisTech; Institut Mines-Telecom; CNRS)*

- **Creating eBooks with Accessible Graphics Content** 89
  Cagatay Goncu, Kim Marriott *(Monash University)*

- **Investigation of Ancient Manuscripts Based on Multispectral Imaging** 93
  Fabian Hollaus, Markus Diem, Stefan Fiel, Florian Kleber, Robert Sablatnig *(TU Wien)*

Scholarly Papers Analysis and Authoring
Session Chair: Peter R. King *(University of Manitoba)*

- **Similarity-Based Support for Text Reuse in Technical Writing** 97
  Axel J. Soto, Abidalrahman Mohammad *(Dalhousie University)*, Andrew Albert *(Innovatia Inc.)*,
  Aminul Islam, Evangelos Milios *(Dalhousie University)*, Michael Doyle *(Innovatia Inc.)*,
  Rosane Minghim, Maria Cristina Ferreira de Oliveira *(Universidade de Sao Paulo)*

- **Exploring Scholarly Papers Through Citations** 107
  Angelo Di Iorio, Raffaele Giannella, Francesco Poggi, Silvio Peroni, Fabio Vitali *(University of Bologna)*

- **Filling the Gaps: Improving Wikipedia Stubs** 117
  Siddhartha Banerjee *(The Pennsylvania State University)*,
  Prasenjit Mitra *(Qatar Computing Research Institute & Hamad Bin Khalifa University)*

- **BBookX: An Automatic Book Creation Framework** 121
  Chen Liang, Shuting Wang, Zhaohui Wu, Kyle Williams, Bart Pursel, Benjamin Brautigam, Sherwyn Saul,
  Hannah Williams, Kyle Bowen, C. Lee Giles *(The Pennsylvania State University)*

- **VEDD: A Visual Editor for Creation and Semi-Automatic Update of Derived Documents** 125
  Kim Marriott, Mingzheng Shi, Michael Wybrow *(Monash University)*

- **Madoko: Scholarly Documents for the Web** 129
  Daan Leijen *(Microsoft Research)*

Logical Structures
Session Chair: Ethan Munson *(University of Wisconsin)*

- **Spatio-temporal Validation of Multimedia Documents** 133
  Joel A. F. dos Santos *(Université Grenoble Alpes)*,
  Christiano Braga, Débora C. Muchaluat-Saade *(Universidade Federal Fluminense)*,
  Cécile Roisin *(Université Grenoble Alpes)*, Nabil Layaïda *(Inria)*

- **Detecting XSLT Rules Affected by Schema Evolution**..143
  Yang Wu, Nobutaka Suzuki *(University of Tsukuba)*

- **Concept Hierarchy Extraction from Textbooks**..147
  Shuting Wang, Chen Liang, Zhaohui Wu, Kyle Williams, Bart Pursel, Benjamin Brautigam, Sherwyn Saul, Hannah Williams, Kyle Bowen, C. Lee Giles *(Pennsylvania State University)*

Document Understanding
Session Chair: Peter R. King *(University of Manitoba)*

- **Combining Advanced Information Retrieval and Text-Mining for Digital Humanities**.......157
  Antoine Widlocher *(Normandie University)*, Nicolas Bechet *(University Bretagne-Sud)*, Jean-Marc Lecarpentier, Yann Mathet, Julia Roger *(Normandie University)*

- **The Delaunay Document Layout Descriptor**...167
  Sébastien Eskenazi, Petra Gomez-Krämer, Jean-Marc Ogier *(Université de La Rochelle)*

- **An Approach to Convert NCL Applications into Stereoscopic 3D**...............................177
  Roberto Gerson de Albuquerque Azevedo, Guilherme F. Lima, Luiz Fernando Gomes Soares *(PUC-Rio)*

Short Papers Presented as Posters

- **AERO: An Extensible Framework for Adaptive Web Layout Synthesis**........................187
  Rares Vernica, Niranjan Damera Venkata *(Hewlett-Packard Labs)*

- **Automatic Text Document Summarization Based on Machine Learning**.......................191
  Gabriel Silva, Rafael Ferreira, Rafael Lins, Luciano Cabral, Hilário Oliveira *(Federal University of Pernambuco)*, Steven J. Simske *(Hewlett-Packard Labs)*, Marcelo Riss *(HP Brazil R&D)*

- **Searching Live Meeting Documents "Show me the Action"**..195
  Laurent Denoue, Scott Carter, Matthew Cooper *(FX Palo Alto Laboratory)*

- **Multimedia Document Structure for Distributed Theatre**...199
  Jack Jansen *(CWI: Centrum Wiskunde & Informatica)*, Michael Frantzis *(Goldsmiths)*, Pablo Cesar *(CWI: Centrum Wiskunde & Informatica)*

- **Change Classification in Graphics-Intensive Digital Documents**................................203
  Jeremy Svendsen, Alexandra Branzan Albu *(University of Victoria)*

- **Fine Grained Access of Interactive Personal Health Records**...................................207
  Helen Balinsky *(Hewlett-Packard)*, Nassir Mohammad *(Hewlett-Packard Labs)*

- **Does A Split-View Aid Navigation Within Academic Documents?**................................211
  Juliane Franze *(Monash University & Fraunhofer ESK)*, Kim Marriott, Michael Wybrow *(Monash University)*

- **An Approach for Designing Proofreading Views in Publishing Chains**.......................215
  Léonard Dumas, Stéphane Crozat, Bruno Bachimont *(UTC)*, Sylvain Spinelli *(Kelis)*

- **High-Quality Capture of Documents on A Cluttered Tabletop with a 4K Video Camera**...219
  Chelhwon Kim *(University of California, Santa Cruz)*, Patrick Chiu, Henry Tang *(FX Palo Alto Laboratory, Inc.)*

- **Segmentation of Overlapping Digits through the Emulation of a Hypothetical Ball and Physical Forces**...223
  Alberto N. G. Lopes Filho, Carlos A. B. Mello *(Universidade Federal de Pernambuco)*

Workshop and Tutorials
Session Chair: Sonja Maier *(University of the Federal Armed Forces, Germany)*

- **Document Changes: Modeling, Detection, Storage and Visualization (DChanges 2015)**...227
  Gioele Barabucci *(Universität zu Köln)*, Uwe M. Borghoff *(Universität der Bundeswehr München)*, Angelo Di Iorio *(Università di Bologna)*, Sonja Maier *(University of the Federal Armed Forces, Germany)*, Ethan Munson *(University of Wisconsin-Milwaukee)*

- **Document Engineering Issues in Document Analysis**...229
  Charles Nicholas, Robert Brandon *(University of Maryland, Baltimore County)*

- **Developing Web Applications with Document Engineering Technologies and Enjoying It!**...231
  Stéphane Sire *(Oppidoc)*

- **What Is This Thing Called Linked Data?**...233
  Manuel Atencia, Jérôme David *(University Grenoble Alpes, LIG, Inria)*,
  Philippe Genoud *(University Grenoble Alpes, LIG)*

Author Index..235

DocEng 2015 Symposium Organization

Symposium Chair: Christine Vanoirbeek *(EPFL, Switzerland)*

Program Chair: Pierre Genevès *(CNRS, France)*

Workshop and Tutorials Chair: Sonja Maier *(University of the Federal Armed Forces, Germany)*

Doctoral Consortium Chair: Cerstin Mahlow *(Institut für Deutsche Sprache, Germany)*

BOF Chair: Charles Nicholas *(University of Maryland, USA)*

Publicity Chair: Tamir Hassan *(Hewlett-Packard, Austria)*

Steering Committee Chair: Steve Simske *(HP Laboratories, USA)*

Steering Committee: David Brailsford *(University of Nottingham, UK)*
Dick Bulterman *(FX Palo Alto Laboratory, USA)*
Matthew Hardy *(Adobe, USA)*
Peter King *(University of Manitoba, Canada)*
Kim Marriott *(Monash University, Australia)*
Ethan Munson *(University of Wisconsin-Milwaukee, USA)*
Charles Nicholas *(University of Maryland, USA)*
Maria da Graca C. Pimentel *(Universidade de Sao Paulo, Brazil)*
Cécile Roisin *(Université Pierre Mendes and INRIA, France)*
Jean-Yves Vion-Dury *(Xerox Research Centre Europe, France)*
Anthony Wiley *(HP Exstream, USA)*

Program Committee: Apostolos Antonacopoulos *(University of Salford, UK)*
Steven Bagley *(University of Nottingham, UK)*
Helen Balinsky *(Hewlett-Packard Laboratories, UK)*
Uwe M. Borghoff *(Universität der Bundewehr München, Germany)*
David F. Brailsford *(University of Nottingham, UK)*
Anne Brüggemann-Klein *(Technische Universität München, Germany)*
Pablo Cesar *(CWI, Netherlands)*
Boris Chidlovskii *(Xerox Research Centre Europe, France)*
Michael Collard *(The University of Akron, USA)*
Niranjan Damera-Venkata *(Hewlett-Packard, USA)*
Stefano Ferilli *(University of Bari, Italy)*
Pierre Genevès *(CNRS, France)*
Gersende Georg *(Haute Autorité de Santé, France)*
C Lee Giles *(Pennsylvania State University, USA)*
Michael Gormish *(Ricoh Innovations Corp., USA)*
Maria da Graca Pimentel *(Universidade de São Paulo, Brazil)*
Matthew Hardy *(Adobe, USA)*
Tamir Hassan *(Hewlett-Packard, Austria)*
Nathan Hurst *(Shutterstock, USA)*

DocEng 2015 Sponsor & Supporters

Sponsor:

Supporters:

Adobe

FX PAL
PALO ALTO LABORATORY

hp

PPIDOC

EPFL
ÉCOLE POLYTECHNIQUE
FÉDÉRALE DE LAUSANNE

Documents as Data, Data as Documents.
What we learned about Semi-Structured Information
for our Open World of Cloud & Devices

Jean Paoli
Microsoft
Redmond, USA
jeanpa@microsoft.com

ABSTRACT

Many of us always believed in a unique vision unifying documents and data through semantically-rich semi-structured information. This vision is even more critical today in our open interconnected world of Clouds and Devices.

The last 20 years represents a real-life worldwide experiment in this area that fueled a massive set of market applications. In this talk, we review the history and trends of a lot of what is enabling today's core interchanges on the internet: from initial research adding document user interfaces to data, to the specification of structured documents, to the generalization of document markup techniques to the wide acceptance of document databases. We will also review our share of historical acronyms such as "Star", "Grif","OpenDoc","WorldWideWeb/Nexus","Amaya","InfoPath '"HTML", "SGML", "XML", "JSON", "YAML","Markdown", "Schema", "Semantics","MongoDB", "Hadoop", "DocumentDB" and many others.

We will then turn, cautiously and humbly, to the future and try to guess: what would the world need? And what do we need to think about to make it happen?

We truly believe in the potential of the open Internet. We see pieces of information (that we once called "Diamonds of the Internet"), being created, shared, re-shaped, re-routed, modified by users or tiny small devices, understood through big data and machine learning, and processed by cloud services. We see the potential of fundamentally designing open platforms connected worldwide. By bridging technologies, we create higher level abstractions and thus more complex organisms (software) that can help everyone. But at the core remains the need for semi-structured open information fundamentally unifying documents and data.

Keywords

Document Model, Document Representation, Document Processing, Document Interaction, Document Database, Semi-Structured Information, Openness.

Short Biography

Jean Paoli is President, Microsoft Open Technologies, Inc. (MS Open Tech), and one of the co-creators of the XML 1.0 standard with the World Wide Web Consortium (W3C). He has long been a strong and passionate advocate of XML and open standards.

In his role as President of Microsoft Open Technologies, a Microsoft subsidiary, Jean leads a diverse team of engineers, standards professionals and technical evangelists to promote interoperability, open platform development and customer choice. Jean's MS Open Tech team has worked closely with many business groups across Microsoft to help develop several technical standards, including W3C's HTML5, IETF's HTTP 2.0, WebRC/ORTC, Cloud standards in DMTF and OASIS. The team also collaborates with a broad variety of open source development communities to contribute tools that promote interoperability between Microsoft technologies within open source environments such as Node.js, MongoDB, Docker, OpenJDK, Apache Cordova, Dash.js, Cocos2d-x, Open edX and Moodle.

Jean jump-started the XML activity in Microsoft Corporation. He created and managed the team that delivered msxml, the software that XML-enabled both Internet Explorer and the Windows operating system. Jean helped architect Office XML support and was instrumental in creating InfoPath, the XML Office Electronic Forms application.

Jean has been a significant player in the worldwide XML community since 1985, when the technology was then known as SGML. Until 1996, when he joined Microsoft, Jean was based in Paris, where he worked in collaboration with European research institutes, including INRIA in France. He designed several systems for major corporations where SGML, in its approach of structuring and storing information, ensured the long life and easy exchangeability of the data across systems. His specialty has been building end-user markup editing tools for semi-structured information. He also participated in ISO/IEC SC34/ WG4 and as co-chair of the TC45 Ecma standards committee that formalized the Office Open XML Format as an international standard.

Jean is the recipient of multiple industry awards for his work on XML, interoperability and the convergence of documents and data.

DocEng'15, September 8-11, 2015, Lausanne, Switzerland.
ACM 978-1-4503-3307-8/15/09.
DOI: http://dx.doi.org/10.1145/2682571.2797070

The Browser as a Document Composition Engine

Tamir Hassan
HP Labs
Vienna, Austria
tamir.hassan@hp.com

Niranjan Damera Venkata
HP Labs
Chennai, Tamil Nadu, India
niranjan.damera-venkata@hp.com

ABSTRACT

Printing has long been a neglected aspect of the Web, and the print function of browsers, when used on documents designed for on-screen consumption, often leads to a poor result. Whereas print CSS goes some way towards optimizing the paper experience, it still does not enable full control over the page layout, which is necessary to obtain a publication-quality print result. Furthermore, its use requires web authors to invest additional resources for a feature that might only be used infrequently. This paper introduces a framework designed to alleviate these issues and improve the print experience on the Web. We describe the technologies that enable us to automatically compose and optimize the layout of a document, and generate a high quality PDF fully within the browser. This functionality can be offered to web publishers in the form of a print button, enabling content to be simultaneously delivered in screen and print formats, and ensuring a publication-quality result that adheres to the publisher's design guidelines.

Categories and Subject Descriptors

I.7.4 [**Computing Methodologies**]: Document and Text Processing: Electronic Publishing

General Terms

Algorithms, Design

Keywords

automated publishing, printing from the Web, HTML, CSS, browser-independent rendering

1. INTRODUCTION

The vast majority of web content today is consumed on the screen of a PC or mobile device, and it is a well known fact that printing web content, in general, often leads to a poor result. Common issues include poorly placed page breaks, missing background colours, low-resolution images

and, in general, a page layout that has not been optimized for the medium.

Whereas developments in web technology over the past years have been geared towards optimizing the on-screen experience, the "on-paper" experience has, at most, been considered as an afterthought, and has suffered as a result. Many web publishers include special "printer friendly" versions of pages; others use the CSS `media="print"` query to separately style and lay out the content for print. Whereas these methods, if implemented properly, can somewhat improve the print experience, they rarely lead to a publication quality result: in most cases, a reader will still immediately notice that the document has been printed from the Web.

Even when using a print stylesheet, commonly referred to as "print CSS", the author does not have full control over the final layout of the document. This is due to several factors, including variations in the way different browser and operating system combinations render fonts, as well as differing output paper sizes and constraints imposed by the printer driver and its configuration.

As a result, print versions of current web pages are not able to take full advantage of the print medium and focus instead generating a simpler, "cleaned up" version of the page (e.g. by removing advertising banners and increasing margins), to reduce the likelihood of serious layout errors occurring across a wide range of systems.

We have addressed these issues by developing a framework for generating publication-quality print documents from web content with automatically generated, optimized layout. All computation, up to the generation of the print-ready PDF, has been coded in JavaScript and can therefore be run directly within the browser, or alternatively on the server. By generating a PDF, we avoid the problem of not having full control over the final layout in HTML. By creating a print button, web publishers are able to use our framework to offer high quality print versions of their content.

This paper is structured as follows: Section 2 presents an overview of related work; Section 3 describes how the document is automatically composed in the browser, and is rendered to HTML for on-screen preview; Section 4 describes the methods and techniques for generating the PDF from this preview; Section 5 describes the steps required to implement our JavaScript methods on the server; and Section 6 illustrates our system in action and compares the result to other ways of printing from the Web. Finally, Section 7 concludes the paper by summarizing the main contributions and presents a direction for future work.

2. RELATED WORK

Browser-based layout is accomplished with HTML and CSS. With the latest versions of these technologies, HTML5 and CSS3, sophisticated responsive web page layouts have become feasible, especially in combination with client side frameworks like Twitter Bootstrap[1] and Zurb Foundation[2]. Bootstrap's grid layout uses a 12 column grid and allows `<div>`s to span an integer number of columns. The span and block level re-flow behavior can be controlled by special classes that allow responsive behavior when device resolution and device orientation is changed.

The problems with CSS as a layout tool are analyzed in [11] and improvements to web and web-based print layouts based on a template specification and filling approach were described in [1] and are still actively being worked on by the W3C [2].

While automated print document composition has been a topic of much research in the document engineering community [10, 7], there has been little work in leveraging the capability of modern browsers as automated print-document composition engines. While there are features of CSS3 such as the multi-column module that allows a developer to set up multi-column text flows (which are very common in high quality print publications), they suffer from poor cross browser support [12] and have restrictions that do not allow a flexible template specification (e.g. multi-column blocks need to be rectangular and images must span all columns). There are efforts by the W3C to create a CSS based replacement for XSL-FO [5], called the CSS Paged Media Module [6] which aims to enable specification and filling a series of print templates to create printable documents. While this approach can work well for well defined static content, highly variable content often requires an intelligent layout algorithm to synthesize optimized layouts.

The most popular print-formatting technology for the Web is still the CSS print stylesheet [8] that must be created on a case by case basis and, as explained in the introduction, is highly sensitive to cross browser, cross operating system variations.

In the following sections of this paper we discuss how we combine HTML5 and CSS3 with our own computational algorithms implemented in JavaScript to create publication-quality print output from content on the Web within the browser.

A prerequisite of achieving a high quality formatted printed document is the ability to select (i.e. extract) and annotate printable content from a web page. For example, Lim et al. [9] propose a tool that attempts to clean and format web pages for an improved print experience, removing advertising, navigation boxes and other auxiliary content fully automatically and formats the document using CSS. The website **www.printfriendly.com** offers similar functionality, which can be accessed via the web interface or downloadable plugin. Both approaches allow the user to make manual adjustments to the initial selection. Chamun et al. [3] propose semi-manual publisher annotation, allowing publishers to annotate printable content in an initial step on an example page. These selections are then used to filter and annotate new content.

For the purpose of this paper, we assume that content extraction and annotation has been performed (for example, using one of the methods described in the previous paragraph). Our focus in this paper is to discuss rendering capabilities of standard web technologies, in particular HTML5, CSS3 and JavaScript along with computational algorithms to create publication-quality print output from content on the Web. We leverage the browser's inbuilt rendering functionality to create a lightweight framework capable of generating high quality print output and accurate onscreen preview across a variety of browser and operating system combinations.

3. DOCUMENT COMPOSITION

In this section we describe our browser-based JavaScript document composition engine, which takes HTML5 content as input and produces a multi-column, multi-page web document. The goal is to achieve publication quality, multi-column print layouts in a lightweight manner within the browser. Our JavaScript engine is adapted from our earlier work on the Probabilistic Document Model (PDM) for layout synthesis [4].

Our layout engine is implemented in JavaScript and takes advantage of the browser's built-in HTML/CSS rendering engine to render all content elements that have been extracted in the previous step. This also gives us a certain amount of tolerance for content extraction errors: For example a `<div>` tag that is styled by a CSS stylesheet may not be correctly recognized (annotated), but might still be presented in a coherent way. In contrast, a heavyweight system running outside of the browser requires perfect content annotation and will not be able to format such a tag correctly. Also, JavaScript enables seamless integration with the browser and allows us to use the same code for in-browser print preview. These advantages come with significant technological challenges in implementing a high quality layout engine in JavaScript.

We highlight the key issues applicable to a browser based environment:

3.1 Content and normalization

The canonical input format is a subset of HTML5. The `<h1>`-`<h5>` tags represent various levels of headings; the `<p>` tags represent re-flowable content which should be capable of breaking and re-flowing across column and page boundaries. The `<figure>` tag is used to represent floating figures. The `<table>` tag represents floating figures. The `<aside>` tag represents a floating sidebar that in turn can contain other HTML5 tags. All other HTML5 tags, although not explicitly supported, are mapped by default to non-floatable, non-reflowable `<div>` tags that are rendered in place[3]. In cases where the input is not in canonical form, we need content normalization methods.

Content normalization fixes format issues with HTML that could throw off the algorithm. We convert HTML tags to a canonical representation. For example, we wrap each `<img>` tag inside a `<figure>` tag, unwrap `<img>` tags embedded in `<p>` tags, and wrap top level `<ul>` and `<li>` tags into `<p>` tags so they can be broken and flowed across columns/pages. We also strip inline styles, inline image width and

---

[1]Bootstrap, **http://getbootstrap.com**
[2]Zurb Foundation, **http://foundation.zurb.com**

[3]Note that we can map any of these to be rendered as floats that may span multiple columns in a layout.

```
<div class="JP_Template JP_FirstPage JP_Odd JP_Even" images="1" sbars="0" name="FP_template">
  <div class="JP_PageContainer">

    <div class ="JP_Header">
      <div class="chapter"></div>
      <img src="Logo.png"/>
      <div class ="JP_Topline"></div>
    </div>

    <div class ="JP_Title title12" startcol="1" endcol="2"></div>
    <div class ="JP_TxtBlock column column1" order="1"></div>
    <div class ="JP_Image Top22"   startcol="2" endcol="2"></div>
    <div class ="JP_TxtBlock column column2" order="2"></div>

    <div class ="JP_Footer">
      <div class ="JP_Bottomline"></div>
      <div class="special" type="pageNumber"></div>
    </div>

  </div>
</div>
```

Figure 1: **Example of a template specification in HTML**

height attributes, clean up empty `<p>` tags, remove non-breaking spaces and trim extra spaces, etc. Hyphenation support is available either by using the CSS `hyphens` property (which is not supported by Chrome) or cross-browser by using the Hyphenator.js library[4].

3.2 The template library

Templates represent possible arrangements of floating elements (e.g. figures, tables, sidebars) and text columns on a page. The basic structure of a template is encoded using empty HTML `<div>` tags with corresponding classes. Figure 1 shows an example template specification in HTML. CSS styles applied to a template determine the width and height of a page, the column widths, margins etc. The CSS also determines the typographical styles of text, colors, and other design attributes required to impart a particular look to a template. We use SASS[5] as a preprocessor for our CSS so that we can generate CSS for various page dimensions using the same basic template. SASS allows variable definitions, functions etc. in the CSS that are resolved at compile time to generate a CSS file. The SASS-generated CSS can be combined with CSS media queries to load versions of a template customized for various target resolutions. Figure 2(a) shows the template specified by Figure 1 with sample content and CSS applied. Figure 2(b) shows the very same template with different (auto-generated by SASS) CSS applied to accommodate a landscape form factor.

The floating page elements have widths that span one or more columns and heights that are initially set to zero in the CSS. A text column may be continuous or broken into segments to accomodate floating sidebars (such as a pull quote). The height of a text column is set to the desired full column height (assuming pure text and no floating elements). An order attribute in each text segment indicates reading order. When content is rendered into a template, the heights of columns adjust to accommodate the content. We will cover this in more detail in the following subsections.

---

[4]Hyphenator.js, https://github.com/mnater/Hyphenator
[5]SASS, http://sass-lang.com

3.3 Scoring content allocations

In PDM we denote by $\Psi(\mathcal{A}, \mathcal{B}, T)$ the maximum score of an allocation of content to a template T. $\mathcal{B}$ denotes content allocated to all pages up to (and including) the previous page while $\mathcal{A}$ denotes content allocated to all pages upto (and including) the current page. Clearly $\mathcal{B} \subset \mathcal{A}$. Thus $\mathcal{A} - \mathcal{B}$ denotes content allocated to the current page template. The score depends on previous content to allow us to consider dangling references, i.e. if a figure or sidebar appearing on the current page is referenced in a prior page.

Given scores $\Psi(\mathcal{A}, \mathcal{B}, T)$ for all possible valid combinations of the arguments[6], the PDM layout synthesis algorithm uses a dynamic programming approach to solve, for the optimal number of pages, the templates to use for each page and the content to be allocated to each page. We compute Ψ as a product of normal distributions each representing the variation of an element/parameter on the page from its most desired value. Furthermore, the variance of the parameters control how much to weight the deviations from ideal values.

In general the procedure to allocate content to a template and score the allocation can take place with (see [13]) or without invoking browser rendering (the choice amounts to a tradeoff between flexibility and complexity). In the latter case we leverage an offscreen pre-rendering step where:

1. Floating elements (images, sidebars, tables) and titles are rendered in an offline buffer with different column spans and their heights are measured (using JQuery's `.height()` method). This results in data tables $height(E^f, span)$) corresponding to each floating element E^f.

2. Stream elements (e.g. subtitles, headings, inine figures, lists and paragraphs) are rendered in a fixed width column. The number of lines for each para is measured.

---

[6]An allocation with too much or too little content is invalid. An allocation of content without any figures to a template with a floating figure slot is also invalid. Conversely, an allocation of content with two figures to a template with only one figure slot is valid since the other image may be rendered as *inline* within a single column.

(a) Portrait

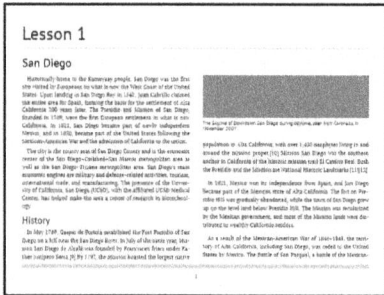

(b) Landscape

Figure 2: Pages derived from the template specification of Figure 1 with (a) portrait and (b) landscape CSS applied. The CSS for each case was automatically generated from a base file using a SASS preprocessor.

An important point to note here is that, in general, one cannot deduce the number of rendered lines of a paragraph from the height and the CSS `line-height` property of the paragraph using:

$$numlines = \frac{\text{height of } \texttt{<p>}}{\text{CSS } \texttt{line-height} \text{ of } \texttt{<p>}} \qquad (1)$$

This is because inline tags such as `<b>,<sup>,<sub>` can cause the line height to increase. To ensure a consistent line-height for measurement we set:

```
b,a,sup { line-height: 1px !important; }
```

in the CSS stylesheet. With this fix, equation (1) yields an accurate estimate of the number of rendered lines when a paragraph is rendered in a column.

Given a template and matching content, we first assign floating elements to their positions in the template. Since we know the span of the floating element slot, we may simply look up the height of the floating element from the data tables $height(E^f, span))$ generated during pre-rendering. The text column heights of columns spanned by the float are reduced accordingly. For each floating element (or title) E^f this results in a column height update for the ith column:

$$h_i \leftarrow h_i - I(E^f, i)\, height(E^f, span) \qquad (2)$$

where $I(E^f, i)$ is the indicator function equal to 1 if E^f spans column i and 0 otherwise. Note that in cases where a column is broken into segments (to accomodate a pull quote, for example) the height update for a column is split proportionally over component column segments.

After the floats have all been positioned, we determine how to place the text inside the columns. The height of text $\mathcal{T}$ can be calculated by summing the heights of partial paragraphs at the beginning and end of the allocation with the heights of the other paragraphs. Next we calculate the approximate bottom whitespace due to the content allocation by:

$$bottom\ space = \frac{\sum_i^N h_i - height(\mathcal{T})}{N} - \delta \qquad (3)$$

The parameter δ is a slack parameter introduced to account for the fact that text is not continuous and hence cannot be expected to break at continuous heights. Instead, column breaks occur at discrete points (most often at line boundaries). For this reason δ is set to the paragraph line height. If the bottom space is negative, the content will overflow the template and $\Psi(\mathcal{A}, \mathcal{B}, T)$ is assigned the value 0.

If content underflows the template, the residual column heights are further updated to account for the bottom white space:

$$h_i \leftarrow h_i - bottom\ space \qquad (4)$$

Finally we can begin pouring text into the residual containers, to create approximately balanced text columns to calculate actual underflow of each column. Breakpoints are located at the line number where the next piece of content will overflow the column container. Thus $N-1$ text breakpoints are located and final column residuals are calculated:

$$h_i \leftarrow h_i - height(\mathcal{T}_i) \qquad (5)$$

where $\mathcal{T}_i$ denotes the height of text in the ith column.

The variations in the residual heights of columns (a measure of how well the columns are balanced), the bottom white space, the dimensions of images/floats, the numbers of missed references and widows/orphans in the column breakpoints are scored using a normal probability distribution for each and the product (or sum when a logarithm is taken) is returned as the template score for a given allocation. In many cases there may be more than one candidate floating element (e.g. a table or an image) that can fill a template's floating slot. In this case, the element that results in the maximum overall page score is selected.

Note that sidebars are scored by recursively running the above steps on the content of each sidebar over matching compatible sidebar templates. The highest "internal" sidebar score is aggregated with the sidebar score, considering the sidebar as a simple float component of a template. This allows multi-column flows inside sidebars in the same way as with main content. An example is shown in Figure 3(b).

3.4 Rendering document pages

Once the layout is computed, the pages are ready to be rendered. For each page, its content is mapped onto a template in much the same way as described in Section 3.3. However this time we must actually invoke browser rendering, so unlike in Section 3.3 where we just had to keep track of partial paras, here we need to simulate paras that break and flow from column to column and page to page.

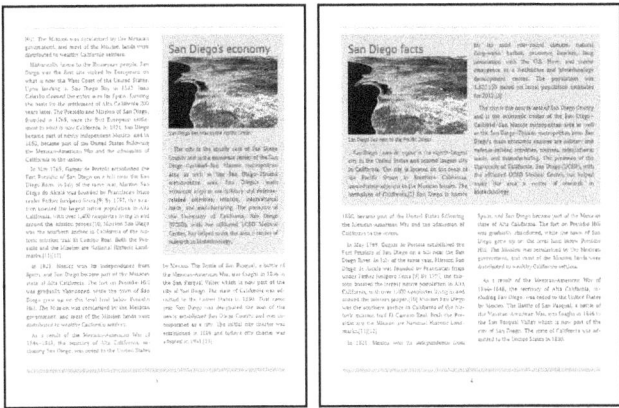

(a) single column sidebar   (b) multi-column sidebar

Figure 3: Sidebars within a template are rendered hierarchically choosing from a library of sidebar templates

It may seem that we could leverage the CSS3 multi-column properties (`column-count`, `column-gap`, `column-fill`) but they are not well supported in most browsers (e.g. `column-fill:balance` is only supported in Firefox) and more importantly the column blocks need to be rectangular, i.e. we cannot have a three-column layout with balanced text flow where a float element spans columns 2 and 3. For these reasons, we have built our own text flow methods that work across browsers and still leverage the browser's native line-breaking functionality.

Columns are styled with `visibility:hidden` so that text that overflows a column is hidden. However, due to bottom whitespace being allowed, text may be required to be broken much earlier than at a column break. To allow partial para rendering in these cases, we append a special column masking `div` (`<div class='column-mask'></div>`) at the end of each column. The height of this `div` is set to the height of the partial para text to be hidden in that column. To render the partial text at the end of a column, the mask is styled as `position:relative` and made to overlap the required partial para lines by setting its inline style in JQuery using:

```
filler.css('top',-partial-end-lines+'px');
```

To simulate a partial para at the top of a column, we render the same para again at the top of the column. After the elements in the column have been placed we shift the entire column contents upward using the JQuery statement:

```
$('.column > *').css('top',
    -partial-start-lines+'px');
```

This has the effect of hiding `partial-start-lines` of the para appended at the top of the column using the `visibility:hidden` property of the column. Figure 4 illustrates how partial paras are simulated at the bottom and top of columns.

We then refine the approximate column balancing by allowing an increase of at most 1 `px` in the para line-spacing.

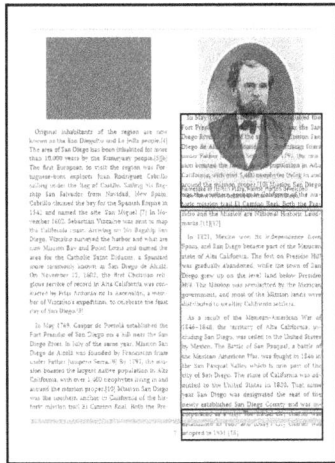

Figure 4: Example of rendering partial text flows. The red box indicates the column boundary of column 2. To render text at the top of column 2, the last para at the end of column 1 is rendered again and the entire column contents are shifted upward to mask the area indicated by the black box at the top of column 2. To render partial text at the end of column 2, a masking filler is rendered as the last element of the column and shifted upward to mask the text at the bottom of the column

This is done using the `knapsack.js` solver[7]. This is a knapsack problem since we need to determine which paragraphs (with weights equal to the number of visible paragraph lines) to *pack* into a knapsack of capacity equal to the residual column height so that the knapsack is filled as close to capacity as possible. After this we may still be left with a small residual height. This is simply distributed among elements in the column by modifying the element padding appropriately. Figure 5 shows the effect before and after fine column balancing.

Where a client-side browsing/print-preview experience is desired (for typical web articles, blog posts etc.), each page is rendered to a Javascript viewer UI that allows a user to preview and browse the HTML pages retaining full link and media interactivity before selecting the print function. Formatting the output on the client side for print (via PDF generation) requires further technical considerations that will be discussed in the next section.

4. PDF GENERATION

In order to ensure a high quality print version of the content, we generate a PDF from the rendered output, which can be either onscreen or in an offscreen buffer. This enables us to leverage the browser's rendering capabilities and design a relatively lightweight system to run in the browser. There is a limited choice of libraries for generating PDF files directly within the browser; we investigated two open-source offerings, jsPDF[8] and HPDF[9], both of which are not as fully-featured as more heavyweight products such as PDFBox and

---

[7]Knapsack.js, https://gist.github.com/danwoods/7496329
[8]jsPDF, https://parall.ax/products/jspdf
[9]hpdf.js, http://manuels.github.io/hpdf.js

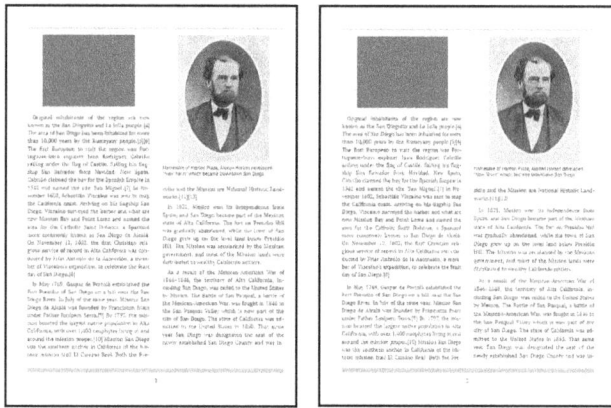

(a) without balancing   (b) with balancing

Figure 5: Effect of column balancing

iText. Initially, the jsPDF library, which is natively coded in JavaScript, was considered, but found not to support custom embedded fonts. Fortunately, this essential functionality was offered by HPDF, which is a JavaScript port of libharu[10]. Because much of the code has been automatically compiled from C bytecode using Emscripten, debugging and modifying the library is more difficult than jsPDF. A notable missing feature of HPDF is Unicode support, although it does support multiple character sets, including several CJK (Chinese-Japanese-Korean) encodings.

Our page content can be represented as a list of graphical content objects (images and vector graphics), filled and unfilled separation boxes, and text blocks, each of which have a rectangular bounding box. Using the `getBounding-ClientRect()` function, we obtain each block's coordinates relative to the page origin, which we then scale to obtain the page coordinates in PDF coordinate space. When using a library such as HPDF, it is necessary to define the PDF structure at a low level: most commands map directly to a single, or a small number of PDF operators. Fortunately, due to the object-oriented nature of PDF, each graphical content object can simply be placed on the page, and there are operators specifically for drawing and filling rectangular boxes.

Textual content presents a more difficult challenge: both `Tj` and `TJ` text operators simply place text along a line, using the font's standard widths for glyphs and spaces, but ignoring any kerning information, as this information does not become part of the embedded font[11].

Recall that we are generating a PDF based on output that has already been laid out for a predetermined page size and displayed on the screen. Regardless of the kerning issue, it is very difficult to ensure that the width occupied by a piece of text rendered using either text operator exactly matches the relative width occupied on screen. A number of issues in the browser's rendering engine could cause this value to differ. For example, the browser might be using integer widths

---

[10]libharu, http://libharu.org
[11]The difference between these two operators is that `TJ` allows individual glyph positioning, and most software creating PDFs inserts kerning adjustments as appropriate at the time of PDF generation.

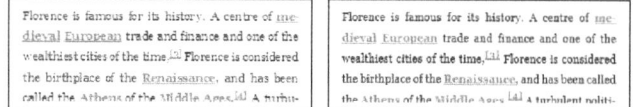

Figure 6: Examples of rendering of the same content in Chrome (left) and Firefox (right) on the Windows operating system

for each character and these rounding errors can add up in the course of a line. Or the overall character height might be rounded up or down to the next integer pixel value (the RGB pixel arrangement on today's monitors generally allows subpixel positioning on the horizontal, but not the vertical axis). Furthermore, there are numerous differences between the way different combinations of operating system, browser and even browser version render fonts. Windows, in particular, is known for its agressive hinting of TrueType fonts, which modifies the shapes, and sometimes also the character widths at small font sizes, in order to improve legibility. Figure 6 shows how the same font can look significantly different in Chrome and Firefox, even though both are running on the same operating system. The differences across operating systems are even greater.

Fortunately, we do know that the deviation in line width between screen and PDF is proportional to the number of characters in the line, and we therefore position small amounts of text, i.e. words or characters, individually, using their scaled coordinates, in order to ensure that the line lengths remain constant and do not differ from the computed result in the render buffer. The `getBoundingClientRect()` function normally only gives us the coordinates at the DOM element level, i.e. the entire block of text; in order to obtain the positions of individual words or characters, it is necessary to wrap each of these substrings in a `<span>` element.

In general, we have found that working on word-level granularity is sufficient for high quality text output with no visible uneven spacing. The spaces between words provide a "buffer" for cumulative differences in character width, and these are small enough not to be noticeable when added to the space amount. Our current solution is based on the latest Chrome version, whose underlying rendering model positions characters in small fractions of pixels, and these fractional values are returned as floating point numbers by `getBoundingClientRect()`. Similarly, the latest Firefox version returns fractional coordinates accurate to 1/60 pixel for each word or character. Older browsers give us less accurate coordinates, however. In cases where only integer coordinates are returned, it is possible to overcome this issue by scaling the font size by a known multiple to obtain more accurate character placement; in our experiments a multiple of 4 was found to be sufficient for 10 point text.

4.1 Hyphenation and lists

Hyphenated words require special treatment when using the above method to output the rendered content to PDF, and the process works for both CSS hyphenation and Hyphenator.js. The chosen granularity (word or character) determines the steps that need to be taken.

In order to display the text properly, we need to determine exactly at which point the word is being split, and the coordinates of both subwords. If word granularity is being used, the `getBoundingClientRect()` function will re-

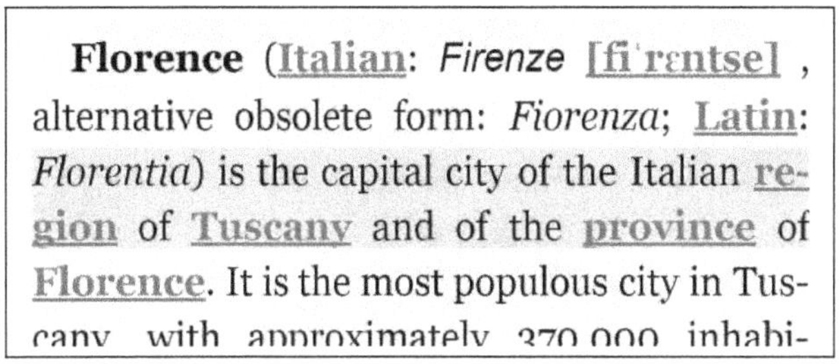

Figure 7: Example of the bounding client rectangle coordinates returned for a hyphenated word

turn the coordinates of a rectangle spanning both subwords, and therefore both lines of text (see Fig. 7). We can use the bottom-left coordinate of this rectangle to position the second subword, but we still need to find out the starting position and number of characters of the first subword.

In order to find the starting position, we first ensure that not only each word, but also the spaces between words, are wrapped in a `<span>` tag. The right coordinate of the previous space is therefore the starting coordinate of the first subword. Determining the split point and hence number of characters in each subword is more difficult. The distance between the starting coordinate of the first subword and the right coordinate (margin) of the paragraph represents the amount of space available. We then try rendering different numbers of characters from the beginning of the word to determine how many fit in the space available.

To do this, we temporarily create a `<br>` tag to move the text insertion point to the following line, followed by a `<span>` tag for the temporary buffer. For $n = 1, 2, 3, ...$ we render the first n characters of the word and measure its width. We continue doing so until the available width is exceeded to find the correct hyphenation point. If Hyphenator.js is being used, this process can be made more efficient by trying only legal hyphenation points, as Hyphenator.js automatically inserts soft hyphen characters at all legal hyphenation points into the text.

For character-level granularity, the hyphenation point is much easier to find, as `getBoundingClientRect()` returns the correct coordinates for all characters apart from the character directly following the hyphen (this single-character `<span>` also contains the hyphen on the previous line and therefore the bounding rectangle encompasses both lines). As the left margin and baseline of the following characters are known, it is not a problem to determine the missing coordinates of this character.

Similarly, lists require special treatment as the marker (bullet or number) is not encompassed by any `<span>` element. Its position can be estimated using the left coordinate (margin) of the parent `<p>` block and the baseline of the following text element. For ordered lists, the index of the item needs to be kept in memory and conversion to the standard HTML types (e.g. alphabetical, Roman numerals) also needs to be implemented manually.

5. SERVER-SIDE EXECUTION

Client-side document composition works well when the document is short (5 pages or less), requiring under 4 seconds. For larger documents (eg. books mashed up from web content), server-side processing is a natural choice. In this

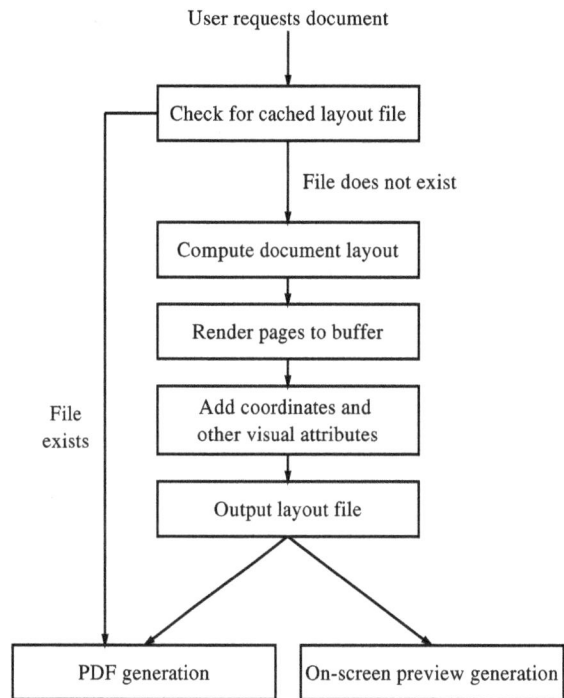

Figure 8: Flowchart for the workflow of the system

case, we benefit from the ability to process and cache longer documents on the server so that viewers can access them immediately. The initial document composition takes a few minutes (under 2 minutes for a 32 page booklet), but this needs to be carried out only once.

With minor modifications, we were able to get the document composition engine running under PhantomJS, a headless browser based on WebKit. The HPDF library used for generating the PDF itself, however, does not currently work in PhantomJS. It does, however, officially run under Node.js, another JavaScript runtime environment designed for server-side processing.

We therefore proceeded with our server-side implementation using both environments; the document composition and HTML rendering is carried out using PhantomJS; only the final PDF generation was be moved to Node.js. As we require a browser environment to obtain the coordinates of the individual content elements on each PDF page, these coordinates are also obtained using PhantomJS before being passed to Node.js for the PDF generation. Both parts of the process use the filesystem to interface with each other: a *layout file*, containing all the elements and their positions, is written to disk.

5.1 A note about platform independence

The PDF generation method described in Section 4 preserves the layout and, in contrast to most browsers' printing functions, guarantees that the line breaks of each paragraph remain unchanged. However, as the methods for in-browser document composition use the browser's rendering engine to measure content heights, minor layout changes can occur between different browsers and systems. Normally, this is not an issue, as the print result still matches the onscreen preview. However, when a cached PDF is downloaded from the server, its layout may not exactly match that of the locally displayed document, if it has also been composed locally.

Therefore, we have developed a *preview mode* to render previously composed documents in a platform-independent way. This is where the layout file, which is used to interface between PhantomJS and Node.js, has a second purpose: Instead of generating a PDF from the elements and their coordinates, these elements are output to an onscreen buffer and positioned using CSS positioning attributes. As well as maintaining the layout of the document, any delay in opening the document due to layout computation is avoided, as the document has already been composed. Fig 8 shows the flowchart of the entire system.

5.2 Issues with PhantomJS

Unfortunately, version 1.9 of PhantomJS was found to have problems rendering certain custom fonts, and would often substitute such fonts with a standard font. As the text was being rendered using an incorrect font, the coordinates that were obtained for PDF generation were inaccurate, leading to uneven character and/or word spacing. The latest version, 2.0, appears to have fixed the font embedding bug, but has introduced new bugs which also lead to irregular character spacing. Thus, PhantomJS is currently considered unsuitable until these issues are resolved. Fortunately, we have found an alternative platform, SlimerJS, on which the code can be run with very little modification. SlimerJS differs from PhantomJS by not being truly headless: it launches an actual instance of the Firefox browser, whose window remains visible if an X server is being used. However, by using xvfb (X Virtual Framebuffer), it is also possible to emulate a headless mode.

6. RESULTS

In order to illustrate the system's abilities, we present a comparison against several popular web printing methods using the web page in Fig. 9 as an example. We used the print functions in Firefox and Chrome, as well as the printfriendly.com plugin and the page's own printer friendly version, to print the web page on A4 ($8\frac{1}{4}$" $\times$ $11\frac{3}{4}$") paper.

The web page uses a print stylesheet, which only makes minor changes to optimize the layout for print. When printing from Chrome in Windows (see Fig. 10), the article fills three pages completely, although the last page contains only auxiliary content. On Firefox, the automatic zoom adjustment results in text that is rather small to read (6.75 pt) and increased whitespace, although the content still takes up three pages (see Fig. 11).

The results from the printfriendly.com Chrome extension and the website's own printer friendly version were very similar, as both removed auxiliary content and formatted the document using a single-column template. The plugin's result (see Fig. 12) took up four pages of A4, although there were large areas of whitespace due to pagination after images. The printer friendly version (see Fig. 13) generated by the website's CMS used a smaller font size, resulting in content that took up just over two pages (the third page was almost blank) and lines of text that were unnaturally long and therefore difficult to read (a two-column layout would have been much more appropriate). Furthermore, the link to the printer friendly version of the page was difficult to find and would likely not have been found by a user wishing to print the page.

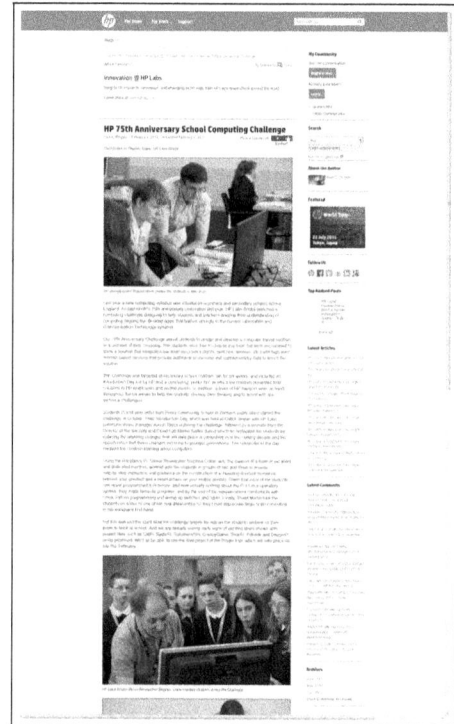

Figure 9: The original web page

Our comparison shows that there is currently a multitude of ways that a web page can be printed to paper. Print CSS alone does not usually suffice, and the user is advised to take the time to experiment with a variety of settings and plugins in order to achieve anything approaching an acceptable result. This is, of course, a frustrating experience for the user and the end result is still clearly not of publication quality – it is immediately obvious that the page has been printed from the Web.

The output of our system using a 3-column template is shown in Fig. 14. In contrast to the alternatives mentioned in this section, we generate a high quality PDF with text set in multiple columns using custom fonts, and a more eye-catching layout with custom fonts and images spanning over multiple columns. Furthermore, the print layout, once generated, can also be rendered to the screen using the method in Section 5.1, and presented as an accurate print preview within the interface of a web application.

7. CONCLUSION AND FURTHER WORK

In this paper, we have presented a framework to generate automatically optimized print versions of marked-up web content within the browser, and have addressed the main technical challenges in achieving a publication quality result. We have also addressed the issue of running the code on the server, enabling longer documents to be pre-cached for immediate loading, and have addressed the issues of previewing such documents in the browser across different systems, ensuring that the layout does not change.

By basing the content markup on a subset of well-known HTML tags and using page templates in HTML and CSS, we have kept the amount of work in adapting existing web content for printing via our framework to a minimum. A further

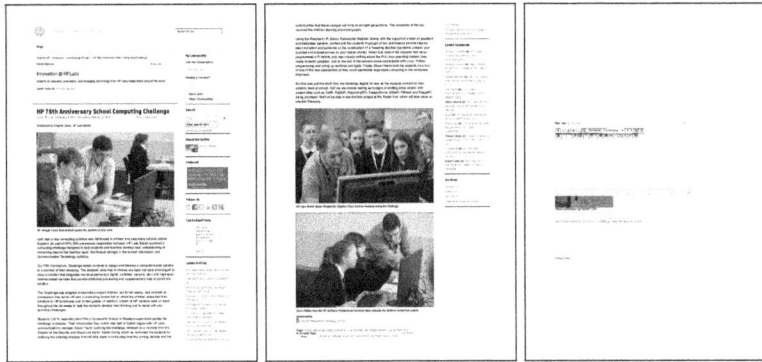

Figure 10: Result obtained by printing from Chrome (all three pages)

Figure 11: Result obtained by printing from Firefox using the "Shrink to fit" function (all three pages)

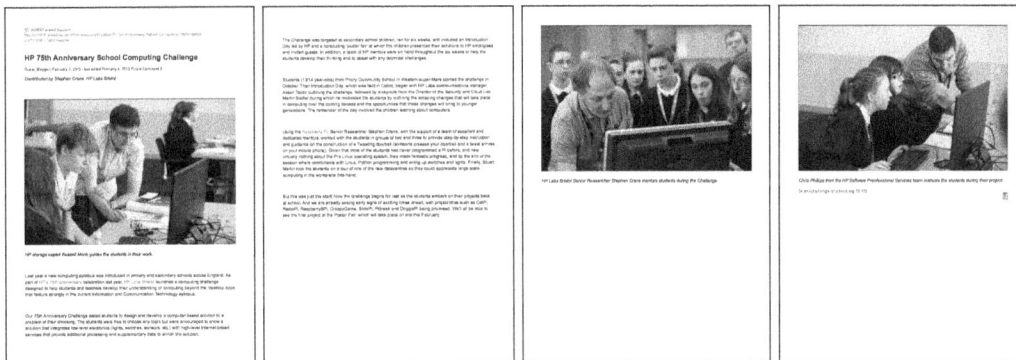

Figure 12: Result obtained by using the Chrome plugin from printfriendly.com (all four pages)

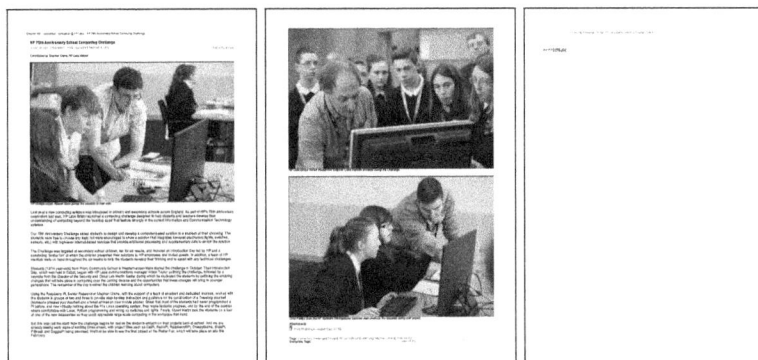

Figure 13: Result obtained by printing the printer friendly version in Chrome (all three pages)

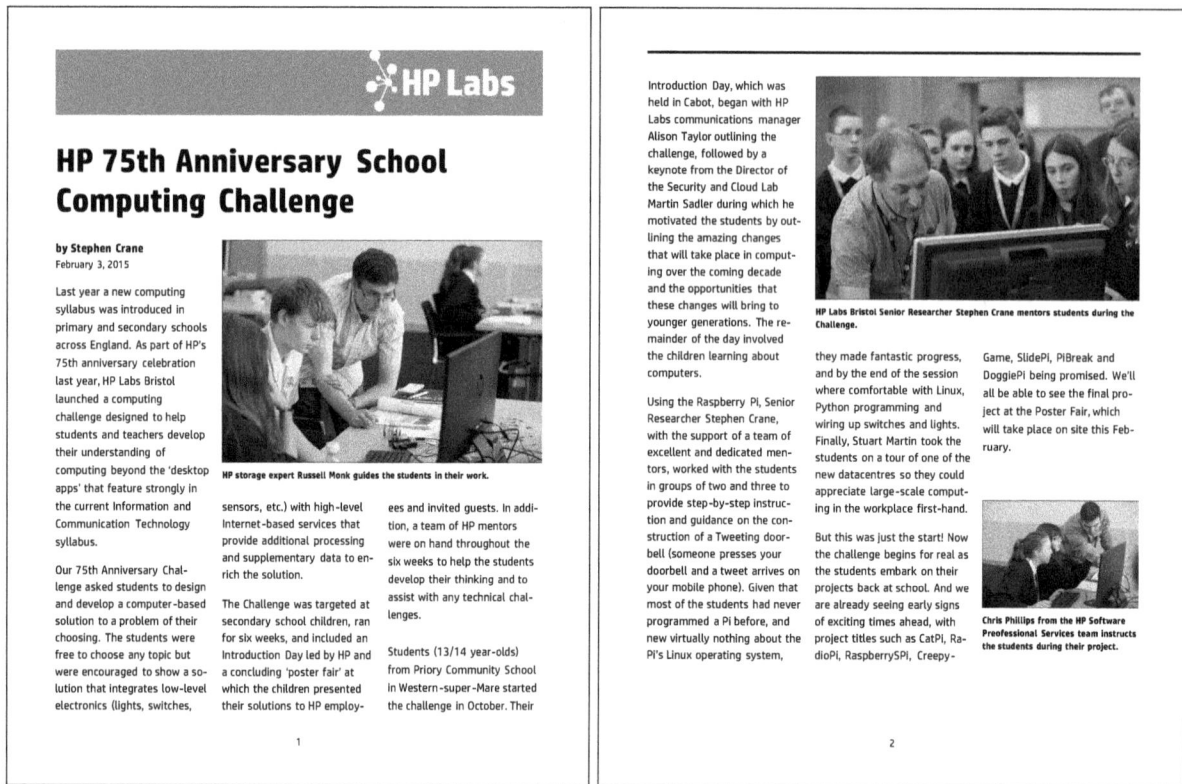

Figure 14: The print-optimized output of our system

direction of research is to make this adaptation automatic or semi-automatic. We hope that the ability to fully tailor the design of the document and add additional content, such as advertising, will make it worthwhile for publishers to start offering high quality print versions of documents using our framework.

8. REFERENCES

[1] C. Acebal, B. Bos, M. Rodríguez, and J. M. Cueva. ALMcss: A JavaScript implementation of the CSS template layout module. In *Proceedings of the 12th ACM Symposium on Document Engineering*, pages 23–32, 2012.

[2] B. Bos and C. Acebal. CSS template layout module. http://dev.w3.org/csswg/css-template-1/. W3C Editor's Draft: 2014-09-30.

[3] R. Chamun, D. Pinheiro, D. Jornada, J. B. S. de Oliveira, and I. H. Manssour. Extracting web content for personalized presentation. In *Proceedings of the 14th ACM Symposium on Document Engineering*, pages 157–164, 2014.

[4] N. Damera-Venkata, J. Bento, and E. O'Brien-Strain. Probabilistic Document Model for automated document composition. In *Proceedings of the 11th ACM Symposium on Document Engineering*, pages 3–12, 2011.

[5] F. Giannetti. XSL-FO 2.0: Automated publishing for graphic documents. In *Proceedings of the 9th ACM Symposium on Document Engineering*, pages 245–246, 2009.

[6] M. Grant. CSS Paged Media Module Level 3. http://www.w3.org/TR/css3-page/. W3C Working Draft: 2013-03-14.

[7] N. Hurst, W. Li, and K. Marriott. Review of automatic document formatting. In *Proceedings of the 9th ACM Symposium on Document Engineering*, pages 99–108, 2009.

[8] C. Krammer. How to set up a print style sheet. http://www.smashingmagazine.com/2011/11/24/how-to-set-up-a-print-style-sheet/. Published: 2011-11-24.

[9] S. H. Lim, L. Zheng, J. Jin, H. Hou, J. Fan, and J. Liu. Automatic selection of print-worthy content for enhanced web page printing experience. In *Proceedings of the 10th ACM Symposium on Document Engineering*, pages 165–168, 2010.

[10] S. Lok and S. Feiner. A survey of automated layout techniques for information presentations. In *Proceedings of the 2nd International Symposium on Smart Graphics*, pages 61–68, 2001.

[11] A. Robinson. In search of the one true layout. http://www.positioniseverything.net/articles/onetruelayout/. Published: 2005.

[12] C. Savarese. Introducing the CSS3 multi-column module. http://www.alistapart.com/articles/css3multicolumn. Published: 2005-10-21.

[13] R. Vernica and N. Damera-Venkata. AERO: An extensible framework for adaptive web layout synthesis. In *Proceedings of the 15th ACM Symposium on Document Engineering*, 2015.

Document Layout Optimization with Automated Paraphrasing

Yusuke Kido
The University of Tokyo
7-3-1 Hongo, Bunkyo-ku
Tokyo, Japan
y.k@is.s.u-tokyo.ac.jp

Hikaru Yokono   Goran Topić   Akiko Aizawa
National Institute of Informatics
2-1-2 Hitotsubashi, Chiyoda-ku
Tokyo, Japan
{yokono, goran_topic, aizawa}@nii.ac.jp

ABSTRACT

We introduce a new concept in document layout optimization. In our approach, *paraphrase-based layout optimization*, layout issues (e.g. widows due to poor page breaking) are automatically fixed by rewording the neighboring sentences. Techniques of paraphrasing are borrowed from the field of natural language processing towards this goal, which is the first attempt in the field of document engineering. We implemented a prototype TeX pre/post-processing system that includes two simple paraphrase generators. The experiment shows that our approach is promising and effective for improving document layout.

Categories and Subject Descriptors

I.7.2 [**Document and Text Processing**]: Document Preparation—*Format and notation, Photocomposition/typesetting*

General Terms

Algorithms, Experimentation, Standardization

Keywords

Document Layout Optimization, Natural Language Processing, Paraphrase, Typesetting, TeX

1. INTRODUCTION

When word processors and computer-based typesetters format text, they must make many decisions automatically; kerning, word spacing, line breaking, page breaking, and many others. Today many people edit documents using computer software, therefore the importance of study on document layout optimization is large.

The idea to formalize layout optimization problems, including line breaking [10] and page breaking [3], as constrained optimization was introduced at the very early stage of its field, and is still popular. With commercial

demands, effective use of a whole page has been also well studied, e.g. page layout including figures, tables, and advertisements [6, 9]. In addition, the rapid growth of the Web and mobile devices requires editors to consider the current situation wherein the same content is viewed in various environments.

Regardless of such increasing needs for document layout optimization, it still cannot be solved completely without human editors' help. One significant problem is that computer software cannot understand the content of text and rewrite it—*even though* a human can do it. This limitation was mentioned as early as 1987 by Knuth and Plass, stating "a properly programmed computer should, in fact, be able to solve the line-breaking problem better than a skilled typesetter could do by hand in a reasonable amount of time (unless we give this person the liberty to change the wording in order to obtain a better fit)" [10].

In this paper, we propose application of natural language processing techniques to this problem, which has been enabled by rapid development in that area in recent decades. The main contribution of this paper is the formalization of paraphrase-based layout optimization. We implemented a prototype system to experiment with our method. This system takes a TeX document as input, and applies our method to it to obtain better layout.ăĂĂ We implemented this prototype system focusing on two kinds of layout issues, hyphenations[1] and widows, and showed that our method is effective in decreasing the number of these issues.

2. RELATED WORK

2.1 Document Layout Optimization

Jacobs et al. [8] pointed out that the ability to adapt document layouts to different display sizes is inevitably required, and proposed the concept of *manifold content*. In their approach to optimize layouts, the user embeds alternative contents (e.g. paraphrases, and images in different sizes) into the document. Then the algorithm selects the best fitting choices from those options and formats the content dynamically to fit the target display device. Such paraphrases and variations of images are not automatically generated, thus the user is required to prepare them while editing. Piccoli and Oliveira [15] proposed

---

[1] Poor handling of the line breaking leads to too much hyphenated words appearing in the paragraph, which is usually advisable to avoid [1]. Thus herein we take decreasing the number of hyphenations as an example of improvements on document layouts.

an automated layout algorithm that combines *guillotine partitioning* of the page and changing font sizes. The algorithm chooses a good partitioning of the page, and then adjusts the font sizes of text, without changing the contents, to fit each particular area of the page. It uses TeX's rendering information to see how the document is currently laid out, and then estimates the area each content is placed into.

2.2 Paraphrasing

Automatic text rewriting, or paraphrasing, is a broad set of tasks in natural language processing. There is a wide range of purposes for text rewriting, e.g. as a simplification preprocess for higher accuracy of various other tasks [13], or as an assistance for people with difficulty in reading [4]. In these tasks, it is necessary to learn paraphrasing rules, or to build a paraphrasing dictionary from a huge corpus. It is quite time-consuming and difficult to produce a resource with sufficient coverage by hand. Therefore, learning rules automatically from various corpora, such as the edit history of Wikipedia [14, 17], the joined resource of Wikipedia and Simple English Wikipedia[2] [18], and parallel corpora[3] [7], has been studied.

3. PROPOSED METHOD

3.1 Overview

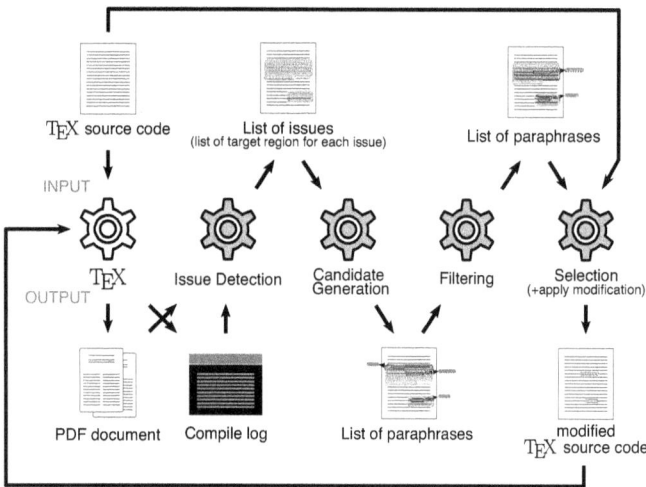

Figure 1: Schema model of our method.

In our method, the input document is processed through four steps: *Issue Detection*, *Candidate Generation*, *Filtering*, and *Selection*. These routines are applied to the document in sequence, repeatedly, until no more improvements can be made. As a prototype, we implemented a small program that applies our method to a TeX document. This system can detect two sample kinds of layout issues in the document, namely hyphenations and widows, and fix them using a simple paraphrasing technique.

[2]Simple English Wikipedia is a special edition of Wikipedia, whose articles are written in Basic English (simplified English). http://simple.wikipedia.org/
[3]A parallel corpus is a set of corpora of different languages, with the same content.

Figure 1 shows the overall workflow of this system. In this section, we present an overview of the proposed method, by showing the high-level overview of the algorithm used in this prototype system.

3.2 Issue Detection

In *Issue Detection*, the input document is scanned for the targeted layout issues. If any are found, then the modification $M(I_i)$ necessary for fixing each issue I_i is calculated. This is represented by two pieces of information: the position $P(I_i)$ where the issue appears in the document, and the amount of required movement $L(I_i)$. To be precise, the position is represented as a region which should be paraphrased in order to fix the issue. For example, assume a word is hyphenated at the end of line. In this case, we can avoid the problem in two ways. One is shortening the preceding phrases (or the hyphenated word itself) to move the starting position of the word backward. The other is lengthening the preceding phrases to move it forward. In either case, the required amount of modification can be calculated from the target word.

In our experimental system, we only target hyphenations and widows. These issues can be detected by extracting bounding box information from compiled PDF documents. In addition, `findhyph` tool, which is included in most TeX distributions, helps find hyphenations. If the detected issue is a hyphenation, it can be fixed by rewriting phrases between the beginning of the paragraph and the hyphenated word. Therefore the algorithm targets this area for paraphrasing. On the other hand, if a widow is found, rewriting any part before the widow may fix it. In our system, however, only the same page as the paragraph (see Figure 2) is searched, in order to reduce processing time.

3.3 Candidate Generation

For each detected issue I_i, the *Candidate Generation* module enumerates all the possible paraphrasing candidates $R = \{(str_j^{\text{before}}, str_j^{\text{after}})\}$ in the region $P(I_i)$ for each I_i. In our preliminary investigation, we used two naive yet practical methods that are based on simple string substitution: *dictionary-based* and *rule-based* methods.

In the dictionary-based method, 66,557 pairs were obtained from PPDB (Lexical), a paraphrase database constructed automatically from bilingual parallel corpora [7]. Since we only used *unigram* paraphrase (or synonym) pairs from this resource, we also built a set of paraphrasing

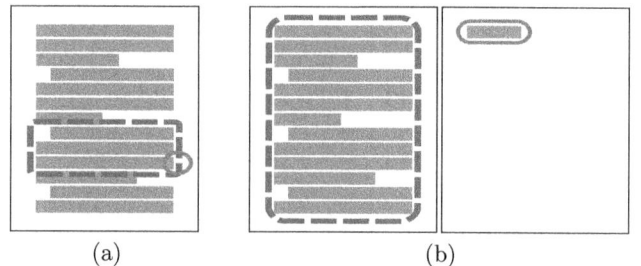

(a)   (b)

Figure 2: Pages with a layout issue detected. The target region for each issue is marked with a dashed rectangle. (a) Page with an end-of-line word break indicated by a red circle. (b) Pages with a widow detected at the top of the second page.

rules which includes several paraphrases for frequently used phrases (e.g. *in order to → to*). Our pattern database contains 142 paraphrase patterns that we obtained from the edit history of Wikipedia. We filtered only paraphrasing edits from the history, among information addition, correction, and spam removal, by using editors' comments (cf. [14, 17]) and the edit distance between revisions. This dataset is relatively small, but can be used for more complex paraphrasing than simply replacing a word with its synonym.

For simplicity, we ignore the possibility of fixing issues by lengthening and just consider shortening in this system. Although we used naive paraphrasing methods in this paper, we plan to incorporate more sophisticated paraphrasing techniques (cf. [2]) in our future implementation.

3.4 Filtering

The *Filtering* module filters out grammatically and semantically inappropriate candidates as much as possible. We implemented two filtering methods.

The first one is based on a 3-gram language model we constructed using Google Ngram Corpus [11], a large dataset of English word n-gram frequency counts obtained from publicly accessible Web pages. Using the language model, we can calculate the estimated probability that a given word sequence appears in real-world text; in other words, we can estimate how likely it is that the phrase is natural and grammatically correct. Based on this, we exclude candidate pairs when the probability of the surrounding text is significantly (more than 90%) decreased by the rewriting.

The second filtering method is based on a vector space model. In this study, we used word2vec [12] with the default configuration, and constructed a 200-dimensional space using the dataset attached to the library for learning. Word vectors are real-valued vectors that map the meaning of words into a continuous multi-dimensional vector space. If two words have similar meanings, then the corresponding word vectors are also likely to be close to each other. Based on this, we exclude candidate paraphrase pairs whose similarity score (cosine similarity) is lower than a pre-set threshold value 0.1.

3.5 Selection

One obvious method to ascertain whether the modification actually fixes the layout issues is to apply the modification to the source file and to compile it again, but this takes a long time. For simplicity, we just re-compile the modified source file after processing each adjacent region to cope with non-local effects in this study. The issue that occurs the first in the document is fixed regardless of its kind. If it is fixed, then the rest of issues are left for the next routine, because rearranging a certain part of the document causes following parts to change their layouts, which is prevented by processing from the beginning of the document to the end.

Given a set of possible rewritings R, the *Selection* module decides a subset of R that successfully resolves the target issue. Since the number of all possible combinations of rewriting candidates is exponential, we employ a greedy algorithm (regarding the size of space saved by adopting each rewriting). If the issue cannot be fixed by employing any of the candidates, the method simply ignores it.

Table 1: Summary of test documents. Documents #1–#8 are double-column layout. The content of documents was taken from Project Gutenberg (PG), English Wikipedia articles (EWP), and arXiv papers (AXV).

	Col.	Cont.	Pp.	Hyphenations		Widows	
1	D	PG	7	31 → 26	(+6, -11)	3 → 3	(+0, -0)
2	D	AXV	7	67 → 58	(+26, -35)	1 → 0	(+0, -1)
3	D	PG	8	47 → 45	(+10, -12)	3 → 1	(+0, -2)
4	D	AXV	9	97 → 92	(+47, -52)	2 → 1	(+1, -2)
5	D	EWP	11	201 → 151	(+56, -106)	0 → 0	(+0, -0)
6	D	EWP	11	194 → 174	(+50, -71)	2 → 1	(+0, -1)
7	D	EWP	11	144 → 120	(+25, -49)	3 → 1	(+1, -3)
8	D	PG	14	113 → 88	(+26, -51)	4 → 4	(+4, -4)
9	S	PG	7	14 → 11	(+4, -7)	2 → 0	(+0, -2)
10	S	EWP	7	19 → 17	(+7, -9)	1 → 1	(+0, -1)
11	S	AXV	8	16 → 10	(+7, -13)	1 → 0	(+0, -1)
12	S	PG	9	15 → 6	(+1, -10)	3 → 3	(+0, -0)
13	S	PG	10	11 → 11	(+0, -0)	3 → 0	(+0, -3)
14	S	AXV	10	22 → 18	(+11, -15)	1 → 0	(+0, -1)
15	S	EWP	11	39 → 26	(+4, -17)	5 → 1	(+0, -4)
16	S	EWP	12	49 → 36	(+20, -33)	3 → 0	(+0, -3)

4. EXPERIMENTAL RESULT

To evaluate our proposed method, we experimented with our prototype system on sample LaTeX documents we prepared ourselves. Unfortunately, most LaTeX source codes are not publicly available, or cannot be built in our environment for lack of dependencies. Also, scientific papers contain many domain-specific terms, which are not likely to be captured by our paraphrase generators. Because of these reasons, we prepared dummy scientific papers, which are 7–14 pages long, contain 3 or 4 figure floats, and are single- or double-column. These were built by first taking English texts from Project Gutenberg, Wikipedia and arXiv Bulk Data Access, and then inserting them into a LaTeX template that imitates a typical scientific paper. We applied our system to these documents, and counted how many layout issues were automatically resolved. In total, we prepared 16 test documents in total.

Table 1 summarizes the results. It shows the number of hyphenations and widows present in each test document before and after processing. Our system decreased the number of hyphenations in every test document. The number of widows is also decreased in some of the documents, and is at least not increased in any of them. Examples of paraphrases generated and used by the system are shown in Table 2.

Not all hyphenations were fixed, which is not only because of the imperfection of the paraphrase generators we used, but also because TeX sets a page flexibly, by stretching and shrinking blank spaces, which makes difficult to control positioning of items in a page [3]. We may overcome this problem by modeling how TeX works to calculate the effect of edits more accurately (cf. [15]). On the other hand, only a few widows were fixed. Our prototype system can only make simple adjustments, i.e. shortening the paragraph to make all lines fit within the same page. It is difficult, however, to shorten a document using only independent replacements by such an amount that a whole line fits into the page. When a human editor wants to fix a widow, he or she may try to lengthen the paragraph instead, so that more than one lines overflow to the next page and thus avoid the widow. Our system's poor handling of widows may be overcome by taking this approach.

Table 2: Examples of paraphrases used for processing a test document, which were generated by (1) the dictionary-based method and (2) the rule-based method.

	Before		After
(1)	accurate	→	exact
	provided an interaction	→	gave an interact
	simply by supplying	→	just by supplying
	significant increases	→	major increases
	book without conversations	→	book without talks
(2)	between 1964 to 1966	→	between '64 to '66
	second edition	→	2nd edition
	in the year 2007	→	in 2007
	never once	→	never
	in order to	→	to

5. DISCUSSION AND FUTURE WORK

In this paper, we presented a framework of paraphrase-based layout optimization. The experimental results show that borrowing techniques from natural language processing field is promising. Although we only dealt with two types of layout issues in this paper, it can be easily extended to other types, such as orphans, rivers, and rags, by implementing a detection algorithm for each kind of issue. This is the first step towards further advancement of paraphrase-based layout optimization.

In the examples shown in Table 2, most paraphrases are appropriate, but some are not; e.g. replacing *interaction* (noun) with *interact* (verb) makes the sentence ungrammatical. Against this problem, two ways of improvements can be made; one is improving paraphrasing technique, and the other is getting human help. First, we used only simple paraphrasing techniques in this study. As already mentioned, paraphrasing is a widely studied area in natural language processing field and is still being actively researched [5, 16]. Therefore the paraphrasing module is expected to be greatly improved by introducing more advanced techniques. Secondly, in order to apply our method in real-world applications, the decision-making on whether or not to adopt the suggested rewriting needs to be more careful. However, our prototype is not yet smart enough to consider e.g. the consistency of writing style and wording. Until these sophisticated decisions would be made possible, our method can be used as a writing assistance. In other words, the system just suggests rewriting candidates for each detected issue, and leaves to the the user to determine whether to adopt them or not. In this way, the system can suggest multiple ("n-best") choices, which decreases the risk of a non-grammatical choice.

6. ACKNOWLEDGMENTS

This work was supported by the Japan Society for the Promotion of Science KAKENHI Grant Number 26540121.

References

[1] *The Chicago manual of style*. The University of Chicago Press Chicago, 16th edition, 2010.

[2] I. Androutsopoulos and P. Malakasiotis. A survey of paraphrasing and textual entailment methods. *Journal of Artificial Intelligence Research*, 38(1), 2010.

[3] K. Bazargan and C. V. Radhakrishnan. Removing vertical stretch—mimicking traditional typesetting with TEX. *TUGboat*, 28(1), 2007.

[4] J. Carroll, G. Minnen, Y. Canning, S. Devlin, and J. Tait. Practical simplification of English newspaper text to assist aphasic readers. In *Proceedings of the AAAI Workshop on Integrating Artificial Intelligence and Assistive Technology*, 1998.

[5] M.-H. Chen, S.-T. Huang, J. Chang, and H.-C. Liou. Developing a corpus-based paraphrase tool to improve EFL learners' writing skills. *Computer Assisted Language Learning*, 28(1), 2015.

[6] G. Gange, K. Marriott, and P. Stuckey. Optimal guillotine layout. In *Proceedings of the 2012 ACM Symposium on Document Engineering*, 2012.

[7] J. Ganitkevitch, B. Van Durme, and C. Callison-Burch. PPDB: The paraphrase database. In *Proceedings of the 2013 Conference of the North American Chapter of the Association for Computational Linguistics: Human Language Technologies*, 2013.

[8] C. Jacobs, W. Li, and D. Salesin. Adaptive document layout via manifold content. In *Proceedings of the 2nd International Workshop on Web Document Analysis*, 2003.

[9] R. Johari, J. Marks, A. Partovi, and S. Shieber. Automatic yellow-pages pagination and layout. *Journal of Heuristics*, 2(4), 1997.

[10] D. E. Knuth and M. F. Plass. Breaking paragraphs into lines. *Software: Practice and Experience*, 11, 1981.

[11] Y. Lin, J.-B. Michel, E. L. Aiden, J. Orwant, W. Brockman, and S. Petrov. Syntactic annotations for the Google Books Ngram Corpus. In *Proceedings of the ACL 2012 System Demonstrations*, 2012.

[12] T. Mikolov, K. Chen, G. Corrado, and J. Dean. Efficient estimation of word representations in vector space. *Computing Research Repository*, abs/1301.3781, 2013.

[13] M. Miwa, R. Saetre, Y. Miyao, and J. Tsujii. Entity-focused sentence simplification for relation extraction. In *Proceedings of the 23rd International Conference on Computational Linguistics*, 2010.

[14] R. Nelken and E. Yamangil. Mining Wikipedia's article revision history for training computational linguistics algorithms. In *Proceedings of the AAAI Workshop on Wikipedia and Artificial Intelligence*, 2008.

[15] R. Piccoli and J. B. Oliveira. Balancing font sizes for flexibility in automated document layout. In *Proceedings of the 2013 ACM Symposium on Document Engineering*, 2013.

[16] W. Xu, C. Callison-Burch, and W. B. Dolan. SemEval-2015 task 1: Paraphrase and semantic similarity in Twitter (PIT). In *Proceedings of the 9th International Workshop on Semantic Evaluation*, 2015.

[17] M. Yatskar, B. Pang, C. Danescu-Niculescu-Mizil, and L. Lee. For the sake of simplicity: Unsupervised extraction of lexical simplifications from Wikipedia. In *Human Language Technologies: The 2010 Annual Conference of the North American Chapter of the Association for Computational Linguistics*, 2010.

[18] Z. Zhu, D. Bernhard, and I. Gurevych. A monolingual tree-based translation model for sentence simplification. In *Proceedings of the 23rd International Conference on Computational Linguistics*, 2010.

Knuth-Plass revisited: Flexible line-breaking for automatic document layout

Tamir Hassan[*]
HP Labs
Vienna, Austria
tamir.hassan@hp.com

Andrew Hunter
HP Labs
Bristol, United Kingdom
andrew.hunter@hp.com

ABSTRACT

There is an inherent flexibility in typesetting a block of text. Traditionally, line breaks would be manually chosen at strategic points in such a way as to minimize the amount of whitespace in each line. Hyphenation would only be used as a last resort. Knuth and Plass automated this optimization procedure, which has been used in various typesetting systems and DTP applications ever since. However, an optimal solution for the line-breaking problem does not necessarily lead us to an optimal document layout on the whole. The flexibility of choosing line breaks enables us, in many cases, to adjust the height of a paragraph by changing the number of lines, without having to make adjustments to font size, leading, etc. In many cases, the word spacing remains within the usual tolerances and visual quality does not noticeably suffer. This paper presents a modification to the Knuth-Plass algorithm to return several results for a given column of text, each corresponding to a different height, and describes steps to quantify the amount of expected flexibility in a given paragraph. We conclude with a discussion on how such "sub-optimal" results can lead to a better overall document layout, particularly in the context of mobile layouts, where flexibility is of key importance.

Categories and Subject Descriptors

I.7.4 [**Computing Methodologies**]: Document and Text Processing:Electronic Publishing

General Terms

Algorithms, Design

Keywords

typesetting, microtypography, automatic layout

---

[*]Parts of this work were carried out during Tamir Hassan's employment at the University of Konstanz and were supported by the EU FP7 Marie Curie Zukunftskolleg Incoming Fellowship Programme (grant no. 291784).

1. INTRODUCTION

Many readers of this paper are likely to be familiar with certain aspects of the Knuth-Plass line-breaking algorithm [3] or have at least encountered it, knowingly or unknowingly, in several situations. It is used to determine the line-breaks of text in the TeX typesetting system, which is commonly used to typeset scientific documents, such as this one. For example, the common `underfull \hbox` warning in TeX is due to the algorithm failing to find an adequate solution to the problem. More recently, a variant of this algorithm has been implemented in the commercial DTP package Adobe InDesign [2].

The algorithm was published in 1981, at a time when computing power was relatively limited and automatic typesetting systems traditionally set line breaks using a first-fit, or greedy approach. The aim of the algorithm was to improve the quality of digitally composed output to approach that of hand-typeset print. The `underfull \hbox` warning was designed to alert the operator in case the algorithm failed to find a solution of sufficient quality, prompting him/her to make manual edits in order to improve the result.

Over thirty years have passed since then, and we therefore need to look at the line-breaking problem from a different angle. First, in today's world of rapidly changing content on mobile devices with various screen sizes, we no longer have the luxury of manual edits to account for layout issues; the layout process must be fully automatic. Secondly, it can be argued that today's readers are less sensitive to microtypographic quality: this is probably due to the relatively poor quality of typesetting on the Web and the fact that most non-Web content that people encounter daily (e.g. Word documents, etc.) is no longer professionally designed.

We must accept that, if we expect fully automatic layout to work on a large variety of screen sizes, microtypography will suffer to some extent. What is of far more importance is the overall appearance of the document, and this can necessitate choosing a non-optimal set of line breaks in order to solve a macrotypographic problem, such as unbalanced columns, excessive whitespace or widows/orphans. In fact, particularly in mobile applications, it is often computationally infeasible to find the global optimum and, as stated by Hurst and Marriott [1], a "Layout Without Obvious Errors" (LWOE) is sufficient.

With this in mind, this paper investigates the problem of line-breaking with the aim of discovering how it can contribute to the flexibility of document layout. In many cases, the typographic parameters for a piece of content (i.e. typeface, font size, tracking, leading) are defined by the designer

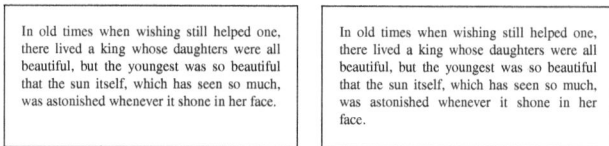

Figure 1: Two possibilities of laying out a paragraph: by breaking the lines accordingly, it is possible to lay out this paragraph in five or six lines.

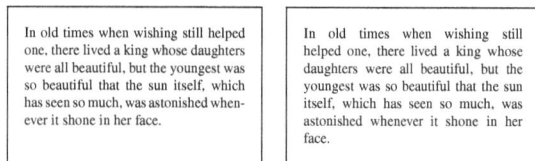

Figure 2: When reducing the column width, only one layout is possible (left). With the expansion threshold doubled to three times the space width, the layout on the right is also possible, but results in excessively wide spaces (particularly in the first line).

and cannot normally be changed. For the interword space, however, a range of widths is considered acceptable (justified text would not be possible otherwise), and this range is arguably larger today than in the print world of the early 1980s. For left-aligned text, the situation is very similar: this time the space width remains fixed, and the variable is the whitespace in the right margin.

With this flexibility, it is possible to typeset a longer paragraph to occupy different numbers of lines, and therefore a different height on the page. We have modified the Knuth-Plass algorithm to do this, and this modification is described in Section 2. Section 3 presents experiments that we have carried out in order to test and quantify the amount of flexibility that the modification gives us, and Section 4 concludes with a discussion and describes further work.

2. MODIFICATION FOR FLEXIBILITY

The Knuth-Plass algorithm uses a box, glue and penalty model to represent the objects within a paragraph of text. In principle, box objects represent characters, glue objects represent the spaces between each word and penalties represent additional, often less-than-ideal, breaking points within the line. Words are thus represented as a string of boxes; with hyphenation enabled, penalty objects are inserted at each potential hyphenation point or "soft hyphen" with the width of a hyphen and a positive penalty value. Lines can only be broken at penalty objects or at glue, provided that it immediately follows a box. Assuming justified text, the quality of each line is measured by the amount of stretching or shrinking applied to each space (glue object) to fill the width of the column and the corresponding penalty is added if the line has been broken at a penalty object.

The algorithm proceeds by first generating a list of all legal breakpoints according to the above definition and then going through these in turn, keeping track of the optimal solution from the beginning of the paragraph up to that point (these partial solutions are termed *feasible breakpoints* in the paper). Due to the principle of dynamic programming, some of these partial solutions are later used to form more complete solutions and, eventually, the complete solution; others get discounted as soon as it becomes evident that they will never lead to the optimal solution. The reader is referred to the paper for a full description of the algorithm.

We have modified the algorithm to store not only one solution, but several solutions for each feasible breakpoint, corresponding to the optimum for each different height, or number of lines (i.e. number of breakpoints − 1) that have been encountered beforehand. The height is simply incremented by 1 each time a partial solution is used to form a solution for a newly encountered legal breakpoint, to account for the new line that has been added.

In the above process, all feasible line breaks are considered that result in lines whose glue objects (spaces) are expanded or shrunk within given thresholds. These thresholds also help to constrain the runtime of the algorithm. The paper suggests thresholds of $\frac{1}{2}$ and $\frac{1}{3}$ of the nominal space width (usually $\frac{1}{3}$ em) respectively, based on typical typesetting rules of the time. If no solution exists within these thresholds, the algorithm returns no result and can either be rerun with a larger expansion threshold or the operator can be asked to intervene. In our case, we don't have the luxury of a human operator and, in order to maximize flexibility, we have found that raising the expansion threshold to three times the suggested value ($1\frac{1}{2}\times$ space width) still yields acceptable looking paragraphs at its limits. This value also corresponds to the default maximum threshold used in Bram Stein's JavaScript implementation of the algorithm[1].

An example of a paragraph typeset in two different heights by the modified algorithm is shown in Figure 1. A further example of a solution where the word spacing exceeds this threshold is shown in Figure 2.

3. EXPERIMENTS

In order to quantify the effectiveness of our modification, we ran experiments on several royalty-free texts downloaded from Project Gutenberg (see Table 1). All texts were in the English language.

Our first goal was to obtain an approximate measure for the amount of flexibility and see whether it varies according to the width of the text column. We carried out this experiment on *Fairy Tales* by the Brothers Grimm, which contained 811 paragraphs of text, translated from the original German. The HyFo Java library[2] with English patterns was used for hyphenation.

The text was set in 18 pt Times Roman using the metrics as defined for the PDF Base 14 Fonts[3] and the column width was varied from 180 pt to 1152 pt, i.e. 10–64 times the font size, in 18 pt increments, thus encompassing both extremes. (Below the limit of 180 pt, it was not possible to typeset all paragraphs in the text within the chosen thresholds).

For each paragraph we recorded the number of results, the largest result (i.e. largest number of lines) and the smallest result. The flexibility (in per cent) was calculated as:

$$\frac{\text{largest number of lines} - \text{smallest number of lines}}{\text{smallest number of lines}}$$

---

[1] TEX line breaking algorithm in JavaScript,
http://www.bramstein.com/projects/typeset/
[2] HyFo Java library, http://sourceforge.net/projects/hyfo/
[3] These are the standard PDF fonts, and their metrics are available at http://www.adobe.com/devnet/font.html

Author	Paragraphs				Average flexibility (10-64)		Average flexibility (16-32)	
	All	Short (<300 chars)	Medium (301-750 chars)	Long (>750 chars)	With hyphenation	Without hyphenation	With hyphenation	Without hyphenation
Grimm	811	261	292	258	12.36%	11.86%	10.63%	9.87%
Dickens	3260	2429	674	157	8.32%	7.83%	7.09%	6.25%
Twain	1859	1494	251	114	7.34%	7.02%	6.77%	6.25%

Table 1: Summary of results

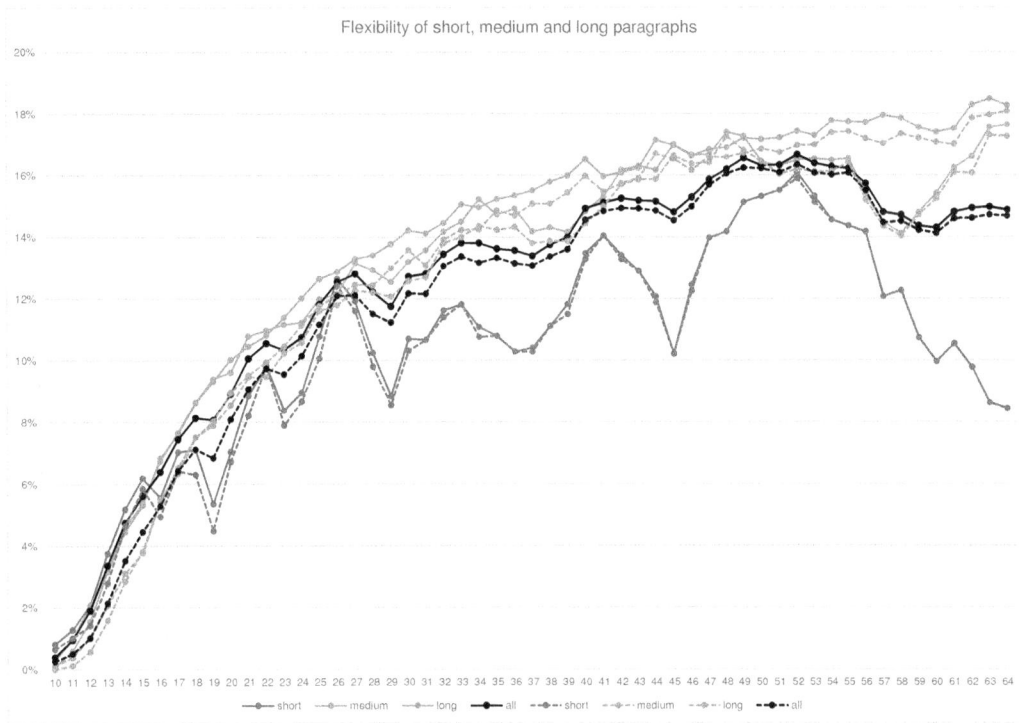

Figure 3: Graph of flexibility vs relative paragraph width for short, medium, long and all paragraphs in the Grimm text. Solid lines are with hyphenation; dashed lines without.

The results were averaged across all the paragraphs in the text and the process was then repeated for each of the column widths. In order to ensure that only paragraphs of content from the original book's text were counted, the downloaded HTML was cleaned up to remove supplementary information such as the table of contents and copyright notices, and all headings were verified to have been included in `<h1>`, `<h2>`, ... tags, and not `<p>` tags, so that they would not distort the result.

The results of this initial experiment are shown in Figure 3 (solid black line). The graph shows a sharp increase in flexibility at the start, with the narrowest paragraphs having almost no flexibility at all. It then begins to level off at around 30 times the font size, which in real-life terms is already a very wide paragraph. Towards the wider end of the scale, the flexibility drops slightly, although such paragraphs are much too wide to be used in practice.

Initially, we found this result counter-intuitive, given that text is often modelled as an area in automatic document layout. By that logic, a paragraph whose length can be increased by one line at a given width would have two lines of flexibility at half the width, and the rest of the paragraph would also be twice as tall. Thus, the flexibility according to the above formula would remain the same.

However, on further inspection of the results, we realized that for narrow columns it is often much more difficult for the algorithm to find a solution within the given thresholds at all, and the results often contain both lines that have been stretched significantly, as well as lines that have been shrunk close to the thresholds. For example, in Figure 2, line 5 in the left example and line 4 in the right example are tightly set, whereas several of the other lines already have very wide inter-word spaces. In such a case, it would not be possible to expand or shrink the paragraph further without causing at least one line to exceed the expansion threshold, and therefore the flexibility of such paragraphs is low.

The aim of our second experiment was to investigate the effect of paragraph length and hyphenation on flexibility. To this end, we categorized each of the 811 paragraphs of the Grimm text into three bins of approximately equal size, based on their length: short, medium and long. Table 1 shows the number of paragraphs in each category and the category definitions. As hyphenation enables inter-word line-breaks, we felt that counting the number of characters instead of words would provide a better indication of paragraph length for our purposes. We then repeated the previous experiment for each individual category and averaged the results over all the paragraphs in each run. All tests were then repeated without hyphenation.

The results are shown in Figure 3: the coloured lines represent each paragraph category; solid lines are with hyphenation and dashed lines without. Here, we can see that longer paragraphs intuitively have a smoother curve and higher flexibility, owing to the troughs in the curve not being present. Disabling hyphenation leads to a slight decrease in flexibility. All results increase steadily up to a paragraph width of around 25× font size; the drop towards the wider end of the scale is most evident in the short category and hardly visible in the long category. A probable reason for this drop is due to the column being so wide that most paragraphs, particularly in the short category, are shorter than a single line of text, and therefore have no flexibility at all.

Finally, we reran the first experiment on two other texts, *A Tale of Two Cities* by Charles Dickens and *The Adventures of Tom Sawyer* by Mark Twain. These texts were significantly longer than the Grimm short stories and resulted in a lower flexibility (around 8% compared to 12.36% for Grimm) on average. The curves are shown in Figure 4. We did, however, notice that the distribution of paragraph lengths was significantly different: whereas the Grimm fairy tales were told in narrative form, the texts of Dickens and Twain featured much dialogue, and it is common practice in English texts to start a new paragraph whenever a person speaks. Figure 5 illustrates the distribution of paragraph lengths in each text.

Finally, we calculated the average flexibility for each text across the entire width range, and across a reduced width range (16×–32× font size), which more realistically represents the column widths found in print today. The results are summarized in Table 1.

4. CONCLUSION AND FURTHER WORK

If we ignore the extremes of the range and consider only the useful column widths, we arrive at a figure of approximately 10% for the Grimm narrative text and approximately 7% for the other two texts, which contain a large number of short paragraphs. This is not an insignificant amount, even though features such as resizable images or headlines, if incorporated into the document, can provide vastly more layout flexibility in terms of area occupied on the page.

It is, however, worth noting that such layouts often have a complex chain of dependencies that must be fulfilled. For example, in a multi-column document, it may not be possible to balance the columns due to an uneven number of lines in the text, or because the column breaks would cause widows or orphans. The added flexibility enables us to shift these breaks to avoid such problems, and initial experiments on multi-column text have shown promising results.

Such dependencies do not only apply to text. For example, in cases where it is not permissible to crop an image, the height is determined by the width, and the number of possible widths is equal to the number of columns on the page. In such a case, the added flexibility in the text can help to "fill in" the discontinuities in the range of layout possibilities.

One thing that we have noticed is that, in cases where a paragraph has been "stretched" to occupy more than its nominal height, the last line always contains a single word,

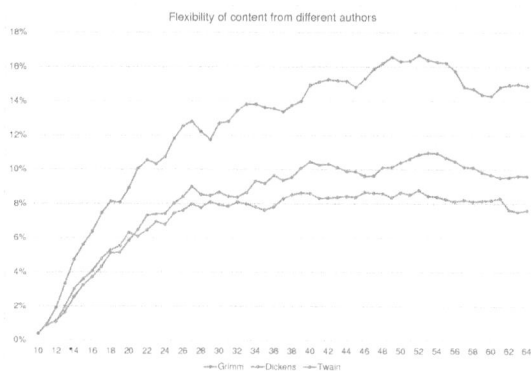

Figure 4: Comparison of the flexibility profiles of texts from three different authors.

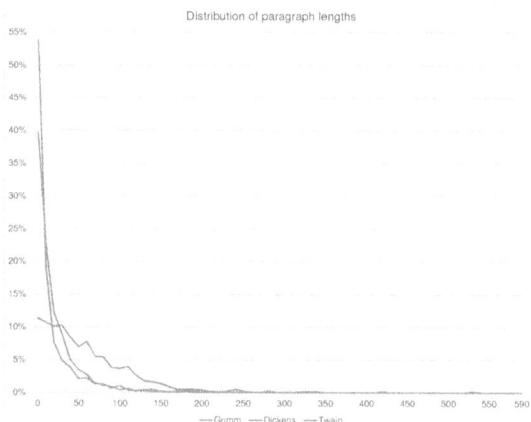

Figure 5: Distribution of paragraph lengths (in characters) in each of the three texts.

due to the algorithm always choosing a solution that minimizes the additional spacing between each word. Similarly, the final line of a paragraph that has been "shrunk" always (almost) runs right up to the right margin. In extreme cases, e.g. where an entire column of text has been stretched, this effect can become noticeable. A possible improvement to the algorithm would be, in such cases, to randomly choose "sub-optimal" solutions with an even higher stretch or shrink factor, to restore the natural variation in the lengths of these lines.

To conclude, we find that ability to vary the height occupied by a block of text is a promising tool for automatic document layout and future work will aim at investigating and quantifying its benefit in the context of an end-to-end automatic document composition and layout system.

5. REFERENCES

[1] N. Hurst and K. Marriott. Satisficing scrolls: A shortcut to satisfactory layout. In *Proceedings of the 8th ACM Symposium on Document Engineering*, pages 131–140, 2008.

[2] E. Kenninga. Optimal line break determination, Jan. 21 2003. US Patent 6,510,441.

[3] D. E. Knuth and M. F. Plass. Breaking paragraphs into lines. *Software — Practice and Experience*, 11(11):1119–1184, 1981.

Hiding Information in Multiple Level-line Moirés

Thomas Walger   Roger David Hersch

École Polytechnique Fédérale de Lausanne (EPFL), Switzerland

{thomas.walger, rd.hersch}@epfl.ch

ABSTRACT

Secure documents often comprise an information layer that is hard to reproduce. Moiré techniques for the prevention of counterfeiting rely on the superposition of an array of transparent lines or microlenses on top of a base layer containing hidden information. Level-line moirés consist of shapes that appear to be beating upon relative translation of a revealing grating on top of a base, in which the desired information is encoded. Usually, the base only contains the information corresponding to one moiré. In order to increase the difficulty of counterfeiting, we use tessellations to incorporate two or more moirés within the same layer. With the method we propose, the information corresponding to up to seven level-line moirés can be embedded within a single base layer. The moirés are recovered with a revealer printed on a transparency or with an array of cylindrical lenses. This method is general and can be extended to other fabrication technologies.

Keywords

Security printing; moiré; tessellation; tiling; level-line moiré

1. INTRODUCTION

The superimposition of gratings often yields astonishing visual effects. Some of these phenomena can easily be observed in the daily life. Moiré fringes can appear when two railings are seen one behind the other, on some translucent curtains or when you photograph a digital screen. In general, moiré effects are undesired when scanning, printing or photographing. However, moiré can also be deliberately used by artists [6] or scientists [1], [4], [5], [7] in order to create surprising effects. In the field of document security, moirés are advantageous since macroscopic effects are produced by superposing layers of microscopic structures. When generated at very high resolutions, these microstructures cannot be easily reproduced. Level-line moirés rely on a theorem from the moiré theory that states that when locally shifting a grating of lines in proportion to an elevation profile and

DocEng'15, September 8-11, 2015, Lausanne, Switzerland.
ⓒ 2015 ACM. ISBN 978-1-4503-3307-8/15/09 ...$15.00.
DOI: http://dx.doi.org/10.1145/2682571.2797078.

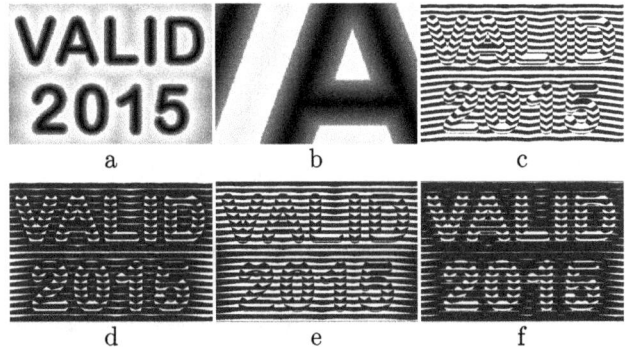

Figure 1: (a) Elevation profile. (b) Enlarged portion of the elevation profile. (c) Base grating. (d), (e) and (f) Level-line moiré obtained for three different translations of the revealer (resp. 0, 20 and 35 pixels upwards). The revealer has a period of 40 pixels and an aperture of 20 pixels.

superposing it with the unshifted grating, the moiré that appears is formed by the level lines of the input elevation profile [2]. Level-line moirés result in shapes that appear to be beating upon displacement of the revealer (see Figure 1). Beginning with two similar gratings, we apply local shifts to one of them (the base) according to the intensity levels of a greyscale image, which we call the elevation profile. The moiré obtained when superposing the two gratings shows level lines of the elevation profile. These level lines follow the gradient of the elevation profile when we translate the revealer. In the context of document security, our goal is to embed several layers of level-line moiré information within a single base. By tessellating the plane with hexagons and thus creating a mask for each layer of information, we can incorporate multiple level-line moirés within one base (see Figure 8). Each moiré appears when a specific revealer is superposed onto the base. The corresponding level lines move when displacing the revealer in its direction of periodicity. We try to maximise the visibility of the level-line moirés while embedding as many moiré information layers as possible. We will therefore express the trade-offs associated with the size of the tiling hexagons, the grating period and the size of the moiré-shape features.

2. MULTIPLE LEVEL-LINE MOIRÉS

To obtain a moiré, a base and a revealer have to be superposed. If several moirés must be obtained, we still have to superpose base and revealer but this time, we must prevent the revealer from exposing the information contained in the other moirés.

For this purpose, as proposed in [2], we superpose bases that have been designed to be revealed by revealers that do not interfere. In this way, each revealer reveals its own moiré. As an example, if we want to embed three level-line moirés in a single base layer, and reveal them by rectilinear gratings, we can create the three single-moiré bases with gratings at angles of 0° (similar to Figure 1c), 60° and 120° and multiply them together. In the example illustrated in Figure 2, we have designed level-line moirés that are revealed by one grating of a specific period at three different rotation angles (one for each moiré). Instead of using rotated instances of the same grating, we could also work with several periods, orientations and geometric transformations of the gratings. Once one of the revealers is superposed on the resulting base, the corresponding moiré appears. However, since the overall base is a superposition of the three single-moiré bases, it becomes darker when increasing the number of embeddings.

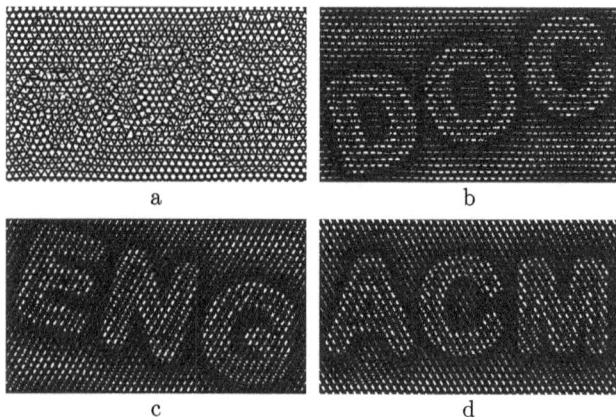

Figure 2: (a) Overall base obtained by superposing the three single-moiré bases in a single image. (b), (c) and (d) Level-line moirés obtained when superposing the revealer formed of line gratings at respectively 0°, 60° and 120°.

As an alternative method, one may tile the space and dedicate a portion of the tiles to each moiré layer. Consequently, the intensity of the base remains unchanged and the hidden information is no longer spread on the whole base but only on certain portions of it. Due to the sparsity of the base, the information cannot be decoded with the naked eye.

The method proposed in this paper therefore relies on tessellating the base in a regular manner. Each tile is filled with the corresponding area from one of the single-moiré bases. With this alternative method, a few challenges have to be met. In order to obtain the desired number of well-visible level-line moirés, one needs to select an appropriate tessellation of the space along with well-thought orientations and periods of the revealing layer.

3. TESSELLATION OF THE SPACE

Many types of tessellations exist. Since we would like all the hidden moirés to be treated similarly, we limit ourselves to regular tilings. The choice has to be made between the only three regular tilings, which are the triangular, the square and the hexagonal tilings [3, Section 1.3]. In order not to favour specific line orientations, we should use tiles that are as close as possible to disks. This is why we decided to use a regular hexagonal tiling. Once the hexagonal tiling is created, we need to assign the hexagons to their moiré and therefore obtain the corresponding tessellation. The tessellations for 3, 5, 7 and 9 embeddings can be seen in Figure 3. For 4, 6, 8 and any other number of embeddings, the tessellations can be created in the same manner. A specific hexagon colour is assigned to each single-moiré base. Once the tessellation is created with hexagons of the desired size, each set of coloured hexagons is used as a mask. The masked areas are filled with the corresponding parts of the associated single-moiré base. Even though in some tessellations the layout of the hexagons is not exactly the same for all the embeddings (e.g. in the case of five embeddings), their distribution is nonetheless close to uniform.

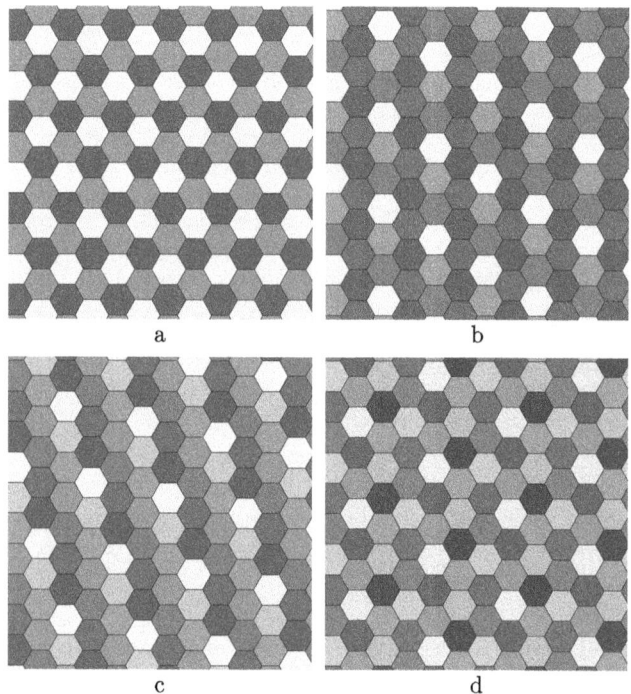

Figure 3: Tessellations for (a) 3, (b) 5, (c) 7 and (d) 9 embeddings.

4. TRADE-OFFS: GENERAL CONSIDERATIONS

Going from one to n level-line moirés in a single base has an effect on the visibility of the moirés. Only $1/n$ of the surface can be assigned to each level-line moiré. While one moiré is revealed on a fraction of the space, the other areas do not show any useful information and, to some extent, mask the revealed moiré. Moreover, the sparsity of the revealed tiles also decreases the visibility of the moiré messages since the sampling by the hexagons can be of rather low frequency compared to the typical sizes of the moiré-shape features. In order to embed as many level-line moirés as possible and to maximise their visibility, trade-offs must be found with respect to the size of the hexagons, the revealing period and the size of the smallest moiré-shape feature.

5. DIMENSIONS OF THE HEXAGONS AND OF THE LINE GRATINGS

The revealing period is directly constrained by the fabrication or the printing technology. Concerning the tiles, we would like to have them small enough to provide a high enough sampling of each moiré (see Figure 4). In order to render the moiré properly, the distance between two tiles sampling the same elevation profile must be shorter than a quarter of the size of the moiré's smallest feature (see Figure 5).

Figure 4: Level-line moirés embedding 3 hidden messages created with hexagons of side-length equal to (a) 12 , (b) 20 and (c) 26 pixels and with a line-grating period of (a) 20, (b) 33 and (c) 43 pixels at 1200dpi. In these images, the left part represents the base alone, the central part represents the superposition of the base and the revealer and the right part represents the revealer alone. The visibility of the moiré decreases as the sampling becomes coarser.

If the tiles are farther from each other, it may still be possible to visually decipher the message. However, parts of the information present in the elevation profile may be lost. Since the distance between two tiles encoding the same elevation profile depends on the number of embeddings (see Figure 3) and on the size of the tiles, these two parameters must be selected in a combined manner. As we increase the number of embeddings, the distance between the hexagons sampling one of the moirés also increases. If we keep the same hexagonal tiles, the limit of a quarter of the size of the moiré's smallest feature can be exceeded. For example, in Figure 6c, it is not possible to correctly embed the 7 different level-line moirés with the chosen tile size. The hexagons are too far apart and we cannot perceive the moiré.

To embed more elevation profiles, the tiles must be of smaller size. In addition, each hexagonal tile needs to cover the line shift that is proportional to the local value of the elevation profile. For a given revealing period, reducing the size of the hexagons decreases the number of periods that can be seen in a tile. Hexagons must contain at least one revealing period and should be as small as possible. As a general rule, the length of the sides of the hexagons should be at

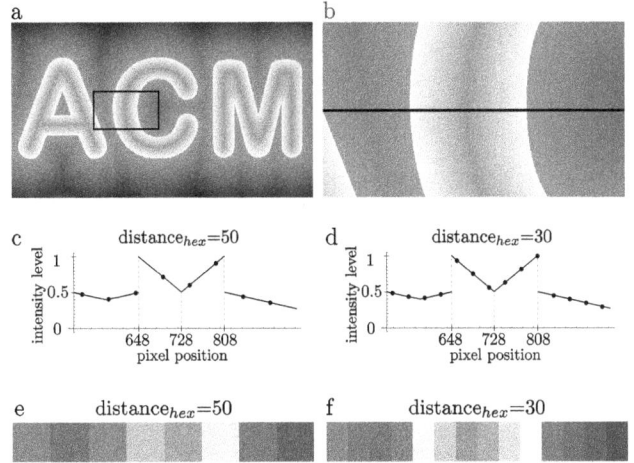

Figure 5: (a) One of the elevation profiles used to create the moiré of Figure 2. (b) Enlargement of the part of (a) with the horizontal line representing the pixels shown in the plots of (c) and (d). (c), (d) Plot representing the elevation profile of the cross-section shown as a line in (b) and the positions where the hexagons sample it, represented by dots, for a distance between hexagons sampling the same moiré equal to 50 pixels, respectively 30 pixels. (e), (f) Resulting sampled elevation-profile values.

least equal to half of the revealing period. This way, one period of the base layer grating will always fit in the hexagons, independently of the orientation. Nevertheless, it is not necessary to always consider the smallest tile dimension. If the moiré's features are large enough, we can also use larger tiles and include more than one period per hexagon. This will lead to a slightly different texture. Similarly, in some applications one may use larger revealing periods in order to obtain a slower displacement of the level lines when moving the revealer. Indeed, the whole cycle of displacement of the level lines is achieved upon translation of the revealer by one period.

6. CONCLUSION

The method that we propose in order to embed more than two level-line moirés within a single base-layer is both effective and efficient. The hidden messages cannot be visually deciphered from the base alone and there are some ways to make it also really hard or even impossible to decipher them by a computer, for example by using revealers that are more sophisticated than simple rectilinear gratings. Another advantage of this method compared to the regular single level-line moiré is that we can use the multiple-moiré embedded bases that we create as dither matrices for halftoning. We can then produce greyscale images incorporating several hidden messages that have the shape of level-line moirés without giving any information about the presence of hidden messages within the apparently random structure of the base (see Figure 7). The described features are independent of the technology. With the current print-based technology, we can easily hide 7 layers and have clearly visible level-line moirés. In the future, higher printing resolution and accuracy may allow hiding even more layers of information.

Figure 6: Level-line moirés obtained with hexagons of side-length equal to 16 pixels and with a line-grating period of 20 pixels at 1200dpi. They embed (a) 3, (b) 5 and (c) 7 hidden messages. In these images, the left part represents the base alone, the central part represents the superposition of the base and the revealer and the right part represents the revealer alone. The feature size to be revealed, e.g. the bar of the M, is of 165 pixels. Therefore, the distance between two tiles sampling the same elevation profile must be smaller than 41 pixels. In these examples, this distance is equal to (a) 16, (b) 28 and (c) 42 pixels. This explains why the moiré is clearly visible in (a) and (b) and only barely visible in (c).

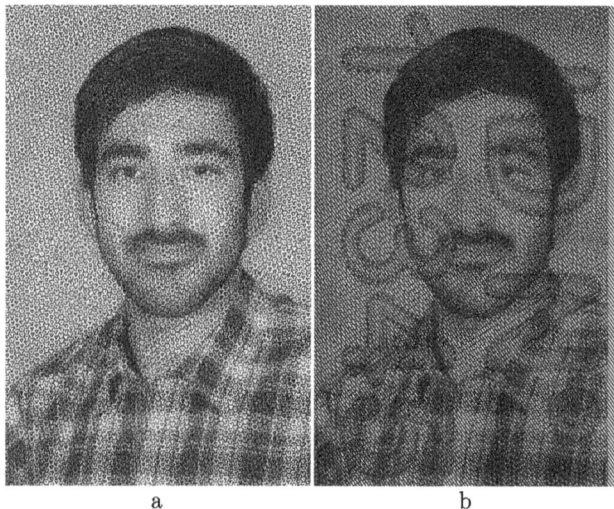

a   b

Figure 7: (a) Image that has been halftoned to incorporate the desired texture that generates the three level-line moirés when a rectilinear revealer of period 16 pixels at 1200dpi is superposed on top of it. (b) The level-line moiré revealed with the revealer at 126°. The other hidden moirés can be revealed by orienting the revealer from Figure 8a at 6° and 66°.

Figure 8: Level-line moirés obtained with hexagons of side-length equal to 12 pixels and with a line-grating period of 16 pixels at 1200dpi. To visualize the moirés, you can print this page on a paper sheet and on a transparency and superpose the revealer (a) that is printed on the transparency and the base (b) that is printed on the paper sheet. You should then be able to see the moirés if you orient the revealer at (c) 36°, (d) 81°, (e) 126° and (f) 171°. Once the moiré appears, you can translate the revealer in its direction of periodicity in order to see the dynamic beating effect. The images should be printed at 1200dpi to obtain the best results.

7. REFERENCES

[1] I. Amidror. *The theory of the moiré phenomenon.* Springer, 2000.

[2] S. M. Chosson and R. D. Hersch. Beating shapes relying on moiré level lines. *ACM Trans. Graph.,* 34(1):9:1–9:11, Dec. 2014.

[3] B. Gruenbaum and G. Shephard. *Tilings and patterns: an introduction.* New York: Freeman, 1989.

[4] R. D. Hersch and S. M. Chosson. Band Moiré Images. *ACM Trans. Graph.,* 23(3):239–247, Aug. 2004.

[5] G. Lebanon and A. M. Bruckstein. Variational approach to moiré pattern synthesis. *J. Opt. Soc. Am. A,* 18(6):1371–1382, Jun 2001.

[6] G. Oster. Optical art. *Appl. Opt.,* 4(11):1359–1369, Nov. 1965.

[7] P.-H. Tsai and Y.-Y. Chuang. Target-driven moire pattern synthesis by phase modulation. ICCV '13, pages 1912–1919, 2013.

TEXUS: A Task-based Approach for Table Extraction and Understanding

Roya Rastan
School of CSE
University of New South Wales
Sydney, Australia
rrastan@cse.unsw.edu.au

Hye-Young Paik
School of CSE
University of New South Wales
Sydney, Australia
hpaik@cse.unsw.edu.au

John Shepherd
School of CSE
University of New South Wales
Sydney, Australia
jas@cse.unsw.edu.au

ABSTRACT

In this paper, we propose a precise, comprehensive model of table processing which aims to remedy some of the problems in the discussion of table processing in the literature. The model targets application-independent, end-to-end table processing, and thus encompasses a large subset of the work in the area. The model can be used to aid the design of table processing systems (We provide an example of such a system), can be considered as a reference framework for evaluating the performance of table processing systems, and can assist in clarifying terminological differences in the table processing literature.

Keywords

Table Extraction, Table Understanding, Task-based Approach, End-to-End Table Processing

1. INTRODUCTION

Tables are a widely-used structure for data presentation and summarisation in documents from many different domains. Tables use layout to arrange information and convey meaning, and are capable of presenting and communicating complex information to human readers. Human readers, in turn, are capable of using layout features as clues for interpreting the logical meaning of the information in tables. Because tables are a rich and widely-available source of inter-related data, it would be useful if their contents could be automatically extracted and manipulated by computers. However, the diversity of layouts and variety of encodings (e.g. HTML, PDF, plain text) of tabular information makes extraction and understanding a challenging problem.

Various research communities, such as machine learning and information retrieval, have worked on the problem of table processing and many approaches have been proposed. However, existing approaches almost always tackle only a subset of the problem (e.g. tables in a specific domain or with particular layout), or focus on sub-tasks of the complete table processing problem (e.g. locating tables). Importantly, most systems are designed as monolithic black-boxes, which makes it difficult to investigate their structure and performance, or to re-use/replace components to advance the state of the art.

There has been some work towards building a coherent, systematic view of the table processing problem. Hurst [12] provided multiple table models, to define tables from different abstraction levels. Silva [5] defined end-to-end table processing as a set of tasks, thus reducing the monolithic, black-box view of the problem. Long [20] proposed an agent-based architecture in which table processing systems are implemented by composing different agents, showing that reusability is relevant to table processing. Taken together, these works almost provide a complete framework for discussion of table processing. However, they were developed independently and do not dovetail well enough nor provide sufficient detail to support the development and evaluation of full end-to-end table processing systems.

In this paper, we propose a task-based approach to table processing (called TEXUS) and provide detailed data and task models that encompass the essential aspects of the above work, and extends it to the point where it *can* be used as a basis for implementation and evaluation of complete end-to-end table processing systems. We make the following contributions: (1) we define table-processing as a set of well-defined tasks with an aim to build a system that produces application-independent table descriptions. (2) we define precise data models to provide standard task interfaces. (3) we show how the models can be used in implementing an end-to-end table processing system.

2. RELATED WORK

In this section, we discuss previous work on table processing techniques and systems, and summarise how we make use of it in developing our models and systems. Before considering the work of others, we need to define precisely what we mean by "end-to-end table processing" (i.e. what are the end points). The starting point for our work is documents in PDF format. We can do this without loss of generality, since PDFs make up a large proportion of the documents we typically encounter, and all other major document formats (e.g. ASCII text, HTML) can be readily converted to PDF. The ending point is an application-independent representation of the table, which could be used for further tasks such as information extraction. The representation we choose is based on Wang's notation [30].

DocEng'15, September 8–11, 2015, Lausanne, Switzerland.
© 2015 ACM. ISBN 978-1-4503-3307-8/15/09 ...$15.00.
http://dx.doi.org/10.1145/2682571.2797069 .

There have been a number of surveys on table processing, although each survey has dealt with just some aspects of the problem. Zanibbi et al. [33] reported on table models, observations and transformations in the table processing literature. Lopresti et al. [22] focused on the definition of "tabularity" and tabular browsing. Embley et al. [6] explored table transformations in semi-automated table processing systems.

We focus on just the work that has attempted to deal with the design and development of an end-to-end table processing solution. The pioneering work in end-to-end table processing is Hurst's PhD thesis [12] which gives a general table model with different abstraction levels (Physical, Functional, Structural, Semantic) to facilitate the interpretation of tables. Although Hurst provided a comprehensive table model, his focus is on the model rather than on the details of the process of table extraction and understanding. Additionally, his discussion of process deals only with determining the internal structure of an identified table, and not with locating the table in the document. Silva [5, 2] was the first to identify the tasks involved in end-to-end table processing. She proposed a design for table processing as a sequence of steps, with feedback loops between the steps to reduce the possibility of errors. Silva's work is important in identifying a set of basic tasks for table processing. However, no formal definition of these tasks and their inputs/outputs was given and only some components of the proposed design were implemented.

As noted above, our end goal for table processing is based on the abstract table model defined by Wang in her PhD thesis [30]. While the thesis focuses on table composition problems, it also provides a table abstraction model which neatly separates a table's logical structure from its layout structure and has been widely cited in the literature [12, 14, 29, 26]. Wang formally defined the notion of an abstract table to describe the logical relationships among table items, and proposed a set of logical operations to manipulate tables based on these logical relationships. Because the model describes tables in a layout-independent way, it has been used as an intermediate model for many table processing systems which aim towards information extraction, such as [14]. While Wang's model is popular, it is still a challenge to develop systems which can automatically derive a Wang-representation from a table in a document.

Long [20] was the first to implement a table processing architecture that encourages collaboration and component re-use. Long defined a multi-agent blackboard architecture, along with guidelines for table boundary identification and table interpretation. Individual agents tackle different partial solutions like processing input characters and processing input lines. Although the system design is sound, and suggests that components from other table processing systems might be incorporated, it is not specified how to achieve this, and the issue of conflict resolution over heterogeneous agents is noted as an open problem.

Our goal is to integrate aspects of the above related work to produce a framework for end-to-end table processing which: (a) identifies the sub-tasks involved (as in [2]), (b) gives precisely defined models to describe the input and output of each sub-task (as in [12]), and (c) packages this as a collection of modules (as in [20]), with well-defined interfaces, to provide a "workbench" for developing tools and techniques

to further the state-of-the-art in table processing. The input of a system built using this framework is a PDF document and the output is a set of abstract table models (as in [30]) describing each of the identified tables in the document. Our original contribution is the integration of these ideas, the development of the models for each sub-task, and extensions to some of the methods/models outlined above.

3. TASK-BASED TABLE PROCESSING

As just described, we view end-to-end table processing as a coherent sequence of tasks that takes a document as input and produces an abstract representation of the tables in the document as the final output.

We define a series of data models to describe the inputs and outputs of the tasks. The input PDF document is initially partitioned into a sequence of *text chunks*, and these form the atomic elements of further processing. The final output of the table processing is represented by an extension of Wang's *abstract table model* [30]).

Our core table processing tasks are as follows: (1) *Document Converting*: convert the PDF input document to our proposed document model, (2) *Locating*: find the tables in the document (their outer boundaries), (3) *Segmenting*: recognise the inner boundaries of each table (cells, rows and columns), (4) *Functional Analysis*: identify the role of each cell in each table (data or access), and (5) *Structural Analysis*: detect the logical relationships between table cells and provide the result as an abstract table. The last four tasks correspond to the first four tasks in Silva [2]. We omit Silva's fifth task (Interpretation), since it is inherently application-dependent, and our end-point is intended to be application agnostic. The tasks would typically be connected in a simple pipeline, but more complex controls such as looping and nested composition can also be considered (although not in this paper). Figure 1 shows a pipeline of these tasks implementing an end-to-end table processing system.

In order to discuss table structures, we use Wang's table terminology [30]. According to Wang, tables are divided into four main regions, delineated by means of a *stub separator* and a *boxhead separator* which are frequently, but not always, shown as physical lines. The lower-right region of the table (the *body*) contains the data. The upper-right region (the *boxhead*) contains column headings and sub-headings. The lower-left region (the *stub*) contains labels which provide access to the data rows. The upper-left region (*stubhead*) contains the headings for the columns in the stub. Figure 2 shows an example table with these regions marked.

Recall that the output of our system is a set of abstract table instances, one for each located table. Wang [30] defines an *abstract table* by an ordered pair (C, δ) where C is a finite set of labelled domains and δ is a mapping from C to the universe of possible data values. The categories appear in the table as headings. The δ mapping relates the categories to the data values in the table body.

We illustrate the various concepts in Wang's notation via the example table in Figure 2. This table has two dimensions and therefore, two top-level categories. The first category is Faculty Cluster, with five subcategories (Sciences, Social Sciences, ... Total). Female Students is the next category with Sample and Population as its subcategories. The following gives examples of the kind of abstract table output obtained by processing this table:

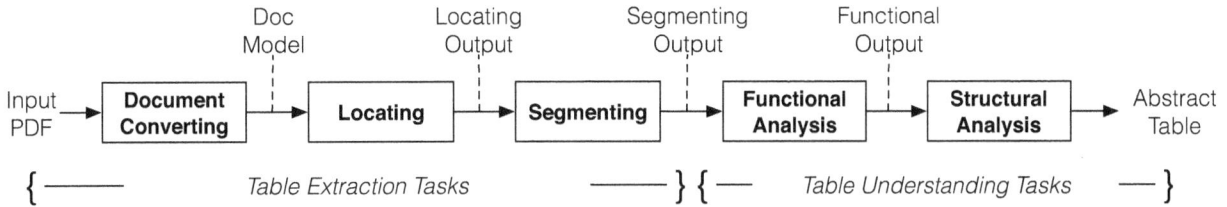

Figure 1: Task-based End-to-end Table Processing Pipeline

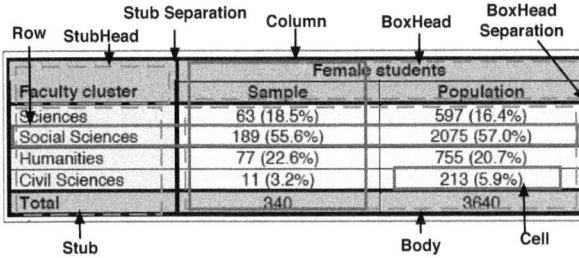

Figure 2: Wang Table Terminology

Category set (hierarchy):
C = { $(Faculty\ cluster, \{(Sciences, \Phi), (Social\ Sciences, \Phi),$
$(Humanities, \Phi), (Civil\ Sciences, \Phi), (Total, \Phi)\}),$
$(Female\ students, \{(Sample, \Phi), (Population, \Phi)\})$ }

Two examples from the δ mapping:
$\delta(Faculty\ cluster.Sciences, Female\ students.Sample) =$
"63 (18.5)%"
$\delta(Faculty\ cluster.Sciences, Female\ students.Population) =$
"597 (16.4)%"

Note that tables typically appear in documents adorned by a title, caption, notes etc. These are not considered as part of the table, and hence do not appear in the abstract table model, but are included in the final output as *table metadata*.

Our goal is to describe end-to-end table processing via a task-based approach where the inputs and outputs of each task are precisely defined. We believe that this approach provides the following benefits: (1) a well-defined decompostion of the task into generally agreed components (2) a consistent vocabulary for describing system scope and goals, (3) reusablity and repeatability in system design and development (4) the opportunity for interoperability of different implementation techniques and approaches. Our end-point is an application-independent model of the tables in the document (a mapping from headings to data cells, in Zanibbi et al's [33] terms). We believe this provides a suitable starting point for semantic analysis and other kinds of domain-dependent analysis, and so we adopt the well-known Wang abstract table model [30], extended to handle tables with no obvious stub.

4. THE BUILDING BLOCKS OF TEXUS

In this section, we give more details on the tasks in the end-to-end table processing framework, and the data models that connect them. We first discuss our data model for input documents. We then consider the four table processing tasks, partitioned into two groups (*Table Extraction* and *Table Understanding*), and give details of their data models. Finally, we briefly discuss table metadata.

4.1 Document Converting

Since our table processing starts with *documents*, we need a suitable model for documents. Both *layout* and *content* are important in analysing tables [17], so our model needs to consider both aspects. Our input documents are PDFs, and there are a range of tools and techniques for extracting layout and text features [11] from PDF documents. We use the pdftohtml tool for our initial processing, followed by pre-processing as described below.

Finding the proper atomic unit of document content for table processing is an important first step. For our purposes, and following from the discussion in [9], individual characters are not a useful atomic unit. Since our primary concern is with the contents of table cells, which typically contain one or more words or numbers, possibly on several lines, we start from the notion of a *text chunk*, which intuitively corresponds to a group of words with a bounding box. In order to identify text chunks, we assume that we can extract properties such as *Left*, *Right*, *Top*, *Bottom* for each element in the document. Fig. 3 shows a document page with some elements of the document model identified (text chunks are indexed as ch_i). While we do not consider

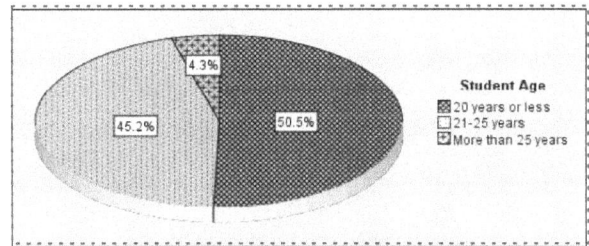

Figure 3: Sample of a document page

individual characters in table processing, they do occur in the document converting step which takes the raw PDF document and produces a tagged document with text chunks as the basic unit. The pre-processor builds text chunks according to the following:

Character: Each `Character` C_i is defined as a tuple of attributes $C_i = (Top, Left, Height, Width, Font, CHAR)$ which describe its position in the document page as well as the actual character. Characters include both visible characters as well as whitespace characters such as space, tab, carriage return, and linefeed.

Word: A `Word` W_j is a sequence of horizontally consecutive `Visible Characters` $\langle C_1, C_2, ..., C_n \rangle$ not containing any whitespace characters. Whitespace characters are also called `Word delimiter`s.

Text Chunk: A `Text Chunk` Ch_j is a sequence of horizontally consecutive `Words` $\langle W_1, W_2, ..., W_n \rangle$ with a bounding box, where the distance between consecutive Text Chunks is greater than the size of the smallest `Word delimiter`. The bounding box is determined by the $Left$ of the leftmost character, the minimum Top value of all characters, the maximum $Bottom$ value of all characters, and the $Right$ of the rightmost character. Text chunks do not overlap.

Line: A `Line` L_j is a sequence of horizontally consecutive `Text Chunk(s)` $L_j = \langle Ch_1, Ch_2, ..., Ch_n \rangle$ with a bounding box based on Ch_1 and Ch_n which ends with an End-of-Line delimiter.

Text Region: A `Text Region` TxR_j is a sequence of `Lines` $TxR_j = \langle L_1, L_2, ..., L_m \rangle$ with a bounding box based on L_1 and L_m. A `Text Region` ends when a `Non-Text Region` or End-of-page is encountered and $\forall i \in \{1, 2, ..., m - 1\}, Bottom(L_i) < Top(L_{i+1})$. The most common type of `Text Region` is a column of text on a single page.

Non-text Region: Any element, such as an image, that is not composed of text is treated as part of a `Non-Text Region`. Such elements can be identified by `pdftohtml`. Consecutive `Non-Text Regions` are merged into a single region.

Page: A `Page` is a sequence of `Text Regions` and `Non-Text Regions`. Page boundaries can be detected by noting the resetting of the Top values of subsequent document elements.

Document: A `Document` Doc is a sequence of `Pages`, $Doc = \langle P_1, P_2, ..., P_q \rangle$.

In above definition, we assume that each table is contained within a `Text Region` (and could be the entire `Text Region`). We also assume that tables do not span multiple pages (although work is currently underway to handle this case).

4.2 Table Extraction

In this section, we detail the *Table Extraction* part of TEXUS. Table extraction goes beyond simply detecting where tables are in a document; it separates tables from the rest of the document and represents each of them in the form of a *Physical* abstraction model. Table extraction consists of two main processes: *Locating* and *Segmenting* and they are mostly described based on the layout attributes of the document and table.

4.2.1 Locating

The aim of locating is to find the starting line and ending line of each table in the document. The location of each table is identified by its boundaries. Lines in the input document are either *table lines* or *text lines*.

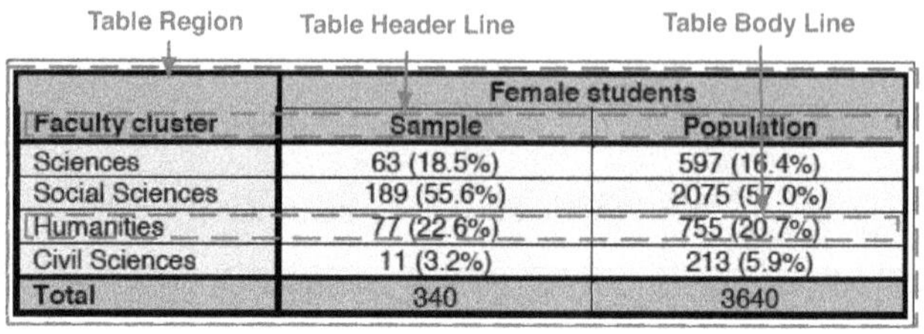

Figure 4: Table Location model

Tables contain two distinct types of `Table Line`:

Table Body Line: A potential `Table body Line` TBL_i is a `Line` containing two or more `Text Chunks` and located in the Table Body Region.

Table Header Line: A `Table Header Line` THL_i is a `Line` containing one or more `Text Chunk(s)` and is placed in Table BoxHead.

The Table location model is then defined in terms of `Table Lines`:

Physical Table Location (T_{Loc}^{Phy}): The model for the ith table $T_{Loc\ i}^{Phy}$ is contained in a `Text Region` and spans a sequence of lines $\langle L_j, L_{j+1}, ..., L_k \rangle$, where zero or more `Table Header Lines` are followed by one or more `Table Body Lines`. $T_{Loc\ i}^{Phy}$ is defined by a `Table Region` TR_i whose bounding box is determined by $(Left(L_j), Top(L_j))$ as `Upper Boundary` UB and $(Bottom(L_k), Right(L_k))$ as `Lower Boundary` LB.

4.2.2 Segmenting

The aim of segmenting is to recognise and detect the inner boundaries of the table (i.e. the rows, columns and individual table cells). Each table cell can be identified by at least a (row,column) position. Table segmentation (e.g. Figure 5) is defined via a `Physical Table Segments` model.

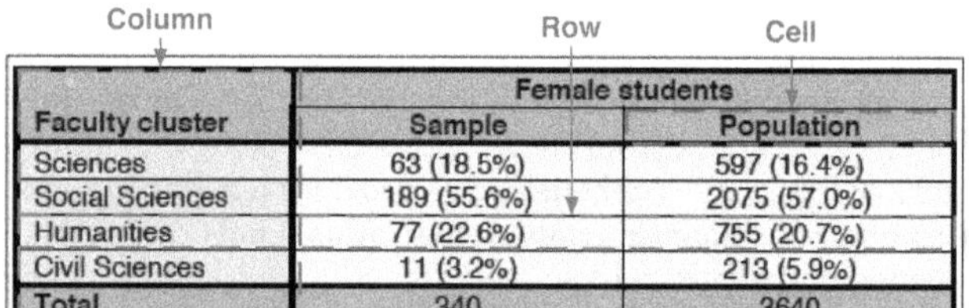

Figure 5: Table Segment model

Physical Table Segments (T_{Seg}^{Phy}): A `Cell` is a `Text Chunk` which is located in a T_{Loc}^{Phy}. A `Row` is a sequence of *horizontally aligned* cells, and a `Col` is a sequence of *vertically-aligned* cells. T_{Seg}^{Phy} is a triple $(Cells, Rows, Cols)$ where $Cells$ is set of two or more `Cells`, $Rows$ is a set of one or more `Rows`, $Cols$ is a set of one or more `Cols`. One cell may span multiple cells in a different row/column either horizontally or vertically.

$Cell_i$ and $Cell_j$ are **horizontally aligned** if either $((|Top(Cell_i)-Top(Cell_j)| \sim 0) \wedge (|Bottom(Cell_i)-Bottom(Cell_j)| \sim 0))$ or spanned vertically.

$Cell_i$ and $Cell_j$ are **vertically aligned** if either $((|Left(Cell_i)-Left(Cell_j)| \sim 0) \wedge (|Right(Cell_i)-Right(Cell_j)| \sim 0))$ or spanned horizontally.

$Cell_i$ **spans horizontally** $Cell_j$ if $((Left(Cell_i)-Left(Cell_j) < 0) \wedge (Right(Cell_i) - Right(Cell_j) \geq 0)) \vee ((Left(Cell_i)-Left(Cell_j) \leq 0) \wedge (Right(Cell_i) - Right(Cell_j) > 0))$.

$Cell_i$ **spans Vertically** $Cell_j$ if $((Top(Cell_i)-Top(Cell_j) < 0) \wedge (Bottom(Cell_i) - Bottom(Cell_j) \geq 0)) \vee ((Top(Cell_i)-Top(Cell_j) \leq 0) \wedge (Bottom(Cell_i)-Bottom(Cell_j) > 0))$. $\square$

4.3 Table Understanding

We now consider the *Table Understanding* part of TEXUS. Understanding a table means going beyond layout features to determine the relationships between the data items. Table understanding consists of two sub-tasks: *Functional Analysis* and *Structural Analysis*.

4.3.1 Functional Analysis

Functional Analysis identifies the role that each cell plays in the table. Cells either contain data or contain indexes for accessing the data (i.e. table headers). In our model, there are two kinds of headers: *attribute cells* which are normally placed in the table Boxhead, as the top-level headers, and *access cells* placed in the stub in the role of indexes. Data cells are contained in the table body and are the target information in the table. Figure 6 gives examples of these.

Figure 6: Table Function model

The functional aspects of cells in a table is described using a **Logical Table Function** model.

Logical Table Function (T_{Func}^{Log}): T_{Func}^{Log} specifies the role of each cell in a table, and identifies the four functional regions: *BoxHead, Stub, StubHead* and *TableBody*. Roles are represented by a set of pairs $(Cell_i, Func_i)$, where $Cell_i$ is an identifier for a cell and $Func_i \in \{Data, Access, Attribute\}$. Each region is defined by the set of cells contained in it.

The following conditions hold on cells in the table:
if $Cell_i \in \{BoxHead, stub, stubHead\}$, $Func(Cell_i) \in \{Attribute, Access\}$,
otherwise $Func(Cell_i) = Data$. $\square$

4.3.2 Structural Analysis

Structural Analysis defines the logical relationships between cells, which determines access paths to the data. Tables are essentially multi-dimensional structures which are presented in two dimensions. Reaching a data value in this multi-dimensional space requires following two paths which intersect at the data cell. One path begins from the top-level *Attribute* (top row in *BoxHead*), the other path begins

from the *StubHead* (topmost/leftmost cell of table). This is essentially the Wang abstract table model [30]. In Wang terminology, the top-level header and *StubHead* are **Categories**. This final output from our end-to-end processing is represented using a **Logical Table Structure** model (or Wang abstract table model). Figure 7 shows examples of the components in such a model.

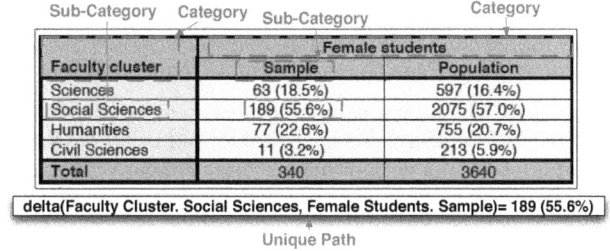

Figure 7: Table Structure model

Logical Table Structure (T_{Struct}^{Log}): A T_{Struct}^{Log} is a pair $(T_{Access}^{Struct}, F_{Map}^{Struct})$. A T_{Access}^{Struct} is a non-empty set of **Access Path** values, where each **AccessPath** is a hierarchical relationship between an **Attribute** or **Access** cell and their subordinate cells. An **AccessPath** $Access_i$ contains an **Attribute** cell **AttrCell** or **AccCell** cell as **Category** and an associated non-empty list of **SubCategory** values $\langle SC_1...SC_n \rangle$. A **SubCategory** SC_i contains an **AttrCell** or **AccCell** cell (and a possibly empty set of **SubCategory** values $\langle SC_{i,1}..SC_{i,n} \rangle$. A **LeafPathCell** is any **AccCell** or **AttrCell** in a **SubCategory** which has an empty set of **SubCategory** values.

F_{Map}^{Struct} is a function that takes a set of access paths and determines the **DataCell** corresponding to those access paths. (Note that examples of access paths were given in Section 3). $\square$

Logical Table Structure models satisfy the following properties: the table must have two or more categories; each category must have a single root header; a category tree cannot contain identical root-to-leaf paths; if a table has n categories, then data cells are accessed via a tuple of n access paths, one through each category tree,

Note that the Wang model does not handle tables where the top row in the *BoxHead* contains more than one cell. We consider a *virtual header* above the top row as a starting point for the access path from the header. Similarly, if a table has an empty *StubHead*, we add a *virtual access* cell to act as the root for the access path from the stub. The names of the virtual cells could either be simple unique identifiers or could be derived based on the names in the header/stub respectively.

Note also that the final data model for our end-to-end processing consists of a set of T_{Struct}^{Log} models, one for each table, along with a set of table metadata entries (discussed in the next section).

In many applications, the logical abstraction obtained from the *Function* and *Structure* views is sufficient to provide effective access to the data. However, other applications may wish to consider domain- and application-specific knowledge. A *Semantic* level allows users to model the meaning of the data contained in the table and to find semantic relationships between table components. This abstraction level is often linked to a domain-specific knowledge base or ontology.

4.4 Table Metadata

The above models are built using the information in the tables. One other kind of information, `Table Metadata`, derived from the document context, can also be potentially useful. In particular, the text regions near the table region often contain useful information about the table. There are three major kinds of table metadata:

Descriptive Metadata consists of table attributes based on layout, presentation and location, and is intended primarily for indexing the table. Examples of such data include Document Type, Page Number, Caption, etc.

Structural Metadata is based primarily on the Function and Structure logical views of the table, and could have potential applications in determining table similarity. Examples of such data include labels and headers on rows and columns, and the semantic categories behind such labels.

Semantic Metadata provides the background semantic structures which are used in interpreting table contents. Examples include knowledge about the domains of data cells and the underlying schema that the table represents.

5. IMPLEMENTATION

Through TEXUS, we intend to facilitate a systematic development and reuse of the concepts and their implementation defined within it. The tasks defined in TEXUS can be implemented and utilised as a set of components. Since the models in TEXUS only specify the expected output of each task, the exact details of how the outcome is achieved are left to the developers. They can easily choose compatible table processing standards, leverage existing component implementations and integrate them to build their own solutions, develop new components, or provide alternative implementation of the same components.

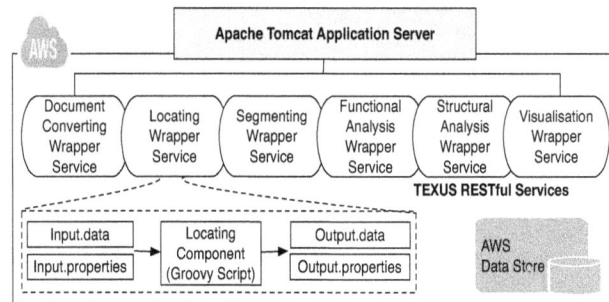

Figure 8: Implementing TEXUS Tasks as Web-based Service Component

5.1 Overall Design

Figure 8 shows our own implementation based on the models in TEXUS. We have implemented each task as a Web-enabled service component. The figure also illustrates that the 'body' part of each component (i.e., implementation of the task) takes two sources of data: an input data model instance and a set of configuration parameters. The outputs are an output data model instance and a set of properties (e.g., header type or error codes if any). To store data model instances, we have chosen to use XML, because (i) it is suitable for describing structured textual information, (ii) it is a platform-independent open standard, and (iii) it is

easily transformable into different formats when necessary. For example, we can visualise the output of any components using a simple XSLT[1] script.

Providing the components as services allows the client applications to be built in a flexible manner. For example, a client application can choose to use one component from the available pool, or use a well-known Web service composition technique to wire the multiple components together.

5.2 Implementation of the Components

We have implemented six components: document converting, locating, segmenting, functional analysis, structural analysis and finally a visualisation component that renders the output of any given component.

Document Converting. The purpose of this component is to create an instance of our document model. We first convert a PDF document to an XML document using a well-known conversion utility named 'pdftohtml[2]' .

This utility partitions the document into a sequence of `<page>`s, where each page is a sequence of `<textChunk>`s, and each `<textChunk>` is an XML `TEXT` element with the following attributes: `top` (vertical distance from top of page); `left` (horizontal distance from left edge of page); `width` (width of text chunk); `height` (height of text chunk); `font` (size, family, and color of text chunk).

We then perform further optimisation on the XML before producing output. First, we tag possible table cells containing multi-lines. Second, recognising multiple page columns (to be distinguished from table columns later). Third, tag text lines, properly recognising lines in each page column.

Locating Component. Taking an instance of TEXUS document model as input, *Locating* first attempts to separate *table lines* from *normal text lines*. It looks for lines with more than one text chunk as a potential table line. *Locating* then uses the transitions from text lines to (potential) table lines, and vice versa, to determine table boundaries. For potential table lines, our implementation also looks for type patterns (numeric, alphabetic, date, etc.), Where a sequence of text chunk categories forms a pattern for that line. A sequence of lines that follows the same, or a similar, type pattern, is a strong candidate for containing the data cells of a table. We also look for spatial patterns. The aim is to determine the left and right boundaries of each table column. Since the text chunks in a column are unlikely to have identical `left` and `right` attributes, we form column extents by considering the left boundaries of chunks in column i and the right boundaries of chunks in column $i+1$. The sequence of chunk extents determined in this way forms a *spatial pattern* for the data in the table. The Locating component outputs XML file which encloses table lines in `<table>` elements, and adds `pattern` attributes to existing `<line>` elements.

Segmenting Component. In this component, the main aim is to detect the inner boundaries of the table as cells, rows and columns. First, we look for dominant table line pattern to determine table rows, and then recognise lines that deviate from the pattern. These lines could be considered potential header lines or uncertain table lines (e.g., summary lines like 'Total'). Using the spatial pattern from Locating, starting from the table's dominant spatial pattern, we build a list of column horizontal boundaries, then scans

---

[1] XSLT, http://www.w3.org/TR/xslt
[2] pdftohtml, sourceforge.net/projects/pdftohtml/

30

the table and checks cell boundaries against these, allowing it to both detect spanned cells and, by considering each cell's `top` and `bottom`, to determine the vertical extent of the column. Finally, we determine table cells. In a table row, each text chunk has boundaries and content data type. Most table cells are clearly delimited from surrounding cells, but we handle two special cases: (i) *span cells*: if the extent of a single text chunk extends across multiple columns, it is labelled as a span cell, (ii) *blank cells*: once rows and columns are determined, the boundaries of cells are known. we detect whether an expected cell location has no corresponding text chunk and labels it as a blank cell. Segmenting produces an XML file which encloses detected cells in `<td>...</td>` and places the text chunks from each table row in `<tr>..</tr>`.

Functional Analysis Component. In this component, the goal is to detect each cell function as data, header or access. A bottom-up and a top-down classification algorithm is used at the same time to detect the boundary of table body containing data cells and the table box head enclosing the header cells. We consider the bottom right most cell in the table boundary as a *data cell*. Then neighbour cells are compared considering spatial and type pattern to find cells with the same functionality. At the same time, the top-most row is assumed as a *potential* header line and hierarchical structure along with spatial and type pattern help to detect the similarity of neighbour cells. The reaching point of the two algorithms is considered as the boxhead separation. The left-most column is always considered as the *access* column. If we encounter a vertical spanned cell in the left-most column, we consider the following column for the access functionality class as well. The functional analysis component adds `function` attribute to each `<td>` element of a table row `<tr>`.

Structural Analysis Component. Having detected the function of cells in the table, the structural analysis component provides two paths for each data cell encompassing one unique *Header Path* and one unique *Access Path*. The root of header rows in the boxhead and the root of access columns in the stubhead (either they exist or we add virtual ones) are considered as the starting point. The path is then constructed for each data cell based on the following rules: (i) For header path, it starts from the root and follows the header cells in the top-down fashion to reach the last header cell in the same column with the related data cell, (ii) For access path, it starts from the stubhead and follows all access cell from left-to-right to reach the last access cell in the same row with the related data cell, (iii) The content of the spanning cells are copied to their underlying contained cells, (iv) The empty cells in the path are replaced with a unique identifier, and (v) Header or access cells with the same content are distinguished by adding unique indices. The component adds `HeaderPath` and `AccessPath` attributes to each data cell in the output. Also the table metadata in three different categories are added to the table representation.

Visualisation Component. Currently, the primary purpose of this component is for debugging. It shows the output data models in a convenient format. It parses the XML output of a component and provides an HTML representation of the content. We used color coding to present different functional regions in the table and also a tree representation of the access and header paths for structural analysis.

5.3 Evaluation

To evaluate our implemented system, we used the dataset introduced in 'ICDAR 2013 Table Competition[3]'. The dataset consists of 67 documents with 156 tables, and contains ground-truth for the locating and segmenting tasks. The tables are in different styles and from various domains.

The performance comparison of seven academic systems and four commercial products (FineReader, Acrobat, OmniPage, Nitro) are presented in the competition. We follow the same evaluation strategy and metrics for reporting our results against the published results of the competition.

The measures *Completeness* and *Purity* are used over the whole dataset. The measures *Recall* and *Precision* are calculated for the unsuccessful cases, counting individual characters for locating, and considering the adjacency relations for segmenting task.

The ICDAR competition reported that in general, the commercial systems performed better than academic ones. Since the details of the algorithms used by commercial systems are not publicly available, it can not be said whether their advantage originates from a better approach to the problem or from having access to a large amount of data which allow them to fine-tune the heuristics in their system overtime.

Overall, TEXUS performed better than most of academic system (except the Nurminen) in all three different evaluations, and even better than Acrobat and Nitro in the commercial system in table extraction. Our performance seems acceptable in locating, however we have difficulties in segmenting especially when the header hierarchy structures are very complex. In the following, we discuss the results of locating and segmenting separately.

Table 1 shows the results of the locating task. Our system has a problem in locating 'small tables' (tables with less than four rows), and tables with summary lines in the middle of the table. However, it is worth pointing out that we performed well in unruled table. It is mentioned that most of the currently available systems do not perform well with unruled tables. Locating floating tables are another category that TEXUS handles well.

Table 1: Result of the Locating task

System	Per-document average			Table Found Total=156	
	Recall	Precision	F-meas.	Complete	Pure
FineReader	0.9971	0.9729	0.9848	142	148
OmniPage	0.9644	0.9569	0.9606	141	130
Silva	0.9831	0.9292	0.9554	149	137
Nitro	0.9323	0.9397	0.936	124	144
Nurminen	0.9077	0.921	0.9143	114	151
Acrobat	0.8738	0.9365	0.904	110	141
TEXUS	**0.9023**	**0.8832**	**0.8926**	**114**	**138**
Yildiz	0.853	0.6399	0.7313	100	94
Stoffel	0.6991	0.7536	0.7253	79	66
Liu et al.2	0.3355	0.8836	0.4864	0	29
Hsu et al.	0.4601	0.3666	0.408	39	95
Fang et al.	0.2697	0.7496	0.3967	28	41
Liu et al.1	0.2207	0.8885	0.3536	0	25

---

[3]http://www.tamirhassan.com/dataset.html

31

Table 2 shows the results of segmenting task based the correct results of locating as input. We performed well in segmenting the vertical spanned cells and multi-line cell boundary detection. However, in some cases when tables have very irregular alignments in cells content, we ended up adding extra blank column in segmenting.

Table 2: Result of the Segmenting task

System	Per-document average		
	Recall	Precision	F-meas.
Nurminen	0.9409	0.9515	0.9460
TEXUS	**0.8423**	**0.8102**	**0.8259**
Silva	0.6401	0.6144	0.6270
Hsu et al.	0.4811	0.5704	0.5220

Finally, Table 3 shows the results of table extraction as a sequence of table locating and segmenting (i.e., segmenting component directly taking input from locating without corrections). Our performance is acceptable compared with other academic systems.

The task-based design of our system provides the opportunity to evaluate and refine the components separately and then try a new composition to improve the performance. It should be mentioned that participants in the ICDAR competition had the opportunity to test their systems beforehand on a practice dataset for bug fixing or training. We did not have access to that dataset and did not use the test dataset before the performance evaluation.

Table 3: Result of Table Extraction

System	Per-document average		
	Recall	Precision	F-meas.
FineReader	0.8835	0.871	0.8772
OmniPage	0.838	0.846	0.842
Nurminen	0.8078	0.8693	0.8374
TEXUS	**0.7823**	**0.8071**	**0.7945**
Acrobat	0.7262	0.8159	0.7685
Nitro	0.6793	0.8459	0.7535
Silva	0.7052	0.6874	0.6962
Yildiz	0.5951	0.5752	0.585

6. FURTHER DISCUSSIONS

Besides providing a basis to design and develop a table processing system, TEXUS may potentially be used as a common ground for evaluating the performance of table processing systems. Although detailing this idea further is our ongoing work, we present a couple of issues in table procesing system evaluation and the relevant concepts in TEXUS for discussion.

6.1 Appropriate Points for Evaluation

It is difficult to adequately compare the quality of results of different table processing system even when they seem to work on the same task [2, 8, 10]. We discuss this issue from two perspectives. First, different terms are used to describe systems that perform table extraction tasks belonging in the same scope. For example, there is much work focused on locating tables in a document. In these works, there is a

TEXUS Name	Synonym Terms
Locating	table identification [19], table detection [7], table area selection [4], table boundary detection [18], table spotting [7]
Segmenting	table recognition [20], table decomposition[19], table text blocks discovery [13], table internal structure detection[28]
Functional Analysis	table header detection [27], table format verification [24], table augmentation[23]
Structural Analysis	table factoring [15], table abstraction [30], detecting table read-wise pattern [32]. table access structure detection[16]

Table 4: TEXUS Tasks and the Synonyms

wide variation in terminology to describe their goals, e.g. *table identification, table detection, table spotting*, etc. In the terms defined in TEXUS, we can describe all of these as *Table Locating*. Since TEXUS defines the atomic tasks involved in a table processing system, each system's goal can either be mapped to one task or a composition of several tasks. Table 4 gives examples of terms that appear in the table processing literature and their mapping to TEXUS atomic tasks.

Some researchers suggest that the appropriate point to evaluate a table processing system is after the final result is produced. For example, if the endpoint is to extract particular information from tables, evaluation is based on how closely the extracted information matches what was expected [25]. However, others claim that, since a table processing system involves many steps, the overall performance of the system often relies on how well the intermediate steps interact, and measuring the performance of intermediate steps is important [20]. In fact, as we have shown above, it would be possible to describe the goals of many table processing systems in terms of logically separated steps. Evaluating table processing at each "step" can also provide a chance to improve each step independently [3], which may lead to increased performance overall. We believe TEXUS, through the well-defined tasks along with concrete data models, can contribute to providing a useful framework to objectively evaluate the systems.

6.2 Proper Unit of Measurement

The characteristics of the appropriate metrics which satisfy the needs of table processing tasks is another discussion in the community. One of the considerations is that the granularity level of the elements at input is not the same as that of output in a table processing task. Different suggestions were made regarding this issue. Silva [2] proposed two new metrics: completeness and purity. Long [21] suggested multi-level evaluation methodology.

However, there is not yet any set unit of measurement in task-based evaluation. Take the locating task as an example, Liu et. al [19] evaluated their system in terms of lines, Wang [31] used cells and Chen [1] considered full tables. In the

ICDAR'13 table competition [9], they defined the measurement unit for locating at an individual character level.

However, the results showed that it was not a proper choice for some cases. This approach gave more weight to the parts of tables that have more characters (e.g., there was a system having a very good precision at the character level, but did not manage to locate even one table completely). Given that the main aim of the locating task, recognising table boundaries should be valued more than say, recognising text areas within a table.

We believe that TEXUS could provide a basis for task-based evaluation measurement metrics, because the table elements (e.g., table boundaries, rows, columns and cells) which may be relevant for measuring performance are explicitly defined in the tasks and their data models. Following the locating task example, we may consider the "text chunks"

as a measuring unit, since cells are the smallest meaningful unit of data in a table structure.

7. CONCLUSION AND FUTURE WORK

We presented TEXUS as a task-based end-to-end table processing system. Our end-to-end table processing starts from a PDF input document and ends with a generic/abstract representation of extracted tables. We define a series of self-contained table extraction tasks in between that transform the input document to its ultimate output format. We have integrated and extended the essential aspects of previous end-to-end table processing systems to produce a framework which clearly identifies the sub-tasks involved, gives precisely defined data models for the input and output of each sub-task. We also have demonstrated that TEXUS is a concrete proposal that can easily be implemented. Our immediate future work includes further advancing the design of the pre-processing task and document model so that it is optimised for table extraction. We are also investigating an application of the TEXUS models as a common ground for table extraction system evaluation framework.

ACKNOWLEDGEMENT

This project was partly supported by the project 'Enabling Market Impact Analysis with Large News Datasets' in Smart Services CRC, Australia, 2013-2014. We thank Owen Peng Yuan and Diyin Zhou for their dedicated efforts spent to implement our prototype system.

REFERENCES

[1] CHEN, H.-H., TSAI, S.-C., AND TSAI, J.-H. Mining tables from large scale html texts. In *Proceedings of the 18th conference on Computational linguistics-Volume 1* (2000), Association for Computational Linguistics, pp. 166–172.

[2] E SILVA, A. C. *Parts that add up to a whole: a framework for the analysis of tables.* PhD thesis, The University of Edinburgh, 2010.

[3] E SILVA, A. C. Metrics for evaluating performance in document analysis: application to tables. *International Journal on Document Analysis and Recognition (IJDAR) 14*, 1 (2011), 101–109.

[4] E SILVA, A. C., JORGE, A., AND TORGO, L. Automatic selection of table areas in documents for information extraction. In *Progress in Artificial Intelligence.* Springer, 2003, pp. 460–465.

[5] E SILVA, A. C., JORGE, A., AND TORGO, L. Design of an end-to-end method to extract information from tables. *International Journal of Document Analysis and Recognition 8*, 2-3 (2006), 144–171.

[6] EMBLEY, D. W., LOPRESTI, D., AND NAGY, G. Notes on contemporary table recognition. In *Document Analysis Systems VII.* Springer, 2006, pp. 164–175.

[7] FANG, J., GAO, L., BAI, K., QIU, R., TAO, X., AND TANG, Z. A table detection method for multipage pdf documents via visual seperators and tabular structures. In *Document Analysis and Recognition (ICDAR)* (2011), IEEE, pp. 779–783.

[8] FANG, J., TAO, X., TANG, Z., QIU, R., AND LIU, Y. Dataset, ground-truth and performance metrics for table detection evaluation. In *Document Analysis Systems (DAS), 2012 10th IAPR International Workshop on* (2012), IEEE, pp. 445–449.

[9] GOBEL, M., HASSAN, T., ORO, E., AND ORSI, G. ICDAR 2013 table competition. In *12th International Conference on Document Analysis and Recognition (ICDAR'13)* (2013), IEEE, pp. 1449–1453.

[10] HU, J., KASHI, R., LOPRESTI, D., NAGY, G., AND WILFONG, G. Why table ground-truthing is hard. In *Document Analysis and Recognition, 2001. Proceedings. Sixth International Conference on* (2001), IEEE, pp. 129–133.

[11] HU, J., AND LIU, Y. Analysis of documents born digital. *Handbook of Document Image Processing and Recognition* (2014), 775–804.

[12] HURST, M. *The interpretation of tables in texts.* PhD thesis, The University of Edinburgh, 2000.

[13] HURST, M. Layout and language: Exploring text block discovery in tables using linguistic resources. In *International Conference on Document Analysis and Recognition* (2001), pp. 523–527.

[14] JHA, P., AND NAGY, G. Wang notation tool: Layout independent representation of tables. In *Pattern Recognition, 2008. ICPR 2008. 19th International Conference on* (2008), IEEE, pp. 1–4.

[15] JIN, D. An algebraic approach to building category parse trees for web tables. *2012 NCUR* (2013).

[16] KIENINGER, T., AND DENGEL, A. Applying the t-recs table recognition system to the business letter domain. In *Document Analysis and Recognition, 2001. Proceedings. Sixth International Conference on* (2001), IEEE, pp. 518–522.

[17] LEE, M.-H., KIM, Y.-S., AND LEE, K.-H. Logical structure analysis: From html to xml. *Computer Standards & Interfaces 29*, 1 (2007), 109–124.

[18] LIU, Y., BAI, K., MITRA, P., AND GILES, C. L. Improving the table boundary detection in pdfs by fixing the sequence error of the sparse lines. In *10th International Conference on Document Analysis and Recognition (ICDAR'09)* (2009), IEEE, pp. 1006–1010.

[19] LIU, Y., MITRA, P., AND GILES, C. L. Identifying table boundaries in digital documents via sparse line detection. In *Proceedings of the 17th ACM Conference on Information and Knowledge Management* (2008), ACM, pp. 1311–1320.

[20] LONG, V. *An Agent-Based Approach to Table Recognition and Interpretation.* PhD thesis, Macquarie University Sydney, Australia, 2010.

[21] Long, V., Cassidy, S., and Dale, R. A multi-level table evaluation method for plain text documents. In *Extended Abstracts of the 7th International Association for Pattern Recognition Workshop on Document Analysis Systems (DAS 2006)* (2006), pp. 21–24.

[22] Lopresti, D., and Nagy, G. A tabular survey of automated table processing. In *Graphics Recognition Recent Advances*. Springer, 2000, pp. 93–120.

[23] Nagy, G., Padmanabhan, R., Jandhyala, R., Silversmith, W., and Krishnamoorthy, M. Table metadata: Headers, augmentations and aggregates. In *Ninth IAPR International Workshop on Document Analysis Systems* (2010).

[24] Nagy, G., and Tamhankar, M. Vericlick: an efficient tool for table format verification. In *IS&T/SPIE Electronic Imaging* (2012), International Society for Optics and Photonics, pp. 1–9.

[25] Oro, E., and Ruffolo, M. Xonto: An ontology-based system for semantic information extraction from pdf documents. In *20th IEEE International Conference on Tools with Artificial Intelligence (ICTAI'08)* (2008), vol. 1, IEEE, pp. 118–125.

[26] Padmanabhan, R. K., Jandhyala, R. C., Krishnamoorthy, M., Nagy, G., Seth, S., and Silversmith, W. Interactive conversion of web tables. In *Graphics Recognition. Achievements, Challenges, and Evolution*. Springer, 2010, pp. 25–36.

[27] Seth, S., Jandhyala, R., Krishnamoorthy, M., and Nagy, G. Analysis and taxonomy of column header categories for web tables. In *Proceedings of the 9th IAPR International Workshop on Document Analysis Systems* (2010), ACM, pp. 81–88.

[28] Shahab, A., Shafait, F., Kieninger, T., and Dengel, A. An open approach towards the benchmarking of table structure recognition systems. In *Proceedings of the 9th IAPR International Workshop on Document Analysis Systems* (2010), ACM, pp. 113–120.

[29] Tao, C., and Embley, D. W. Automatic hidden-web table interpretation, conceptualization, and semantic annotation. *Data & Knowledge Engineering 68*, 7 (2009), 683–703.

[30] Wang, X. *Tabular abstraction, editing, and formatting*. PhD thesis, University of Waterloo, 1996.

[31] Wang, Y., and Hu, J. Detecting tables in html documents. In *Document Analysis Systems V*. Springer, 2002, pp. 249–260.

[32] Yang, Y. *Web table mining and database discovery*. PhD thesis, Simon Fraser University, 2002.

[33] Zanibbi, R., Blostein, D., and Cordy, J. R. A survey of table recognition. *Document Analysis and Recognition 7*, 1 (2004), 1–16.

Multi-oriented Text Extraction from Information Graphics

Falk Böschen
Kiel University
Olshausenstraße 40
24118 Kiel, Germany
fboe@informatik.uni-kiel.de

Ansgar Scherp
Leibniz Information Centre for Economics - ZBW
Düsternbrooker Weg 120
24105 Kiel, Germany
asc@informatik.uni-kiel.de

ABSTRACT

Existing research on analyzing information graphics assume to have a perfect text detection and extraction available. However, text extraction from information graphics is far from solved. To fill this gap, we propose a novel processing pipeline for multi-oriented text extraction from infographics. The pipeline applies a combination of data mining and computer vision techniques to identify text elements, cluster them into text lines, compute their orientation, and uses a state-of-the-art open source OCR engine to perform the text recognition. We evaluate our method on 121 infographics extracted from an open access corpus of scientific publications. The results show that our approach is effective and significantly outperforms a state-of-the-art baseline.

Categories and Subject Descriptors

I.7.5 [**Document and Text Processing**]: Document Capture—*Optical Character Recognition*

General Terms

Experimentation; Measurement

Keywords

infographics; OCR; multi-oriented text extraction

1. INTRODUCTION

Scientific publications often include information graphics (short: *infographics*) to visualize statistics, survey data, and research results in an easy to perceive way. Retrieval over infographics is typically based on the surrounding text. However, information graphics often contain textual information that is *frequently not present in surrounding text* [2]. Therefore, ignoring the textual information encoded in graphics discards a big opportunity to improve retrieval and understanding of the content.

Existing research on analyzing infographics such as [17, 7, 15, 5, 8, 4] just simply assume that a perfect OCR is

readily available. However, as illustrated by the example in Figure 1, OCR on infographics poses several challenges that are insufficiently addressed by current solutions: (i) First, the text contained in infographics is often rotated at different angles to fit axes or graphical components. (ii) Second, the textual elements often have different fonts, sizes, and typographic emphases. (iii) Third, we find text elements that partially cover some graphical components in the infographics or have different background colors. This makes it difficult to identify the text elements and separate them from the graphical components.

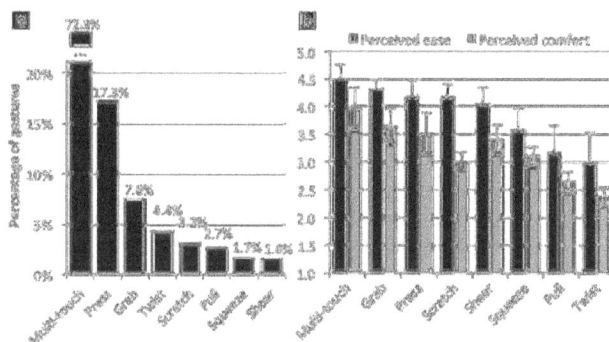

Figure 1: Challenges for text extraction from infographics (example taken from [18]).

In this paper, we propose an initial version of a novel infographics processing pipeline and conduct a first evaluation to proof its concept. The pipeline makes use of a combination of methods from data mining and computer vision to identify and extract text from infographics. The evaluation over 121 infographics extracted from an open access corpus of scientific publications demonstrates its effectiveness. It significantly outperforms a reasonable baseline applying the state-of-the-art OCR engine Tesseract[1].

The remainder of the paper is organized as follows: Subsequently, we discuss the related work. Section 3 presents our pipeline for text extraction. Section 4 specifies the experiment set-up and dataset used. The results are presented in Section 5 and discussed in Section 6, before we conclude.

2. RELATED WORK

Research on infographics typically focused on the classification task [17], i.e., determining the diagram type of a

---

[1] https://code.google.com/p/tesseract-ocr/

graphic, or finding areas of text in the infographics [1, 14]. However, due to the huge variety of infographics, it shows to be hard to train such a classifier. Kataria et al. [7] address this issue by focusing on 2D plots and using the coordinates of the image regions as support to distinguish between text and graphics. Only few works deal with the identification of text elements in infographics with the purpose to extract the structural layout of text and graphics [9]. Chester [4] developed the VEM framework for extracting graphical symbols and their associated text but it is still very limited and only applicable to bar charts, pie charts, and line charts. The most advanced analysis techniques for infographics are provided by ReVision [15] and VIEW [5] that aim at reengineering data from bar charts and pie charts with the goal to render it in some other form. The SIGHT system extracts the core message of bar charts to make them accessible to visually impaired users [3].

All these approaches assume to have perfect OCR results from infographics. However, having high-quality OCR results from infographics is unrealistic. Thus, they use data sets with manually entered text labels. The lack of perfect OCR for infographics is also shown by the limitations of existing works on rotation-invariant OCR that require a single character in high resolution and perfectly cropped boundary [12] or are tailored to a particular problem, e.g. cartographic material [10].

Our approach aims to fill the gap by defining a robust text extraction pipeline for infographics containing text of various emphases, size, color, and multiple orientations.

3. TX PROCESSING PIPELINE

The pipeline for Text eXtraction from infographics (short: TX) comprises six steps as illustrated in Figure 2.

(1) Adaptive binarization and labeling. The first step performs a novel adaptive binarization based on a quadtree that hierarchically divides the infographic into tiles. For each tile, we determine an optimal binarization threshold by applying Otsu's method [11], which outperforms standard approaches based on a fixed threshold or histogram. For each tile, we apply the popular Sobel operator to determine the edges. We compute the Hausdorff distance over the edges of the current tiles and their parent tile. We further subdivide a tile if a certain empirical threshold is not reached. The final threshold is computed by averaging over all tiles. The resulting binary image is then labeled using the Connected Component Labeling method [13]. The output of this step is a set of labeled regions of the infographic.

(2) Grouping regions to text elements. The regions produced in step (1) are categorized into "text elements" and "graphic symbols". To this end, we calculate for each region a feature vector with the center of mass coordinates (based on the first order moments), bounding box (width and height), and mass-to-area-ratio. We apply the density-based clustering algorithm DBSCAN to categorize regions into "text elements" and noise ("graphic symbols" and others), since we do not know the number of clusters beforehand. Output of this step is a clustering where each cluster is a set of regions representing a candidate text element.

(3) Computing of text lines. Clusters created by DBSCAN do not necessarily represent text lines. Thus, we apply a second clustering based on a Minimum Spanning Tree (MST) on top of the DBSCAN results. The rationale is that regions belonging to the same text lines a) tend to be closer together

(than other regions) and b) the edges between those regions are of similar orientation. For each cluster, the MST is build using the regions' center of mass coordinates. We compute a histogram over the angles between the edges in the tree and discard those edges that differ from the main orientation.

(4) Estimating the orientation of text lines. While the MST applied in step (3) can well produce potential text lines, it is not well suited for estimating the orientation of the text lines as it is computed on the center of mass coordinates. Thus, in the fourth step we apply a standard Hough line transformation to estimate the actual text orientation. This estimation is known to be error tolerant with regards to deviations in the orientations for small number of regions.

(5) Rotate regions and apply OCR. Based on the text lines computed in step (3) and their orientation in step (4), we crop rotated sub-images from the input infographic and apply OCR. In our current implementation, we use the state of the art OCR engine Tesseract without layout analysis (i.e., in single text block mode).

The last step (6) is the evaluation of the results, which is described in detail below.

4. EVALUATION SETUP

We compare the performance of our infographics analysis pipeline TX with a baseline based on Tesseract. We compute the results over 1-, 2- and 3-grams as well as words. A word is a series of alpha-numeric characters, i. e., it does not contain any white space characters. The n-grams are computed over the words. Below, we first describe the evaluation procedure and dataset used. Subsequently, we introduce our baseline and evaluation metrics.

4.1 Evaluation Procedure

We match the results of TX and the baseline with some gold standard to conduct our evaluation. The matching considers both the position of the text elements as well as their orientation in the infographics. We take each word from TX and baseline and calculate the intersection of its bounding box with the bounding box of all words in the gold standard. The pair with the maximum intersection is taken for evaluation. Therefore, we assign each extracted word to either one or zero words from the gold standard. All words from TX/baseline that were not assigned are considered to be false positives. All words from the gold standard without pairing are considered as false negatives. The n-grams are computed over the words of each set.

4.2 Dataset and Gold Standard

In our initial evaluation, we use a dataset of 121 infographics. We obtained them from a large corpus of 288,000 open access publications in the domain of economics we collected earlier. From this corpus, we extracted 200,000 candidate images by applying aggressive thresholds: We require a minimum width/height of 500 pixels as OCR is infeasible on smaller images. We also removed images of size above 2000 pixels as these were not individual graphics but rather scans of entire pages. From the candidate set, we randomly picked images - one at a time - and presented them to a human viewer to confirm that it is an infographic. For creating the gold standard, we have developed a web-based selection tool and manually annotated the infographics' text elements. Each text element contains the information about

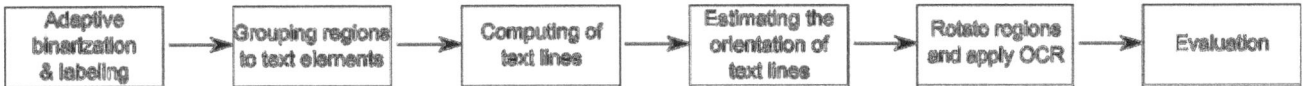

| Adaptive binarization & labeling | → | Grouping regions to text elements | → | Computing of text lines | → | Estimating the orientation of text lines | → | Rotate regions and apply OCR | → | Evaluation |

Figure 2: Novel processing pipeline for text extraction from infographics

its position, dimension, rotation, and alpha-numeric characters.

4.3 Baseline

Currently, there are no special tools freely available that are capable of performing text extraction from infographics. Related works such as rotation-invariant OCR [12, 10] are too limited to be applicable in a general context of extracting text from infographics (for details see Section 2). Thus, we use the state-of-the-art OCR engine Tesseract in its default mode, i.e., including layout analysis over the entire infographic, as a reasonable baseline. It is appropriate to apply Tesseract as baseline as it is capable of multi-oriented text extraction. Tesseract supports a rotation margin of $\pm 15°$ [16]. In addition, it can detect text rotated at $\pm 90°$.

4.4 Evaluation Metrics over Multisets

As mentioned in Section 4, we evaluate our pipeline over n-grams and words. For the n-grams, we apply the standard evaluation metrics precision (P), recall (R), and F_1-measure (F) as defined below:

$$P = \frac{|Extr \cap Rel|}{|Extr|}, \quad R = \frac{|Extr \cap Rel|}{|Rel|}, \quad F = \frac{2 \cdot P \cdot R}{P + R}$$

Extr refers to the n-grams as they are computed from text elements that are extracted from an infographic by TX and the baseline, respectively. *Rel* refers to the relevant n-grams from the gold standard. Both *Extr* and *Rel* are multisets, so we need to adjust the definitions of P and R. Multisets can appear insofar as the same n-gram can appear multiple times in both the extractions result from TX and the baseline as well as gold standard. To properly account for the number of occurrences of an n-gram in *Extr* or *Rel*, we define the counter function $\mathbf{C}_A(x) := |\{x | x \in A\}|$ (as an extension of a set indicator function) over a multiset A. For an intersection of multisets A and B, the counter function is defined as follows:

$$\mathbf{C}_{A \cap B}(x) := \min\{\mathbf{C}_A(x), \mathbf{C}_B(x)\} \quad (1)$$

Based on $\mathbf{C}_{A \cap B}(x)$, we define P and R for multisets:

$$P = \frac{\sum_{x \in Extr \cup Rel} \mathbf{C}_{Extr \cap Rel}(x)}{\sum_{x \in Extr} \mathbf{C}_{Extr}(x)} \quad (2)$$

$$R = \frac{\sum_{x \in Extr \cup Rel} \mathbf{C}_{Extr \cap Rel}(x)}{\sum_{x \in Rel} \mathbf{C}_{Rel}(x)} \quad (3)$$

In addition, it can happen that one of the sets *Extr* and *Rel* are empty. This refers to the situation when a) our TX pipeline or baseline do not extract a text where they should, i.e., $Extr = \emptyset$ and $Rel \neq \emptyset$. In this case, we define following Groot et al. [6] that $P := 0$ and $R := 0$ (false negative). In the situation b) where TX or the baseline find some text where they should not, i.e., $Extr \neq \emptyset$ and $Rel = \emptyset$, we define $P := 0$ and $R := 1$ (false positive).

For evaluating the results on level of individual words (i. e. sequences of alpha-numeric characters separated by blank or carriage return), we use standard Levenshtein distance.

5. RESULTS

Table 1 shows the average number of 1-, 2-, and 3-grams obtained from our extraction pipeline (TX), baseline (BL), and gold standard (GS) from the 121 infographics in our dataset. In addition, we show the average number of words extracted from the dataset and the average length of the words in number of characters. Standard deviations are provided in brackets.

	1-grams	2-grams	3-grams	Words	Length
TX	177.20 (128.20)	127.34 (100.51)	89.34 (79.35)	50.07 (31.95)	3.63 (2.69)
BL	106.30 (87.71)	80.17 (69.12)	60.79 (54.54)	25.21 (22.12)	4.15 (2.25)
GS	150.65 (122.28)	115.93 (103.09)	84.95 (85.61)	35.46 (22.24)	4.22 (1.48)

Table 1: Average number of n-grams and words extracted from the 121 infographics and average word length.

As one can see, our novel multi-oriented text extraction pipeline TX detects about 50% more n-grams and twice as many words as the baseline. However, the average length of the words is quite similar. In addition, TX extracts slightly more n-grams and words than the gold standard actually contains. Also, both the TX pipeline and baseline extract words that are shorter than the gold standard. Overall, we observe quite high standard deviations including the gold standard. Thus, the textual content of the 121 infographics is quite diverse.

The results of our comparison between the TX pipeline and baseline in terms of average P, R, and F measures (standard deviation in brackets) for the 1-, 2-, and 3-grams are reported in Table 2. In addition, we show the relative improvement of TX over the baseline, which is on average about 20% higher (all statistically significant except F-measure on 3-grams, details omitted here for reasons of brevity). In particular for R, the novel TX pipeline can achieve results of at least 35% above the baseline. One can also observe that in general the performance degrades from 1-grams to 3-grams. Finally, the results show a high standard deviation as well.

Regarding the Levenshtein distance, the results for our TX pipeline are on average 2.23 (SD=1.29). Thus, about two characters need to be changed for an exact match. For the baseline we report an average Levenshtein distance of 2.53 (SD=1.59). The difference of 0.3 is significant ($t(120) = 2.1, p < .04$) using a standard significance level of $\alpha = 5\%$.

Finally, for our pipeline one observes on average 12.94 false negatives (SD=17.88) as well as 49.87 false positives (SD=31.52). In comparison, we report on average 17.01 false negatives (SD=17.40) and 5.67 false positives (SD=9.42) for the baseline. Thus, the TX pipeline produces significant less

	n-gram	P	R	F
	1	.50 (0.41)	.68 (0.36)	.47 (0.39)
TX	2	.41 (0.41)	.60 (0.41)	.39 (0.39)
	3	.29 (0.38)	.49 (0.43)	.27 (0.36)
	1	.37 (0.36)	.48 (0.36)	.36 (0.35)
BL	2	.32 (0.35)	.44 (0.37)	.32 (0.35)
	3	.24 (0.32)	.36 (0.37)	.24 (0.32)
	1	35.32%	42.15%	28.95%
Diff.	2	28.15%	37.97%	20.86%
	3	18.00%	36.81%	11.94%

Table 2: Average P, R, F measures for TX and baseline.

false negatives ($V(120) = 4503.5, p < .01$). However, TX produces significantly more false positives than the baseline ($t(120) = -16.6, p < .001$).

6. DISCUSSION AND CONCLUSION

The results of our evaluation show the general effectiveness of the novel TX pipeline for the multi-oriented text extraction from infographics. This is especially documented by the increase in recall for the n-grams compared to the baseline. The increase in recall results from finding more text elements at different orientations. Also the precision increases, which results in an higher performance of TX as documented in the F-scores. We observe a quite high standard deviation in the results of both TX and baseline. This can be explained by the already high standard deviation in the gold standard. With other word, the infographics in our dataset are quite diverse in terms of the number of text elements they contain. Thus, the observed standard deviation is not an issue of our extraction pipeline (or the baseline) but an artefact of the dataset. One potential negative influence on the results of our evaluation is the decreasing number of 3-grams in the infographics. On average, we find only about half as many 3-grams than 1-grams. However, as the results in Table 1 show, there are still on average 80 3-grams in the gold standard. Enough to produce reasonable results.

Comparing the extracted words using Levenshtein distance shows that we can detect them significantly better than the baseline. Our TX engine has less false negatives, i.e., it extracts more text elements from the gold standard than the baseline can do. However, the TX pipeline makes more mistakes in terms of extracting text elements where there are none in the gold standard. This is documented in Table 1, where one can see that our TX pipeline extracts on average more text elements as there are actually in the infographics (defined by the gold standard). A detailed analysis of these false positives shows that those falsely extracted text elements mostly contain special characters. Thus, it should be possible to remove these false positives in a future extension of our work.

So far, we have used the state-of-the-art OCR software Tesseract in our pipeline. In the future, we will also apply alternative OCR engines like Ocropus[2]. Most importantly, we will extend the dataset used in this paper by annotating infographics at large scale using a crowd-sourcing approach.

Acknowledgment. We thank Chifumi Nishioka for collecting the open access publications used in our experiments.

---

[2] https://github.com/tmbdev/ocropy

7. REFERENCES

[1] P. Agrawal and R. Varma. Text extraction from images. *IJCSET*, 2(4):1083–1087, 2012.

[2] S. Carberry, S. Elzer, and S. Demir. Information graphics: an untapped resource for digital libraries. In *SIGIR*, pages 581–588. ACM, 2006.

[3] S. Carberry, S. E. Schwartz, K. F. McCoy, S. Demir, P. Wu, C. Greenbacker, D. Chester, E. Schwartz, D. Oliver, and P. Moraes. Access to Multimodal Articles for Individuals with Sight Impairments. *TiiS*, 2(4):21:1–21:49, January 2013.

[4] D. Chester and S. Elzer. Getting Computers to See Information Graphics So User Do Not Have to. In *Foundations of Intelligent Systems*. Springer, 2005.

[5] J. Gao, Y. Zhou, and K. E. Barner. VIEW: Visual information extraction widget for improving chart images accessibility. In *Image Processing*. IEEE, 2012.

[6] P. Groot, F. van Harmelen, and A. ten Teije. Torture tests: A quantitative analysis for the robustness of knowledge-based systems. In *EKAW*, 2000.

[7] S. Kataria, W. Browuer, P. Mitra, and C. L. Giles. Automatic extraction of data points and text blocks from 2-dimensional plots in digital documents. In *Advancement of Artificial Intelligence*. AAAI, 2008.

[8] Z. Li, S. Carberry, H. Fang, K. McCoy, and K. Peterson. Infographics Retrieval: A New Methodology. In *Natural Language Processing and Information Systems*. Springer, 2014.

[9] Z. Li, M. Stagitis, S. Carberry, and K. F. McCoy. Towards retrieving relevant information graphics. In *SIGIR*. ACM, 2013.

[10] R. Mariani, M. P. Deseilligny, J. Labiche, and R. Mullot. Algorithms for the hydrographic network names association on geographic maps. In *Document Analysis and Recogn.* IEEE, 1997.

[11] N. Otsu. A threshold selection method from gray-level histograms. *Systems, Man and Cybernetics, IEEE Transactions on*, 9(1):62–66, Jan 1979.

[12] P. M. Patil and T. R. Sontakke. Rotation, scale and translation invariant handwritten devanagari numeral character recognition using general fuzzy neural network. *Pattern Recogn.*, 40(7):2110–2117, July 2007.

[13] H. Samet and M. Tamminen. Efficient component labeling of images of arbitrary dimension represented by linear bintrees. *IEEE TPAMI*, 10(4):579–586, 1988.

[14] J. Sas and A. Zolnierek. Three-stage method of text region extraction from diagram raster images. In *CORES*. Springer, 2013.

[15] M. Savva, N. Kong, A. Chhajta, L. Fei-Fei, M. Agrawala, and J. Heer. ReVision: Automated Classification, Analysis and Redesign of Chart Images. In *UIST*, pages 393–402. ACM, 2011.

[16] R. Smith. A simple and efficient skew detection algorithm via text row accumulation. In *Document Analysis and Recogn.*, volume 2, Aug 1995.

[17] F. Wang and M.-Y. Kan. NPIC: Hierarchical synthetic image classification using image search and generic features. In *Image and Video Retrieval*. Springer, 2006.

[18] M. Weigel, V. Mehta, and J. Steimle. More than touch: understanding how people use skin as an input surface for mobile computing. In *CHI Conference*, pages 179–188. ACM, 2014.

Interlinking English and Chinese RDF Data Using BabelNet

Tatiana Lesnikova
Univ. Grenoble Alpes & INRIA
Grenoble, France
tatiana.lesnikova@inria.fr

Jérôme David
Univ. Grenoble Alpes & INRIA
Grenoble, France
jerome.david@inria.fr

Jérôme Euzenat
INRIA & Univ. Grenoble Alpes
Grenoble, France
jerome.euzenat@inria.fr

ABSTRACT

Linked data technologies make it possible to publish and link structured data on the Web. Although RDF is not about text, many RDF data providers publish their data in their own language. Cross-lingual interlinking aims at discovering links between identical resources across knowledge bases in different languages. In this paper, we present a method for interlinking RDF resources described in English and Chinese using the BabelNet multilingual lexicon. Resources are represented as vectors of identifiers and then similarity between these resources is computed. The method achieves an F-measure of 88%. The results are also compared to a translation-based method.

Categories and Subject Descriptors

H.3.1 [**Content Analysis and Indexing**]: Linguistic processing, Dictionaries; I.2.4 [**Knowledge Representation Formalisms and Methods**]: Semantic networks; E.2 [**Data Storage Representations**]: Linked representations

General Terms

Semantic Web, Cross-lingual Data Interlinking

Keywords

Cross-lingual Instance Linking, Cross-lingual Link Discovery, owl:sameAs

1. INTRODUCTION

Linked Data enables the extension of the Web based on Semantic Web technologies. RDF (Resource Description Framework) is a W3C data model according to which a resource is described by triples (subject, predicate, object). The RDF statements form a directed labeled graph where the graph nodes represent resources and the edges represent relations between these resources. A set of statements about a resource constitutes a description set which contains certain characteristics of a resource and thus can ground the resource "identity".

Knowledge can be expressed in different languages. DBpedia[1] provides a semantic representation of Wikipedia in which multiple language labels are attached to the individual concepts. It has become the nucleus for the Web of Data. Though there are interlingual links between different language versions of Wikipedia, there are knowledge bases in other languages which are not interlinked. For example, XLore [8] is an RDF Chinese knowledge base which provides a semantic representation of national knowledge sources (Baidu baike, Hudong baike).

Cross-lingual interlinking consists in discovering links between entities across knowledge bases of different languages. It is particularly difficult due to several reasons: (1) the structure of graphs can be different and the structure-based techniques will not be much of help; (2) even if the structures are similar to one another, the properties themselves and their values are expressed in different natural languages. In this regard, we adopt a Natural Language Processing (NLP) approach to address the problem of finding the same object described in two different languages. Our hypothesis is that if two resources denote the same real-world object, then the descriptions of these resources should overlap with each other.

In this paper, we propose an instance interlinking method based on a multilingual lexicon which serves as a pivot language in order to make two resources comparable. We describe an experiment on interlinking resources with English and Chinese labels across data sets and compare it with a translation-based method. Given two RDF data sets, our goal is to find the identical resources and to interlink them with owl:sameAs link. This type of link is important for tracking information about the same resource across different data sources. The paper answers the following questions:

- Is a multilingual lexicon an appropriate medium to identify resource in two different languages?
- What method performs better: a method based on translation technology or multilingual lexicon?

The remainder of the paper is structured as follows. Section 2 presents related work on interlinking methods. Section 3 describes the proposed approach based on multilingual lexicon. Section 4 describes a corpus used in the experiments and evaluation scenarios. Results of the experiments are shown in Section 5. We outline our contributions and propose directions for future work in Section 6.

---

[1]http://wiki.dbpedia.org

DocEng'15, September 8–11, 2015, Lausanne, Switzerland.
© 2015 ACM. ISBN 978-1-4503-3307-8/15/09 ...$15.00.
DOI: http://dx.doi.org/10.1145/2682571.2797089.

2. RELATED WORK

The problem of finding the same object across heterogeneous data sources has many names: duplicate matching (deduplication), record linkage (in the database field), entity matching, entity resolution, object identification, instance matching. In the Semantic Web, data interlinking is the task of finding the same entity within different RDF graphs. The challenges for multilingual Web of data and linking procedures have been highlighted in [2]. In a cross-lingual context, interoperability involves linking identical resources described in different languages. A comprehensive survey of techniques for data linking can be found in [6]. The use of string matching is a widespread technique to identify similarity between entities, however, in a cross-lingual context, string matching algorithms will not work.

Datasets can be described by ontologies. Even if the ontologies are in the same language, the difference in granularity of categories can complexify the process of ontology matching. Recent developments have been made also in cross-lingual ontology matching [4]. A common approach to break the natural language barrier consists in transforming a cross-lingual problem into a monolingual one by translating the elements of one ontology into the language of the other ontology using machine translation [1]. After translation, monolingual matching strategies are applied.

In previous experiments [3], we described an interlinking method which has been relying both on language elements in a graph and machine translation. In this method, given two RDF graphs with resources described in different languages, each resource has been represented as a virtual document containing textual information from n neighboring nodes. Once constructed, these documents have been translated and standard text processing techniques have been applied. The similarity computed between documents is taken for similarity between resources. The pair of documents with the highest similarity score has been considered as a correspondence between identical resources.

Furthermore, instead of translation, it is possible to use multilingual lexical resources to compute semantic relatedness between entities. In the next section, we detail how an external multilingual resource can be used in interlinking RDF data across languages.

3. CROSS-LINGUAL INTERLINKING METHOD

We assume that resources in RDF are described with labels in different natural languages: properties and their values are usually natural language words. We adopt a linguistic interlinking approach where the textual description of a resource is very important: the similarity score highly depends on the overlapping text.

The framework that we designed for interlinking cross-lingual RDF resources is depicted in Figure 1, extending the process presented in [3].

In the present approach, we use a multilingual lexicon which serves as a basis for resource comparison. The interlinking method is schematized in Figure 2.

In particular, the method is the following:

1. Constructing a **Virtual Document** per resource. Due to the graph structure of RDF, we collect literals up to a specific distance (that we call level). The triples of an RDF graph can have simple strings (literals) as

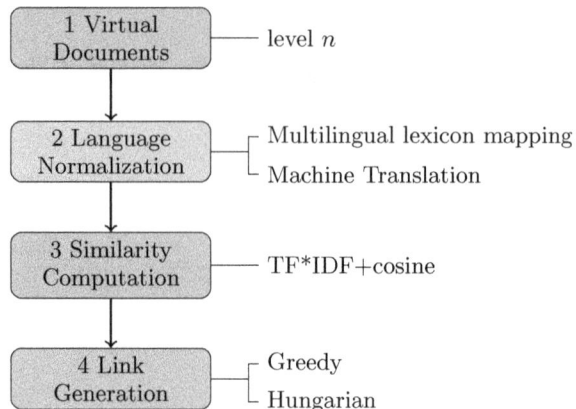

Figure 1: Framework for Cross-lingual RDF Interlinking.

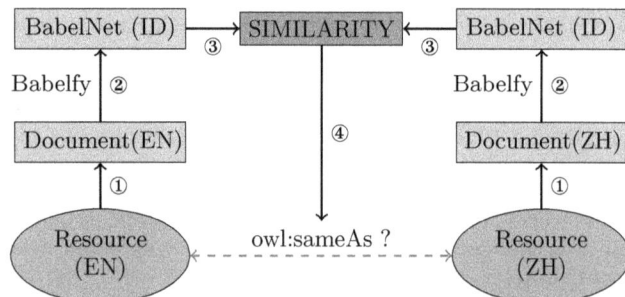

Figure 2: Interlinking Method Using Multilingual Lexicon. Multilingual terms are mapped to a common identifier. Similarity is computed between identifiers. Numbers correspond to the steps of the method.

an object which serve as a descriptor for a subject. We collect literals from all resource properties, the names of the properties themselves are not considered. In the example of Figure 3, the subject is "dbpedia:Lucerne" which has several literals, e.g., the label "Lucerne". These collected literals will constitute the body of a virtual document. We work with level 1 and 2 only.

2. Replacing document terms by identifiers from a **Multilingual Lexicon** in order to project the words of each language onto the same semantic space. At this step, we represent original documents as vectors of identifiers (IDs). A corresponding identifier (ID) is retrieved for a term. An identifier stands for a sense of a term and very often there are many senses (IDs) per term. If more that one sense exists, word sense disambiguation techniques shall be applied in order to select the best sense. The terms not found in a multilingual lexicon are discarded and we do not work with them in our experiments. To compute semantic relatedness, multilingual lexical knowledge resources can be used, e.g., BabelNet [5] or DBnary [7].

3. **Computing Similarity** between documents. We use a standard term weighting scheme (TF*IDF) and apply cosine similarity. These are classical techniques for finding similar documents, moreover, they showed good performance in our previous experiments. The

output of this step is a set of similarity values between pairs of virtual documents.

4. **Generating Links** between identical resources. At this stage, an algorithm extracts links on the basis of the similarity between documents. We use the Hungarian or greedy methods to extract links.

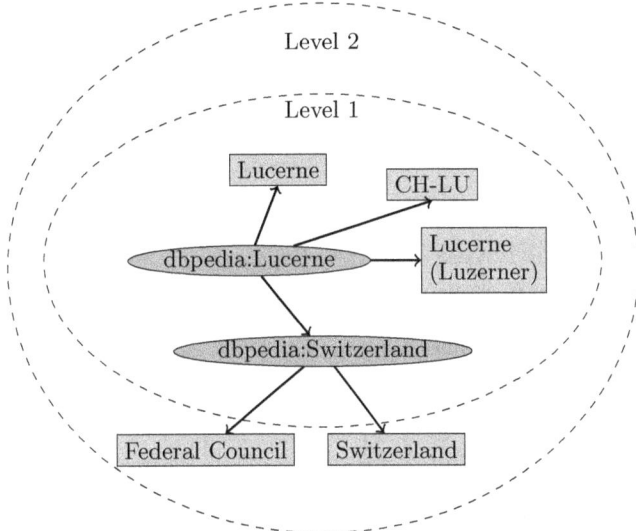

Figure 3: Creation of Virtual Documents by Levels.

4. EVALUATION SETUP

Our goal is to evaluate how the method, described in the previous section, works and what parameters are important. We particularly focus on four parameters: the presence or absence of non-matching entities in a data set, the presence or absence of rdfs:label property values in a virtual document, the amount of text in a virtual document per resource and the link extraction mechanism. We also evaluate the suitability of multilingual lexicon for identifying identical resources.

4.1 RDF Data

The experiment has been conducted on two separate RDF data sets with resources represented in English and Chinese respectively. Thus, the data consist of the English and Chinese parts. For the English part, we used DBpedia 3.9[2], for the Chinese part – Xlore.org[3]. We restricted our experiment to named entities, e.g, presidents, sportsmen, geographical places.

The original data set is the same as described in [3], however we have enhanced it in several aspects. The Chinese data has already been linked to the English version of DBpedia and we used a list of owl:sameAs links as our reference link set at the evaluation step. Two datasets have been constructed:

- Original set: contains 100 entities in one-to-one correspondence in English and Chinese languages.

[2]http://wiki.dbpedia.org/Downloads39
[3]http://xlore.org/index.action

- Original set + noise: we added 10 entities into each language side which do not have a match in the other language. This has been done in order to observe how similarity works when entities do not have matches.

The Chinese Xlore data set has been already linked to the English DBpedia. We used reference links (existing owl:sameAs links between resources) in order to select a list of entities per category. We selected entities that appeared in a reference link set and contained textual information at both levels and in both languages. The result of this selection is a relatively clean corpus which contains textual description of resources at both levels. This allowed us to test the level at which the performance is better. Entities used as noise are entities which have been present only in one language side and have been selected from the same categories as entities from the original set.

Each of these datasets contains virtual documents of two kinds: with an rdfs:label property value or without it. Thus, we have two variations of each dataset per language: Label and NoLabel.

Since we are linking named entities, an rdfs:label property value is usually a name of the entity which can be highly discriminative. By constructing a virtual document without this property value, we estimate the importance of this element in a resource description. The average number of words in virtual documents of the Original set is 230 at level 1 and 2100 at level 2 for the English language, the numbers do not vary much when noise is added. No such statistics is available for Chinese since we do not use Chinese tokenization (it is done at lexicon-mapping step by Babelfy).

4.2 Experimental parameters

Multilingual lexicon mapping.

We use BabelNet 2.5.1 which is a multilingual lexicon which connects concepts and named entities in a large network of semantic relations called synsets. Each synset represents a given meaning and contains synonyms which express that meaning in a range of different languages. Since many terms can have several synsets, we also made use of Babelfy 0.9 [4] in order to retrieve the best meaning per term. By design, Babelfy had a limit of 3500 characters for input text, so we had to cut documents at level 2 only. The impact of this is that we missed additional textual information which could have been useful for similarity computation.

Machine translation.

We also apply machine translation on the experimental data. We translate virtual documents using Machine Translation in order to transform documents into the same language. We use Bing Translator[5] to translate Chinese documents into English. Once the documents are translated, we preprocess data to prepare it for similarity computation. Virtual documents are treated as "bags of words", and we use standard NLP preprocessing techniques: transform cases into lower case + tokenize + filter stop words. Once the documents are preprocessed, we apply TF*IDF and cosine similarity.

[4]http://babelfy.org/
[5]https://www.bing.com/translator/

Table 1: Comparison of MT and BabelNet Methods. Similarity between Entities Using TFIDF. The numbers represent precision (P), recall (R) and F-measure (F) for the Hungarian extraction method.

	Hungarian	Machine Translation						BabelNet					
		level 1			level 2			level 1			level 2		
		P	F	R	P	F	R	P	F	R	P	F	R
Label	Original set	1	**1**	1	0.94	0.94	0.94	0.88	**0.88**	0.88	0.83	0.83	0.83
	Original set + noise	0.9	0.94	0.99	0.83	0.87	0.91	0.73	0.76	0.80	0.7	0.73	0.77
NoLabel	Original set	0.93	0.93	0.93	0.92	0.92	0.92	0.81	0.81	0.81	0.78	0.78	0.78
	Original set + noise	0.8	0.84	0.88	0.78	0.82	0.86	0.71	0.74	0.78	0.65	0.68	0.71

5. RESULTS

In the current evaluation, we have compared the results obtained using both methods: MT-based and BabelNet, see Table 1. We have compared the results using two popular assignment algorithms: the Hungarian and greedy. The best results have been achieved by the Hungarian algorithm so we do not report the results of the greedy one. The best results are obtained at level 1 on data sets with the rdfs:label property. Results at level 2 decrease for both algorithms: this is because information at level 2 becomes less discriminative and more noisy. Results are also lower when non-matching entities are added. In general, the translation approach outperformed the approach based on multilingual lexicon. This might be due to the better development of MT capability and unavailability of identifiers for some terms as well as errors in disambiguation in BabelNet. Since the terms not found in BabelNet have been discarded (as per step 2 Section 3), we know neither the nature of the missing terms nor the distribution of the number of missing terms per entity. If missing terms are preserved, the absence of identifiers may be compensated by translating those terms using machine translation. The results at level 2 may have been affected by the input text limit of Babelfy.

6. CONCLUSIONS

With the growing amount of heterogeneous data on the Web, it is important to make these data machine processable. In the Semantic Web, RDF data sets can be published with labels in different languages. In this context, data interlinking requires specific approaches to tackle cross-lingualism. We have evaluated two approaches based on machine translation and multilingual lexicon. Our results show that the best results are obtained using machine translation with an F-measure of 100%, while the results obtained with the multilingual lexicon are slightly lower with an F-measure of 88%. The highest results have been obtained on datasets with the rdfs:label property which shows that a name of a named entity is a discriminative feature in the interlinking process. Overall, both approaches seem to be promising for cross-lingual RDF data interlinking. However, the limitation would be the availability of language resources for a given pair of languages. The present work can be extended in the following directions:

- Test if both approaches can be complementary: errors made by one method can be corrected by the other method;
- Explore the suitability of Wikipedia for comparing resources.

ACKNOWLEDGMENTS

This work is partially supported by the ANR Lindicle[6] (12-IS02-0002) project in cooperation with Tsinghua University, China.

7. REFERENCES

[1] B. Fu, R. Brennan, and D. O'Sullivan. A Configurable Translation-Based Cross-Lingual Ontology Mapping System to adjust Mapping Outcome. *Journal of Web Semantics: Science, Services and Agents on the World Wide Web*, 15(3):15–36, 2012.

[2] J. Garcia, E. Montiel-Ponsoda, P. Cimiano, A. Gómez-Pérez, P. Buitelaar, and J. McCrae. Challenges for the Multilingual Web of Data. *Journal of Web Semantics*, 11:63–71, 2012.

[3] T. Lesnikova, J. David, and J. Euzenat. Interlinking English and Chinese RDF Data Sets Using Machine Translation. In *Proceedings of the 3rd Workshop on Knowledge Discovery and Data Mining Meets Linked Open Data (Know@LOD 2014)*, volume 1243. CEUR-WS, 2014.

[4] C. Meilicke, R. García-Castro, F. Freitas, W. R. van Hage, E. Montiel-Ponsoda, R. R. de Azevedo, H. Stuckenschmidt, O. Svab-Zamazal, V. Svatek, A. Tamilin, C. Trojahn, and S. Wang. MultiFarm: A Benchmark for Multilingual Ontology Matching. *Journal of Web Semantics*, 15:62–68, 2012.

[5] R. Navigli and S. P. Ponzetto. Babelnet: The automatic construction, evaluation and application of a wide-coverage multilingual semantic network. *Artif. Intell.*, 193:217–250, 2012.

[6] A. Nikolov, A. Ferrara, and F. Scharffe. Data linking for the semantic web. *Int. J. Semant. Web Inf. Syst.*, 7(3):46–76, July 2011.

[7] G. Sérasset and A. Tchechmedjiev. Dbnary: Wiktionary as Linked Data for 12 Language Editions with Enhanced Translation Relations. In *3rd Workshop on Linked Data in Linguistics: Multilingual Knowledge Resources and Natural Language Processing, LREC 2014*, pages 68–71, 2014.

[8] Z. Wang, J. Li, Z. Wang, S. Li, M. Li, D. Zhang, Y. Shi, Y. Liu, P. Zhang, and J. Tang. XLore: A Large-scale English-Chinese Bilingual Knowledge Graph. In *Proceedings of the ISWC 2013 Posters & Demonstrations Track*, volume 1035, pages 121–124. CEUR-WS, 2013.

---

[6]http://lindicle.inrialpes.fr/

Efficient Computation of Co-occurrence Based Word Relatedness [*]

Jie Mei, Xinxin Kou, Zhimin Yao, Andrew Rau-Chaplin,
Aminul Islam, Abidalrahman Moh'd, Evangelos E. Milios
Dalhousie University
Halifax, Nova Scotia
{jmei, kou, yao, arc, islam, amohd, eem}@cs.dal.ca

ABSTRACT

Measuring document relatedness using unsupervised co-occurrence based word relatedness methods is a processing-time and memory consuming task. This paper introduces the application of compact data structures for efficient computation of word relatedness based on corpus statistics. The data structure is used to efficiently lookup: (1) the corpus statistics for the Common Word Relatedness Approach, (2) the pairwise word relatedness for the Algorithm Specific Word Relatedness Approach. These two approaches significantly accelerate the processing time of word relatedness methods and reduce the space cost of storing co-occurrence statistics in memory, making text mining tasks like classification and clustering based on word relatedness practical.

Categories and Subject Descriptors

H.3.3 [**Information Search and Retrieval**]: Retrieval models

Keywords

Co-occurrence, Document Relatedness, Word Relatedness

1. INTRODUCTION

Many document relatedness methods are based on word relatedness [7,10]. Corpus-based word relatedness methods use co-occurrence statistics to compute relatedness [1,3,4, 10–13]. The advantages of these methods are: (1) they capture the semantic relatedness of different words, whereas in vector-based similarity only identical words present in documents contribute to the similarity between them. (2) generally, they are unsupervised and do not require other resources than a corpus; (3) the flexibility of applying them in different domains by using domain specific corpora; (4) they

---

[*] The research was funded in part by the Natural Sciences and Engineering Research Council of Canada (NSERC), and The Boeing Company.

Permission to make digital or hard copies of all or part of this work for personal or classroom use is granted without fee provided that copies are not made or distributed for profit or commercial advantage and that copies bear this notice and the full citation on the first page. Copyrights for components of this work owned by others than ACM must be honored. Abstracting with credit is permitted. To copy otherwise, or republish, to post on servers or to redistribute to lists, requires prior specific permission and/or a fee. Request permissions from Permissions@acm.org.
DocEng'15, September 8-11, 2015, Lausanne, Switzerland.
© 2015 ACM. ISBN 978-1-4503-3307-8/15/09 ...$15.00.
DOI: http://dx.doi.org/10.1145/2682571.2797088.

can be easily updated when corpora are updated. However, there are factors that affect using them on real-world applications, including the scalability and real-time performance in addition to the availability of using large corpora.

This paper aims to improve the scalability and real-time performance of co-occurrence based word relatedness methods. The features of these methods are explored to find the common co-occurrence components, which are used in two different approaches. One is a general framework, which makes lookup of co-occurrence statistics efficient and scalable through compact data structures and applicable to all methods. The other approach aims to improve the performance of a specific method by precomputing and storing the word relatedness of all word pairs in the corpus in compact data structures. In order to optimize the performance, both approaches make use of off-line pre-processing to standardize different corpora into structural statistics as well as compact data structures to support fast lookup of co-occurrence statistics and word pair relatedness respectively.

The experimental results using the Google web 1T n-gram corpus [2] show that both of the proposed approaches significantly improve the performance of word relatedness computation by aggregating co-occurrence statistics off-line.

2. CO-OCCURRENCE BASED WORD RELATEDNESS METHODS

In this section, six widely used word relatedness methods are summarized and put into a common efficient framework that is likely to support other similar methods. The common notations are: N is the total number of documents. H is the total number of web pages. The frequency of a word ω in a corpus and the document frequency of a word ω are $C(\omega)$ and $D(\omega)$, respectively.

Jaccard Coefficient measures the relatedness of two words by *the ratio of co-occurrence to individual presence.* It is commonly used in information retrieval as a measure of association. In some word relatedness estimation methods, web page count [1] or document frequency [6] can be used to measure word presence in a corpus.

$$\text{Jaccard}(\omega_1, \omega_2) = \frac{D(\omega_1, \omega_2)}{D(\omega_1) + D(\omega_2) - D(\omega_1, \omega_2)}$$

Simpson Coefficient measures the relatedness of two words by *the ratio of co-occurrence to the minimum individual presence* [1]. This method is useful in minimizing the

(a) Common word relatedness approach.

(b) Algorithm specific word relatedness approach.

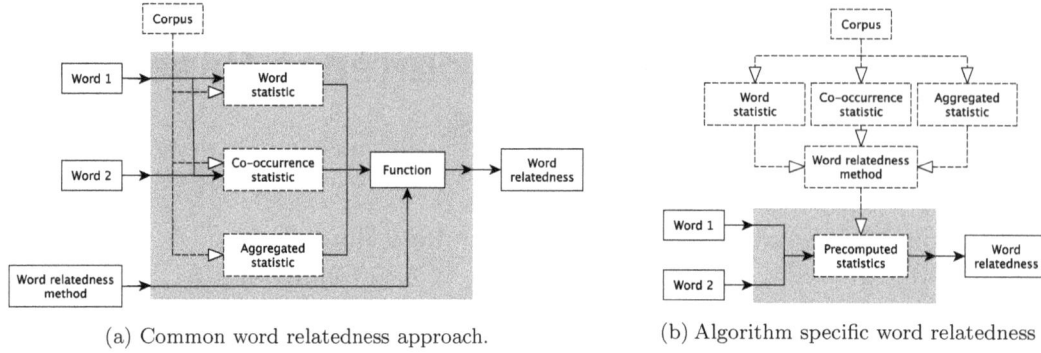

Figure 1: Proposed computational approaches. The shadowed boxes encapsulate the online processing steps. The objects on the left and right are the inputs and outputs. The dashed objects and relations are involved in the off-line processing.

effect of unequal presence [9].

$$\text{Simpson}(\omega_1, \omega_2) = \frac{H(\omega_1, \omega_2)}{\min(H(\omega_1), H(\omega_2))}$$

Dice Coefficient measures the relatedness of two words by *the ratio of the co-occurrence to the average individual presence*. Similar to Jaccard Coefficient, web page count [1] or document frequency [6] can be used to measure word presence in the corpus.

$$\text{Dice}(\omega_1, \omega_2) = \frac{2D(\omega_1, \omega_2)}{D(\omega_1) + D(\omega_2)}$$

Pointwise Mutual Information (PMI) measures the relatedness of two words by *comparing the probability of observed co-occurrence to the probability of independent co-occurrence* [3]. This method represents the variation between two probabilistic events [1,6].

$$\text{PMI}(\omega_1, \omega_2) = \log_2\left(\frac{\frac{D(\omega_1, \omega_2)}{N}}{\frac{D(\omega_1)}{N}\frac{D(\omega_2)}{N}}\right)$$

Normalized Google Distance (NGD) measures the distance of two words by *a page-count-based distance metric between given words* [4]. It is based on normalized information distance [11], where N_{norm} is a normalizing factor that can have any reasonable value greater than $H(\omega)$.

$$\text{GND}(\omega_1, \omega_2) = \frac{\max(\log H(\omega_1), \log H(\omega_2)) - \log H(\omega_1\omega_2)}{\log N_{norm} - \min(\log H(\omega_1), \log H(\omega_2))}$$

Google Trigram Method measures the relatedness of two words by *considering the frequency of the trigrams that start and end with the given pair of words normalized by their unigram frequencies* [10], where $\mu_T(\omega_1, \omega_2)$ is the mean frequency of trigrams which either start with ω_1 and end with ω_2, or start with ω_2 and end with ω_1 and $C_{\max}$ is the maximum frequency among all unigrams.

$$\text{GTM}(\omega_1, \omega_2) =$$

$$\begin{cases} \frac{\log \frac{\mu_T(\omega_1, \omega_2) C_{\max}^2}{C(\omega_1)C(\omega_2)\min(C(\omega_1)C(\omega_2))}}{-2\times\log\frac{\min(C(\omega_1), C(\omega_2))}{C_{\max}}} & \text{if } \log\frac{\mu_T(\omega_1,\omega_2)C_{\max}^2}{C(\omega_1)C(\omega_2)\min(C(\omega_1),C(\omega_2))} > 1 \\ \frac{\log 1.01}{-2\times\log\frac{\min(C(\omega_1),C(\omega_2))}{C_{\max}}} & \text{if } \log\frac{\mu_T(\omega_1,\omega_2)C_{\max}^2}{C(\omega_1)C(\omega_2)\min(C(\omega_1),C(\omega_2))} \leq 1 \\ 0 & \text{if } \mu_T(\omega_1, \omega_2) = 0 \end{cases}$$

The unigram count $C(\omega)$ and trigram count $C(\omega_1, \omega_2)$ can replace the page count and document frequency in all other methods in this section [9].

3. WORD RELATEDNESS APPROACHES

This section describes two efficient approaches with different applicability and efficiency. These approaches map to two use cases for using word relatedness methods in applications: (1) Using multiple methods at the same time, such as combining the result of several existing methods in a certain proportion or comparing result from different methods to find a best fit.(2) A single specific method is required as is typical in applications such as clustering which uses word relatedness as a preliminary step in other NLP tasks.

3.1 Common Word Relatedness

The Common Word Relatedness (CWR) approach exploits the underlying pre-computation opportunities that are generally available in the methods mentioned in Section 2. As illustrated in Figure 1a, different corpora will be considered, including raw text corpus, n-gram corpus [8], and web search engine based corpus [4, 13], to demonstrate the generality of this approach. The statistics used by the co-occurrence based methods can be categorized into three types: *Word statistics* is the information for individual word, including document frequency ($D(\omega)$ in Section 2), occurrence frequency ($C(\omega)$). *Co-occurrence statistics* is the information for co-occurrence word pair, including document frequency ($D(\omega_1, \omega_2)$), occurrence frequency ($C(\omega_1, \omega_2)$), mean frequency ($\mu_T(\omega_1, \omega_2)$). *Aggregated statistics* is the information for the corpus, including number of document (N), maximum frequency ($C_{\max}$). This type of statistics is usually used as a normalization factor.

Intuitively, every co-occurrence based method makes use of the word, co-occurrence, and aggregated statistics can be expressed with the following generalized expression:

$$Rel(\omega_1, \omega_2) = f(w(\omega_1), w(\omega_2), c(\omega_1, \omega_2), a) \quad (1)$$

In this expression, a word relatedness method is a function f, with three parameters: $w(\omega_1)$ and $w(\omega_2)$ are the word statistics for word ω_1 and ω_2, $c(\omega_1, \omega_2)$ is the co-occurrence statistics, and a is the aggregated statistics. Notice that all the statistical aggregation is performed by getting $w(\omega_1)$, $w(\omega_2)$ and $c(\omega_1, \omega_2)$. The function f performs only basic algebraic operations and no statistics aggregation. Given $w(\omega_1)$, $w(\omega_2)$, $c(\omega_1, \omega_2)$ and a, any co-occurrence based word relatedness method f can be computed efficiently.

3.2 Algorithm Specific Word Relatedness

This subsection describes the Algorithm Specific Word Relatedness Approach (ASWR) to more efficiently compute

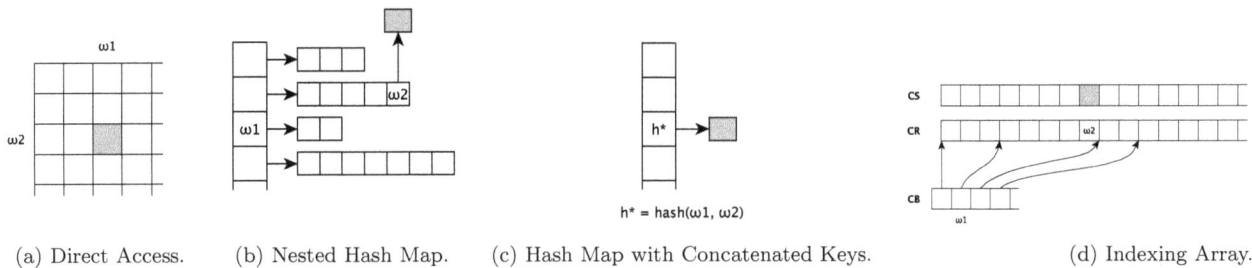

(a) Direct Access.   (b) Nested Hash Map.   (c) Hash Map with Concatenated Keys.   (d) Indexing Array.

Figure 2: Co-occurrence indexing data structures.

specific word relatedness methods. Observed from Equation 1, given a corpus, the two words ω_1 and ω_2, variables $w(\omega_1)$, $w(\omega_2)$ and $c(\omega_1,\omega_2)$ are constant statistics related to that corpus. The word relatedness method f is the *only* factor that changes the result $Rel(\omega_1,\omega_2)$.

This observation motivates us to aggressively exploit the pre-computation to be a method specific word relatedness approach. As illustrated in Figure 1b, given a corpus for a specific word relatedness method and a word pair ω_1,ω_2, the relatedness value can be returned directly instead of the corpus statistics. This can be expressed as:

$$Rel(\omega_1,\omega_2) = rel(\omega_1,\omega_2) \qquad (2)$$

Compared to Equation 1, this expression does not refer to the statistics (w, c, a) and the method (f), because these variables are pre-computed to be rel in Equation 2.

4. EFFICIENT INDEXING STRUCTURES

The key idea to accelerate the performance of the proposed word relatedness approaches on massive amount data is to pre-compute the intermediate data off-line, so that the intermediate data can be looked up rather than having to be computed on-line. In essence, efficient implementations of the classic data structures [5] are required for retrieving co-occurrence statistics. Time, space efficiency, and the trade-off between them should be taken into consideration. Four potential data structures for retrieving word statistic are described in this section.

Direct Access(DA) uses a co-occurrence statistics matrix implemented by a two-dimensional array as shown in Figure 2a. This design has the optimal retrieving speed, but it reserves space for every possible word pairs. The memory cost of the two-dimensional array grows quadratically with the growth of the number of words n. It is infeasible to maintain this data structure in-memory for a large n.

Nested Hash Map(NHM) uses a more space-efficient representation of a sparse matrix with expected constant lookup time. As showed in Figure 2b, NHM is implemented by a two-level structure consisting of a primary hash table indexed by row indices of the matrix and each secondary hash table storing the non-zero entries in the row.

Hash Map with Concatenated Keys(HMCK) uses a one-level hash table, which further reduces the memory used to store the co-occurrence statistics. As shown in Figure 2c, this data structure uses the concatenation of two words as the keys in the hash table.

Parallel Blocking Array(PBA) uses arrays illustrated in Figure 2d, which cost less memory space than hash tables. *Co-occurrence Block (CB)* declares the blocks range. When searching for the co-occurrence statistics in corpus, the two words are the key attributes to uniquely identify

record. In this design, the first word in a pair is chosen as the *blocking key* and the second word as the *reference key* for every record in the block. Starting and ending values in each cell refer to the starting position and the end position of the corresponding reference keys of each blocking key. *Co-occurrence Reference (CR)* stores the reference keys for each record. CR is divided into blocks of which the ranges are defined in CB. *Co-occurrence Statistics (CS)* stores preprocessed co-occurrence statistic. CS is parallel with CR.

5. EXPERIMENTAL EVALUATION

The experiments were conducted on a Linux server containing 32 Intel Xeon E5-2650 @ 2.00GHz cores and 256 Gigabytes main memory. The evaluation is performed using the unigrms and trigrams of the Google n-gram corpus. To test the resource usage for all implementations, 35 million word pairs are randomly generated from the abstracts of $43,542$ ACM articles.

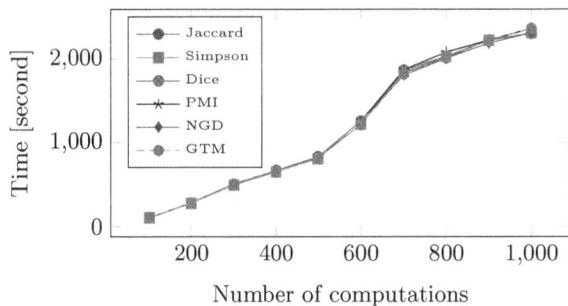

Figure 3: Performance of naïve in-memory approach.

A naïve in-memory approach is used as a baseline. It maintains Google web 1T corpus in a lexicographically sorted array and performs binary search to fetch statistics. Its data structure takes 98.35 Gigabytes making its use infeasible in many applications. Figure 3 shows the time taken in second as a function of the number of word relatedness computation performed. All methods in Section 2 have similar performance, because most of the processing time is used for fetching statistics from corpus and this step is identical for all methods. The naïve in-memory approach can compute only 0.42 word relatedness computation per second, which is too slow to be used in most applications.

We compare the performance of four data structures in CWR approach in terms of time and space usage. DA cannot fully index Google web 1T n-gram corpus in the memory of the testing server (256GB). To get a baseline timing for our experiment, a smaller vocabulary with $100,000$ words is used. The time taken for retrieving statistics is the same

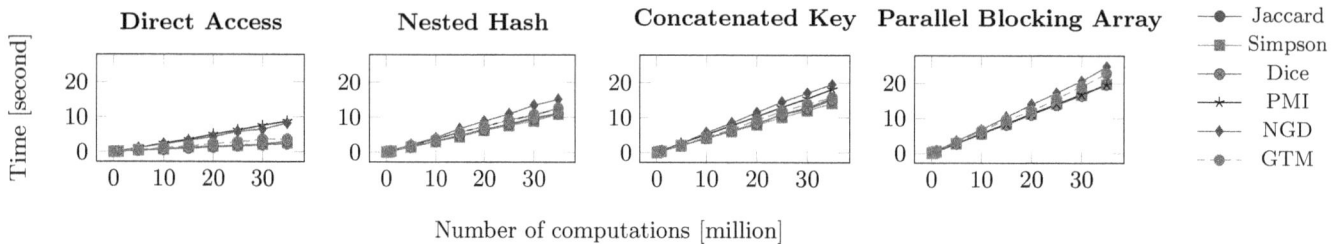

Figure 4: Computation time for word relatedness methods with index structures in CWR approach.

and the difference of performance between methods is due to their formula computation.

Data structure	Computation per second$[10^6/s]$						Space [GB]
	Jaccard	Simpson	Dice	PMI	NGD	GTM	
DA	15.178	13.672	11.494	3.977	4.276	9.642	1.4×10^6
NHM	3.136	3.192	3.163	2.771	2.311	2.770	8.151
HMCK	2.264	2.473	2.319	1.924	1.795	2.221	8.649
PBA	1.783	1.769	1.770	1.783	1.409	1.529	1.983

Table 1: Performance for each data structure

Table 1 shows the performance of all the combination of co-occurrence data structures and word relatedness methods in millions computation per second. DA is the most time efficient data structure in this test and is more than two times faster than other data structures. It computes more than 15 millions of word relatedness computation per second with Jaccard word relatedness. The rest three data structures are competing. The performance of NHM is about 50% better than HMCK and 80% better than PBA. PBA takes 1.983 Gigabytes to maintain the data structure for word relatedness computation. HMCK and NHM exceed 411% and 336% comparing with PBA, respectively.

Figure 5 illustrates the computation time for GTM with PBA in CWR and ASWR approaches. 17% speed up is achieved using ASWR compare to CWR approach. Empirically, the proposed approaches using the four data structures perform several orders of magnitude better than the naïve in-memory approach, which makes them more suitable for different applications. DA is the most time efficient but cost incredible large memory than other data structures due to the statistics sparsity. It is suitable for small vocabularies or extremely large corpus. PBA is the most space efficient solution, while NHM is the most applicable time efficient solution. Compare with CWR approach, ASWR approach is method specific but achieves better performance.

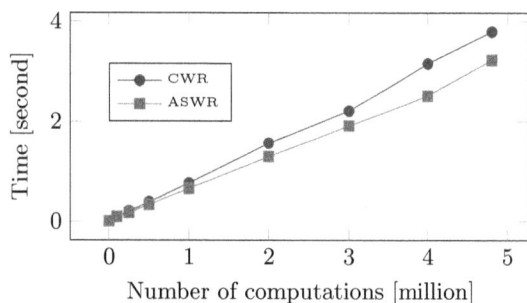

Figure 5: The computation time for GTM using PBA.

6. CONCLUSION

This paper has demonstrated that with careful algorithmic engineering, co-occurrence based word relatedness methods can be engineered for high performance. The proposed

word relatedness computation approaches make the common co-occurence word relatedness methods applicable and achieve a huge improvement on time and space. The compact data structure further accelerates processing time and reduces memory space cost. The proposed approaches can be parallelized on multi-core machines or clusters for further speed-up.

7. REFERENCES

[1] D. Bollegala, Y. Matsuo, and M. Ishizuka. A web search engine-based approach to measure semantic similarity between words. *Knowledge and Data Engineering, IEEE Trans. on*, 23(7):977–990, 2011.

[2] T. Brants and A. Franz. Web 1T 5-gram corpus version 1.1. Technical report, Google Research, 2006.

[3] K. W. Church and P. Hanks. Word association norms, mutual information, and lexicography. *Comput. Linguist.*, 16(1):22–29, Mar. 1990.

[4] R. Cilibrasi and P. Vitanyi. The Google similarity distance. *Knowledge and Data Engineering, IEEE Trans. on*, 19(3):370–383, March 2007.

[5] T. H. Cormen, C. E. Leiserson, et al. *Introduction to algorithms*, volume 2. 2001.

[6] E. Iosif and A. Potamianos. Unsupervised semantic similarity computation between terms using web documents. *Knowledge and Data Engineering, IEEE Trans. on*, 22(11):1637–1647, Nov 2010.

[7] A. Islam and D. Inkpen. Semantic text similarity using corpus-based word similarity and string similarity. *ACM Trans. Knowl. Discov. Data*, 2(2):10:1–10:25, July 2008.

[8] A. Islam and D. Inkpen. Managing the Google web 1t 5-gram data set. In *Natural Language Processing and Knowledge Engineering, 2009. NLP-KE 2009. International Conference on*, pages 1–5. IEEE, 2009.

[9] A. Islam, E. Milios, and V. Kešelj. Comparing word relatedness measures based on Google n-grams. In *COLING 2012, 24th International Conference on Computational Linguistics, 2012*, pages 495–506, 2012.

[10] A. Islam, E. Milios, and V. Kešelj. Text similarity using Google tri-grams. In *Advances in Artificial Intelligence*, volume 7310, pages 312–317. Springer, 2012.

[11] M. Li, X. Chen, X. Li, B. Ma, and P. Vitanyi. The similarity metric. *Information Theory, IEEE Trans. on*, 50(12):3250–3264, Dec 2004.

[12] G. Salton and M. J. McGill. *Introduction to Modern Information Retrieval*. McGraw-Hill, Inc., New York, NY, USA, 1986.

[13] P. D. Turney. Mining the web for synonyms: Pmi-ir versus lsa on toefl. In *Proceedings of the 12th European Conference on Machine Learning*, EMCL '01, pages 491–502, London, UK, UK, 2001. Springer-Verlag.

Automatic Extraction of Figures from Scholarly Documents

Sagnik Ray Choudhury
Information Sciences and
Technology
Pennsylvania State University
sagnik@psu.edu

Prasenjit Mitra
Information Sciences and
Technology
Pennsylvania State University
pmitra@ist.psu.edu

Clyde Lee Giles
Information Sciences and
Technology
Pennsylvania State University
giles@ist.psu.edu

ABSTRACT

Scholarly papers (journal and conference papers, technical reports, etc.) usually contain multiple "figures" such as plots, flow charts and other images which are generated manually to symbolically represent and illustrate visually important concepts, findings and results. These figures can be analyzed for automated data extraction or semantic analysis. Surprisingly, large scale automated extraction of such figures from PDF documents has received little attention. Here we discuss the challenges of how to build a heuristic independent trainable model for such an extraction task and how to extract figures at scale. Motivated by recent developments in table extraction, we define three new evaluation metrics: figure-precision, figure-recall, and figure-F1-score. Our dataset consists of a sample of 200 PDFs, randomly collected from five million scholarly PDFs and manually tagged for 180 figure locations. Initial results from our work demonstrate an accuracy greater than 80%.

Categories and Subject Descriptors

H.4 [**Document Analysis**]: Information Extraction; D.2.8 [**PDF processing**]: machine learning

General Terms

figure extraction; machine learning; PDF processing

Keywords

figure extraction; PDF; document analysis

1. INTRODUCTION

Scholarly papers often contain multiple "figures" some of which are generated from data which is not reported anywhere else in the paper, making them invaluable sources of information, available only there. These figures can be manually extracted from PDF documents using free software such as Inkscape. However, a batch extractor is necessary

for extraction at scale, say for a search engine. Previous research explored automatic classification and data extraction from specific types of figures, mostly line graphs and scatter plots [2,11](see section 2). But, these methods have not yet been applied to large scale datasets.

One possible way to extract such figures is to segment a page image (a PDF page converted into an image or a scanned image of a document page) into text and graphics region. This is a well-known research problem dating back to the 1980s [13]. These algorithms assume a considerable difference in pixel densities in the text and graphics regions. While that is true for most newspaper/magazine documents, engineering drawings, and scholarly papers are different [3].

There is an abundance of "born digital" scholarly documents, mostly in the PDF format. It is certainly possible to convert a born digital PDF document into page images and apply existing image segmentation algorithms [4,14]. But, PDF to image conversion can be computationally expensive. Our experiments suggest that the average CPU time for PDF page to image conversion is more than two seconds, while our PDF processing-based approach takes half of that.

Figures are embedded in PDF documents in raster (PNG, JPEG) or vector formats (SVG, EPS). Typically, raster images are embedded in the PDF as separate content streams (XObjects). Therefore, it is easy for a PDF parser to extract them but it is hard to extract vector graphics as PDF documents themselves are written in the same format. In a PDF document, graphics and textual elements are often interleaved in the content stream and can not be easily segregated. Previous work by Futrelle et al. [8], Shao et al. [15] and very recently, Clark et al. [7] have reported heuristic methods for this task. But as these methods depend strongly on heuristics, they are often hard to reproduce since they require elaborate manual tuning. More importantly, most previous work has not discussed any strategy or results for the evaluation the extraction accuracy (with the exception of Clark et al. [7]).

We report a machine learning based method that does not depend on heuristics to extract figures from PDF documents. We also define metrics to evaluate the extraction accuracy and create a tagged dataset for use and future evaluation. We show that our method is more scalable with regards to existing approaches. Plus, our average F1-score is higher than 80%.

2. RELATED WORK

In earlier work, we described machine learning based algorithms for figure metadata extraction [5] and a search engine on the extracted metadata [6]. Here, we focus on figure extraction, especially vector graphics.

This problem can be solved in a two-step process: 1. Convert a PDF page into an image, and 2. Segment that image into text and graphics regions. There has been considerable work in such page segmentation. The approaches can be broadly classified into three classes: 1. A top-down block based approach where the image is segmented into blocks, and these blocks are classified as text or graphics region [13]; 2. A bottom up pixel-based approach where each pixel is classified as image or text and finally grouped together to form larger blocks [16]; and 3. A morphological operation based approach where a "graphics mask" is created through a set of morphological operations [1]. As discussed in section 1, these approaches suffer from a scalability problem. Also, these methods assume that the pixel density of a figure region is significantly different from that of a text region, which is usually not true for scholarly documents [3]. Our previous work [14] improved the morphological segmentation but suffered from scalability.

Little work([7,8,15]) has explored figure extraction from PDF documents by processing the PDF primitives. As mentioned before, they suffer from problems such as manual tuning of heuristics and lack of standardized evaluation metrics and data sets.

3. USING PDF OBJECT MODEL FOR FIGURE EXTRACTION

At an abstract level, a PDF document can be described using three types of primitives: text, path (vector elements such as lines and curves) and raster (bitmap) images. Each primitive is painted on the screen using a set of operations, the graphics state, and a transformation matrix.

We output bounding boxes for figure regions on a page merging paths and bitmap images. These bounding boxes contain the text inside the figure.

Extraction of bitmap images is relatively easy because there are only four operators for painting the image, and the painting locations can be extracted easily as well. The scenario is more complicated For the vector elements. Three types of operators are used to render a path:

1. **Path construction**: Operators c (curveto), l (lineto) and others are used to define start and end points of a path.

2. **Path painting**: Operators S (stroke path), s (close and stroke path) are used to paint a path on the screen. These operators determine the color, width and other esthetic details.

3. **Clipping paths**: Operators W and W^* are used to construct clipping paths. A clipping path defines a region of the page which should be used for painting the vector elements.

Extracting the locations for "paths" can be difficult because the parser needs to consider various elements of the graphics environment, as described before. Therefore, it is beneficial to have a higher level representation of the PDF. Recent work by Hassan et al. [10] introduced an "object level" representation of PDF documents. Their software (pdfXtk) produces bounding boxes of vector and raster graphic elements from a PDF document, combining several small subpaths. The goal of the software is to "obtain a simplified representation of the most important lines and

boxes which are of material importance for layout analysis, i.e. they are likely to be noticed immediately by a human reader just scanning through the page and are at the level of granularity required for performing document analysis" [10]. Our system uses the output of this software.

The output from pdfXtk are the bounding boxes for paths, but not all of them belong to graphics regions. For example, most tables have lines, symbols can be drawn by curves. These paths need to be filtered out before the grouping. Surprisingly, previous works don't discuss that. We propose models learned from the data to remove these "noisy paths". Also, we show that the grouping can be done using clustering algorithms, removing the need for heuristics. Once paths are classified and clustered, their bounding boxes can be merged to produce final figure regions.

3.1 Classification of Raster Graphics and Paths

We considered a binary classification problem where we classified each path/raster graphic as a member of a figure region (positive) or not (negative). We observed that most large raster graphics (area of the graphic > 10% of the page area) belonged to the positive class. Paths pose a greater challenge and determining such heuristic is hard. We extracted following features for each path:

- **Character density ratio**: It is intuitive that the paths inside the figure regions will have less text around them whereas paths inside table/equation region will have a higher amount of text. Therefore, for each path, we extract the character density within a region around it. Character density is defined as the number of characters inside a region / area of the region. We also extract the character density for the whole document. The feature value is defined as CD_p/CD_{pdf}(character density of the path / character density of the PDF).

- **Distance from boundary**: PDF pages usually contain paths which acts as demarcations or used for decorative purposes. For example, footnotes are usually separated from the main content by a straight line near the boundary of the page. On the contrary, paths inside figure regions are far from the page boundary. We define the distance of a path from a boundary as the minimum of distances from all axes.

- **Number of paths in ϵ neighborhood**: This feature is motivated from DBSCAN algorithm where a point is classified as noise if it has less than N points in its ϵ neighborhood. Often, paths are used to paint symbols such as ratio (/), summation (Σ). As these paths should be inside the text regions and not the figure regions, ideally they should have less number of paths around them.

- **Area**: We observed that the paths inside the figure regions had smaller area compared to the other paths.

We experimented with four classifiers, and the results are reported in section 4.3.

3.2 Combining Paths into Figure Regions

Paths classified as positive instances can be grouped by heuristics to create figure regions. A popular way for such grouping is optimized X-Y cut, [12] but the parameters for the algorithm need to be tuned. Therefore, our system uses a clustering algorithm.

A clustering algorithm such as K-means has three parameters: 1. The number of clusters, 2. Distance function and 3.

Initialization. Most scholarly documents contain figure captions. Therefore, number of clusters can be estimated easily using regular expressions. From our previous work [14], it was evident that the best distance function is the Euclidean distance between the centers of the bounding boxes. In the usual implementations of K-means algorithm, the initial points are chosen randomly, which can lead to arbitrary results. We experimented with two initialization methods:

- **Nearest point to a figure caption (NFC)**: Points nearest to the figure captions were used as initialization points. The distance is measured by Manhattan distance between two rectangles.

- **K-means++**: In this method, cluster centers are chosen to be far away from each other. The first initial cluster center is chosen at random. The second cluster center x is chosen with a probability proportional to the distance of the point x from the first cluster center. This process is repeated until K cluster centers are chosen.

4. EXPERIMENTS AND RESULTS

4.1 Dataset

We randomly sampled 200 PDF files from CiteSeerX repository and split them into pages, yielding approximately 1800 pages. 85 pages each having more than one figure and more than five paths/images were randomly selected as test data.

From the rest, we randomly selected 50 pages containing at least one figure to generate the data for the classification experiment. We extracted approximately 3000 paths, but more than 85% of these paths belonged to the positive class. This is not surprising, given that most paths would belong to some figure. However, this could create highly overfitted models, especially in decision trees. To solve this data imbalance problem, we further sampled 50 pages that contained no figure but tables. The final data for classification (approximately 4000 paths) had 2:1 positive to negative ratio.

Since figure regions had to be manually tagged from the page images, and we only investigated the harder cases (pages with minimum two figures), the dataset is relatively small. A completely random selection would include pages with one figure. Though that would increase the accuracy, there would be no clustering evaluation.

4.2 Evaluation

For the classification problem, we use well-known evaluation metrics: precision, recall, and F1-score. For our problem, it is important to have high recall for the negative class, even at the expense of the positive class. Because, even if some positive samples belonging to a figure region are wrongly classified, they would possibly be merged into the region due to the correctly classified samples. Figure 1 shows an example of that case.

The clustering evaluation is tricky. Standard metrics such as adjusted rand index are not suitable because even a single point clustered wrongly can change the region size dramatically. Suppose the location of the actual figure is given by a rectangle R_g and the predicted location is given by a rectangle R_p. The evaluation metrics are defined as:

1. **Figure-precison**: $\frac{\text{Area overlap between } R_g \text{ and } R_p}{\text{Area of } R_p}$

2. **Figure-recall**: $\frac{\text{Area overlap between } R_g \text{ and } R_p}{\text{Area of } R_g}$

3. **Figure-F1-score**: Harmonic mean of figure-precison and figure-recall.

Given the gold standard data for a page (i.e. set of all R_gs for that page) and the predicted locations for the same page (set of all R_ps for that page) we first calculate the correspondence between the sets. A correspondence configuration is defined as a one to one mapping between two sets. We calculate the total area overlap for all such possible configurations and the one having the maximum value is considered to be the final mapping. Once the mapping is defined, we calculate the "figure-precision", "figure-recall" and "figure-F1-score" values between (R_p, R_g) pairs. Our metrics are motivated by ICDAR 2013 table localization competition [9].

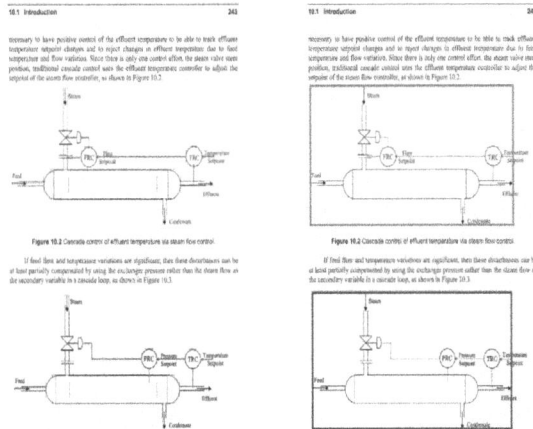

(a) Classification results on a sample page.

(b) Clustering results on the classified paths.

Figure 1: An example where some instances of the positive class (green) are classified as negative class (red). However, that doesn't change the clustering quality.

4.3 Classification: Results and Discussions

We experimented with four classifiers for the classification problem: 1. A Linear Kernel SVM (penalty parameter value=1), 2. A Gaussian Naïve Bayes classifier, 3. A Decision Tree classifier with depth=3 and Gini index as the splitting criterion and 4. A Logistic Regression classifier. The data (4000 paths) was splitted in 70:30 ratio for training and testing, maintaining the class balance. Each classifier was run 200 times, and the metrics were calculated on the test data. The results of the experiments are presented in table 1. Note that the experiment process is equivalent to stratified cross-validation but more robust as it is done for 200 times. The decision tree performed better in classifying the negative class. More importantly, the recall is the highest when we use decision trees. Inference in decision trees is rule-based, hence scalable. We experimented with multiple combinations of the features, but the results didn't improve.

4.4 Clustering: Results and Discussions

We used the decision tree model learned from the training data to classify each path in test data. Positively classified paths were clustered using K-means, and finally merged into figure regions. For the clustering problem, we experimented

Classifier	Recall		Precision		F1-Score	
	(-)ve	(+)ve	(-)ve	(+)ve	(-)ve	(+)ve
SVM	53.9	87.7	65.4	82.0	58.7	84.7
Naïve Bayes	45.5	92.0	70.4	80.1	55.1	**85.7**
Decision Tree	73.2	73.1	53.7	86.8	**61.7**	79.1
Logistic Regression	72.4	69.1	49.5	85.7	58.8	76.5

Table 1: Classification results for used classifiers.

with two initialization parameters. The results are presented in table 2. For the first method of initialization (Nearest point to a figure caption), clustering is deterministic because the choice of the initial cluster centers is deterministic. For the second method (K-means++), the choice is probabilistic. Therefore, we ran the clustering process ten times and chose the fifth output. We ran the clustering and merging process on 85 pages, each having more than one figure region and five paths. Figure precision, recall, and F1-scores were calculated as described in section 4.2. We had 180 figures in the gold standard. Table 2 presents the average values for the metrics. As expected, the first initialization method outperforms the K-means++ method.

Initialization method	Figure-precison	Figure-recall	Figure-F1-score
Nearest point to a figure caption	81.9	85.0	80.9
K-means++	78.4	80.4	76.6

Table 2: Figure-precison,recall and F1-scores on test data.

5. CONCLUSION AND FUTURE WORK

We propose a machine learning based approach to extract figures from scholarly PDF documents. Our system builds on recent developments in document processing. Contrary to most work in this area, our approach is heuristic independent and achieves good accuracy and scalability. We have also designed evaluation metrics and created a labeled dataset. Future work would be to improve the clustering algorithm and explore the table extraction problem using a similar approach.

6. ACKNOWLEDGEMENTS

We gratefully acknowledge partial support from the National Science Foundation and NPRP grant # 4-029-1-007 from the Qatar National Research Fund (a member of Qatar Foundation).

7. REFERENCES

[1] D. S. Bloomberg. Multiresolution morphological approach to document image analysis. In *Proc. of the International Conference on Document Analysis and Recognition, Saint-Malo, France*, 1991.

[2] W. Browuer, S. Kataria, S. Das, P. Mitra, and C. L. Giles. Segregating and extracting overlapping data points in two-dimensional plots. In *Proceedings of the 8th ACM/IEEE-CS joint conference on Digital libraries*, JCDL '08, pages 276–279, New York, NY, USA, 2008. ACM.

[3] S. S. Bukhari, F. Shafait, and T. M. Breuel. Improved document image segmentation algorithm using multiresolution morphology. In *IS&T/SPIE Electronic Imaging*, pages 78740D–78740D. International Society for Optics and Photonics, 2011.

[4] H. Chao and J. Fan. Layout and content extraction for pdf documents. In *Document Analysis Systems VI*, pages 213–224. Springer, 2004.

[5] S. R. Choudhury, P. Mitra, A. Kirk, S. Szep, D. Pellegrino, S. Jones, and C. L. Giles. Figure metadata extraction from digital documents. In *Document Analysis and Recognition (ICDAR), 2013 12th International Conference on*, pages 135–139. IEEE, 2013.

[6] S. R. Choudhury, S. Tuarob, P. Mitra, L. Rokach, A. Kirk, S. Szep, D. Pellegrino, S. Jones, and C. L. Giles. A figure search engine architecture for a chemistry digital library. In *Proceedings of the 13th ACM/IEEE-CS joint conference on Digital libraries*, pages 369–370. ACM, 2013.

[7] C. Clark and S. Divvala. Looking beyond text: Extracting figures, tables and captions from computer science papers. In *Workshops at the Twenty-Ninth AAAI Conference on Artificial Intelligence*, 2015.

[8] R. P. Futrelle, M. Shao, C. Cieslik, and A. E. Grimes. Extraction, layout analysis and classification of diagrams in pdf documents. In *2013 12th International Conference on Document Analysis and Recognition*, volume 2, pages 1007–1007. IEEE Computer Society, 2003.

[9] M. Gobel, T. Hassan, E. Oro, and G. Orsi. Icdar 2013 table competition. In *Document Analysis and Recognition (ICDAR), 2013 12th International Conference on*, pages 1449–1453. IEEE, 2013.

[10] T. Hassan. Object-level document analysis of pdf files. In *Proceedings of the 9th ACM symposium on Document engineering*, pages 47–55. ACM, 2009.

[11] X. Lu, S. Kataria, W. J. Brouwer, J. Z. Wang, P. Mitra, and C. L. Giles. Automated analysis of images in documents for intelligent document search. *IJDAR*, 12(2):65–81, 2009.

[12] J.-L. Meunier. Optimized xy-cut for determining a page reading order. In *ICDAR*, volume 5, pages 347–351, 2005.

[13] G. Nagy and S. Seth. Hierarchical representation of optically scanned documents. In *Proceedings of International Conference on Pattern Recognition*, volume 1, pages 347–349, 1984.

[14] S. Ray Choudhury and C. L. Giles. An architecture for information extraction from figures in digital libraries. In *Proceedings of the 24th International Conference on World Wide Web Companion*, pages 667–672. International World Wide Web Conferences Steering Committee, 2015.

[15] M. Shao and R. P. Futrelle. Recognition and classification of figures in pdf documents. In *Graphics Recognition. Ten Years Review and Future Perspectives*, pages 231–242. Springer, 2006.

[16] S. N. Srihari. Document image understanding. In *Proceedings of 1986 ACM Fall Joint Computer Conference*, ACM '86, pages 87–96, Los Alamitos, CA, USA, 1986. IEEE Computer Society Press.

Generating Abstractive Summaries
from Meeting Transcripts

Siddhartha Banerjee
The Pennsylvania State
University
College of IST
PA, USA
sub253@ist.psu.edu

Prasenjit Mitra
Qatar Computing Research
Institute
Hamad Bin Khalifa University
Doha, Qatar
pmitra@qf.org.qa

Kazunari Sugiyama
National University of
Singapore
School of Computing
Singapore
sugiyama@comp.nus.edu.sg

ABSTRACT

Summaries of meetings are very important as they convey the essential content of discussions in a concise form. Both participants and non-participants are interested in the summaries of meetings to plan for their future work. Generally, it is time consuming to read and understand the whole documents. Therefore, summaries play an important role as the readers are interested in only the important context of discussions. In this work, we address the task of meeting document summarization. Automatic summarization systems on meeting conversations developed so far have been primarily extractive, resulting in unacceptable summaries that are hard to read. The extracted utterances contain disfluencies that affect the quality of the extractive summaries. To make summaries much more readable, we propose an approach to generating abstractive summaries by fusing important content from several utterances. We first separate meeting transcripts into various topic segments, and then identify the important utterances in each segment using a supervised learning approach. The important utterances are then combined together to generate a one-sentence summary. In the text generation step, the dependency parses of the utterances in each segment are combined together to create a directed graph. The most informative and well-formed sub-graph obtained by integer linear programming (ILP) is selected to generate a one-sentence summary for each topic segment. The ILP formulation reduces disfluencies by leveraging grammatical relations that are more prominent in non-conversational style of text, and therefore generates summaries that is comparable to human-written abstractive summaries. Experimental results show that our method can generate more informative summaries than the baselines. In addition, readability assessments by human judges as well as log-likelihood estimates obtained from the dependency parser show that our generated summaries are significantly readable and well-formed.

DocEng'15, September 8-11, 2015, Lausanne, Switzerland.
© 2015 ACM. ISBN 978-1-4503-3307-8/15/09 ...$15.00.
DOI: http://dx.doi.org/10.1145/2682571.2797061.

Table 1: Two sets of extractive summaries along with the corresponding gold standard human generated abstractive summaries from a meeting in the AMI corpus [5]. Set 2 follows Set 1 in the actual meeting transcript. "A," "B" and "D" refer to three distinct speakers in the meeting.

Set 1: Human-generated extractive summary
D: um as well as uh characters.
D: um different uh keypad styles and s symbols.
D: Well right away I'm wondering if there's um th th uh, like with DVD players, if there are zones.
A: Cause you have more complicated characters like European languages, then you need more buttons.
D: I'm thinking the price might might appeal to a certain market in one region, whereas in another it'll be different, so
D: kay trendy probably means something other than just basic
Abstractive summary: The team then discussed various features to consider in making the remote.
Set 2: Human-generated extractive summary
B: Like how much does, you know, a remote control cost.
B: Well twenty five Euro, I mean that's um that's about like eighteen pounds or something.
D: This is this gonna to be like the premium product kinda thing or
B: So I don't know how how good a remote control that would get you. Um.
Abstractive summary: The project manager talked about the project finances and selling prices.

Categories and Subject Descriptors

I.2 [**ARTIFICIAL INTELLIGENCE**]: Natural Language Processing—*Language generation*

Keywords

Abstractive meeting summarization; Integer linear programming; Topic segmentation

1. INTRODUCTION

Meeting summarization helps both participants and non-participants by providing a short and concise snapshot of the most important content discussed in the meetings. While previous work on meeting summarization was primarily extractive [14, 15], a recent study showed that people generally prefer abstractive summaries [29].

Table 1 shows the human-written abstractive summaries along with the human-generated extractive summaries from the AMI cor-

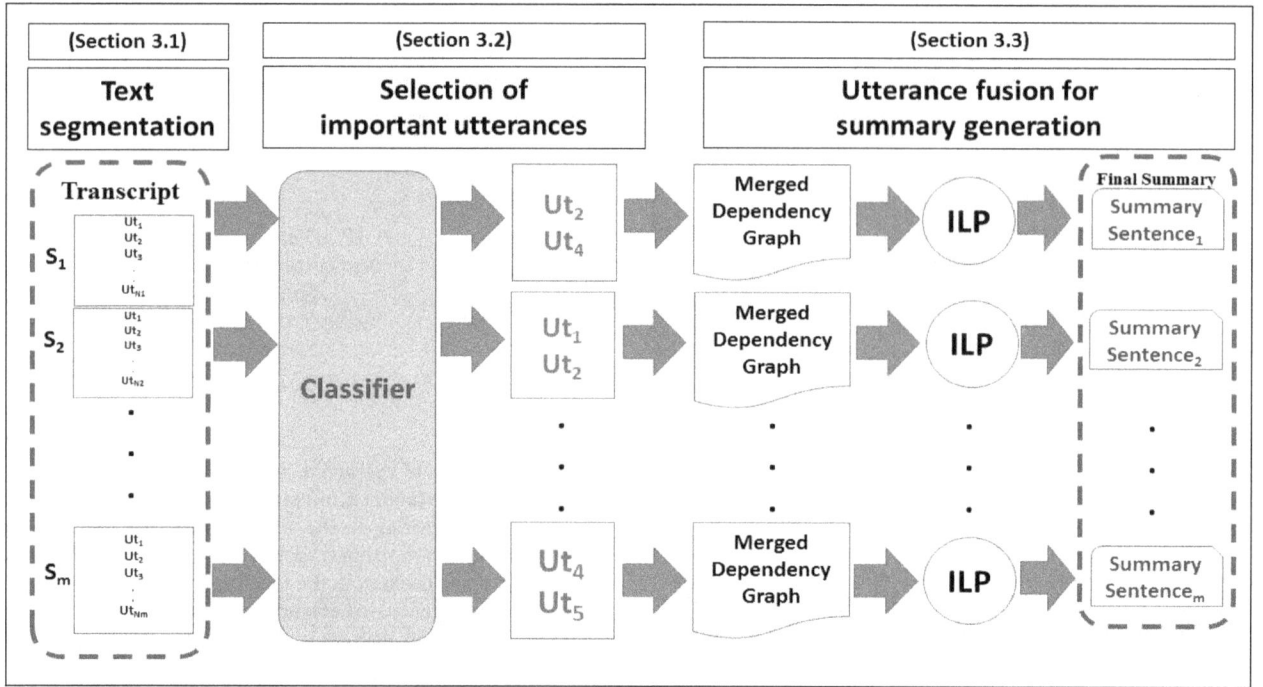

Figure 1: Our meeting summarization system overview.

pus [5]. Set 1 and Set 2 show two different topics discussed in the meeting – *design features* and *finances*. We have skipped other intervening utterances not included in the extractive summary. As shown in Table 1, the utterances are highly noisy and contain unnecessary information. Even if an extractive summarizer can accurately classify these utterances as "important" and generate a summary, it is usually hard to read and synthesize information from such summaries. In contrast, the human written summaries are compact and written in non-conversational style. They are more readable than the extractive summaries and preserve the most important information.

Previous approaches to abstractive meeting summarization have relied on template-based [36] or word-graph fusion-based [26] methods. The template-based method was applied to the generation of *focused summaries*.[1] Template-based generation is feasible in the case where the type of the summary is known apriori; however, our work does not make any assumptions on the type of the summary to be generated. The word-graph fusion-based technique, on the contrary, used an unsupervised approach to fuse a cluster of utterances generated using an entailment graph-based approach. However, this method did not take into consideration any grammatical dependencies between the words, resulting in ungrammatical output in several cases.

In this work, we propose an automatic way of generating short and concise abstractive summaries of meetings. Every meeting is usually comprised of several sub-topics [19]. As shown in Table 1, the participants discuss different aspects in Set 1 and Set 2. A well-formed abstractive summary should identify the most important aspects discussed in the meeting. In other words, if we can summarize the important information from every aspect, we can generate an informative summary that highlights the salient elements of the meeting. Therefore, we need to determine the boundaries where significant topic changes happen to isolate different aspects. Fur-

ther, to generate a summary for each segment (topic), we should be able to fuse information from multiple utterances on that topic and retain the most informative constituents. Simultaneously, we should also generate grammatical output to ensure that the final summaries are well-formed and readable.

Figure 1 shows the overview of our proposed meeting summarization system. As shown in Figure 1, initially, a meeting transcript is divided into several topic segments S_i ($i = 1, 2, \ldots, m$), where each segment contains N_i utterances ($Ut_{N_1}, \ldots, Ut_{N_i}$) on a specific topic. Previous work on meeting summarization [28] has shown that *lexical cohesion* is an important indicator in topic identification in meetings. We experiment with two different lexical-cohesion based text segmentation algorithms: LCSeg [13] and unsupervised Bayesian topic segmentation [8]. Only a few utterances contain information that is worthy of being included in the summary. Therefore, we introduce an extractive summarization component. To identify the most important (summary-worthy) utterances, we employ a supervised learning approach to construct a classifier by using content and discourse-level features. We parse the important utterances in each segment using a dependency parser, and then fuse the corresponding dependency graphs together to form a directed graph (*merged dependency graph*). The directed graph consists of the words in the utterances as the nodes, while the edges represent the grammatical relations between the words. Such a graph construction method ensures fusion of common information elements from utterances within the same topic segment. We introduce an *anaphora resolution* step when merging dependency graphs. We also introduce an *ambiguity resolver* that takes into consideration the context of words when fusing several utterances. Consider the following two utterances:

"um there's a sample sensor and there's a sample speaker unit",

"I'm not sure how the sample unit gonna work."

Once the first utterance is added into the graph, two nodes containing the word "*sample*" are created. The ambiguity resolver

---

[1]Focused summary refers to summaries on specific aspects of the meeting such as actions, decisions, etc.

maps the word "*sample*" from the second utterance to the second node ("*sample*" node adjacent to "*unit*") to account for the correct context of the words. Our goal is to retain the most informative nodes (words) in the graph. Further, linguistically well-formed grammatical relations should be retained. We formulate the sub-graph generation problem as an Integer Linear Programming (ILP) problem by adapting an existing sentence fusion technique [10]. The solution to the ILP problem generates a sub-graph that satisfies several constraints to maximize information content and linguistic quality. Information content is measured using Hori and Furui's word informativeness formula [18] while the linguistic quality is estimated using probabilities of grammatical relations from the Reuter's corpus [1]. Grammatical relations extracted from the Reuter's corpus assign higher preferences to non-conversational style of text, thereby resulting in summaries that mirror the flair of human-written abstracts. In the ILP problem, we introduce constraints to limit the length of the sentences. Further, we ensure connectivity in the graph. We introduce several linguistic constraints to generate grammatical output. The sub-graph generated from each segment is linearized [11] using a bottom-up approach to generate a one-sentence summary. The one-sentence summaries from all the segments are combined in the final summary. Note that we do not introduce any new phrases or words in the process of combining information from multiple utterances. Instead, we consider utterances that are associated with the same topic and apply the ILP-based fusion technique to identify grammatical relations that contains more informative phrases, at the same time leading to generation of summaries that are fairly readable.

To the best of our knowledge, this is the first work that addresses the problems of readability, grammaticality, and content selection jointly for meeting summary generation without employing a template-based approach. Experimental results on the aforementioned AMI corpus that consists of meeting recordings show that our approach outperforms the comparable systems. ROUGE-2 and ROUGE-SU4 [20] scores from our abstractive model (0.048 and 0.087) are significantly better than that of the extractive summaries (0.026 and 0.044) as well as the word-graph based abstractive summarization method [26] (0.041 and 0.079). We also assess readability of the summaries using a human judge, demonstrating that the summaries generated by our method are fairly well-formed.

2. RELATED WORK

In the field of meeting summarization, while extractive techniques have been widely employed so far [22, 24], abstractive techniques, including sentence compression, template and graph-based approaches, have been focused on recently.

Liu and Liu [23] used sentence compression to generate summaries of meetings. However, they reported that the quality of the generated summaries are not so good and there is a potential limit to apply such methods to summarization. Murray *et al.* [30] mapped conversations to an ontology that was complemented with a Natural language generation (NLG) component used for transforming utterances to summaries. The corresponding full summarization system was later presented in [29], where a user study was conducted on the abstractive summaries that were generated. However, the full summarization system involved extensive manual labor to set specific speakers, entities, etc. in a template before using an NLG realizer to generate the summaries. Lu and Cardie [36] proposed a method that learns templates from the human written summaries and generates the summaries of decisions and actions of meetings by using the best set of templates for a particular summary ranked using a greedy approach. In contrast, we cannot use templates be-

cause we assume that the type of a conversation (action, decision, etc) is not known apriori.

Mehdad *et al.* [26] developed a method that first over-generates multiple fused utterances in an entailment graph, and then chooses one based on the final path ranking. The fusing of the utterances only considers words, and ignores the grammatical relations between them. This results in generation of summaries with poor linguistic quality. More recently, Oya *et al.* [32] used the same fusion technique to generate summaries of meetings. Both of the methods developed by Mehdad *et al.* and Oya *et al.* mentioned above relied on using multi-sentence compression (MSC) [9] that combines information from sentences that are similar or connected using some common entity. The MSC technique is a word-graph based method where multiple sentences or utterances can be represented as a network of words. A directed graph is generated where the nodes represent the words while edges exist if two words are adjacent in the utterances. From the graph, several paths between the start and end points can be generated. The new paths can represent content that can be different from the original utterances. Oya *et al.*'s proposed approach requires significant effort to generate the templates using hypernym information for creating slots in the templates. Our framework also consists of a similar segmentation module as employed in Oya *et al.*'s work, which ensures that we divide the meeting transcript into several topics. Our proposed method is fundamentally different from most of the aforementioned techniques (except Oya *et al.*'s work) in that it considers individual segments to generate a summary sentence.

Our previous work [2] has briefly described the effectiveness of the fusion-based technique, which is also employed in this work. Our preliminary results demonstrated that the fusion based model can combine and convey useful information, generating reasonable abstractive meeting summaries. Hence, we extend this work using topic segments to build an end-to-end framework. We address the issue of readability of the generated summaries by modeling the strength of grammatical relations in the optimization problem. Our approach does not require creation of templates. Instead, our model aims to generate a sentence on each topic by identifying relevant grammatical relations and informative words from a collection of important utterances in a meeting.

3. PROPOSED APPROACH

As explained in Section 1, our proposed approach consists of three steps: First, we segment an entire conversation between participants into multiple text segments. Second, we apply an extractive summarizer that extracts important utterances from each segment. Finally, we fuse all the utterances in a segment using an ILP based approach to generate a summary sentence. All the generated sentences are appended to create the final summary. In the following, we detail each step.

3.1 Text Segmentation

Topic segmentation has been used in summarization of news articles [21, 4]. Generally, lexical cohesion-based measures work well for topic segmentation [27]. As the primary focus of our work is to generate summaries, we experiment with two different text segmentation algorithms: **LCSeg** and **Bayesian unsupervised topic segmentation**.

LCSeg: Galley *et al.* [13] developed a topic segmentor, LCSeg, based on lexical cohesion, which is considered to be a good indicator of the discourse structure of the text. The intuition behind this algorithm is that major term repetitions occur when the underlying topics in the text start or end. It takes into consideration multiple

Table 2: Features to select important utterances. Most of them are adopted from previous works [12, 37]. The most important speaker refers to the one that utters maximum number of words. Our work introduces the segment-based features. The content words include nouns, adjectives, verbs and adverbs.

(1)	Basic features
	– Length of a dialogue
	– Number of content words
	– Portion of content words
	– Number of new nouns introduced
(2)	**Content features**
	– Cosine similarity with entire meeting transcript
	– Presence of proper nouns
	– Most important speaker in meeting
	– Content words in previous dialogue act
(3)	**Segment based features**
	– Most important speaker in segment
	– Cosine similarity of dialogue with entire segment

features such as discourse cues and overlaps. LCSeg is applied to meeting corpora and achieved promising results. Hence, this approach is suitable for our segmentation step.

Bayesian unsupervised topic segmentation: This is also promising approach to topic segmentation. Eisenstein and Barzilay [8] proposed an unsupervised approach to topic segmentation based on lexical cohesion modeled by a Bayesian framework. The cohesion arises through a generative process. The words are modeled from a multinomial language model and the observed likelihood is maximized to generate a lexically-cohesive segmentation. This algorithm requires a user to specify the desired number of segments.

3.2 Selection of Important Utterances

Our second step is to identify the set of important utterances in each topic segment. As shown in Table 2, we use multiple features to identify the important set of utterances in a meeting. We adopt basic and content features from previous works [12, 37]. In addition to the above mentioned features, we introduce two segment-based features:

(i) The most important speaker in a segment.

(ii) Cosine similarity between the utterance and all of the other utterances in a segment.

We construct classifiers using all the features on the training set. We conduct experiments to evaluate the impact of our introduced segment-based features in addition to the basic and content features. Moreover, constructing a model using the meeting summarization data also suffers from the unbalanced data problem as only few utterances are considered to be important to generate the final summary. In order to address this problem, we apply the following techniques to oversample the minority data:

Weight: Let $npRatio$ be $\frac{\#negative}{\#positive}$. For the training instances, we assign weights of one and $npRatio$ to the negative and positive examples, respectively.

Resampling: We reproduce a random subsample of the training data using sampling with replacement. In this case, the new training data has the same total number of samples as the old one. However, they contain equal populations in both of the classes.

SMOTE: In synthetic minority oversampling technique (SMOTE) [6], the minority class is randomly oversampled. This algorithm forms new examples of minority class by interpolating between several minority class examples that lie together and thereby can avoid the overfitting problem.

3.3 Fusion of Utterances for Summary Generation

The final step in our approach is to combine information from multiple extracted utterances in each segment that the classifier identifies as summary-worthy. Several techniques have been proposed for sentence fusion tasks [3]. However, fusion on meeting utterances requires an algorithm that is robust for noisy data as utterances often have disfluencies. We adapt a sentence fusion technique [10] to meeting utterances. The dependency parse trees of the individual utterances within a topic segment are combined together. The best sub-graph that satisfies several constraints and maximizes the propagated information is selected using as an integer linear programming (ILP) formulation. ILP has been applied successfully to many natural language processing tasks [7, 34]. The formulation of the objective function in the ILP function takes into consideration the informativeness of the words, weights of the edges along the dependency tree and a factor that assigns more weights to utterances that are more closer to topic shifts, *i.e.*, towards the end of a segment. We also introduce an additional step of pronoun resolution. We observe that a lot of pronominal references are used in utterances and resolving such references would produce more relevant fusion by merging dependency graphs. Finally, the solution of the ILP problem is linearized to produce a sentence. In this section, we explain all of the details using a simple example. Suppose that the following three utterances within a topic segment are labeled as important by the classifier:

(Ut_1) *"Um well this is the kick-off meeting for our project."*

(Ut_2) *"so we're designing a new remote control and um."*

(Ut_3) *"Um, as you can see it's supposed to be original, trendy and user friendly."*

As can be seen, there are the introductory statements in a meeting that discusses the purpose of the meeting. We apply pre-processing to get rid of words such as *"um," "ah"* that cause disfluencies and do not contribute to any information content in the utterances.

Anaphora resolution. Our final goal is to generate a one-sentence summary from these utterances. To obtain a summary for each segment, we fuse the dependency graphs of the utterances by merging them on the common words that represent the nodes in the graph. However, in the above example, there are no common words in the three utterances. As can be seen from the utterances, the *"it"* in utterance (Ut_3) refers to *"a new remote control"* in (Ut_2). To ensure accurate dependency graph merging, where the graphs are merged on the nodes (words in an utterance), it is important to resolve such pronominal references. Without resolving such references, it would be impossible to fuse the above utterances, even though they are referring to the same entity. We use the publicly available Stanford CoreNLP package[2] [25] that has a co-reference resolution module. We resolve pronouns only if there is a pronominal reference to the previous utterance.

Dependency graph merging. Once anaphora resolution has been applied, the extracted utterances in each segment are parsed using

---

[2] http://nlp.stanford.edu/software/corenlp.shtml

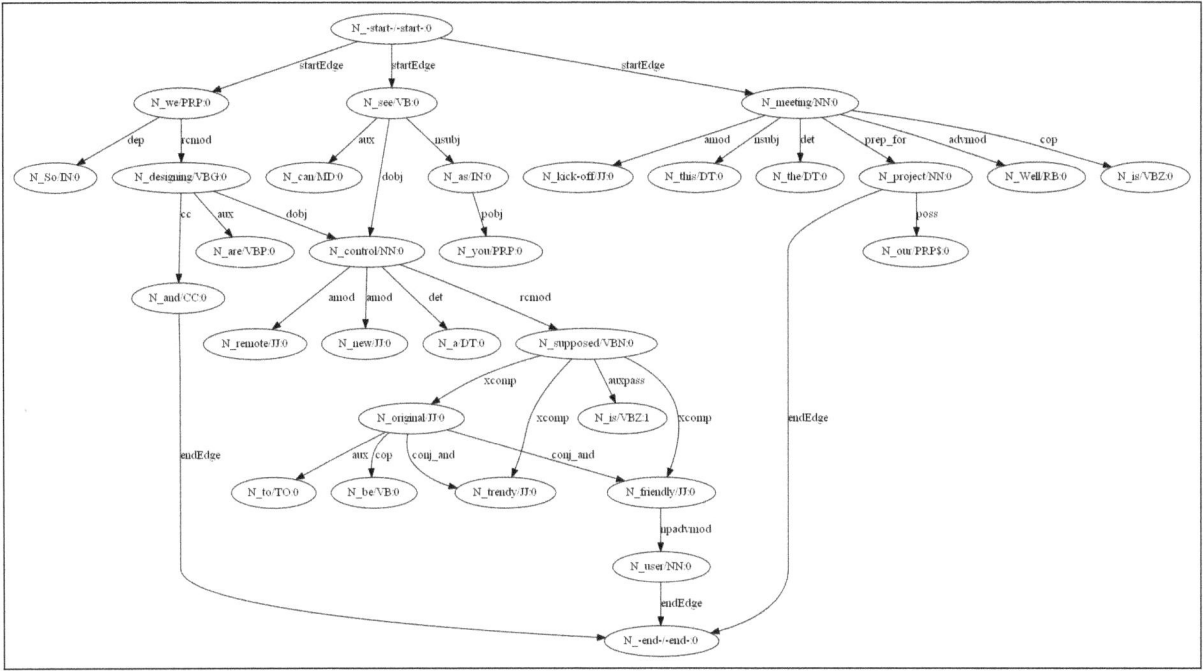

Figure 2: A merged dependency graph generated from several utterances. Note that only a section of the entire graph is shown. The nodes are shown as "*N_word*" and the labels are placed on the edges.

the Stanford dependency parser that is also a part of the CoreNLP package. Every individual utterance has an explicit ROOT vertex. We add two dummy nodes in the graph: the *start* node and the *end* node. The ROOT nodes from the utterances are all connected to the *start* node and the last word of every utterance is connected to the *end* node. The words from the utterances are iteratively added onto the graph. The words that have the same word form and the parts of speech (POS) tag are assigned to the same nodes. While only content words are merged, stopwords are not merged. The use of POS information prevents ungrammatical mappings. Hereafter, we refer to a word as the tuple of "{word, POS}." We also address ambiguities in the word mappings. If a new word that needs to be merged onto the graph has multiple mapping candidates, we introduce an ambiguity resolver.

Ambiguity resolver. Suppose that a new word w_i that has k ambiguous nodes where it can be mapped to. The k ambiguous nodes are referred to as mappable nodes. For every ambiguous mapping candidate, we first find the words to the left and right of the mappable word of the sentences, and then compute the number of words in both of the directions that are common to the words in either direction of the word w_i. We define the directed context as follows:

$$dirContext = \#CommonWords(dir, window),$$

where *dir* and *window* denote the direction of context (*left*/*right*) and the number of words to be considered in either direction, respectively. We calculate the directed context in both of the directions upto a window size of two words. Finally, w_i is mapped to the node that has the highest directed context. If a tie cannot be broken or no common context can be found with any of the existing nodes, a new node for w_i is created. An example of the ambiguity resolution has been provided in Section 1.

We use the JGrapht[3] package for the generation of the graph structure. Figure 2 shows a snapshot of the merged dependency graph generated from the three utterances, Ut_1, Ut_2, and Ut_3 in Section 3.3. The three utterances have been combined together in a common structure, with various possible paths between the *start* and the *end* dummy nodes. To obtain the dependency relations, we use the "collapsed dependency representation" from the Stanford parser that collapses edges of conjunctions and prepositions and places the corresponding information on the edge labels (*e.g.*, conj_and, prep_at, etc).

ILP formulation. The next step is to solve and generate a subgraph from this structure that satisfies a number of syntactic constraints and maximizes the information content simultaneously.

Similar to the fusion technique by Fillipova and Strube [10], we model the problem as an integer linear programming (ILP) formulation. However, the formulation of our objective function and the constraints are significantly different from their system. We add a lexical cohesion component in the ILP formulation. Moreover, our constraints leverage linguistic knowledge to generate grammatical output. Furthermore, they applied it to German language only. The directed edges in the graph are represented as $x_{g,d,l}$ in the ILP problem where g, d and l denote the governor node, dependent node and the label of an edge, respectively. The edges represent the variables in the objective function which can either take value of 1 or 0 depending on whether the edge has to be preserved or deleted.

We maximize the following objective function:

$$\sum_x x_{g,d,l} \cdot p(l \mid g) \cdot I(d) \cdot \frac{p_x}{N}. \qquad (1)$$

As shown in Equation (1), we introduce three different terms: $p(l \mid g)$, $I(d)$ and $\frac{p_x}{N}$. The term $p(l \mid g)$ denote the probabilities of the labels given a governor node, g. We can calculate these probabilities from any given corpora. For every node (word and POS)

[3] http://jgrapht.org/

55

Table 3: Probabilities of outgoing edges from a node for "produced/VBN."

aux-pass	nsubj-pass	aux	prep_with	agent	prep_in	adv-mod
0.286	0.214	0.214	0.071	0.071	0.071	0.071

in the entire corpus, the probabilities are represented as the ratio of the sum of the frequency of a particular label and the sum of the frequencies of all the labels emerging from a node. In this work, we calculate these values using Reuters corpora [33] in order to obtain dominant relations from non-conversational style of text. For example, Table 3 shows the probabilities of outgoing edges from a node ("*produced/VBN*"). The term $I(d)$ denotes the informativeness of a node. In order to compute $I(d)$, we improve the word significance score [18] as follows:

$$I(d) = f_s \cdot \log \frac{F_A}{F_d}, \tag{2}$$

where f_s, F_A, and F_d denote the frequency of a word in a text segment, the sum of the frequencies of all the words in the corpus, and the frequency of the dependent word d in the entire Reuters corpus, respectively. The last term $\frac{p_x}{N}$ in Equation (1) is based on the idea of lexical cohesion. Our intuition is that important decisions in a meeting are taken just before a topic concludes. Therefore, to model the relative importance of such utterances, we introduce the term $\frac{p_x}{N}$, where N and p_x denote the total number of extracted utterances in a segment and the position of the utterance (the edge x belongs to) in the set of N utterances, respectively. As a result of this term, utterances more closer to topic boundaries are assigned higher weights.

In order to solve the above ILP problem, we impose a number of constraints. Some of the constraints have been directly adapted from the original ILP formulation [10]. For example, we use the same constraints for restricting one incoming edge per node, as well as we impose the connectivity constraint to ensure a connected graph structure. The other constraints we impose are defined as follows:

$$\forall l \in startEdge, \sum_l x_{g,d,l} = 1, \tag{3}$$
$$\forall l \in endEdge, \sum_l x_{g,d,l} = 1$$

$$\sum_x x_{g,d,l} \leq \gamma \tag{4}$$

$$\sum_{g,d} (x_{g,d,l} + x_{d,g,l}) \leq 1 \tag{5}$$

$$\forall l_{out} \in \{aux, cop, det\}, \sum_{u,l_{in}} x_{g,u,l_{in}} - x_{u,d,l_{out}} = 0 \tag{6}$$

$$\forall g, l_{out} \in aux \lor cop \lor det, \sum_{l_{out}} x_{g,d,l_{out}} \leq 1 \tag{7}$$

Equation (3) limits the subtree to compulsorily have just one start edge and one end edge. This helps in preserving one ROOT node, as well as it limits to one *end* node for the generated subtree. Equation (4) limits the generated subtree to have a maximum of γ nodes. The start nodes and end nodes are still a part of the subtree that is generated by solving this optimization problem. Hence, the value of γ needs to be set to 2, which is more than the desired number of maximum words in the summary sentence. In order to prevent bidirectional relations between two nodes, we impose Equation (5) as a constraint. To maintain the linguistic quality of the generated sentence, by using Equations (6) and (7) as constraints, we

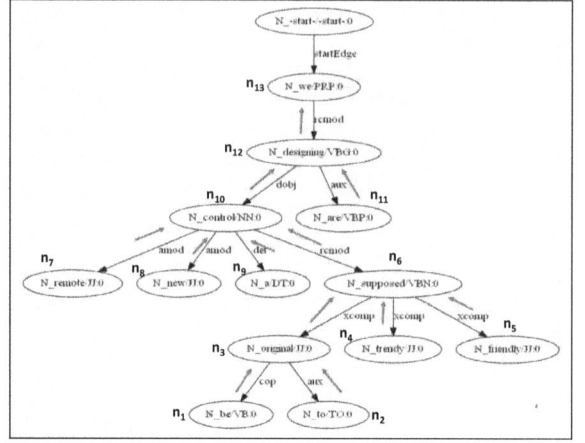

Figure 3: Dependency graph linearization process.

always include a maximum of one auxiliary verb (aux), copular verb (cop) and determinant (det) if they exist. We use the Gurobi software[4] [16] for the optimization tasks. Figure 3 shows the final graph that is retained from the graph in Figure 2 after solving the ILP problem.

Linearization: The purpose of linearization is to generate a sentence from the final subtree generated by solving the ILP problem. We take a relatively straightforward bottom-up approach to tackle the problem. We keep adding the leaf nodes to their governing nodes until it reaches the ROOT node. We maintain the same order of the words as in the source sentences during the merging process.

As shown in Figure 3, the nodes *to/TO* (n_2) and *be/VB* (n_1) are added to the node *original/JJ* (n_3). After merging these words, they are reordered so that the ordering resembles the one in the source sentences. The sequence of the nodes is changed only during the merge with the governing node: they are kept fixed for the future operations. Hence, the nodes *to/TO* (n_2) and *be/VB* (n_1) are memorized along with the node *original/JJ* (n_3). In the next step, the ordering of the node *original/JJ* (n_3) matters with respect to the other leaves the governing node (n_6) has. However, this might be a problem in the case where there are leaf nodes from a governor node at some higher level. In this example, *trendy/JJ* (n_4) and *friendly/JJ* (n_5) will get merged to *supposed/VBN* (n_6) before the node *original/JJ* (n_3) as they are leaf nodes. To prevent such merging, we only allow to merge the leaf nodes to the governing node that is at the farthest distance from the ROOT vertex. We apply Dijkstra's algorithm [35] to calculate the path length. Thus, in Figure 3, the nodes *trendy/JJ* (n_4) and *friendly/JJ* (n_5) are added only after *to/TO* (n_2) and *be/VB* (n_1) are merged to *original/JJ*. The final sentence after linearization is as follows:

> *We are designing a new remote control supposed to be original trendy and friendly.*

4. EXPERIMENTAL RESULTS

4.1 Dataset and Evaluation Metrics

The AMI Meeting corpus [5] contains 139 meeting transcripts along with their corresponding extractive and abstractive summaries. The standard test set of this corpus includes 20 meetings. Our extractive summarization component is trained using the training set,

---

[4] http://www.gurobi.com/

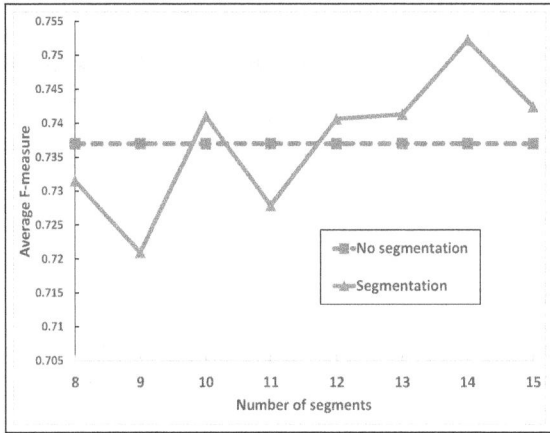

Figure 4: Average F-measures obtained by varying the number of segments. Also shows the impact of addition of segment-based features.

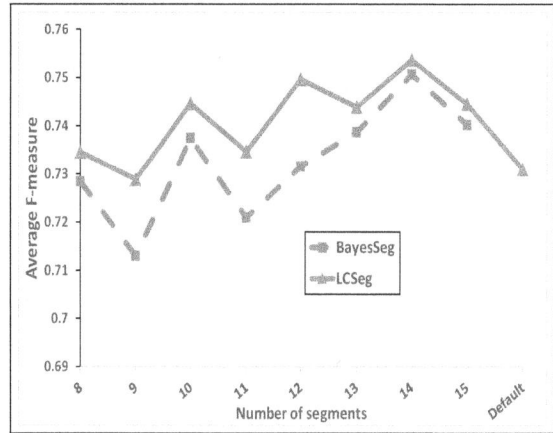

Figure 5: Comparison of performance obtained by text segmentation algorithms: Bayesian segmentation (BayesSeg) and LCSeg. "Default" setting does not require the number of segments to be explicitly stated when computing segment boundaries using LCSeg.

i.e., the remaining 119 meetings. We evaluate the accuracy of the classifiers using standard metrics: Precision, Recall and F-measure. We also evaluate the impact of introducing segment-based features. To evaluate the quality of the summaries, we verify the effectiveness of content selection using ROUGE, which has been widely used as a standard technique to evaluate information content in document summarization tasks by comparing system-generated summaries to human-written abstractive summaries. Further, we also evaluate the linguistic quality of the generated summaries using human judgments.

4.2 Classifier Evaluation

As described in Section 3.1, we used two different text segmentation algorithms: LCSeg and Bayesian unsupervised topic segmentation. Furthermore, we employed three classifiers: Support Vector Machines (SVM), Random Forest (RF) and Naive Bayes (NB). To overcome the problem of unbalanced data, we used three different sampling techniques (Weight, Resampling, and SMOTE) as described in Section 3.2. We evaluated all the possible configurations on the training dataset to determine the best configuration suitable for our summary generation. We used Weka [17] for all the classification tasks with the default set of parameters. We perform 10-fold cross validation on the training set. First, we try to find the optimal number of segments that provides the best classification accuracy. Simultaneously, we also evaluate the contribution of adding segment-based features during training the classifiers. Second, we also identify the text segmentation algorithm that works best on this dataset. Finally, based on the above decisions, we compare the performances of the classifiers to decide our extractive summarization component (*i.e.*, classifier that gives the the best) and the best sampling strategy to avoid any bias due to the unbalanced dataset.

Number of segments: We optimize the number of segments for each meeting by varying it from 8 to 15 on the training data. Figure 4 shows the average F-measure obtained by the classifiers constructed from the set of all features ("Segmentation") and the features excluding the segment-based features ("No segmentation"). The graph shows the average F-measure obtained by all combinations of the classifiers and the sampling strategies with respect to the various number of segments. As expected, the average F-measures do not show any change when we skip the segment-based features. However, we observe slight differences when we introduce the segment-based features. Generally, when the number of segments is between 12 to 15, we observe about 1% improvement

Table 4: Precision (Pre), Recall (Rec), and F-measure (F) obtained by classifiers along with each of the three sampling strategies. We set the number of segments to 14.

Classifier	Sampling	LCSeg			BayesSeg		
		Pre	Rec	F	Pre	Rec	F
NB	Weight	0.792	0.787	0.786	0.788	0.784	0.783
	Resampling	0.796	0.790	0.789	0.791	0.787	0.786
	SMOTE	0.831	0.804	0.811	0.830	0.807	0.813
RF	Weight	0.726	0.722	0.721	0.730	0.727	0.727
	Resampling	0.892	0.889	**0.888**	0.880	0.877	**0.877**
	SMOTE	0.817	0.821	0.819	0.817	0.820	0.818
SVM	Weight	0.623	0.591	0.563	0.601	0.584	0.566
	Resampling	0.752	0.741	0.739	0.690	0.689	0.689
	SMOTE	0.660	0.694	0.667	0.691	0.711	0.697

in F-measure by adding the segment-based features over the basic set of features. According to Figure 4, we observe the highest average F-measure of 0.752 when we segment the meeting transcript into 14 topics. We set the number of segments to 14 for our following experiments.

LCSeg vs Bayesian unsupervised topic segmentation: Figure 5 shows the comparison of average F-measures of the classification models for each of the topic segmentation algorithms. As can be seen, LCSeg generally outperforms Bayesian segmentation. The *default* setting of the number of segments refers to the setting for LCSeg, which does not require to specifying the number of text segments. According to Figure 5, the default setting does not perform well. Both of the segmentation algorithms achieve similar F-measure in classification accuracies when we set the number of segments to 14. Note that the optimal number of segments were obtained by applying 10-fold cross validation using both the segmentation algorithms.

Evaluation of classifiers and sampling strategy: Table 4 shows the results of classification evaluation. The scores in the table were obtained by setting the number of segments to 14. As can be seen from the table, the NB and RF classifiers significantly outperform SVM. The best system is obtained by combining the RF classifier with the Resampling strategy. In both of the segmentation algorithms, the combination of RF and Resampling gives the best F-measure (0.888 and 0.877). Resampling and SMOTE sampling

Table 5: ROUGE scores obtained by several configurations in content selection. We compute ROUGE-1 (R-1) and ROUGE-2 (R-2) without any limit on summary length for comparison.

Classifier	Sampling	LCSeg		BayesSeg	
		R-1	R-2	R-1	R-2
NB	Weight	0.660	0.141	0.663	0.142
	Resampling	0.666	0.142	0.674	0.145
	SMOTE	0.673	0.145	0.675	0.147
RF	Weight	0.679	0.147	0.702	0.144
	Resampling	**0.705**	**0.158**	**0.703**	**0.157**
	SMOTE	0.694	0.152	0.695	0.153
SVM	Weight	0.490	0.114	0.473	0.112
	Resampling	0.563	0.143	0.556	0.139
	SMOTE	0.525	0.123	0.567	0.141

Table 6: Content selection evaluation. We compute ROUGE-2 (R-2) and ROUGE-SU4 (R-SU4) scores by comparing the system generated summaries and the human-written summaries for all the meetings in the test set.

Method	R-2	R-SU4
Our abstractive model	**0.048**	**0.087**
Our abstractive model (no anaphora resolution)	0.036	0.071
MSC model [9]	0.041	0.079
Extractive model (baseline)	0.026	0.044

strategies outperform the Weight strategy when using RF and SVM. However, when using NB, the performance using Weight and Resampling strategy is very similar.

4.3 Content Selection

In text summarization, it is also important to evaluate to what extent a classifier retains valuable information that should exist in a summary. Therefore, system generated summaries should be compared to human-written summaries automatically. We evaluate content selection using ROUGE.

Training Set: Table 5 shows the experimental results of content selection on the training set. We compare extractive summaries with human-generated abstracts for all the meetings in the training set and compute ROUGE-1 (R-1) and ROUGE-2 (R-2) scores. We do not impose any length constraints during ROUGE evaluation on the training data. Similar to Table 4, the combination of RF with Resampling strategy outperforms other techniques in terms of R-1 and R-2 scores. We use the RF classifier trained using Resampling strategy as our extractive component. This classifier is used on the test set to identify important utterances in the meeting transcripts. We segment each meeting transcript into 14 (optimal) segments using the LCSeg algorithm as it slightly outperform Bayesian unsupervised topic segmentation.

Test-set evaluation: We generate abstractive summaries from the meeting transcripts in the test set using our ILP-based approach. To evaluate our abstractive summaries, we compare them to the extractive summaries generated by the best performing classifier. We also compare the summaries to the MSC method proposed by Fillipova [9] that has been adapted for abstractive meeting summarization [26] develped earlier. As an input to the MSC model, we use the same set of utterances per segment that was extracted by the classifier. The sentence in each segment that obtains the highest score using MSC is used in the final generated summary. The human-written abstracts, on average, contain close to 300 words. Therefore, we applied a length constraint while performing ROUGE evaluation to limit summary comparison upto 300 words.

Table 7: Readability estimates of summaries.

Method	Readability score	Log likelihood
Our abstractive model	0.74	**-125.73**
MSC model [9]	0.62	-141.31
Extractive model	0.67	-136.22

We use ROUGE-2 (R-2) and ROUGE-SU4 (R-SU4) recall scores to compare all approaches. Both the ROUGE scores have been found to correlate well with human judgments [31]. Table 6 shows that our abstractive model can effectively maximize information content, resulting in better summaries compared with the other models. Furthermore, the ROUGE scores of the MSC model also significantly outperforms the extractive model, indicating that MSC results in more informative summaries. To evaluate the impact of anaphora resolution, we run our abstractive summarization model without performing the pre-processing step of pronoun resolution. ROUGE-2 score obtained by the abstractive model with anaphora resolution (0.048) is significantly better than the model without anaphora resolution (0.036). This indicates that anaphora resolution significantly contributes to content selection. Due to pronoun resolution, there are more chances of fusing information from various utterances within a topic segment. The extractive model obtains the lowest ROUGE scores as we restrict comparison to the first 300 words. In contrast, the abstractive methods (our methods and MSC) can effectively integrate the information from multiple utterances within the first 300 words.

ROUGE comparison: In general, shorter summaries are preferred by human readers. Extractive meeting summaries tend to be very long. In contrast, human-written summaries are very short and contain 300 words on average. To take this preference of shorter summaries into account, we evaluate summaries using only the first 300 words. The extractive summaries are fairly long and contain 2000-5000 words. Including several utterances distracts a reader's focus on the salient aspects, resulting in low readability of the summaries. Therefore, we set the length parameter in ROUGE (l) to 300 to limit the comparison to only the first 300 words.

4.4 Readability Analysis

To evaluate the linguistic quality of the generated summaries, we perform readability analysis. We asked one human judge to mark sentences in the generated abstractive summaries as either readable or not readable. Readability indicates how well the idea in the sentence is conveyed to the reader. Excessive presence of disfluencies or ill-formed utterances should be marked as not readable. We provided these instructions to the human judge. Out of 261 summary sentences generated for the 20 abstractive summaries, 67 sentences were found to be *not readable* (∼26%). We also manually evaluated the extracted utterances and found that 33% of the utterances contained various disfluencies, making them difficult to read. We also performed another readability analysis for the summaries generated using MSC and found that only 62% of the generated sentences in the summaries are readable. The readability of MSC summaries (0.62) is even worse than that of the extractive summaries (0.67), showing that, while the generated sentences in MSC model are informative (high ROUGE scores), they suffer from serious grammatical issues as no factor of linguistic quality is considered in the model. Generally, several utterances in extractive summaries were marked as not readable due to excessive use of disfluencies. Furthermore, there were incomplete utterances that created confusion in the minds of the reader. For example, an extracted utterances – "Ah eagle , right okay ." – although gram-

Table 8: Examples of summary sentences that our system generated (S) and corresponding human–written (H) summary sentences. Note that they are only small portions of the summaries and not the entire summaries.

S: Slightly curved around the sides like up to the main display as well. It was voice activated .
H: The remote will be single-curved with a cherry design on top. A sample sensor was included to add speech recognition.
S: The market trends and our traditional usual market research study suggests the use of rechargeable batteries.
H: He suggested substituting a kinetic battery for the rechargeable batteries and using a combination of rubber and plastic for the materials.
S: And in this detailed design the usability interface meeting we will discuss our final design the look-and-feel.
H: All these components were re-arranged in a revised prototype.

matical, does not tell us anything about what is being spoken about. To obtain a coarse estimate of grammaticality, we also calculate the average log-likelihood score provided by the Stanford Parser. We compute the average log-likelihood scores of the confidence of the dependency parses for each type of summaries. Table 7 shows the average scores.[5]

Table 8 shows some examples of summaries generated by our system. The table indicates that the summaries generated by our system are relatively well-formed and they reflect the formal style of non-conversational text. We aligned sentences from the human-written abstracts and the corresponding sentences selected from each segment that our algorithm generates.

Error Analysis: In some cases the linearization component does not produce relevant ordering of words. For example, in the third summary sentence in Table 8, the system-generated summary lacks certain conjunctions and the ordering of words is inappropriate. The phrase "detailed design the" can be removed to maintain clarity. In addition, the entity – *design* has been repeated. To solve these problems, we plan to introduce intra-sentence level constraints to improve generated summaries.

Our algorithm is designed to retain informative words as well as grammatical dependencies that are more probable in any given corpus. However, the grammatical dependencies that we choose might not necessarily lead to well-formed grammatical sentences. Furthermore, our ILP-based model is unable to understand long-term dependencies of entities within a generated sentence. For example, consider the following output:

"Decided important reflect our budget our the product accessible a wide range of consumers limiting anyone know that kind ."

As can be seen, it is really hard for a reader to identify what the summary sentence is trying to convey although certain words or phrases hint at the topic of *deciding the budget based on the range of consumers*. Our model at present does not memorize previous choices of entities referred in the utterances. Furthermore, our linearization component is based on the ordering of words in the source utterances. However, using the same ordering as the source sentences might not necessarily work well. In the context

---

[5]Lower the magnitude of the log-likelihood scores, the higher is the confidence associated with the dependency parse.

of an entirely new generated summary sentence, lexical or phrasal reordering and other transformations might be required. In such cases, it might be more effective to use language model based confidence scores to determine the best ordering of words. Improvement in the ILP formulation is possible by including confidence of the sequence of words in addition to the incorporation of knowledge about the entities. Optimizing such a complete model can help generate summaries that are much easier to read. Further, such summaries would contain coherent elements on the same entities in the summary sentences. We might also hope to optimize the model by including the number of segments as a parameter in the model. Currently, the maximum number of sentences in the summary is dependent on the number of topic segments. We can improve the formulation such that model itself decides the optimal length of the summaries ensuring that all the informative points in the meeting discussion are included in the system generated summary.

5. CONCLUSIONS AND FUTURE WORK

In this work, we have proposed an approach to generate abstractive summaries from meeting conversations. We proposed a method for dividing a conversation into multiple topic segments. We used an extractive summarizer to identify the important set of utterances, and then applied ILP-based utterance fusion to generate one sentence summary from every topic segment. We leveraged the grammatical relations in the fusion technique that are more dominant in non-conversational style of text. The experiments on content selection and readability indicate that our method can generate relevant abstractive summaries from meeting transcripts without any templates. However, as we have already pointed out, not all generated summaries are usable due to the lack of coherence among several entities discussed within the same summary sentence. We plan to improve the generation using knowledge of entities and also refine readability using a language model. In future work, we plan to develop better linearization techniques. We also plan to improve our algorithm by not limiting one sentence per segment but allowing the ILP model to decide the optimal number of sentences for a complete summary.

6. REFERENCES

[1] C. Apté, F. Damerau, and S. M. Weiss. Automated Learning of Decision Rules for Text Categorization. *ACM Transactions on Information Systems (TOIS)*, 12(3):233–251, 1994.

[2] S. Banerjee, P. Mitra, and K. Sugiyama. Abstractive Meeting Summarization Using Dependency Graph Fusion. In *Proc. of the 24th International Conference on World Wide Web Companion (WWW '15 Companion)*, pages 5–6, 2015.

[3] R. Barzilay and K. R. McKeown. Sentence Fusion for Multidocument News Summarization. *Computational Linguistics*, 31(3):297–328, 2005.

[4] B. K. Boguraev and M. S. Neff. Discourse Segmentation in Aid of Document Summarization. In *Proc. of the 33rd Annual Hawaii International Conference on System Sciences (HICSS-33)*, pages 1–10, 2000.

[5] J. Carletta, S. Ashby, S. Bourban, M. Flynn, M. Guillemot, T. Hain, J. Kadlec, V. Karaiskos, W. Kraaij, M. Kronenthal, et al. The AMI Meeting Corpus: A Pre-announcement. In *Proc. of the 2nd International Workshop on Machine Learning for Multimodal Interaction (MLMI 2005)*, pages 28–39, 2006.

[6] N. V. Chawla, K. W. Bowyer, L. O. Hall, and W. P. Kegelmeyer. SMOTE: Synthetic Minority Over-sampling

Technique. *Journal of Artificial Intelligence Research (JAIR)*, 16(2002):321–357, 2002.

[7] J. Clarke and M. Lapata. Global Inference for Sentence Compression: An Integer Linear Programming Approach. *Journal of Artificial Intelligence Research (JAIR)*, 31(2008):399–429, 2008.

[8] J. Eisenstein and R. Barzilay. Bayesian Unsupervised Topic Segmentation. In *Proc. of the Conference on Empirical Methods in Natural Language Processing (EMNLP 2008)*, pages 334–343, 2008.

[9] K. Filippova. Multi-sentence Compression: Finding Shortest Paths in Word Graphs. In *Proc. of the 23rd International Conference on Computational Linguistics (Coling 2010)*, pages 322–330, 2010.

[10] K. Filippova and M. Strube. Sentence Fusion via Dependency Graph Compression. In *Proc. of the Conference on Empirical Methods in Natural Language Processing (EMNLP 2008)*, pages 177–185, 2008.

[11] K. Filippova and M. Strube. Tree Linearization in English: Improving Language Model Based Approaches. In *Proc. of the Human Language Technology Conference of the North American Chapter of the Association for Computational Linguistics (HLT-NAACL 2009)*, pages 225–228, 2009.

[12] M. Galley. A Skip-Chain Conditional Random Field for Ranking Meeting Utterances by Importance. In *Proc. of the 2006 Conference on Empirical Methods in Natural Language Processing (EMNLP 2006)*, pages 364–372, 2006.

[13] M. Galley, K. McKeown, E. Fosler-Lussier, and H. Jing. Discourse Segmentation of Multi-party Conversation. In *Proc. of the 41st Annual Meeting on Association for Computational Linguistics (ACL '03)*, pages 562–569, 2003.

[14] N. Garg, B. Favre, K. Riedhammer, and D. Hakkani-Tür. ClusterRank: A Graph Based Method for Meeting Summarization. In *Proc. of the 10th Annual Conference of the International Speech Communication (INTERSPEECH 2009)*, pages 1499–1502, 2009.

[15] D. Gillick, K. Riedhammer, B. Favre, and D. Hakkani-Tur. A Global Optimization Framework for Meeting Summarization. In *Proc. of the IEEE International Conference on Acoustics, Speech, and Signal Processing (ICASSP 2009)*, pages 4769–4772, 2009.

[16] Gurobi Optimization, Inc. Gurobi Optimizer Reference Manual, 2014.

[17] M. Hall, E. Frank, G. Holmes, B. Pfahringer, P. Reutemann, and I. H. Witten. The WEKA data mining software: an update. *ACM SIGKDD Explorations Newsletter*, 11(1):10–18, 2009.

[18] C. Hori and S. Furui. A New Approach to Automatic Speech Summarization. *IEEE Transactions on Multimedia*, 5(3):368–378, 2003.

[19] P.-Y. Hsueh and J. D. Moore. Automatic Topic Segmentation and Labeling in Multiparty Dialogue. In *Spoken Language Technology Workshop*, pages 98–101, 2006.

[20] C.-Y. Lin. ROUGE: A Package for Automatic Evaluation of Summaries. In *Proc. of the ACL-04 Workshop on Text Summarization Branches Out*, pages 74–81, 2004.

[21] C.-Y. Lin and E. Hovy. The Automated Acquisition of Topic Signatures for Text Summarization. In *Proc. of the 18th Conference on Computational Linguistics (COLING '00)*, pages 495–501, 2000.

[22] H. Lin, J. Bilmes, and S. Xie. Graph-based Submodular Selection for Extractive Summarization. In *Proc. of the IEEE Workshop on Automatic Speech Recognition & Understanding (ASRU 2009)*, pages 381–386, 2009.

[23] F. Liu and Y. Liu. From Extractive to Abstractive Meeting Summaries: Can It Be Done by Sentence Compression? In *Proc. of the 47th Annual Meeting of the Association for Computational Linguistics (ACL-IJCNLP 2009)*, pages 261–264, 2009.

[24] Y. Liu, S. Xie, and F. Liu. Using N-best Recognition Output for Extractive Summarization and Keyword Extraction in Meeting Speech. In *Proc. of IEEE International Conference on Acoustics Speech and Signal Processing (ICASSP 2010)*, pages 5310–5313, 2010.

[25] C. D. Manning, M. Surdeanu, J. Bauer, J. Finkel, S. J. Bethard, and D. McClosky. The Stanford CoreNLP Natural Language Processing Toolkit. In *Proc. of 52nd Annual Meeting of the Association for Computational Linguistics (ACL 2014): System Demonstrations*, pages 55–60, 2014.

[26] Y. Mehdad, G. Carenini, F. W. Tompa, and R. T. NG. Abstractive Meeting Summarization with Entailment and Fusion. In *Proc. of the 14th European Workshop on Natural Language Generation*, pages 136–146, 2013.

[27] J. Morris and G. Hirst. Lexical Cohesion Computed by Thesaural Relations as an Indicator of the Structure of Text. *Computational Linguistics*, 17(1):21–48, 1991.

[28] G. Murray and G. Carenini. Summarizing Spoken and Written Conversations. In *Proc. of the Conference on Empirical Methods in Natural Language Processing (EMNLP 2008)*, pages 773–782, 2008.

[29] G. Murray, G. Carenini, and R. Ng. Generating and Validating Abstracts of Meeting Conversations: a User Study. In *Proc. of the 6th International Natural Language Generation Conference (INLG 2010)*, pages 105–113, 2010.

[30] G. Murray, G. Carenini, and R. Ng. Interpretation and Transformation for Abstracting Conversations. In *Proc. of the Human Language Technology Conference of the North American Chapter of the Association for Computational Linguistics (HLT-NAACL 2010)*, pages 894–902, 2010.

[31] A. Nenkova and K. McKeown. A Survey of Text Summarization Techniques. *Mining Text Data*, pages 43–76, 2012.

[32] T. Oya, Y. Mehdad, G. Carenini, and R. Ng. A Template-based Abstractive Meeting Summarization: Leveraging Summary and Source Text Relationships. In *Proc. of the 8th International Natural Language Generation Conference (INLG 2014)*, pages 45–53, 2014.

[33] T. Rose, M. Stevenson, and M. Whitehead. The Reuters Corpus Volume 1-from Yesterday's News to Tomorrow's Language Resources. In *Proc. of the 3rd International Conference on Language Resources and Evaluation Conference (LREC'02)*, pages 827–832, 2002.

[34] D. Roth and W.-T. Yih. A Linear Programming Formulation for Global Inference in Natural Language Tasks. In *Proc. of the 8th Conference on Natural Language Learning (CoNLL-2004)*, pages 1–8, 2004.

[35] S. Skiena. Dijkstra's algorithm. *Implementing Discrete Mathematics: Combinatorics and Graph Theory with Mathematica, Reading*, pages 225–227, 1990.

[36] L. Wang and C. Cardie. Domain-Independent Abstract Generation for Focused Meeting Summarization. In *Proc. of the 51st Annual Meeting of the Association for Computational Linguistics (ACL 2013)*, pages 1395–1405, 2013.

[37] S. Xie and Y. Liu. Using Corpus and Knowledge-based Similarity Measure in Maximum Marginal Relevance for Meeting Summarization. In *Proc. of IEEE International Conference on Acoustics, Speech and Signal Processing (ICASSP 2008)*, pages 4985–4988, 2008.

Enhancing Exploration with a Faceted Browser through Summarization

Grzegorz Drzadzewski
David R. Cheriton School of Computer Science
University of Waterloo
Waterloo, ON, N2L 3G1, Canada
gdrzadze@cs.uwaterloo.ca

Frank Wm. Tompa
David R. Cheriton School of Computer Science
University of Waterloo
Waterloo, ON, N2L 3G1, Canada
fwtompa@cs.uwaterloo.ca

ABSTRACT

An enhanced faceted browsing system has been developed to support users' exploration of large multi-tagged document collections. It provides summary measures of document result sets at each step of navigation through a set of representative terms and a diverse set of documents. These summaries are derived from pre-materialized views that allow for quick calculation of centroids for various result sets. The utility and efficiency of the system is demonstrated on the New York Times Annotated Corpus.

Categories and Subject Descriptors

H.2.4 [**Systems**]: Textual databases; H.4.3 [**Communications Applications**]: Information browsers

General Terms

Algorithms, Design

Keywords

document repository, faceted browser, tags, result diversification, bursty terms

1. INTRODUCTION

Faceted browsing and search has emerged as a valuable technique for information access in many e-commerce sites, including Wal-Mart, Home Depot, eBay, and Amazon [15]. Faceted search has also been shown to be effective in helping users navigate document repositories, including the document collection at the University of North Carolina library, and it was preferred by users over traditional search interfaces based on text content alone [10].

With faceted browsing a user can navigate through a document collection by using facets as filters for specifying a document set of interest. Once the result set is narrowed down to a manageable size, the user can examine individual documents. Other than the count of items associated with each metadata tag for each facet in the result set, faceted browsers do not usually provide any tools to help users understand the contents of the result set. Alternatively, systems such as Scatter/Gather display a link to the medoid document and the top-k most frequently occurring terms [1], which gives a hint at the scope of each sub-collection. If the information provided is not particularly informative, the user must arbitrarily choose individual documents to examine in an attempt to understand what is in the isolated sub-collection.

When navigating through many document sets, however, it is too time consuming to examine many documents from each set to determine whether the set as a whole or some subset may be of interest. As a user aid, document sets may be summarized to provide a quick overview of their contents. Common summaries for sets of documents include a representative set of terms [7, 8], a ranked list of representative documents [1, 2, 5], and a natural language abstract [9]. Each of these approaches relies on being able to compute the centroid for any given document set.

We have developed an enhanced faceted browser interface that, in addition to letting a user perform traditional faceted browsing and searching, provides a user with summary information about the resulting document set. In our implementation, the summary includes a diverse set of representative documents and a well-chosen set of representative terms. In addition, the information scent [6] is enhanced by providing a set of representative terms for each of the important *sub-collections* of the result set (cf. multi-menus [11]). With these summary measures in place, a user is able to quickly grasp the topics covered by large result sets. This additional summary information can be especially useful in situations when the documents are not ordered in a favourable way (such as when using PubMed, where result sets are ordered by date rather than by relevance to the query).

We demonstrate the system on the New York Times (NYT) annotated corpus [12], which consists of 1.5 million tagged documents. The assigned tags are treated as facet values over which the user can search and browse.

2. BASIC MEASURES OF INTEREST

2.1 Set Centroid

Following standard practice in information retrieval, we model a document as a *bag of terms* represented by a document term vector (DTV), which is a vector of values where each entry corresponds to a term together with the term's (normalized) frequency in that document. A set of DTVs can be aggregated together to obtain a *set centroid* for the corresponding documents, which can be used by set summarization procedures. A set centroid C is represented by a vector of term frequencies equal to the mean of all the DTVs for documents that belong to that set.

2.2 Representative Terms

Given a document set of interest S_c and a superset $S_p \supseteq S_c$ (its context), the *burstiness* of a term w is measured using $B_+(w, C_{S_c}, C_{S_p})$ as defined in Equation 1, where C_{S_c} is the centroid of set S_c and C_{S_p} is the centroid of its context S_p:

$$B_+(w, C_{S_c}, C_{S_p}) = \frac{C_{S_c}[w].freq}{C_{S_p}[w].freq^{0.95}} \quad (1)$$

A term is considered *bursty* if it has a sufficiently higher frequency of occurrence in set S_c than its frequency of occurrence in the context set S_p: $B_+(w, C_{S_c}, C_{S_p}) > t$, where t is pre-defined threshold (set to 1 in our system). The top k or fewer (if fewer than k terms are above the threshold) bursty terms found in C_{S_c} constitute the set of representative terms $\mathbb{B}_k(S_c, S_p)$ for S_c relative to S_p.

Since the absence of terms may often be as informative as their presence, we also want to show terms that occur significantly less in the set than in its superset. Therefore, we define negative burstiness, denoted $B_-(w, C_{S_c}, C_{S_p})$, as defined in Equation 2.

$$B_-(w, C_{S_c}, C_{S_p}) = \frac{C_{S_p}[w].freq}{C_{S_c}[w].freq^{0.95}} \quad (2)$$

The top k or fewer terms in C_{S_c} with $B_-(w, C_{S_c}, C_{S_p}) > t$ are then displayed as part of the summary, representing a set of rare terms (denoted $\mathbb{B}_k^-(S_c, S_p)$) for S_c relative to S_p.

As an example, Table 1 shows the set of positive and negative bursty terms (labelled "representative terms" and "rarely occurring terms," respectively) for the document set returned in response to the query "Music," along with the bursty terms associated with its two largest subsets: "Music AND Recordings (Audio)" and "Music AND Opera." The representative terms for the query "Music" are derived using $\mathbb{B}_{20}(S_{Music}, S_G)$, where S_G corresponds to all documents in the corpus, and those for "Music AND Recordings (Audio)" and "Music AND Opera" are defined with respect to "Music" using $\mathbb{B}_{20}(S_{Music \wedge Recordings(Audio)}, S_{Music})$ for the former and $\mathbb{B}_{20}(S_{Music \wedge Opera}, S_{Music})$ for the latter; the rarely occurring terms use the corresponding negated formulae.

3. REPRESENTATIVE DOCUMENTS

3.1 Approaches to Diversification

There is a large body of research on search result diversification [14]. However, that work deals with diversification of results to ambiguous queries, for which different results are optimal depending on the interpretation of the query. That body of work is not directly applicable to our scenario since we do not deal with queries over text, but rather with navigation over tags. Because documents are assigned single instances of tags (we are not considering folksonomies, where the same tag can be assigned to a document by many users), documents matching a query over tags cannot be ordered based on the tag frequency in a similar fashion as term frequency is used to rank documents in a standard text search. Instead, in situations where documents are equal members

Table 1: Summary generated for the query "Music" in the NYT.

Query	Music
Doc. Count	57,192
Rep. Doc.	*Anniversaries Fill the Halls With Melody*
Repres. Terms	sonata*,orchestra*,album*,concerto*, beethoven*,guitar*,brahm*,quartet*, philharmon*,melodi*,schubert*,mezzo*, bassist*,melod*,saxophonist*,pianist*, symphoni*,saxophon*,bariton*,cello*
Rarely Occurring Terms	report*
Subquery	**Music AND Recordings (Audio)**
Subset Count	7,728
Rep. Doc.	*A Once Proud Industry Fends Off Extinction*
Repres. Terms	cassett*,cd*,reissu*,emi*,disk*, grammophon*,bmg*,soni*,label*,disc*,rca*, record*,album*,analyst*,nonesuch*,releas*, chart*,parel*,billion*,soundtrack*
Rarely Occurring Terms	tulli*,pm*,averi*,intermiss*,tomorrow*, ticket*,tonight*,fisher*,carnegi*,saturdai*, hall*,alic*,costum*,metropolitan*,sundai* recit*,auditorium*,lincoln*,festiv*,concert*
Subquery	**Music AND Opera**
Subset Count	6,408
Rep. Doc.	*Rossini, Hold the Pasta Sauce*
Repres. Terms	opera*,libretto*,figaro*,puccini*,donizetti*, verdi*,metropolitan*,coloratura*,costum*, wagner*,operat*,luciano*,aria*,rossini*,und* stage*,scene*,tenor*,la*,dramat*
Rarely Occurring Terms	saxophonist*,bassist*,guitarist*,rapper*, drummer*,guitar*,album*,songwrit*,band*, sonata*,jam*,rap*,punk*,drum*,jazz* improvis*,funk*,hop*,saxophon*,rock*
⋮	⋮

of a set, representative documents are picked based on the centroid of the set, and the set is represented through a medoid [1] or through a set of documents that provide coverage of important concept terms stored in the centroid [2].

Using multiple documents to cover all the important concept terms found in the centroid of a set may be appropriate for representing a flat set, but in a collection with multi-tagged documents, as is the case with NYT, most sets can be partitioned into coherent subsets. For example, a set of documents defined by the "Music" tag can be partitioned into subsets, such as "Music AND Opera," derived by intersecting multiple dominant tags found in the set. These subsets impose a hierarchy over the set, which can be used for choosing a diverse representative set of documents, similarly to what was proposed by Vee et al. [16]. A set generated through this approach has documents that represent concepts found in many centroids of various subsets in the set of interest, and so will have a richer diversity than is possible with the coverage approach whose documents are optimized to cover a single centroid. This approach parallels the use of query reformulations to provide diverse sets of results for web searches [13].

Table 2: Analysis of documents returned for a query on bursty terms with respect to the corresponding tags (where only result sets of size greater than 100 are considered)

Query Type	Instance Count	Mean Precision at 100	Mean Rank of Top Relevant Doc.
t_x	1,015	$62.4_{\sigma=23.0}$	$1.44_{\sigma=1.42}$
$t_x \wedge t_y$	5,179	$70.7_{\sigma=20.6}$	$1.25_{\sigma=0.98}$

Instead of calculating the medoid directly from the cosine distance of each document from the centroid, we take advantage of the infrastructure provided by a standard information retrieval system such as Lucene. Given a query, Lucene's ranking function ranks a document highly if the terms specified in a query appear frequently in the document and the document contains many of the terms specified in the query. This aligns well with the properties used for evaluating whether or not a document is a good representative of a set (i.e., it provides good coverage of the important concept terms of the centroid and those terms occur frequently in the document). As a result, the highest ranked document to a query consisting of the bursty terms of a set centroid makes a good representative document for the corresponding set. Since bursty terms are all relatively rare in the corpus, the ranking function will not likely have a strong bias towards documents that represent only some of the query terms.

We have examined the quality of this mapping between tags and the top 20 bursty terms describing the corresponding centroids (Table 2) to determine whether documents that contain the bursty terms tend to be in the expected subset (having the corresponding tag). The mapping was evaluated over all sets that have at least 100 documents and are defined by a single tag or by a conjunction of two tags. The top 20 bursty terms representing each of those sets were used to formulate queries. For each of those queries, a large proportion of the top 100 documents in the ranked lists of results are annotated with the corresponding tag or tags. Thus, there is a high correlation between the tags and the content text. In addition, the highest ranked result to the query on the bursty terms predominantly comes from the same set as the bursty terms. The existence of the required tags on many of the top 100 documents returned by a bursty terms query confirms the influence of the identified bursty terms in defining a document set. Furthermore, since many relevant documents are found in the top 100 results, various IR optimization techniques that take advantage of early termination can be used without fear of missing a representative document.

3.2 Finding Representative Documents

Given a query Q defining a set of documents S_Q, let $t_1, t_2, ..., t_n$ be a ranked sequence of tags for which the rank of tag t_i is based on $|S_{Q \wedge t_i}|$ and the dissimilarity of $S_{Q \wedge t_i}$ with respect to both S_Q and other subsets $S_{Q \wedge t_j}$ where $j < i$. (Details of the tag ranking algorithm are given in the full description of the system [3].) The $N+1$ diverse representative documents for S_Q, denoted by $\mathbb{D}_Q(N, k)$, are defined

using Equation 4.

$$D_Q(i,k) = \begin{cases} R(\mathbb{B}_k(S_Q, S_G)) & \text{if } i = 0 \\ R(\mathbb{B}_k(S_{Q \wedge t_i}, S_Q)) & \text{if } i > 0 \end{cases} \quad (3)$$

$$\mathbb{D}_Q(N,k) = \bigcup_{i=0}^{N} D_Q(i,k) \quad (4)$$

where S_G corresponds to all documents in the corpus and $R(x)$ returns the document in S_Q that is top ranked when posing the text query using the terms in the set x.

For example, $D_{Music}(0, 20)$ is found by taking the top 20 positive bursty terms, which include stemmed words such as *sonata, orchestra, album, concerto,* and *beethoven,* and issuing a text query with those terms. The highest ranked document in set S_{Music} is chosen as a representative document, which happens to be the document with title *Anniversaries Fill the Halls With Melody* as shown in Table 1. $D_{Music}(1, 20)$ is found using the bursty terms in the largest subset, "Music∧Recordings (Audio)," and $D_{Music}(2, 20)$ uses the subset "Music∧Opera." For our example, $\mathbb{D}_{Music}(2, 20)$ is displayed in Table 1, and these three documents together form a diverse representative document set for S_{Music}.

4. SYSTEM ARCHITECTURE

The architecture of the faceted browsing system is shown in Figure 1. The system relies on the Partial Materialization Module, described by Drzadzewski and Tompa [4], which is central to efficient system performance. The module is designed to ensure fast access to requested centroids of document sets defined through Boolean operations over tags, while consuming minimal storage. Fast access to the centroid measure for document sets makes it feasible to produce the proposed summary measures for many sets within a short amount of time, so that a user can interactively explore large document collections. For example, with the help of the Partial Materialization Module, a centroid for a document set consisting of 142,000 documents can be obtained in under two seconds, whereas it would take 120 seconds to calculate the same centroid by aggregating individual documents.

When a user specifies a query over tags, the system produces a summary for the resulting documents by first accessing the Tag-Tag Index and a Tag-Document Index found in the Partial Materialization Module to produce a ranked sequence of N tags, such that each chosen tag produces a large subset that is dissimilar from both the document set of interest and subsets produced by other selected tags. These tags are then individually combined with the original query as a conjunction in order to produce N sub-queries. (For the query "Music," sub-queries such as "Music AND Recordings (Audio)" and "Music AND Opera" are generated.) The original query along with the N sub-queries are then fed into the Partial Materialization Module, which produces a centroid for each of the queries along with the centroid for the whole corpus.

The resulting centroids are compared against each other to derive both positive and negative bursty terms (Eqns. 1 and 2) for the result set and principal subsets. The positive bursty terms are then used to form multiple text queries (a separate query for each set of bursty terms) (Eqns. 3 and 4). The highest ranked documents returned from each search

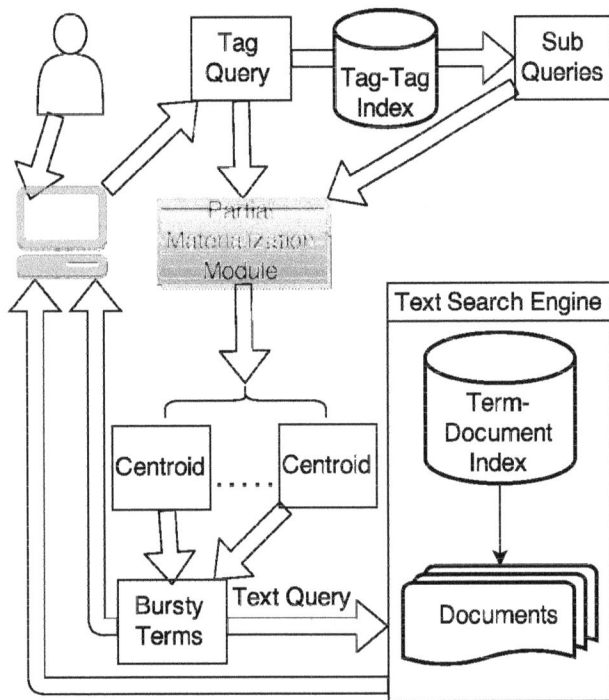

Figure 1: System for supporting faceted browsing

along with the corresponding bursty terms are returned to the user to produce the summary of the resulting set similar to Table 1.

The user interface is developed as a web app, and Lucene is used for indexing the documents and for supporting text queries through the standard ranking function. Additional information about the system is provided in the full system description [3] and on our website[1].

5. CONCLUSIONS

Whereas a standard faceted browser in response to a user's query on a tag (e.g., "Music") would produce a list of all documents that have that tag (which happen to be 57,192 documents) as well as a list of facets and the number of documents associated with each facet ("Recordings (Audio)" with 7,728 documents, and "Opera" with 6,408 documents), our system also provides a set of diverse representative documents that come from the various subsets (defined by queries "Music AND Recordings (Audio)", and "Music AND Opera") as well as representative terms for the result set and each principal subset. This information provides a useful summary and an information scent so users can make informed decisions as to which subset(s) they may want to explore further.

Acknowledgements

Financial assistance from NSERC, Mitacs, and the University of Waterloo is greatly appreciated.

---

[1]http://www.db.uwaterloo.ca/TagBrowser2015/

6. REFERENCES

[1] D. R. Cutting, J. O. Pedersen, D. R. Karger, and J. W. Tukey. Scatter/Gather: A cluster-based approach to browsing large document collections. In *Proc. 15th Ann. Int. ACM SIGIR Conf. Res. Dev. Inf. Retr.*, pages 318–329, 1992.

[2] V. Deolalikar. Distance or coverage?: Retrieving knowledge-rich documents from enterprise text collections. In *Proc. 23rd ACM Int. Conf. on Inf. Knowl. Manage.*, CIKM 2014, pages 1771–1774, 2014.

[3] G. Drzadzewski. *On-Line Analytical Systems for Multi-Tagged Document Collections*. PhD thesis, Cheriton Sch. Comp. Sci., Univ. Waterloo, 2015. in preparation.

[4] G. Drzadzewski and F. W. Tompa. Partial materialization for on-line analytical processing over multi-tagged document collections. *Knowl. Inf. Syst.*, 2015. to appear.

[5] A. F. Gelbukh, M. Alexandrov, A. Bourek, and P. Makagonov. Selection of representative documents for clusters in a document collection. In *8th Int. Conf. Applic. Nat. Lang. Inf. Sys.*, pages 120–126, 2003.

[6] J. C. Goodwin, T. Cohen, and T. C. Rindflesch. Discovery by scent: Discovery browsing system based on the Information Foraging Theory. In *2012 IEEE Int. Conf. Bioinf. Biomed. Worksh.*, BIBMW 2012, pages 232–239, 2012.

[7] S. Goorha and L. Ungar. Discovery of significant emerging trends. In *Proc. 16th ACM SIGKDD Int. Conf. Knowl. Disc. Data Min.*, KDD '10, pages 57–64, 2010.

[8] A. Popescul and L. H. Ungar. Automatic labeling of document clusters. unpublished, http://citeseer.nj. nec.com/popescul00automatic.html, 2000.

[9] D. R. Radev, H. Jing, M. Styś, and D. Tam. Centroid-based summarization of multiple documents. *Inf. Process. Manage.*, 40(6):919–938, Nov. 2004.

[10] S. Ramdeen and B. M. Hemminger. A tale of two interfaces: How facets affect the library catalog search. *J. Am. Soc. Inf. Sci. Technol.*, 63(4):702–715, 2012.

[11] D. R. Raymond. Personal data structuring in videotex. Technical Report CS-84-7, Cheriton Sch. Comp. Sci., Univ. Waterloo, February 1984.

[12] E. Sandhaus. The New York Times Annotated Corpus. Linguistic Data Consortium, Univ. Penn., http://www.ldc.upenn.edu/Catalog/catalogEntry.jsp? catalogId=LDC2008T19, 2008.

[13] R. L. T. Santos, C. Macdonald, and I. Ounis. Exploiting query reformulations for web search result diversification. In *Proc. 19th Int. Conf. World Wide Web*, WWW '10, pages 881–890, 2010.

[14] R. L. T. Santos, C. Macdonald, and I. Ounis. Search result diversification. *Found. Trends Inf. Retr.*, 9(1):1–90, 2015.

[15] D. Tunkelang. *Faceted Search*. Synthesis Lectures on Information Concepts, Retrieval, and Services. Morgan & Claypool Publishers, 2009.

[16] E. Vee, U. Srivastava, J. Shanmugasundaram, P. Bhat, and S. Yahia. Efficient computation of diverse query results. In *Proc. 24th IEEE Int. Conf. Data Engin.*, ICDE 2008, pages 228–236, April 2008.

A Quantitative and Qualitative Assessment of Automatic Text Summarization Systems

Jamilson Batista,
Hilário Oliveira,
Rafael Dueire Lins
UFPE, Recife, PE, Brazil
{jba, rdl}@cin.ufpe.br

Steven J. Simske
HP Labs
Fort Collins, CO 80528, USA
steven.simske@hp.com

Rafael Ferreira,
Rodolfo Ferreira,
Gabriel Silva
UFRPE, Recife, PE, Brazil
{rflm, gfps}@cin.ufpe.br

Marcelo Riss
HP Brazil R&D
Porto Alegre, RS, Brazil
marcelo.riss@hp.com

ABSTRACT

Text summarization is the process of automatically creating a shorter version of one or more text documents. This paper presents a qualitative and quantitative assessment of the 22 *state-of-the-art* extractive summarization systems using the CNN corpus, a dataset of 3,000 news articles.

Categories and Subject Descriptors

I.2.7 [**Natural Language Processing**]: Text analysis.

General Terms

Algorithms, Experimentation

Keywords

Text Summarization; Summarization Evaluation; Survey

1. INTRODUCTION

Text Summarization (TS) is the process of automatically creating a compressed versions of one or more documents, preserving their information [19]. Although the research in summarization started in 1958 with Luhn [15] the recent increase in the amount of text documents available, especially regarding to the expansion of the web, boosted the amount of research and systems developed in the last 15 years. TS methods can be classified as *Extractive* and *Abstractive* [13]. *Extractive* summarization systems select a set of the most significant sentences from a document, exactly as they appear, to form the summary, being usually performed in three steps ([16]):

- Create an intermediate representation of the text;

- Score the most important sentences;

- Select the highest score sentences.

Abstractive systems attempt to improve the coherence among the sentences in the summary by eliminating redundancies and clarifying their context. Summarization systems can also be classified as *single-* or *multi-document*.

This paper presents a qualitative and quantitative assessment of the 22 state-of-the-art summarization systems using the CNN corpus [11], which encompasses 3,000 documents extracted from CNN website(www.cnn.com). Such texts are high quality and for each of them there is a summary of 3 or 4 sentences provided by the original authors, the *highlights*. The summarization rate of 90% was adopted for all tools and systems tested.

2. THE EVALUATED SYSTEMS

The systems evaluated and the abbreviations used are presented in Table 1.

2.1 Qualitative Analysis

The systems evaluated are classified into different dimensions traditionally used to categorize summarization systems:

- *Input:* The system is able to generate a summary from *single-* or *multi-documents*.

- *Output:* The type of the summary generated is *extractive (Ext)* (i.e. the original sentences of the documents are selected to generate the summary) or *abstractive (Abs)* (some processing is done to compress or fuse the information of the sentences).

- *Purpose:* The system produces *generic or oriented summaries*.

- *Language:* The system is *mono-lingual* or works with several languages (*Multi-lingual*).

- *License:* The tool is a *commercial or a free* service.

- *Platform:* The system platform is *desktop* or is available on the *Web*.

Table 2: *Classifications of the systems evaluated based on different summarization dimensions.*

System	Input	Output	Purpose	Language	License	Platform
Almus	Single/Multi	Ext	Generic or update	Mono	Free	Desktop
AutoS	Single	Ext	Generic	Mono	Free	Web
Aylien	Single	Ext	Generic	Multi	Commercial	Web
Classifier4J	Single	Ext	Generic	Mono	Free	Desktop
Compendium	Single/Multi	Ext/Abs	Generic	Mono	Free	Web
			Query-focused			
			Sentiment-based			
Custom Writing	Single	Ext	Generic	Mono	Free	Web
HP-FS	Single/Multi	Ext	Generic	Multi	Commercial	Desktop
Free Summarizer	Single	Ext	Generic	Mono	Free	Web
OpenText Summarizer	Single	Ext	Generic	Multi	Free	Desktop/Web
Py Teaser	Single	Ext	Generic	Multi	Free	Desktop
Sumy	Single	Ext	Generic	Multi	Free	Desktop
SweSum	Single/Multi	Ext	Generic	Multi	Free	Web
Text Compactor	Single	Ext	Generic	Mono	Free	Web
Sumplify	-	Ext	Generic	-	Free	Web
Tools4Noobs	-	Ext	Generic	Multi	Free	Web
Findwise Summarizers	Single/Multi	Ext	Generic	-	Free	Web
Text Analysis Online	Single	Ext	Generic	-	Free	Web
TextSummarization	-	Ext	Generic	-	Free	Web

Table 1: *Abbreviations used for the systems tested.*

System	Abbreviations
Almus: Automatic Text Summarizer [20]	Almus
Auto Summarizer [2]	AutoS
Aylien Text Analysis API [3]	Aylien
Baseline First N Sentences [17]	FirstNSent
HP-Functional Summarization [6, 7]	HP-FS
Classifier4J [14]	C4J
Compendium [12]	Compend
Custom Writing [27]	CW
Findwise Biclique [8]	FindBI
Findwise MultipleKernelLearning [8]	FindMKL
Findwise Submodular Optimization [8]	FindSMO
Findwise TextRank [8]	FindTR
Free Summarizer [1]	FS
Open Text Summarizer [18]	OTS
Pyteaser [24]	PyT
Sumplify [21]	Sump
Sumy [22]	Sumy
SweSum: Automatic Text Summarizer [5, 9]	SweSum
TAO Simple Text [23]	TAO
Text Compactor [4]	TC
Text Summarization [25]	TextS
Tools4Noobs [26]	T4N

Table 2 classifies the systems using the presented dimensions.

1. The majority of systems are only single document, only five are extensible to deal with multi-document.

2. Only Compendium performs some degree of abstractive summarization.

3. Six systems are multi-language, the other ones are for one specific language.

4. The only commercial system evaluated was Aylien.

5. Some systems run on desktops, but the majority are available on the web.

3. PERFORMANCE EVALUATION

This section describes: (i) the dataset used; (ii) the methodology followed in the experiments to assess the quality of summaries; (iii) the results of the performance evaluation.

3.1 Evaluation Methodology

Two quantitative evaluations are used to assess the effectiveness of the systems evaluated. The first evaluation is performed by counting the numbers of sentences selected by the system that match the human gold standard. In the second evaluation, the well-know ROUGE (Recall-Oriented Understudy for Gisting Evaluation) [10] is used. ROUGE measures the content similarity between system-developed summaries and the gold standards. ROUGE-2 was used here as it claims to achieve the best correlation with human annotators [10].

As the summaries of CNN corpus have 10% of the original text, this compression rate was used in the performed experiments. Some of the evaluated systems allow the user to define the summary size in three ways: *(i)* number of sentences, *(ii)* number of words, and *(iii)* compression rate.

3.2 Performance Evaluation

Table 3 shows the results of the first quantitative evaluation performed by counting the numbers of sentences selected by the systems to create the summary that matches with the human gold standard. The 3,000 documents of the CNN corpus used in this evaluation have a total of 10,753 sentences into the gold standard. The five highest scores were obtained by: AutoS (3029), C4J (3014), FirstNSent (2882), HP-FS (2842), PyT (2825) and Aylien (2657).

The best two systems AutoS and C4J achieved very similar results with 0.50% of difference. In fact, the best five systems obtained relatively close results, only differing within a range of 7.72%. Comparing C4J with FindTR, system

Table 3: *Number of summaries sentences into gold standard.*

System	Correct Sentences Selected
Human GoldStandard	10,753
AutoS	3,029
C4J	3,014
FirstNSent	2,882
HP-FS	2,842
PyT	2,825
Aylien	2,657
TAO	2,513
TextS	2,481
Almus	2,406
FS	2,399
Sump	2,224
SweSum	2,145
TC	2,137
Sumy	2,090
Compendium	2,064
OTS	2,060
FindSMO	2,052
T4N	1,994
CW	1,901
FindBI	1,851
FindMKL	1,825
FindTR	1,810

Table 4: *Systems performance comparison using ROUGE-2 recall, precision and f-measure (%).*

System	Recall	Precision	F-Measure
C4J	35.74	34.19	**34.95***
FirstNSent	31.22	**36.25***	**33.55***
Aylien	33.65	31.94	32.77
HP-FS	34.67	30.72	32.57
AutoS	**39.29***	26.94	31.96
FS	32.60	30.22	31.36
T4N	27.71	34.09	30.57
TextS	27.00	33.55	29.92
TC	28.00	31.89	29.81
OPTS	27.75	31.00	29.26
FindSMO	24.87	32.38	28.13
Sump	28.39	27.46	27.91
SweSum	25.86	30.07	27.81
PyT	31.19	23.55	26.84
CW	25.05	25.87	25.45
Sumy	28.00	23.30	25.43
Almus	26.78	23.77	25.18
FindTR	21.73	28.44	24.64
TAO	30.11	20.82	24.62
FindMKL	20.96	28.83	24.28
FindBI	21.01	28.11	24.05
Compendium	21.96	26.14	23.87

[1]* Means that the result is statistically significant than the others systems

with worst result, a difference of 67.35% was found. These results show that evaluated systems create a wide variety of summaries.

The baseline *FirstNSent* even being a simple heuristic has a good performance. This corroborates the previous works that pointed out the importance of sentence position as feature to sentence importance mainly in news articles [17, 6].

The overall accuracy was low for all systems, AutoS achieve 28.16%. It happens because in news documents the authors use a wide variety of sentences to present the same fact. Thus, the summarizer select sentence different from the gold standard; however similar in the meaning.

As aforementioned, ROUGE-2 has the highest agreement with manual evaluations, due this a detailed results of precision, recall and f-measure sorted by f-measure are showed in Table 4. A statistical significance test using a two-sided Wilcoxon signed-rank with a $p \leq 0.05$ is used and the statistical differences are highlighted in Table 4.

In each measure a different system reached the best results. AutoS (39.29%) reached the best recall, and FirstNSent (36.25%) the best precision. Both systems achieved statistically superior results than others. C4J (34.95%) and FirstNSent (33.55%) obtained the two best f-measure, despite the difference between them, it was not statistically significant. Compared to the others, both systems showed statistically superior f-measure results.

Aylien and HP-FS also reach interesting results, achieving only 2.38 percentage point less than C4J in relation to the f-measure.

Based on the two experiments performed, we conclude that C4J is the best summarization tool in our evaluation. It reached the best performance in Rouge-2 f-measure (Table 4) and the second best performance in the first experiment (Table 3) with a small difference 0.50% in relation to AutoS (best system).

C4J provides an extractive single-document summarization based on word frequency method [6]. It computes the frequency of all words in the document and selects the 100 most frequent words. Then it selects the first **N** sentences of the document which contain at least one of the 100 most frequent words to compose the summary. **N** depends of the required summary compression rate. This approach can be seen as combination of sentence position strategy and word frequency method.

4. CONCLUSIONS

This papers presents a qualitative analysis of the 22 *state-of-the-art* extractive summarization tools under six aspects:

1. *Input*: single- or multi-documents;

2. *Output*: extractive or abstractive;

3. *Purpose*: generic or oriented summaries;

4. *Language*: mono- or multi-lingual;

5. *License*: commercial or free;

6. *Platform*: desktop or Web-use.

The analysis of the 22 studied tools shows that the majority of those summarization systems are: single-document, extractive, generic, mono-lingual, free and web-use. Such analysis also points that the main direction of research in summarization is the creation of summarization solution for: (i) multi-documents summarization; (ii) creation of abstractive summaries; (iii) oriented based summaries, such as: update-, query-, sentiment-based; (iv) summarization of multi-lingual documents.

The two quantitative evaluation assessments performed showed that Classifier4J, Autosummarizer, Aylien and HP-Functional Summarization are the four best systems analyzed. It is important to remark that the results obtained claim for a much deeper evaluation as the either number of sentences from the gold standard selected or the ROUGE results obtained in the best cases provide a result of around 30% precision rate, which may be considered low. Some sort of human evaluation of the quality of summaries is also needed, even if it is not performed in the whole CNN test set, as the evaluation must involve at least two or three people to check the quality of each of the 66,000 summaries, a tedious task of huge dimension. One possibility is offered by trying to automatically measure the degree of similarity of the sentences in the gold standards and the summaries, as such measure seems to offer more accurate results than ROUGE, as they take into account semantic information besides lexical and syntactic ones.

One of the problems already identified that remains to be addressed is that most of the systems analyzed perform extractive summarization, the major drawback of such systems is the lack of cohesion of the generated summaries. Unresolved coreferences and discourse relations were often identified in the generated summaries, decreasing their level of understanding. Strategies on how to estimate and to improve the degree of coherence of the generated summaries is left an important point for further investigation.

5. ACKNOWLEDGMENTS

The research results reported in this paper have been partly funded by a R&D project between Hewlett-Packard do Brazil and UFPE originated from tax exemption (IPI - Law number 8.248, of 1991 and later updates).

6. REFERENCES

[1] Free summarizer. http://freesummarizer.com/, 2011. Last acess: Mar. 2015.

[2] Autosummarizer. Automatic text summarizer. http://autosummarizer.com/, 2014. Last acess: Mar. 2015.

[3] Aylien. Aylien text analysis api. http://aylien.com/text-api-doc, 2011. Last acess: Mar. 2015.

[4] T. Compactor. Text compactor. http://www.textcompactor.com, 2015. Last acess: Mar. 2015.

[5] H. Dalianis and et al. From swesum to scandsum: Automatic text summarization for the scandinavian languages. pages 153–163. Museum Tusculanums Forlag, 2003.

[6] R. Ferreira and et al. Assessing sentence scoring techniques for extractive text summarization. *Expert Systems with Applications*, 40(14):5755–5764, 2013.

[7] R. Ferreira and et al. A context based text summarization system. In *DAS 2014*, pages 66–70, Apr., 2014.

[8] Findwise. Findwise multi-document summarizers. http://labdemos.findwise.com/demomds, 2015. Last acess: Mar. 2015.

[9] M. Hassel and H. Dalianis. Swesum - automatic text summarizer. http://swesum.nada.kth.se/index-eng.html, 2003. Last acess: Mar. 2015.

[10] C.-Y. Lin. Rouge: A package for automatic evaluation of summaries. In *ACL-04 Workshop*, pages 74–81, Barcelona, Spain, July 2004. Association for Computational Linguistics.

[11] R. D. Lins and et al. A multi-tool scheme for summarizing textual documents. In *IADIS - WWW/INTERNET*, pages 1–8, July 2012.

[12] E. Lloret and et al. COMPENDIUM: A text summarization system for generating abstracts of research papers. volume 88, pages 164–175. Data Knowl. Eng., 2013.

[13] E. Lloret and M. Palomar. Text summarisation in progress: a literature review. *Artif. Intell. Rev.*, 37(1):1–41, Jan. 2012.

[14] N. Lothian. Classifier4j. http://classifier4j.sourceforge.net/, 2003. Last acess: Mar. 2015.

[15] H. P. Luhn. The automatic creation of literature abstracts. *IBM J. Res. Dev.*, 2(2):159–165, Apr. 1958.

[16] A. Nenkova and K. McKeown. A survey of text summarization techniques. In *Mining Text Data*, pages 43–76. Springer, 2012.

[17] Y. Ouyang and et al. A study on position information in document summarization. In *Proceedings of the 23rd International Conference on Computational Linguistics: Posters*, pages 919–927. Association for Computational Linguistics, 2010.

[18] N. Rotem. Open text summarizer. http://libots.sourceforge.net/, 2003. Last acess: Mar. 2015.

[19] K. Spärck Jones. Automatic summarising: The state of the art. *Information Processing Management*, 43(6):1449–1481, Nov. 2007.

[20] J. Steinberger and K. Ježek. Text summarization and singular value decomposition. ADVIS'04, pages 245–254, Berlin, Heidelberg, 2004. Springer-Verlag.

[21] Sumplify. Sumplify. http://sumplify.com/, 2015. Last acess: Mar. 2015.

[22] Sumy. Sumy. https://github.com/miso-belica/sumy, 2015. Last acess: Mar. 2015.

[23] TAO. Text analysis online (). http://textanalysisonline.com/simple-text-summarizer, 2015. Last acess: Mar. 2015.

[24] D. Teaser. Py teaser. https://github.com/xiaoxu193/PyTeaser, 2013. Last acess: Mar. 2015.

[25] TextSummarization. Text summarization. http://textsummarization.net/text-summarizer, 2015. Last acess: Mar. 2015.

[26] Tools4Noobs. Tools4noobs. http://www.tools4noobs.com/summarize/, 2015. Last acess: Mar. 2015.

[27] C. Writing. Custom writing summarizer. http://custom-writing.org/writing-tools/summarizer, 2006. Last acess: Mar. 2015.

Automatic Document Classification using Summarization Strategies

Rafael Ferreira,
Rafael Dueire Lins,
Luciano Cabral,
Fred Freitas
U.F.PE, Recife, Brazil
{rflm, rdl}@cin.ufpe.br

Steven J. Simske
Hewlett-Packard Labs
Fort Collins, CO 80528, USA
steven.simske@hp.com

Marcelo Riss
Hewlett-Packard Brazil
Porto Alegre, RS, Brazil
marcelo.riss@hp.com

ABSTRACT

An efficient way to automatically classify documents may be provided by automatic text summarization, the task of creating a shorter text from one or several documents. This paper presents an assessment of the 15 most widely used methods for automatic text summarization from the text classification perspective. A naive Bayes classifier was used showing that some of the methods tested are better suited for such a task.

Categories and Subject Descriptors

I.7.0 [**Document and Text Processing**]: General

General Terms

Algorithms, Experimentation

Keywords

Automatic Text Summarization; Text Classification.

1. INTRODUCTION

The amount of data available today in the Internet has reached an unprecedented volume as is still growing fast every day. Text documents such as news articles, electronic books, scientific papers, and blogs are the majority of such data [1]. The huge volume of data has made it difficult to sieve useful information from the Internet.

Text Classification (TC) is a valuable way of organizing a large number of documents [2] into a number of pre-defined categories. Machine learning algorithms such as decision trees [4], neural network [7] and Bayesian classifiers [9] have been used for such a purpose. Automatic Text Summarization (TS) [13] aims at creating a shorter version of a document keeping its essential content. Thus, it can be also seen

[1] http://www.worldwidewebsize.com/

DocEng'15, September 8-11, 2015, Lausanne, Switzerland.
© 2015 ACM. ISBN 978-1-4503-3307-8/15/09 ...$15.00.
DOI: http://dx.doi.org/10.1145/2682571.2797077.

as a technique to eliminate irrelevant information from a text, making it smaller and improving its classification process [15]. The methods for evaluating TS techniques are [13]: (i) *Intrinsic Evaluation* (IE) attempts to measure the quality of summaries. For instance, how summarization can improve the user understanding of a text. (ii) *Extrinsic Evaluation* (EE) tests the effectiveness of a summarization system in applications, such as text classification. In this case this is the accuracy of the classification of the summary in relation to the classification of the original document.

Although the technical literature reports the use of TS as a way to improve TC [21], the analysis of the TS methods that are more suitable for such a purpose has never been made before. This paper proposes an extrinsic evaluation of the 15 most widely used automatic text summarization methods aiming at text classification. The assessment performed here used 1,000 texts from the CNN dataset [11], each of which is classified in several subject areas using a naive Bayes classifier. The experiments performed here show that the different automatic text summarization methods achieve better results in intrinsic [6] and extrinsic scenarios.

2. AUTOMATIC TEXT SUMMARIZATION

TS [13] aims at automatically creating a compressed version of one or more documents, extracting the essential information in them. TS techniques are classified as *Extractive* and *Abstractive*. Extractive systems select a set of the most significant sentences from a document, exactly as they appear, to form the text summary. Abstractive systems attempt to improve the coherence among the sentences in the summary by eliminating redundancies and clarifying their context; sentences that are not in the original text may be introduced. Extractive summaries are of more widespread use today, as they are easier to create. Extractive methods are usually performed in three steps [19]: (i) Creating an intermediate representation of the text; (ii) Sentence scoring; and (iii) Selection of sentences, according to some criteria.

The first of the steps above creates a representation of the document. Usually, it divides the text into paragraphs, sentences, and tokens. Sometimes some preprocessing, such as stop words removal, is also performed. The second step tries to determine which sentences are important to the document or to which extent it combines information about different topics, by sentence scoring. The score measures how relevant a sentence is to the "understanding" of the text as a whole. The last step combines the scores provided by the previous steps and generates a summary.

The first reference to text summarization using extractive summarization dates back to 1958 [14]. The focus of sentence scoring is to determine which sentences are representative of a given text. In general, three approaches are followed: (i) *Word Scoring*: assigning scores the words; (ii) *Sentence Scoring*: position in the document, similarity to the title, etc. *Graph Scoring*: relationship between sentences.

2.1 Word Scoring

The initial methods in sentence scoring were based on words. Each word receives a score and the weight of each sentence is the sum of all scores of its constituent words.

- **Word Frequency**: As the name of the method suggests, the more frequently a words occurs in the text, the higher its score[14, 1].

- **TF/IDF**: It uses TF/IDF formula 1 in order to give score to sentences [18].

$$TF/IDF(w) = (NumTS) * log(\frac{(NumS)}{(MenST)}) \quad (1)$$

where $NumTS$ is the occurrences of term t in sentence S, $NumS$ is the total number of sentences, and $MenST$ is the number of sentences with mention to term t).

- **Word Co-occurrence**: Word Co-occurrence measures the probability of two terms from a text appear alongside each other in a certain order [12].

- **Lexical Similarity**: Assumes that the important sentences are identified by strong chains [18]. In other words, it relates sentences that employ words with the same meaning (synonyms) or other semantic relation.

- **Upper Case**: This method assigns higher scores to words that contain one or more upper case letters [20]:

$$CPTW(j) = \frac{NCW(j)}{NTW(j)} \quad (2)$$

NCW = Number of first letter capital words, and
NTW = Total number of words present in sentence.

$$UCf = \frac{CPTW(j)}{MAX(CPTW(j))} \quad (3)$$

UCf = Uppercase feature value.

- **Proper Noun**: Usually the sentences that contain a higher number of proper nouns are more important [5].

2.2 Sentence Scoring

This approach analyzes the features of the sentence itself and was used for the first time in 1968 [3] analyzing the presence of cue words in sentences. The main approaches are described below.

- **Cue-Phrases**: Sentences started by "in summary", "in conclusion", etc., as well as domain-specific terms are indicators of significant content of a text document [20]. The score is assigned using the formula:

$$CP = \frac{CPS}{CPD} \quad (4)$$

CPS = Number of cue-phrases in the sentence,
CPD = Total number of cue-phrases in the document.

- **Sentence Position**: The position of a sentence indicates its importance; the most important ones tend to be at the beginning of the text. [5, 1].

- **Sentence Resemblance to the Title**: word overlap of a sentence with the document title [5, 1].

- **Sentence Centrality**: The vocabulary overlap between a sentence and all the other sentences in the document [5, 1].

$$Score = \frac{Ks \cap KOs}{Ks \cup KOs} \quad (5)$$

Ks = Keywords in s, and
KOs = Keywords in other sentences.

- **Sentence Length**: Penalize sentences that are either too short or long [5, 1].

- **Sentence Inclusion of Numerical Data**: Numerical data are important, thus likely to be included in the summary [5, 1, 20].

2.3 Graph Scoring

In graph-based methods the score is generated by the relationship among the sentences. When a sentence refers to another it generates a link with a similarity value between them, which are used to generate the scores of sentence.

- **Text Rank**: It extracts keywords and weights the "importance" of words by using a graph-based model[16].

- **Bushy Path of the Node**: is defined as the number of links connecting a sentence (node) to sentences on the map [5].

- **Aggregate Similarity**: sums the weights (similarities) on the links [5].

Reference [6] presents an assessment of the techniques above using an intrinsic measure [13]. It evaluates those techniques using text classification (extrinsic measure) and to improve the text classification process.

3. SUMMARIZATION / CLASSIFICATION

This section evaluates the suitability of each of the methods in Section 2 for text classification.

The CNN corpus developed by Lins *et al.* [11] consists of 1,000 news texts extracted from *www.cnn.com*. This test corpus has texts in grammatically correct standard English, on general interest subjects, but there is also the *highlights*, a summary 3 to 5 sentences long written by the original authors. The highlights were the basis for the development of the *gold standard*, which was obtained by the injective mapping of each of the sentences in the highlights onto the original sentences of the text. The *gold standard* was formed with most voted mapped sentences chosen. Every text was originally tagged in one out of ten subject areas: Asia, business, Europe, Latin America, Middle East, sports, tech, travel, US and world. Each of these subject areas has 100 texts, each of them 41-sentence long on average.

In this work the Naive Bayes Network classifier [8] was used. Such probabilistic classifier, relies on the Bayes Theorem [17], which assumes that all attributes of the training data are independent of each other given the context of the

Table 1: *Results of Text Classifications Applied to: 1- Original Texts from CNN Dataset (in boldface) and 2- Summaries Using Proper Noun Method.*

	Asia	bness	Europe	L.Amec	M.East	sports	tech	travel	US	world
Asia	**23**-26	**4**-5	**0**-1	**0**-1	**2**-2	**1**-0	**0**-1	**11**-3	**5**-2	**4**-9
business	**1**-2	**36**-32	**0**-0	**0**-0	**0**-1	**1**-2	**2**-3	**2**-3	**5**-3	**3**-4
Europe	**0**-5	**2**-2	**18**-21	**4**-2	**3**-4	**1**-1	**0**-1	**1**-3	**13**-2	**8**-9
L.America	**1**-3	**1**-0	**1**-2	**27**-27	**0**-2	**2**-2	**0**-0	**4**-1	**5**-3	**9**-10
M.East	**1**-3	**1**-2	**1**-1	**0**-0	**38**-35	**1**-1	**0**-0	**4**-0	**0**-1	**4**-7
sports	**0**-0	**1**-3	**0**-2	**1**-0	**0**-0	**46**-41	**0**-0	**0**-1	**2**-2	**0**-1
tech	**0**-0	**10**-10	**0**-0	**0**-1	**0**-0	**1**-2	**22**-20	**3**-3	**12**-11	**2**-3
travel	**1**-2	**3**-9	**4**-4	**0**-0	**1**-2	**1**-1	**0**-0	**29**-20	**8**-10	**3**-2
US	**0**-2	**6**-6	**1**-0	**0**-1	**3**-2	**0**-1	**0**-2	**16**-14	**23**-20	**1**-1
world	**1**-3	**4**-5	**9**-7	**2**-7	**4**-3	**1**-0	**3**-1	**5**-5	**16**-13	**5**-6

class. The algorithm works as follows: first, in a preliminary learning phase, it generates a list of words with their frequencies from the input corpus. Each word in this generated list is labeled with the class it belongs to; resulting in a sort of "dictionary" for each class. Then, from this class dictionary, a tree is constructed whose leaves are the class labels and the intermediate nodes indicate probabilities calculated according to the Bayes theorem. Finally, when a new text is submitted to the classifier, it traverses the generated tree until it finds a leaf that indicates the class that best matches the words in the input text. The classifier undergoes a training phase before the real tests are performed. It is important to remark that before classifying a document some processing is performed to remove all stop words such as articles and pronouns.

3.1 Classifying the Original Documents

In order to assess the effectiveness of the different text summarization strategies for text classification one needs to assess the performance of the classifier itself. This was done by training the Naive Bayes classifier with a percentage of the original (non-summarized) documents and testing the accuracy of the classification with the remaining ones. Thus, the training set varied between 10% to 90% of the original set of documents. The best classification accuracy of 0.534 was reached when the training and test sets were halved in the number of documents. Table 1 presents the confusion-matrix of the classification of the documents of the CNN-corpus using 50 original documents of each class for training and 50 other for testing. The analysis of the data in boldface in Table 1 allows a number of conclusions: (i) Although the CNN-corpus is the largest corpus available today for text summarization the original subject tagging has a high degree of overlap; (ii) The tag "world" is too general in such a way that only 10 % of the texts tagged as such were recognized; (iii) More specific subjects, such as "sports" yielded a more accurate classification reaching 82%.

3.2 Classifying Summaries

Each of the 500 text documents used for testing (50 documents from 10 different classes) were summarized using each of the 15 methods described above yielding 7,500 summaries in total, each of them 6-sentences long. The results for the overall accuracy are shown in Table 2.

As already remarked the original classification encompasses a high degree of overlap between some categories. Having the original text as a reference, whose global classification

Table 2: *Results of Text Classifications Applied to a 6-sentence Summary From CNN Dataset.*

	Accuracy
Complete Text	0.534
Aggregate Similarity	0.432
Bushy Path	0.454
Cue-Phrase	0.404
Lexical Similarity	0.440
Numerical Data	0.416
Proper Noun	0.496
Resemblance-Title	0.444
Sentence Centrality	0.324
Sentence Length	0.450
Sentence Position	0.436
TextRank	0.460
TF/IDF	0.480
Upper Case	0.480
Word Co-Occurrence	0.430
Word Frequency	0.472

accuracy is 0.534 some of the text summarization techniques are not too far behind, as the most accurate of them, Proper Noun, reaches 0.496. The confusion matrix for the text classification using Proper Noun as a summarization strategy is presented in non-boldface font in Table 1.

The joint analysis of the two values that belongs in each slot of the classification Table 1 for the original and summarized documents using the Proper Noun method yields a global view of the misclassification degree in the process. The difference in the classification of the original text and the summarized one using Proper Noun is of 158 documents in 1,000.

3.3 Comparison with the Intrinsic Evaluation

This section presents a comparison between the performance of extrinsic and intrinsic text summarization. Extrinsic evaluation uses the results presented in Section 3.2 while intrinsic evaluation uses the results obtained from reference [6], which reports on two quantitative assessments of the same sentence scoring methods analyzed here.

ROUGE (Recall-Oriented Understudy for Gisting Evaluation) [10] was used for the first quantitative assessment comparing a summary with a given reference or a set of references, and examining the number of n-grams of words they all have in common. The second qualitative evaluation is done by counting the numbers of sentences selected by the system that match the gold standard. Reference [6] points out that the top five summarization methods using intrinsic evaluation are: sentence length, sentence position, resemblance-title, word frequency and TF/IDF.

Differently from the experimental results presented in Section 3.2, in relation to intrinsic text summarization evaluation, the sentence scoring methods achieve good results. Sentence length and sentence position appear as efficient summarization methods. This is because, for such a task, the user needs sentences that are easier to understand and that cover the text subject. Thus,for news articles, the size of the sentence and the position in relation to the text are relevant. Generally, in well written news texts, the important phrases are at the beginning and end of document and they are consistent. For text classification, the summary needs not to be understandable, it only supposes to contain the main information (in general, it means main words) from the text.

Resemblance-title, word frequency and TF/IDF achieve good results both for EE and IE. The documents used in the tests (CNN news) have well-formed words and the journalists usually provide titles containing the main information of the news. These methods provide relevant sentences for both text summarization and text classification.

It is important to notice that upper case and proper noun methods do not perform as well in the summarization task as in text classification. Thus, the best text summarization methods used to create summaries are different from those used for text classification.

4. CONCLUSIONS

This paper presents an extrinsic evaluation of document classification using the 15 most widely used text summarization methods. Tests were performed using the CNN-corpus, a high-standard test set with 1,000 news articles tagged into 10 different subject categories. The texts in CNN-corpus have on average 41 sentences. A Naive Bayes classifier was trained with 500 documents and used to perform the automatic classification of the 7,500 summaries obtained to assess the suitability of each of those methods in text classification.

The results show that the best summarization techniques for document classification are word scoring methods. Preliminary performance tests showed that text classification using summaries are almost twice faster than using the original document. This work opens a new research perspective on the influence of text summarization in automatic document classification. The development of a document classification system using the results shown here and an assessment of the relation between automatic text summarization and information retrieval are research initiatives on progress.

Acknowledgments

The research results reported in this paper have been partly funded by a R&D project between Hewlett-Packard do Brazil and UFPE originated from tax exemption (IPI - Law number 8.248, of 1991 and later updates).

5. REFERENCES

[1] A. Abuobieda, N. Salim, A. Albaham, A. Osman, and Y. Kumar. Text summarization features selection method using pseudo genetic-based model. In CAMP, pages 193 –197, 2012.

[2] C. C. Aggarwal and C. Zhai. A survey of text classification algorithms. In *Mining Text Data*, pages 163–222. 2012.

[3] H. P. Edmundson. New methods in automatic extracting. *J. ACM*, 16(2):264–285, Apr. 1969.

[4] D. M. Farid, L. Zhang, C. M. Rahman, M. Hossain, and R. Strachan. Hybrid decision tree and naive bayes classifiers for multi-class classification tasks. *Expert Systems with Applications*, 41(4, Part 2):1937 – 1946, 2014.

[5] M. A. Fattah and F. Ren. Ga, mr, ffnn, pnn and gmm based models for automatic text summarization. *Comput. Speech Lang.*, 23(1):126–144, 2009.

[6] R. Ferreira, L. de Souza Cabral, R. D. Lins, G. de Franca Silva, F. Freitas, G. D. C. Cavalcanti, R. Lima, S. J. Simske, and L. Favaro. Assessing sentence scoring techniques for extractive text summarization. *Expert Systems with Applications*, 40(14):5755–5764, 2013.

[7] M. Ghiassi, M. Olschimke, B. Moon, and P. Arnaudo. Automated text classification using a dynamic artificial neural network model. *Expert Systems with Applications*, 39(12):10967 – 10976, 2012.

[8] M. J. Islam, Q. M. J. Wu, M. Ahmadi, and M. A. Sid-Ahmed. Investigating the performance of naive- bayes classifiers and k- nearest neighbor classifiers. In ICCIT '07.

[9] L. H. Lee, D. Isa, W. O. Choo, and W. Y. Chue. High relevance keyword extraction facility for bayesian text classification on different domains of varying characteristic. *Expert Systems with Applications*, 39(1):1147 – 1155, 2012.

[10] C.-Y. Lin. Rouge: A package for automatic evaluation of summaries. *Text Summarization Branches Out: Proceedings of the ACL-04 Workshop*, pages 74–81, 2004.

[11] R. D. Lins, S. J. Simske, L. de Souza Cabral, G. de Silva, R. Lima, R. F. Mello, and L. Favaro. A multi-tool scheme for summarizing textual documents. In *Proc. of 11st IADIS WWW/INTERNET 2012*, pages 1–8, 2012.

[12] X. Liu, J. J. Webster, and C. Kit. An extractive text summarizer based on significant words. In ICCPOL '09, pages 168–178, 2009. Springer-Verlag.

[13] E. Lloret and M. Palomar. Text summarisation in progress: a literature review. *Artif. Intell. Rev.*, 37(1):1–41, 2012.

[14] H. P. Luhn. The automatic creation of literature abstracts. *IBM J. Res. Dev.*, 2(2):159–165, 1958.

[15] R. Mihalcea and S. Hassan. Using the essence of texts to improve document classification. In *(RANLP)*, 2005.

[16] R. Mihalcea and P. Tarau. TextRank: Bringing Order into Texts. In *CEMNLP*, 2004.

[17] T. Mitchell. *Machine Learning*. McGraw-Hill Education, 1st edition, 1997.

[18] V. G. Murdock. *Aspects of sentence retrieval*. PhD thesis, University of Massuchetts Amherst, 2006.

[19] A. Nenkova and K. McKeown. A survey of text summarization techniques. In *Mining Text Data*, pages 43–76. Springer, 2012.

[20] R. S. Prasad, N. M. Uplavikar, S. S. Wakhare, V. Jain, and T. A. Yedke. Feature based text summarization. In *International Journal of Advances in Computing and Information Researches*, volume 1, 2012.

[21] D. Shen, Q. Yang, and Z. Chen. Noise reduction through summarization for web-page classification. *Information Processing and Management*, 43(6):1735–1747, 2007.

The Venice Time Machine

Frédéric Kaplan
EPFL
frederic.kaplan@epfl.ch

ABSTRACT

The Venice Time Machine is an international scientific programme launched by the EPFL and the University Ca'Foscari of Venice with the generous support of the Fondation Lombard Odier. It aims at building a multidimensional model of Venice and its evolution covering a period of more than 1000 years. The project ambitions to reconstruct a large open access database that could be used for research and education. Thanks to a parternship with the Archivio di Stato in Venice, kilometers of archives are currently digitized, transcribed and indexed setting the base of the largest database ever created on Venetian documents. The State Archives of Venice contain a massive amount of hand-written documentation in languages evolving from medieval times to the 20th century. An estimated 80 km of shelves are filled with over a thousand years of administrative documents, from birth registrations, death certificates and tax statements, all the way to maps and urban planning designs. These documents are often very delicate and are occasionally in a fragile state of conservation. In complementary to these primary sources, the content of thousands of monographies have been indexed and made searchable.

The documents digitised in the Venice Time Machine programme are intricately interweaved, telling a much richer story when they are cross-referenced. By combining this mass of information, it is possible to reconstruct large segments of the city's past: complete biographies, political dynamics, or even the appearance of buildings and entire neighborhoods. The information extracted from the primary and secondary sources are organized in a semantic graph of linked data and unfolded in space and time in an historical geographical information system. The resulting platform can serve for both research and education. About a hundred researchers and students collaborate already on this programme. A doctoral school is organised every year in Venice and several bachelor and master courses currently use the data produced in the context of the Venice Time Machine. Through all these initiatives, the Venice Time Machine explores how "big data of the past" can change research and education in historical sciences, hopefully paving the way towards a general methodology that could be applied to many other cities and archives.

Keywords: Digital Humanities

SHORT BIOGRAPHY

Prof Frédéric Kaplan holds the Digital Humanities Chair at Ecole Polytechnique Federale de Lausanne (EPFL) and directs the EPFL Digital Humanities Laboratory (DHLAB). He conducts research projects combining archive digitisation, information modelling and museographic design. He is currently directing the "Venice Time Machine", an international project in collaboration with the Ca'Foscari University in Venice and the Venice State Archives, aiming to model the evolution and history of Venice over a 1000 year period. He is also conducting projects with the Bibliothèque Nationale de France, the Bibliothèque Nationale Suisse, the Bodmer Foundation, the Musée de l'Elysée and participated to exhibitions in several museums including the Centre Pompidou in Paris and the Museum of Modern Art in New York.

Frederic Kaplan graduated as an engineer of the Ecole Nationale Supérieure des Telecommunications in Paris and received a PhD degree in Artificial Intelligence from the University Paris VI. Before founding the Digital Humanities Laboratory, he worked ten years as a researcher at the Sony Computer Science Laboratory and six years at the EPFL pedagogical research laboratory. He was also the founder and president of OZWE, a company that designed and produced innovative interfaces, now one of the world leading studios in immersive gaming.

Frederic Kaplan published more than a hundred scientific papers, 6 books and about 10 patents. He is the chief editor of Frontiers in Digital Humanities and co-directs the Digital Humanities book collection at EPFL Press. He created the first Digital Humanities Master course in Switzerland and is now taking an active role for shaping a complete new curriculum at EPFL. He was the co-local organizer of the Digital Humanities 2014 conference in Lausanne, the largest scientific meeting ever conducted in this domain.

DocEng'15, September 8-11, 2015, Lausanne, Switzerland.
ACM 978-1-4503-3307-8/15/09.
DOI: http://dx.doi.org/10.1145/2682571.2797071

Towards Mobile OCR:
How To Take a Good Picture of a Document Without Sight

Michael P. Cutter
University of California, Santa Cruz
mcutter@soe.ucsc.edu

Roberto Manduchi
University of California, Santa Cruz
manduchi@soe.ucsc.edu

ABSTRACT

The advent of mobile OCR (optical character recognition) applications on regular smartphones holds great promise for enabling blind people to access printed information. Unfortunately, these systems suffer from a problem: in order for OCR output to be meaningful, a well-framed image of the document needs to be taken, something that is difficult to do without sight. This contribution presents an experimental investigation of how blind people position and orient a camera phone while acquiring document images. We developed experimental software to investigate if verbal guidance aids in the acquisition of OCR-readable images without sight. We report on our participant's feedback and performance before and after assistance from our software.

Categories and Subject Descriptors

H.5.2 [**Information Interfaces and Presentation**]: User Interfaces–Input devices and strategies, Interaction styles

General Terms

Design, Experimentation, Human Factors

Keywords

Visual Impairment, Optical Character Recognition, Document Processing

1. INTRODUCTION

There is increasing interest in mobile applications that can allow a blind person to access printed information such as restaurant menus, bills, signs on a door, etc. The ever increasing computational power of modern smartphones, combined with high quality on-board cameras, is enabling the development of OCR-based, low-cost applications that have great potential for benefiting the blind community. The fact that these software systems run on mainstream platforms (Android and iOS), rather than on customized devices, is an important bonus, since the latter are often expensive, lack support, and, like many assistive technology tools, are sometimes not well accepted due to the associated "stigma". However,

DocEng'15, September 8-11, 2015, Lausanne, Switzerland.
© 2015 ACM. ISBN 978-1-4503-3307-8/15/09 ...$15.00.
DOI: http://dx.doi.org/10.1145/2682571.2797066.

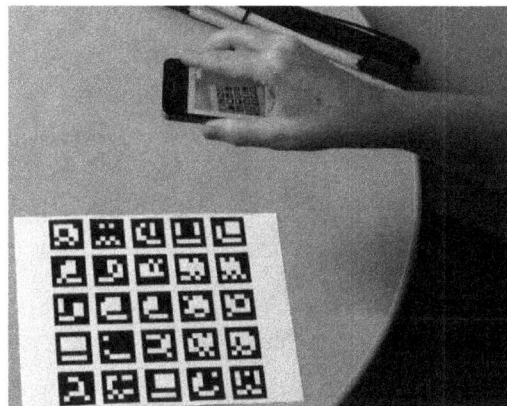

Figure 1: A participant positioning an iPhone over a document printed with ArUco fiducials.

as utilities for consumer mobile devices such as the Voice Over feature on iPhones proliferate, we can expect more wide spread adoption for accessibility applications.

Unfortunately, even the best OCR algorithm fails if the text in the image is cropped, the image has low resolution, is blurred, or badly lit. For sighted users, this is not a problem: one just needs to look at the scene through the screen, moving and orienting the phone until the desired text document is correctly framed and exposed before taking a shot. Even the best systems on the market can only provide post-facto indirect confirmation that a picture was actually readable – normally after producing garbled or incomplete text. The latency associated with OCR processing only makes things worse: one may have to wait for several minutes just to find out that the image was not OCR-readable and another snapshot of the document needs to be taken.

This contribution presents an experimental study with 12 blind participants. We first investigate how they hold and position the camera during image acquisition. Then they use our software that provides feedback while he or she tries to take an OCR-readable picture of a document. This experimental tool offers two modalities of usage. The first modality provides real-time confirmation when the user has reached a *compliant pose*, that is, when he or she has moved the camera to a position from which an OCR-readable image of the whole document can be taken. The second modality utters spoken directions to the user about where to move the phone next in order to increase the likelihood of reaching a compliant pose. After trying out our software we measure how they hold the camera again without assistance from our system.

This experimental study addresses two important research issues, concerning: (1) the ability of blind people to correctly position a smartphone in order to obtain an OCR-readable picture of a document; (2) the potential for increasing the success of this task by means of system-generated feedback. These results will hopefully inspire more research into mechanisms that could enable more efficient use of mobile OCR applications, and thus allow better access to printed information for blind users.

2. RELATED WORK

Document scanners coupled with OCR and text-to-speech have been used successfully by many blind people to access printed text [19]. Kane et al. [9] developed an augmented reality digital desk assistive environment which allows blind people to interact with complex paper documents. Their acquisition technology is a mounted desktop camera, which captures a live stream of images. The largest contour in the image is assumed to be the document and processed by optical character recognition. One of their user interface contributions is an "edge menu", inspired by the author's previous work [10]. The edge menu displays an alphabetical list of detected words. By clicking on an word on the list translational guidance is spoken to the image coordinate where the word was detected.

In recent years, a number of mobile OCR applications have been introduced to the market, to enable quick text access "on the go". The KNFB Mobile reader [2] and Blindsight's Text Detective [3] iPhone app are perhaps the best known such systems. The KNFB reader, which runs on the Nokia N82 phone, generates an optional "field of view report" via synthetic speech a few seconds after a picture has been taken of a document. This report contains information about the angle of the camera relative to the page and about whether all corners are visible or some text is cut off. By carefully holding the phone in position after the first picture has been taken, the user may be able to re-position the camera, if needed, so as to take a better framed picture. In practice, after taking a snapshot with KNFB, one has to wait for OCR to be completed before realizing that the shot was not compliant. Since multiple shots are normally needed, the whole process may be intolerably slow (possibly several minutes). However, KNFB just released an iOS version of their application which might remedy some of the latency issues. Unlike the KNFB Reader, Text Detective lets the user move the phone over the document, processing images continuously as they are taken by the phone's camera. As soon as an image is found containing text-like patterns, the phone vibrates briefly and the OCR process (which takes a few seconds) is started. This "opportunistic" approach is made possible by a fast text detection algorithm that is used to select promising images to be passed to the more computationally intensive OCR. However, their text spotter does not measure compliance: it will take a picture as soon as some text-like pattern is seen, possibly resulting in truncated lines etc. Only after OCR processing will the user find out that the shot was not compliant and that the hovering operation needs to be restarted. Often multiple hovering-OCR iterations are necessary, resulting in a long acquisition time. A similar opportunistic strategy is taken by an iPhone app named Prizmo [1], which processes each input image to find the edges of a rectangular document.

None of these smartphone OCR applications ensure that a blind user will be able to take a well-framed image of the document. In order to help a person take a good picture of a document, the use of mechanical stands has been proposed (e.g. the Optical Scan Stand tool that is available for the Galaxy Core Advance handset). These devices may be very useful for fixed-size documents, but do not allow the user to reduce or increase the distance to the document, which is often necessary to account for small font size or large document size.

Shilkrot et al. [11] created a wearable device to support reading on the go. Their system is worn on the finger and like Text Detective reads small blocks of text. They explored continuous tone and haptic feedback to alert the user that they have reached the end of a textblock; or have veered too far from the textline. There is also a commercial product worn as glasses called OrCam [17] that provides real time OCR by users pointing their head and finger at the block of text they wish to be read. However, neither of these approaches ensure that the user has captured the entire document and both require that the person buy a dedicated piece of technology.

The difficulty of taking good pictures without sight represents a hurdle not only for mobile OCR, but also for other applications of camera-based information access, as well as for recreational photography. For example, Bigham et al. [18] used simple computer vision techniques along with crowdsourcing to help a blind user point the camera correctly to an object (for example, to better identify it or to get closer to it). Brady et al [6] analyzed the type of objects blind people take photos of in a crowd sourcing answer seeking scenario. Their analyis also includes photo quality assessment. They found that 46% of the questions asked by their recent power users regarded 'reading'. The use of remote sight operators, who can look at the image taken by a blind person and provide advice on how to orient the camera to take a better picture, was also considered by Kutiyanawala et al. [21] in a tele-assistance system for shopping. TapTapSee [15] is another popular app that uses crowdsourcing for text reading from an image taken by an iPhone. Zhong et al. [14] developed a key-frame selection algorithm and combined it with a cloud based visual search engine to help blind people identify objects continuously.

EasySnap and the next iteration, PortraitFramer, are mobile applications developed by Jayant et al. [8], that give feedback to a blind photographer about the scene light, or about the presence and location in the picture of an object or of a person. The use of real-time feedback to help a blind person photo document transit accessibility was also studied by Vazquez and Steinfeld [12]. In this scenario, there is no clearly defined "target" (e.g., a face) that could be used to guide framing. Instead, a general–purpose saliency map is used to select a region of interest. A camera-based system for barcode access, equipped with a guidance mechanism that suggests how to move the camera in order to precisely center a detected barcode, was developed by Tekin and Coughlan [22]. The process of taking a precisely framed picture of a document for OCR processing could potentially be facilitated by stitching together multiple pictures, each containing a partial view of the document, into a panoramic image (or mosaic) of the whole document, as suggested by Zandifar et al. [13].

Experiments with sighted, blindfolded participants using a system similar to the one discussed in this contribution were conducted in a study by Cutter and Manduchi [7]. This study used a naive guidance algorithm, and included experiments that were meant only to validate the feasibility of such an approach. In fact, sighted people are likely to develop, through daily experience with vision-mediated camera handling, mechanisms and skills that are very different from those available to blind people, and thus cannot, even when blindfolded, be considered representative of blind users for the tasks considered in the experiments. With respect to the preliminary study in [7], we re-designed the guidance algorithm, the experiments, and the evaluation criteria, and only considered blind participants.

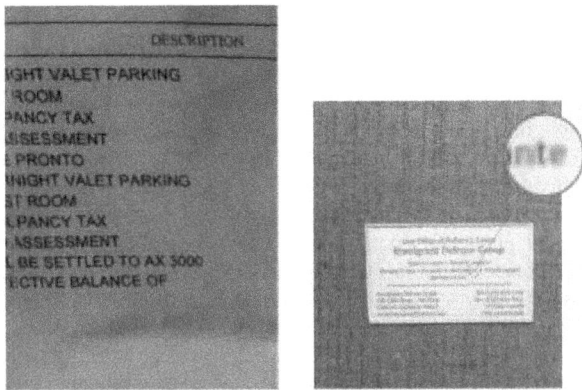

Figure 2: Non-OCR-compliant images (detail). Left: Text lines were successfully identified by the TextDetective app (blue rectangles), but parts of the lines are not visible. Right: The business card was correctly framed (yellow rectangle) by the Prizmo app, but the resolution is too low for OCR (see zoomed-in inset).

3. METHOD

3.1 Overview and Rationale

Our goal in this work was to shed light on the process by which a blind person can operate a hand-held camera (embedded in a smartphone) to access text data printed on a document. We assume that the user can rely on OCR software capable of decoding printed text provided that: (1) the entirety of the page is visible, and (2) text is imaged with a certain minimum size. Furthermore, we assume that the OCR software is able to decode text at any orientation and even with noticeable perspective distortion (due e.g. to camera slant), as these factors can be corrected by proper image processing. In these conditions, text access can be obtained as long as the user is able to take a proper (*compliant*) picture of the document, in a way that is precisely formalized in a later section.

The main questions driving our investigation are:

1. *How difficult is it to take a compliant picture of a document without sight?* To the best of our knowledge, there are no published studies about the ability of blind people to maneuver a camera in order to take a readable picture of a document. Our research seeks to establish a baseline against which any proposed assistive technology for mobile OCR can be compared.

2. *Could this process be facilitated by proper system-generated feedback?* We considered two different approaches to provide feedback to the user. In the first approach, the system continuously takes images (frames) and analyzes each image to verify whether the imaged document is readable; as soon as a compliant (readable) image is taken, the user is notified and the process is stopped. In the second approach, the system additionally provides instructions to the user about where to move the phone to increase the likelihood of a compliant picture being taken.

To address these questions, we developed the necessary experimental software tools and designed experiments. We decided to emulate an "ideal" OCR software and feedback mechanism by means of an image processing system based on augmented reality (AR) markers. Rather than dealing with a regular printed document, our participants interacted with a sheet of paper on which a number of AR markers (*fiducials*) were printed. Based on the image taken by the iPhone camera of these fiducials, the system quickly and robustly identifies its own position and orientation (collectively called *pose*) with respect to the document. This information is sufficient to establish whether the image of a "real" document of known size taken from the same camera pose would be OCR-readable (i.e., the pose is compliant), and to provide feedback and guidance to the user. This almost-Wizard-of-OZ mechanism allows us to abstract from the actual OCR software employed and to concentrate on the user interaction component of the system, under the assumption of an "ideal" image processing software. Using this tool, we can ascertain whether feedback mechanisms have potential for improving the user experience with mobile OCR without sight, which would justify further research in this direction; additionally, this system allows us to investigate the most promising strategies to present feedback to the user.

3.2 Population

Twelve blind participants (four females and eight males) were recruited through announcements on newsletters and word of mouth. All but one participant had at most some residual light perception. The participant who had some residual vision left had acuity of 20/3800 in one eye; the other eye had no vision (prosthetic). In order to remove any possibility that the little residual vision could bias results, this participant was blindfolded during the test. The participants were of age between 18 and 65, with a median age of 53. Of these participants, two were congenitally blind, two became blind at age three, and all others lost their sight after the age of ten. Two of the participants had lost their sight less than five years prior to the experiment. Seven participants were regular iPhone users, and four participants had tried mobile OCR systems before (but were not regular users of this technology).

3.3 The Compliant Pose Space of a Document

A *compliant* picture of a document is a picture that contains all of the text in the document, at enough resolution that it can be read by OCR. More precisely, a picture of a letter-sized (8.5" by 11") document is considered compliant for the sake of this study if: (1) all four corners of the printable area are visible, where in our case the printable area has top and bottom margins of 1.5" and left and right margins of 0.5"; and (2) a small letter placed anywhere in the printable area is seen in the picture at enough resolution that it can be read accurately by OCR. A "small letter" could be, for example, a lowercase 'x' character typed in 12 point Arial font, which has height of 4.23 mm. By "accurately readable by OCR" , we mean that the height of the letter in the image should be of at least 12 pixels [13]. This is based on the readability constraint discussed in [7] calculated at 8MP photo resolution of the iPhone. Thus, a compliant image of a document is such that the whole content can be read via OCR. Note that we define compliance only in geometric terms: factors such as bad illumination or blur certainly contribute to the quality of OCR reading, but are neither considered in this definition nor in this study.

We define *compliant pose* as the pose (3-D location + camera orientation, with respect to a reference system fixed with the document) of a camera that takes a compliant picture. Note that the compliance of a pose depends on the camera's optical/imaging characteristics (intrinsic parameters [20]). For example, a pose that is compliant using a wide field-of-view lens may be non-compliant using a longer lens (because the document may not be seen in its entirety in the second case). Likewise, a compliant pose for a narrow field-of-view lens may be non-compliant for a shorter lens due to reduced angular resolution.

For a given camera, the set of all compliant poses form the *compliant pose space*. The compliant pose space of a document can be computed based on geometry. In addition, given a non-compliant pose, one could predict whether moving the camera in a certain direction and rotating it around a certain axis will result in a compliant pose. This information may be used in a guidance mechanism to provide hints to the user about how to move the camera in order to take an OCR-readable image. Of course, this assumes that the camera pose can be somehow computed – a difficult problem in itself. Several techniques are available for image-based pose estimation, ranging from stereo triangulation (when a system with two cameras is available), to structure from motion/SLAM, to methods that use fiducials printed on the page at known locations.

In our study, we used printed fiducials for camera pose estimation. In fact, in our experiments we give away completely with textual information, and use a document containing solely well-calibrated fiducials instead (see Fig. 1). This approach is justified by the fact that the goal of this investigation is to study the mechanisms that can facilitate reaching a compliant pose and thus obtaining an OCR-readable image of the document. In this way, we are able to separate the *technical* difficulties of pose estimation from the *human factors* that pertain to holding a camera and taking a compliant picture.

3.4 Interaction Modalities

We considered three different interaction modalities in our study. Each modality represents a mechanism by which the user may try to take a compliant picture of a document using a smartphone. The three considered modalities are described below.

3.4.1 Snapshot

In the *snapshot* modality, the user simply takes a snapshot of the document (e.g. by pressing a button or tapping the screen), from a position and orientation that, in his or her judgment, results in a compliant picture. No feedback is provided by the system, except to confirm (via synthetic speech) that a snapshot action was registered.

3.4.2 Hovering: Just Confirmation

In this case, the user moves the camera over the document ("hovering") while the system takes and processes pictures continuously. As soon as a compliant picture is detected, the system notifies the user and the process is stopped. The user is not required to take any action (such as pressing a button) besides moving the camera around the position that he or she expects to be the most appropriate for a compliant picture.

3.4.3 Hovering: Guidance

This represents a more interactive version of the "hovering" modality. The system continuously takes and processes pictures, and in addition produces hints (in the form of short synthetic speech sentences) advising the user about where to move the camera next in order to increase the likelihood of reaching a compliant pose.

3.5 Apparatus

3.5.1 Pose Estimation

The application developed for this experiment runs on an iPhone 4S (with a 4:3 aspect ratio and video resolution of 640x480). To compute the camera pose from a picture of the printed fiducials, we use the ArUco [4] Augmented Reality library, implemented

with OpenCV [5]. A letter-size sheet is printed with ArUco's fiducial patterns in known locations (see Fig. 1). The software detects the location of the fiducials in the camera's field of view and computes the pose of the camera (previously calibrated off-line). Only a single fiducial is necessary for pose estimation, but accuracy is increased when multiple fiducially are seen. The software is able to process 20 images per second on average, although in practice the effective frame rate is smaller due to other concurrent processing on the phone. Given the camera's pose (computed with respect to a reference system centered at the paper sheet), one can obtain the homography (perspective transformation [20]) that maps points in the paper sheet to pixels. This information is used to compute compliance of the current pose, based on the criteria discussed above (visibility of all corners of the document's printable area, minimum resolution). Note that pose compliance detection (along with proper user confirmation) is all that is needed for the *hovering: just confirmation* modality. The *guidance* modality requires further processing and a more complex user interface, as explained below.

3.5.2 Guidance

The goal of the *guidance* mechanism is to give clear instructions as to where to move the camera to reach a compliant pose. This algorithm produces a *correction vector* that takes the camera to a compliant pose if the same orientation is maintained. The correction vector links the current camera position with the closest point in the *compliant segment* (see Fig. 3), which is the set of points on a line through the center of the sheet, parallel to the optical axis of the camera, such that each point in the segment is a compliant camera location under the current orientation. The compliant segment for a given camera orientation is defined by two endpoints, $\mathbf{p}_1$ and $\mathbf{p}_2$, where $\mathbf{p}_2$ is higher (with respect to the document) than $\mathbf{p}_1$.

However, if the slant of the camera with respect to the sheet normal is too large (*non–compliant orientation*), the compliant segment for the current camera orientation may contain no points, meaning that, in order to reach a compliant pose, the camera needs to be rotated.

Correction information is communicated to the user through synthetic speech. Synthetic speech capabilities are provided by the Flite [16] library. Each short sentence contains directions along at most two Cartesian axes, and precisely those in need of the largest correction (e.g., "Move up 5 and forward 3" or "Move left 4"). We felt that specifying three vector coordinates (e.g., "Move up 5, forward 3 and left 8") would generate exceedingly long sentences and possibly become confusing. Units are expressed in centimeters, and the reference system is fixed with respect to the paper sheet (not the user). This could create a conflict if the user construes the direction as if in reference to his or her body; however, we noted that most participants kept the paper sheet aligned with their body, reducing the risk of conflicting frames of reference. Note that the camera pose is monitored in real time, and directions are produced continuously (with a minimum gap of 1 second between two sentences).

If a non–compliant orientation is detected, the system utters the sentence "Reset orientation", which prompts the user to re-orient the phone, ideally bringing the phone parallel to the document. Upon detection of a compliant pose, the system utters the sentence "Pose compliant", terminating the trial.

Our strategy for determining the correction vector was inspired by a similar algorithm originally proposed by Cutter and Manduchi [7]. Their algorithm does not consider camera orientation: it always produces a correction vector that would bring the camera to a compliant pose *under the assumption that the sheet is seen front-to-parallel*. With the system used in their study, the heights

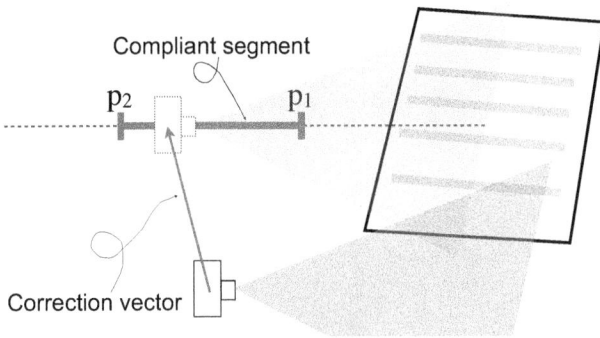

Figure 3: A simple guidance example. The current camera pose (shown in solid line) is not compliant, because part of the document is outside of its field of view. If the camera is moved by the correction vector, it will reach a position in the compliant segment. If the orientation is kept constant, any position on the compliant segment is compliant.

of $\mathbf{p}_1$ and $\mathbf{p}_2$ are of 28 cm and 42 cm, respectively and centered at the orgin. In practice, this means that the correction vector is potentially incorrect as soon as the iPhone is not held parallel to the sheet (i.e. at non-null *off-axis angles*). As shown in Fig. 7, off-axis angles of 10 degrees or more are to be expected, which highlights the need for explicit orientation reasoning as in the new algorithm proposed here. With our algorithm $\mathbf{p}_1$ and $\mathbf{p}_2$ and set dynamically given the current orientation and position.

3.6 Procedure

Participant were given an introduction to the goals of the experiment and to its procedures. They were informed that, in order to take a "good" (compliant) picture of the document, the camera should be at a height of between approximately one foot and one and a half feet over the document, with the iPhone level (horizontal) and well aligned with the document. Each participant was asked to sit on a chair in front of a small desk, and invited to adjust the height of the chair to ensure that he or she was able to raise his or her iPhone-holding hand comfortably at least 40 cm above the desktop. Participants were informed that they could stand up during the experiment, if they felt that this would increase their comfort, and that they could use either or both hands to hold the phone. Most participants decided to sit for the duration of the experiment, although three participants decided to stand for all or some of the trials. Several of the participants experimented with multiple positions of the phone holding hand throughout the experiment.

After this preliminary phase, each participant performed the experiment, structured as an ordered sequence of sessions: Pre-intervention, Intervention, and Post-intervention. Each session was comprised of 12 identical trials; participants were informed that the first three trials of each session were to be considered practice trials. At the beginning of each trial, the paper sheet was slightly moved and rotated on the desktop, and the iPhone was placed flat (the camera facing downwards) over the document's left corner closest to the participant. In this way the participants frame of reference was reset; each trial simulates a fresh document scanning scenario. Each participant was assigned a Group ID (0 or 1), such that the IDs were evenly distributed across participants.

3.6.1 Pre-Intervention

The goal of each trial was to take a compliant picture of the document using the *snapshot* modality described earlier. The partici-

pant was asked to pick up the iPhone, and position it where he or she thought a good picture of the document could be taken. Once they were confident of the position they took a picture by pressing either of the two small volume buttons on the side of the iPhone. Participants were free to re-position the document on the desktop if they wanted to, and could take as much time as they wanted before taking the snapshot.

Several participants found the action of pressing one of the volume buttons difficult to execute, especially when holding the phone with one hand, although others found it very natural. Two participants expressed concern about the possibility that while reaching with a finger for these buttons, the phone may be inadvertently moved, generating blur or resulting in the picture taken from an incorrect location; however, this didn't seem to be the case, and all snapshots taken this way were correctly processed by the system.

3.6.2 Intervention

The goal of these trials was to move the iPhone over the document so as to reach a compliant pose using one of the *hovering* modalities described earlier. Participants in Group 0 used the *hovering: guidance* modality, while participants in Group 1 used the *hovering: just confirmation* modality. The starting procedure at each trial was the same as for the pre-intervention trials. A time-out period T_{to} of 150 seconds was set for each trial: if a compliant pose was not reached within the time-out period, the trial was terminated.

3.6.3 Post-Intervention

This session was identical to the Pre-intervention session. All participants used the *snapshot* modality to try to take compliant pictures of the document. These trials were meant to investigate whether experience with a hovering modality in the Intervention trials could increase the user's awareness of the compliant space, and thus facilitate taking a compliant snapshot of a document without system assistance. At the end of the three sessions, participants were asked to answer a short questionnaire, described in detail in the Results section.

The experiments described in [7] also consider similar interaction modalities to those considered here, albeit under different names. However, the experiment design in [7] and in the study presented here are very different. Participants in the experiments of [7] all underwent the same sequence (Snapshot; Hovering:Just Confirmation; Hovering:Guidance). This design does not allow one to evaluate whether experience with a hovering modality can increase one's skill at taking compliant snapshots without system assistance (which is the reason for the Pre- and Post-Intervention phases of the new design). In addition, the experiment design from [7] did not balance the order of the hovering modalities, resulting in a potentially biased analysis.

3.7 Metrics

3.7.1 Accuracy

Each *snapshot* trial can be characterized by a binary variable (*success*) that is equal to 1 if the snapshot resulted in a compliant picture, 0 otherwise. The *success rate* (*SR*) represents the average success value over all trials in a session.

We also derive a measure of accuracy (*proportion legible*) defined as the number of equivalent 12-point characters in the printable area that are OCR-readable from the image, divided by the total number of characters in the printable area, assuming the the printable area is filled with 12-point characters in an ordered grid. (This grid is designed based on standard inter-character and inter-

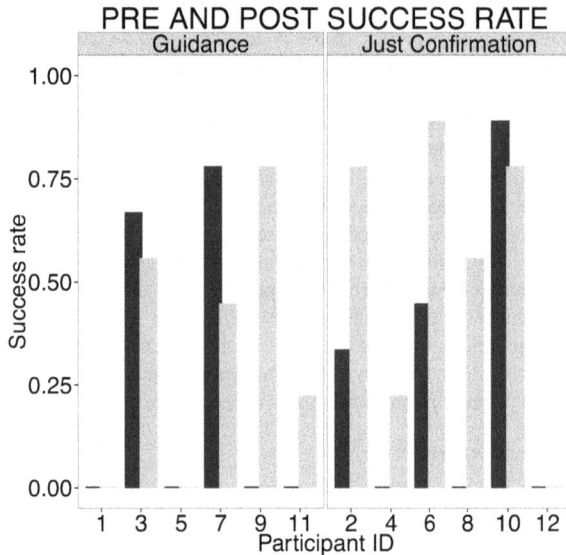

Figure 4: Success rate for all participants in the snapshot-type trials. Left: Group 0 (Guidance). Right: Group 1 (Just confirmation). Black: pre-intervention. Gray: post-intervention.

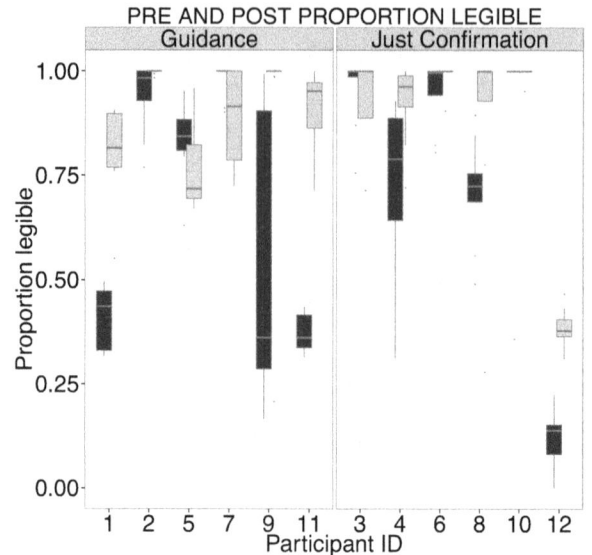

Figure 5: Proportion legible for all participants in the snapshot-type trials, shown as box plots. Left: Group 0 (Guidance). Right: Group 1 (Just confirmation). Black: pre-intervention. Gray: post-intervention.

line spacing.) The proportion legible metric gives an indication of the document area that can be accessed by OCR. Note, however, that this does not translate directly into "readable portion of a document": if, for example, the right half of a text column is outside of the camera's FOV, the whole column is not "readable" (even though individual words in the left half can be decoded by OCR). A more useful metric, which we will consider in future work, would take the document structure into account. For each session, we computed the *median proportion legible* over all trials in the session.

3.7.2 Time

For the *hovering* trials, we measure the time from the beginning of the trial until a compliant pose is reached (*time-to-completion*, T_c). If a compliant pose is not reached before the time-out period T_{to}, we simply set $T_c = T_{to}$.

4. RESULTS

4.1 Snapshot Modality

4.1.1 General Results

Figs. 4 and 5 show the results, in terms of success rates and proportion legible, for the pre- and post-intervention trials using the *snapshot* modality. From these plots, it results clear that, while some participants were quite proficient at this task, others had serious difficulties. In particular, seven participants could not take a single compliant picture in the pre-intervention trials; three of them could not take any compliant picture in the post-intervention trials either.

To investigate the main causes of failure, we need to consider all conditions that can result in a non-compliant pose. The space of poses PS can be divided into four disjoints sets:

PS1: Poses that can be made compliant by simply re-positioning the camera (orientation unchanged) but not by simply re-orienting the camera (position unchanged).

PS2: Poses that can be made compliant by simply re-orienting the camera (position unchanged) but not by simply re-positioning the camera (orientation unchanged).

PS3: Poses that can be made compliant by simply re-orienting the camera or re-positioning the camera.

PS4: Poses that can be made compliant only by re-orienting and re-positioning the camera.

We analyzed the poses of the non-compliant snapshots, in order to obtain proportion of occurrence of the different types of poses above. This is expressed as probabilities (see Tab. 1.)

Pr(PS1)	Pr(PS2)	Pr(PS3)	Pr(PS4)
0.35	0.1	0.49	0.06

Table 1: The probability distribution of non-compliant poses across the four conditions considered.

This data suggests that in most cases ($\Pr(PS1) + \Pr(PS3) = 0.84$) a simple re-positioning of the camera would have led to a compliant snapshot. In a smaller proportion of cases ($\Pr(PS2) + \Pr(PS3) = 0.59$), a compliant pose would have been reached by simply re-orienting the phone. The more serious situation of a pose requiring both orientation and position adjustment occurs only 6% of the time.

Fig. 6 shows the location of the camera at the time of the snapshot for compliant poses (black dots) and non-compliant poses (grey dots). (Remember that locations higher than 42 cm and lower than 28 cm with respect to the document are non-compliant.) The plot suggests that in many cases, non-compliance was due to the participant keeping the phone too close to the document (the difference in height means between compliant and non-compliant poses is significant at $p < 0.001$). Fig. 7 shows the histogram of *off-axis angles* (defined as the angle between the camera's optical axis and the normal to the document) at the time of the snapshot. (Note that

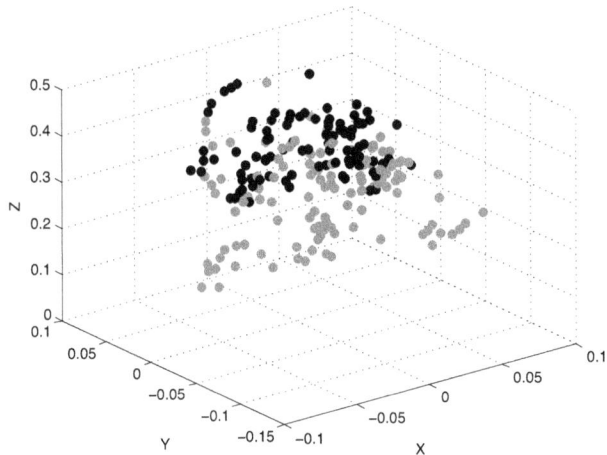

Figure 6: 3-D locations of camera pose in the pre- and post-intervention trials, with respect to a reference system centered at the center of the paper sheet (units are in meters). Black: compliant pose. Gray: non-compliant pose.

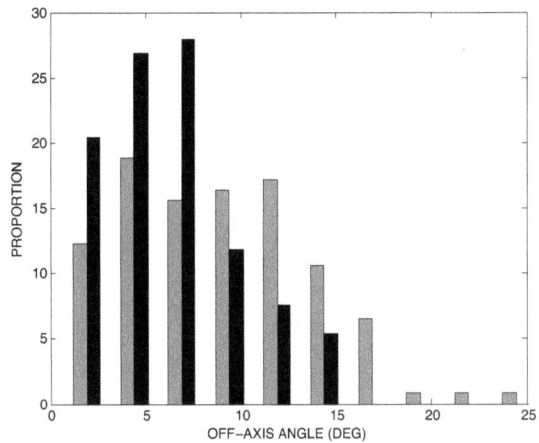

Figure 7: Histogram of off-axis angles for compliant (black) and non–compliant (gray) terminal poses in the pre- and post-intervention trials.

the off-axis angle, by itself, does not determine compliance: if the camera is located to the side of the document, a moderately large off-axis angle may be required for compliance.) This histogram shows that, on average, non-compliant poses were characterized by a larger off-axis angle than compliant poses (the difference in means is significant at $p < 0.001$).

The median time to take a snapshot (over all trials in a pre- or post-intervention session) ranged from 5.6 sec. to 39.3 sec., with a mean of 12.4 sec.

4.1.2 Pre- and Post-Intervention Comparison

We compared the success rate and median proportion legible for pre- and post-intervention sessions using a standard 2×2 mixed factorial design model. Note from Fig. 4 that among those participants who were able to take compliant pictures in the post-intervention trials, two in Group 0 and four in Group 1 improved their success rate after the intervention session, while two in Group 0 and one in Group 1 worsened their performance. The difference in mean success rate between pre- and post-intervention and across groups was not found to be significant at $\alpha = 0.05$.

The difference in mean between the pre- and post-treatment median proportion legible is significant at $p = 0.04$ (mean equal to 0.72 for pre-treatment, 0.89 for post-treatment). However, the main effect of intervention type (guidance vs. just confirmation) was not found to be significant at $\alpha = 0.05$. No significant difference was found between the means of camera height, horizontal offset (distance to the line perpendicular to and centered at the sheet), or off-axis angle at the time snapshots were taken for the pre- and post-intervention trials. However, for the participants that were not able to take a single compliant snapshot in the pre-intervention trials (participants 1,4,5,8,9,11,12; see Fig. 4), we noted that the median (across trials) of the horizontal offset decreased from 5.5 cm to 3.7 cm (paired one-sided t-test; $p = 0.03$). This may help explain why all but one of these participants performed better (in terms of proportion legible) in the post-intervention trials.

4.2 Hovering Modalities

4.2.1 Time-to-Completion

Fig. 8 shows a box plot of the logarithm of the time-to-completion values for all hovering-type trials (Intervention session). The median (over all trials) time-to-completion ranged from 3.6 sec to 48.1 sec, with an average value of 13.9 sec.

Multiple-sample repeated measurements ANOVA analysis did not find a significant difference in the mean time-to-completion between participants in Group 0 (guidance) and Group 1 (just confirmation).

4.3 Participant Surveys

At the end of the experiment, each participant was asked to complete a short survey. Participants were asked to comment on a number of statements using a five-point Likert scale (with 'strongly disagree' represented by '1' and 'strongly agree' represented by '5'). The statements, reported verbatim below along with the median response, differed slightly across the two participant groups.

Questions for Group 0 (*Hovering: Guidance*)	Median response
I feel that, after interacting with the system, I am now able to take better pictures of the document by myself.	4
It was easy to follow the directions from the system.	5
The directions from the system helped me take better pictures of the document.	4
If the guidance system were available as an application, I would be interested in using it.	5

Questions for Group 1 (*Hovering: Just Confirmation*)	Median response
The system helped me take better pictures of the document.	4
It was easy to follow the directions from the system.	5
If this system were available as an app, I would be interested in using it.	5

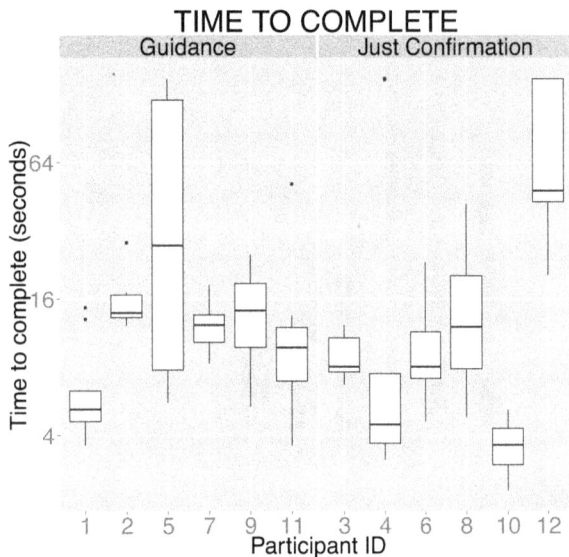

TIME TO COMPLETE

Figure 8: Time-to-completion values for all participants shown as a box plot on logarithmic scale. Left: Group 0 (Hovering: Guidance). Right: Group 1 (Hovering: Just Confirmation).

5. DISCUSSION

Participants exhibited a wide diversity of skill taking compliant snapshots without help from the system (Figs. 4 and 5). By observing the participants during the experiment, it was clear that some were much more "methodical" than others in the way they moved the phone to take a snapshot. Interestingly, as shown by Fig. 6, participants tended to take snapshots at a short distance from the document: the maximum recorded height of a snapshot was 44 cm, which is slightly above the maximum compliant height (42 cm). As mentioned earlier, participants were informed that the correct height was approximately between one foot and one and a half feet, but it seems that they preferred to err on the lower end. Of course, since no feedback was provided in the pre-intervention session, participants did not have a means to correct what could be a biased perception of the camera height. However, this tendency did not change even after the Intervention phase, in which participants had a chance to experiment first-hand the range of compliant heights.

Can the proprioception skills that are necessary to correctly position a camera be taught? We note that during the trials performed as part of the pre and post-test, we observed no trend of improvement between the first and the second half of the trials. This makes sense since there is no feedback during the snapshot trials. However, for many participants we observed improvement between the the pre and post-test. In addition, our quantitative results with the experimental system, along with the outcomes from the participant surveys, supports this observation. However, these results do not provide a clear indication of what exactly was learned through the Intervention phase.

As mentioned above, participants in the post-test trials continued to take snapshots from a relatively low height, something that undoubtedly contributed to a fair portion of failures. However, anecdotally a participant in the guidance group said after several trials of the intervention "ahah now i've got it". Similar "aha" moments occurred for other participants during the intervention; at which point the subsequent intervention trials were quickly completed.

We were surprised by the discovery that both the *guidance* and the *just confirmation* intervention modalities produce comparable results. We carefully designed a complex guidance modality, and expected that it would help the user reach a compliant pose faster. This expectation was supported by preliminary results using a similar system with sighted blindfold participants presented in [7]. Although as discussed earlier, the experimental design and the chosen metrics in [7] may have been inappropriate for this type of analysis.

Why is it, then, that the guidance modality, with its rich system feedback, did not prove superior to the just confirmation modality in terms of time-to-completion in the present study? We believe that the reason for this lies in the sub-optimal design of the user interface used in these prior experiments. Upon careful analysis of the videos collected during the trials, we determined two main pitfalls of the current design:

Lack of explicit orientation guidance. As shown in Fig. 7, non-OCR-complaint images are often associated with excessive off-axis angles. Our original guidance system gave directions in terms of translation but not of orientation; this was a deliberate choice in order to keep the complexity of directions low. Participants were advised to keep the iPhone horizontal; only upon detection of a large off-axis angle was a synthetic speech warning produced. However, most participants found it difficult to re-orient the phone correctly (horizontally), resulting in the off-axis warning being re-issued several times before the orientation of the iPhone was properly adjusted. When this happened, the whole process was slowed down, which generated frustration among some participants. We now believe that some form of orientation correction guidance would be very beneficial. Indeed, as discussed earlier, in 59% of the non-compliant snapshot cases, a simple camera re-orientation would have been sufficient to make the pose compliant, and in 6% of the cases this correction would in fact have been necessary.

Disruptive guidance modality. The synthetic speech directions produced by the system contained precise metric indication of where to move the phone next. Ideally, the user would move the phone exactly as directed, ending at a compliant pose. In fact, this was rarely the case, due to the difficulty of moving the phone precisely as directed. This resulted in participants following a discrete sequence of movements; after each movement, they would pause and wait for the system to produce the next direction. In contrast, participants in the group that did not use the guidance system moved the phone in continuous motion; this allowed for a larger portion of space to be explored in the same amount of time. The difference in behavior for the two hovering modalities can be noticed in Fig. 9. The path marked in blue (*hovering:guidance*) is characterized by non-uniform velocity and several abrupt turns in response to a direction, whereas the path marked in red (*hovering:just confirmation*) shows a more uniform motion. In future work we will explore different types of acoustic interface that require less information processing by the user and encourage smooth trajectories.

6. CONCLUSIONS

We have presented an experimental study that investigated modalities to help a blind person take better pictures of a document faster through the use of image processing software. The overarching goal of this project is to facilitate the use of mobile OCR for printed text access.

The proposed mechanisms have been implemented using special printed fiducials, and could not be used directly with regular printed documents. This investigation explores the "best case scenario" of a perfectly functioning device; similar functionalities on regular printed documents are not out of reach.

Camera orientation can be computed from the device accelerometers and by measuring orientation of detected parallel text lines. By detecting the endpoints of text lines, one can make inferences about whether the text is fully visible (e.g. a line ending at the edge of the image is likely truncated) or, if not, where the camera should be moved for better visibility. Readability of characters can be computed by a fast text spotter (e.g. if characters in a line cannot be spotted, the camera is too far). Localization features could be approximately inferred by computer vision algorithms with heuristics about the visual structure of typical documents. These vision-based algorithms can obtain functionalities similar (albeit less accurate) to using fiducials with real-world documents.

Acknowledgments

Research reported in this publication was supported by the National Eye Institute of the National Institutes of Health under award number 1R21EY025077-01 The authors would like to thank Corinne Olafsen who assisted during the experiments.

7. REFERENCES

[1] Prizmo. `http://www.creaceed.com/prizmo`. Accessed: 2013-11-09.

[2] Knfb reader mobile. `knfbReadingTechnology, Inc`, 2008. http://www.knfbreader.com/.

[3] Text detective (blindsight inc.). `http://blindsight.com/textdetective`, 2011.

[4] Aruco: a minimal library for augmented reality applications based on opencv. Universidad D Cordoba, 2012. http://www.uco.es/investiga/grupos/ava/node/26.

[5] G. Bradski. The OpenCV Library. *Dr. Dobb's Journal of Software Tools*, 2000.

[6] E. Brady, M. R. Morris, Y. Zhong, S. White, and J. P. Bigham. Visual challenges in the everyday lives of blind people. In *Proceedings of the SIGCHI Conference on Human Factors in Computing Systems*, CHI '13, pages 2117–2126, New York, NY, USA, 2013. ACM.

[7] M. P. Cutter and R. Manduchi. Real time camera phone guidance for compliant document image acquisition without sight. In *Document Analysis and Recognition (ICDAR), 2013 12th International Conference on*, pages 408–412. IEEE, 2013.

[8] C. Jayant, H. Ji, S. White, and J. P. Bigham. Supporting blind photography. In *The proceedings of the 13th international ACM SIGACCESS conference on Computers and accessibility*, ASSETS '11, pages 203–210, New York, NY, USA, 2011. ACM.

[9] S. K. Kane, B. Frey, and J. O. Wobbrock. Access lens: A gesture-based screen reader for real-world documents. In *Proceedings of the SIGCHI Conference on Human Factors in Computing Systems*, CHI '13, pages 347–350, New York, NY, USA, 2013. ACM.

[10] S. K. Kane, M. R. Morris, A. Z. Perkins, D. Wigdor, R. E. Ladner, and J. O. Wobbrock. Access overlays: Improving non-visual access to large touch screens for blind users. In *Proceedings of the 24th Annual ACM Symposium on User Interface Software and Technology*, UIST '11, pages 273–282, New York, NY, USA, 2011. ACM.

[11] R. Shilkrot, J. Huber, C. Liu, P. Maes, and S. C. Nanayakkara. Fingerreader: A wearable device to support text reading on the go. In *CHI '14 Extended Abstracts on Human Factors in Computing Systems*, CHI EA '14, pages 2359–2364, New York, NY, USA, 2014. ACM.

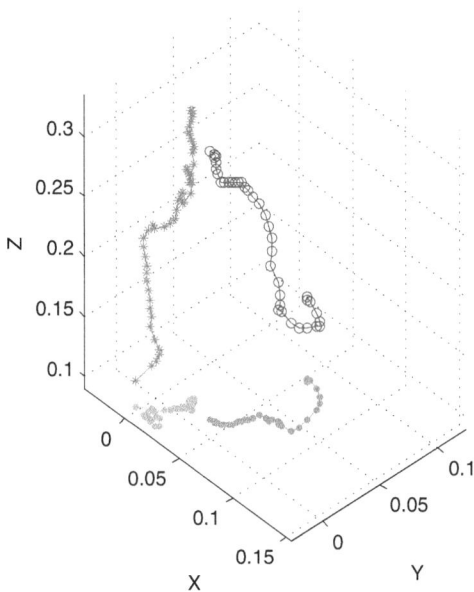

Figure 9: The paths represent camera locations during two trials, using the hovering:just confirmation modality (red) and the hovering:guidance modality (blue). Units are in meters. The projection of the paths on the horizontal plane are shown with faded color. Circular blue marks and red asterisks are placed at constant time periods of 0.1 s. Only the portion of the path after a certain time lag is shown as measurements cannot be taken when the camera is too close to the document. This lag was of 6.8 s for the path marked in red and of 3.9 s for the path marked in blue.

[12] M. Vázquez and A. Steinfeld. Helping visually impaired users properly aim a camera. In *Proceedings of the 14th international ACM SIGACCESS conference on Computers and accessibility*, ASSETS '12, pages 95–102, New York, NY, USA, 2012. ACM.

[13] A. Zandifar and A. Chahine. A video based interface to textual information for the visually impaired. In *Proceedings of the 4th IEEE International Conference on Multimodal Interfaces*, ICMI '02, pages 325–, Washington, DC, USA, 2002. IEEE Computer Society.

[14] Y. Zhong, P. J. Garrigues, and J. P. Bigham. Real time object scanning using a mobile phone and cloud-based visual search engine. In *Proceedings of the 15th International ACM SIGACCESS Conference on Computers and Accessibility*, ASSETS '13, pages 20:1–20:8, New York, NY, USA, 2013. ACM.

[15] TapTapSee. `www.taptapseeapp.com`.

[16] A. Black and K. Lenzo Flite: a small fast run-time synthesis engine In *SSW4-2001*, paper 204. 2001

[17] ORCAM. `www.orcam.com`.

[18] J. Bigham, C. Jayant, A. Miller, B. White, and T. Yeh. Vizwiz::locateit — enabling blind people to locate objects in their environment. In *Proc. Workshop on Computer Vision Applications for the Visually Impaired*, 2010.

[19] J. Coughlan and R. Manduchi. Camera-based access to visual information. In R. Manduchi and S. Kurniawan, editors, *Assistive Technology for Blindness and Low Vision*. CRC Press, 2013.

[20] R. I. Hartley and A. Zisserman. *Multiple View Geometry in Computer Vision*. Cambridge University Press, ISBN: 0521540518, second edition, 2004.

[21] A. Kutiyanawala, V. Kulyukin, and J. Nicholson. Teleassistance in accessible shopping for the blind. In *Proc. ICOMP'11*, 2011.

[22] E. Tekin and J. Coughlan. A mobile phone application enabling visually impaired users to find and read product barcodes. In Proc. International Conference on Computers Helping People with Special Needs *ICCHP '10*, 2010.

MSoS: A Multi-Screen-Oriented Web Page Segmentation Approach

Mira Sarkis, Cyril Concolato, Jean-Claude Dufourd
Telecom ParisTech; Institut Mines-Telecom; CNRS LTCI
{sarkis, concolato, dufourd}@telecom-paristech.fr

ABSTRACT

In this paper we describe a multiscreen-oriented approach for segmenting web pages. The segmentation is an automatic and hybrid visual and structural method. It aims at creating coherent blocks which have different functions determined by the multiscreen environment. It is also characterized by a dynamic adaptation to the page content. Experiments are conducted on a set of existing applications that contain multimedia elements, in particular YouTube and video player pages. Results are compared with one segmentation method from the literature and with a ground truth manually created. With a 81% precision, the MSoS is a promising method that is capable of producing good segmentation results.

Categories and Subject Descriptors

C.2.4 [**Distributed Systems**]: Distributed Applications; H.3.3 [**Information Search and Retrieval**]: Clustering, Information Filtering; H.3.4 [**Systems and Software**]: Distributed Systems

Keywords

Web Application, Page Segmentation, Automatic Processing, Application Distribution, Multiscreen

1. INTRODUCTION

Understanding and analyzing web content at the Internet scale requires automatic processing techniques. These techniques try to simulate the human understandability in terms of visualization, semantic meaning and interaction. Among the existing techniques for web content analysis, web page segmentation techniques are widely used. They consist in decomposing a page into blocks that englobe coherent and related content. Segmentation is used in the adaptation of content to mobile, printing devices or in applications performing information extraction, among others.

In a multi-screen environment, where multiple devices are used to display and to interact with related content, users

DocEng'15, September 08 - 11, 2015, Lausanne, Switzerland.
© 2015 ACM. ISBN978-1-4503-3307-8/15/09 ...$15.00.
DOI: http://dx.doi.org/10.1145/2682571.2797090.

want to have their applications distributed among their devices. For instance, using the touch-screen of a smart-phone to control the smart-TV functions, while the large screen of the smartTV displays the multimedia content. In order to efficiently exploit the features of each device, the distribution is achieved by splitting the application into multiple pieces and by associating each piece to a proper device. The challenges here are: (1) to identify coherent blocks of content that can be separated from the rest without breaking the web page structure, (2) to know the device features wherein the content is efficient for the end-user and (3) to automatically map the content blocks to the 'best-match' device.

With this motivation, this paper has one principal objective: *To propose a segmentation method that is automatic and guided by the multi-screen environment, based on: (1) visual analysis, (2) DOM analysis, and (3) analysis of content functions in order to achieve the application distribution in a multiscreen environment.* A content function refers to the type of interaction between a user and a block of content, e.g., 'display' for multimedia content and 'interaction' for interactive content. In contrast to existing works, our intention is to guide the segmentation based on the features of target devices to facilitate the mapping of blocks to devices. We call our approach multiscreen-oriented segmentation and we refer to it as MSoS. The validation of MSoS is performed in the virtual splitting system [5] that re-factors web pages to create multi-screen applications and hereinafter referred to as VSplitter. We have tested MSoS on a set of pages featuring video elements and interactive content, e.g., YouTube pages and video-player applications. Through experimentation, we show how the MSoS adapts to the page content to produce better results when compared to Block-o-Matic[4], a method in the literature and to a ground truth.

This paper is organized as follows. Section 2 introduces our MSoS approach within the state-of-the-art. In Section 3 MSoS is described. The implementation and the evaluation of MSoS in the VSplitter are described in Section 4. Finally conclusions are drawn in Section 5.

2. STATE OF THE ART

Segmentation techniques: Hybrid segmentation techniques can get better results compared to techniques that are based only on one type of analysis, i.e., DOM, visual or content analysis. For instance the hybrid VIPS [1], based on the joint DOM and visual analysis, utilizes both structural information in the DOM tree and visual cues to semantically segment a page. The hybrid Block-o-Matic (BoM) platform [4], based also on the joint DOM and visual analysis, addi-

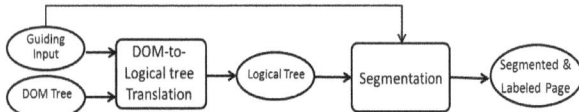
Figure 1: Modified BoM segmentation model

tionally abstracts the segmentation from the DOM tree and works at higher levels. This abstraction facilitates the understanding and the processing of the page structure. BoM starts by filtering the DOM structure based on the W3C content classification[1] and on the geometrical features to form a logical tree. Afterwards, the logical tree is processed based on Gestalt laws, i.e., proximity, similarity, closure and simplicity, and on the degree of granularity for merging nodes. At the end of the segmentation, the final blocks are represented in the logical tree by leaf nodes that mainly contain information about the node geometry and the corresponding DOM elements. This link between logical nodes and DOM elements makes the segmentation results easily exploitable by other applications.

Though the processing of BoM is totally automatic, its configuration with a granularity parameter (pG) is manual and has to be tailored for each page. The pG value determines the threshold under which a logical node automatically produces a block and above which the node's children are processed individually. This value dictates the segmentation results. Configuring BoM with an inadequate pG value leads to a page not correctly segmented, and applying BoM with the same pG value on a heterogeneous page does not always create coherent blocks similarly on the whole page.

Identifying block functions: BoM does not separate the blocks based on their functions, but it labels blocks with labels that are not relevant for our multi-screen environment, e.g., header, content, image, logo, etc.[4]. A function-based object model (FOM) for website adaptation is introduced by Chen et al.[2]. The segmentation model defines a block as a set of information that have a specific function, i.e., information, navigation, interaction, decoration or others. In FOM, even if a function reflects the intention of the author for using this object, it does not reflect the type of interaction with the end-user.

Positioning our approach: In our work, we reuse the hybrid approach and the abstraction model proposed by BoM but we adapt the segmentation to make it completely automatic and multiscreen-oriented. We propose in particular to update the pG value based on the content. Additionally, our approach reuses the idea of identifying the block functions from the page content as in FOM, but we define functions from the end-user perspective and not the author.

3. THE MULTISCREEN-ORIENTED-SEGMENTATION APPROACH

3.1 Overview

Our method segments a raw page based on input which guides: (1) the behavior analysis of DOM elements, (2) the labeling of logical leaf nodes with a function and (3) the production of blocks from logical leaf nodes. Specifically, the functions we use, i.e., "multimedia" and "interactive", are derived from the device features. The following sections

[1]http://www.w3.org/TR/html5/dom.html#content-categories

describe each phase of the MSoS approach that is depicted in Figure 1.

3.2 DOM to partially-labeled logical tree

The goal of this phase is to abstract the DOM tree and to represent the page in the form of a logical tree specific to our approach, in which we seek to label each node with a function and to minimize the number of leaf nodes to optimize the segmentation process.

Similar to BOM, the DOM tree is first filtered and for each retained DOM element a logical node is created and added to the logical tree. To then label a logical node with a function, we analyze the static and dynamic behavior of the corresponding DOM element. The element behavior is identified through its tag name, its HTML attributes and its JS properties. In particular, we check the properties that can alter the static behavior of an HTML element, e.g., event listeners, and the HTML5 attributes that identify the role of an element, e.g., 'role'. If the function of a DOM element corresponds to one of the guiding input functions, we label the logical node with this function. There are elements whose behavior does not satisfy any of the functions. In this case, their corresponding logical node remains non-labeled. Thus, the leaf nodes of the resulting logical tree are not all labeled and their number is relatively big.

To reduce their number, the logical tree is optimized to form geometrically bigger labeled blocks. This optimization will serve the next segmentation phase. The optimization procedure is as follows: (1) the tree is traversed from the root to the leaf nodes in a breadth-first manner. (2) If a node is labeled, we check whether its siblings are labeled with the same function. If positive, we merge them to form one node. (3) After analyzing all siblings, if only one labeled child remains, we propagate its label to its parent. The output of this first phase is a logical tree with a smaller number of nodes but with bigger geometry. It should be noted that some nodes may still be non-labelled.

3.3 Segmentation

The segmentation consists of producing labeled blocks from the partially-labeled logical tree. A trivial segmentation that produces one block from each logical leaf node, results in creating an excessive number of blocks. A better segmentation can be obtained by (1) merging logical nodes according to the Gestalt laws and the pG value, (2) while keeping blocks with different functions separated and (3) making all leaf nodes labeled with the adequate function.

In this work, we consider the notions of global and local pG as defined in BoM[4]. The global pG is set before starting the segmentation. The local pG is updated during runtime, as described in the next paragraph, to adapt the segmentation of the node subtree to its content. Both the global and local pG values are calculated automatically by considering the geometry of the labeled descendants respectively in the entire logical tree and in a local subtree as follows: for all the labeled nodes, we calculate the ratio of their areas over the relevant page area. We define the relevant page area as the rectangular area defined by the top-left corner of the page, a width equal to the page width, and a height set to the minimum between the page height and five times the screen height. We set the pG value of a subtree to the biggest pG value in this subtree, or to the global pG if the subtree does not have labeled descendants. Intuitively, the bigger the lo-

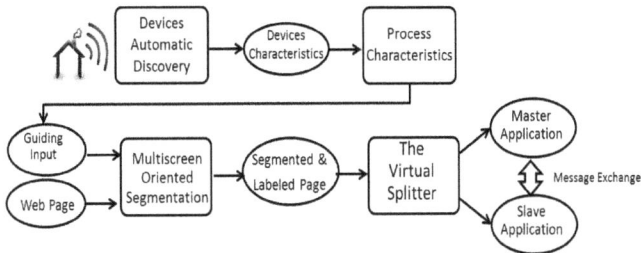

Figure 2: The fully automatic virtual splitting system

cal pG is, the fewer final blocks will be produced and the better the segmentation results are.

Then, we proceed with the processing of the logical tree in a depth-first manner starting from the root node and using the global pG value, as follows: (1) if a node is labeled, we try to merge it with its siblings, as described below. (2) if a node is non-labeled and its descendants have different labels, we process its subtree. (3) if a node is non-labeled and its descendants have only one function and its relative area is bigger than the pG, then we process its subtree; otherwise, we investigate the possibility of merging it with its siblings.

We try to merge a node with its next siblings, as follows: if the node does not have any sibling, it produces a block. Otherwise, for each sibling, if one of the functions of the sibling descendants is different from the current node function, the nodes are not merged even if the Gestalt laws and geometrical conditions are satisfied, and the current node produces a block. Otherwise, if the functions are the same, the merging of nodes is tested using the Gestalt laws and the geometrical conditions, as used in BoM. At the end of the merging, at least one labeled block is produced.

4. EXPERIMENTATION

4.1 Deployment and integration aspects

To deploy our approach and validate that it produces results that are useful in the context of multi-screen applications, we integrated it with the COLTRAM platform [3] and the VSplitter [5].

We developed a COLTRAM web service to automatically discover devices available in the network and to get a list of their features. We limit the number of devices to two. We characterize each device based on: (1) its screen size, i.e., large or small display, (2) its means of interaction, i.e., touch input, keyboard, mouse or non-interactive, (3) its type, i.e., TV, portable device or desktop. Then, for each device we identify their dominant feature that we consider as the function of the device. For instance, a smartTV is better used for displaying "multimedia" content, e.g., image, video, etc., a smart phone with a touch-screen is adequate for "interaction" purposes. As depicted in Figure 2 the guiding input, formed as a json object that associates each device with a function, and the application DOM tree are fed to MSoS.

Based on this input, we statically classify the element tags. For instance, the 'audio', 'video' and 'object' tags are used to embed multimedia content in a web document. In the W3C content categories, the interactive content is limited to the HTML tags that are initially intended for the user interaction. In our classification, we did not adopt the interactive content definition given by W3C because:(1) some tags in the category are more multimedia than interactive, e.g., video and audio elements with a control bar, (2) some

elements can become interactive after event listeners are registered on them to listen to user interaction events. In consequence, we analyze first the HTML attributes that are set statically in the HTML document, or dynamically on document load. And second, we capture event listeners by instrumenting the addEventListener native method.

The VSplitter refactors single-screen applications, delivers a multi-screen application, and maintains the application functionality across devices by monitoring the application updates and synchronizing the content between two devices, the master and the slave. The VSplitter uses an annotated DOM tree with annotations indicating to which device a DOM element should belong. In order to annotate the application DOM tree, we exploit the fact that the logical nodes contain a reference to their corresponding DOM elements. We annotate DOM elements based on the label of their corresponding logical node. If this label refers to the selected function of the master device, then we annotate the element as 'device1'. Otherwise, if it refers to features of the slave device, we annotate it as 'device2'. Since the logical tree does not cover the complete DOM tree, but only the retained elements during the abstraction phase, the DOM tree is not totally annotated. The annotation is then resolved as denoted in our previous work [5] and the content is distributed over the master and slave applications. Each of these applications is wrapped in a COLTRAM application and exposes a service for communication. Both master and slave applications are discoverable by each other, thus allowing a communication channel. Using this channel, updates and synchronization messages are exchanged continuously between the master and slave applications.

4.2 Results and Discussion

In this section, we illustrate the MSoS results by comparing them to BoM results and we evaluate our MSoS by comparing it to a ground truth that we refer to as GT. The procedure is based on the evaluation of three performance parameters: the visual coherence of blocks, the correctness of the function attributed to each block, and finally that blocks do not have content with different functions.

To test our method, we selected ten existing pages with multimedia and interactive content, classified as follows: (1) social applications i.e., YouTube, (2) video player applications, i.e., mediaElement[2], videojs[3], jplayer[4], (3) web synchronized applications, e.g., semantic video[5]. Applications and results are accessible from our site [6].

Comparing to BoM: We illustrate the MSoS results by comparing them to the same page segmented by BoM. Figure 3 presents the two segmentation results on a YouTube page [7]. Note that we cropped the comments section to better illustrate the segmentation results. Figure 3(a) represents the segmentation results using BoM with a pG value set manually to 0.31. Note here that the block colors are internal to BoM. Figure 3(b) represents the segmentation results with MSoS. During the segmentation, two main values were computed: 0.36 (global and local) and 0.31 (local). Most of the logical nodes were processed with the 0.31 value, this

---

[2] http://mediaelementjs.com/

[3] http://www.videojs.com/

[4] http://jplayer.org/

[5] http://popcornjs.org/demo/semantic-video

[6] http://download.tsi.telecom-paristech.fr/gpac/MSoS

[7] http://bit.ly/1eue6i3

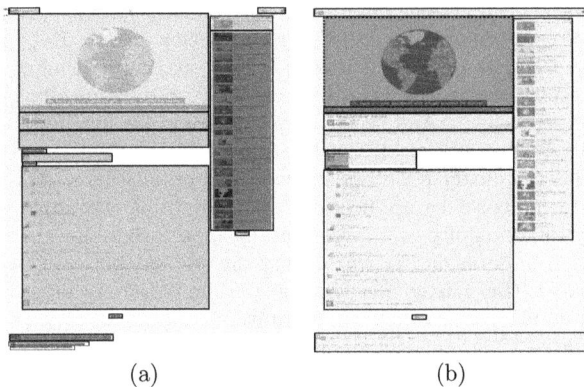

(a)   (b)

Figure 3: Segmentation results on a YouTube page (a) BoM with pG = 0.31 (b) MSoS with pG = 0.31 and 0.36

is why we decided to configure BoM with this value. Comparing the two figures, the blocks generated from MSoS are more coherent than those of BoM, in particular, the header, footer and the sidebar section. Note that BoM did not consider the search bar on the top of the page, while our algorithm did. In Figure 3(b) the YouTube video controls are identified as a block separated from the video block. This proves that content functions were taken into consideration during the segmentation. The grey blocks refer to interactive blocks and the unique purple block refers to the multimedia content. Note that video subtitles are judged as multimedia content since they overlap the video element. Our method ensured the separation of blocks with different functionality, thus facilitating the content mapping to the 'best-match' device in the context of multi-screen environment.

Applications	Precision	Recall	Non-Matching	
			Over-Segmented	Non-Related
YouTube pages	0.38	0.67	0.08	0.46
Video player pages	0.74	0.80	0.056	0.18
Video Sync	0.72	0.96	0.035	0.21

Table 1: Evaluation of the MSoS approach

Comparing to a ground truth: In order to evaluate our MSoS approach a GT was created manually, where coherent blocks were created and assigned a function between 'Multimedia' and 'Interactive'. Afterwards, we compared the MSoS results to the GT and we provide the comparison results in Table 1 in the form of precision and recall rates. We define the precision and recall rates as follows:
$Precision = Nb\ of\ Matching\ Blocks/Nb\ of\ MSoS\ Blocks$,
$Recall = Nb\ of\ Matching\ Blocks/Nb\ of\ GT\ Blocks$.
The Recall is equal to one if the MSoS could identify correctly all the blocks of the GT. The Precision is equal to one if the MSoS did not produce any non-matching block. The non-matching column refers to the average number of blocks that: 1) are over-segmented by the MSoS, 2) have no correspondence with any block in the GT or they are not correctly labeled.

As Table 1 shows, the precision and recall rates for YouTube pages are the lowest (0.38 and 0.67 resp.). This is due to the high average of non-related blocks. These non-related blocks are due to the identification of additional interactive blocks that are present in YouTube pages but are not visible for users, e.g., the guiding block that appears when we click on the button next to the YouTube logo in the top of the

page. The tests conducted on the applications from video-player libraries always lead to the separation of the control bar from the video element. This is validated by the high precision and recall values (0.74 and 0.80 respectively). The non-related blocks here refer to the cases where the MSoS could not label some blocks since they were not merged with any labeled blocks. In addition in one application the subtitles were merged with the control bar while they should have been merged with the video element. For the third set of applications, the precision rate is 0.96 and it indicates that almost all the blocks of the GT were identified by MSoS. Though the average number of the over-segmented blocks is small for the three set of applications (0.08, 0.056 and 0.035 resp.), it is important to note here that the over-segmentation is the drawbacks of using a pG value that is calculated according only to the labeled nodes.

5. CONCLUSION

This paper proposed a multiscreen-oriented segmentation approach. The segmentation method is hybrid and aims at creating coherent blocks and separating blocks of different functionalities given as a guiding input. MSoS is completely automatic and characterized by a dynamic adaptation to the page content. It is inspired by an abstraction model proposed in BoM. To validate our work, MSoS was integrated within the virtual splitting system for application distribution in the multi-screen context. Experiments were conducted on a set of existing multimedia applications. We compared the MSoS results to BoM[4] and to a manually created ground truth. With our adaptive method, better segmentation results were obtained especially in critical regions of the page and blocks with different function were kept separated. With a 81% precision, the MSoS is a promising method. As a perspective, we are planning to enlarge our application dataset to compare our MSoS qualitatively and quantitatively to different segmentation methods. In addition, we want to extend the evaluation plan to consider the importance of the block position on block identification.

6. REFERENCES

[1] D. Cai, S. Yu, J.R. Wen, and W.Y. Ma. Vips: A vision-based page segmentation algorithm. Technical report, Microsoft, MSR-TR-2003-79, 2003.

[2] J. Chen, B. Zhou, J. Shi, H. Zhang, and Q. Fengwu. Function-based object model towards website adaptation. In *Proceedings of the 10th International Conference on World Wide Web*, WWW '01, pages 587–596, New York, NY, USA, 2001. ACM.

[3] J.C. Dufourd, M. Tritschler, L. Bassbouss, R. Bouazizi, and S. Steglich. An open platform for multiscreen services. In *the 11th European Interactive TV conference EuroITV*, Como, Italy, June 2013.

[4] A. Sanoja and S. Gançarski. Block-o-matic: A web page segmentation framework. In *Multimedia Computing and Systems (ICMCS), 2014 International Conference on*, pages 595–600. IEEE, 2014.

[5] M. Sarkis, C. Concolato, and J.C. Dufourd. The virtual splitter: Refactoring web applications for the multiscreen environment. In *Proceedings of the 2014 ACM Symposium on Document Engineering*, DocEng '14, pages 139–142, New York, NY, USA, 2014. ACM.

Creating eBooks with Accessible Graphics Content

Cagatay Goncu
Faculty of IT
Monash University, Australia
cagatay.goncu@monash.edu

Kim Marriott
Faculty of IT
Monash University, Australia
Kim.Marriott@monash.edu

ABSTRACT

We present a new model for presenting graphics in eBooks to blind readers. It is based on the GraViewer app which allows an accessible graphic embedded in an iBook to be explored on an iPad using speech and non-speech audio feedback. We also introduce a web-based tool, GraAuthor, for creating such accessible graphics and describe the workflow for including these in an iBook. Unlike previous approaches our model provides an integrated digital presentation of both text and graphics and allows the general public to create accessible graphics.

Categories and Subject Descriptors

I.7.1 [**Document And Text Processing**]: Electronic Publishing; K.4.2 [**Computers And Society**]: Social Issues—*Assistive technologies for persons with disabilities*

General Terms

Design, Human Factors

Keywords

eBook, accessible graphics, authoring

1. INTRODUCTION

One of the most disabling consequences of being blind (by whom we mean any person whose level of vision does not allow them to easily read printed text or graphics even when magnified) is a lack of access to information presented graphically. Computer applications like DAISY or Apple's VoiceOver screen reader allow blind people to access digital textbooks, web pages and other textual material by using speech or refreshable braille displays. However, reading graphic elements with VoiceOver or DAISY is still limited to reading an alternative textual description associated with the graphics.

Despite accessibility guidelines the vast majority of on-line graphics either do not include an alternative text description of the graphic or the text is very general and not helpful [11]. Even when provided such a description can only summarise the information in the graphic and necessarily loses information contained in the original graphic. It is also difficult to use a textual description to build a mental model of the layout of the graphic's elements. For these reasons accessibility guidelines recommend the use of tactile graphics for presenting graphics in which spatial relationships are important, e.g. maps, plans, technical drawings etc [17].

Tactile graphics are usually printed on swell or embossed paper and allow the blind reader to feel the graphic elements and to understand their spatial layout. Unfortunately they suffer from three significant disadvantages. The first is that they form a bulky, separate addendum to the main text. The second is that they use Braille which most blind people cannot easily read [8]. The third disadvantage is that they require special purpose printers or paper for their production, and so are relatively expensive (around US $5 a sheet.)

Tactile graphics were combined with an eBook for, we believe, the first time in 2014. The Space Telescope Science Institute (STScI) partnered with the SAS Corporation, the National Braille Press, and the National Federation of the Blind to create an accessible iBook "Reach for the Stars" [12]. VoiceOver is used to read the book while tactile overlays can be laid over selected graphics on the iPad and the reader obtains audio feedback when they touch the overlay. While this certainly provides a more integrated presentation of text and graphics the need for expensive tactile overlays remains a significant disadvantage of this approach.

Here we present a new model for combining accessible graphics with eBooks that does away with the need for tactile overlays. Rather than using an overlay we use the GraViewer app [5] to present an accessible version of the graphic on an iPad using audio feedback. Here, we extend our previous research into GraViewer by considering how it can be used to present graphics from eBooks. Our main technical contributions are to present a web-based authoring tool, GraAuthor, for creating accessible graphics that can be viewed using GraViewer on the iPad and the workflow for integrating these graphics into an iBook.

An important feature of GraAuthor is that it is designed to be used by the general public. This is in contrast to the current state of affairs for tactile graphics where most tactile graphics (including the tactile overlays in "Reach for the Stars") are created by trained transcribers. While GraAuthor can be used by transcribers it has been designed so that it can be used by teachers, friends, colleagues and family of a person who is blind. In combination with iBooks Author this allows these people to easily create eBooks with fully integrated accessible graphics.

DocEng'15, September 8-11, 2015, Lausanne, Switzerland
Copyright is held by the owner/author(s). Publication rights licensed to ACM.
ACM 978-1-4503-3307-8/15/09 ...$15.00.
DOI: http://dx.doi.org/10.1145/2682571.2797076.

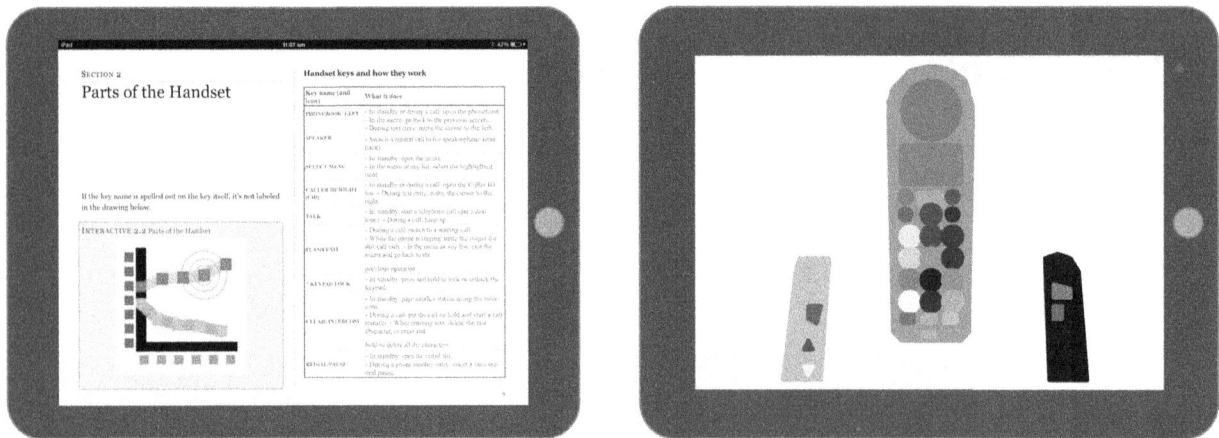

Figure 1: Reading an iBook with an embedded accessible graphic. The image on the left shows the iPad screen as a blind person uses iBooks with VoiceOver to read an instruction manual. A standard placeholder image indicates that the graphic can be opened in GraViewer. When the user double taps on the image the graphic is shown on the iPad using GraViewer (on the right.) As the reader touches the graphic elements the associated text is read aloud. The user returns to the iBook using the Home button.

To illustrate the usefulness of this approach, our running example is an accessible version of the instruction manual for a cordless phone. Better access to the illustrations in such manuals is a frequent request by blind people. Unfortunately, at present the use of trained transcribers and tactile graphics makes the cost of producing such an accessible instruction manual prohibitive. GraAuthor addresses this by allowing a friend or family member to quickly construct an accessible digital version for no cost apart from their time. Board game layouts, fictional and non-fictional maps and plans are examples of other material that might also be usefully transcribed using GraAuthor.

2. RELATED WORK

Presentation technologies for accessible graphics fall into four main categories: tactile graphics, e.g. [2], audio only presentation which is either based on a textual description of the graphic or sonification, e.g. [10]; tactile overlay on top of a pressure-sensitive screen which provides audio feedback when a graphic element is pressed, e.g. [13]; haptic presentation using devices like the phantom, e.g. [14]; or presentation on a touchscreen device using a mixture of haptic or audio feedback as the user explores the graphic, e.g. [6, 4]. The advantage of the last approach is that it does not rely on expensive tactile graphics or overlays but still allows the user to use both hands to explore the graphic and build up a mental model of it. This is the approach that we use.

Currently most tactile graphics are created by trained transcribers using tools like CorelDraw. Production is a time consuming iterative process in which the graphic is tested with blind proof readers. Researchers at the University of Washington have built an image processing tool (TGA) that can be used by transcribers to extract and replace text from scanned graphics by the equivalent braille [7]. There has been some previous research into automatic generation of accessible graphics from on-line images. This has focussed on automatically generating a textual summary or audio presentation of on-line bar charts (Interactive SIGHT) [1] and (iGraph-LITE) line graphs [3]. Recently a tool for automatically generating an accessible floor plan from an on-line floor plan was described in [5].

Our work differs in its focus on creating an authoring tool that can be readily used by non-professionals to create graphics for a blind friend, colleague or family member and by the ability to tightly integrate the accessible graphic into an eBook.

3. READING AN ACCESSIBLE EBOOK

Screen readers like Apple's VoiceOver and eBooks and new standards like ePub 3.0 are revolutionising access to books and other textual material by blind readers. However, access to graphics in these materials is currently not well supported. In this section we give a new model in which accessible graphics are embedded in the eBook, allowing a fully integrated reading experience as shown in Figure 1. Our implementation utilises iBooks because Apple products are widely used in the blind community due to their comprehensive accessibility support.

Our model makes use of an application called GraViewer which we previously developed for accessible presentation of information graphics on the iPad [5]. It is based on prior research into audio and audio-haptic presentation of graphics on touch screen devices [6, 5] and street maps on mobile devices [15, 9]. GraViewer's user interface is designed to be consistent with the iOS accessibility framework: it utilises standard iOS accessibility gestures for menu navigation and application control as well as using VoiceOver for speech.

GraViewer allows a blind user to explore the graphic with both hands, much like a tactile graphic. Whenever a graphic element is first touched or subsequently queried, audio feedback describes the element. A sharp click indicates when a graphic element is entered or left and a volume gradient along the boundary helps the blind user follow the boundary of a shape or a line. When a graphic is first opened a textual overview of the graphic is read to the user. This is in line with guidelines for tactile graphics which recommend providing a Braille overview to help the blind reader quickly build up a mental model of the graphic.

GraViewer displays graphic content specified in SVG (the W3C standard for Scalable Vector Graphics) and uses metadata associated with the shapes to control the interaction. The metadata associated with a shape is: its ID, audio volume level for the interior of the shape and for its boundary, the text string to be read out when the shape is queried, and the name of a (non-speech) audio file and/or the color code for generating the sound associated with the shape during navigation.

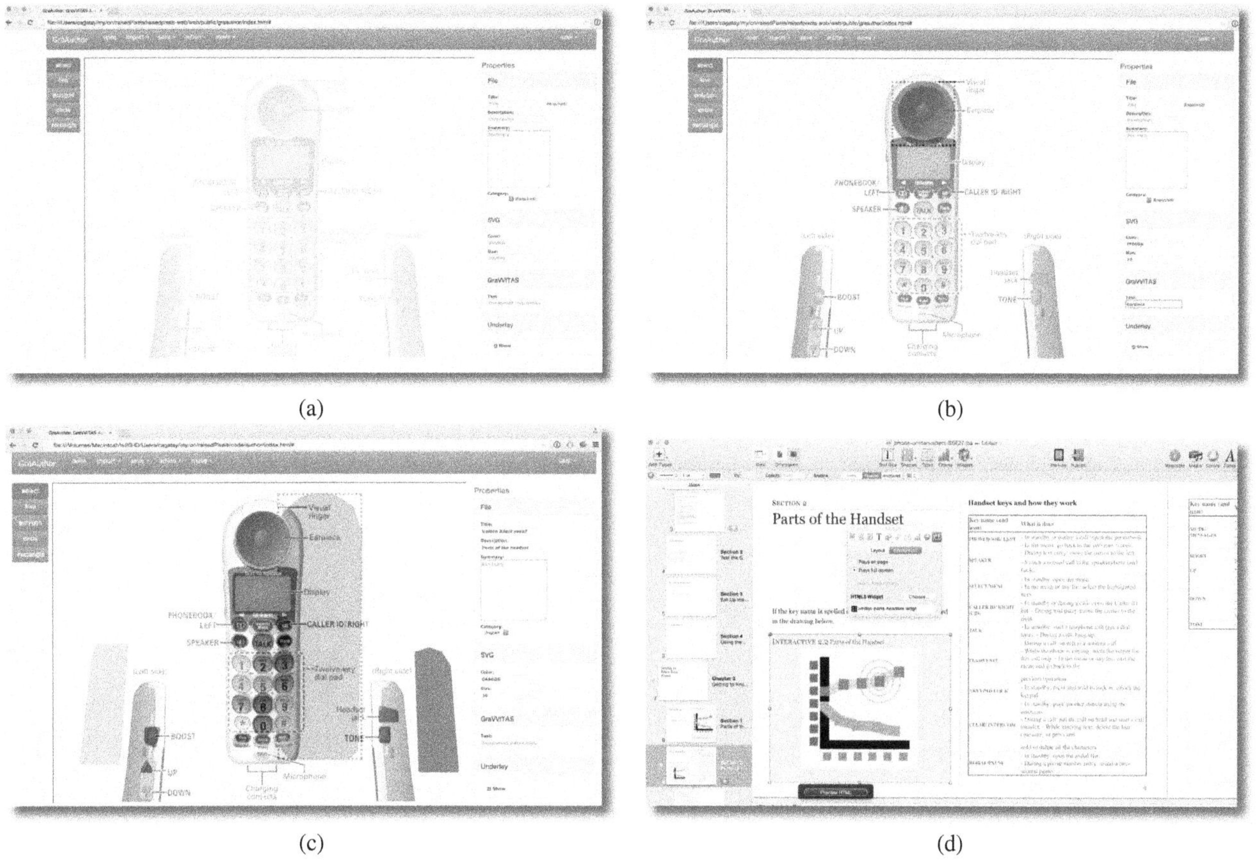

Figure 2: Creating an accessible graphic of the controls on a telephone handset (https://www.uniden.com.au) with GraAuthor. (a) The original image is imported and displayed as an underlay. (b) The author creates simple polygons and lines and overlays these on the image to create the accessible graphic. The author can associate a textual description with each shape which will be read aloud when the shape is touched. (c) The almost complete graphic which is ready to be saved as an HTML widget. (d) The HTML widget can be embedded in an iBook using iBooks Author.

Because GraViewer displays an SVG file, it fits well with HTML5 and ePub 3.0. In our implementation, an accessible graphic is embedded in a iBook as an HTML widget.

When reading an iBook the blind user can select the widget by double tapping on it and it will be displayed using GraViewer as shown in Figure 1. Once they have finished viewing the graphic they can use the home button to exit from GraViewer and return to their current location in the iBook. For the first time accessible graphics are fully integrated with text presentation.

4. ACCESSIBLE EBOOK CREATION

Accessible graphics are created by trained transcribers. However we wanted to "democratise" their production so as to allow teachers, friends, colleagues and family of the blind person to easily create eBooks with fully integrated accessible graphics. The intent is to support access to the many graphics that are encountered day-to-day like diagrams in instruction manuals, maps in travel guides, board game instructions etc that are currently not available to blind people because of prohibitive production cost.

Our model for creation is built around GraAuthor which is shown in Figure 2. This is a web-based graphics authoring tool that allows a sighted person to quickly create an accessible graphic suitable for display with GraViewer. GraAuthor has two interesting features.

The first is that the author can import an image of the visual graphic for which they wish to create the accessible version and use this to guide the construction. The faded out image is shown in the background and by tracing lines and shape boundaries the author can quickly create the accessible version.

The second interesting feature is that GraAuthor allows the author to provide a textual overview of the graphic and to associate a textual description and non-speech audio file with each graphic element. These are the basis for the audio feedback provided by GraViewer when the graphic is displayed.

Once the graphic has been created in GraAuthor, it can be exported as an HTML widget. Then when authoring an iBook using iBooks Author, the HTML widget can be inserted into the page at whatever location the author desires – see Figure 2(d). Once the iBook is finished it can be exported to the iPad of the blind reader as an email attachment, through a file sharing service like DropBox, or published through the iBooks store.

It is worth pointing out that creating an understandable accessible graphic is not straightforward. Obviously colour and texture must be replaced by a textual description while the much lower resolution of touch means that the accessible version must abstract and simplify the original graphic. Furthermore, devices like perspective are not easily understood by blind people and so should be replaced by an orthogonal view [16].

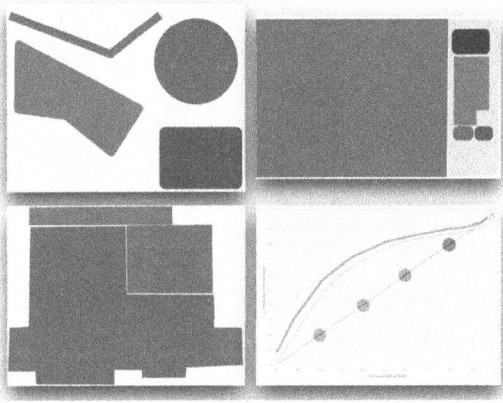

Figure 3: Some examples of different graphics which have been created with GraAuthor: (i) Simple geometric shapes, (ii) Front view of a microwave, (iii) Overview of an airport floor plan, (iv) Annotated image of a line graph.

To help the novice author, GraAuthor comes with examples of common kinds of information graphics: tables, floor plans, maps, line graphs which can be used as the basis for creating new graphics. Furthermore our model allows the person creating the graphic to quickly publish the graphic to an iPad and obtain feedback from the blind reader, and modify or improve it as necessary.

5. EVALUATION

Both GraViewer and GraAuthor were developed using a participatory design methodology with blind end-users and transcribers. Blind users have used GraViewer to understand a wide variety of graphics including line charts and floor plans, some of which are shown in Figure 3. In [5], 8 participants were presented with floor plans of large houses with 10 rooms, and asked questions to determine whether they could find the number of the rooms, point to a particular room, show the path from one room to another, and describe the overall layout. All participants answered all the questions correctly, except two who made a mistake in the first question.

6. CONCLUSION

We have provided a new model for presenting graphics in eBooks to blind readers and described two tools, GraViewer and GraAuthor, that support this model for iBooks. Unlike previous approaches our model provides integrated delivery of both text and graphics and allows non-professionals to create accessible graphics. We believe our model and tools have the potential to dramatically improve access to a wide range of digital information graphics.

However there is still considerable work to be done. This includes more extensive user studies trialling the use of GraViewer and GraAuthor in real-world contexts, such as school or work, and integration of image processing and OCR into GraAuthor so as to semi-automate transcription.

7. ACKNOWLEDGMENTS

We acknowledge the support of ARC through LP110200469 and of our project partners the Statewide Vision Resource Center, Vision Australia, jTribe and the Catholic Education Office (Melbourne). In particular we wish to thank Deb Lewis, Armin Kroll, Leona Holloway and the participants for their help.
Disclosure: Cagatay Goncu is co-founder of RaisedPixels, a company which is commercialising GraViewer and GraAuthor.

8. REFERENCES

[1] S. Demir, D. Oliver, E. Schwartz, S. Elzer, S. Carberry, K. F. Mccoy, and D. Chester. Interactive sight: textual access to simple bar charts. *New Review of Hypermedia and Multimedia*, 16(3):245–279, 2010.

[2] Y. Eriksson. *Tactile Pictures: Pictorial Representations for the Blind 1784-1940*. Gothenburg Uni. Press, 1998.

[3] L. Ferres, G. Lindgaard, L. Sumegi, and B. Tsuji. Evaluating a tool for improving accessibility to charts and graphs. *ACM Transactions on Computer-Human Interaction (TOCHI)*, 20(5):28, 2013.

[4] N. A. Giudice, H. P. Palani, E. Brenner, and K. M. Kramer. Learning non-visual graphical information using a touch-based vibro-audio interface. In *Proc. of the 14th Int. ACM SIGACCESS Conference on Computers and Accessibility*, pages 103–110. ACM, 2012.

[5] C. Goncu, A. Madugalla, S. Marinai, and K. Marriott. Accessible on-line floor plans. In *Proceedings of the 24th International World Wide Web Conference*. ACM, 2015.

[6] C. Goncu and K. Marriott. Gravvitas: Generic multi-touch presentation of accessible graphics. In *Proc. INTERACT'11*, pages 30–48. Springer, 2011.

[7] C. Jayant, M. Renzelmann, D. Wen, S. Krisnandi, R. Ladner, and D. Comden. Automated tactile graphics translation: in the field. In *Proc. of the 9th Int. ACM SIGACCESS Conference on Computers and Accessibility*, pages 75–82. ACM, 2007.

[8] The Braille Literacy Crisis in America: Facing the Truth, Reversing the Trend, Empowering the Blind. Technical report, Jernigan Institute, 2009.

[9] N. Kaklanis, K. Votis, and D. Tzovaras. Touching openstreetmap data in mobile context for the visually impaired. In *Proc. of the 3rd Workshop on Mobile Accessibility-ACM SIGCHI Conf. on Human Factors in Computing Systems*, 2013.

[10] A. R. Kennel. Audiograf: a diagram-reader for the blind. In *Proceedings of the second annual ACM conference on Assistive technologies*, pages 51–56. ACM, 1996.

[11] J. Lazar, A. Allen, J. Kleinman, and C. Malarkey. What frustrates screen reader users on the web: A study of 100 blind users. *International Journal of human-computer interaction*, 22(3):247–269, 2007.

[12] A. Lopez, E. Sabbi, and E. Summers. *Reach for the Stars: Touch, look, listen, learn*. SAS Institute, 2015. Available through iBooks.

[13] D. Parkes. Nomad: An audio-tactile tool for the acquisition, use and management of spatially distributed information by visually impaired people. In *Proc. of the Second International Symposium on Maps and Graphics for Visually Handicapped People*, 1988.

[14] H. Petrie et al. TeDUB: A system for presenting and exploring technical drawings for blind people. *Computers helping people with special needs*, pages 47–67, 2002.

[15] B. Poppinga, C. Magnusson, M. Pielot, and K. Rassmus-Gröhn. Touchover map: audio-tactile exploration of interactive maps. In *Proc. of the 13th Int. Conf. on Human Computer Interaction with Mobile Devices and Services*, pages 545–550. ACM, 2011.

[16] Purdue University. *Tactile Diagram Manual*, 2002.

[17] Round Table on Information Access for People with Print Disabilities Inc., Australia & New Zealand. *Guidelines on Conveying Visual Information (2005)*, 2005.

Investigation of Ancient Manuscripts based on Multispectral Imaging

Fabian Hollaus
Computer Vision Lab
TU Wien, TUW
Vienna, Austria
holl@caa.tuwien.ac.at

Markus Diem
Computer Vision Lab
TU Wien, TUW
Vienna, Austria
diem@caa.tuwien.ac.at

Stefan Fiel
Computer Vision Lab
TU Wien, TUW
Vienna, Austria
fiel@caa.tuwien.ac.at

Florian Kleber
Computer Vision Lab
TU Wien, TUW
Vienna, Austria
kleber@caa.tuwien.ac.at

Robert Sablatnig
Computer Vision Lab
TU Wien, TUW
Vienna, Austria
sab@caa.tuwien.ac.at

ABSTRACT

This work is concerned with the digitization and analysis of historical documents. The investigation of the documents has been conducted in three successive interdisciplinary projects. The team involved in the projects consists of philologists, chemists and computer scientists specialized in the field of digital image processing. The manuscripts investigated are partially degraded since they have been infected by mold, are corrupted by background clutter or contain faded-out or even erased writings. Since these degradations impede a transcription by scholars and worsen the performance of automated document image analysis techniques, the documents have been imaged with a portable multispectral imaging system. By using this non-invasive investigation technique, the contrast of the faded out characters can be increased, compared to ordinary white light illumination. Post-processing techniques, such as dimension reduction tools, can be used to gain a further legibility increase. The resulting images are used as a basis for further document analysis methods. These methods have been especially designed for the historical documents investigated and involve Optical Character Recognition and writer identification. This paper presents an overview on selected methods that have been developed in the projects.

Categories and Subject Descriptors

I.4 [**Computing Methodologies**]: Enhancement; I.4 [**Image Processing and Computer Vision**]: Applications

Keywords

Document Image Analysis; Optical Character Recognition; Writer Identification; Multispectral Imaging

DocEng'15, September 8-11, 2015, Lausanne, Switzerland.
© 2015 ACM. ISBN 978-1-4503-3307-8/15/09 ...$15.00.
DOI: http://dx.doi.org/10.1145/2682571.2797072.

1. INTRODUCTION

This work presents efforts that have been taken to examine historical documents. The documents have been investigated in the course of three interdisciplinary projects, in which philologists, chemists and computer scientists are involved. The objects investigated have been created in the middle ages and are partially in a poor condition, which impedes a transcription by the scholars involved in the project. In order to facilitate the work of the scholars, the objects are imaged with a portable MultiSpectral Imaging (MSI) system, since MSI can be used to gather image details that are invisible to the human eye [6].

Several researchers [10] [6] have shown that MSI can be used to enhance the visibility of such degraded writings and to improve the legibility. For example in [2] the famous Archimedes Palimpsest[1] is imaged with an MSI system and the authors show that this non-invasive investigation method can be used to enhance the visibility of the original text. Additionally it is shown in [2] and [10] that dimension reduction techniques can be used in a post-processing step to further enhance the contrast of the faded-out writings, compared to the unprocessed multispectral images.

In order to further support the work of the scholars, various document image analysis techniques have been developed during the projects - involving methods for Optical Character Recognition (OCR) and writer identification. The methods are suited for the challenging documents investigated and will be introduced in the following sections.

This work is structured as follows: In Section 2 the MSI system is introduced as well as an enhancement method. The OCR approach for degraded handwritings is described in 3.1 and the writer identification method detailed in Section 3.2. Finally, the paper is summarized in Section 4.

2. MULTISPECTRAL IMAGING

Our MSI system is portable, since it is most often used in libraries. The acquisition setup is illustrated in Figure 1. The system consists of two different cameras: (1) A Hamamatsu C9300-124 NearInfraRed (NIR) grayscale cam-

---

[1] A palimpsest is an ancient document that has been reused by overwriting the original text. The parchment has been reused, since it was a precious material in former times.

era with a spectral response between 300nm and 1000nm and (2) a Nikon D4 SLR camera, which is used for white light photographs and UltraViolet (UV) fluorescence imaging. A filter wheel is mounted in front of the Hamamatsu camera and it contains 7 different optical filters. The historical documents are illuminated with two multispectral LED panels (Eureka!Light - Equipoise imaging), which enable an imaging in 11 different narrow-band spectral ranges between UV and NIR. The usage of the LED panels reduces the heat - compared to broadband tungsten illumination, which might damage the historical documents [10].

In Figure 2 a portion of an ancient manuscript is shown. The historical text is written in Glagolitic, which is the oldest Slavonic [8] script. The image in Figure 2 (left) has been taken under white light and the image in Figure 2 (right) is an UV fluorescence image. The visibility of the text in the white light image is limited, because of the varying background. On the contrary, in the UV fluorescence image, the contrast between the fore- and background regions is increased and the text is better visible.

While the imaging in selected narrow-band spectral ranges can be used to gain a contrast enhancement, several post-processing techniques can be used to gain a further legibility increase: Several researchers [6] [10] have shown that dimension reduction techniques, such as Principal Component Analysis (PCA), can be successfully applied on multispectral images of ancient documents. Thus, the dimensionality of the multispectral data is reduced and the contrast of the degraded writing is also often increased. In our case the multispectral data is stored in a matrix, where the number of rows is equal to the number of pixels in one multispectral image ($4000 \times 2672px$) and the number of columns is equal to the number of channels. This number is varying, but the minimum number of channels is 16. By making use of dimension reduction methods the number of columns of the transformed data is reduced, but it is not predefined, how many dimensions are necessary to enhance the writing. For instance, we noted in [5] that for a particular manuscript the writing was usually enhanced by one of the first 5 principal components.

We have suggested an enhancement approach in [5] that makes use of Linear Discriminant Analysis (LDA) in order to enhance the contrast of the faded-out text. Since LDA is a supervised dimension reduction technique, it is necessary to label a subset of the multispectral observations as belonging to the fore- or background. In order to label such a training set automatically, we propose to make use of document image analysis techniques - namely a text line detection based on Local Projection Profiles [13] and a document image binarization method [12]. By using those two methods, the enhancement technique can be applied in an automated manner.

It should be noted that by using the labeling procedure, a certain amount of pixels is falsely labeled, due to low contrast of the text and background variation. While this decreases the quality of the resulting images, the images are still partially superior compared to the often used PCA approach and to unprocessed multispectral images: A qualitative analysis conducted by the scholars belonging to our project team showed that the enhancement results were superior to the other images in 5 out of 8 cases.

One example output of the algorithm is shown in Figure 3. It can be seen that the text is partially visible under

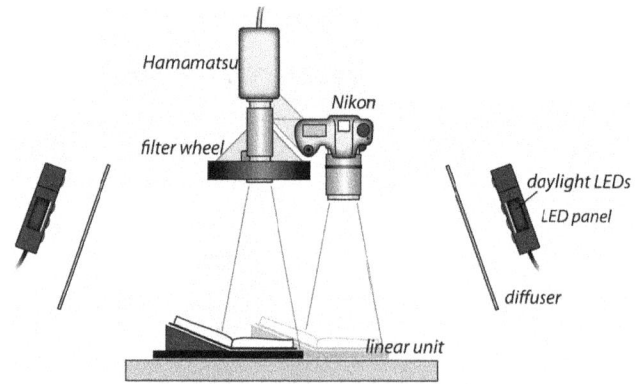

Figure 1: Illustration of the MSI system.

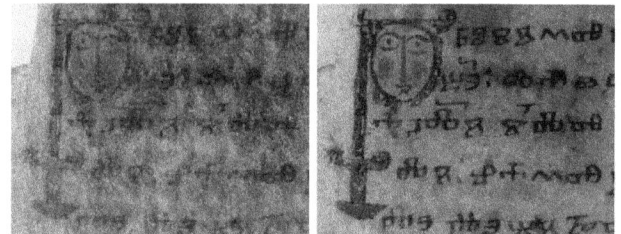

Figure 2: Manuscript portion illuminated with white light (left) and UV light (right).

UV light and also in the NIR range. However, the overall visibility of the text is still limited compared to the resulting image of the enhancement method.

3. DOCUMENT IMAGE ANALYSIS

The images taken are not only investigated by the scholars, but are also used to develop new document image analysis techniques. Two of these methods are detailed in the following, namely a method for OCR and a writer identification technique.

3.1 Optical Character Recognition

In order to support the work of the philologists an OCR approach has been suggest in [11]. The method is designed for strongly degraded documents. Due to the degradations, a successful application of a document image binarization method is not possible. Therefore, the OCR method does not make use of a binarization method, but instead makes use of local feature descriptors that are calculated on grayscale images: Therefore Scale Invariant Feature Transform (SIFT) [7] features are directly calculated on a test image and the features found are then compared to SIFT features that have been calculated on a training database. Afterwards, the Euclidean distances between features in the training set and features found on the test image are calculated. The most similar training features are found and are assigned to the characters found in the test image. The interested reader is referred to [11] for more details on the algorithm.

The method has been applied on 15 different test panels containing Glagolitic writings. The OCR system gained an overall F-Measure of 0.88 on non-degraded test panels and

Figure 3: Multispectral images and enhancement result. Top row: White light image (left) and UV fluorescence image (right). Bottom row: NIR image (left) and enhancement result (right).

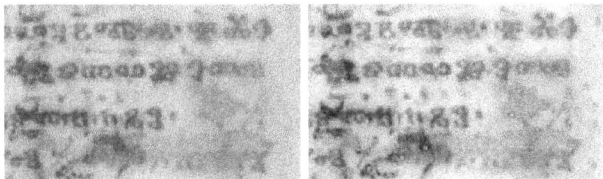

Figure 4: Output of the OCR method. (Left) Input image. (Right) Output image. Green indicates correct classified characters and red depicts incorrect classified characters.

an F-measure of 0.61 on degraded ones. An example output of the method is shown in Figure 4.

3.2 Writer Identification

The philologists of our project team are not only concerned with the transcription of the texts, but also with the identification of scribes. This writer identification is fulfilled by paleographers, who are performing this task mainly manually in order to localize or authenticate the ancient texts [13], [1]. In order to make this task applicable to a large amount of data, we suggested an automated writer identification in [3].

The method is originally designed for modern handwritings [4] and has been adopted for the historical writings imaged in our projects. The method makes use of local SIFT [7] feature descriptors and visual vocabularies in order to describe handwriting characteristics. In the original method the SIFT algorithm is directly applied on the input images. In the case of the historical writings, the documents are partially degraded by clutter and water stains. Therefore, SIFT features are also found on the document background and the overall performance of the writer identification method is decreased. In order to resolve this drawback, a preprocessing step is applied: At first text lines are found by applying the algorithm in [13] and the text lines are used for the identification of the main text block. The input image is then cropped so that only the main text region is contained in the output image. Afterwards, the document image binarization method is applied to identify foreground pixels and the sub-

sequent writer identification method is directly applied on the foreground regions found. For this purpose the SIFT approach is applied on the binarized image and a visual vocabulary is built. The features are clustered by applying a Gaussian Mixture Model and the Fisher Kernel [9]. More details on the algorithm can be found in [4].

The method has been tested on 361 document images, containing Glagolitic handwritings. The writings are belonging to five different manuscripts and the philologists in our project team identified seven different writers as authors. Each of the images has been used as an input image and the method identified the most similar image in the remaining dataset. In 98.9% of all cases, the method found an image that was written by the same author as the input image. This result indicates that the method is suited for the historical documents investigated in the projects.

4. CONCLUSION

This paper presents efforts that have been taken in interdisciplinary projects, devoted to the investigation of historical documents. The overall aim of the projects is to support to work of philologists who are analyzing ancient manuscripts. These manuscripts have been imaged with a MSI system in order to raise the visibility of the hardly legible writings. In order to gain a further legibility increase a post-processing method is suggested that is based on dimension reduction. Furthermore, two document image analysis techniques are presented: The first one is an OCR method that is especially designed for historical and degraded writings. The second technique is a writer identification method that is originally designed for modern writings and has been adopted for the historical manuscripts imaged in the projects. Numerical results are given in the cited papers, which show that the methods are at least partially superior to other state-of-the-art techniques. Additionally, the results show that the methods can be used successfully as a supporting technology for philologists.

5. ACKNOWLEDGMENTS

The research was funded by the Austrian Federal Ministry of Science, Research and Economy.

6. REFERENCES

[1] M. Bulacu, R. van Koert, L. Schomaker, and T. van der Zant. Layout Analysis of Handwritten Historical Documents for Searching the Archive of the Cabinet of the Dutch Queen. In *Proc. of the Ninth ICDAR 2007 Vol 1*, pages 357–361, Washington, DC, USA, 2007. IEEE Computer Society.

[2] R. Easton, W. Christens-Barry, and K. Knox. Spectral Image Processing and Analysis of the Archimedes Palimpsest. In *19th EUSIPCO*, pages 1440–1444, 2011.

[3] S. Fiel, F. Hollaus, M. Gau, and R. Sablatnig. Writer identification on historical glagolitic documents. In *Document Recognition and Retrieval XXI, San Francisco, California, USA, February 5-6, 2014.*, pages 902102–902102–10, 2014.

[4] S. Fiel and R. Sablatnig. Writer identification and writer retrieval using the fisher vector on visual vocabularies. In *2013 12th International Conference on Document Analysis and Recognition, Washington, DC, USA, August 25-28, 2013*, pages 545–549, 2013.

[5] F. Hollaus, M. Gau, and R. Sablatnig. Enhancement of multispectral images of degraded documents by employing spatial information. In *ICDAR*, pages 145–149, 2013.

[6] M. Lettner, M. Diem, R. Sablatnig, and H. Miklas. Registration of Multispectral Manuscript Images as Prerequisite for Computer Aided Script Description. In *12th Computer Vision Winter Workshop*, St.Lambrecht, Austria, 2007.

[7] D. G. Lowe. Distinctive image features from scale-invariant keypoints. *International Journal of Computer Vision*, 60(2):91–110, 2004.

[8] H. Miklas, M. Gau, F. Kleber, M. Diem, M. Lettner, M. Vill, R. Sablatnig, M. Schreiner, M. Melcher, and E. Hammerschmid. St. catherine's monastery on mount sinai and the balkan-slavic manuscript-tradition. *Slovo. Towards a Digital Library of South Slavic Manuscripts*, pages 13–36, 2008.

[9] F. Perronnin and C. R. Dance. Fisher kernels on visual vocabularies for image categorization. In *2007 IEEE Computer Society Conference on Computer Vision and Pattern Recognition (CVPR 2007), 18-23 June 2007, Minneapolis, Minnesota, USA*, 2007.

[10] K. Rapantzikos and C. Balas. Hyperspectral imaging: potential in non-destructive analysis of palimpsests. *ICIP*, 2:II–618–21, 11-14 Sept. 2005.

[11] S. Saleem, F. Hollaus, M. Diem, and R. Sablatnig. Recognizing glagolitic characters in degraded historical documents. In *14th International Conference on Frontiers in Handwriting Recognition, ICFHR 2014, Crete, Greece, September 1-4, 2014*, pages 771–776, 2014.

[12] B. Su, S. Lu, and C. L. Tan. Binarization of historical document images using the local maximum and minimum. In *DAS*, pages 159–166, 2010.

[13] I. B. Yosef, N. Hagbi, K. Kedem, and I. Dinstein. Line segmentation for degraded handwritten historical documents. In *ICDAR*, pages 1161–1165, 2009.

Similarity-Based Support for Text Reuse in Technical Writing

Axel J. Soto
Faculty of Computer Science
Dalhousie University
Halifax, Canada
soto@cs.dal.ca

Abidalrahman
Mohammad
Faculty of Computer Science
Dalhousie University
Halifax, Canada
amohd@cs.dal.ca

Andrew Albert
Innovatia Inc.
St. John, Canada
andrew.albert@innovatia.net

Aminul Islam
Faculty of Computer Science
Dalhousie University
Halifax, Canada
islam@cs.dal.ca

Evangelos Milios
Faculty of Computer Science
Dalhousie University
Halifax, Canada
eem@cs.dal.ca

Michael Doyle
Innovatia Inc.
St. John, Canada
michael.doyle@innovatia.net

ABSTRACT

Technical writing in professional environments, such as user manual authoring for new products, is a task that relies heavily on reuse of content. Therefore, technical content is typically created following a strategy where modular units of text have references to each other. One of the main challenges faced by technical authors is to avoid duplicating existing content, as this adds unnecessary effort, generates undesirable inconsistencies, and dramatically increases maintenance and translation costs. However, there are few computational tools available to support this activity. This paper investigates the use of different similarity methods for the task of identification of reuse opportunities in technical writing. We evaluated our results using existing ground truth as well as feedback from technical authors. Finally, we also propose a tool that combines text similarity algorithms with interactive visualizations to aid authors in understanding differences in a collection of topics and identifying reuse opportunities.

Categories and Subject Descriptors

I.2.7 [**Natural Language Processing**]: Text Analysis; I.7.1 [**Document and Text Editing**]: Document Management

Keywords

Text Similarity, Document Analysis, Authoring Tools and Systems, Visual Text Analytics

1. INTRODUCTION

Technical writing or technical communication is a broad field that can be defined differently depending on the con-

DocEng'15, September 8–11, 2015, Lausanne, Switzerland.
Copyright is held by the owner/author(s). Publication rights licensed to ACM.
ACM 978-1-4503-3307-8/15/09.
DOI: http://dx.doi.org/10.1145/2682571.2797068.

text. In this paper, we broadly define it as the written communication about technical or specialized subjects, such as computational systems, medical procedures, or environmental regulations. This task is performed by companies and government agencies for writing manuals, websites and procedures on a regular basis.

In general, technical writing follows a modular approach for content creation. *Topic-based* authoring is a common approach for the creation of technical documents, where content is structured around topics. Note that we refer to the term 'topic' in a completely different sense here to the one that is commonly used within the text mining community. In this paper, we refer to topics as text fragments that "...are typically about a specific subject, have an identifiable purpose and can stand alone". The Darwin Information Typing Architecture (DITA) [1, 22] is the most common topic-based data model for authoring and publishing.

The main idea behind topic-based authoring (also typically referred as *single-source* writing) is to keep modular units of text that are stored in a single centralized repository, so that this allows an effective reusing of content [11] in different contexts. For example, assume a company has technical manuals, release notes, and an online help web page about a specific device. Very likely, a large part of the content of these documents will be shared. A new edition of a device being released typically leads to changes in the text referring to the updated features of the device. By keeping the writing modular and single-sourced, not only is the text to change easier to pin-point, but it is updated once and reused by any other resources that require that information. This reduces maintenance costs and the chances of inconsistencies. Another useful scenario for highlighting the importance of topic-based writing is language translation, where it is desirable to avoid translating the same text more than once.

One challenge in topic-based writing is identifying opportunities for topic reuse. In other words, given a set of topics, the task is to identify topics or subsets of topics, such as sentences or paragraphs, with similar text content, so that the common text can be referenced and reused, and thus unnecessary repetition is avoided. Note that the problem requires identifying not just the same sequence of text in two topics, but also similar enough content that can be slightly modified to allow reuse. In addition, similar or exact content may not always be a good case for reuse, due to the common content being too short, or due to texts that while similar, are likely to mean different things.

Text mining algorithms can help to find topics that are good candidates for reuse. Therefore, one of our goals is to better understand the impact of different similarity approaches for identifying topic reuse candidates. Furthermore, from initial interactions with technical writers we recognized that the actual modification of topics by rewriting or reusing of content is a task that cannot be accomplished in a fully automated manner. For this reason, we are also interested in investigating the design of appropriate tools that allow technical authors to explore the collection of topics, in such a way that they can integrate the results of the similarity methods, and hence make more informative writing decisions.

This paper is organized as follows. The next section reviews related work and methods in this area. In Section 3 we present the different similarity methods we investigated, while Section 4 describes the evaluations we applied on them. The proposal of two interactive visualizations is described in Section 5. Finally, Section 6 summarizes the main contributions of this work and discusses future extensions.

2. RELATED WORK

There are several commercial and non-commercial computational tools that aim at supporting topic-based authoring, such as DITA-optimized XML editors or DITA Content Management Systems. Despite technical writing not being a new area and the DITA standards have been first proposed in 2001, the computer science research community has not looked much into this area. Some exceptions are the work of Paris et al. [20], where a support tool for technical writers of multi-lingual instructions is described, or Baptista's description of the adoption of DITA into a project [2].

While topic-based writing and DITA standards allow and facilitate the reuse of content, technical authors are faced with a difficult task when they need to create or modify technical content, so that they can find similar topics, and hence make the most out of single-sourced type of writing. However, to the best of our knowledge, we have found no research paper that looks into this very concrete problem of how to identify reuse opportunities more easily in the context of technical writing.

Our hypothesis is that text similarity algorithms can provide a powerful basis for detecting potential reuse cases among topics. Many types of text similarity algorithms have been proposed in the literature. An organization of these algorithms can be broadly characterized depending on whether word order is considered or not, whether merely syntactic similarity (word matching) or semantic similarity (matching of words that convey similar meanings) is captured, and whether real-based similarity or binary-based near-duplicate identification is performed [17, 18, 19]. While not in the context of technical writing, some studies have benchmarked and proposed several similarity methods for paraphrasing and plagiarism detection in social media, news and Wikipedia, such as [3], [23], and [26].

Given the lack of studies in the domain of technical text reuse, our goal is to investigate the use of different sim-

ilarity methods that can be categorized differently in the taxonomy we just described. Therefore, in this paper we experimented with Cosine similarity [18], Longest Common Subsequence [6], Google TriGram similarity method [15] and Locality Sensitive Hashing [24]. Cosine similarity is one of the most basic, yet popular, methods that has been used in very different domains. It captures syntacting matching of words assuming a bag-of-words model (i.e. without considering word order). In Longest Common Subsequence the order of words is important, as the algorithm finds the longest ordered sequence of matching words between two texts. This method has been applied for plagiarism detection in different works [3, 10, 7]. Google Trigram Method is a semantic similarity algorithm that has been proven to be the state-of-the-art in capturing the semantic meaning between texts. It uses a corpus-based approach to capture relatedness between words, which has shown to be superior to many knowledge-based methods [15]. Finally, Locality-Sensitive Hashing represents a family of methods for detecting near-duplicates in very large corpora efficiently. Some applications on finding duplicate content in the web include [12, 21]. In the next section we will describe these similarity algorithms in more detail.

Outside the technical writing domain, several research papers have investigated the modeling and identification of text reuse along time. Researchers have studied ways in which text is copied from one literary work to another, such as in ancient Greek texts [5], newspapers [25] and in the web [21]. It is worth noting that a common aspect in all these papers is the use of visualizations to reflect the findings and allow further understanding of how text components are replicated. Additionally, the work by Janicke et al. [16] presented various interesting visualization strategies to understand how different versions of a document or even different documents share commonalities. Another related domain that has matured greatly both in reuse strategies and in the use of visual aids is that of software. For instance, the work by Druzinski et al. [8] presents a framework, based on the concept of variant analysis, that supports visualizing the commonalities as well as variations amongst software components.

A second hypothesis we consider in this paper is that the proper deployment of any computational tool for topic reuse has to consider the author in the loop, so that the findings of the algorithms can be verifiable and applicable by non text mining experts. The presence of visual strategies and metaphors in most of the content reuse papers that we have reviewed support this hypothesis. However, as opposed to most of these works our focus is not on visualizing existing reuses of content, but rather on using the visualization as a tool to enable an interactive data exploration that facilitates the identification of reuse opportunities.

3. TEXT SIMILARITY METHODS

In this section we describe the four similarity methods that we have experimented with in this work. We chose algorithms of different characteristics so that we could better understand their benefits and limitations in this context.

3.1 Cosine Similarity

Cosine similarity is one of the most popular similarity algorithms that have been applied to text. It measures the degree of similarity of two documents as the correlation between their corresponding vector representations, which can be quantified as the cosine of their angle. Given two documents $\vec{d_1}$ and $\vec{d_2}$, their cosine similarity is:

$$COS(\vec{d_1}, \vec{d_2}) = \frac{\vec{d_1}.\vec{d_2}}{\parallel \vec{d_1} \parallel \parallel \vec{d_2} \parallel}.$$

Despite its simplicity and the fact that it ignores the relative order of the words in the document, it offers a competitive baseline for text similarity [18].

3.2 Longest Common Subsequence

Longest Common Subsequence (LCS) is another widely employed technique to measure similarity between texts. It measures the total length of the longest matching substrings in both texts, where these substrings are allowed to be non-contiguous as long as they appear in the same order [6, 14]. While the original algorithm was applied to find substrings of characters, a natural extension is to consider it for words, i.e. the longest common substring has to be composed by a sequence of full words only. The final similarity score can be obtained by dividing the number of words of the longest common subsequence by the length in words of the shortest document under comparison.

3.3 Google Tri-gram Similarity

The Google Tri-gram similarity method (GTM) is an unsupervised corpus-based approach for measuring semantic relatedness between text. GTM uses unigrams and trigrams from the Google Web 1T N-gram corpus[1] to compute the relatedness between words [15], and also extends this concept to quantify the relatedness between text documents. The Google Web 1T N-gram corpus counts the frequency of English word n-grams (unigrams to 5-grams) calculated over one trillion words of web page texts collected by Google in 2006.

The relatedness of two words is computed by considering the trigrams that start and end with the given pair of words, and normalized by their mean frequency using the unigram frequency of each of the words as well as the most frequent unigram in the corpus, as shown in Equation 1. In this equation $C(\omega)$ stands for the frequency of the word ω, $\mu_T(\omega_1, \omega_2)$ is the mean frequency of the trigrams that either start with ω_1 and end with ω_2, or start with ω_2 and end with ω_1, and $C_{\max}$ is the maximum frequency among all unigrams.

$$\text{GTM}(\omega_1, \omega_2) = \begin{cases} \dfrac{\log \frac{\mu_T(\omega_1, \omega_2) C_{\max}^2}{C(\omega_1) C(\omega_2) \min(C(\omega_1) C(\omega_2))}}{-2 \times \log \frac{\min(C(\omega_1), C(\omega_2))}{C_{\max}}} \\ \quad \text{if } \log \frac{\mu_T(\omega_1, \omega_2) C_{\max}^2}{C(\omega_1) C(\omega_2) \min(C(\omega_1) C(\omega_2))} > 1 \\ \dfrac{\log 1.01}{-2 \times \log \frac{\min(C(\omega_1), C(\omega_2))}{C_{\max}}} \\ \quad \text{if } \log \frac{\mu_T(\omega_1, \omega_2) C_{\max}^2}{C(\omega_1) C(\omega_2) \min(C(\omega_1) C(\omega_2))} \leq 1 \\ 0 \quad \text{if } \mu_T(\omega_1, \omega_2) = 0 \end{cases}$$

$$(1)$$

GTM computes a score between 0 and 1 to indicate the relatedness between two texts based on the relatedness of the words within the texts. For given texts P with m words (i.e., $P = \{p_1, p_2, \cdots, p_m\}$) and R with n words (i.e., $R = $

$\{r_1, r_2, \cdots, r_n\}$), where $m \leq n$, first all the common words (the number of common words is δ) are removed, and then a matrix is built, where each entry $a_{ij} \leftarrow GTM(p_i, r_j)$ is the relatedness between words p_i and r_j taken from P and R, respectively.

$$M = \begin{pmatrix} a_{11} & a_{12} & \cdots & a_{1(n-\delta)} \\ a_{21} & a_{22} & \cdots & a_{2(n-\delta)} \\ \vdots & \vdots & \ddots & \vdots \\ a_{(m-\delta)1} & a_{(m-\delta)2} & \cdots & a_{(m-\delta)(n-\delta)} \end{pmatrix}$$

From each row $M_{i:} = \{a_{i1} \cdots a_{i(n-\delta)}\}$ in the matrix, the significant elements $A_i = \{a_{ij} | a_{ij} > \mu(M_{i:}) + \sigma(M_{i:})\}$ are selected, where $\mu(M_{i:})$ and $\sigma(M_{i:})$ are the mean and standard deviation of row i. The summation of the means of all the $m - \delta$ rows is $\sum_{i=1}^{m-\delta} \mu(A_i)$. Then, we can compute the document relatedness using the following equation:

$$Rel(P, R) = \frac{(\delta + \sum_{i=1}^{m-\delta} \mu(A_i)) \times (m + n)}{2mn}$$

GTM similarity can be computed online[2].

3.4 Similarity based on Locality-Sensitive Hashing

The last similarity method that we applied relies on a general framework for computing similarity functions known as Locality-Sensitive Hashing (LSH), which was first proposed by Gionis et al. [9]. The main goal of LSH is to avoid the combinatorial comparison of all pairs of instances to find those that are near-duplicates. A good introduction to the topic can be found elsewhere [24, 17].

LSH-based methods typically rely on creating low-dimensional signatures of data instances so that the similarity of the signatures approximates that of the original data instances. A key characteristic of the signature creation process is that it is computationally inexpensive in comparison to dimensionality reduction methods, such as multi-dimensional scaling or methods based on singular-value decomposition. In this paper, we make use of min-hashing [4], which aims at creating signatures that approximate Jaccard distance in the context of sparse data representations.

Once the signatures are generated, they are divided in pieces of equal size called "bands". Then, the idea of the approach is to hash the bands of each signature into buckets, so that bands of different signatures that are hashed into the same buckets are likely to correspond to similar data instances.

We applied this same principle to allow the identification of near-duplicate documents in a time that grows linearly with the data. Note that this is a non-deterministic process (dependent on the hash functions) that can generate both false positives, i.e. collisions of signature bands that occur by chance and not because the data instances are similar, as well as false negatives, i.e. signatures of near-duplicates being different and hence not colliding into the same buckets.

For our implementation, we extracted bag of word trigrams as our vector representation. This generates a high-dimensional and sparse representation that is suitable for the application of LSH, whilst simultaneously being able to capture the occurrence of words and their relative order. We chose signatures with a dimensionality equal to 100. We set

---

[1] https://catalog.ldc.upenn.edu/LDC2006T13

[2] http://ares.research.cs.dal.ca/gtm/

the number of bands to 50 (i.e. bands of size 2), so that we get more chances for near-duplicates to have similar bands. The similarity score we applied is proportional to the number of times the two signatures bands collide into the same bucket. We also give it a boost to the score when the units that collide are also contiguous in the topic.

4. AUTOMATIC IDENTIFICATION OF REUSE CASES

Our first attempts on the application of the similarity algorithms were carried out by using the whole text of both topics under comparison. However, this approach did not succeed in identifying good reuse candidates, as it failed to provide a high similarity score when only parts of the content were shared. Therefore, this led us to split our topics into smaller units, so that we can compare the text of these units, and hence capture these finer-grain similarities within the topics.

One major challenge we have with LCS, COS and GTM is that the number of comparisons grows quadratically with the number of units to be compared. This means that in some cases, in order to keep the methods within a desirable running time, it may be necessary to constrain the number of topics to be considered in the dataset. This problem gets aggravated by using a finer granularity as our units of reuse, since this further increases the number of comparisons. This was one of our main motivations for incorporating LSH as part of our analysis.

In this section we describe the datasets, the corresponding preprocessing, and the different experiments that we carried out. Due to the different nature of LSH with respect to the other similarity methods, we divided our evaluation by presenting first the results on LCS, COS and GTM, while results using LSH are shown afterwards. We conclude this section discussing another alternative evaluation.

4.1 Datasets and Preprocessing

We conducted our experiments on four different datasets. The first three datasets are books named *CORDAP Content Developer*, *CORDAP Product Owner*, and *CORDAP Reviewer*, which were made available online[3]. The fourth dataset is a proprietary book that we will refer to it as *PropA*. The reason for including this fourth dataset is that it contains a larger number of topics than the first three ones, and hence some computational challenges can be identified due to the large number of comparisons required.

Prior to the similarity computation, books were preprocessed as follows. The DITA topics were parsed so that the text can be extracted from the XML structure. This extracted text is tokenized to allow the application of the different similarity algorithms. In addition to the text extraction, each topic is split into smaller chunks of text, which are considered as our textual units for comparison. These textual units are the ones to be compared in a pairwise manner using the different similarity methods described in Section 3. Thus, when comparing a pair of topics, the actual topic similarity is an aggregate of the pairwise unit similarities. For this aggregate we used the maximum among all pairwise unit similarities between the two topics.

We experimented with two different granularities for the textual units: the *coarse* one, which consists of splitting the

---

[3]http://web.cs.dal.ca/~soto/topicreuse.html

topics using the first level of element tags of the hierarchical DITA topic structure[4], and the *fine* granularity, which consists of splitting the content of topics according to the lowest level of the DITA element tags.

4.2 Evaluation of Similarity Algorithms

We applied different evaluation methods to our similarity algorithms. We first evaluated the results of our similarity algorithms by comparing them to existing reuse references that are present in the topics of our datasets. These references point to a specific element in another topic, where this element can encompass from as little as a single sentence to as much as the whole topic. In the DITA terminology, these type of references are called *conref*, and we will consider them as our ground-truth of a reuse between the two topics. LCS, COS and GTM are evaluated first, while the evaluation on LSH using different granularities is done afterwards.

The idea of the evaluation is that after calculating the pairwise comparison of all topics and ranking them in descending order of similarity, the ground-truth references should be among the top-ranked pairs. This evaluation can be accomplished by borrowing metrics from information retrieval [18]. We used precision at n ($P@n$), which is the percentage of true positives among the top n most similar pairs. This allows us to know how accurate the method is when suggesting a low number of candidates for reuse. Precision at 3, 4, and 5 for three different datasets can be examined in Tables 1–3. Unless otherwise indicated, we used the coarse granularity for our comparisons.

Table 1: Precision at 3, 4 and 5 for three similarity methods using CORDAP Content Developer

	LCS	COS	GTM
P@3	1.00	1.00	1.00
P@4	1.00	1.00	1.00
P@5	1.00	1.00	0.80

Table 2: Precision at 3, 4 and 5 for three similarity methods using CORDAP Product Owner

	LCS	COS	GTM
P@3	1.00	1.00	1.00
P@4	0.75	1.00	1.00
P@5	0.80	1.00	1.00

Table 3: Precision at 3, 4 and 5 for three similarity methods using CORDAP Reviewer

	LCS	COS	GTM
P@3	0.67	0.67	0.33
P@4	0.75	0.50	0.25
P@5	0.60	0.40	0.40

In order to evaluate the accuracy of the methods in detecting the whole number of reuse cases, we also report the

---

[4]A DITA topic can be thought as an XML document where content is contained in hierarchical element tags

true positive rate in terms of all ranked pairs. These curves can be found in Figure 1 using one panel for each dataset. The performance of each similarity method can be analyzed by the area under the curve (AUC), i.e. the larger this area is, the higher the true positives are ranked, and hence the better the method is.

As an analysis of these results, we can see in Tables 1–3 that the similarity methods are fairly accurate in detecting reuse cases when a small number of candidates are presented. The true positive rate curves of Figure 1 show that LCS achieves the best performance as far as detecting existing reuse cases is concerned. However, to better interpret these results, it is important to understand our ground truth. These instances of text reuse are not necessarily comprehensive in the sense that not every pair of topics that could have been reused is annotated as such. Section 5.1 shows some cases that highlight this scenario. Also the textual unit we considered for our comparisons is not necessarily the same as the one used in the ground-truth, and hence existing reuse instances that are smaller to our units are not likely to be selected among the top-ranked pairs. The next subsection further analyzes this granularity issue in more detail.

4.2.1   *Results with Locality-Sensitive Hashing (LSH)*

We recall that LSH allows identifying near-duplicate text using an algorithm with a time complexity that grows linearly with the number of textual units to be compared. Yet this is at the expense of a higher likelihood of failing to detect similar instances that are not identical, i.e. false negatives, and even getting some poor candidates for reuse, i.e. false positives.

A comparison between the best performing algorithm, LCS, and LSH is shown in Figure 2. When we used the coarse granularity, results show that LSH is able to find 70% of the reuse cases, while the remaining reuse cases, which are likely to reference finer-grain elements, go completely unnoticed to LSH. However, when the finer granularity is used, all the reuse instances are found at a rate similar to LCS. Yet, the time needed to find these instances with LSH is several orders of magnitude lower, from minutes to seconds.

The full strength of LSH is highlighted when a larger set of topics is used. In this case we used the dataset PropA, which has around 1,400,000 pairs of coarse units and around 6,000,000 pairs of fine units to be compared. This dataset is interesting due to its size and to the fact that its topics have a large number of reuses at very different granularities. Results in Figure 3 show that LSH can detect around 75% (when using coarse units) and 82% (when using fine units) of the existing reuse instances using far less attempts than the other methods, but then the true positive rate diminishes considerably. Clearly, the cost of the pairwise comparison using the finer units is prohibitive for LCS, COS and GTM, considering that running GTM using the coarse units took more than a day, whereas running LSH took less than 5 minutes.

These results should be also taken with care as merely optimizing these curves considering our current ground-truth would imply in disregarding semantically similar instances that can also represent important reuse opportunities. Also, while a finer granularity analysis is important in some cases, this unavoidably generates more false positive instances. As discussed in the next section, small units of text are not al-

ways good candidates for reuse as they may generate more overhead that outweighs its actual benefits.

5.   INTERACTIVE ANALYSIS OF REUSE CASES

This research work also included meetings and surveys with domain experts and technical authors. One key point that was drawn from these interactions is that no matter how good a similarity algorithm can be, authors feel reluctant to trust a fully-automatic method that can do a "search & replace" on similar topics. Authors commented that it is important for them to manually read and assess whether similar text is supposed to convey the same idea, or whether texts are coincidentally similar but likely to evolve differently in the future.

In this section, we first present a small study that aimed at understanding how authors evaluate whether an opportunity for reuse exist between a pair of presented topics. Then, we describe and assess two different interactive tools aimed at supporting technical authors in their work.

5.1   Presentation of highly-ranked pairs to technical authors

The evaluation so far only considered the accuracy of different algorithms in identifying existing reuse references in the text. However, this does not take into account the cases when a pair of topics (or textual units) conveys a similar message with a slightly different wording. Therefore, we took five top ranked pairs of topics in our multiple datasets that were not annotated with an existing reuse case between them, and we presented those to four technical authors. As an illustration, one of the pairs presented is the following (Case 2 in Table 4):

> Topic 1: Adding work packages to an iteration. Iterations can group work packages with the same due dates. At least one iteration must exist. Group all work packages due for the same milestone into one iteration. In My Products, expand the desired product. Click the desired release. Click Iterations. Select the box around the iteration to which the work package belongs. Work packages that are not yet added to an iteration are shown in Unscheduled. All work packages in the selected iteration appear. Drag and drop the work package into the desired iteration. The work package is now part of the selected iteration.

> Topic 2: Adding an iteration. Iterations can group your work packages by due dates. Know the due date for your iteration. Use iterations to easily track a group of work packages with similar due dates. In My Products, expand the desired product. Click the desired release. Click Iterations. Click Create new iteration. Enter a name and description for the iteration. Set the start and end dates. Click Save. The iteration is set and ready for work packages. If you need to edit an iteration, click the iteration name. The iteration details window opens for editing.

It is clear that the second sentence in both pairs conveys the same message despite not using the exact same words.

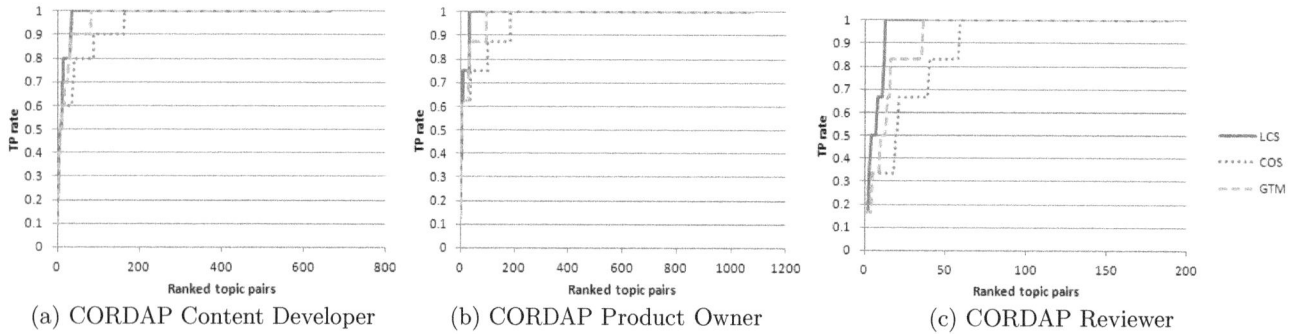

(a) CORDAP Content Developer (b) CORDAP Product Owner (c) CORDAP Reviewer

Figure 1: True positive rate for different datasets. Area under the curves: (a) LCS: 655.50, COS: 631.60, GTM: 648.80; (b) LCS: 1070.25, COS: 1039.75, GTM: 1060.25; (c) LCS: 184.17, COS: 167.17, GTM: 177.33

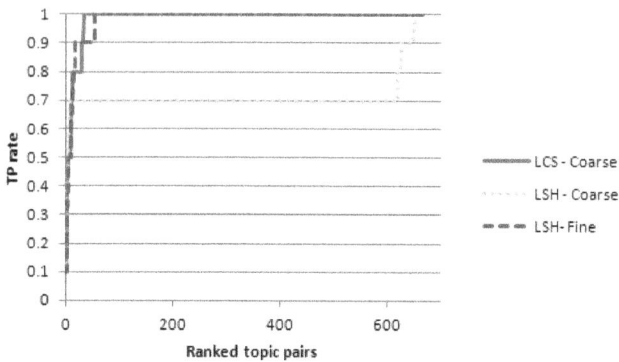

Figure 2: True positive rate using LSH (with a coarse and fine textual unit granularity) on CORDAP Content Developer. LCS performance is the same as the one reported in Figure 1 (a) but included here as a reference.

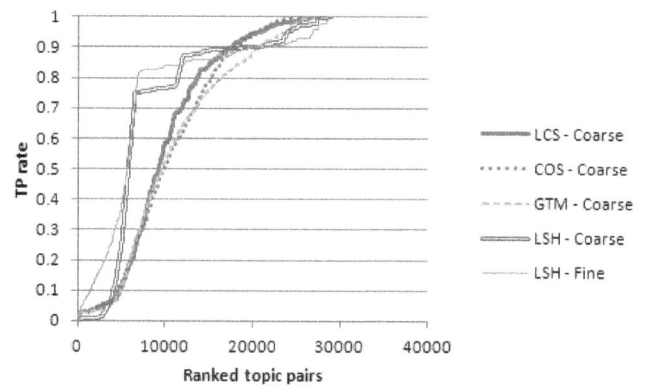

Figure 3: True positive rate using LCS, COS and GTM (coarse units) and LSH (coarse and fine) on PropA.

Overall, upon the presentation of the five selected pairs and the question of whether authors see a reuse opportunity, the responses can be found in Table 4.

Table 4: Author responses upon the presentation of five selected topic pairs and the question of whether authors see a reuse opportunity.

	Author 1	Author 2	Author 3	Author 4
Case 1	Yes	Yes	Yes	Yes
Case 2	Yes	Yes	No	Yes
Case 3	Yes	Yes	Yes	Yes
Case 4	Yes	No	No	No
Case 5	Yes	No	No	Yes

From the authors' feedback on this rather small sample of topic pairs, we could draw some preliminary conclusions. First, whether a case should be reused or not seems to be author-dependent. Some authors may prefer highly modularized topics, while others consider that if there is little text to be shared, then the overhead of reuse does not overcome the benefits, and hence it is not worth the effort. At least there was always one author who considered that each presented topic pair contains a topic reuse opportunity. Also, authors stated that in some cases some sort of restructuring or rewriting was required, which may affect other topics

too. All these facts support our hypothesis that a fully automatic tool may not be appropriate and hence some sort of interactive tool may be necessary to address this problem.

5.2 Overall Topic Similarity

Our first visualization was designed to provide an overview of several topics and their similarity. Ideally, these topics are supposed to be presented to an author for creating or updating one or more related books. The use case we had in mind for this visualization is of an author who is assigned to work on a book where several topics already exist. In the beginning this author would be interested in an overview of the set of topics and how they are clustered (groups of topics related to each other). Alternatively, a writer may want to focus on a specific topic and check what other related topics to this one exist, so as to avoid possible inconsistent text repetition.

In order to support this use case we have developed an interactive tool that incorporates the similarity algorithms described in Section 3 in a visual manner. A screenshot of this tool is shown in Figure 4. The interface contains three main components: a force-based topic similarity graph layout (left), a topic search panel (bottom right) and additional options (top right).

In the topic similarity graph, nodes represent topics and edges connect topics in such a way that the length of edges is inversely related to their similarity. Nodes also encode the topic type[5] and their text length using different marker types and sizes, respectively. The topic search panel allows ordering topics in different ways as well as searching topics by keyterms. There are additional options that allow modifying the graph view in different ways:

1. Thresholding the topic similarity graph, i.e. removing edges below a certain similarity value. In this way authors can interactively focus on different levels of similarity.

2. Filtering of connections incident to certain topic types. This is known to be a common requirement as authors are interested in finding similarities among specific topic types, e.g. looking for similarities among task-type topics only.

These different ways of filtering edges combined with the force-based layout of the graphs facilitate the exploration of sets with several hundred topics, as those disconnected topics get repelled to the borders decluttering graph connections.

There are several other interactions that can be applied on the graph. One of them is to overlay existing (conref) reuse references, which are added as directed links (starting from the topic that has the reference) and in a different color. These existing reuses help indicate for instance which topics would be affected if a referenced topic changed. Another important interaction is the possibility of identifying the most similar topics with respect to a specific topic (i.e. the *focus* topic or node). In this way all edges are hidden except the ones incident to the focus node. This action can be achieved either by shift-clicking a node in the graph or a row in the topic search result table. One final important option is the possibility to use the "Compare" button to bring up the visualization described in Section 5.3 using the topics connected in the graph (up to the top five most similar topics). Readers can experiment with this online tool[6]. Source code has been made available online[7].

5.3 Multiple Topic Text Comparison

Our second visualization was designed as a complement to the previous one to provide an easy way of comparing the text of one topic against other candidate topics for reuse. While this visualization resembles typical interfaces for the popular diff algorithm [13] a key difference here is that we are interested in commonalities, rather than in differences. Furthermore, text is split into smaller units, as explained in Section 4.1, which are compared combinatorially where the relative order of the paragraphs is not important. A screenshot of this interface is shown in Figure 5.

The interface is organized as follows. At the top of the screen there is one topic, which we call the focus topic. This is the one that was shift-clicked in the previous visualization. At the bottom there are up to five topics, which we call the neighboring topics. These are the most similar topics and they are connected to the focus topic as indicated by the previous graph. When hovering over each paragraph of the focus topic, the most similar paragraph in the neighboring topics are also highlighted. A bar chart on the right of the

focus topic allows quick identification of similar paragraphs, which in turn indicate potential topics for reuse. On the top left of the screen, the number of neighboring topics shown at the bottom can be adjusted, and the context graph of this panel shows the subset of the topic graph that is being explored.

The visualization shows different similarities depending on the context in which they are applied, namely: "topic similarity" and "paragraph similarity". The topic similarity is just the maximum paragraph similarity of the topic. The paragraph similarity that is shown below the neighboring topics corresponds to the highlighted paragraph. The paragraph similarity shown in the histogram corresponds to the maximum paragraph similarity between the paragraph aligned with the histogram bar and the most similar paragraph in the neighboring topics. This visualization can be accessed from the previous one after the clicking of the "Compare" button. Source code has been made available online[8].

5.4 Preliminary Feedback on the Tools from Technical Authors

The interactive tools were presented to the previously mentioned four technical authors to obtain a preliminary feedback on the tool. Due to the fact that technical authors were distributed geographically in different cities and countries, interaction was through a web survey and not in real time. Although the similarity algorithm underlying the visual interfaces can be changed interactively, for the author evaluation we restricted ourselves to LCS, as this was the method that performed the most consistently in our experiments.

A negative aspect we noticed was that some authors expressed a rather general concern for the tool, especially with the graph, of being distracting as opposed to a feature that could potentially improve efficiency. One author reported on using command line tools, such as the unix command "grep", to manually find similar instances of text in other topics. Future designs could integrate some of these text-oriented functionalities so that authors can get the best out of visual and non-visual types of interaction. One author reported a lack of a clear understanding of what the graph was representing. We think that this could have been alleviated by providing a real time interaction with the author and providing a basic level of training for the tool. In addition, making the interfaces intuitive and hiding any unnecessary complexity seem to be an important aspect for authors to embrace this type of technology.

We also had some encouraging comments, such as: "*This would be useful for large user docs with many procedures and similar GUIs that you could quickly discover similarities and opportunities to reuse content. Often these topics are redundant but over the course of 100+ pages you may not catch all the opportunities to reuse content unless you compared each topic side by side. An option like this interface would save a lot of time both in discovering reuse opportunities and in updating books for future releases*". Interestingly, this same author, who indicated in three out of the five cases in Section 5.1 that the pairs did not present any reuse opportunity, when presented these same cases using the visual text comparison, i.e. the interface of Figure 5, he or she replied

---

[5]Topics are typically classified in different types depending on their content e.g. task, reference, concept, etc.

[6]http://web.cs.dal.ca/~soto/topicreuse.html

[7]https://github.com/axelsoto/DITA-Topic-Graph

[8]https://github.com/axelsoto/DITA-one-on-many-comparison

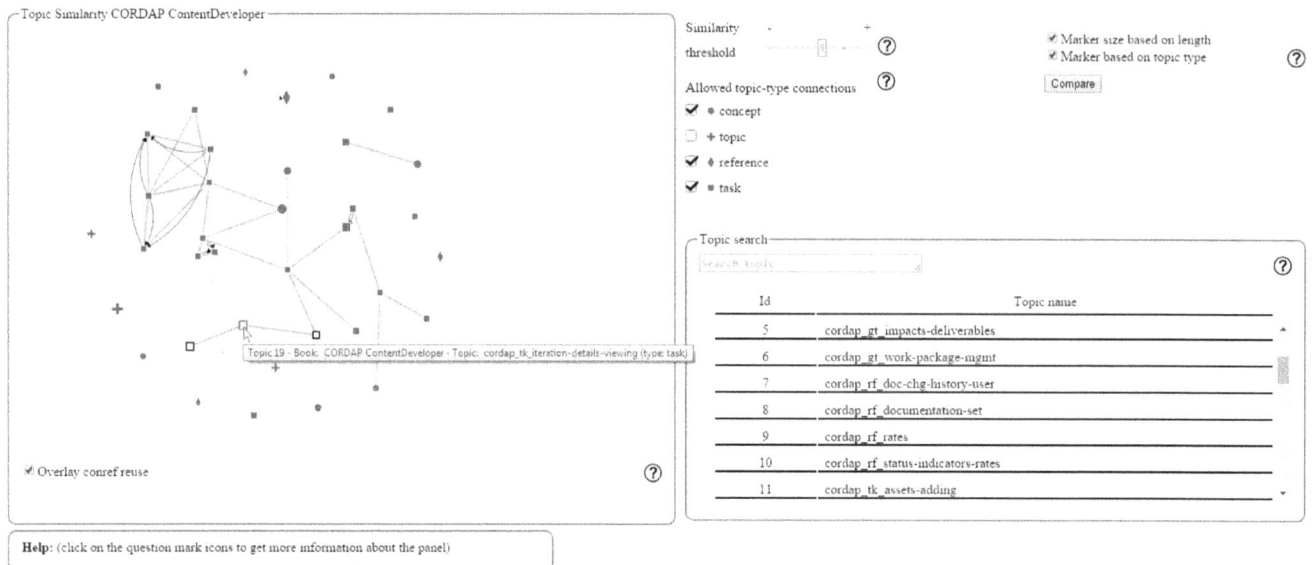

Figure 4: Overall Topic Similarity interactive visualization. Authors can interact with topics and see how they relate to each other.

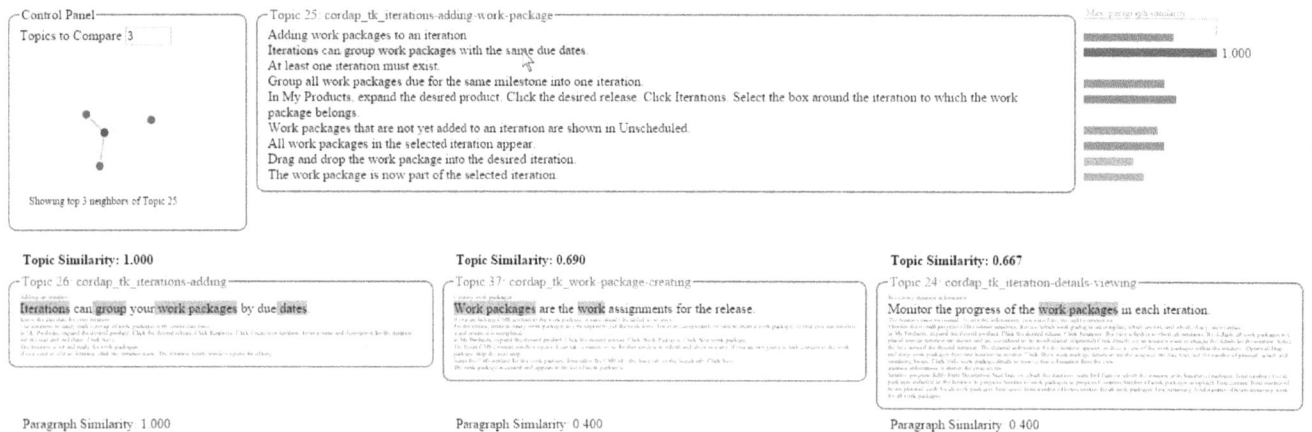

Figure 5: Multiple topic text comparison. Authors can analyze one topic against several ones and identify pieces of text within the topics that are candidate for reuse. For example, topics 25 and 26 seem to have paragraphs that are candidate for reuse despite not being identical.

that all these cases were a good opportunity for reuse. This would suggest that the visual highlighting was helpful in identifying reuse opportunities more easily.

5.5 Design Guidelines for Prospective New Visualizations

The proposed visualizations constitute an innovative approach towards the analysis of an existing set of technical topics. While these interfaces were implemented at a proof-of-concept level, we envision them as a tool to be integrated into the author's regular writing workflow. In this way, possible topics for reuse should be suggested to the author while writing, as opposed to the scenario presented here where topics similarities are analyzed in retrospective. However, appropriate interfaces should be designed so that the visual aids are suggested in a non-obtrusive manner. In addition, after the identification of similar topics, proper interactions should be facilitated for the generation of the

necessary metadata to establish the reuse of a topic with minimal manual effort.

These visualizations would encompass multiple benefits for technical authors, especially for junior authors or those unfamiliar with the topics they may be working on. They would provide ways of identifying at a glance potential topics for reuse, and hence reducing time spent reading and searching for reuse opportunities. In addition, a network visualization of existing topic reuses raises the awareness of the impact on the modification of reused topics.

6. CONCLUSIONS

This paper presented the application of different similarity algorithms in the domain of topic-based technical authoring for text reuse. These similarity algorithms are representative and state-of-the-art approaches within the taxonomy described in Section 2. This study allowed us to compare and to determine the advantages and benefits of different similarity methods for the task of topic reuse. In addition, we have proposed two interactive visualizations that aim at supporting technical writers in their tasks. The first one allows the interactive exploration of a collection of topics and their similarity, while the second one allows comparing and inspecting commonalities of a topic against other similar topics.

We found LCS to be the best performing algorithm to detect existing (conref) reuse cases. While GTM performed slightly worse for our ground-truth, its capacity of capturing semantic similarity allows finding potential reuse candidates between topic pairs that may be missed by the other methods. LSH finds a high-percentage of near-duplicates in a considerably lower complexity time. Regarding the interactive visualizations, preliminary feedback suggested that this type of technologies could have an important impact on authors' productivity, considering that much of their work is manually intensive, and also that they would not trust on any fully automatic tool.

As future work we plan to combine the different strengths of the similarity algorithms. In this way, a hybrid approach that takes the output of all methods can be obtained. This is in alignment with other approaches presented elsewhere for the tasks of plagiarism and paraphrase identification [3, 26]. One important challenge to address is to obtain first a high-quality ground-truth dataset that goes beyond the use of existing reused topics. This can be achieved from the manual annotation of a large set of topic pairs or from a time-stamped repository, where the evolution of topics at different points in time can be captured. In the latter case, we could determine how topics look before and after reuse. Such a high-quality ground-truth dataset would allow us to experiment with different parameterizations for the similarity methods, without the risk of overfitting to the particular case we considered in this paper.

Another important extension would be to study whether authors could also take a more important role in controlling certain method parameters, such as the acceptable rate of false positives or false negatives. For instance, a lower false positive rate can be obtained by increasing the granularity of the textual units, while a lower false negative rate can be obtained by giving more importance to a semantic-based similarity algorithm, like GTM, or by increasing the number of bands in LSH. Finally, another interesting research direction would be to study the application of our approaches in a real-time context, where users get support as they write, as opposed to an *a posteriori* analysis as presented here.

7. ACKNOWLEDGMENTS

This work was carried out with the aid of grant 2013-LACREG-07 from the International Development Research Centre, Ottawa, Canada and a CALDO-FAPESP grant (Proc. 2013/50380-0). Brazilian researchers are also supported by grants from CNPq (205291/2014-7) and FAPESP (2011/22749-8), and researchers based in Canada by grants from NSERC and a contract from Innovatia Inc.

8. ADDITIONAL AUTHORS

Additional authors: Rosane Minghim (Instituto de Ciências Matemáticas e de Computação, Universidade de São Paulo, email: rminghim@icmc.usp.br) and Maria Cristina Ferreira de Oliveira (Instituto de Ciências Matemáticas e de Computação, Universidade de São Paulo, email: cristina@icmc.usp.br).

9. REFERENCES

[1] Darwin information typing architecture (DITA) version 1.2 - OASIS standard http://docs.oasis-open.org/dita/v1.2/spec/DITA1.2-spec.html.

[2] J. Baptista. Pragmatic DITA on a budget. In *Proceedings of the 26th Annual ACM International Conference on Design of Communication*, pages 193–198. ACM, 2008.

[3] D. Bär, T. Zesch, and I. Gurevych. Text reuse detection using a composition of text similarity measures. In *Proceedings of the International Conference on Computational Linguistics*, volume 1, pages 167–184, 2012.

[4] A. Z. Broder, M. Charikar, A. M. Frieze, and M. Mitzenmacher. Min-wise independent permutations. In *Proceedings of the 30th Annual ACM Symposium on Theory of Computing*, pages 327–336. ACM, 1998.

[5] M. Büchler, A. Geßner, T. Eckart, and G. Heyer. Unsupervised detection and visualisation of textual reuse on ancient greek texts. *Journal of the Chicago Colloquium on Digital Humanities and Computer Science*, 1(2), 2010.

[6] F. Y. L. Chin and C. K. Poon. A fast algorithm for computing longest common subsequences of small alphabet size. *Journal of Information Processing*, 13(4):463–469, 1991.

[7] P. Clough and M. Stevenson. Developing a corpus of plagiarised short answers. *Language Resources and Evaluation*, 45(1):5–24, 2011.

[8] S. Duszynski, J. Knodel, and M. Becker. Analyzing the source code of multiple software variants for reuse potential. In *18th Working Conference on Reverse Engineering (WCRE) 2011*, pages 303–307, Oct 2011.

[9] A. Gionis, P. Indyk, and R. Motwani. Similarity search in high dimensions via hashing. In *Proceedings of the 25th International Conference on Very Large Data Bases*, pages 518–529, 1999.

[10] B. Gipp and N. Meuschke. Citation pattern matching algorithms for citation-based plagiarism detection: greedy citation tiling, citation chunking and longest common citation sequence. In *Proceedings of the 11th ACM Symposium on Document Engineering*, pages 249–258. ACM, 2011.

[11] N. Harrison. The Darwin information typing architecture (DITA): Applications for globalization. In *Proceedings of International Professional Communication Conference*, pages 115–121. IEEE, 2005.

[12] M. Henzinger. Finding near-duplicate web pages: A large-scale evaluation of algorithms. In *Proceedings of the 29th Annual International ACM SIGIR Conference on Research and Development in Information Retrieval*, pages 284–291. ACM, 2006.

[13] J. W. Hunt and M. MacIlroy. *An algorithm for differential file comparison*. Bell Laboratories, 1976.

[14] R. W. Irving and C. Fraser. Two algorithms for the longest common subsequence of three (or more) strings. In *Proceedings of the Third Annual*

Symposium on Combinatorial Pattern Matching, CPM '92, pages 214–229. Springer-Verlag, 1992.

[15] A. Islam, E. Milios, and V. Kešelj. Text similarity using google tri-grams. In *Advances in Artificial Intelligence*, pages 312–317. Springer, 2012.

[16] S. Jänicke, A. Geßner, M. Büchler, and G. Scheuermann. Visualizations for text re-use. In *Proceedings of the 5th International Conference on Information Visualization Theory and Applications*, pages 59–70, 2014.

[17] J. Leskovec, A. Rajaraman, and J. D. Ullman. *Mining of massive datasets*. Cambridge University Press, 2014.

[18] C. D. Manning, P. Raghavan, and H. Schütze. *Introduction to information retrieval*, volume 1. Cambridge University Press Cambridge, 2008.

[19] R. Mihalcea, C. Corley, and C. Strapparava. Corpus-based and knowledge-based measures of text semantic similarity. In *Proceedings of the 21st National Conference on Artificial Intelligence*, volume 6, pages 775–780, 2006.

[20] C. Paris, K. Vander Linden, M. Fischer, A. Hartley, L. Pemberton, R. Power, and D. Scott. A support tool for writing multilingual instructions. In *International Joint Conference on Artificial Intelligence*, volume 14, pages 1398–1404, 1995.

[21] M. Potthast, M. Hagen, M. Völske, and B. Stein. Crowdsourcing interaction logs to understand text reuse from the web. In *Proceedings of the 51st Annual Meeting of the Association for Computational Linguistics*, pages 1212–1221, 2013.

[22] A. Rockley, S. Manning, and C. Cooper. *DITA 101: Fundamentals of DITA for Authors and Managers*. Soc. Technical Communication, FAIRFAX, VA, USA, 2010.

[23] M. Sanchez-Perez, G. Sidorov, and A. Gelbukh. The winning approach to text alignment for text reuse detection at PAN 2014. *Notebook for PAN at CLEF*, pages 1004–1011, 2014.

[24] M. Slaney and M. Casey. Locality-sensitive hashing for finding nearest neighbors. *Signal Processing Magazine, IEEE*, 25(2):128–131, 2008.

[25] D. Smith, R. Cordell, and E. Dillon. Infectious texts: Modeling text reuse in nineteenth-century newspapers. In *2013 IEEE International Conference on Big Data*, pages 86–94, Oct 2013.

[26] N. P. Vo, S. Magnolini, and O. Popescu. Paraphrase identification and semantic similarity in twitter with simple features. In *The 3rd International Workshop on Natural Language Processing for Social Media*, page 10, 2015.

Exploring Scholarly Papers Through Citations

Angelo Di Iorio
Department of Computer
Science and Engineering
University of Bologna, Italy
angelo.diiorio@unibo.it

Raffaele Giannella
Department of Computer
Science and Engineering
University of Bologna, Italy
raffaele.giannella@studio.unibo.it

Francesco Poggi
Department of Computer
Science and Engineering
University of Bologna, Italy
fpoggi@cs.unibo.it

Silvio Peroni
Department of Computer
Science and Engineering
University of Bologna, Italy
silvio.peroni@unibo.it

Fabio Vitali
Department of Computer
Science and Engineering
University of Bologna, Italy
fabio.vitali@unibo.it

ABSTRACT

Bibliographies are fundamental components of academic papers and both the scientific research and its evaluation are fundamentally organized around the correct examination and classification of scientific bibliographies. Currently, most digital libraries publish bibliographic information about their content for free, and many include the citations (outgoing and in some cases even incoming) to the papers they manage. Unfortunately no sophistication is spent for these lists: monolithic pieces of text where it is even difficult to tell automatically the authors, the title and publication details, and where users are provided with no mechanisms to filter and access full context of each citation. For instance, there is no way to know in which sentence a work was cited (the *citation context*) and why (the *citation function*).

In this paper we introduce a novel environment for navigating, filtering and making sense of citations. The interface, called BEX, exploits data freely available in a Link Open Dataset about scholarly papers; end-user testing proved its efficacy and usability.

Categories and Subject Descriptors

H.5.2 [**Information Systems**]: Information Interfaces and Presentations—*User Interfaces (D.2.2, H.1.2, I.3.6)*

Keywords

Scholarly data visualization; Information interfaces and presentation; Semantic publishing; Citations

1. INTRODUCTION

Bibliographies are the most distinguishable peculiarity of the scientific communication. Researchers as a habit situate their work within a community of like-minded colleagues whose contribution is revered, appreciated, criticized, or possibly even ridiculed, but in any case explicitly acknowledged and mentioned, and the accuracy and completeness of such mentions constitute a substantial means to evaluate the soundness and acceptability of the scientific communication itself.

In fact, researchers spend a lot of time exploring bibliographies: when approaching new research areas, when reviewing papers, when writing papers, they use bibliographies for exploring a discipline and for building the network of semantic connections of its topics. It is not a case that digital libraries of scholarly papers - such as ACM DL, IEEE Xplore DL, etc. - show bibliographic references and incoming citations in separate lists that can be freely examined often even when the full text of the paper is not publicly available.

Yet, digital libraries publish bibliographies as monolithic units that cannot be easily processed as separate and autonomous items. Consider, for instance, the frequent task of checking the freshness of references of an academic paper: there is no better way to do this than inspecting each reference and manually filtering outdated ones. Similarly, counting self-citations requires users to manually inspect the references and item by item compare the authors to those of the one providing the bibliography. While these tasks are not a big deal for a single paper, they become fairly time-consuming and difficult when dealing with a big number of papers, such as when dealing with the full set of submissions to a conference or a special issue of a journal. An aggravating factor is that these checks and evaluate tasks often have to be completed under some serious pressure: who cannot confess of having written a review right before the (extended) deadline? Or having made the initial selection of accepted papers for a conference just a few hours before delivering the acceptance letter? Or even arranged a related works section in short time?

In this paper we discuss how to support researchers and academics in these daily tasks, making it easy to access data in bibliographies that otherwise are hard to find, inspect and filter. We break the problem in two parts.

- *Rich data*: on the one hand, we need to identify and classify bibliographics so that rich data can be published about papers (e.g. author list, publication year, venue, etc.) and citation networks, both incoming and outgoing references.

DocEng'15, September 8-11, 2015, Lausanne, Switzerland.
© 2015 ACM. ISBN 978-1-4503-3307-8/15/09 ...$15.00.
DOI: http://dx.doi.org/10.1145/2682571.2797065.

In particular, in the last few years we witnessed an ever increasing interest in making bibliographic data available as Linked Open Data (LOD): DBLP++[1], JISC OpenCitation corpus (OCC) [20] and Nature Publishing Group Linked Data Platform (NPG LDP)[2] are just some representative examples of such effort. Unfortunately, although a lot of information is available in these datasets, the landscape is still fragmented and a lot of useful data are still missing or unevenly provided by publishers.

For instance, none of the datasets we are aware of contains information about the *citation contexts* - defined in [16] as "the sentences of the original papers where a particular work was cited" - or the *citation functions*, defined in [22] as "the reasons why papers are cited". Having such data can be very helpful to understand the nature of citations and to give them more or less importance.

- *Intuitive interfaces* allowing users to read and make sense of the bibliographic data - for instance, to filter data, to navigate paper collections, to explore citations, along with their functions and contexts, in an easy and intuitive way.

This work builds upon a framework for extracting and describing rich data about bibliographies presented in previous works and focuses on the second aspect, introducing a novel environment for accessing rich data about citations. To do so, we briefly present the Semantic Lancet Triplestore, a LOD dataset used as backend for BEX.

The structure of the paper is as follows. Section 2 describes some related works; some issues in daily tasks on citations, along with possible improvements, are investigated in Section 3; Section 4 gives some background on the Semantic Lancet Triplestore; BEX is fully describe in Section 5; the evaluation of the current prototype is presented in Section 6 before concluding the paper.

2. RELATED WORKS

A large variety of systems support the exploration of scholarly data, some of them providing an interface to a specific repository of bibliographic information, others integrating multiple data sources to provide access to a richer set of data and navigation functionalities. The most famous academic search engine is probably Google Scholar[3], which provides search and citation services, supporting access to the scholarly literature. DBLP[4] is another well-known computer science bibliography portal. CiteSeerX[5] focuses instead on large-scale integration and indexing of research papers, and includes mechanisms for suggesting relevant papers. These systems mainly focus on providing a good interface for publication search and are not designed to support sensemaking tasks in the academic domain.

On the contrary, Microsoft Academic Search[6] provides a variety of visualizations, including co-authorship graphs,

publication trends, and co-authorship paths between authors. In a similar way Arnetminer[7] also offers different visualizations and provides support for expert search and trend analysis. [10] is another visual analytics tool that provides multiple coordinated views in order to reveal trends, support the investigation of connections, and describe activities throughout conference communities.

BiblioViz [18] is based on the principle of minimal visual representation, and provides a compact, comprehensive and extensible system for visualizing bibliography information based on two techniques: a bidimensional tabular view, and a tridimensional network representation. Action Science Explorer [4] is another interesting example of visual analytic tool that leverages statistics, citation text extraction, natural language summarization, advanced filtering capabilities and network visualization to see citation patterns and identify clusters.

3. RESEARCH-RELATED TASKS ON BIBLIOGRAPHIES

Several experimental studies have confirmed their importance of bibliographies for the research community. Just to name a few: [13] surveyed more than two thousand American researchers working on natural science, engineering and medical science and showed that their primary search tools are citation databases, followed by general search engines; [12] showed similar results by interviewing social science faculty members in Taiwan.

The community has also investigated how citations and papers are read, and how they are actually exploited for research-related tasks. [2] surveyed thousands of faculty members for a long period (28 years, since 1977 to 2005). The results were very interesting: the number of papers being read is constantly increasing but people tend to cite a limited set of papers. One of the reasons is that they rely more on searching than on browsing and give priority to those papers highly ranked in digital libraries. The same paradox was noticed by [5]: ranking papers by their incoming citations made researchers cite the same papers that others have cited, thus narrowing the overall citation patterns. The research also showed how the amount of time spent for reading each paper is ever decreasing. This is also connected to the large number of digital publications available today: the overall time for reading increases but people have to deal with a huge amount of information and cannot help reading them rapidly [7].

In this section we focus on some of these tasks, in particular to those that researchers perform on bibliographies. This set of tasks is the results of an analysis based on the experience of our research group and some discussions with colleagues of our department. We organized our discussion around the roles played by a researcher and the tasks performed for each role. The researcher is first of all a *reader*, who reads articles and navigate them through citations. The process of finding relevant works is very common when writing new papers and project proposals: indeed, a researcher is also an *author*. The research community also relies on peer-review processes, which require researchers to also act as *reviewers* or *editors*. When reviewing papers, a researcher uses citations and checks, for instance, the number of self-citations or the publication year of cited papers.

[1]http://dblp.l3s.de/dblp++.php
[2]http://data.nature.com
[3]http://scholar.google.com
[4]http://www.informatik.uni-trier.de/~ley/db/
[5]http://citeseerx.ist.psu.edu/
[6]http://academic.research.microsoft.com/
[7]http://arnetminer.org/

Table 1: Common tasks on bibliographies, for different classes of users.

No.	Role	Goal/Task
1	reader/author	**Goal (G1)** : build/update a bibliography [of recent papers] on a given topic • **T1a:** find authoritative papers on a given topic • **T1b:** find recent papers on a given topic • **T1c:** navigate citation networks to find other interesting/relevant papers
2	reviewer	**Goal (G2)** : evaluate if a paper is up-to-date • **T2a:** check the publication year of the cited papers • **T2b:** check if relevant papers are missing in the bibliography
3	reviewer, editor	**Goal (G3):** evaluate how much a work is self-referential • **T3:** count self-citations
4	reviewer, editor	**Goal (G4):** evaluate if a paper fits the scope of a journal/conference • **T4a:** read the abstract; if possible, the whole paper • **T4b:** check the bibliography and search cited papers published in the same venue • **T4c:** check the relevance of the other cited papers (published in other venues)
5	evaluator	**Goal (G5):** evaluate the impact of a paper • **T5a:** check how many times a paper is cited • **T5b:** how citations have evolved • **T5c:** check why a paper is cited
6	evaluator	**Goal (G6):** evaluate the impact of a researcher • **T6a:** check how many times the work of a candidate is cited • **T6b:** check how citations have evolved • **T6c:** check why a candidate is cited
7	event organizer	**Goal (G7):** find potential participants • **T7a:** find papers about topics relevant to the event • **T7b:** check authors of relevant papers

Citations are also increasingly used for evaluation purposes. Researchers are then asked to be part of academic boards in charge of evaluating research products. Our analysis covers such a scenario with a specific role: *evaluator*. Researchers are involved in organizing scientific events, thus we added the role of *event organizer*. Note that there are many other tasks characterizing each of these roles but they are left out of discussion, since they are not specific on bibliographies.

Table 1 summarises our analysis. The discussion uses the well-known terminology of [8]: the term *goal* is used to indicate a final objective a user wishes to achieve, a *task* is a sequence of one or more activities the user thinks are required to achieve a goal. Each task is specific of a peculiar user *role*. Note also that we did not decompose each task in hierarchical subtasks, for the sake of simplicity.

The first goal (G1) consists in building or updating a bibliography on a given topic. A common approach is to use keyword-based search tools, scan the list of returned papers and filter potentially relevant ones (T1a, T1b). Researchers might read abstracts to have a clearer idea of each paper. Further candidates are often searched by analysing citation networks (T1c), as shown by several experimental studies [12] [23]: starting from a list of relevant papers, incoming and outgoing citations are scanned and, in turn, new candidates are analysed and, if relevant, added to the list. The criteria used to discern among papers may vary a lot: considering the total number of citations may be a suitable indicator to identify seminal papers, whereas it may fail when searching for recent developments or cutting edge works. In the second case, other criteria such as the publication date are more convenient. In all cases, the researchers have to

inspect the list of citations and to manually find relevant information.

The second group of tasks are performed by researchers as reviewers. To evaluate if a paper is up-to-date (G2), they inspect the bibliography and look at the publication year of each item (T2a). Furthermore they check if any relevant recent paper is not cited (T2b). These operations are still manual. One of the reasons is that, in almost all cases, papers under revision are PDFs and the bibliographic references cannot be processed as separate units.

The same applies to following two tasks. The first one covers the analysis of self-citations in order to understand how much a work is self referential (G3): in fact, the reviewers/editors check how many cited papers are written by the same authors, or some of them (T3). The editors/reviewers might also want to check the number of papers cited by a paper submitted to a journal and published in the same journal (T4b). That might be an indicator of the suitability of that paper for that journal (G4).

The evaluation of research works (G5) and researchers (G6) is often performed by counting the incoming citations to each research work and by aggregating them for further analysis. Thus, evaluators need to easily access information about the number of times each paper is cited (T5a). It is also interesting to know how citations are distributed over time (T5b). Tasks 5 and 6 are widely supported today. One aspect that is still under-estimated is the nature of the citations. In fact, not all citations are equal: some are given just for information, some as necessary background, some refers to a work the citing paper is an extension of. It would be useful to store and be able to analyse citations together with the sentence to which they belong to (*citation context*), or together with information about the reason why a paper is cited (*citation function*, T5c). A time perspective is helpful here. For instance, we can expect that an important work is referenced for information or used as background for many years, but if it keep being extended, or some methods therein contained are used for a long time, it means it still plays an active and important role.

There is a further common task that researchers perform by exploring papers and citations: finding experts in a given topic or simply people who are interested in that topic (T7a, T7b). These people usually are searched among the authors of relevant papers — that, as discussed so far, are found by exploiting citations too. Such expert finding task might be useful, for instance, when searching for potential participants to a scientific events (G7).

3.1 Performing tasks with existing tools

These tasks are successfully performed today by accessing digital libraries and databases of bibliographic records. Nonetheless searching the relevant information for a given task is not always simple and direct. The problem can be studied from two orthogonal perspectives: *availability of data* and *interface*.

First of all, it depends on the way data are structured and made available. In fact, most of the existing repositories do not offer APIs to access data (e.g. Google Scholar) or offer partial APIs that do not cover all needed information (e.g. ScienceDirect and Scopus). Consider, for instance, the case of citation contexts and functions. Such data would be valuable tools to better characterize citations and to assess their impact. Though, none of the platforms we are aware of make these data available.

Even if some information is stored in the repositories, it is not directly processable by the users. Let us consider the list of bibliographic references. These lists are often made available as separate content from the full-text of the papers, for instance in ACM or IEEE Xplore DLs (where they can be freely accessed even if the PDF is subject to payment); on the other hand, they are treated as 'monolithic' units: the users can export citations and navigate to the cited/citing papers but they are not allowed to show only some references or to quickly access some information. If a researcher wants to read the abstract and the bibliography of a cited paper, for instance, he/she has to open it a separate tab and to interrupt the navigation. Similarly, there is no way to filter items in bibliographies automatically.

Some filtering capabilities on bibliographies are actually already available to the users. For instance, Elsevier's Scopus allows users to order the lists of references and to apply various filters. Such ordering options, on the other hand, are available only on lists of papers returned by a search (for instance, papers on a given topic, or written by a given author, etc.) or lists of papers citing a given one. It is not possible to work on the whole bibliography of a paper or to keep filters active while surfing bibliographies.

In the next sections we present a novel interface, called BEX, that makes all these actions straightforward and that helps researchers in completing most of the tasks discussed so far. To do so, we also need to introduce the Semantic Lancet Triplestore, a rich knowledge-base on scholarly papers and citations that is used as backend for BEX.

4. EXTRACTING AND MODELLING CITATIONS: SPAR AND SEMANTIC LANCET

In the last few years, different research groups in both academia and industry have started to work for pushing the research communication and the scholarly publishing to the next step of evolution of the whole publishing domain, characterised by the *Semantic Publishing* movement. Basically speaking, Semantic Publishing stands for the use of Web and Semantic Web technologies to enhance a published document such as a journal article so as to enable the definition of formal representations of its meaning, facilitate its automatic discovery, enable its linking to semantically related articles, provide access to data within the article in actionable form, and allow integration of data between papers [14].

Along the lines of the Semantic Publishing movement and guidelines, we have started the *Semantic Lancet Project* (`http://www.semanticlancet.eu`), which is focused on building a Linked Open Dataset of scholarly publications. The aim of the project is twofold. On the one hand, we have developed a series of scripts that allow us to produce proper RDF data compliant with the *Semantic Publishing and Referencing* (*SPAR*) *Ontologies* (http://www.sparontologies.net) [14], which are a suite of orthogonal and complementary ontology modules for creating comprehensive machine-readable RDF metadata for all aspects of publishing domain. On the other hand, we have made publicly-available the *Semantic Lancet Triplestore* (*SLT*), i.e., a freely available LOD dataset that includes rich data about scholarly papers, that range from a large network of citations (that also includes citation contexts and functions) to semantically-enriched abstracts, from provenance data to time-aware descriptions of the scientific production. Currently the STL contains data about all papers in the Web Semantics journal published by Elsevier, but our plan is to extend it incrementally.

The SPAR Ontologies that are used in the SLT for describing the particular aspects of interest for this paper (i.e., citations and abstracts of papers) are the following:

1. the *Citation Typing Ontology* (*CiTO*)[8] is an ontology that enables the characterisation of the nature or type of citations, both factually and rhetorically;

2. the *Citation Counting and Context Characterisation Ontology* (*C4O*)[9] is an ontology that permits the number of in-text citations of a cited source to be recorded, along with the number of citations a cited entity has received globally on a particular date;

3. the *Document Components Ontology* (*DoCO*)[10] is an ontology that provides a structured vocabulary of document components, both structural (e.g., block, inline, paragraph, section, chapter) and rhetorical (e.g., abstract, introduction, discussion, acknowledgements, reference list, figure, appendix), enabling these components, and documents composed of them, to be described in RDF.

As shown in Fig. 1, several entities defined in the aforementioned ontologies have been used in the SLT for modelling citations and abstracts of papers in a semantic fashion.

---

[8]http://purl.org/spar/cito
[9]http://purl.org/spar/c4o
[10]http://purl.org/spar/doco

In particular, they allow us to describe four different kinds of objects that are relevant for this work:

- *in-text reference pointer*, i.e., the entity present in the body text (e.g., "[5]") of a citing work that denotes a particular bibliographic reference in the reference list or a footnote. In scientific literature, this in-text reference pointer can be presented in different forms;

- *citation context*, i.e., the textual content of that component of the published paper (i.e., the sentence) within which an in-text reference pointer appears, which provides the rhetorical rationale for the existence of that citation;

- *citation function*, i.e., the author's reason for citing a given paper, that can be either factual (e.g., if the author of the citing entity describes work that uses a method detailed in the cited entity) or rhetorical (e.g., if the author of the citing entity agrees with statements or ideas presented in the cited entity);

- *abstract*, i.e., the text of papers abstract and its representation in RDF according to ontology design patterns and linguistic frames.

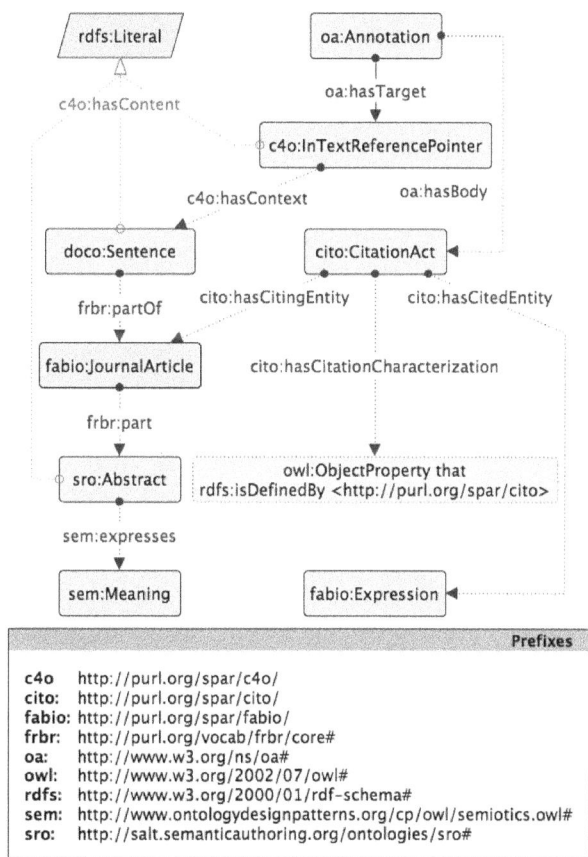

Figure 1: The Graffoo diagram [6] of the ontological entities used in the SLT for describing citation functions, in-text reference pointers and papers abstract.

As example, the RDF representation (in Turtle) of the abstract of a paper included in the SLT and of one of its citation (including its function) is available on-line[11].

The semantic characterisation of abstracts and the specification of citation functions are created automatically starting from the actual content of the paper in consideration. The semantic abstracts are generated by a module of the Semantic Lancet Project developed for this purpose. In particular it relies on FRED[12] [15], which is a tool that implements deep machine reading methods based on Discourse Representation Theory, Linguistic Frames, and Ontology Design Patterns, for deriving a logical representation (expressed as OWL) of natural language sentences. The output of this module is then used by the *Abstract Finder* (`http://www.semanticlancet.eu/abstractfinder`), which is a service for searching relevant papers according to their textual and semantic abstracts, by exploiting the semantic information about concepts, events, roles and named entities included in the semantic abstract.

The citation functions are extracted by another module that allows one to capture them by means of *CiTalO* [3]. CiTalO is a chain of tools for identifying automatically the nature of citations according to CiTO, in a way that is comparable with humans. A run of this module queries the SLT by finding all the in-text reference pointers (and the related citation sentences) and links them to their related citation functions as returned by CiTalO. The output of this module together with the Abstract Finder service are used by BEX for supporting the navigation of the SLT.

5. EXPLORING SEMANTIC LANCET DATA ON CITATIONS: BEX

The Bibliography EXplorer (BEX)[13] is an interactive web-based tool aimed at supporting the analysis, exploration and sense-making process of papers and citations available in the Semantic Lancet Triplestore. The BEX design and the consequent user interaction are driven by Shneiderman's Information Seeking Mantra [19]: "Overview first, zoom and filter, then details-on-demand".

The navigation starts with two search functionalities: besides searching a title, the user can also search relevant papers according to their content. This search is performed by calling the Abstract Finder service[14] described above. Other services, for instance based on full-text search or other mining techniques, can be integrated with a few modifications to BEX. Thus, through BEX a researcher can write in the search box a tentative abstract for her/his paper to retrieve meaningful papers that match with it from a pure textual but also semantic point of view. Fig. 2 shows the main interface of BEX and the output of a search.

Search results are organized as a list of papers, ordered by default from the most recent to the oldest one. Through the sorting box at the top of the interface, the user can easily define custom criterion to order the results (i.e. year, number of citations) and the order type (i.e. ascending or descending). For each returned paper, BEX shows a summary of basic information (e.g. title, publication year, author list,

---

[11]http://eelst.cs.unibo.it/DOCENG-2015/slt-example.ttl
[12]FRED: http://wit.istc.cnr.it/stlab-tools/fred
[13]http://eelst.cs.unibo.it:8089/
[14]http://www.semanticlancet.eu/abstractfinder

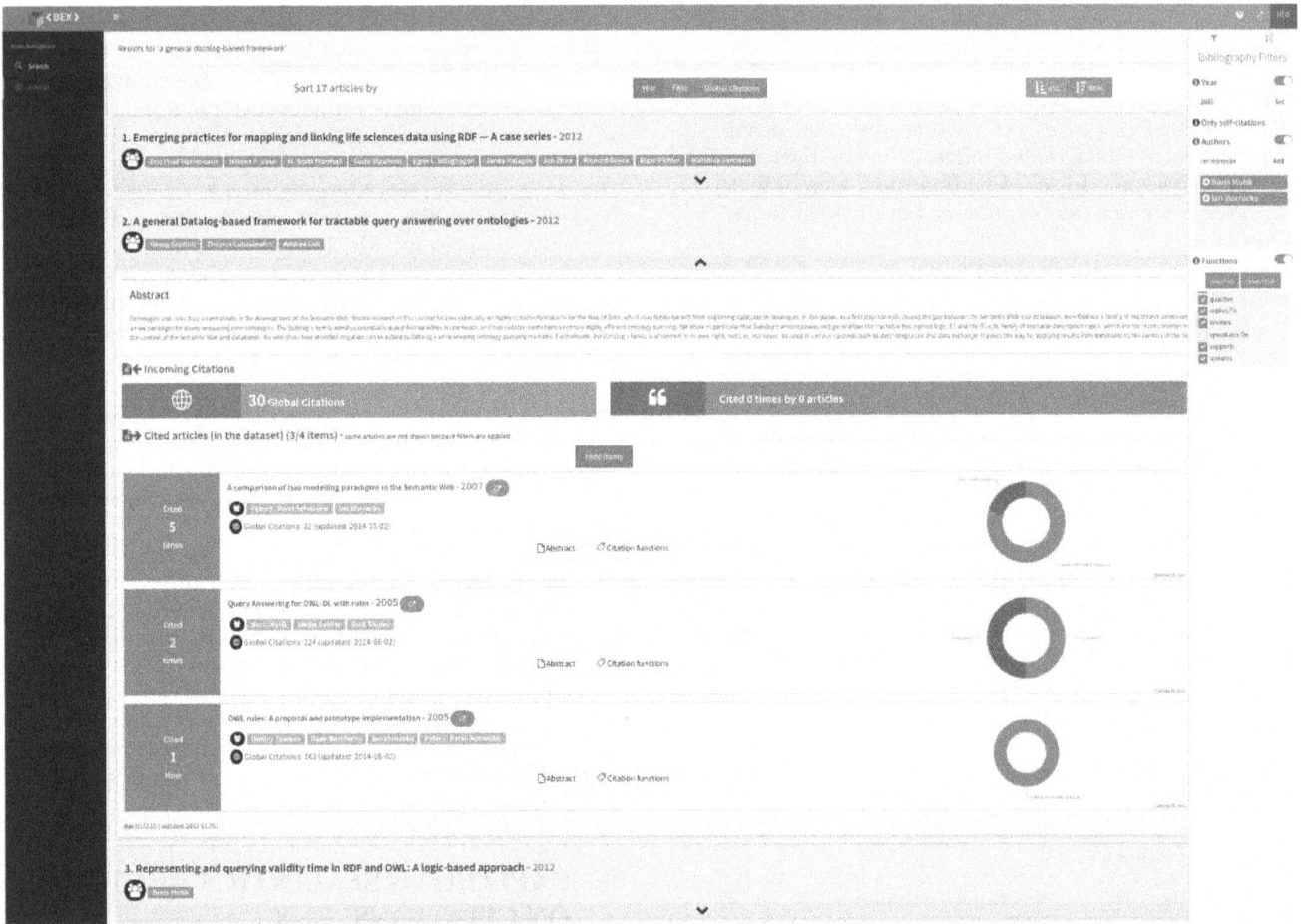

Figure 2: The main interface of BEX and the list of papers returned by a search. Abstracts and data on citations can be collapsed/expanded on the user's demand.

etc.) and a link to the paper official page on Elsevier's ScienceDirect.

In order to gather more information about a paper in the list, the user can open a sliding box showing the full abstract and data about citations, organized in two separate sections: *outgoing* and *incoming*.

By clicking on the "Show Items" button, the user can get access to the information about the *outgoing citations*, as shown in the central part of Fig. 2. BEX organizes the cited papers in a vertical list, and for each paper it shows, from left to right, the following information: the number of times in which the paper is referenced by the paper under examination, some general information about the paper, and a piechart summarizing the number and type of citations received from the focus paper. Moreover, abstract and citation contexts are shown in popups windows.

In the *incoming citation* section, two counters show the number of *global* and *internal* citations received by the paper under examination. The term 'global' here indicates citations for a paper as counted by external services (Scopus); the term 'internal' indicates the citations given by papers described in our dataset (published in the Journal of Web Semantics).

Further details about the citation functions of incoming internal citations are available. This information is pre-sented in a popup window organized in three parts: a pie chart gives an overview of the number and type of incoming citations (top left), a column chart shows the distribution of the citation functions on a time axis (top right), and details about the citation contexts are presented in the bottom. In the two charts at the top of the page, different colors are used to encode the function of each single citation, and citations with the same function are grouped together. Finally, the last component shows, for each paper citing the paper under focus, the list of the citation contexts.

6. EVALUATION

We performed an experimental evaluation in order to assess the efficacy and users' satisfaction in using BEX for research tasks. The tests involved 19 users, with different background and skills.

The testers were asked to use the system[15] to complete four assignments and to fill some questionnaires about their experience. The real test was preceded by a warm-up task, in which the testers were asked to read a short-guide about BEX and to explore it. They were given exactly 5 minutes to become confident with the system.

---

[15]Testers were asked to only use BEX, without any other external tool.

The test included four assignments, each mapped to one of the goals discussed in Section 3 and summarized below:

A1. **Build a bibliography of recent papers on a given topic (Goal G1)** : the testers were asked to find the most cited and the most recent paper about a given topic, together with a list of five papers citing/cited by those two and relevant to the same topic. We expected users to search papers by abstract similarity and to read their bibliographic information (title, publication year and abstract) to complete the assignment.

A2. **Check if a paper is up-to-date (G2)**: the testers were given the title of a paper and were asked to indicate how many of the papers cited by that one have been published since a given date. The assignment could be then completed by searching the paper in BEX and inspecting its bibliography. As discussed in Section 3, such a task is very common when reviewing papers. On the other hand, papers are usually submitted as PDF and BEX cannot be used directly. This is not an issue for the purpose of our test, since we aimed at evaluating the interface only. We used one random paper, already loaded in the dataset. The issue is anyway very interesting and challenging. It could be addressed by implementing automatic processes that extract relevant information on-the-fly and produce a set of (semantic) data to be shown in BEX. We are investigating the integration of existing services like PDFX[16] towards this goal. Note also that these observations are valid for the next assignment as well.

A3. **Evaluate how much a work is self-referential (G3)**: given the title of a paper, the testers were asked to indicate how many self-citations it contains and how many times it was cited by papers written by the same authors (or some of them). Even this assignment can be completed by searching the paper by title and inspecting both the bibliography and the list of papers citing it or using filters.

A4. **Evaluate the impact of a paper (G5)**: the testers were asked to indicate how many times a paper with a given title was cited and for which reasons (in some specific years and overall). The citation counters and functions provided by BEX were expected to help users to complete this assignment.

Note that we have not included any assignment for goal G4 (evaluate if a paper fits the scope of a journal) since SLT only contains the papers published in one single journal at this stage. We also decided to exclude goals G5 and G6 for this test session. The reason was that the corresponding assignment would be too long, requiring users to iterate the same operations on all papers written by a given author, and we wanted to reduce the effort and time required to the testers. The current implementation of BEX, in fact, is mainly focused on the exploration of papers instead of authors. That exploration is anyway very interesting and one of future directions of our research.

Note also that the assignments here are numbered and presented in the same order of their corresponding goals. They were actually given in a different order (by increasing

---

difficulty and duration) but this does not affect the final result.

We also asked testers to indicate which features of BEX they used to complete each assignment, by filling a list of options shown at the end of each assignment – equal for all assignments, thus containing even non-required features, with no suggestion to the testers. The answers to these questions gave us very interesting indications about the use of the interface. These results will be discussed at the end of the section, after investigating BEX efficacy and usability.

6.1 Efficacy

We first studied if testers could complete the assignments with BEX, by manually comparing the answers given by each tester to the expected answers. Though some participants failed to complete some assignments, the overall efficacy was high. Results are summarized in Table 2.

Table 2: Testing efficacy on all four assignments. The values for assignment A1 are partial since there was no fixed expected output (open assignment).

Assign.	Success	Partial	No answer
A1	75,33% *	9,00% *	15,67%
A2	79,00%	21,00%	0,00%
A3	84,50%	10,50%	5,00%
A4	80,67%	12,33%	7,00%

The efficacy on assignment A2 (check if a paper is up-to-date) was lower than we expected. Some users, in fact, listed all papers in bibliography without taking into account their publication year. Only one tester listed one single paper, probably due to a wrong interpretation of the question. Nonetheless, no one complained that the available information was not enough to complete the assignment.

The efficacy on assignment A3 (check if a work is self-referential) was very high. Though not shown in the table, in fact, all users apart from one identified correctly the number of self-citations given by the input paper. The testers confirmed that the presence of visual hints and clear information about self-citations was very helpful to complete the task. The overall score decreases to 84.50% since some users failed in identifying self-citing papers among those citing the input one. Since 4 testers over 19 gave the same value, lower than the expected one, we believe that the testers did not wait for having the full list of citing papers or received only a partial list from the server. A clearer hint about the loading process and some more control is then needed, as discussed in the next section.

The efficacy on assignment A4 (evaluate the impact of a paper) is worth discussing in detail. The overall score is quite high (80.67%). Nonetheless some testers misinterpreted the question about the overall number of citations and used different counters to answers: some reported the number of global citations, others the number of internal citations. Only 13 testers over 19, in fact, answered correctly. This affected the overall efficacy for this assignment. Considering only the questions about citation functions, in fact, the success is higher than 90%.

We discuss A1 at the end since it is the most critical one. The efficacy was acceptable, though not very high. One user

---

[16]http://pdfx.cs.man.ac.uk/

experienced some problems in completing the assignment, due to technical problems in loading the content. Apart from that, all others were able to find the most cited and the most recent papers. Limiting to these two questions, in fact, the efficacy score is 90%. Nonetheless, 8 users had some difficulties in searching relevant papers on a given topic and navigating the large amount of information available in the platform. In the next section we will discuss these usability issues in more detail.

6.2 Usability

After the completion of all assignments, the testers were asked to fill two questionnaires. The first one was a *System Usability Scale* (*SUS*) [1], a well-known questionnaire used for the perception of the usability of a system. It has the advantage of being technology independent and it is reliable even with a very small sample size [17]. The mean SUS score was 64.5 (in a 0 to 100 range). The value shows how the users' satisfaction was quite high though there are still some open issues as discussed in the rest of this section.

In addition to the main SUS scale, we also examined the sub-scales of pure *Usability* and pure *Learnability* [11]. They gave us a more precise characterization of the users' feedback. The mean values for Usability was 62.5 and Learnability was 72.4. This means that the system was perceived as easy to learn but some of its functionalities were not completely clear and users experiences some difficulties in completing the tasks.

In order to go deeper, we also included four open questions in the test:

- What were the most useful features of BEX to help you realise your assignments?

- What were the main weaknesses that BEX exhibited in supporting your assignments?

- Would you suggest to modify any part of BEX?

- Can you think of any additional features that would have helped you to accomplish your assignments?

We subjected the text answers to a qualitative analysis based on *grounded theory* methods. Grounded theory [21] is a method often used in social science to extract relevant concepts from unstructured corpora of natural language resources. In opposition to traditional methods aiming at fitting (and sometimes forcing) the content of the resources into a predefined model, grounded theory aims at having the underlying model emerge "naturally" from the systematic collection by rephrasing, reorganising and interpreting the actual sentences and terms of the resources. We thus believe it is a reasonable tool to examine our questionnaires in order to let important concepts emerge from the text.

We proceeded first with *open coding*, with the purpose of extracting actual relevant sentences – called *codes* – from the texts, and subsequently performed the so-called *axial coding*, which is the rephrasing of the original codes so as to have semantic connections emerge from them and generate concepts. We finally analysed the respective frequency of each emerged concept (defined as the number of codes which contributed to the concept's existence) so as to consider the most important issues arising from the answers. Figure 3 shows the codes that were mentioned by the users.

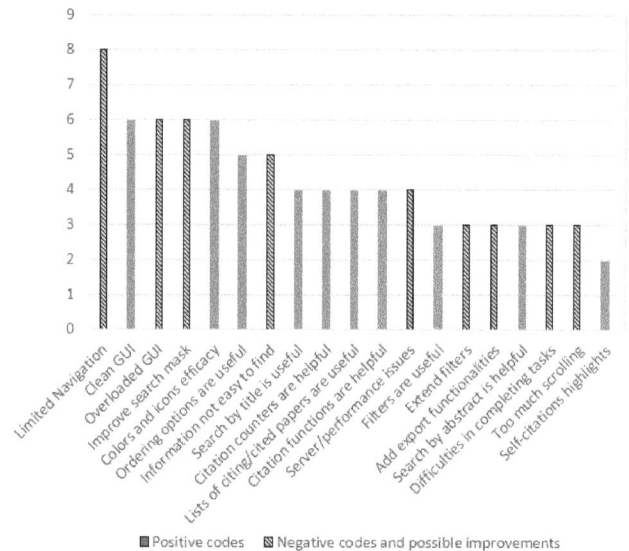

Figure 3: The codes mentioned by at least two users, ordered by their frequency and grouped in positive and negative codes. Negative codes also include suggestions for possible improvements.

We characterized codes as 'positive' (highlighting strengths and functionalities appreciated by the users) and 'negative' (highlighting current limitations and possible improvements).

The overall impression of the testers is encouraging, as shown by the distribution of positive/negative codes.

Some other interesting observations can be distilled from our analysis:

- **Clean GUI with several functions**. Several users appreciated the interface and the set of functionalities made available. In fact they classified as 'useful' most of the features: self-explaining icons (in particular, those on self-citations), citation counters and lists of citations, filters and search options, etc.. The presence of citation contexts and functions was also identified as a key and innovative contribution.

- **Information not easy to find**. The great amount of data and functionalities, on the other hand, confused some testers. Some of them complained that they had to do a lot of actions in order to get the information they were looking for. The fact that some boxes are collapsed by default (so that users have to manually open them) and some content is shown with a large font (and users have to scroll down and risk to get lost) was perceived as a strong limitation.

- **Limited navigation**. One of the most critical issues was the fact that tabs are disabled, so that users are not allowed to open multiple views and to freely surf the knowledge-base. The fact that details of the papers citing a given one are shown in a fixed modal window (that cannot be moved and resized, and requires users to scroll) was also criticized. Overall, the navigation was considered too basic by some users. The possibility of bookmarking papers and surfing the history were also suggested as possible improvements. This also

FEATURE	A1			A2			A3			A4			TOTAL	
search by title	10	53%		19	100%	X	18	95%	X	17	89%	X	64	112%
search by abstract	12	63%	X	0	0%		0	0%		0	0%		12	63%
ordering options on search results	16	84%	X	2	11%		2	11%		3	16%		23	121%
icons and tooltips	11	58%	X	4	21%	X	13	68%	X	12	63%	X	40	53%
paper publication info box	7	37%	X	3	16%	X	2	11%	X	3	16%		15	26%
abstract	3	16%		0	0%		0	0%		0	0%		3	
clickable list of authors	0	0%		0	0%		1	5%		0	0%		1	
bibliography filters	2	11%		2	11%	X	2	11%	X	0	0%		6	16%
bibliography ordering options	3	16%		0	0%	X	0	0%	X	0	0%		3	8%
breadcrumbs	0	0%	X	0	0%		0	0%		0	0%		0	0%
charts	3	16%		0	0%		0	0%		9	47%	X	12	63%
motivations for citations in textual form	2	11%		0	0%		0	0%		8	42%	X	10	53%
citation counters	12	63%	X	4	21%		6	32%		10	53%	X	32	84%
in-line help guide	0	0%	X	1	5%	X	0	0%	X	0	0%		1	1%
other	0	0%		2	11%		1	5%		0	0%		3	

Figure 4: The features of BEX used by the testers to accomplish the assignments.

tell us that the breadcrumb is not evident and should be made available during all navigation phases.

- **Improve search and filters.** Search capabilities were largely used during the test sessions. Nonetheless several users confirmed that the search mask needs to be extended (as a matter of fact we have already implemented further search options, not available at the time of the test). The suggestion is to include a *faceted search*, as already available in most of the existing digital libraries. Filters were also well appreciated and users suggested to extend them to also work on the list of papers citing a given one, the list of papers returned by a search or written by a given author.

- **Add export functionalities**. An interesting extension – that we admittedly had not taken into consideration – is to give users the possibility of exporting information about citations. Not only the lists of papers (both citing and cited by a given one) but also the citation functions and contexts. The idea is to process such information separately and to integrate it with other sources of data. The availability of a public SPARQL end-point for Semantic Lancet LOD, though not visible and relevant for the test, goes exactly in that direction.

- **Server/performance issues.** During some tests the system was particularly slow in loading content, making some tasks very difficult – and in a few cases impossible – to complete. It was due to some technical problems on the SPARQL end-point, since the current installation is not optimized to handle a large volume of requests (indeed we are migrating to a different platform).

6.3 Use of BEX features

The participants were also asked to indicate which features of BEX they used to complete the test. Fig. 4 summarizes their answers, indicating how many testers used each feature for each assignment. For each assignment we also indicate, in the third column, which features we expected testers to use. Note that some of these features were strictly required to complete the assignment (for instance, the "search by title" for assignment A2) while others were

optional (for instance, the in-line guide might be helpful but the assignment could be completed without accessing it).

It is interesting to notice that the behaviour of the testers was not uniform. Let us consider for instance the assignment A2: although all users started searching by title, some of them exploited only the information provided by icons and tooltips, while a few others activated filters. Furthermore, it is interesting to investigate the cases in which testers did not behave as we expected. In the assignment A3, for example, all users searched the paper and most of them looked at the self-citation icon to recognize those written by the same authors, but only two testers used filters. An explanation of such a behavior is that, since the list of paper under examination was very short (only 6 items), the testers have preferred to scan it manually. It is also interesting to notice that the citation functions have been read in two alternative ways (for assignment A4): some users preferred the aggregated information available in charts, while others have accessed the citation contexts and motivations in textual form.

Finally, the last column of the table gives us very useful clues about the overall use of BEX features in performing different tasks. The first comforting consideration concerns BEX functionalities: citation counters, icons, charts and motivations for citations have been largely used by most of the testers. Another consideration is about some possible improvements of BEX interface. For example, none of the testers used bredcrumbs, that are the only mechanism provided by BEX to surf through the navigation history. This is a clear weakness that we have to take in consideration in the next version of the tool. Moreover, by comparing the wide use of the ordering options on search results (available by default in the center of the interface) to bibliography filters and ordering options (that have to be activated by clicking on a small icon), we understand that we should give more emphasis to these last useful functionalities.

7. CONCLUSIONS

In this paper we have introduced the *Bibliography Explorer* (*BEX*), i.e., an interactive web-based tool aimed at supporting the analysis, exploration and sense-making of papers and citations available in the Semantic Lancet Triplestore. In particular, after discussing the most common tasks that researchers perform on bibliographies of a research paper (according to their actual role, e.g., author, reader, reviewer), we have introduced the main features of BEX and we have described the results of an user testing session. The evaluation of such results had shown that BEX is quite good in supporting researchers to address the aforementioned tasks, even if a few of issues still have to be solved in order to use the full potential of the tool appropriately. We are working to refine the tool, and we plan to perform a full comparative analysis with existing solutions.

We also plan to focus on two new development directions. On the one hand, we want to allow the use of BEX also with (RDF-based) datasets that do not comply with the models used in the Semantic Lancet triplestore, such as DBLP++, OpenCitation Corpus and NPG Linked Data Platform. On the other hand, we want to focus on enabling users to address the tasks typically associated with the evaluation of authors (related to goals G6 and G7).

8. REFERENCES

[1] Brooke, J. (1996). SUS: a "quick and dirty" usability scale. In Usability Evaluation in Industry: 189-194.

[2] Carol Tenopir, Donald W. King, Sheri Edwards, Lei Wu, 2009. Electronic journals and changes in scholarly article seeking and reading patterns, Aslib Journal of Information Management, 61:1, pp. 5-32.

[3] Di Iorio, A., Nuzzolese, A. G., & Peroni, S. (2013). Towards the automatic identification of the nature of citations. In A. Garcia Castro, C. Lange, P. Lord, & R. Stevens (Eds.), Proceedings of 3rd Workshop on Semantic Publishing (SePublica 2013), CEUR Workshop Proceedings 994: 63–74. Aachen, Germany.

[4] Dunne, C., Shneiderman, B., Gove, R., Klavans, J., Dorr, B. (2012). Rapid understanding of scientific paper collections: Integrating statistics, text analytics, and visualization. JASIST, 63(12), 2351-2369.

[5] Evans, James A. "Electronic Publication and the Narrowing of Science and Scholarship." Science 321, no. 5887 (2008): 395-99.

[6] Falco, R., Gangemi, A., Peroni, S., & Vitali, F. (2014). Modelling OWL ontologies with Graffoo. In ESWC 2014 Satellite Events - Revised Selected Papers, Lecture Notes in Computer Science 8798: 320–325. Berlin, Germany: Springer.

[7] Hélène de Ribaupierre and Gilles Falquet. 2011. New trends for reading scientific documents. In Proceedings of the 4th ACM workshop on Online books, complementary social media and crowdsourcing (BooksOnline '11). ACM, New York, NY, USA, 19-24.

[8] J. Preece, J., Carey, T. , Rogers, Y., Holland,S. , Sharp, H. Benyon,D. Human-Computer Interaction. Ics Series. Addison-Wesley Publishing Company, 1994.

[9] Juliane Franze, Kim Marriott, and Michael Wybrow. 2014. What academics want when reading digitally. In Proceedings of the 2014 ACM symposium on Document engineering (DocEng '14). ACM, New York, NY, USA, 199-202.

[10] Lee, B., Czerwinski, M., Robertson, G., Bederson, B. (2005). Understanding research trends in conferences using PaperLens. In CHI extended abstracts on Human factors in computing systems (pp.1969-1972). ACM.

[11] Lewis, J. R., & Sauro, J. (2009). The Factor Structure of the System Usability Scale. In Proceedings of the 1st International Conference on Human Centered Design (HCD 2009): 94-103.

[12] Mei-Ling Wang, Scholarly journal use and reading behavior of social scientists in Taiwan, The International Information & Library Review, Volume 42, Issue 4, 2010, Pages 269-281, ISSN 1057-231.

[13] Niu, X., Hemminger, B. M., Lown, C., Adams, S., Brown, C., Level, A., McLure, M., Powers, A., Tennant, M. R. and Cataldo, T. (2010), National study of information seeking behavior of academic researchers in the United States. J. Am. Soc. Inf. Sci., 61: 869–890.

[14] Peroni, S. (2014). Semantic Web Technologies and Legal Scholarly Publishing. Law, Governance and Technology Series 15. Springer. http://dx.doi.org/10.1007/978-3-319-04777-5

[15] Presutti, V., Francesco D., & Aldo G. (2012). Knowledge extraction based on discourse representation theory and linguistic frames. In Proceedings of the 18th International Conference on Knowledge Engineering and Knowledge Management (EKAW 2012): 114–129. Berlin, Germany: Springer.

[16] Qazvinian, V., Radev, D. (2010). Identifying Non-explicit Citing Sentences for Citation-based Summarization. In Proceedings of the 48th Annual Meeting of the Association for Computational Linguistics (ACL 10): 555–564.

[17] Sauro, J. (2011). A Practical Guide to the System Usability Scale: Background, Benchmarks & Best Practices. CreateSpace. ISBN: 1461062707

[18] Shen, Z., Ogawa, M., Teoh, S. T., Ma, K. L. (2006). BiblioViz: a system for visualizing bibliography information. In Proceedings of the 2006 Asia-Pacific Symposium on Information Visualisation-Volume 60 (pp. 93-102).

[19] Shneiderman, B. (1996). The Eyes Have It: A Task by Data Type Taxonomy for Information Visualizations. In Proceedings of the IEEE Symposium on Visual Languages, pages 336-343,Washington. IEEE Computer Society Press, 1996.

[20] Shotton, D. (2013). Publishing: Open citations. Nature, 502(7471): 295–297.

[21] Strauss, A. Corbin, J. (1998). Basics of Qualitative Research Techniques and Procedures for Developing Grounded Theory (2nd edition). Sage Publications. ISBN: 0803959408

[22] Teufel, S., Siddharthan, A., Tidhar, D. (2006). Automatic classification of citation function. In Proceedings of the 2006 Conference on Empirical Methods in Natural Language Processing (EMNLP 06): 103–110.

[23] Yichen Jiang, Aixia Jia, Yansong Feng, and Dongyan Zhao. 2012. Recommending academic papers via users' reading purposes. In Proceedings of the sixth ACM conference on Recommender systems (RecSys '12). ACM, New York, NY, USA, 241-244.

Filling the Gaps: Improving Wikipedia Stubs

Siddhartha Banerjee
The Pennsylvania State University
Information Sciences and Technology
University Park, PA, USA
sbanerjee@ist.psu.edu

Prasenjit Mitra
Qatar Computing Research Institute
Hamad Bin Khalifa University
Doha, Qatar
pmitra@qf.org.qa

ABSTRACT

The availability of only a limited number of contributors on Wikipedia cannot ensure consistent growth and improvement of the online encyclopedia. With information being scattered on the web, our goal is to automate the process of generation of content for Wikipedia. In this work, we propose a technique of improving stubs on Wikipedia that do not contain comprehensive information. A classifier learns features from the existing comprehensive articles on Wikipedia and recommends content that can be added to the stubs to improve the completeness of such stubs. We conduct experiments using several classifiers - Latent Dirichlet Allocation (LDA) based model, a deep learning based architecture (Deep belief network) and TFIDF based classifier. Our experiments reveal that the LDA based model outperforms the other models (~6% F-score). Our generation approach shows that this technique is capable of generating comprehensive articles. ROUGE-2 scores of the articles generated by our system outperform the articles generated using the baseline. Content generated by our system has been appended to several stubs and successfully retained in Wikipedia.

Categories and Subject Descriptors

I.2 [**ARTIFICIAL INTELLIGENCE**]: Natural Language Processing—*Language generation*

Keywords

Wikipedia Generation; Text Summarization; Topic Modeling

1. INTRODUCTION

Wikipedia – the online encyclopedia has become very popular as it provides comprehensive information on various topics and satisfies the information needs of readers across the globe. On an average, at least 700 new articles are added everyday to Wikipedia. However, several categories on Wikipedia either do not have decent coverage or the articles are not of acceptable quality. Creating new articles and editing older ones usually consume significant amount of time and hence is expensive. To address the above mentioned issues, we propose a framework that can generate content automatically by leveraging available web sources to improve already exist-

DocEng'15, September 8-11, 2015, Lausanne, Switzerland.
© 2015 ACM. ISBN 978-1-4503-3307-8/15/09 ...$15.00.
DOI: http://dx.doi.org/10.1145/2682571.2797073.

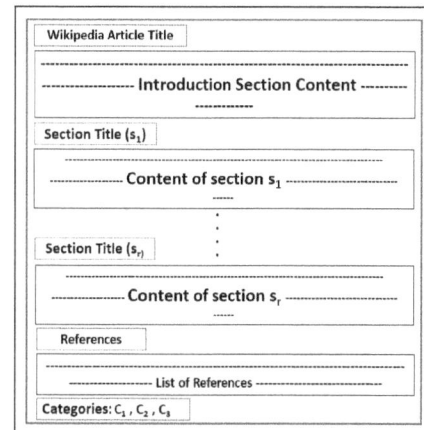

Figure 1: Page structure of a sample Wikipedia article

ing articles on Wikipedia that do not have encyclopedic coverage[1]. Consider Figure 1, that shows the general structure of Wikipedia articles. In case of stubs, generally the sections ($s_1, ..., s_r$) are not present. We aim to create the content in those sections by leveraging already existing information in the stubs, namely the introductory content and also by learning from other comprehensive articles belonging to the same Wikipedia category.

In our prior work [1], we proposed a technique using extractive summarization [11] to generate articles on drama and plays. Only a few of the automatically generated articles were accepted because Wikipedia policies have become stricter over the years and violation of copyright is not acceptable. A Wikipedia article generator that can summarize content in an abstractive [11] manner is desired such that content from the web is rewritten automatically. An example of our system generated output can be found on Wikipedia[2].

We argue that to improve a stub on Wikipedia, we can learn from articles within the same category as they generally contain similar sections. We train a classifier that can assign excerpts extracted from the web into specific sections on an article that belongs to a particular category. The training data contains content from the specific sections on Wikipedia as the instances and their corresponding section titles as the labels. We restrict to only one category of articles at a time to avoid any ambiguity in section titles. Further, we consider only the top 10 most frequent sections in the category as the most representative sections in any category. We experiment with two different classifiers. The first approach is based

---

[1] Such articles are known as stubs in Wikipedia (https://en.wikipedia.org/wiki/Wikipedia:Stub)

[2] https://en.wikipedia.org/wiki/Actinic_conjunctivitis - Sections on *Causes* and *Symptoms* were added on 5th January, 2015 were added using our automatic content generator

on topic-modeling using Latent Dirichlet Allocation (LDA) [3] that has proven to be very effective in classification tasks. Every excerpt from the web is represented as a vector of topics and the classifier (we used Random Forest) is used to predict the class (section title) of the excerpt. The second approach is based on deep learning, that uses a deep-belief network (DBN) [4] to build a generative model from the document vectors to classify the excerpts into their respective classes. The classification models assign multiple excerpts collected from the web into each section. Previous work only considered the most informative excerpt; however, this choice leads to the possibility of loss of useful information. To build a comprehensive summary of an article, we need to synthesize information from multiple sources. Hence, we apply LexRank [6], which is a popular unsupervised multi-document summarization technique, and then apply sentence compression [5] to rewrite the web content.

To the best of our knowledge, this work is the first to address the issue of generating content for Wikipedia stubs. We also address the issue of text summarization for Wikipedia content generation. Our experiments reveal that the classification model trained using topic vectors outperform the model trained using deep learning (F1-score - 88% Vs 82%). To evaluate the quality of the articles generated by our approach, we generate the content of several articles on diseases that already exist in Wikipedia using our method. We evaluate the articles using ROUGE [10]. ROUGE-2 scores indicate that our method (0.33) generates more informative summaries than the baseline [12] (0.19). Further, we added content to several articles on Wikipedia, most of which have been retained by reviewers.

2. RELATED WORK

The problem of generating content to populate an Wikipedia article to transform it into a more comprehensive source of information has not been addressed well. Learning structures of templates from the Wikipedia articles have been attempted in the past [12, 14]. However, both the approaches use queries to extract excerpts from the web and the excerpts ranked as the most relevant are added into the article. However, as already pointed out, current standards of Wikipedia requires rewriting of web content to avoid copyright violation issues.

In order to address the issue of copyright violation, multi-document abstractive summarization is required. Various abstractive approaches have been proposed till date [11]. However, no method is full proof. A recent work from our group in this field has led to the development of an abstractive summarization technique for Wikipedia article generation that is based on fusion of information from multiple sentences [2]. Template-based methods for summarization work well but it assumes prior domain knowledge [9] and hence cannot be applied to generation of Wikipedia pages as domain specific template generation will require a huge manual effort. On the contrary, we can use text-to-text generation (T2T) techniques, and more specifically, sentence compression, in which a sentence is shortened but the actual meaning of the original is retained. Our method applies LexRank [6] followed by sentence compression [5] for text-to-text generation.

3. PROPOSED APPROACH

We need to address two sub-problems. First, we need to ensure that we retrieve salient content from the web that fit into the various sections of the article. Second, our method should be able to synthesize and present the content to the reader using automatic text summarization. Thus, we deploy a two-stage process – **Content Extraction** and **Content Summarization**.

3.1 Content Extraction

The goal of this stage is to retrieve content that is relevant to the topic of the stub. This section highlights all the steps we applied for relevant content extraction.

Classification Model: The classification problem can be formulated as follows: Let C, a category on Wikipedia has k Wikipedia articles (W).

$$(C) = \{W_1, W_2, W_3, W_4, ..., W_k\}$$

Each article W_j has several sections denoted as $s_{ji}c_{ji}$ where s_{ji} is the section title of the ith section in the jth article. Similarly, c_{ji} refers to the content in the ith section in the jth article. Let us denote the 10 most frequent sections as $S = \{S_1, S_2, ..., S_{10}\}$. If any of the s_{ji} from W_j matches any section title in S, the content (c_{ji}) is appended to the training set along with the section title (s_{ji}) as the corresponding label. These steps are repeated for all the articles in the category. We build two different classification models – (i) *LDA based classification* and (ii) *Deep Learning using DBN*.

[i] LDA based classification: Latent Dirichlet Allocation (LDA) [3] is based on the idea that every document is a mixture of several topics. Any topic is represented as a vector of probabilities of words. Each section content is represented as a vector of topic distributions. Our objective is to learn topic representations that are unique to any class so that we can accurately classify any web excerpt by inferring the topics in the excerpt. We denote the number of topics as m. Each data point is then represented as follows:

$$c_{ji} = \{p_{ji}^{t_1}, p_{ji}^{t_2}, p_{ji}^{t_3}, ..., p_{ji}^{t_m}\}$$

where the set of topics are t_1, t_2, t_3,... , t_m, and $p_{ji}^{t_m}$ refers to the probability of topic m of the ith content in the jth article. We experiment with several values of m and use the value that generates the best classification model. We use 2000 iterations to compute the topic probabilities. The topic vectors retrieved from the section contents are used to train a Random Forest (RF) classifier.

[ii] Deep Belief Network: We also build another classification model using deep learning architecture. More specifically, we use a Deep Belief Network (DBN) [4] with 300 hidden layers. DBN's are stacked Restricted Boltzmann Machines (RBM). These can be trained in a greedy manner to extract a deep hierarchical representation of the training data. DBN models the joint distribution between observed vector x and the ℓ hidden layers h^k as follows:

$$P(x, h^1, \ldots, h^\ell) = \left(\prod_{k=0}^{\ell-2} P(h^k|h^{k+1})\right) P(h^{\ell-1}, h^\ell)$$

where $x = h^0$, $P(h^{k-1}|h^k)$ is a conditional distribution for the visible units conditioned on the hidden units of the RBM at level k, and $P(h^{\ell-1}, h^\ell)$ is the visible-hidden joint distribution in the top-level RBM. We use 100 epochs when training the DBN. Document representations were created using paragraph vectors [8]. We used 100 dimensional paragraph vectors that were fed into the DBN network.

Web excerpt extraction: We extract multiple excerpts from the web on the stub topic using search queries and classifying the excerpts in three steps as follows:

[i] Query Generation: We generate useful queries by combining the stub title and keyphrases extracted from the introductory content of the stub. Using focused queries increases relevance as well as disambiguation of content. We use the KEA algorithm [13] to extract keyphrases from the introductory section content of an Wikipedia article. The query is used to retrieve the top 20 search results from Google.

[ii] Boilerplate removal: Web pages contain a lot of clutter in addition to relevant content. The content from the search results obtained in the previous step needs pruning to remove unimportant content. Removal of such content is done using boilerplate detection [7].

[iii] Classification of excerpts: The two classification models require two different feature representations of the excerpts to predict their class. For the topic model based prediction, each excerpt is represented as a topic vector by inferring the topic distributions from the same LDA model generated earlier. On the contrary, for

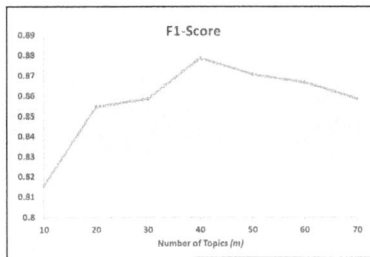

Figure 2: F-Score Vs Number of Topics for Topic based Content Classification

Table 1: Classification Performance Comparison [All our experiments were run on a machine with Intel i7 processor and 16GB of RAM]

Method	Precision	Recall	F1-Score	*Time to train*
LDA-RF	0.879	0.879	**0.879**	4 minutes
DBN	0.820	0.820	0.820	360 minutes
Bag-of-NGrams NB	0.740	0.760	0.749	10 minutes

prediction using DBN, word vector representations are used. The classifier predicts the class (section title) for each content. To prevent potential misclassifications, we use only the predictions that have a confidence of at least 0.5.

3.2 Content Summarization

The content assigned to each section requires summarization to ensure that only the most important information is conveyed in the article. Further, the generator must not violate copyrights and should revise the original text. Ideally, we also want to apply an unsupervised summarization model so that the technique can be applied to all Wikipedia categories without any domain specificity.

Multi-excerpt summarization: LexRank [6] has been particularly very effective in multi-document text summarization and considered to be one of the state-of-the-art unsupervised summarizers. In our case, the set of multiple documents are the set of excerpts retrieved for each section. In a collection of excerpts on the same topic, all sentences do not always carry equal value. LexRank computes scores of sentences considering all the sentences from the excerpts in the form of a matrix. The continuous version of LexRank relies on the strength of the similar links. Similarity is computed using cosine similarity. Equation (1) assigns a score of the salience of a node in the graph, which implies the importance of the sentence in the whole network. Let $p(u)$ be the centrality of node u. Continuous LexRank is then defined as follows:

$$p(u) = \frac{d}{N} + (1-d) \sum_{v \in adj[u]} \frac{\text{idf-modified-cosine}(u,v)}{\sum_{z \in adj[v]} \text{idf-modified-cosine}(z,v)} p(v),$$

(1)

where $adj[u]$ and N are the set of nodes that are adjacent to u and the total number of nodes in the graph, respectively. We set d, the damping factor, to 0.85 as this value gave us the best results in our experiments. The computation convergences to generate the final scores of the sentences. The extractive summary is obtained by ordering the sentences based on their LexRank scores. The URLs from where the sentences are extracted are retained to generate citations in Wikipedia.

Sentence compression: We apply sentence compression to rewrite the summarized sentences. The model that we use is based on an ILP formulation [5]. Sentence compression is formulated as an optimization problem where the words are considered to be binary variables. The solution to the integer linear programming problem decides which words to retain and which to discard, by imposing certain constraints on the desired compression length and other syntactic constraints. The objective function of the optimization problem was formulated by considering trigram probabilities. In addition, word informativeness was also taken into consideration in the objective function. A trigram language model was used to find the best sequence of words that maximized the objective function and generate the best possible compression. We apply a minimum compression rate of 0.7, which means that the number of tokens in the final sentence would be at least 70% of that of the original sentence. The summarized content is entered into the Wikipedia stubs.

4. EXPERIMENTAL RESULTS

To evaluate the effectiveness of our proposed approach, we conducted several experiments. Our experiments were designed to answer the following questions: In this section, we first describe the dataset that we constructed to conduct the experiments followed by the results of our classification experiments. We also performed ROUGE evaluation, normally used in summarization evaluation, to compare the content of the articles generated using our approach and the already existing articles on Wikipedia. Further, we also appended generated content into several stubs on Wikipedia.

Dataset: We extracted around 6000 articles and 560 stubs from the category of *diseases and disorders*[3]. To identify the most representative set of sections available in the full articles, we computed the frequencies of the section titles. The most frequent 10 sections in these articles were the following: *Prevention, Treatment, Prognosis, Pathophysiology, Classification, Causes, Diagnosis, History, Epidemiology* and *Symptoms*. Content from only these sections were included in the final dataset. We had 9692 instances to train the classifier. Further, we applied re-sampling to take the imbalance of the dataset into consideration.

Number of topics: Any LDA model requires a predefined number of topics, m, to calculate the topic distributions. The number of topics that work best in a certain situation can vary. For this reason, we experimented with multiple values of m and determined the best configuration from the F1-score values obtained using the classification experiments. As mentioned earlier, we used Random Forest (RF) classifier trained using the topic distributions and applied 10-fold cross validation. As can be seen from the Figure 2, the F1-score obtained using the classifier depends on the number of topics. The best results were obtained using 40 topics on the particular category we considered for our experiments. We will use the model trained using 40 topics as the final classification model using topic vectors. We used the MALLET API[4] to generate topic models.

Comparison of Classification Models: We compared the classification accuracy of the two classification models - (i) LDA based model with 40 topic features and trained using RF (**LDA-RF**), and (ii) Deep Belief Network with 300 hidden layers, each fold running for 100 epochs (**DBN**).

As can be seen from the table 1, the topic model based classification approach outperforms the deep-learning model by ~6% in terms of the F1-score. Moreover, training the deep learning model consumes a lot of time compared to the RF classifier. The probabilistic distribution of words in the web excerpts as inferred using LDA seems to be a reasonable approach and the classifier trained on the dataset can be used to predict the sections of web excerpts. Moreover, the sections that have more coverage in our dataset generally ended up having higher accuracies, suggesting that training using more articles will help build better classifiers. We compared both the approaches with the baseline, that uses a Naive Bayes (NB) classifier trained using n-gram features with the TFIDF values as the feature values. Our experiments show that both the LDA based

---

[3]https://en.wikipedia.org/wiki/Category:Diseases_and_disorders
[4]http://mallet.cs.umass.edu/api/

Table 2: Content Selection Evaluation

Method	ROUGE-1	ROUGE-2
Our method	**0.551**	**0.332**
ILP (Sauper and Barzilay, 2009)	0.431	0.191

Table 3: Statistics of Wikipedia generation

Statistics	Count
Number of stubs edited	39
Number of stubs where edits were retained without any changes	20
Number of stubs that required minor editing	6
Number of stubs where edits were modified by reviewers	4
Number of stubs in which content was removed	9
Average change in size of stubs	315 bytes
Average number of edits made post content-addition	~3

method and DBN outperform the NB classifier by a significant margin.

Wikipedia article generation: To evaluate the effectiveness of our generation approach, we generated the content of around 80 articles that currently exist in Wikipedia and are labeled as belonging to the *diseases* category. Automatic evaluation of generated content is hard; however, ROUGE [10] has been used in summarization tasks to measure content selection. We use ROUGE to compare the current version of the articles on Wikipedia and the articles generated by our system. Further, we compared the scores with that generated by Sauper and Barzilay's [12] system. For their system, we provided as input the first 20 excerpts retrieved from the web using the keyword strategy mentioned in their work. As can be seen from the table 2, the ROUGE scores of our system are significantly better than the ILP based technique. Unigram and bigram ROUGE scores show that our method can be used to generate articles on Wikipedia with high accuracies and are able to generate a significant chunk of the content without any human intervention. Further, the content that we generate does not use a single excerpt but combines information from multiple sources implying that more information is conveyed on any topic.

Stub content generation: To evaluate whether our technique is able to improve existing stubs, we have already posted the generated content using our technique into 39 stubs under the *diseases* category on Wikipedia. In most cases, the content has been retained along with the references. In some cases, the references did not seem as reliable sources to the Wikipedia reviewers and the information from such websites have been removed from Wikipedia. Further, in some stubs, the reviewers rephrased content in some pages to fit the information according to Wikipedia guidelines. An example of a modified page is the article on *2014 Enterovirus D68 outbreak*[5]. The stub contained the introduction and the history section (version 631382537). Our method created three new sections and appended the articles with the content and the references (version 641838267). As can be seen from the article, the section titles are appropriate and correctly identify with the content in those sections.

Table 3 shows some statistics of the Wikipedia page generation. Overall, the results were encouraging showing the effectiveness of the approach. The content was removed in 9 cases because of the presence of unreliable sources of information or due to the presence of irrelevant information. In 4 stubs, we had to do minor revision as the reviewer pointed out that the content was very similar to the original source. We also measured the change in the size of the contents of the stubs and also number of edits made after our content addition. On an average, the size of each stub increased by 315 bytes and received 3 edits from other collaborators.

---

[5] https://en.wikipedia.org/wiki/2014_Enterovirus_D68_outbreak

5. CONCLUSIONS AND FUTURE WORK

In this work, we proposed a technique to generate content for Wikipedia stubs automatically and eventually improve such articles. Our experiments show that the topic modeling based classification outperforms a deep belief network model. Both the methods are significantly superior than the baseline method of text classification using TFIDF vectors. Our method also successfully recreated the content of full articles already existing on Wikipedia and outperformed other existing methods in literature on this task. Further, the content that we generated for the stubs, were entered into Wikipedia and most of the content has been retained, with minor changes by the reviewers in a few cases. In future, we plan to develop more robust rewriting techniques by learning grammar rules from Wikipedia so that we can do better paraphrasing while generating content in such pages.

6. REFERENCES

[1] S. Banerjee, C. Caragea, and P. Mitra. Playscript classification and automatic wikipedia play articles generation. In *Proceedings of the 22nd International Conference on Pattern Recognition (ICPR)*, pages 3630–3635. IEEE, 2014.

[2] S. Banerjee and P. Mitra. Wikikreator: Improving wikipedia stubs automatically. In *Proceedings of the Joint Conference of the 53rd Annual Meeting of the ACL and the 7th International Joint Conference on Natural Language Processing of the AFNLP*. Association for Computational Linguistics, 2015.

[3] D. M. Blei, A. Y. Ng, and M. I. Jordan. Latent dirichlet allocation. *the Journal of machine Learning research*, 3:993–1022, 2003.

[4] Y.-l. Boureau, Y. L. Cun, et al. Sparse feature learning for deep belief networks. In *Advances in neural information processing systems*, pages 1185–1192, 2008.

[5] J. Clarke and M. Lapata. Global inference for sentence compression: An integer linear programming approach. *J. Artif. Intell. Res.(JAIR)*, 31:399–429, 2008.

[6] G. Erkan and D. R. Radev. Lexrank: Graph-based lexical centrality as salience in text summarization. *J. Artif. Intell. Res.(JAIR)*, 22(1):457–479, 2004.

[7] C. Kohlschütter, P. Fankhauser, and W. Nejdl. Boilerplate detection using shallow text features. In *Proceedings of the third ACM international conference on Web search and data mining*, pages 441–450. ACM, 2010.

[8] Q. Le and T. Mikolov. Distributed representations of sentences and documents. In *Proceedings of the 31st International Conference on Machine Learning (ICML-14)*, pages 1188–1196, 2014.

[9] P. Li, Y. Wang, and J. Jiang. Automatically building templates for entity summary construction. *Information Processing & Management*, 49(1):330–340, 2013.

[10] C.-Y. Lin. Rouge: A package for automatic evaluation of summaries. In *Text Summarization Branches Out: Proceedings of the ACL-04 Workshop*, pages 74–81, 2004.

[11] A. Nenkova, S. Maskey, and Y. Liu. Automatic summarization. In *Proceedings of the 49th Annual Meeting of the Association for Computational Linguistics: Tutorial Abstracts of ACL 2011*, page 3. Association for Computational Linguistics, 2011.

[12] C. Sauper and R. Barzilay. Automatically generating wikipedia articles: A structure-aware approach. In *Proceedings of the Joint Conference of the 47th Annual Meeting of the ACL and the 4th International Joint Conference on Natural Language Processing of the AFNLP: Volume 1-Volume 1*, pages 208–216. Association for Computational Linguistics, 2009.

[13] I. H. Witten, G. W. Paynter, E. Frank, C. Gutwin, and C. G. Nevill-Manning. Kea: Practical automatic keyphrase extraction. In *Proceedings of the fourth ACM conference on Digital libraries*, pages 254–255. ACM, 1999.

[14] C. Yao, X. Jia, S. Shou, S. Feng, F. Zhou, and H. Liu. Autopedia: automatic domain-independent wikipedia article generation. In *Proceedings of the 20th international conference companion on World wide web*, pages 161–162. ACM, 2011.

BBookX: An Automatic Book Creation Framework

Chen Liang‡, Shuting Wang†, Zhaohui Wu†, Kyle Williams‡, Bart Pursel‡*,
Benjamin Brautigam*, Sherwyn Saul*, Hannah Williams*, Kyle Bowen*,C. Lee Giles‡†

‡Information Sciences and Technology
†Computer Science and Engineering
*Teaching and Learning with Technology
The Pennsylvania State University, University Park, PA 16802, USA
cul226@ist.psu.edu, sxw327@cse.psu.edu,
{zzw109,kwilliams,bkp10,bjb40,sps20,hrw115,kbowen}@psu.edu, giles@ist.psu.edu

ABSTRACT

As more educational resources become available online, it is possible to acquire more up-to-date knowledge and information. We propose BBookX, a novel computer facilitated system that automatically and collaboratively builds free open online books using publicly available educational resources such as Wikipedia. BBookX has two separate components: one creates an open version of existing books by linking different book chapters to Wikipedia articles, while another with an interactive user interface supports interactive real-time book creation where users are allowed to modify a generated book from explicit feedback.

Categories and Subject Descriptors

H.3.3 [**Information Storage and Retrieval**]: Information Search and Retrieval; I.7.m [**Document and Text Processing**]: Miscellaneous

Keywords

Automatic book creation; personalization; open educational resources

1. INTRODUCTION

In an era of ubiquitous learning where information is rapidly increasing and changing, creating a contemporary personalized book has many advantages. To facilitate learning in such an environment, customized and personalized educational options and learning resources have been proposed, including MOOCs, Wikibooks[1], Wikiversity[2], etc. While they provide choices and flexibility in learning, creating and maintaining high-quality up-to-date learning resources on a large scale is still a challenging problem, especially for fast changing domains such as computer science. For example,

[1] http://en.wikibooks.org/wiki/Main_Page
[2] http://en.wikiversity.org/wiki/Wikiversity:Main_Page

the latest version of the popular book "Pattern Recognition and Machine Learning" misses much of the recent development of certain machine learning methods such as deep learning. However, much of this content is publicly available online in high-quality open formats.

To deal with this we propose the BBookX system which utilizes information retrieval techniques to intelligently harvest online resources and reorganize them in a format of a personalized learning resource similar to a textbook using open access textbooks and Wikipedia. By automatically linking book chapters to Wiki articles, BBookX is able to utilize the knowledge available on Wikipedia and create an open version of existing classic textbooks.

With an interactive user interface, BBookX supports collaborative real-time book creation whereby an open book is generated from user content and queries. An explicit relevance feedback mechanism allows user feedback to reformulate the query for additional searches.

Such a tool has many advantages for open educational resources: reduce the cost of creating and maintaining learning resources, contribute to open educational resources, and provide more up to date information for fast changing fields.

The rest of this paper is organized as follows: Section 2 introduces the system overview of BBookX; Section 3 discusses the construction of open book repository; Section 4 describes the interactive book creation; Section 5 presents related work and Section 6 concludes.

2. SYSTEM OVERVIEW

The system overview of BBookX shown in Figure 1 consists of two major components: the open book repository construction and the interactive book creation tool. The open book repository is built from two resources. First, existing online open access textbooks are collected. Second, for other textbooks, it is possible to create a Wiki-based open version by linking chapters to Wikipedia articles. Both open access books and Wiki-based open books are stored in the open book repository and indexed using Solr/Lucene[3]. The interactive book creation component allows users to specify the information of the book which they want to build using queries. The system will then retrieve a list of indexed educational resources ranked by the relevance to the query. An interactive user interface provides easy click selection and drag/drop functions allowing users to evaluate the returned resources. User feedback is utilized by an explicit relevance

[3] http://lucene.apache.org/solr/

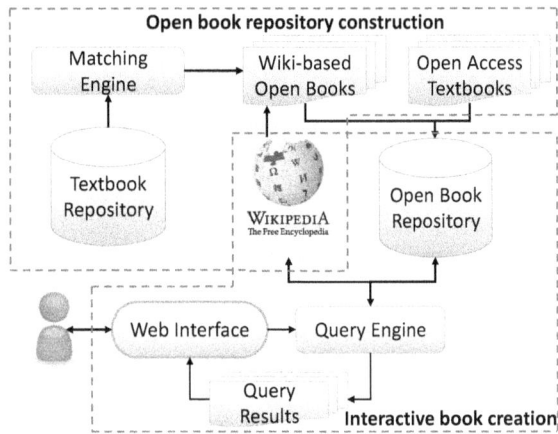

Figure 1: BBookX system overview.

Textbook	P@1	P@3	P@5	MAP@10
Computer networks	0.84	0.52	0.42	0.37
Macroeconomics	0.83	0.54	0.42	0.34
Precalculus	0.83	0.46	0.39	0.34

Table 1: Performance of the candidate ranking on three different textbooks.

3. The Application Layer	3. The Application Layer
3.1 Principles	3.1 Principles
3.1.1 The Peer-to-peer Model	3.1.1 Peer-to-peer
3.1.2 The Transport Services	3.1.2 Connectionless-mode Network Service
3.2 Application-level Protocols	3.2 Application-level Protocols
3.2.1 The Domain Name System	3.2.1 Domain Name System
3.2.2 Electronic Mail	3.2.2 Email
3.2.3 The HyperText Transfer Protocol	3.2.3 Hypertext Transfer Protocol
5. The Network Layer	5. The Network Layer
5.2 Internet Protocol	5.2 Internet Protocol
5.2.1 IP Version 4	5.2.1 IPv4
5.2.2 ICMP Version 4	5.2.2 Internet Control Message Protocol

Figure 2: Example of a Computer Networking book created using Wikipedia. The left part is the table of contents of the original book. The right part is the generated table of contents.

feedback mechanism to reformulate the query to generate a new list of results. The generated book will be refined through such an interactive search process. Details of these two components are discussed later.

3. OPEN BOOK REPOSITORY

3.1 Collecting Open Access Textbooks

In order to construct our open book repository, we first create a collection of existing online open access textbooks by crawling different websites. Our available data sources include Wikibooks, Saylor Academy[4], MIT OCW[5], Open-Stax College[6], etc. So far we have collected more than 3000 open access textbooks.

3.2 Generating Open Books Using Wikipedia

In order to provide high-quality and well-structured open books, we also utilize classic textbooks created by experts. Here we create an open version of existing books using Wikipedia. Our method is to link book chapters to Wiki articles. Specifically, for each chapter we provide users a list of Wiki articles which are most relevant to the topics covered in the book. Our method consists of three modules: concept identification, candidate selection and candidate ranking.

Concept Identification identifies the important concepts discussed in each book chapter. First, we build a domain-specific dictionary which contains the concepts related to the book topic. A depth-first search method is used to crawl Wikipedia with the seed set to be the main Wiki page related to the topic. Titles of Wiki articles visited by our crawler will be added to the concept dictionary [9]. Second, we match concepts from the dictionary in the book chapter and calculate the importance score for each concept using term frequency-inverse document frequency (tf-idf).

Candidate Selection selects the candidate Wiki articles related to the concepts in the book chapter. Two approaches are applied to collecting the candidate set. The similarity between the title of the book chapter and the title of Wiki articles is determined whereby if the Wiki title also appears in the chapter title, then the Wiki article is added to the

candidate set. In addition, the similarity between the content of Wikipedia articles and that of the book chapter when each book chapter and Wikipedia article is represented as a tf-idf vector using all vector space concepts in the dictionary. The content similarity is calculated by the cosine similarity between tf-idf vectors and top N Wiki articles with high similarity are included in the candidate set.

Candidate Ranking ranks the candidates for the most relevant Wiki articles. Using a learning to rank model, SVM^{rank} [4], different features are extracted for training including local features, such as content similarity and the Jaccard distance between titles, and global features such as redundancy features and consistency features[7]. While local features are able to capture the relatedness between the book chapter and Wiki candidates, global features are used to ensure global coherence between Wiki candidates. SVM^{rank} is tested on three textbooks from different domains. For each book chapter, three graduate students label each Wiki candidate as "relevant" or "irrelevant" with evaluation of 5-fold cross-validation on all chapters of the three books. As listed in Table 1, the performance of the proposed ranking method is consistent on three different textbooks.

Figure 2 shows a part of the book generated for an existing textbook "Computer Networking: Principles, Protocols, and Practice". The left side of the figure is the table of contents of the original book. Our method of the subsections (e.g. 3.1.1, 3.1.2) show the top candidate Wiki article for each section on the right side and link the book chapter sections to the relevant Wiki article.

3.3 Indexing Subsystem

The indexing subsystem indexes all open educational resources collected by the system, including Wikipedia articles, open access textbooks, and Wiki-based open books cre-

---

[4]http://www.saylor.org/books/
[5]http://ocw.mit.edu/courses/online-textbooks/
[6]http://openstaxcollege.org/

[7]More details of the proposed candidate ranking method can be found in our recent work[12].

ated by BBookX. A Wikipedia dump of Dec 8, 2014 is used. Each Wikipedia article and book chapter indexed is first preprocessed, which includes tokenization, stop word and punctuation removal, conversion to lower case, and stemming. Then Solr/Lucene is used to build a full text index for the content of each document. To calculate the similarity score, key phrases of each document are also extracted and indexed [11]. Specifically, anchor texts are extracted from each Wiki article as key phrases. For book chapters, the Maui tool [6] is used to extract keyphrases. Besides full text and key phrases, the metadata of each document is also indexed, such as Wiki title, book chapter title, document source, etc.

4. INTERACTIVE BOOK CREATION

Parts of the user interface for the interactive book creation tool are shown in Figure 3.

4.1 User Interface

After logging into the system, users can choose either to edit a book in "My books", which stores books previously created, or start creating a new book. The book creation process can start with creating a book title and a short description (<50 words) of the book (as shown in Figure 3a). Next users add chapters. For each chapter, a title and a short description is also created. Figure 3b shows the interface for adding chapters. The system also allows users to add subchapters or remove an existing chapter. When users finish adding chapters, they can click the "Query" button to retrieve a list of candidate items for each chapter, which could be sections of open books or Wiki articles. Users can review the returned results, reorder the list, and delete items which are not appropriate (as shown in Figure 3c). If several items under a chapter are deleted, users can regenerate the results for that chapter by clicking "Query". Explicit feedback is utilized by BBookX to reformulate the query for improved ranking. Finally, all resources that users think are relevant are combined as a book, which can be stored in "My books". In addition, the built book can be exported to HTML or text files for offline editing.

4.2 Query Subsystem

The query subsystem receives the information of a chapter/subchapter as a query and returns a ranked list of relevant educational resources, including Wiki articles and sections of open books. It mainly consists of the following three processes:

Querying: For a query $q = (t_q, c_q)$, where t_q is the chapter title and c_q is the associated descriptive text, BBookX retrieves a set of candidate relevant resources D by querying t_q and c_q in the pre-built full text index. The key phrases of q, denoted as k_q, are also extracted for the following ranking process.

Ranking: For each candidate resource d in D, BBookX calculates the similarity score between q and d, denoted as $sim(q, d)$, by considering features similar to local features described in Section 3.2, such as title similarity and text similarity. D is sorted by similarity score in descending order as a ranked list.

In our system, $sim(q, d)$ is calculated as

$$sim(q, d) = \alpha_1 \cdot cosSim(c_q, c_d) + \alpha_2 \cdot cosSim(k_q, k_d)$$
$$+ \alpha_3 \cdot Jaccard(t_q, t_d)$$

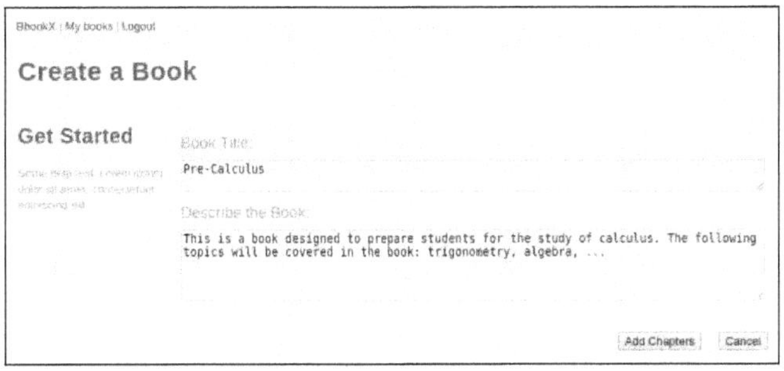

(a) Interface for creating a book title and a short description.

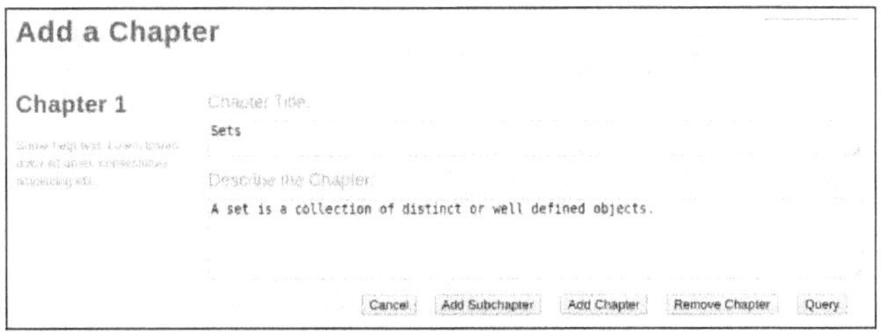

(b) Interface for creating chapters.

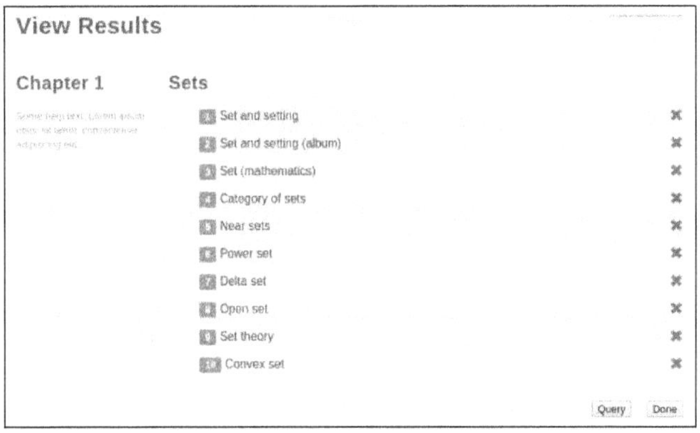

(c) Initial results for the chapter.

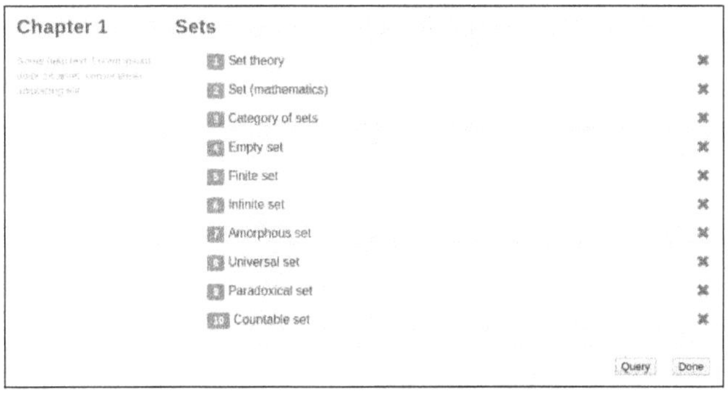

(d) New results using user feedback.

Figure 3: Interactive user interface.

where $cosSim(c_q, c_d)$ is the cosine similarity between the word vectors of the content of q and d, $cosSim(k_q, k_d)$ is the cosine similarity between key phrase vectors of q and d, and $Jaccard(t_q, t_d)$ is the Jaccard similarity between the title of q and d. Specifically, $\alpha_1 = 0.2$, $\alpha_2 = 0.2$, and $\alpha_3 = 0.6$.

Relevance feedback: Users can decide whether to keep a returned item or retrieve a new ranked list of items. BBookX incorporates a relevance feedback mechanism, which includes three steps: 1) Store the results kept by users as relevant results; 2) Select the top 20 key phrases from these results using term frequency weights; 3) Perform query expansion by adding these selected key phrases to the description c_q. A new query q' is then used to retrieve relevant results. Since users usually will not write a detailed chapter description, the relevance feedback will help users to find relevant results. Of course, other methods can be used and are currently being explored.

4.3 Case Study

We use several case studies to test the performance of the proposed query subsystem. In general, BBookX can generate a satisfactory result using no more than two iterations of user feedback. Figure 3 shows an example of the creation process for the chapter "Sets" for a precalculus book. With the chapter title and descriptive text shown in Figure 3b, users first get 10 educational resources from BBookX, as shown in Figure 3c. However, some results are not relevant, such as "Set and setting" and "Set and setting (album)". If users decide to only keep the results "Set theory", "Set (mathematics)" and "Category of sets", the feedback is used to retrieve a new list of results (as shown in Figure 3d). In this case, the new returned resources are all related to "set" in mathematics.

5. RELATED WORK

FlexBook[8] is a textbook authoring platform where users can produce and customize the book content by re-purposing educational content. Wikibooks provides a wiki-based platform which allows different users to collaboratively create books [2]. To our knowledge, existing systems do not support the automatic retrieval and organization of relevant educational resources to facilitate the book creation process.

The method used in the interactive query subsytem of BBookx is related to relevance feedback [10]. Three types of feedback can be utilized: explicit feedback, which is collected by users explicitly marking relevant and irrelevant documents [13]; implicit feedback, which is inferred by the system based on users' observable behaviors such as clicks and votes [1, 5]; and pseudo feedback, which is gathered by assuming the top-k ranked documents are relevant [3]. Currently, BBookX uses only explicit feedback.

Our methods is also similar to wikification [7, 8], which automatically identifies concept mentions in text and links them to referents in Wikipedia. The difference is our focus is on extracting the most important concepts for each book chapter, not named entities mentioned in the general text.

6. CONCLUSIONS

BBookX is an automatic book creation system that assists users in creating personalized online books. by constructing an open book repository from existing open access textbooks, Wiki-based open books, and other open educational resources. We propose and evaluate methods for linking built book chapters to relevant Wiki articles. An interactive user interface supports real-time book creation from user queries which incorporates explicit relevance feedback.

To our knowledge BBookX is the first system that automatically and collaboratively creates books from open edu-

cational resources. Promising applications would be to reduce the cost of creating and maintaining learning resources and instructional content and readily incorporating rapidly changing information. New books entirely different from others can also be built. Students could also build books associated with their courses.

Acknowledgments

We gratefully acknowledge partial support from the National Science Foundation.

7. REFERENCES

[1] E. Agichtein, E. Brill, and S. Dumais. Improving web search ranking by incorporating user behavior information. In *Proceedings of SIGIR*, pages 19–26, 2006.

[2] C. J. Bonk, M. M. Lee, N. Kim, and M.-F. G. Lin. The tensions of transformation in three cross-institutional wikibook projects. *The Internet and Higher Education*, pages 126–135, 2009.

[3] C. Buckley, G. Salton, J. Allan, and A. Singhal. Automatic query expansion using SMART: TREC 3. In *Proceedings of TREC*, pages 69–80, 1994.

[4] T. Joachims. Training linear svms in linear time. In *Proceedings of SIGKDD*, pages 217–226, 2006.

[5] T. Joachims, L. Granka, B. Pan, H. Hembrooke, and G. Gay. Accurately interpreting clickthrough data as implicit feedback. In *Proceedings of SIGIR*, pages 154–161, 2005.

[6] O. Medelyan, E. Frank, and I. H. Witten. Human-competitive tagging using automatic keyphrase extraction. In *Proceedings of EMNLP*, pages 1318–1327, 2009.

[7] R. Mihalcea and A. Csomai. Wikify!: linking documents to encyclopedic knowledge. In *Proceedings of CIKM*, pages 233–242, 2007.

[8] D. Milne and I. H. Witten. Learning to link with wikipedia. In *Proceedings of CIKM*, pages 509–518, 2008.

[9] L. Ratinov, D. Roth, D. Downey, and M. Anderson. Local and global algorithms for disambiguation to wikipedia. In *Proceedings of ACL*, pages 1375–1384, 2011.

[10] G. Salton and C. Buckley. Improving retrieval performance by relevance feedback. *Readings in information retrieval*, 24(5):355–363, 1997.

[11] R. Shams and R. E. Mercer. Investigating keyphrase indexing with text denoising. In *Proceedings of the 12th ACM/IEEE-CS joint conference on Digital Libraries*, pages 263–266, 2012.

[12] S. Wang, C. Liang, Z. Wu, K. Williams, B. Pursel, B. Brautigam, S. Saul, H. Williams, K. Bowen, and C. L. Giles. Concept hierarchy extraction from textbooks. In *Proceedings of ACM symposium on Document engineering*, 2015.

[13] R. W. White, I. Ruthven, and J. M. Jose. The use of implicit evidence for relevance feedback in web retrieval. In *Advances in Information Retrieval*, pages 93–109. Springer, 2002.

---

[8]CK-12 Foundation: http://www.ck12.org/

VEDD: A Visual Editor for Creation and Semi-Automatic Update of Derived Documents

Kim Marriott
Faculty of IT
Monash University, Australia

Mingzheng Shi
Faculty of IT
Monash University, Australia

Michael Wybrow
Faculty of IT
Monash University, Australia

{Kim.Marriott, Mingzheng.Shi, Michael.Wybrow}@monash.edu

ABSTRACT

Document content is increasingly customised to a particular audience. Such customised documents are typically built by combining content from selected logical content modules and then editing this to create the custom document. A major difficulty is how to efficiently update these derived documents when the source documents are changed. Here we describe a web-based visual editing tool for both creating and semi-automatically updating derived documents from modules in a source library.

Categories and Subject Descriptors

H.5.2 [**Information Interfaces And Presentation**]: User Interfaces—*Graphical user interfaces (GUI)*; I.7.1 [**Document And Text Processing**]: Document and Text Editing—*Version control*

Keywords

Design, human factors; custom documents

1. INTRODUCTION

Document content is increasingly tailored to a particular audience. For example, instruction manuals can be customised to take into account the purchaser's choice of options or textbooks can be customised to the needs of a particular school. Typically the customised document is built by combining selected logical content modules from a *source* library and then editing this to create a *derived document*. A significant difficulty is how to efficiently update these derived documents when the source documents are changed. Here we describe a web-based visual editing tool for both creating and semi-automatically updating derived documents from modules in a source library.

The software, VEDD, is designed for creating and updating customised textbooks. It has been developed using a user-centered design methodology [1] with production staff from a publishing house that specialises in such books. In their existing workflow, source and derived documents are separate files and all updating from source documents is done manually. This is time consuming

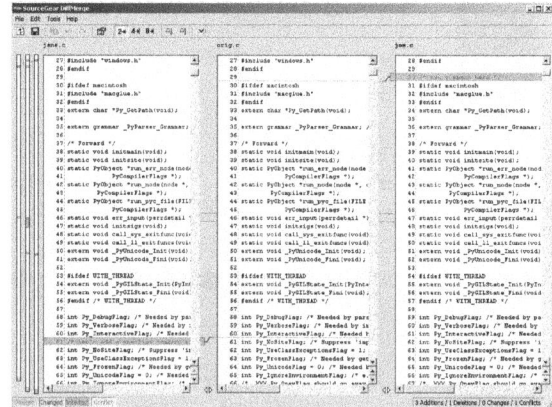

Figure 1: Many SCM systems provide visual tools like this to help with three way merging. This screenshot is from [7] and was created with "SourceGear DiffMerge." The middle pane shows the original file while the left and right panes show the two different modified versions with a visual indication of the differences between each version and the original as well as highlighting potential update conflicts. The user then approves or rejects the updates and resolves conflicts. As she does so, the changes are propagated to the pane in the middle which shows the emerging merged file. Note how the two modified versions are treated and shown in a completely symmetric manner.

and error prone. VEDD considerably reduces the time required for both creation and update as well as reducing the chance of errors.

There has been considerable research into version control systems for software and text [4] and more recently hypermedia [3]. Most support parallel editing and merging of different versions of documents. The most common approach is to use a semi-automatic three way merge in which the two different versions are compared to their most recent common ancestor. Changes are automatically included in the merged version if they are to different parts of the document. Where changes are to the same part of the document and they conflict then the user is asked to choose. The standard tool is **diff3**. Many software configuration management (SCM) systems provide visual tools to help with such three way merging, e.g. see Figure 1.

The process of updating of the derived document is also a kind of three way merge since the updated derived document is made by merging changes made to the source with the changes made when the derived document was created. However, in a standard three way merge the two different versions are treated symmetrically as there is no *a priori* semantic difference between the reasons for introducing changes in each. In our context this is not true: changes

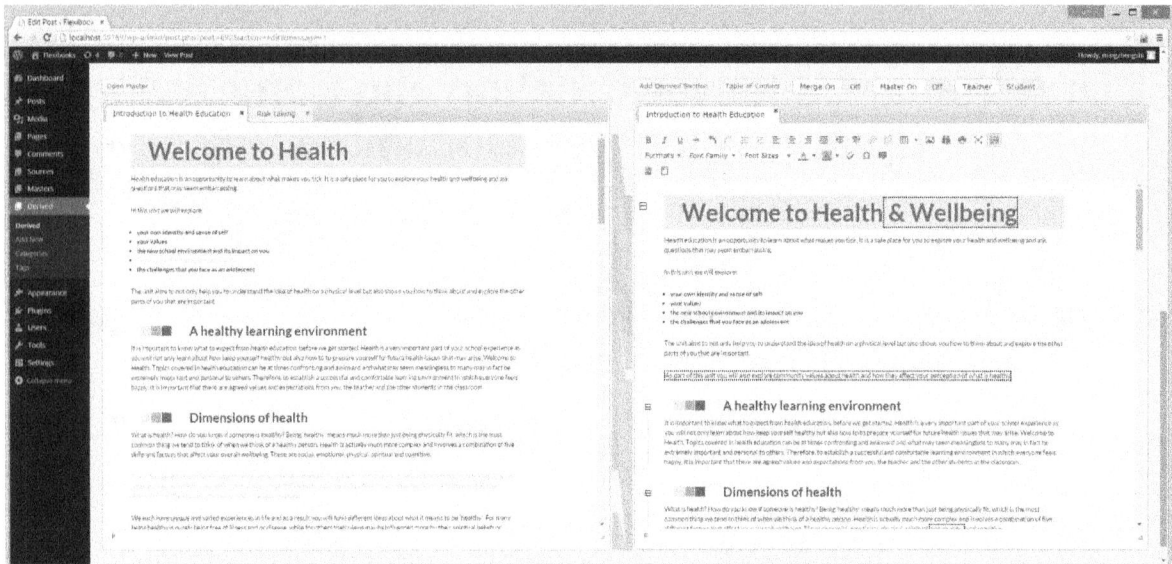

(a) To create a new derived document the user opens the source modules (left) and copies content to the new chapter (right). The navigation bar in the middle of the display allows the user to see the relationship between source and derived content. The colour indicates if it is a verbatim copy (green) or a modified copy (red).

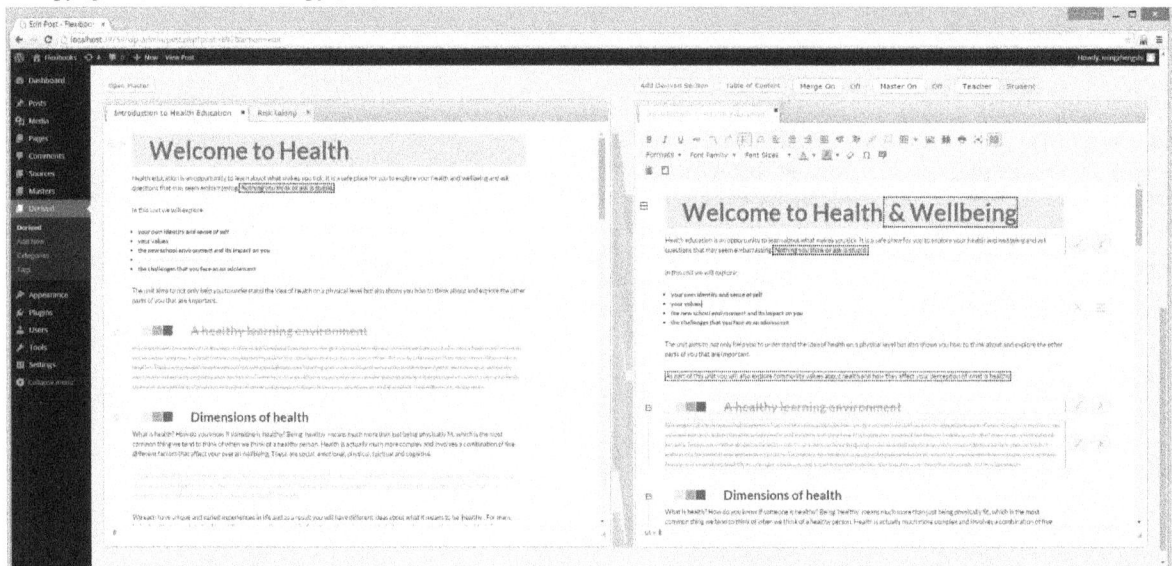

(b) When the derived document is opened after changes have been made to the source modules, the user can choose to update the derived chapters. The source module and changes are shown (left) and the suggested propagated changes/conflicts are shown for the derived document (right). The user can accept/reject each change and edit the derived chapter to resolve conflicts. Different visual encodings distinguish between differences due to derivation and to updates.

Figure 2: Creating and updating a derived document with VEDD.

made to the source are conceptually quite different to those made when the derived document was created from the original source. The main novelty in our tool is the need to handle this asymmetry. In a sense we wish to apply the changes made to the source as a kind of fuzzy patch [2] to the derived document. Our main technical contributions are:

- A novel two-screen visual representation of this 3-way merge that uses different visual conventions to distinguish differences between the source and derived documents and the updates to the source.

- A technique for doing this asymmetric merge that relies on tracking identity of document elements.

Figure 2 shows the use of our tool and this visual representation.

2. CONTEXT

The publishing company we have worked with specialises in customised educational material for schools called Flexibooks. The company has a large collection of source modules. These introduce a logically distinct topic and are about 1–5 pages long. The school specifies their tailored textbook by choosing which modules to include in it. The school can further customise the content from the modules by, for instance, requesting different examples or images, by rewriting or reordering the content, and by providing their own material, such as school images or regulations, for inclusion. The resulting customised textbook is arranged into chapters and has a title page and other front matter including a table of contents. The chapters often interleave content from more than one source module and are typically 5–30 pages long. They also have their own table of contents.

The source modules and derived document have a standard logical structure. They contain paragraphs, various kinds of lists and list items including exercises and questions, figures which are typically images, and section and subsection headers. Modules and chapters are made up of hierarchically organised sections and subsections. Each of these has a header and may contain lists, figures and paragraphs while lists contain list items. The company uses various standard styles for the different components.

Each year the publishing company updates the source modules. Usually the changes are limited, for instance reflecting changes in laws and regulations, updated census data, changes in who holds a particular office such as that of Prime Minister, and the use of recent topical case studies. However, on occasion the changes are much more extensive because of changes in curriculum.

Each year the school is given the option of updating their custom textbooks. The derived document is updated based on changes made to the source module. The school may also request additional changes. These are made after the updates from the source module.

In the current workflow source modules and derived chapters are separate Microsoft Word files. File and directory naming conventions encode the dependencies and version number. Updating from the source documents is done manually using change tracking to identify changes. This is time consuming and must be carefully checked by another team member because it is error prone. It is worth pointing out that while the production staff are well-trained in the use of traditional publishing tools like Word they do not have a strong technical background and, for instance, have no experience in version control systems beyond change tracking in Word.

3. VEDD: A VISUAL EDITOR FOR DERIVED DOCUMENTS

We have worked closely with staff from the company to develop a tool that semi-automates the update process. We employed a user-centered design methodology [1] in the development of the tool which we called VEDD. We met regularly to discuss the requirements and design, then to allow production staff to provide feedback on their use of the evolving tool. As far as possible we wanted VEDD to use concepts that production staff were familiar with. As the company was moving to replace Word by ePub 3.0 we chose to work with HTML5 as our document format.

3.1 Creating Derived Documents

It was clear from talking to production staff they thought about document in terms of its logical hierarchy and tracked dependencies in terms of that hierarchy. Thus for instance, they might say that a section, sub-section, paragraph or list is derived from that in a source module. We therefore annotated the HTML in the source modules and sections with class attributes to explicitly represent this hierarchy and allowed the user to manipulate the document in terms of this hierarchy.

In version control systems such as **Git**, the file name is used to implicitly track dependencies and identity. The tool knows that if a later file has the same name as an earlier file then they are different versions of the same file. As discussed in [8], equating file names with object identity while straightforward can be problematic. In our context dependency tracking is more difficult as a derived chap-

ter can depend upon more than one module, only some parts of a module may be included, and the parts may be reordered.

Based on discussions with production staff we decided that paragraphs, images, captions, list items were the lowest level of granularity at which to track identity and dependency between the module and chapter content. We call these the *base elements*. In order to track these more complex dependencies each of these base elements in the source module was given a unique identifier (using the HTML id attribute). During creation of a chapter the author copies base elements from each source module into the chapter and as part of the copying process VEDD adds an attribute to the element recording the dependency upon the source element with this id. This dependency is preserved during subsequent editing unless the element is completely deleted. If part of a base element is copied, such as a sentence from a paragraph it is marked as being dependent upon the source base element it is part of.

Figure 2(a) show how a new derived textbook is created with VEDD. The left pane contains source modules that have been opened by the author. There is a tab for each source module. The right pane shows the chapters in the derived textbook, one tab for each chapter plus a tab for the front matter including the title page and automatically generated table of contents.

VEDD allows content to be viewed and placed in the derived document at different levels of granularity. The logical hierarchy of the module or chapter is shown in the left margin using a control widget and vertical line to show the extent of the section/subsection. These are nested and allow the user to collapse/expand the section/sub-sections. Widgets allow entire sections, sub sections or paragraphs to be easily copied across to the currently open chapter. Conventional copy and paste can also be used. The user can then use standard editing controls to modify the derived content.

A vertical navigation bar between the left and right pane shows the dependencies using a thin parallelogram connecting source and derived content. It also allows the user to quickly align derived content with the source from which it is derived by clicking on the parallelogram associated with the derived element. This will open the tab of the corresponding source (if not already open) and horizontally align the source and derived element.

A green parallelogram indicates the derived content is unmodified while red means the derived content has been modified. Differences between the source and derived content are shown in a non-standard way. Source content that does not occur in the derived chapters is faded out, while content in the derived chapters that does not occur in a source module is enclosed in a rectangle with a very thin border. We chose these visual indicators so as to distinguish changes due to derivation from those due to updates.

3.2 Updating Derived Documents

The main reason for developing VEDD was to semi-automate update of derived textbooks. As the first step, production staff use VEDD to update the source modules. In this stage the source module is shown in a single pane and production staff use standard editing controls to make changes. They can turn change tracking on or off. Differences are shown in standard fashion: deleted text is struckthrough, new text is highlighted in yellow.

The tool keeps track of different versions of the source modules. Whenever production staff open a derived textbook, VEDD checks to see if the modules on which the textbook depends have been modified. If the textbook is out of date w.r.t. the latest version of some module the user is given the option of updating the derived textbook and the tabs for the chapters are highlighted if a source module for that chapter has been modified.

Figure 2(b) shows how the derived document is updated with VEDD. The user interface and visualisation is a natural extension of that for derived document creation. The right pane shows the textbook. In the example, the user has indicated they wish to update the textbook and clicked on a tab to update one of the chapters. As in creation, the navigation bar can be used to open and align source elements with derived element.

A custom merge policy [5] is used to propagate changes from the source modules to the derived chapter. In most cases propagation is straightforward and the suggested change is shown to the user for them to accept or reject, much like accepting changes in Word. Updates to source that has been modified result in a conflict which the user must edit to resolve the conflict.

The difference between the original source module and the updated source are shown using a Word-like track change conventions (yellow highlight for new text, strikethrough for deleted text) that are familiar to the editorial staff. This visual convention is also used to show the proposed changes to the derived document. This means that update changes are visually distinct from changes arising from derivation, clearly showing the asymmetry between the two kinds of difference. These visual conventions allows us to show the merge using only two panes and is visually quite different from symmetric three-pane visualisations like that of Figure 1.

As we have discussed we do not use a standard symmetric three way merge. The merge policy for base elements is:

	source change		
derived content	addition	deletion	modification
copied element	propagate	propagate	propagate
modified element	propagate	conflict	conflict
new element	—	—	—

The first column lists the different kinds of content that can occur in the derived chapter: verbatim copy of a base element, modified copy of a base element, or completely new content. If it is a verbatim copy all changes made to the corresponding element in the source module are marked for propagation to the derived document. If the source for a modified copy is modified or deleted this is marked as a conflict but if new content is added to the element then this is marked for propagation.

The remaining case is when new base elements are added to the source module. These are marked for propagation to the derived document only if their parent element has had content copied to the derived document. New content whose parent has not had content copied to the derived chapter is not marked for propagation. Thus a list element will not be copied if no parts of the list are present in the derived document, a sub-section will not be copied if no part of the surrounding section occurs in the derived document, while a new section will always be copied to the derived document.

A consideration when identifying changes in text is the level of granularity: this could be at the level of words, sentences or paragraphs [6]. We compare text at the word level as this is what Word does and so was what the editorial staff were used to. In contrast we track dependencies at the paragraph level.

3.3 Implementation

VEDD was implemented in WordPress (http://wordpress.com/). It contains about 5000 lines of code in PHP, JavaScript, and CSS excluding third-party packages. VEDD mainly contains two parts. One part is a WordPress plug-in where two custom post types had been defined to represent the source and derived documents. As can be seen in Figure 2(a), both source and derived documents have a menu item on the control panel on the left of the web page. The standard user interface such as list view and edit view

are inherited from a standard WordPress post type. In addition, we extended the editor for derived modules to track dependencies between source and derived modules, identify the difference between source and derived modules, and identify the changes in the source modules that require attention in the derived chapters during change tracking. We used an open-source JavaScript differencing algorithm (https://github.com/tnwinc/htmldiff.js) to find the difference between two base elements.

The other part of VEDD is a TinyMCE plugin. TinyMCE (http://www.tinymce.com/) is the default text editor in WordPress. We created a TinyMCE plug-in to enhance the functionalities of the text editor. For example, we added control widget and vertical lines in the left margin of the editor to present a hierarchical view of the document and buttons in the right margin of the editor for users to easily move or delete a paragraph, or to accept/reject a change during change tracking. We also added custom styles and custom buttons in the tool bar.

4. CONCLUSION

We have presented VEDD, a web-based tool for creating and updating customised textbooks. While intended for textbooks, the tool could also be used to support other kinds of customised documents such as instruction manuals, etc. The main novelty in the tool results from the need to handle and visualise asymmetric merging of changes resulting from both the derivation and updates to the source document.

Acknowledgments

It is a pleasure to thank the Macmillan Flexibooks staff who have collaborated in the design of VEDD: Nat Andrews, Luke Gray, Lauren McGregor, Oliver Smith and Elizabeth Thorne. We also acknowledge the support of the Victorian Government through the DSDBI Technology Development Voucher Program.

5. REFERENCES

[1] C. Abras, D. Maloney-Krichmar, and J. Preece. User-centered design. *Bainbridge, W. Encyclopedia of Human-Computer Interaction. Thousand Oaks: Sage Publications*, 37(4):445–456, 2004.

[2] N. Fraser. Fuzzy Patch. https://neil.fraser.name/writing/patch/. Accessed: 2015-04-15.

[3] D. L. Hicks, J. J. Leggett, P. J. Nürnberg, and J. L. Schnase. A hypermedia version control framework. *ACM Transactions on Information Systems (TOIS)*, 16(2):127–160, 1998.

[4] T. Mens. A state-of-the-art survey on software merging. *Software Engineering, IEEE Transactions on*, 28(5):449–462, 2002.

[5] J. P. Munson and P. Dewan. A flexible object merging framework. In *Proceedings of the 1994 ACM conference on Computer supported cooperative work*, pages 231–242. ACM, 1994.

[6] C. M. Neuwirth, R. Chandhok, D. S. Kaufer, P. Erion, J. Morris, and D. Miller. Flexible diff-ing in a collaborative writing system. In *Proceedings of the 1992 ACM conference on Computer-supported cooperative work*, pages 147–154. ACM, 1992.

[7] E. Sink. Source Control HOWTO. http://ericsink.com/scm/source_control.html. Accessed: 2015-04-15.

[8] M. Zukowski. Track changes: Identity in version control. Master's thesis, University of Toronto, 2014.

Madoko: Scholarly Documents for the Web

Daan Leijen
Microsoft Research

1. INTRODUCTION

Madoko [8] is a novel authoring system for writing complex documents. It is especially well suited for complex academic or industrial documents, like scientific articles, reference manuals, or math-heavy presentations. It started out as a project to take a fresh look at how we write academic articles. In particular, we would like to satisfy the following requirements when writing complex documents:

- *Structured*: The semantic content is most important and the input should be clearly structured in a way that is easy to process and transform by a computer.
- *Readable*: The plain text should be easy to read on its own without any special rendering. As a writer, most time is spend *writing* and the actual input should be pleasant to read.
- *Independent*: There should be multiple ways to render the actual structured content; in particular, for academic documents it is very important to generate high-quality PDF while being able to use the required publishing style (usually through a LaTeX package). However, it should also be possible to generate high quality HTML that can be re-scaled and can re-flow on various reading devices.
- *Styled*: The rendering should be styled separate from the content, much like CSS is used to style HTML.
- *Programmable*: Finally, it should be easy to transform and process the content for complex documents. For example, doing syntax highlighting on code, inserting special symbols, providing custom content, or generating graphs from input data. Moreover, this includes things like numbering figures, tables, and sections, internal references, footnotes, citations, and an index.

There are very few systems that satisfy these requirements. One of the most widely used tools that comes close to meet the requirements is LaTeX [6, 7]. However, there are some serious drawbacks besides the initial learning curve:

- TeX was created for fixed page-oriented layouts and it is exceedingly difficult to generate re-scalable and re-flowable HTML for example (despite many attempts [5, 10, 11, 13]).

- Even though LaTeX tries to present a document using structured commands, it is still in essence a linear stream of macros and very difficult to process by other tools.
- Many documents quickly become hard to read with many commands interspersed with actual content.

We created Madoko as a new system that addresses these drawbacks. In particular, Madoko is based on *Markdown* [4] as its input format. The main design goal is to enable lightweight creation of high-quality scholarly and industrial documents for the web and print, while maintaining John Gruber's Markdown philosophy of simplicity and focus on plain text readability.

Since the Markdown input format is well-structured, this allows Madoko to generate both high quality HTML *and* PDF (through LaTeX and BibTeX); see Figure 2 for a side-by-side view. There has been a lot of effort in Madoko to make the LaTeX generation robust and customizable while integrating well with the various academic document- and bibliography styles. This is also fully supported in HTML and therefore an article written in Madoko can both be rendered for final publication in high-quality PDF, but also as a high-quality HTML file. The latter is much better for reading on modern devices like tablets and phones since it can scale and reflow dynamically. A study by Franze et al. [2] showed that the most desired features when reading papers is being able to change the font size, alter margins, or have a single column layout; all of these are trivial in a web browser. Of course, this article itself was written in Madoko, and the HTML version can be viewed at http://tinyurl.com/p4bm62o. Others have tried to create re-scalable and re-flowable content from paginated PDF [12], or the other way around, paginating dynamic content [3], but we believe starting from a more high-level structured input format is a better way of approaching this problem.

The move to Markdown makes the the documents *structured*, *readable*, and *independent*. The final ingredients that Madoko adds are to make the documents *styleable* through standard CSS rules (Section 2.2), and *programmable* through transformation rules (Section 2.4). These additions also makes it easy to add custom domain specific document elements, like *exercise* or *answer*, that can be transformed, numbered, and styled in a declarative manner.

Finally, the online version at madoko.net (see Figure 1) integrates seamlessly with Dropbox, GitHub, and OneDrive, making documents available anywhere on any device. Madoko synchronizes automatically and multiple authors can work concurrently on the same document. Madoko uses robust three-way merges on concurrent updates. This means that updates by others are not quite real-time as in other collaborative environments (although they are performed fre-

DocEng'15, September 8-11, 2015, Lausanne, Switzerland.
Copyright is held by the owner/author(s). Publication rights licensed to ACM.
ACM 978-1-4503-3307-8/15/09 ...$15.00.
DOI: http://dx.doi.org/10.1145/2682571.2797097.

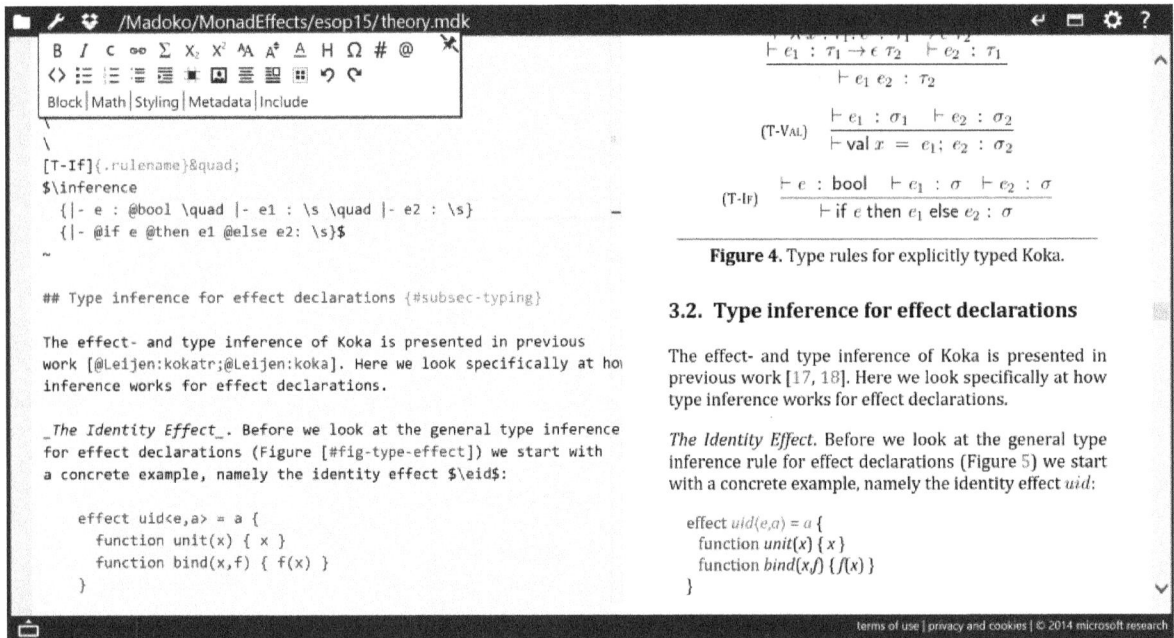

Figure 1: A screenshot of an article in the Madoko.net environment.

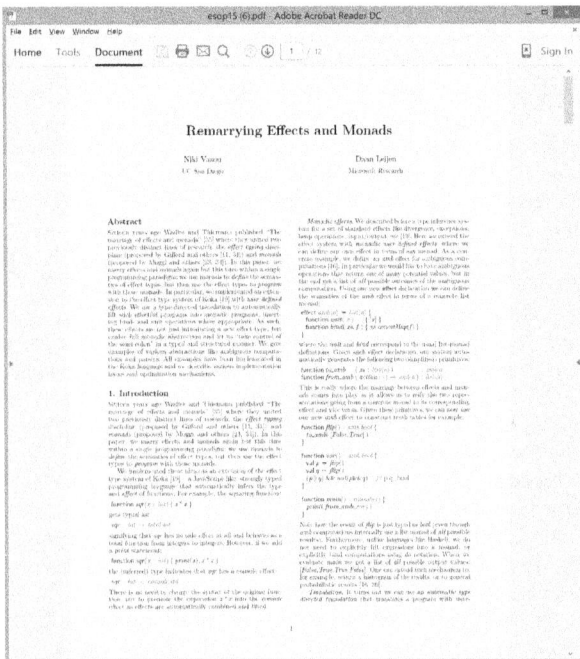

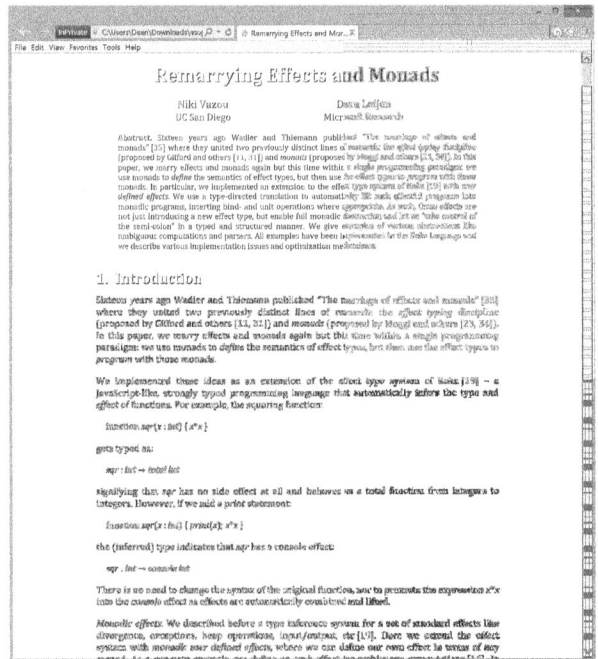

Figure 2: Output in PDF (left) and HTML (right)

quently), but anyone can now work off-line and still reliably merge when connecting again. Madoko.net is itself a HTML5 web application and the editor continues to work in the browser even when offline. Of course, you can always use the plain command line version of Madoko locally (`npm install -g madoko`).

2. OVERVIEW

Given the space constraints, we will highlight various novel features of Madoko in the following sections and compare against other approaches.

2.1 Structured content through Markdown

The input format of Madoko is based on Markdown [4]. This is widely used by writers to create content for the web without having to write explicit HTML. The format is straightforward and based on plain text. Here is a small example:

```
The _grocery_ list:

* [Milk].
* Banana.
* and some math: $e = mc^2$.

[Milk]: http://en.wikipedia.org/wiki/Milk
```
↝

The *grocery* list:

- Milk.
- Banana.
- and some math: $e = mc^2$.

Markdown is carefully designed to be easy to write, but also to be easily readable on its own. Note for example how the link to the Wikipedia article is defined outside of the text to enhance readability. We feel that in practice reading Markdown directly is very pleasant and perhaps a big part of its popularity among writers.

Even though the markup is minimal, it is actually straightforward to parse into its high-level document structure. This makes Markdown much closer to a markup language like XML or HTML, and quite different from a stream processor like TeX. The explicit logical structure makes it possible to easily process and transform Madoko documents for features like custom blocks or code layout for example.

2.2 Styling content through CSS

Unfortunately there has been a plethora of Markdown extensions in recent years that each address different features for different audiences. In the design of Madoko, we try to limit the extensions to just few judiciously chosen generic mechanisms. One of them is the use of standard CSS attributes for document styling. Most Markdown elements can be followed by a set of attributes in between braces[1]. For example,

```
This is [red]{color=red}
```
↝

This is red

---

[1] Currently, the syntax of the CSS attributes follows the HTML style of declaring attributes (i.e. a `=` instead of a `:`) for historical reasons. This is unfortunate and we are working to use fully standard CSS in future releases.

$$e^{ix} = \cos x + i \sin x$$

Figure 3: Euler's formula

Almost all of the CSS 2.0 style attributes are supported. This of course works immediately when generating HTML, but also for PDF output: all the attributes are carefully emulated using LaTeX commands. For most people using CSS attributes for styling works much easier than remembering specific LaTeX commands.

The style attributes work especially well in combination with another extension of Madoko, namely *custom blocks*. As an example, we create a custom *callout* block:

```
~ Callout
The formula $e=mc^2$ is famous.
~
```
↝

Note: The formula $e = mc^2$ is famous.

Note how the callout is indented with a background color and preceded by "Note:". The styling of such custom block is done using a Madoko metadata rule at the start of the document:

```
~Callout: margin-left=1em background-color=#FFC966
         padding=0.5ex before="**Note**: "
```

This makes it very easy to style the final output while still being able to write the content in pleasant Markdown. As of now, Madoko does not yet support regular CSS matching rules but we plan to support that in a future version. The **before** attribute is an example of the rewriting abilities of Madoko where we insert some text before the content. In general, arbitrary regular expression transformations can be applied as shown in Section 2.4.

2.3 References and citations

References, citations, footnotes, table-of-contents, etc. are all supported through standard attributes. Following CSS, we can use #*id* to assign an identity to an element. We re-use the standard brackets in Markdown to refer to such elements. Here is an example of a reference to a figure (together with a citation).

```
See Figure [#fig-euler] for an example of Euler's
formula [@Euler:formula].

~ Figure { #fig-euler caption="Euler's formula" }
$e^{ix} = \cos x + i \sin x$
~
```
↝

See Figure 3 for an example of Euler's formula [1].

As we can see in the previous example, figures are supported through the **Figure** custom block. Citations are referenced using @*id*. The identifier refers to a standard BibTeX entry: Madoko reads standard `.bib` files and integrates seamlessly with BibTeX style files (including for HTML output).

2.4 Transforming content

In complex documents, we often need to transform the input in various ways. Madoko has various mechanisms that allow this. The **replace** attribute transform the element by replacing regular expression matches. For example, in a

Haskell code fragment we may want replace an arrow `->` by an arrow symbol ($\rightarrow$) to make it more pretty. We can do this by adding a metadata rule that matches all code fragments:

```
~code: replace=/->/\(&rarr;\)/g
```

The regular expression actually replaces the symbol `->` with `\(&rarr;\)` where `\(` and `\)` escape out of verbatim mode into regular Markdown. Here is an example of this rule in action:

```
The type of 'map' is 'forall a. a -> a -> a'.
```
$\rightsquigarrow$
```
The type of map is forall a. a → a → a.
```

2.5 Recursive replacements

In general, replacement rules can be nested, chained, and recursive which makes them quite expressive. For example, we can actually calculate Fibonacci numbers. In the following sample, n number of x characters are replaced by $fib(n)$ y characters:

```
How many 'y''s is the Fibonacci of 5 'x''s?
~ Fib
xxxxx
~
```
$\rightsquigarrow$

How many y's is the Fibonacci of 5 x's?yyyyyyyy

This is done through the following metadata rule:

```
~Fib: replace='/^x?$/y/'
      replace='/xx(x*)/~Fib&nl;x\1&nl;~&nl;~Fib&nl;\1&nl;~/'
      notag tight
```

The first replacer will replace a single optional x with a y. The second one matches 2 or more x's, and replaces these recursively by two new `Fib` blocks: one with $n-1$ and one with $n-2$ x characters. These blocks will now get processed recursively. Finally, by using the `notag` attribute we suppress the inclusion of many `div` elements in the HTML, while the `tight` attribute suppresses the addition of paragraph elements.

This example shows the replacement facility of Madoko is quite powerful. It is even possible to define a generic SKI combinator expander which makes Madoko's replacement mechanism (almost) Turing complete[2].

2.6 Typesetting code

Madoko has an internal extension mechanism where we can execute JavaScript code that transforms the content[3]. This is used for example to provide powerful syntax highlighting based on lexical specifications. Most common languages are provided and it is easy to extend existing definitions.

For example,

```
``` javascript
function hello() { return "hello world!"; }
```
```
$\rightsquigarrow$
```
function hello() { return "hello world!"; }
```

---

[2] Almost, since Madoko expands only up to a certain limit and since regular expressions cannot express arbitrarily deep nesting levels.

[3] At this time this mechanism is not yet generically exposed but we plan on doing this in a future version of Madoko.

Moreover, Madoko has another extension that allows typesetting of *pretty* code: here code is rendered in a proportional font where any items starting with 2 or more spaces are vertically aligned (following the excellent `lhs2tex` tool [9]). Combined with replacement rules, this makes it easy to typeset code in a sophisticated way using proportional fonts:

```
``` Haskell
rep_alg    = ( \_            -> \m ->  Leaf m
             , \lfun rfun -> \m ->  let  lt = lfun m
                                         rt = rfun m
                                    in Bin lt rt "hi"
             )
rep_min t  = (cata_tree rep_alg t) (cata_tree min_alg t)
```
```
$\rightsquigarrow$
```
rep_alg   = (λ_   → λm → Leaf m
             , λlfun rfun → λm → let lt = lfun m
                                        rt = rfun m
                                   in Bin lt rt "hi"
)
rep_min t = (cata_tree rep_alg t) (cata_tree min_alg t)
```

In this example we also used a replacement rule to render a `\` as a lambda.

3. CONCLUSION

Try Madoko at madoko.net. Madoko is still a young project and any feedback is much appreciated. We hope that we will see more and more academic articles that also come with a high quality HTML version – being able to resize and reflow makes it much more pleasant to read on screens.

4. REFERENCES

[1] Leonhard Euler. Introductio in analysin infinitorum. 1748.

[2] Juliane Franze, Kim Marriott, and Michael Wybrow. What academics want when reading digitally. In *DocEng '14*, pages 199–202, 2014.

[3] Fabio Giannetti. Paginate dynamic and web content. In *DocEng '11*, pages 143–152, 2011.

[4] John Gruber. Markdown. 2004. URL http://daringfireball.net/projects/markdown.

[5] Eitan Gurari. tex4ht. 2004. URL https://www.tug.org/tex4ht.

[6] Donald E. Knuth. *The TeX book*. AW, 1984.

[7] Leslie Lamport. *LaTeX: A Document Preparation System (2nd Edition)*. Addison-Wesley, 1994.

[8] Daan Leijen. Madoko. 2015. URL https://www.madoko.net.

[9] Andres Löh. lhs2tex. 2004. URL http://www.andres-loeh.de/lhs2tex.

[10] John MacFarlane. Pandoc. 2006. URL http://pandoc.org.

[11] Luc Maranget. On using Hevea, a fast LaTeX to HTML translator. In *Eutypon, proceedings of the Greek TeX friends group*, 11-12, 2004.

[12] Simone Marinai. Reflowing and annotating scientific papers on ebook readers. In *DocEng '13*, pages 241–244, 2013. doi:10.1145/2494266.2494311.

[13] Bruce Miller. LatexML. 2012. URL http://dlmf.nist.gov/LaTeXML.

Spatio-temporal Validation of Multimedia Documents

Joel A. F. dos Santos
Univ. Grenoble Alpes, Inria,
LIG - Grenoble, France
MídiaCom Lab, Univ. Federal
Fluminense - Niterói, Brazil
joel.ferreira-dos-
santos@inria.fr

Christiano Braga
Computer Science Dep.
Univ. Federal Fluminense
Niterói, Brazil
cbraga@ic.uff.br

Débora C.
Muchaluat-Saade
MídiaCom Lab, Computer
Science Dep., Univ. Federal
Fluminense - Niterói, Brazil
debora@midiacom.uff.br

Cécile Roisin
Univ. Grenoble Alpes
Inria, LIG
F-38000 Grenoble, France
cecile.roisin@inria.fr

Nabil Layaïda
Inria, LIG
Univ. Grenoble Alpes
F-38000 Grenoble, France
nabil.layaida@inria.fr

ABSTRACT

A multimedia document authoring system should provide analysis and validation tools that help authors find and correct mistakes before document deployment. Although very useful, multimedia validation tools are not often provided. Spatial validation of multimedia documents may be performed over the initial position of media items before presentation starts. However, such an approach does not lead to ideal results when media item placement changes over time. Some document authoring languages allow the definition of spatio-temporal relationships among media items and they can be moved or resized during runtime. Current validation approaches do not verify dynamic spatio-temporal relationships. This paper presents a novel approach for spatio-temporal validation of multimedia documents. We model the document state, extending the Simple Hypermedia Model (SHM), comprising media item positioning during the whole document presentation. Mapping between document states represent time lapse or user interaction. We also define a set of atomic formulas upon which the author's expectations related to the spatio-temporal layout can be described and analyzed.

Categories and Subject Descriptors

D.2.4 [**Software Engineering**]: Software/Program Verification—*Validation*; F.3.2 [**LOGICS AND MEANINGS OF PROGRAMS**]: Semantics of Programming Languages—*Program analysis*

General Terms

Verification

DocEng'15, September 8–11, 2015, Lausanne, Switzerland.
Copyright is held by the owner/author(s). Publication rights licensed to ACM.
ACM 978-1-4503-3307-8/15/09 ...$15.00.
DOI: http://dx.doi.org/10.1145/2682571.2797060.

Keywords

Multimedia document validation; Spatial validation; Temporal validation

1. INTRODUCTION

One approach for authoring multimedia documents is using a declarative authoring language. Following such an approach, an author describes the spatial and temporal layout of a multimedia presentation in terms of media items and relations (in time and/or space) among them. We consider user interaction as a special case of temporal relation.

Although the use of a declarative authoring language is intended to make the authoring effort easier, it is still possible that the resulting spatio-temporal[1] layout does not fit the author's expectations due to the incorrect use of constructions available in the authoring language in use. We call an *undesired behavior* every mismatch between "what the author wants" and "what the author gets". It is important, thus, that authors are able to identify undesired behaviors in the created multimedia document prior to its deployment.

An attempt to identify undesired behaviors is usually simulation of the document presentation. This process, however, is usually not *effective* since several executions would be necessary for the verification of undesired behaviors, and may be *incomplete*, from a correctness perspective, since the computations representing the document presentation may be infinite. Moreover, multimedia documents can be automatically generated inside a production pipeline. In this case, simulating the execution of the document before deploying it would be costly, if possible.

In previous work [8, 9], we presented a state space [1] approach aiming at the temporal validation of multimedia documents. Our approach relies on a formal representation of the behavior of multimedia documents with *SHM* (Simple Hypermedia Model). *SHM* captures the general behavior of multimedia documents as a rewrite theory $\mathcal{R}_{SHM}$. The description of a given document d in *SHM* as a rewrite theory $\mathcal{R}_{SHM}(d)$ induces a transition system $\mathcal{S}_{SHM}(d) = (S, \rightarrow)$,

---

[1]From now one we use the term *spatio-temporal layout* to represent a combination of both the spatial and temporal layout, the same holds for the term *spatio-temporal relation.*

where each state in S represents the state of d as a whole in a given moment of its execution, and each transition in $\rightarrow$ models a user interaction or a time lapse.

In our previous work, and also in related work, the validation of the spatial layout was performed separated from the temporal layout of a multimedia document. Spatial validation is usually offered by indicating possible overlapping of media items. In our previous work, this was done in a two-step approach, where we first verified if media items would overlap based on their initial position and then verified if they were presented together.

As an example of spatio-temporal validation, consider the document in Figure 1, which has media items A and B^2. In the beginning of the document execution, media A is presented in the *left position*[3]. t_1 time units after the beginning of the presentation, A begins to slide to the *right position*. t_2 time units after t_1, A arrives at the *right position* and then B is presented in the *left position*.

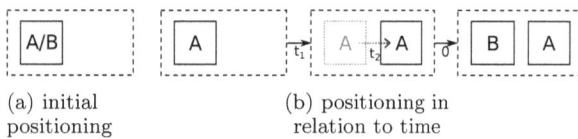

(a) initial   (b) positioning in
positioning   relation to time

Figure 1: Spatial layout of document example

If we consider just the initial positioning for A and B, and not the relative positions they occupy later on, we may infer that they overlap in space, since both have the same initial positioning (Figure 1a) and both are presented together. However, when the position of media items changes in time, as it can be seen in Figure 1b, reasoning about space separate from time gives incorrect results. Therefore we need to consider the position of media objects during the whole document execution.

We propose a novel spatial validation by extending *SHM* such that the document state now comprises media positioning. Positioning information may change over time (if applicable) according to the document specification. We also create a set of atomic formulas upon which the author's expectations, related to the spatio-temporal layout, can be described.

The remainder of this paper is structured as follows. Section 2 discusses our understanding of spatio-temporal validation. Section 3 presents related work considering the validation of multimedia documents. Section 4 discusses our approach for modeling of the spatio-temporal layout of a multimedia document in order to perform validation. Section 5 discusses limitations and future directions to our work. Section 6 concludes this paper and presents future work.

2. SPATIO-TEMPORAL VALIDATION

The spatio-temporal layout of a multimedia presentation is commonly defined as two disjoint sets of definitions. In the temporal axis, media items are placed in time either with absolute values or in relation to other media items or event occurrences, such as user interaction. In the spatial axis, as

---

[2]For simplicity, from now on we may refer to a media item just by media or by its name (A or B in this example).
[3]We describe media positioning by *left position* and *right position*, with respect to the device screen, since a specific value is not important for this example.

presented in [13], media items are placed in relation to the screen, another media or into predefined channels. Usually, media positioning is defined in relation to the screen, in absolute values (pixels) or relative (percentage) values.

A media position may change over time. Some authoring languages allow the author to change media position in response to the occurrence of events in the presentation. Such a change may comprise: moving a media around by changing, for example, its left/top attributes; or scaling a media by changing, for example, its width/height attributes. It is worth mentioning that such changes may occur incrementally over a time interval, as it happens in the example of Figure 1.

In this section we present a series of small examples of a multimedia document d that presents two media items A and B. The author of such examples defines the position of A and B in absolute values. Each figure represents an example, where the dashed rectangle represents the screen (at some moment) and solid rectangles represent the region where a media item is presented. Arrows between two screens represent a time lapse and arrows between regions inside the same screen represent movement, which can be done incrementally over a time period whose duration is presented over the arrow.

Case 1. This example describes a static spatial layout, i.e. A and B do not change their position over time. This case is a pure temporal example, where A is presented (just) before B in time. Figure 2 presents the spatio-temporal layout the author perceives from document d.

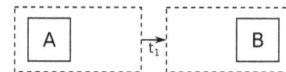

Figure 2: Case 1 spatio-temporal layout

considering a temporal layout example, most of the author's expectations can be described with temporal properties. For example, the author may want to ensure that, for this document, A *before* B, or that *not*(A *together* B). However, it is also possible for the author to express spatial properties. For example, the author may wish to ensure that A *sideof* B, or A *samesize* B. Since the spatial layout is static, spatial validation can be done over the initial position of media items.

Case 2. This example involves the change over time of the spatial layout of a multimedia document. In this example, A has a fixed position and B moves across the screen, changing its position incrementally over t_1 time units. Figure 3 presents the spatio-temporal layout the author perceives from document d.

Figure 3: Case 2 spatio-temporal layout

Validating the spatio-temporal layout of such an example is not so simple as statically validating the spatial layout and, in parallel, validating the temporal layout. For example, suppose the author wish to ensure that at some point, while moving across the screen, B will overlap A. This requires verifying if, in at least one moment during the document execution, A and B will overlap. Such kind of property has to be encoded by composing temporal and spatial properties, such as *somepoint(A overlap B)*.

Case 3. This example, as in case 2, involves change of the spatial layout of a multimedia document over time. However, more than one change in the spatial layout occur in sequence. Figure 4 presents the spatio-temporal layout the author perceives from document d.

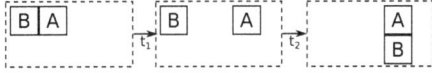

Figure 4: Case 3 spatio-temporal layout

In this example, we have two sequential changes in the position of media items A and B. First, A after t_1 time units changes its position getting detached from B. After A and B are detached for t_2 time units, B changes its position to be below A and, once again, attached to A. The author may wish to enforce, in this case, for example, that *somepoint(A detached B)*, or yet *A together B*. Interesting properties to be verified, however, involve the sequencing of states, such as: *given that we reach a state where A is at the side of B, can we reach another state where A is above B?* To encode such kind of property, one could use a temporal connector such as *(A side B) then (A above B)*.

3. RELATED WORK

The literature is rich on the discussion of spatio-temporal validation of multimedia documents. Some of the approaches discussed in this section do not primarily address validation but could be considered in such a task. We classify them according to coverage in either spatial or temporal dimensions, as follows: (i) purely temporal, (ii) both temporal and spatial but with the spatial dimension static, and (iii) both spatial and temporal dimensions (*spatio-temporal*). We also classify them according to the reasoning principle applied for document validation. The first group of papers (first line of Table 1) relates to validation of a multimedia document by investigating the document state over its presentation. This may be done by reachability analysis or the application of axioms over the document state. The second group of papers (second line of Table 1) relates to validation of a multimedia document by checking the consistency of a set of constraints.

	Purely Temporal	Temporal + Spatial (static)	Spatio-Temporal
Doc. State	[20, 7, 12, 5]	[15]	[16]
Constraint	[4, 11, 17]		[3]*

Table 1: Related work classification

Santos et al. in [20] discuss an approach for the temporal validation of multimedia documents by translating them into the real-time process algebra framework RT-LOTOS. It combines processes that specify the document presentation with other processes that model the available platform. A minimum reachability graph is built from the RT-LOTOS formal specification such that each node in the graph represents a reachable state and each edge the occurrence of an event or temporal progression. The validation is achieved by verifying, for example, if the state corresponding to the end of the document presentation can be reached from the

document's initial state. Similarly, verifying if a media item will be executed is performed by determining if a state where it is being executed is reachable from the document's initial state. The tool presented in [20] can validate NCM (Nested Context Model) [22] and SMIL (Synchronized Multimedia Integration Language) [23] documents.

Oliveira et al. in [7] introduce HMBS (Hypermedia Model Based on Statecharts). An HMBS multimedia application is described by a statechart, where states represent pages (i.e. the information presented to the user) and transactions and events represent a set of possible link activations. The validation of an HMBS application is performed over a reachability tree, which is built from the application statechart. From the reachability tree, it is possible to determine if a given page is reachable or not and also if a group of pages is presented simultaneously or not. The reachability graph also allows the detection of configurations from which no other page may be reached or that present cyclical paths.

Felix in [12] presents an approach for the validation of temporal properties of NCL documents through the application of model checking techniques. He presents a notation for the description of NCL's temporal characteristics. Such a description is transformed into a timed automata net that indicates the document temporal behavior. The transformation creates a state machine for each media item and a synchronizer machine for each link declared in the document. A synchronizer machine is used for tying together the occurrence of events in media state machines. The validation of an NCL document is performed over the timed automata net representing the document using temporal logic formulas created by the author.

Bossi and Gaggi in [5] define a formal semantics for SMIL through a set of inference rules inspired by Hoare logic. The rules describe the document state before and after the execution of a given SMIL construction. Thus, in the authoring phase, the structure of a SMIL document may be enriched with assertions expressing temporal properties. Another application resulting from the defined formal semantics is the concept of equivalence, which guarantees that two sets of SMIL constructions may be replaced, without changing the presentation behavior. The validation of a document is performed by the application of axioms, also defined in the proposed semantics, that verify if a given construction or set of constructions correctly change the document state. Otherwise, it presents to the author the problem found so it can be corrected.

As can be seen in Table 1, the works presented in [20, 7, 12, 5] present a purely temporal approach, where the validation of a multimedia document is performed by investigating the document state over its presentation. In [20, 7, 12], it is done by reachability analysis and in [5] by analyzing if the document state changes according to some axioms. Validation of the spatial layout of a document is not discussed in those papers.

Júnior et al. in [15] use a model-driven approach for the presentation behavior validation of NCL documents. The validation is achieved by transforming an NCL document into a Petri Net. This transformation is done in two steps. In the first step, the document is represented in a language called FIACRE as a set of components and processes (representing the behavior of a component). The second step transforms the FIACRE representation into a Petri Net. The validation uses a model-checking tool and temporal logic formulas representing the properties to be validated. Spatial validation is briefly discussed in [15] and is performed over the document initial positioning. As presented in Table 1, their approach covers both temporal and spatial dimensions, however the spatial dimension is static.

King et al. in [16] define extensions for the SMIL language allowing authors to describe how the spatio-temporal layout should change in reaction to events. Changes in position and size are described by a set of expressions, which may consider the state of the document. The paper presents an approach for calculating at runtime the value of such expressions, and therefore the change in the spatial layout to be performed. Although such an approach does not refer to document validation, it is an interesting example on how to parameterize by time or an event occurrence the rules that specify the spatial layout of a presentation.

Bertino et al. in [4] propose an authoring model based on constraints. A multimedia application in that model consists of several topics, where each topic is composed by semantically-related media items. The system automatically group media items into topics according to the constraints defined by the author. The application generation process is responsible for three main tasks: consistency checking, presentation structure generation and topics generation. The system enlarge the set of constraints with others that, even not defined explicitly, are consequences of the constraints defined by the author. Consistency checking is then performed over the constraint set. If an inconsistency arises, the system applies relaxation techniques, to reduce the constraint set to a consistent one. When such a reduction is not possible, the author review is required. The presentation structure generation process creates a direct graph that represents the application structure. Each vertex of such graph represents a topic and each edge a connection between topics. After this step, the system relates media items to topics and builds, for each topic, the spatial layout and the temporal sequence of media items belonging to it.

Elias et al. in [11] also propose an authoring model based on constraints. It defines two operators *TEMPORAL* and *SPATIAL*, to model temporal and spatial relations, respectively. Each operator allows the author to define a priority value. In order to maintain the consistency of the constraint set, whenever necessary, constraints are removed according to this priority value. In case two inconsistent constraints present the same priority, relaxation techniques are applied to determine the constraint to be removed. Besides the verification of inconsistencies among constraints, this approach also enables the author to verify if the constraint set is incomplete, that is, if there is one or more media items that are not reached during presentation. The consistency checking is done by finding the minimum spanning tree T in the constraint graph. Constraints that create cycles are removed to maintain the acyclic nature of T. Completeness checking is done by searching all media items reachable from the first media item. If this search returns the vertex set of T, then all items are reached directly or indirectly from the initial one. Otherwise, the author has to define constraints to make the constraint set complete. With the use of the *SPATIAL* operator, it is possible to determine if A overlaps B and vice versa. The spatial consistency is checked the same way as the temporal one.

Laborie et al. in [17] presents an approach for the automatic adaptation of the layout of a multimedia presentation according to the display used for its presentation. The approach creates an abstract description of the author's document as a set of objects and constraints representing temporal and spatial relations among objects. It also takes into account a profile comprising device constraints together with user preferences. Given the set of potential document executions $\mathcal{M}_s$ given by the abstract description and the set of potential executions $\mathcal{M}_p$ given by the profile, the adaptation process calculates $\mathcal{M}_s \cap \mathcal{M}_p$ to determine if some adaptation is required or not. In case the document has to be adapted, the goal is to change document relations such that it now complies with the profile and the (behavioral) distance from the previous declaration is minimum.

As can be seen in Table 1, the works presented in [4, 11, 17] cover both temporal and spatial dimensions, where the validation of a multimedia document is performed by consistency checking over a set of constraints. In each work, however, the spatial dimension is static, since spatial constraints do not change over time. Moreover, reasoning about time and space in [4, 11, 17] is performed as two separated problems.

Belouaer and Maris in [3] present a SAT Modulo Theory (SMT) [2] approach for solving spatio-temporal planning problems. A set of constraints modeling the spatial disposition of items and their hierarchy is used to describe both the initial state of a given problem and its goal. Other constraints model actions that change the spatial position of items. Such actions may define an inherent duration and also at each moment (in time) they should be applied. By solving the problem, taking into account the constraints representing actions, it is possible to verify if the goal can be achieved or not. Although this work does not refer to multimedia documents, it is an interesting example on how spatial constraints can be parameterized by time in order to cover both spatial and temporal dimensions.

4. MODELING SPATIO-TEMPORAL LAYOUT

In our work, we use a state space approach for the validation of multimedia documents. We rely on the representation of the behavior of multimedia documents as a rewrite theory, which we call *SHM* [9]. In Section 4.1 we briefly describe the *SHM* model. The proposed extensions to allow spatio-temporal validation are presented in Section 4.2. Next, Section 4.3 discusses how the author expectation can be described in *SHM*. Section 4.4 presents the use of *SHM* with a real document. Finally, Section 4.5 presents an evaluation of our approach.

4.1 SHM

This section gives a brief description of *SHM*. Our intention is to equip the reader with sufficient tools to understand our validation approach and its extensions in Section 4.2. A more comprehensive description of *SHM* is available in [9].

Essentially, multimedia documents describe the spatio-temporal layout of a multimedia presentation in terms of media items and relations (in time and/or space) among them. The presentation as a whole can be parameterized by variables inherent to media items or global to the document.

SHM captures the general behavior of multimedia documents as a rewrite theory $\mathcal{R}_{SHM} = (\Sigma, E, R)$, where (Σ, E)

defines the constructs [4] to be used to represent the document state (in a given moment during its execution), and R defines rules that induce transitions among states.

The document state is represented by the composition of the states of all media fragments declared inside a document and the value of variables. A media fragment represents a subpart of a media item, possibly the whole item. State information for a given fragment or variable is represented by means of state machine configurations ($SMConf$). An $SMConf$ has the general form $\langle id, ty, st, oc, cl, v \rangle$, where id is a fragment or variable identifier, ty is the state machine type, st its state, oc its occurrences counter, cl its countdown clock and v its value (in case $SMConf$ represents a variable). The type of an $SMConf$ can be either *[pre]sentation* when it represents the presentation state of a fragment, *[sel]ection* when it represents user selection over a fragment and *[att]ribution* when it represents changes in the value of variables. The state of an $SMConf$ has the following possible values: *sleeping*, *occurring* and *paused*.

Every state machine configuration starts in the *sleeping* state. As the presentation goes on, the st component will eventually change to the *occurring* state. If we suppose an $SMConf$ associated with a media item representing a video object, as the first frame of the video begins its presentation, the st component of the $SMConf$ representing its presentation transits to the *occurring* state. The st component of an $SMConf$ remains in the *occurring* state for a given period of time, represented by the $SMConf$'s countdown clock. As soon as the last frame of the video finishes its presentation (i.e. its countdown clock reaches zero), the st component of $SMConf$ goes back to the *sleeping* state. This is what we call the *natural end* of a media presentation. It is important to highlight that not all media items may have a natural end. One example is a media item representing an image, which does not have an inherent duration. In this case, the st component of the $SMConf$ representing that media item will remain in the *occurring* state indefinitely.

Relations in SHM may be defined among fragments, variables or a combination of both. Every relation is represented by an equation with the general form $[l]\ C_o \rightarrow C_f\ if\ P$, where l is a label to the relation, C_o and C_f represent (part of) the document configuration and P is a predicate over the state of fragments or the value of variables. Given that the document state reaches a configuration that contains C_o and predicate P is evaluated as *true*, we rewrite C_o by C_f, thus changing the document configuration according to a given relation. Relations are triggered by state changes in an $SMConf$ and, as an effect, produce changes in the state of other $SMConf$s (possibly the same). Labels in Figure 5 correspond to the state changes considered by SHM.

Relations may be applied from time to time, whenever the presentation reaches a configuration where a relation can be applied. Those configurations are reached either by a time lapse (when the natural end of a fragment occurs) or by user interaction with a fragment. Therefore, we model time lapse and user interaction by rules *step* and *interact* in R. Rule *step* fast-forwards the presentation by decrementing countdown clocks of every $SMConf$ in the *occurring* state. Given that at least one $SMConf$ clock will reach zero, the resulting state change (possibly) triggers the application of

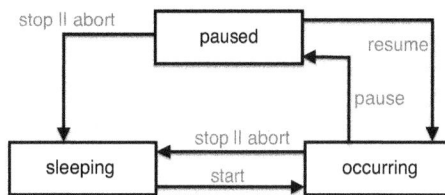

Figure 5: State changes

relations further changing the document state as a whole. Given that the presentation state of a fragment is in the *occurring* state, rule *interact* changes its selection state at any point during its presentation. The non-determinism induced by the interleaving of both rules produces different traces of the document presentation.

For a given document d, we extend theory $\mathcal{R}_{SHM}$ into a rewrite theory $\mathcal{R}_{SHM}(d)$ such that $\mathcal{R}_{SHM}(d)$ declares all fragments inside d and variables considered in relations. For each relation in d one or more rewrite rules are created to represent such a relation. Moreover, additional rewrite rules are created to model relations among fragments of a media item and the media item as a whole, and relations among media items and their parent composition, if there is one. Transformation τ_{SHM} automates such process creating rewrite theory $\mathcal{R}_{SHM}(d)$ from a multimedia document d.

In [8, 9] we have used SHM for the temporal validation of multimedia documents through model checking. Theory $\mathcal{R}_{SHM}(d)$ induces a transition system $\mathcal{S}_{SHM}(d) = (S, \rightarrow)$, where each state in S represents the state of d as a whole in a given moment of its execution, and each transition in $\rightarrow$ models the user interaction or a time lapse. Moreover, a set of predefined expected behaviors were formalized as LTL [18] (Linear Temporal Logic) formulas, such as: *reachability* (will a media be presented?), *media termination* (given that a media is presented, does it end?) and *document termination* (does the document as a whole end?).

4.2 SHM extension for Spatio-Temporal Validation

In our previous work, we have attempted to offer spatial validation by indicating possible overlapping of media items. This was done in a two-step approach, where we first verified if media items might overlap based on their initial position and then verified if they were presented together.

In this work, to enhance the spatio-temporal validation, we extend SHM in two ways: (i) the document state now stores the position of a media item (or a fragment of it) and (ii) given that the position of a media changes over time this behavior has to be captured by SHM.

The former is achieved by representing every positioning attribute - *left*, *top*, *width* and *height* - as a variable, so that the document state is able to store its value during the execution. In order to be able to relate a given variable to a media item attribute, we extend SHM with the following functions:

$$left, top, widht, height : MedId \rightarrow VarId$$

where *MedId* and *VarId* are sets of identifiers for media items and variables in SHM, respectively. With such approach, we

---

[4]As presented along this section, such constructs declare state machine configurations, their composition into the whole document and operations for changing their state.

137

can evaluate the value of the *left* attribute of media A, by evaluating the value of variable $left(A)$.

During the document presentation, it is possible that media items change their position. A common way to achieve it is to declare relations that change the value of the positioning attributes in response to an event occurrence. This change can be either *discrete*, or *incremental* over a time interval. In the latter, the relation provides, together with the new values, the duration for the change and the increment by which values have to be changed.

In order to model such behavior, we extend transformation τ_{SHM} so that for every relation in d that changes the value of positioning attributes of media items, one or more equations perform the same change in $\mathcal{R}_{SHM}(d)$. For example, suppose the following causal relation declared in d^5.

$$[r1] \; A.begin \rightarrow B.left := 400 \; if \; \top$$

It states that whenever the document reaches a configuration where media A begins its presentation, we change the value of attribute *left* of media B to 400.

Transformation τ_{SHM} will create the following rewrite rule for representing relation *r1*, where *pre* and *att* is the short for presentation and attribution, respectively.

$$[r1] \; A.pre.begin \rightarrow \left\{ \begin{array}{l} left(B).att.start, \\ left(B).value = 400 \end{array} \right\} \; if \; \top$$

The relation presented above exemplifies a discrete change of the positioning attributes of media B. It is possible that this change is incremental over a time interval. For example, suppose the following causal relation *r2*.

$$[r2] \; A.begin \rightarrow \left\{ \begin{array}{l} B.left := 400 \\ during : 4s \; by : 10px \end{array} \right\} \; if \; B.left == 0$$

It extends relation *r1*, such that, given A beginning its presentation and B's left position is equal to 0, the positioning attribute *left* changes its value by an increment of 10 *pixels* for 4 *seconds*. The *left* value changes 400 *pixels*, with an increment of 10 *pixels*, thus 40 incremental changes are produced over 4 seconds. Therefore each change occurs at each 0.1 seconds.

Transformation τ_{SHM} will create the following rewrite rules for representing relation *r2*.

$$[r2\_init] \; A.pre.begin \rightarrow \left\{ \begin{array}{l} left(B).att.start, \\ left(B).value \; + = \; 10, \\ C.pre.start \end{array} \right\}$$
$$if \; left(B).value == 0$$

$$[r2\_inc] \; C.pre.end \rightarrow \left\{ \begin{array}{l} left(B).att.start, \\ left(B).value \; + = \; 10, \\ C.pre.start \end{array} \right\}$$
$$if \; C.pre.occur < 40$$

where C has a duration of 0.1 seconds and is used to represent the delay between two incremental changes. Operation $+ =$ represents an increment operation over the value of variables.

---

[5]We use the same notation of *SHM* for simplifying the example.

4.3 Describing the author's expectation

Multimedia documents can be created by an author with a range of available authoring tools. Depending on the multimedia language in use, tools may be able to provide the author with different views of the document, besides a preview of its spatio-temporal layout. Moreover, multimedia documents can be automatically generated, making it difficult for an author to know all of its spatio-temporal layout specifications. Our approach is intended to be used after the authoring phase, where the author wants to verify if the spatio-temporal layout of a given existing document is the expected one.

As presented in Section 4.1, in [8, 9] we formalized a set of predefined expected behaviors, such as: *reachability* (will a media be presented?), *media termination* (given that a media is presented, does it end?) and *document termination* (does the document as a whole end?). For each document to be validated those properties were verified.

With the *SHM* extensions presented in Section 4.2 we are able to represent media item position and their change across the document presentation. In order to enable the description of the author's expectation about the spatio-temporal layout he/she might perceive, we define a set of atomic formulas in either temporal or spatial axis. The description of a spatio-temporal layout, therefore, is achieved by a combination of both.

In the temporal axis, formulas represent Allen's relations [1] between time intervals as presented in Figure 6, where rectangles represent time intervals.

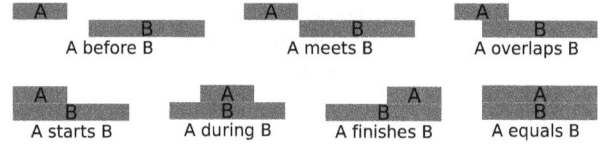

Figure 6: Allen's relations between time intervals

In the spatial axis, formulas represent RCC spatial relations between regions [19] as presented in Figure 7, where rectangles represent regions.

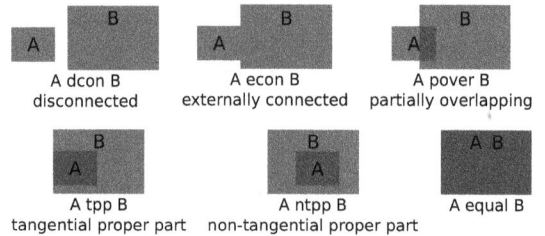

Figure 7: RCC spatial relations between active regions

Although RCC relations enable to relate media items in space, they may not be enough to represent the exact spatial layout expected by an author. Suppose, for example, the three configurations presented in Figure 8. Each example represents a spatial layout relating media items A and B.

It is worth noticing that every example can be described by relation *pover*, since in each example A partially overlaps B. However, they can not be considered the same spatial layout since A and B assume different relative positions in each example.

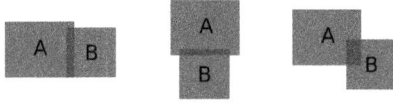

Figure 8: Possible cases of A *pover* B

To be able to describe the relative position between media items, we extend RCC spatial relations (except *equal*), so that relations are parameterized by the angle between media items. The angle between two media items is calculated as presented in Figure 9. It presents two *disconnected* media items A and B with A being at an angle α with respect to B.

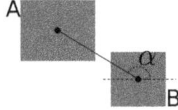

Figure 9: Angle between media items with respect to B

We represent such an example by the formula A $dcon(\alpha)$ B.

Angle α can be described in degrees or, if such precision is not necessary, by a cardinal direction as presented in Figure 10.

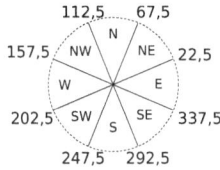

Figure 10: Cardinal direction

Thus, the example of Figure 9 may also be represented by formula A $dcon(NW)$ B.

We formalize the properties we want to validate in LTL [18]. An LTL formula φ is defined as follows, where X, F, G, U, W and R are called temporal operators.

$$\varphi \quad ::= \quad \top \mid \bot \mid p \mid \neg(\varphi) \mid (\varphi \wedge \varphi) \mid (\varphi \vee \varphi) \mid (\varphi \rightarrow \varphi) \mid$$
$$(X\varphi) \mid (F\varphi) \mid (G\varphi) \mid (\varphi \ U \ \varphi) \mid (\varphi \ W \ \varphi) \mid (\varphi \ R \ \varphi)$$

$X\varphi$ (*next*) states that a formula φ must be valid for the following state. $F\varphi$ (*future*) states that a formula φ must be valid for some future state. $G\varphi$ (*global*) states that a formula φ must be valid for all states in a path. $\varphi_1 \ U \ \varphi_2$ (*until*) states that a formula φ_1 must be valid until a formula φ_2 becomes valid. $\varphi_1 \ W \ \varphi_2$ (weak until) states that a formula φ_1 must be valid until a formula φ_2 becomes valid or φ_1 must be valid for all states in the path. $\varphi_1 \ R \ \varphi_2$ (release) states that a formula φ_1 must be valid until a formula φ_2 becomes valid and both φ_1 and φ_2 must be valid at the same time for some state.

It is worth noticing that formulas in the temporal axis describe the evolution of (part of) the document state through several states. For example, formula A *meets* B is described by the following LTL formula.

$$i_1 \ meets \ i_2 = \quad F((i_1.pre.occurring \wedge i_2.pre.sleeping) \wedge$$
$$X(i_1.pre.sleeping \wedge i_2.pre.occurring))$$

On the other hand, formulas in the spatial axis consider the values of positioning attributes inside a given state. They

are combined with a temporal operator for representing a spatio-temporal layout. As an usage example of a spatial formula, suppose we want to verify in **case 2** of Section 2 if at some point A and B will overlap in space. Thus we write the following formula

$$F(A \ pover \ B)$$

where we combine spatial relation *pover* with temporal operator F (future).

4.4 Modeling in practice

Both the *SHM* model and transformation τ_{SHM} are implemented using the Maude system [6]. The verification of LTL formulas is performed by the Maude model-checker tool. Transformation τ_{SHM} has been implemented for both NCL [14] and SMIL [23] documents. The extensions of τ_{SHM} presented in this paper have been implemented only for NCL document transformation.

Figure 11, adapted from [21], presents the spatio-temporal layout of an excerpt of document *First João* used as case-study. It presents a main video (media item *video*) about a soccer player. At some point during the video presentation, an advertisement icon is presented (media item *icon*) at the upper right corner (as seen in Figures 11a and 11b). If the user interacts with the icon, the video is downsized and repositioned (upper left corner) and a video of a kid thinking about shoes (media item *kid*) starts playing (as seen in Figure 11c).

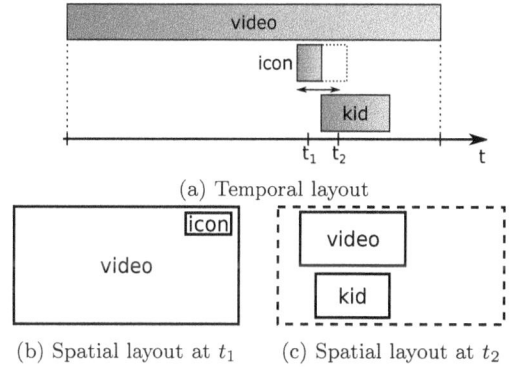

(a) Temporal layout

(b) Spatial layout at t_1 (c) Spatial layout at t_2

Figure 11: First João spatio-temporal layout

In such an example the author may want to ensure either temporal properties, spatial properties or both. For example, suppose the author wants to ensure that media items *video* and *kid* will never overlap (in space). The author may also want to ensure that media *video* is presented above *kid*.

This expected spatio-temporal layout can be described, by using the formulas presented in Section 4.3 as follows

$$kid \ during \ video \rightarrow G(kid \ dcon(S) \ video) \qquad (1)$$

where, given that *kid* is presented while *video* is presented, then *kid* has to be disconnected from *video* and below it (at its south).

Using *SHM* we can validate Formula 1 by using the Maude model-checker as follows, where [] is used to represent the temporal operator G (global).

```
1  Maude> red modelCheck(run, ('kid pre during 'video pre) −>
2                                      []('kid dcon[S] 'video)) .
3  reduce in NCLDOC : modelCheck(run, 'kid pre during 'video pre −>
4                                      []'kid dcon[S]'video) .
5  rewrites: 2036 in 39ms cpu (48ms real) (51323 rewrites/second)
6  result Bool: true
```

Formula 1 holds since, as can be seen in Figure 11, *kid* and *video* do not overlap. However, if just their initial position and size were considered, they would overlap and the spatial-temporal analysis would not be correct.

4.5 Evaluation

We performed two tests to evaluate our proposal, in order to indicate a reasonable performance for our approach. Test results are presented in Figure 13. Tests were performed in a Centos 6.7 virtual machine running on four cores of an Intel E5-2650v2, 2.6 GHz with 16 GB of memory.

In the first test we have a document d with two media items A and B. Both A and B start their presentation as d's presentation begins. Media A changes its position and size until it has the same position and size of B and then it remains that way. Document d's presentation ends when both A and B finish their presentation. Figure 12 presents the spatio-temporal layout for this test.

Figure 12: Spatio-temporal layout for the first test

The first test consists in incrementing the number n of steps for changing A's position and size until it reaches the same position and size of B. For each value of n we ran the following Maude command and gathered the statistics provided by Maude.

```
1  red modelCheck(run, <>('A equal 'B)) .
```

As the number of steps grows, the number of states in $\mathcal{S}_{SHM}(d)$ grows linearly with it. The impact in increasing the number of steps in the time Maude takes to perform the above command is presented in Figure 13a. As it can be seen, time also increases linearly with the number of steps.

In the second test, we fixed the number of steps to 10 and increased the number n of media items inside the document changing their position. For each value of n we ran the following two Maude commands and gathered the statistics provided by Maude.

```
1  red modelCheck(run, <>('A1 equal 'B)) .
2  red modelCheck(run, <>('A1 equal 'B /\ ... /\ 'An equal 'B)) .
```

The impact in increasing the number of media items in the time Maude takes to perform the two commands above is presented in Figure 13b. As it can be seen, time grows exponentially with the number of items and the size of the formula to be tested has almost no impact in time. Testing the execution of each test document alone indicated that approximately all the time spent by validating the above formula was spent by Maude in building the transition system where the temporal formulas were verified.

Comparing our approach presented in this paper to our previous works indicates that time increases mostly because of the growth in the number of state machines required for

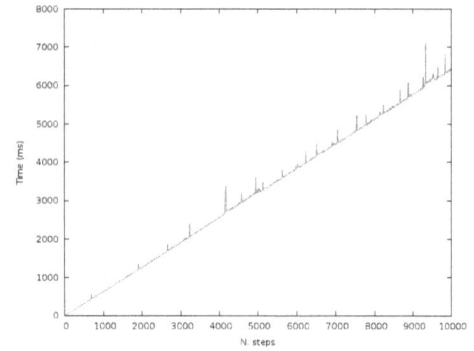

(a) Number of steps X time (ms)

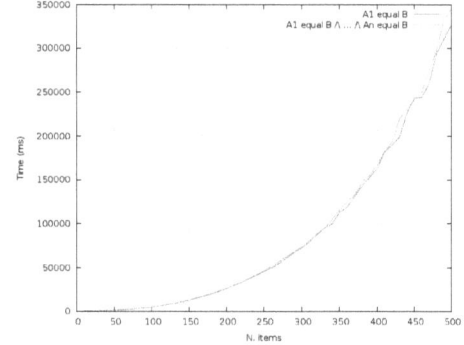

(b) Number of items X time (ms)

Figure 13: Test results

representing the document's spatial layout. In our tests, for each state machine representing a media item, five more (four for the positioning attributes and one for the increment delay) were created. Comparing the time spent to run each document with a similar one, regarding the number of state machines, but without spatial information, indicates a small increase in time.

From the graph in Figure 13a we see a linear growth of time related to the number of steps for changing the position and size of a media item. For a document with 10000 steps the validation is performed in about 6.5 seconds. It is worth mentioning that, in common multimedia documents, movements of media items take a few seconds, thus, even with a precision of milliseconds we are still able to give an answer to the author in a reasonable time. In general, such a huge number of steps is not necessary and can be abstracted to decrease the overall duration of the validation.

Increasing the number of steps for changing the positioning attributes of media items will linearly increase the number of states, as seen above. A real problem of state explosion arrives, on the other hand, when user interaction is possible. Depending on the document, the time interval when a user can interact with a media item may be very long. Moreover, it is possible for media items to be selected more than once. Since in *SHM* when the user interacts with a media item, a new branch is created when that selection occurred, it is easy to see that as selection grows, more states there will be. To handle such a problem, we enable the author to define a maximum number of user interactions for each media item during transformation τ_{SHM}. Other possible solution for avoiding such increase in the number of states is to create abstractions in the state representation.

5. DISCUSSION

In Section 4.5 we presented test results, which indicate a reasonable performance of our validation approach. Together with the results we discussed some limitations of our work. In this section we present a possible direction for our approach regarding such limitations.

Our validation is performed by model-checking over a transition system representing the document state evolution over time. In our approach, the document state represents current values for information about media items, e.g its state, countdown clock, top position or width. Taking into consideration the spatial layout, the document state describes "the whole" layout (i.e. all positioning attributes) in a given instant.

Another interesting approach would be to validate the spatio-temporal layout of a multimedia document even when "a partial" layout description is provided, for example, by a set of spatial constraints. Thus, the author does not need to provide specific positioning for each media item, but instead, spatial relations among them.

A future direction for our work is to provide a constraint approach for the spatio-temporal validation of multimedia documents. In such an approach, both the temporal and spatial layouts are described through a set of constraints. Spatial constraints may be parameterized by time, such that they are enforced just in a given moment (or interval) during the document execution. By the combination of both approaches, we will be able to perform the spatio-temporal validation presented here but even when a partial description of the presentation spatial layout is provided.

We have been working in this new approach by representing constraints as formulas in the SMT solver Yices [10]. Temporal constraints relate begin and end times of intervals. Spatial constraints relate the borders of rectangular regions. Whenever it is possible to build the layout from the set of constraints, the solver presents a valuation for it.

In the temporal dimension, media items are represented as intervals. Each interval is represented as a tuple $\langle i, e, d, b \rangle$, where i and e represent its initial and end times, respectively, d its duration and b is a boolean that indicates if a given interval is considered or not to be part of the temporal layout.

Using that approach we describe the example in Figure 11. The intervals initial time, end time and duration are gathered from the document declaration, whenever possible. We also have an interval called $selec$, to represent the user interaction over media $icon$ such that $selec$, if it occurs, has to occur inside the interval for $icon$.

We model the causal relation specifying that, once $icon$ is selected, end media $icon$ presentation and start media kid presentation as follows, where I^i and I^e represent the initial and end times of interval I, I^d its duration and I^b if it is considered or not as part of the temporal layout.

$$(selec^b \wedge kid^b \wedge (icon^e = selec^e) \wedge (kid^i = selec^e)) \quad \vee$$
$$(\neg selec^b \wedge \neg kid^b \wedge (icon^e = icon^i + icon^d))$$

Therefore, the interval for media kid occurs only if $selec$ occurs and not otherwise. Whenever $selec$ occurs it causes the end of $icon$.

In such an approach we can verify if it is possible for kid to end after $video$ (as exemplified above) by adding the following constraint,

$$kid^b \wedge (kid^e > video^e)$$

that, as expected, yields an $unsatisfiable$ temporal layout. Yices takes around 5ms for presenting this answer.

In the spatial dimension, media items are represented as rectangles by their projection in either x and y dimensions. Each projection is represented as a tuple $\langle i, c, e \rangle$, where i and e represents its initial and end border and c its center in that dimension. We define a set of constraints to organize media items in space. Constraints are able to $align$ two items, $distribute$ items inside a region, compare the size of two items and also arrange items in a $flow$ inside a region.

To present a reasonable performance for that approach we used Yices to verify if it was possible to organize 49 items inside a 450×450 canvas. Sizes of items represent the combinations of width and height ranging from 10 to 70. The result is $satisfiable$ and Yices presents a possible valuation for item regions. It is worth noticing that smaller canvas sizes yielded $unsatisfiable$ spatial layouts. The evaluation of such an example in Yices takes around 3s.

The direction of this work, aiming at enhancing the multimedia validation we provide is to combine our existing model-checking approach with such SMT approach. For problems involving conditions over events and specific instances of media items (such as looping media items), it seems straightforward to use model-checking. On the other hand, problems involving numerical dependencies, such as placing media items in time and space, it seems straightforward to use SMT.

In our approach, media items are represented in space by their rectangular region. However, it is possible that the visible amount of a media item has a different form. One solution for improving the precision in media items representation (in space) is to represent it by the composition of several small rectangles. The greater the number of rectangles, the greater the representation precision is. On the other hand, more rectangles means more time for validating a document. An approximation, therefore, is necessary. We believe the best solution is to leave such option for the user.

6. CONCLUSION

Although the use of a declarative authoring language is intended to make the authoring effort easier, it is still possible that the resulting spatio-temporal layout does not fit the author's expectations due to the incorrect use of constructions available in the authoring language in use.

This work proposes an approach for the temporal and spatial validation of multimedia documents such that positioning information may change over time (if applicable) according to the document specification.

The extension of SHM for enabling spatio-temporal validation, as verified by tests, increases the time necessary to perform the validation. It occurs mainly because of the increase in the number of state machines necessary for storing the positioning attributes of media items. Moreover, although small, increasing the number of steps in an incremental change of position and/or size also contributes to increase time. As discussed, such an increase, however, is not considered a problem for validating common multimedia documents.

By the combination of formulas in the temporal and in the spatial axis the author may describe the desired spatio-temporal scenario. An ongoing work is to provide a tool where the author may create a description of the desired spatio-temporal scenario. Moreover, this tool enables the author to create a set of tests to be validated over a given multimedia document.

This paper also discussed future directions for our multimedia validation approach. Future directions point towards using a constraint-based approach for representing the spatio-temporal layout of a document and also performing the document validation. Initial results indicate the soundness of such an approach.

7. ACKNOWLEDGEMENTS

We thank the support of both the Brazilian agency CNPq and Inria in the context of Science without Borders Program. We also thank the Brazilian agencies FAPERJ and CAPES for their support.

8. REFERENCES

[1] J. F. Allen. Maintaining Knowledge about Temporal Intervals. *Communications of the ACM*, 26(11):832–843, 1983.

[2] C. W. Barrett, R. Sebastiani, S. A. Seshia, and C. Tinelli. Satisfiability modulo theories. *Handbook of satisfiability*, 185:825–885, 2009.

[3] L. Belouaer and F. Maris. SMT Spatio-Temporal Planning. In *ICAPS 2012 Workshop on Constraint Satisfaction Techniques for Planning and Scheduling Problems (COPLAS 2012)*, pages 6–15, 2012.

[4] E. Bertino, E. Ferrari, A. Perego, and D. Santi. A Constraint-Based Approach for the Authoring of Multi-Topic Multimedia Presentations. In *IEEE International Conference on Multimedia and Expo*, pages 578–581, Amsterdam, Netherlands, July 2005. IEEE Computer Society.

[5] A. Bossi and O. Gaggi. Analysis and verification of SMIL documents. *Multimedia Systems*, 17(6):487–506, 2011.

[6] M. Clavel, S. Eker, F. Durán, P. Lincoln, N. Martí-Oliet, and J. Meseguer. *All about Maude - A High-performance Logical Framework: how to Specify, Program, and Verify Systems in Rewriting Logic*, volume 4350. Springer-Verlag New York Inc, 2007.

[7] M. de Oliveira, M. Turine, and P. Masiero. A statechart-based model for hypermedia applications. *ACM Transactions on Information Systems (TOIS)*, 19(1):52, 2001.

[8] J. A. F. dos Santos, C. Braga, and D. C. Muchaluat-Saade. A Model-driven Approach for the Analysis of Multimedia Document. In *SLE (Doctoral Symposium)*, pages 37–44, Dresden, Germany, 2012.

[9] J. A. F. dos Santos, C. Braga, and D. C. Muchaluat-Saade. An Executable Semantics for a Multimedia Authoring Language. In *Formal Methods: Foundations and Applications*, pages 67–82. Springer, Brasília, Brazil, 2013.

[10] B. Dutertre. Yices 2.2. In A. Biere and R. Bloem, editors, *Computer-Aided Verification (CAV'2014)*, volume 8559 of *Lecture Notes in Computer Science*, pages 737–744. Springer, July 2014.

[11] S. Elias, K. Easwarakumar, and R. Chbeir. Dynamic consistency checking for temporal and spatial relations in multimedia presentations. In *Proceedings of the 2006 ACM symposium on Applied computing*, pages 1380–1384, Dijon, France, 2006. ACM.

[12] M. F. Felix. *Formal Analysis of Software Models Oriented by Architectural Abstractions*. PhD thesis, Pontifícia Universidade Católica do Rio de Janeiro, 2004. in Portuguese.

[13] H. L. Hardman. *Modeling and Authoring Hypermedia Documents*. PhD thesis, Universität Amsterdam, 1998.

[14] ITU. Nested Context Language (NCL) and Ginga-NCL for IPTV services. http://www.itu.int/rec/T-REC-H.761-200904-S, 2009. ITU-T Recommendation H.761.

[15] Júnior, D. P. and Farines, J. and Koliver, C. An Approach to Verify Live NCL Applications. In *Proceedings of the 18th Brazilian Symposium on Multimedia and the Web*, pages 223–232, São Paulo, Brazil, 2012. ACM.

[16] P. King, P. Schmitz, and S. Thompson. Behavioral reactivity and real time programming in xml: functional programming meets smil animation. In *Proceedings of the 2004 ACM symposium on Document engineering*, pages 57–66. ACM, 2004.

[17] S. Laborie, J. Euzenat, and N. Layaïda. Semantic adaptation of multimedia documents. *Multimedia tools and applications*, 55(3):379–398, 2011.

[18] A. Pnueli. The temporal logic of programs. In *18th Annual Symposium on Foundations of Computer Science*, pages 46–57, Providence, USA, 1977. IEEE.

[19] D. A. Randell, Z. Cui, and A. G. Cohn. A spatial logic based on regions and connection. *Principles of Knowledge Representation and Reasoning*, pages 165–176, 1992.

[20] C. Santos, L. Soares, G. de Souza, and J. Courtiat. Design methodology and formal validation of hypermedia documents. In *Proceedings of the sixth ACM International Conference on Multimedia*, pages 39–48, Bristol, United Kingdom, 1998. ACM.

[21] L. F. G. Soares and S. D. J. Barbosa. *Programming in NCL 3.0: developing applications for the Ginga middleware, Digital TV and Web*. Elsevier, 2009. in Portuguese.

[22] L. F. G. Soares, R. F. Rodrigues, and D. C. Muchaluat-Saade. Modeling, authoring and formatting hypermedia documents in the HyperProp system. *Multimedia Systems*, 2000.

[23] W3C. Synchronized Multimedia Integration Language - SMIL 3.0 Specification. http://www.w3c.org/TR/SMIL3, 2008. World-Wide Web Consortium Recommendation.

Detecting XSLT Rules Affected by Schema Evolution

Yang Wu
University of Tsukuba
1-2 Kasuga, Tsukuba 305-8850, Japan
wuyang65432@yahoo.co.jp

Nobutaka Suzuki
University of Tsukuba
1-2 Kasuga, Tsukuba 305-8850, Japan
nsuzuki@slis.tsukuba.ac.jp

ABSTRACT

In general, schemas of XML documents are continuously updated according to changes in the real world. If a schema is updated, then XSLT stylesheets are also affected by the schema update. To maintain the consistencies of XSLT stylesheets with updated schemas, we have to detect the XSLT rules affected by schema updates. However, detecting such XSLT rules manually is a difficult and time-consuming task, since recent DTDs and XSLT stylesheets are becoming more complex and users do not always fully understand the dependencies between XSLT stylesheets and DTDs. In this paper, we consider three subclasses based on unranked tree transducer, and consider an algorithm for detecting XSLT rules affected by a DTD update for the classes.

Categories and Subject Descriptors

I.7.1 [**Document and Text Processing**]: Document Management

Keywords

XML, XSLT, schema evolution

1. INTRODUCTION

In general, schemas of XML documents are continuously updated according to changes in the real world. If a schema is updated, then XSLT stylesheets are also affected by the schema update. To maintain the consistencies of XSLT stylesheets with updated schemas, we have to detect the XSLT rules affected by schema updates in order to determine whether the XSLT rules need to be updated accordingly. However, detecting such XSLT rules manually is a difficult and time-consuming task, since recent DTDs and XSLT stylesheets are becoming larger and more complex and users do not always fully understand the dependencies between XSLT stylesheets and old/updated schemas. In this paper, we consider an algorithm for detecting XSLT rules affected by a DTD update automatically.

DocEng'15, September 8–11, 2015, Lausanne, Switzerland.
© 2015 ACM. ISBN 978-1-4503-3307-8/15/09 ...$15.00.
DOI: http://dx.doi.org/10.1145/2682571.2797086 .

Let us give a small example of XSLT rules affected by a DTD update. Consider the following fragments of old/new DTDs and an XSLT stylesheet.

```
DTD_old:
<!ELEMENT items (book*,music*)>
<!ELEMENT book  (meta,title,authors)>
<!ELEMENT music (info,title,artist)>
<!ELEMENT meta  (id,date,(pages|length),format?)>
<!ELEMENT info  (meta,description?)>

DTD_new:
<!ELEMENT items (book*,music*)>
<!ELEMENT book  (meta,title,authors)>
<!ELEMENT music (meta,description?,title,artist)>
<!ELEMENT meta  (id,date,(pages|length),format?)>

XSLT:
<xsl:template match="meta">
...
</xsl:template>

<xsl:template match="info/meta">
...
</xsl:template>
```

`DTD_old` has two `meta` elements: one is a child of `book` and the other is a child of `info`. The first XSLT rule is applied to the former `meta` element, while the second rule is applied to the latter `meta` element. Here, suppose that the `info` element is unnested, i.e., `info` in the content model of `music` is replaced by "`meta,description?`" (`DTD_new`). Then the first XSLT rule is now applied to the latter `meta` element as well as the former, and we have no `meta` element to which the second XSLT rule is applied. These two XSLT rules are *affected* by the DTD update.

In this paper, we propose an algorithm for detecting XSLT rules affected by a DTD update. We consider three subclasses of XSLT: UTT, UTT^{pat}, and UTT^{pat,sel}. UTT coincides with the standard unranked tree transducer [5], and UTT^{pat} and UTT^{pat,sel} are extensions of UTT, where *pat* denotes XSLT pattern and *sel* denotes `select` of `apply-templates`. We first give a polynomial-time algorithm for detecting XSLT rules affected by a DTD update assuming UTT/UTT^{pat} as XSLT. We next show that the problem becomes undecidable if UTT^{pat,sel} is assumed as XSLT.

2. PRELIMINARIES

In this section, we give some definitions related to DTD and tree transducer.

DTD and Update Operations to DTDs

Let Σ be a set of labels. For a node v in a tree t, by $l(v)$ we mean the label of v. The language specified by a regular

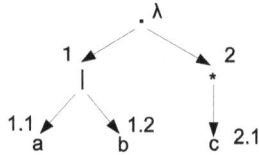

Figure 1: Tree structure of r

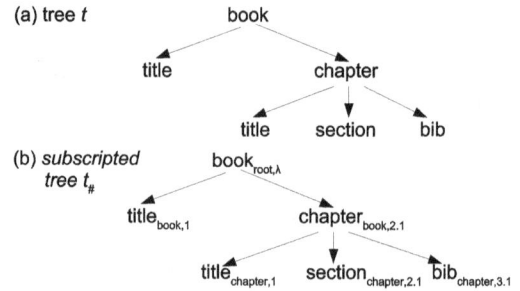

Figure 2: Tree t and its subscripted tree $t_\#$

expression r is denoted $L(r)$. A DTD is a tuple $D = (d, sl)$, where d is a mapping from Σ to the set of regular expressions over Σ, and $sl \in \Sigma$ is the start label. For a label $a \in \Sigma$, $d(a)$ is the *content model* of a. A tree t is *valid* against $D = (d, sl)$ if $l(v) = sl$ for the root v of t and for any node n in t, $l(v_1) \cdots l(v_n) \in L(d(l(v)))$, where $v_1, \cdots, v_n$ are the child nodes of v.

EXAMPLE 1. *Consider the following DTD, where* book *is the start label. Then this DTD is denoted* $(d, book)$, *where* $d(\text{book}) = \text{title chapter}^+$, $d(\text{chapter}) = \text{title section}^+ \text{ bib}?$, $d(\text{title}) = d(\text{section}) = d(\text{bib}) = \epsilon$.

```
<!ELEMENT book     (title,chapter+)>
<!ELEMENT chapter  (title, section+, bib?)>
<!ELEMENT title    (#PCDATA)>
<!ELEMENT section  (#PCDATA)>
<!ELEMENT bib      (#PCDATA)>
```

To define update operations to DTDs, we need to define the positions of elements/operators in a content model. Thus, we represent a content model as a tree and specify the position of each node by Dewey order. For example, Fig. 1 shows the tree structure of $r = (a|b)c^*$, where each node is associated with its position. For a regular expression r, the label at position u in r is denoted $l(r, u)$ and the subexpression at position u of r is denoted $sub(r, u)$. For example, in Fig. 1, $l(r, 1) = '|'$, $l(r, 1.1) = a$, $sub(r, 1) = (a|b)$.

Let $D = (d, sl)$ be a DTD. *Update operations* to D are defined as follows.

- $ins\_elm(a, b, u)$: inserts a label b at position u in $d(a)$.

- $del\_elm(a, u)$: deletes the label at position u in $d(a)$.

- $nest(a, b, u)$: nests the subexpression at u in $d(a)$ by b. This operation replaces the subexpression at u in $d(a)$ by b and sets $d(b) = sub(d(a), u)$.

- $unnest(a, u)$: this is the inverse operation of $nest$, and replaces the label $l' = l(d(a), u)$ at u in $d(a)$ by regular expression $d(l')$.

By $op(D)$ we mean the DTD obtained by applying an update operation op to D. An *update script* is a sequence of update operations. For an update script $s = op_1 op_2 \cdots op_n$, we define $s(D) = op_n(\cdots(op_2(op_1(D))))$.

Tree Transducer

A *pattern* is defined as $pat = ls_1 / \cdots / ls_n$, where $ls_i = ax_i :: l_i$, $ax_i \in \{\downarrow, \downarrow^*\}$, and $l_i \in \Sigma$. $\downarrow$ and $\downarrow^*$ denote child and descendant-or-self axes, respectively. Let t be a tree and v be a node of t. We say that v *matches* pat if there is a sequence $v_1, \cdots, v_n$ of nodes in t such that $v_n = v$, $l(v_i) = l_i$ $(1 \leq i \leq n)$, and that for any $2 \leq i \leq n$, if $ax_i = \downarrow$, then t has edge $v_{i-1} \to v_i$, otherwise (i.e., $ax_i = \downarrow^*$) there is a path from v_{i-1} to v_i in t.

A *hedge* is a finite sequence of trees. The set of hedges is denoted by H_Σ. For a set Q, by $H_\Sigma(Q)$ we mean the set of Σ-hedges such that leaf nodes can be labeled with elements from Q. A *tree transducer* is a quadruple (Q, Σ, q_0, R), where Q is a finite set of *states*, $q_0 \in Q$ is the *initial state*, and R is a finite set of *rules* of the form $(q, pat) \to h$, where $q \in Q$, pat is a pattern, and $h \in H_\Sigma(Q)$. For example, $(q, a/b/c) \to c(p)$ corresponds to the following XSLT template.

```
<xsl:template match="a/b/c" mode="q">
  <c>
    <xsl:apply-templates mode="p" />
  </c>
</xsl:template>
```

Let v be a node in a tree t. The translation defined by a tree transducer $Tr = (Q, \Sigma, q_0, R)$ at v in state q, denoted by $Tr^q(t, v)$, is inductively defined as follows.

R1: If there is a rule $(q, pat) \to h \in R$ such that v matches pat, then $Tr^q(t, v)$ is obtained from h as follows: for each leaf node u in h, if $l(u)$ is a state, say p, then replace u with hedge $Tr^p(t, v_1) \cdots Tr^p(t, v_n)$, where $v_1, \cdots, v_n$ are the children of v.

R2: Otherwise, $Tr^q(t, v) = \epsilon$.

The transformation of t by Tr, denoted by $Tr(t)$, is defined as $Tr(t) = Tr^{q_0}(t, v_0)$, where v_0 is the root node of t. The class of the tree transducers defined above is denoted UTT^{pat}. In particular, if for every rule $(q, pat) \to h \in R$ pat is a single label, then the restricted class is denoted UTT, which coincides with that of the standard unranked tree transducer[5]. Finally, $\text{UTT}^{pat,sel}$ is the class obtained by extending UTT^{pat} with select of apply-templates (details are omitted).

Rules Affected by DTD Updates

A DTD may contain more than one element having the same name, and we have to distinguish such elements when detecting the rules affected by DTD updates. By $a_{b,u}$ we mean the element a at position u in $d(b)$. We say that $a_{b,u}$ is a *subscripted* label. If a is the root element, then the corresponding subscripted labels is $a_{root,\lambda}$. By $D_\#$ we mean the DTD obtained from D by replacing each label in a content model with its corresponding subscripted label. For a tree t valid against D, $t_\#$ is a *subscripted tree* of t if $t_\#$ is obtained by replacing each label in t with its corresponding subscripted label so that $t_\#$ is valid against $D_\#$ (see Fig. 2).

Let $D = (d, sl)$ be a DTD, s be an update script to D, and $s(D) = (d', sl)$. For a subscripted label $a_{b,u}$ in $D_\#$, if $a_{b,u}$ is not deleted by s, then $a_{b,u}$ also appears in $s(D)_\#$ (its

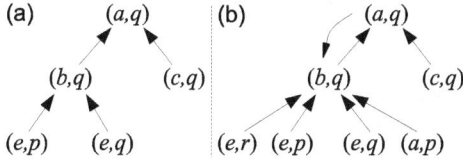

Figure 3: Dependency graphs

parent b and position u may change). Thus, this element in $s(D)_\#$ can be denoted by $a_{b',u'}$ for some element b' and position u', and we say that $a_{b,u}$ *corresponds* to $a_{b',u'}$[1].

Let $Tr = (Q, \Sigma, q_0, R)$ be a tree transducer. For a subscripted label $a_{b,u}$ and a rule $rl \in R$, rl is *applicable* to $a_{b,u}$ in a tree t if for some node v in t, (1) rl is applied to v during the transformation of $Tr(t)$, and, (2) for some subscripted tree $t_\#$ of t, the label of v is $a_{b,u}$ in $t_\#$.

Let $a_{b',u'}$ be a subscripted label in $s(D)_\#$ and $a_{b,u}$ be its corresponding element in $D_\#$. We define two sets of rules *affected* by s at $a_{b',u'}$, denoted $R^+(a_{b',u'})$ and $R^-(a_{b',u'})$, as follows. (1) $R^+(a_{b',u'})$ is the set of rules $rl \in R$ such that rl is not applicable to $a_{b,u}$ in $D_\#$ but becomes applicable to $a_{b',u'}$ in $s(D)_\#$. (2) $R^-(a_{b',u'})$ is the set of rules $rl \in R$ such that rl is applicable to $a_{b,u}$ in $D_\#$ but not applicable to $a_{b',u'}$ in $s(D)_\#$. In particular, if $D_\#$ has no subscripted label corresponding to $a_{b',u'}$, then $R^-(a_{b',u'}) = \emptyset$.

3. ALGORITHM

In this section, we present an algorithm for computing $R^+(a_{b',u'})$ and $R^-(a_{b',u'})$ for every $a_{b',u'}$, assuming a tree transducer belongs to UTT/UTT^{pat}.

To compute these sets, we have to find the rules applicable to each element. To do this, we use label-state pairs and find dependencies of such pairs. In short, pair (a, q) means that a rule can be applied to a in state q. Consider the rule R1 in the definition of UTT/UTT^{pat}, and suppose that the antecedent of the rule R1 holds. This means that a rule $(q, pat) \to h$ is applied to a node v in state q, and thus we have a pair (a, q) with $l(v) = a$. Then consider the consequence of the rule R1. Each state p in h is replaced by $Tr^p(t, v_1) \cdots Tr^p(t, v_n)$. Let $b = l(v_i)$. Then $Tr^p(t, v_i)$ means that a rule is (possibly) applied to b in state p, thus we obtain (b, p). Since (b, p) is obtained by (a, q), we denote this dependency by an edge $(b, p) \to (a, q)$. A *dependency graph* is a graph $G_D = (V_D, E_D)$ consisting of such nodes and edges.

EXAMPLE 2. *Let $D = (d, a)$ be a DTD, where $d(a) = bc$, $d(b) = e$, $d(c) = d(e) = \epsilon$. Let $Tr = (Q, \Sigma, q, R)$ be a tree transducer, where $Q = \{p, q, r\}$, $\Sigma = \{a, b, c, e\}$, and $R = \{(q, a) \to a(q), (q, c) \to c, (q, b) \to b(pq), (q, b/a/b) \to b(r)\}$. Since the root element is a and the initial state is q, we obtain (a, q). Since $d(a) = bc$ and $(q, a) \to a(q)$ can be applied to a in state q, we obtain nodes (b, q), (c, q) and edges $(b, q) \to (a, q)$ and $(c, q) \to (a, q)$. By applying rules in R similarly, we obtain the dependency graph in Fig. 3(a).*

To define the algorithm formally, we need some definitions. By $St(h)$ we mean the set of states in a hedge h. For example, if $h = a(pq)$, then $St(h) = \{p, q\}$. Let $pat = ax_1 ::$

---

[1] In some cases the update script between old and new DTDs is not given explicitly. In such cases, the algorithms in [4, 3] can generate update scripts between DTDs.

$l_1 / \cdots / ax_n :: l_n$ be a pattern. A rule $(q, pat) \to h$ is *applicable* to (a, q) in G_D if there is a sequence $(a_1, q_1), \cdots, (a_n, q_n)$ such that (M1) $(a, q) = (a_n, q_n)$, (M2) $a_i = l_i$ ($1 \leq i \leq n$), and that (M3) for every $2 \leq i \leq n$, if $axis_i =\downarrow$, then $(a_i, q_i) \to (a_{i-1}, q_{i-1}) \in E_D$, otherwise (i.e., $axis_i =\downarrow^*$) there is a path from (a_i, q_i) to (a_{i-1}, q_{i-1}) in G_D.

We present algorithm FINDDEP for constructing a dependency graph. $R(a, q)$ denotes the set of rules applied to (a, q) so far. S maintains a set of label-state pairs that should be examined, which is initially $\{(sl, q_0)\}$ (line 3). Then the following is repeated until S becomes empty. First, the algorithm chooses an arbitrary pair (a, q) from S (line 5), then finds a rule $rl = (q, pat) \to h$ such that rl is applicable to (a, q) in G_D and that rl is not applied to (a, q) so far (line 6). According to rl and the consequence of the rule R1, for every $q' \in St(h)$ and every child element b of a, if (b, q') is a newly found pair, then (b, q') is added to V_D (and S) and $(b, q') \to (a, q)$ is added to E_D (lines 9 to 13). On the other hand, if (b, q') is already in V_D, only $(b, q') \to (a, q)$ is added to E_D (lines 14 to 15). Due to this edge addition, some rule may become applicable to a pair (c, q'') if (a, q) becomes reachable from (c, q'') via $(b, q') \to (a, q)$ (see Example 3 below). Thus we find such pairs and add to S (lines 16 to 18).

Algorithm FINDDEP

Input: DTD $D = (d, sl)$, tree transducer $Tr = (Q, \Sigma, q_0, R)$.
Output: Dependency graph $G_D = (V_D, E_D)$.

1. $V_D \leftarrow \{(sl, q_0)\}$; $E_D \leftarrow \emptyset$
2. $R(sl, q_0) \leftarrow \emptyset$;
3. $S \leftarrow \{(sl, q_0)\}$;
4. **while** $S \neq \emptyset$ **do**
5.   Choose a pair $(a, q) \in S$. Delete (a, q) from S.
6.   **if** there is a rule $rl = (q, pat) \to h \in R$ such that rl is applicable to (a, q) in G_D and that $rl \notin R(a, q)$ **then**
7. $R(a, q) \leftarrow R(a, q) \cup \{rl\}$
8.   **for** each element b appearing in $d(a)$ and each state $q' \in St(h)$ **do**
9.   **if** $(b, q') \notin V_D$ **then**
10. $V_D \leftarrow V_D \cup \{(b, q')\}$
11. $E_D \leftarrow E_D \cup \{(b, q') \to (a, q)\}$
12. $R(b, q') \leftarrow \emptyset$
13. $S \leftarrow S \cup \{(b, q')\}$
14.   **else if** $(b, q') \to (a, q) \notin E_D$ **then**
15. $E_D \leftarrow E_D \cup \{(b, q') \to (a, q)\}$
16.   **for** each $(c, q'') \in V_D$ such that (a, q) becomes reachable from (c, q'') via $(b, q') \to (a, q)$ **do**
17.   **if** there is a rule $rl \in R$ such that rl is applicable to (c, q'') in G_D and that $rl \notin R(b, q')$ **then**
18. $S \leftarrow S \cup \{(c, q'')\}$;
19. **return** $G_D = (V_D, E_D)$

EXAMPLE 3. *Consider the DTD and the tree transducer in Example 2. Then suppose that D is slightly modified so that $d(b) = ea$ instead of $d(b) = e$. Since element a is now a child of b, by rule $(q, b) \to b(pq)$ we obtain a new node (a, p) and new edges $(a, p) \to (b, q)$ and $(a, q) \to (b, q)$ (Fig. 3(b)). Moreover, since rule $(q, b/a/b) \to b(r)$ is now applicable to (b, q) due to path $(b, q) \to (a, q) \to (b, q)$, we obtain new node (e, r) and new edge $(e, r) \to (b, q)$.*

To present an algorithm for computing $R^+(a_{b',u'})$ and $R^-(a_{b',u'})$, we need a definition. A rule $(q, pat) \to h$ is *applicable* to (a, q) with *parent b* in G_D if there is a sequence $(a_1, q_1), \cdots, (a_n, q_n)$ that satisfies the following condition as well as the conditions M1 to M3.

M4) If $axis_n = \downarrow$, then $a_{n-1} = b$. Otherwise (i.e., $axis_n = \downarrow^*$), there is a path from (a_n, q_n) to (a_{n-1}, q_{n-1}) whose first edge is $(a_n, q_n) \to (b, q')$ for some $q' \in Q$.

The following algorithm computes $R^-(a_{b',u'})$ for every $a_{b',u'}$ ($R^+(a_{b',u'})$ can be obtained similarly). This algorithm constructs dependency graphs G_D and G'_D for old/new DTDs, and then takes "diff" between G_D and G'_D to obtain $R^-(a_{b',u'})$.

Algorithm MAIN

Input: DTD $D = (d, sl)$, update script s to D, tree transducer $Tr = (Q, \Sigma, q_0, R)$.

Output: $R^-(a_{b',u'})$ for every $a_{b',u'}$ in $s(D)$.

1. $G_D \leftarrow \text{FindDep}(D, Tr)$
2. $G'_D \leftarrow \text{FindDep}(s(D), Tr)$
3. **for** each subscripted element $a_{b',u'}$ in $s(D)$ **do**
4. $R^-(a_{b',u'}) \leftarrow \emptyset$
5.   **if** D has a subscripted element $a_{b,u}$ corresponding to $a_{b',u'}$ **then**
6. $M \leftarrow \{rl \in R \mid rl \text{ is applicable to } (a, q) \text{ with parent } b \text{ in } G_D, q \in Q\}$
7. $M' \leftarrow \{rl \in R \mid rl \text{ is applicable to } (a, q) \text{ with parent } b' \text{ in } G'_D, q \in Q\}$
8. $R^-(a_{b',u'}) \leftarrow M \setminus M'$
9. **return** $\{R^-(a_{b',u'}) \mid a_{b',u'} \text{ is a subscripted element in } s(D)\}$

Let $M_c = \max_{a \in \Sigma} |d(a)|$ and $M_s = \max_{(q,pat) \to h \in R} |St(h)|$, where $|d(a)|$ denotes the number of labels appearing in $d(a)$. Then algorithm MAIN runs in $O(|R|^5 (M_c M_s)^3)$. In particular, assuming a tree transducer belongs to UTT, the algorithm runs in $O(|R|^2 (M_c M_s))$. We also have the following.

THEOREM 1. *Let D be a DTD, s be an update script to D, T_r be a tree transducer belonging to UTT/UTT^{pat}, and $a_{b,u}$ be a subscripted element in $s(D)$. Then $rl \in R^-(a_{b',u'})$ iff $rl \in R'^-(a_{b',u'})$, where R'^- is the result of MAIN.*

Finally, consider the case of $UTT^{pat,sel}$. The following result comes from the fact that tree transformation can proceed in arbitrary direction due to `select` of `apply-templates`.

THEOREM 2. *Let D be a DTD, s be an update script to D, T_r be a tree transducer belonging to $UTT^{pat,sel}$, and $a_{b,u}$ be a subscripted element in $s(D)$. Then deciding if there exists a rule of T_r affected by s at $a_{b,u}$ is undecidable.*

4. EVALUATION EXPERIMENT

We implemented our algorithm in Java and conducted a preliminary experiment. The DTDs used in our experiment are version 2.1.1 and version 2.2.2 of MSRMEDOC[2]. We denote the former as D and the later as $s(D)$, respectively. MSRMEDOC is a format for information interchange in the development process of production and supply. The numbers of elements in D and $s(D)$ are 183 and 204, respectively. The number of update operations between D and $s(D)$ is 106 (68 *ins_elms*, 11 *del_elms*, 27 *nests*, 0 *unnest*).

Since we didn't find any XSLT stylesheet for the DTDs, we made an XSLT stylesheet for XML to HTML transformation. The stylesheet has 10 rules and the average length of the patterns is 4. In the experiment, we have two examinees who are both graduate students and are familiar with DTD and XSLT. We explained the definitions of the

---
[2]http://www.msr-wg.de/medoc/downlo.html

DTDs, R^+ rule, and R^- rule, and related examples to the examinees in advance. Then, we presented the stylesheet to the examinees and asked them to find R^+/R^- rules manually. For both examinees 18 minutes was required to find all the R^+/R^- rules. On the other hand, the execution time of our algorithm is 2135ms under a mobile PC with Intel Core i3 2.60GHz. This result suggests that our algorithm can save much time to maintain the consistencies of XSLT stylesheets. However, the stylesheet used above is rather small, and we expect that it will take even more time to detect the R^+/R^- rules manually in larger XSLT stylesheets. We will investigate this further.

5. RELATED WORK

The algorithm in [2] transforms XPath expressions according to a schema update. Although XPath expressions are used as XSLT patterns, their algorithm cannot be applied to our problem since XSLT rules affected by a schema update cannot be detected by checking each XSLT pattern independently. To the best of our knowledge, there is no study on detecting XSLT rules affected by a schema update. On the other hand, there are several studies dealing with XML schema updates. For example, the algorithms in [4, 3] extract "diffs" between two schemas. In [6] a taxonomy of possible problems for XQuery induced by a schema update is introduced, and an algorithm for detecting such problems is proposed. The system in [1] checks the forward and backward compatibility between old and new schemas w.r.t. a given XPath query.

6. CONCLUSION

In this paper, we proposed an algorithm for detecting XSLT rules affected by schema update. As a future work, we would like to conduct more experiments by using more DTDs and XSLT stylesheets.

7. ACKNOWLEDGMENT

This work is partially supported by JSPS KAKENHI Grant Number 26330126.

8. REFERENCES

[1] GENEVÈS, P., LAYAÏDA, N., AND QUINT, V. Identifying query incompatibilities with evolving xml schemas. *SIGPLAN Not. 44*, 9 (2009), 221–230.

[2] HASEGAWA, K., IKEDA, K., AND SUZUKI, N. An algorithm for transforming XPath expressions according to schema evolution. In *Proc. DChanges 2013* (2013).

[3] HORIE, K., AND SUZUKI, N. Extracting differences between regular tree grammars. In *Proc. ACM SAC* (2013), pp. 859–864.

[4] LEONARDI, E., HOAI, T. T., BHOWMICK, S. S., AND MADRIA, S. DTD-Diff: A change detection algorithm for DTDs. *Data & Knowledge Engineering 61* (2007), 384–402.

[5] MARTENS, W., AND NEVEN, F. Typechecking top-down uni- form unranked tree transducers. In *Proc. ICDT* (2002), pp. 64–78.

[6] OLIVEIRA, R., GENEVÈS, P., AND LAYAÏDA, N. Toward automated schema-directed code revision. In *Proceedings of the 2012 ACM symposium on Document engineering* (2012), DocEng '12, pp. 103–106.

Concept Hierarchy Extraction from Textbooks

Shuting Wang[†], Chen Liang[‡], Zhaohui Wu[†], Kyle Williams[‡],
Bart Pursel[‡*], Benjamin Brautigam[*], Sherwyn Saul[*], Hannah Williams[*],
Kyle Bowen[*], C. Lee Giles[‡†]

[†]Computer Science and Engineering
[‡]Information Sciences and Technology
[*]Teaching and Learning with Technology
Pennsylvania State University, University Park, PA 16802, USA
sxw327@cse.psu.edu, cul226@ist.psu.edu,
{zzw109,kwilliams,bkp10,bjb40,sps20,hrw115,kbowen}@psu.edu, giles@ist.psu.edu

ABSTRACT

Concept hierarchies have been useful tools for presenting and organizing knowledge. With the rapid growth of online knowledge resources, automatic concept hierarchy extraction is increasingly attractive. Here, we focus on concept extraction from textbooks based on the knowledge in Wikipedia. Given a book, we extract important concepts in each book chapter using Wikipedia as a resource and from this construct a concept hierarchy for that book. We define local and global features that capture both the local relatedness and global coherence embedded in that textbook. In order to evaluate the proposed features and extracted concept hierarchies, we manually construct concept hierarchies for three well used textbooks by labeling important concepts for each book chapter. Experiments show that our proposed local and global features achieve better performance than using only keyphrases to construct the concept hierarchies. Moreover, we observe that incorporating global features can improve the concept ranking precision and reaffirms the global coherence in the book.

Categories and Subject Descriptors

I.2.6 [**Learning**]: Knowledge acquisition; Concept learning; I.7.5 [**Document and Text Processing**]: Document Capture—*Document Analysis*; H.3.3 [**Information Storage And Retrieval**]: Information Search and Retrieval

Keywords

Open education; concept hierarchy; textbooks; Web knowledge;

1. INTRODUCTION

A concept hierarchy is a powerful tool for representing and organizing knowledge; it has been widely used in learning

and education [16, 17]. It forms a valuable component for numerous science education tasks, including documenting and exploring concept change [26], knowledge sharing [24, 4, 11] and knowledge acquisition [9, 8]. Early work on concept hierarchy construction relied heavily on human expertise. However, with more open educational resources, many available online, we feel automatic concept hierarchy extraction from these resources can be very useful for knowledge extraction and creation.

Textbooks provide organized units of knowledge and a balanced and chronological presentation of information. As such they are a high-quality information resource for concept hierarchy extraction. However, most previous work on concept hierarchy extraction from textbooks has only made use of the textual information within the textbooks, not leveraging the rich structure of textbooks or connect the inside-the-book knowledge to external knowledge resources [21, 14].

We propose a method for extracting concept hierarchies from digital books using Web knowledge. Our work fits into the growing amount of Web knowledge which offers significant opportunities to enhance learning for students by encouraging knowledge sharing and supporting dynamic interactions among learners [25, 6].

Specifically, we leverage Wikipedia, a free-access Web knowledge base that contains more than 4 millions concepts, to assist in concept hierarchy extraction. For brevity we abbreviate Concept Hierarchy Extraction from Books as (*CHEB*). In the *CHEB* task, we are given a digital textbook with its lexical content and table of contents (TOC) with the goal to extract and output a concept hierarchy for that book. To do this we extract a set of related important Wikipedia concepts for each book chapter and organize them as a concept hierarchy using the book's TOC.

To extract the concept hierarchy, we utilize a Learning-to-Rank approach which considers both *local relatedness* and *global coherence*. We propose local features to extract related concepts for each chapter separately, utilizing measures such as textual similarity between a book chapter and candidate concepts. We also expect the extracted concept hierarchy to be globally coherent, i.e. the concept in a given chapter should also be related to other concepts in current/different subchapter(s). Based on this, we argue that a useful concept hierarchy should have:

• **Less redundancy in the sense that chapters do not always discuss all of the same concepts**: The concept hierarchy is a possible summary of the book. Thus, information overlap between concepts in different subchapters should be small. For instance, if subchapter 1.1 covers "Gross Domestic Product" in detail, subchapter 2.1 should not cover this concept in detail again.

- **Consistency with other concepts in the same chapter**: Concepts within in a subchapter should be highly correlated to each other. For instance, our concept hierarchy will put "Interest Rate" and "Real Interest Rate" together rather than putting "Interest Rate" and "Unemployment" in the same subchapter.

- **Consistent learning order in that concepts follow each other as with prerequisites**: For each concept, the concept hierarchy should follow the learning order of concepts. Given a concept, prerequisite concepts should be introduced before this concept and subsequent concepts should be introduced after the concept. For example, the concept hierarchy should discuss "Gross Domestic Product" before "Real Gross Domestic Product".

In order to capture the global coherence, *CHEB* utilizes the Wikipedia link graph and page content to estimate the pairwise Wikipedia candidate relatedness and learning order. Corresponding to the three characteristics of an our concept hierarchy, three sets of global features are proposed based on their estimated relatedness and learning order.

To evaluate the quality of the extracted concept hierarchy, we conduct experiments on three well used textbooks. By manually labeling the important concepts for each chapter in the books, we obtain a concept hierarchy for each book. We empirically train the concept hierarchy extractor using the proposed features and perform extraction on the testing data. Our results show that incorporating both local and global features achieves significantly better performance and confirms our definition of global coherence in the book.

To the best of our knowledge, this work represents the first attempt to combine the properties of local relatedness and global coherence to automatically extract concept hierarchies from textbooks. Our the major contributions are:

- Automatic extraction of concept hierarchies from textbooks using Web knowledge.

- Propose three sets of global features, which ensure less redundancy, consistency and appropriate learning order for a concept hierarchy that captures the global coherence embedded in a book.

- Manually build concept hierarchies for three well used books and utilize a Learning-to-Rank approach to train and test our concept hierarchy extractor.

The paper is organized as follows. We first define the **Concept Hierarchy Extraction from Books (CHEB)** approach and introduce its work flow in Section 2. Local and global features are introduced in Section 3. In Section 4, we discuss the data preparation and evaluation metrics. In Section 5 analyzes the experimental results for three well used textbooks and presents an example of the generated concept hierarchy. Related work is in Section 6 followed by conclusion and future work in Section 7.

2. PROBLEM DEFINITION & APPROACH

We first formalize our **Concept Hierarchy Extraction from Books (CHEB)** approach and then briefly introduce our local and global *CHEB* features which consider both the relatedness between extracted concepts and books and the global coherence among the extracted concepts.

SYMBOL	DESCRIPTION
B	the input book
N	number of subchapters
tb_i	title of ith subchapter
cb_i	content of ith subchapter
cs_{ip}	p^{th} important concepts in i^{th} subchapter
$\lambda(i)$	chapter number of the ith subchapter
W	domain specific dictionary
w_i	i^{th} Wikipedia concept in the dictionary
$L(w_i, w_j)$	prerequisite relation between w_i and w_j
$I(i,j)$	order of subchapter i and subchapter j
Γ	extracted concept hierarchy

Table 1: Symbol Notation

2.1 Concept Hierarchy Extraction from Books

Essentially, *CHEB* utilizes the TOC of the book to construct a concept hierarchy by extracting related concepts in each chapter. Instead of performing keyword extraction on the book's contents [21], we use Web knowledge to improve the concept extraction and enrich the book content. We use Wikipedia to identify important concepts in the book. For simplicity, we consider each Wikipedia title as a concept.

The input to a *CHEB* framework is a book B with a list of titles $TB = \{tb_1, tb_2, ..., tb_N\}$ and contents $CB = \{cb_1, cb_2, .., cb_N\}$. tb_i and cb_i are the title and the content for the ith subchapter in the TOC respectively, and N is the total number of subchapters in the book. Here we use the term "subchapter" to refer to all the headings in the TOC and ignore the level of the headings. For instance, both 1.1 and 1.1.1 are subchapters. As for the term "chapter", we use it to refer to a set of subchapters whose first level chapter numbers are the same. For instance, chapter 1 may include subchapter 1, subchapter 1.1 and subchapter 1.2.

Given a book B and a set of Wikipedia titles $W = \{w_1, w_2, ..., w_{|W|}\}$, our goal is to produce a concept hierarchy which lists a set of important Wikipedia concepts for each subchapter. We represent the output hierarchy as $\Gamma = \{cs_1, cs_2, ..., cs_N\}$ where $cs_i = \{w_1, w_2, ..., w_K\}$ is a K-tuple and $w_j \in cs_i$ is an important concept for subchapter j. *CHEB* constructs a concept hierarchy for the book by organizing the concepts extracted from each subchapter using the book's TOC. Figure 1 gives an example of the input and output of *CHEB*. The left side is the TOC of a macroeconomics book and the right side is the concept hierarchy extracted from the book.

2.2 Local and Global Concept Hierarchy Extraction from Books

Since the concept hierarchy uses the inherent structure of the book, our goal is to devise an algorithm that extracts a set of concepts which are related to the book chapter and also forms a "coherent" knowledge hierarchy which is consistent with the book structure. A necessary attribute of the concept hierarchy is **local relatedness**, i.e., the extracted concepts for a specific subchapter need to be related to the subchapter in some way. For instance, they share similar keywords or key phrases.

The *local CHEB* approach extracts important concepts for each subchapter independently. Specifically, given a subchapter i, its title tb_i and content cb_i, let $\Phi(cs_{ij}|tb_i, cb_i)$ be

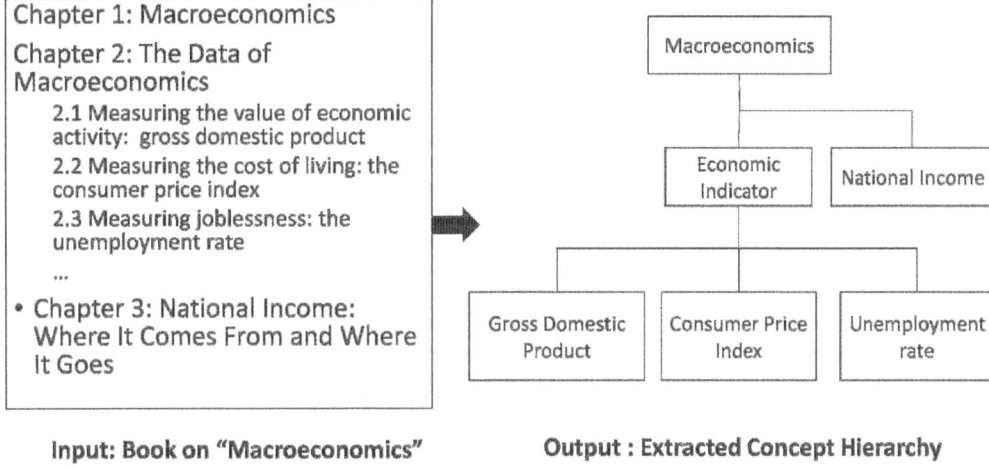

Input: Book on "Macroeconomics"   **Output : Extracted Concept Hierarchy**

Figure 1: Example of an extracted concept hierarchy

the score function such that concept cs_{ij} is the jth related concept in this subchapter. The local approach solves the following optimization problem:

$$\Gamma^*_{local} = \arg\max_\Gamma [\sum_{i=1}^{N} \sum_{p \in cs_i} \Phi(cs_{ip}|tb_i, cb_i)] \quad (1)$$

Besides having *local relatedness*, we also expect that the concept hierarchy is **globally coherent**. Whether to put a concept in a specific subchapter is not only decided by the relatedness between the concept and the subchapter, but also by the coherence between this concept and the concepts in the same/different subchapter(s). For instance, given a book about macroeconomics, if we already rank "Gross Domestic Product" as an important concept for subchapter 1.1, we may want to lower the rank of this concept in subchapter 1.2. Therefore, we expect that the extracted concept hierarchy not only considers the *local relatedness*, but also preserves the *global coherence*. In genera for *global coherence*, *CHEB* is expected to extract a concept hierarchy with the following attributes: **less redundancy in the sense chapters do not always talk about all of the same concepts, consistency with other concepts in the same chapter** and a **consistent learning order in that concepts follow each other as with prerequisites**, as discussed in Section 1.

Based on above three assumptions, global optimization for concept hierarchy occurs when the solve the following equation:

$$\Gamma^* = \arg\max_\Gamma \sum_{i}^{N} \sum_{p \in cs_i} [\Phi(cs_{ip}|tb_i, cb_i) - \Psi(\Gamma) + \Theta(\Gamma) + \gamma(\Gamma)] \quad (2)$$

where $\Phi(\cdot)$ is the local optimization function and $\Psi(\cdot)$, $\Theta(\cdot)$ and $\gamma(\cdot)$ are three functions corresponding to the features proposed above.

$\Psi(\cdot)$ captures the redundancy of concept hierarchy by calculating the total pairwise information overlap between con-

cepts in different subchapters, which should be minimized. $\Theta(\cdot)$ corresponds to the consistency feature and captures the pairwise relatedness between concepts within the same subchapter. The global consistency feature proposed above requires this function to be maximized. $\gamma(\cdot)$ ensures that the hierarchy orders the concepts following pairwise learning order on the book level. For any concept in the hierarchy, introducing its prerequisite concept after it or its subsequent concept before it should be avoided.

Eq. 2 is NP-hard and approximations are needed to solve this as an optimization problem. The common approach is to estimate the pairwise relation $\Psi(\cdot)$, $\Theta(\cdot)$, and $\gamma(\cdot)$ and generate *approximated concept hierarchy contexts* Γ_1, Γ_2, and Γ_3 for $\Psi(\cdot)$, $\Theta(\cdot)$, and $\gamma(\cdot)$ respectively. In this work, Wikipedia content and link information are utilized to estimate the relatedness and the learning order between concepts w_i and w_j, which brings two benefits: 1) a good estimation of pairwise concept relation and relatedness due to the rich semantics residing in Wikipedia content and links, and 2) an easy way for computing the features because Wikipedia has a unified template for most concepts and links.

Given the estimated relation between concepts, we then solve Eq. 3 in an approximate form:

$$\Gamma^* \approx \arg\max_\Gamma \sum_{i=1}^{N} \sum_{p \in cs_i} [\Phi(cs_{ip}|tb_i, cb_i) - \sum_{cs_{jq} \in \Gamma_1} \Psi(cs_{ip}, cs_{jq})$$
$$+ \sum_{cs_{jq} \in \Gamma_2} \Theta(cs_{ip}, cs_{jq}) + \sum_{cs_{jq} \in \Gamma_3} \gamma(cs_{ip}, cs_{jq})] \quad (3)$$

As we discussed above, function $\Psi(\cdot)$ captures the redundancy in the concept hierarchy and therefore, given a concept w_j that serves as a candidate concept in the ith subchapter, the concept hierarchy context considered for this concept (Γ_1 in Eq. 3) should be those concepts in different chapters. Notice that we are using chapters but not subchapters here. The reason is that some books present relatively different concepts in different subchapters while some do not. To generalize our solution, we consider concepts in different chapters when we deal with the issue of concept redundancy.

Similarly, we can simplify Γ_2 and Γ_3 for Θ and γ respectively. Basically, for each candidate concept w_j in the ith subchapter, Γ_2 only includes w_k from subchapter i since we focus on the consistency of concepts within the same subchapter; as for Γ_3, which considers the learning order, we include concepts from all subchapters except for those from the current subchapter. Therefore, we can rewrite Eq. 3 as the following form:

$$\Gamma^* \approx \arg\max_{\Gamma} \sum_{i=1}^{N} \sum_{p \in cs_i} [\Phi(cs_{ip}|tb_i, cb_i)$$

$$- \sum_{CN(j) \neq CN(i)}^{N} \sum_{q=1}^{|cs_j|} \Psi(cs_{ip}, cs_{jq}) + \sum_{q=1}^{|cs_i|} \Theta(cs_{ip}, cs_{iq}) \quad (4)$$

$$+ \sum_{i \neq j}^{N} \sum_{q=1}^{|cs_j|} \gamma(cs_{ip}, cs_{jq})]$$

where $\lambda(\cdot)$ is defined as a function which returns the chapter number of given a subchapter. For instance, $\lambda(1.1.1)$ and $\lambda(1.1)$ return both 1 which is the chapter number of subchapter 1.1.1 and 1.1. Therefore, $\sum_{\lambda(j) \neq \lambda(i)}^{N} \sum_{q=1}^{|cs_j|} \Psi(cs_{ip}, cs_{jq})$ is the total information overlap between candidate cs_{ip} and all candidates in different chapters. We want to minimize this overlap to reduce redundancy in the concept hierarchy. $\sum_{q=1}^{|cs_j|} \Theta(cs_{ip}, cs_{iq})$ corresponds to the second global feature of the book such that concepts within one subchapter should be consistent. $\sum_{i \neq j} \sum_{q=1}^{|cs_j|} \gamma(cs_{ip}, cs_{jq})$ is used to capture the consistency between the learning order of the candidate concepts and the order of subchapters in the book. It can be expanded as $L(cs_{ip}, cs_{jq}) \times I(i,j)$. L is a pre-extracted matrix of size $|W| \times |W|$ where $|W|$ is the size of domain specific dictionary. $L(cs_{ip}, cs_{jq})$ denotes the prerequisite relationship between concepts cs_{ip} and cs_{jq}. $I(i,j)$ represents the order of subchapter i and subchapter j. L an I are formally defined as:

$$L(w_i, w_j) = \begin{cases} 1 & \text{if } w_i \text{ is the prerequisite concept of } w_j \\ -1 & \text{if } w_i \text{ is the subsequent concept of } w_j \\ 0 & \text{otherwise} \end{cases} \quad (5)$$

$$I(i,j) = \begin{cases} 1 & \text{if } i \text{ is a subchapter before } j \\ -1 & \text{if } i \text{ is a subchapter after } j \\ 0 & i = j \end{cases} \quad (6)$$

Given a concept i, we want its prerequisite concepts to appear before it and its subsequent concepts to appear after it in the extracted concept hierarchy.

Eq. 4 can be solved by finding each cs_{ip} for the ith subchapter independently, and still enforce some degree of *global coherence* by adding function Φ, Θ and γ in the optimization function.

3. CONCEPT HIERARCHY EXTRACTION FROM BOOKS

In this section we present our method, *CHEB*, for solving the optimization problem defined in Eq. 4. *CHEB* combines a local model and a global model which capture three characteristics of an our concept hierarchy: less redundancy, content consistency and a appropriate learning order. Each function in the equation can be represented as a weighted sum of local and global features which capture chapter-concept or concept-concept pairwise relatedness. For instance, the local relatedness function Φ is defined as:

$$\Phi(w|tb, cb) = \sum_i \omega_i \phi_i(w|tb, cb)$$

where $\phi_i(w|tb, cb)$ is the ith local feature that captures the relatedness between the candidate concept w and the book chapter given its title tb and content cb. Details of the local features utilized in *CHEB* will be introduced in following sections. The coefficient ω_i is learned using a Support Vector Machine over training data from the constructed data set, described in Section 4.1.

Similarly, the redundancy function Ψ and consistency function Θ are defined as the weighted sums of the features which capture the relatedness between two candidates from different chapters and within the same subchapter respectively. The learning order function γ defines that whether two are appropriately ordered in the concept hierarchy based on the pre-estimated learning order relationship extracted from Wikipedia.

In general, *CHEB* is a three-stage method as shown in Figure 2. It first extracts a domain-specific dictionary for a given book topic and then performs candidate selection for each chapter. Finally, by re-ranking the candidates based on the local and global features, it generates the concept hierarchy which arrives at coherent sets of important concepts for a given book.

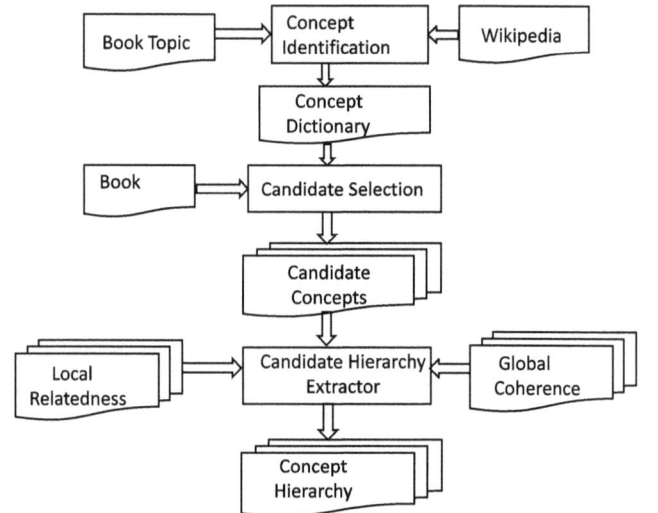

Figure 2: Workflow of the CHEB system

In the following sections, we will describe three modules of *CHEB* as suggested in Fig 2. We first present a domain-specific concept dictionary construction method using Wikipedia and then introduce our candidate selection method based on title and content similarity. Finally, we discuss our concept hierarchy extraction method and present the details of the proposed local and global features.

3.1 Domain Specifc Concept Identifcation

The first step of our method is to build a domain-specific dictionary which contains all the possible concepts related to the topic of a book. Specifically, we depth-first search crawl Wikipedia starting from the Wikipedia page of the topic. For instance, Wikipedia page "Macroeconomics" is set as the starting page to perform crawling for a macroeconomics book. For every page visited by our crawler, we extract all the Wikipedia pages that are linked to by anchor texts in the current page and add their titles into the concept dictionary [23]. Thus the dictionary is supposed to consist of a set of Wikipedia titles related to a given domain.

During the crawling process, there would be Wikipedia concepts which have low relatedness to the domain being accessed. For instance, "Salt Lake City" would be crawled since it is linked by concept "Packet Switching". However, this concept is not related to the "Computer Network" domain. Therefore, we perform a filter on the extracted dictionary which removes the unrelated concepts using Wikipedia category information. A category is considered to be a "weak category" if the number of Wikipedia pages in the dictionary which belong to this category is below some threshold. Notice that a concept may belong to multiple categories. If half of its categories are weak categories, the concept will be removed from the dictionary.

3.2 Candidate Selection

The next step of our method is to select all related candidate concepts for each book chapter and construct a candidate concept hierarchy for the book. It is intuitive that a Wikipedia concept is related to a book chapter if their titles or contents are similar. Therefore, we first define **titleMatch** as a function measuring the relatedness between a candidate concept and a chapter. Given the book chapter title tb and a Wikipedia candidate title tw, if the Wikipedia title is in the book chapter title, $titleMatch(tb, tw) = 1$; Otherwise, $titleMatch(tb, tw) = 0$. For example, for title "Inflation and Interest Rates", Wikipedia candidates "Inflation" and "Interest Rates" are found and their $titleMatch$ score over the book chapter is 1.

The next measure designed for candidate selection is **cosineSim** which measures the cosine similarity between the content of Wikipedia candidate and that of the book. Given a chapter, we first match concepts from the dictionary in the chapter content and obtain a list of Wikipedia concepts which appears in the chapter. Then all the anchor texts in these Wikipedia pages and all the concepts in the dictionary are used as a vector space to calculate the normalized term frequency-inverse document frequency (tf-idf) vector for the book subchapter and each Wikipedia candidate. The $cosineSim$ score between c and each candidate is then calculated as the consine similarity between word vectors.

Our candidate set consists of the top N candidates based on $cosineSim$ score and those candidates whose $titleMatch$ equals 1, i.e., the candidates whose title appears in the chapter title. These two simple but powerful features are able to capture most of the related and important concepts for each

book chapter. They are also used in the relatedness feature set, which will be introduced in the following section.

3.3 Concept Hierarchy Generation

In this section, we present the details of the local and global features proposed.

3.3.1 Local Features

In addition to the two features used in the candidate selection, we also make use of the Jaccard distance between the chapter title tb_i and the Wikipedia candidate title w_i as a feature.

$$Jaccard(tb_i, w_i) = 1 - \frac{|tb_i \cap w_i|}{|tb_i \cup w_i|}$$

3.3.2 Global Features

Global features contain three subsets which correspond to the three characteristics of a concept hierarchy: less redundancy, content consistency and an appropriate learning order.

Redundancy features and Consistency features.

In order to resolve the redundancy issue in the concept hierarchy, we reduce the information overlap between the concepts in different chapters, which can be approximated by calculating the pairwise relatedness between the candidate being considered and candidates in different chapters. Similarly, whether a Wikipedia candidate is "consistent" in this chapter can be approximated by calculating the pairwise relatedness between the candidate being considered and the concepts in the same chapter.

Therefore, for both redundancy and consistency features, it is necessary to capture the relatedness between two Wikipedia candidates. Given two candidates w_i and w_j, three relatedness measures are utilized:

- **cosineSim**, which considers the cosine similarity between contents of w_i and w_j.
- **Jaccard**, which considers the Jaccard distance between titles of w_i and w_j.
- **semSim**, which computes the semantic similarity of a pair of articles from the links they make [28]. Let L_i be the set of Wikipedia concepts which link to w_i and W_{all} be the total number of concepts in Wikipedia, $semSim$ is defined as

$$semSim(w_i, w_j) = 1 - \frac{\max(\log |L_i|, \log |L_j|) - \log |L_i \cap L_j|}{W_{all} - \min(\log |L_i|, \log |L_j|)}$$

The redundancy that a candidate can possibly bring into the concept hierarchy is captured by the following features:

$$cosSimRed(cs_{ip}) = \sum_{\lambda(j) \neq \lambda(i)}^{N} \sum_{q=1}^{min(|cs_j|, K)} cosineSim(cs_{ip}, cs_{jq})$$

$$JaccardRed(cs_{ip}) = \sum_{\lambda(j) \neq \lambda(i)}^{N} \sum_{q=1}^{min(|cs_j|, K)} Jaccard(cs_{ip}, cs_{jq})$$

$$semSimRed(cs_{ip}) = \sum_{\lambda(j) \neq \lambda(i)}^{N} \sum_{q=1}^{min(|cs_j|, K)} semSim(cs_{ip}, cs_{jq})$$

where K is a pre-specified parameter and $min(|cs_j|, K)$ is number of candidates to be considered in subchapter j when computing the redundancy. We want to minimize the information overlap for candidates in different concepts. However, if a candidate is not an important concept for a subchapter, it makes no sense to minimize the information overlap between this concept and other candidates in different chapters. Therefore, when calculating redundancy features, we only want to consider those concepts with higher probability of being important candidate concepts. Empirically, we find that the local features are very powerful and the candidates ranked by *titleMatch* and *cosineSim* have relatively high ranking precisions. Therefore, we assume that top-K candidates have higher probability of being important and only consider these K concepts.

Consistency features are defined by the following measures:

$$cosSimCons(cs_{ip}) = \sum_{q=1}^{min(|cs_j|,K)} cosineSim(cs_{ip},cs_{iq})$$

$$JaccardCons(cs_{ip}) = \sum_{q=1}^{min(|cs_j|,K)} Jaccard(cs_{ip},cs_{iq})$$

$$semSimCons(cs_{ip}) = \sum_{q=1}^{min(|cs_j|,K)} semSim(cs_{ip},cs_{iq})$$

Similarly, we only consider top-K candidates in a subchapter when calculating consistency features.

Learning Order features.

In order to represent the learning order between two Wikipedia candidates w_i and w_j, we define L as a $|W| \times |W|$ matrix where $L(w_i,w_j)$ is the learning order relationship between w_i and w_j as suggested in Section 2.2. At issue is how do we know the prerequisite relationship between two concepts?

Since Wikipedia pages have a relatively uniform format, we try to extract the learning order based on two heuristics. The first sentence of most of the Wikipedia pages, if not all, gives a succinct and general definition for the concept. And the first heuristic used is: given two Wikipedia concepts w_i and w_j and their first sentences s_i and s_j, w_i is the prerequisite of w_j if w_i appears in s_j. For example, the first sentence of the Wikipedia concept **Hyperinflation** is *In economics, hyperinflation occurs when a country experiences very high and usually accelerating rates of* **inflation***, rapidly eroding the real value of the local currency, and causing the population to minimize their holdings of the local money.* We thus consider concept *inflation* a prerequisite of *hyperinflation*.

Also, most Wikipedia pages have a TOC which links to related concepts. The second heuristic used is based on the TOC: given two Wikipedia concepts w_i and w_j and their TOC toc_i and toc_j, w_i is the prerequisite of w_j if w_j appears in toc_i. For example, the TOC of Wikipedia concept **Money** contains **Money supply** and we thus treat concept *Money* as a prerequisite of *Money supply*. However, this heuristic may have some problems. One is that two Wikipedia concepts can appear in each other's TOC, such as **Inflation** and **Monetary policy**. It is difficult to figure out which concept we should learn first. For these cases, these two concepts are considered to have no learning order. Since the TOC based rule is not as strong as the definition based rule, it is considered as a complementary of the defini-

tion rule, i.e., if the definitions already suggest some learning orders, we will not consider the TOC.

After quantifying the learning order between two concepts, the next step is to capture the global coherence of the concept hierarchy. Given a concept cs_{ip} in subchapter i, we hope that all cs_{ip}'s prerequisites introduced in the book appear in subchapters before i and all cs_{ip}'s subsequent concepts introduced in the book appear in subchapters after i. In order to achieve this goal, we define feature **preCorr** and **subCorr** to capture the global learning order of the concept hierarchy given the candidate cs_{ip} in the ith subchapter:

$$preCorr(cs_{ip}) = \frac{\sum\limits_{j<i}^{N} \sum\limits_{q=1}^{min(|cs_j|,K)} L(cs_{ip},cs_{jq})=-1}{\sum\limits_{j\neq i}^{N} \sum\limits_{q=1}^{min(|cs_j|,K)} L(cs_{ip},cs_{jq})=-1}$$

$$subCorr(cs_{ip}) = \frac{\sum\limits_{j>i}^{N} \sum\limits_{q=1}^{min(|cs_j|,K)} L(cs_{ip},cs_{jq})=1}{\sum\limits_{j\neq i}^{N} \sum\limits_{q=1}^{min(|cs_j|,K)} L(cs_{ip},cs_{jq})=1}$$

Similarly, we consider only top-K candidates in a subchapter when calculating the learning order features. Eq. 3.3.2 and Eq. 3.3.2 compute the percentage of concepts that are appropriately ordered based on the prerequisite relationships for cs_{ip}'s and capture the consistent learning order of a useful concept hierarchy.

3.3.3 Concept Hierarchy Extractor Training

After generating the features for concept hierarchy extraction, we learn the coefficients for the extractor using SVM^{rank} [12] on a data set with manually labelled rankings of Wikipedia candidates for each chapter in three classic textbooks. We use different combinations of features to train our extractor in order to study the importance of different features.

4. DATA SETS AND EVALUATION METRICS

In this section, we first discuss the data preparation for testing *CHEB* approach and then introduce the evaluation metrics.

4.1 Data Preparation and Experiment Setup

We evaluate *CHEB* on three high quality textbooks: "Computer networking: a top-down approach featuring the Internet" (hereafter, the computer network book) [1], "Principles of macroeconomics" (hereafter, the macroeconomics book) [2], and "Precalculus: Mathematics for calculus" (hereafter, the precalculus book) [3]. We apply *CHEB* on these three books to see how it performs on textbooks in different domains.

The general procedure to build test bed for *CHEB* includes four steps: 1) remove the subchapters with less than

---

[1]Kurose, James. F. (2005). Computer networking: a top-down approach featuring the Internet. Pearson Education India.
[2]Mankiw, N. Gregory.(2014). Principles of macroeconomics. Cengage Learning.
[3]Stewart, James, Lothar Redlin, and Saleem Watson. Precalculus: Mathematics for calculus. Cengage Learning, 2015.

100 words or no important concepts; 2) extract domain specific dictionary for each book; 3) select the *top-30* candidates for each subchapter; and 4) manually label the candidates as "important" or "unimportant". **Book Subchapter Preprocessing** Besides subchapters with less than 100 words are removed, the "Introduction" and "Conclusion" subchapters which summarize the concepts in other subchapters are also removed.

Domain Specific Dictionary Construction To construct our data sets for *CHEB*, we first perform domain specific dictionary construction as described in Section 3.1 for each book. Here we use "Computer Network" as the root Wikipedia page for the computer network book, "Macroeconomics" for the macroeconomics book, and "Precalculus" for the precalculus book. A filter is then applied on the dictionary as described in Section 3.1. If a Wikipedia category contains less than 15 pages in the dictionary, it is considered as a weak category. The number of Wikipedia titles in the dictionary for the three books are: 29689 for the Computer network book, 7981 for the Macroeconomics book and 11766 for the the Precalculus book.

Candidate Selection The *top-30* Wikipedia candidates are selected using the two features described in Section 3.2 (*titleMatch* feature and *cosineSim* feature).

Data Labeling Based on the extracted candidates, we manually label each Wikipedia candidate as "important" or "unimportant". For each book, three graduate students with corresponding background knowledge are recruited to label the data. The correlation between the annotators is quite high. For instance, for the computer network book, the three annotators achieve a 79% correlation. This high agreement shows that our manually constructed data set is reliable. Moreover, we use a majority vote to solve the cases where there is not a unanimous agreement. The books also have different structures including the depth of the TOC, the number of subchapters and the average number of concepts in each subchapter. Table 2 and Figure 3 provide some statistics for the book structures.

4.2 Evaluation Metrics

To evaluate the performance of our extractor, we use the metrics **precision@n** and **Mean-Average-Precision(MAP)**. *Precision@n* measures the fraction of the important concepts in *top-n* ranking results. As shown in Figure 3, most of the book subchapters have less than five important concepts. Therefore, for *Precision@n*, we set $n = 1, 3, 5$. We also use Mean Average Precision@10 *MAP@10* to demonstrate an average precision over *top-10* ranking results.

5. EXPERIMENTS AND RESULTS

We conduct experiments to extract concept hierarchies from books in different domains. Specifically, we test whether the proposed local and global features are effective for identifying important concepts in each subchapter.

We conduct two sets of experiments by comparing our method with baselines. The book-level experiment uses two books as training data and the other book as testing data, and the subchapter-level experiment conducts experiments on three books separately by using part of the subchapters of a book as training data and the remaining chapters as testing data. We finally given a case study on a concept hierarchy extracted from the computer network book.

5.1 Baseline Method

SimSeerX [27] is a similar document search engine and we use the keyphrase method implemented as the baseline model. It receives a whole document as a query, performs automatic information extraction on the document, and then uses several similarity functions to identify and rank similar documents in an indexed collection. *SimSeerX* has been designed in order to work with multiple document collections and offer multiple similarity functions. It currently supports similarity functions based on keyphrases [18], sequences of terms, and overall word similarity in documents. *SimSeerX* provides a generic architecture for similarity search and has been used with several document collections, such as the *CiteSeerX* collection, Wikipedia dataset and a plagiarism dataset in which it was the best plagiarism detector. In this study, we use the keyphrase similarity function in *SimSeerX* as a baseline.

When using keyphrase similarity in *SimSeerX*, two documents are considered potentially similar if they share at least one automatically extracted keyphrase or if the keyphrase exists in the text. For each document indexed by *SimSeerX*, keyphrases are automatically extracted using the *Maui tool* [18]. *Maui* begins by identifying candidate keyphrases in the text based on n-grams of words, and then features [18] for each word are inputs to a machine learning model and with the output the probability that the candidate keyphrase is a keyphrase. *SimSeerX* indexes the *top-10* keyphrases identified by *Maui*. At query time, the *top-10* queries are extracted from the query document using the same procedure and indexed documents with at least one matching keyphrase are retrieved. This candidate set of results is then ranked based on the full text cosine similarity of each document with the query document. For what we believe to be a fair comparison, we remove the concepts which are not in the domain specific dictionary from the ranking results of the baseline method.

5.2 Book-Level Concept Hierarchy Extraction

In this section, a book-level concept hierarchy extraction is first performed by using two of the books as training data and the third one as testing data. Table 3 shows the ranking precisions on computer network book, macroeconomics book and precalculus book respectively. As shown, we test different combinations of features, with the local features derived from different aspects of relatedness between book subchapter and Wikipedia candidates, and global features which consider the global coherence of the book structure. The results show that incorporating our proposed local and global features into the extractor does achieve significantly higher precision than the baseline model. Recall that different books vary significantly in terms of their structure and the number of important concepts in each subchapter, but our results appear robust across all of them.

From the experimental results, we see that local features, namely *titleMatch*, *cosineSim* and *Jaccard*, are effective in the concept hierarchy extraction. However, the *titleMatch* feature is not very robust because its usefulness depends on type of book title. A title that is an analogy or has too little information can make this not very useful. For instance, the title of subchapter 1.1.1 of the computer network book is *A Nuts-and-Bolts Description*, making it difficult for the *titleMatch* feature to obtain meaningful information. Moreover, information contained in the title is usually limited

	Computer Network	Macroeconomics	Precalculus
toc depth	3	2	2
# subchapters	50	21	17
avg # important concepts per subchapter	3.6	4.5	4.3
avg # candidate concepts per subchapter	69.933	80.1071	69.2903
avg length of title (words)	3.34	6.19	2.53

Table 2: Physical characteristics of books

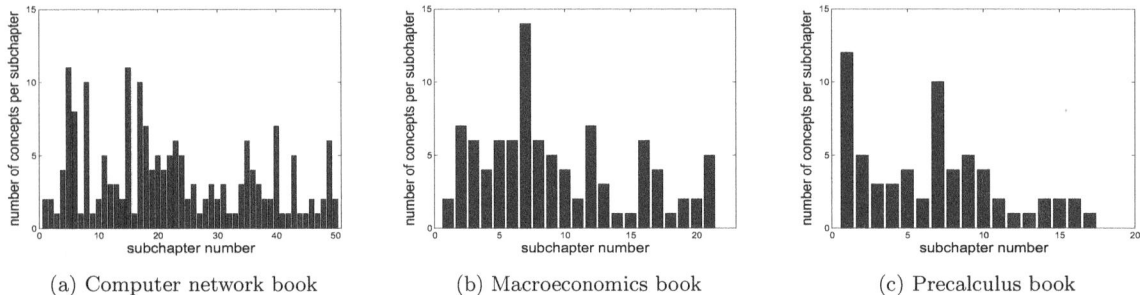

(a) Computer network book (b) Macroeconomics book (c) Precalculus book

Figure 3: Number of important concepts in each book subchapter

and thus the *titleMatch* feature has a very low recall which leads to the low *MAP@10* score. As shown in the results, the *titleMatch* feature has the lowest *MAP@10* score among all the features on three books. The feature achieves a best *MAP@10* score of 0.12 on the macroeconomics book, which has the largest average number of words in the title as shown in Table 2.

Incorporating global features does achieve better results for the computer network book and the macroeconomics book, but not so on the precalculus book. A potential reason for this is that the precalculus book is an entry-level book and splits each concept into more than one subchapter in order to present more details. For instance, Chapters 2,3,4,5, and 6 all discuss functions. Therefore, it is hard for *CHEB* to capture the book structure and thus the global features.

5.3 Subchapter-Level Concept Hierarchy Extraction

From the numbers in Table 2, we see the book structures are quite different. In order to capture their different structures, we also conduct experiments on each book separately.

Parts of the subchapters are used as training data to train the extractor and the remaining subchapters are used as testing data using 5-fold cross validation. From the results, we observe that out model outperforms the baseline method for the overall performance on three books and the results obtained using different feature sets are consistent with the findings in the overall experimental results (See Table 3).

Although the gains in the global features are marginal, global features are especially helpful in predicting the *top-1* important concept. As we can observe, adding global features improves *precision*@1 from 0.79 to 0.84 for the computer network book, 0.8 to 0.83 for the macroeconomics book, and 0.80 to 0.83 for the precalculus book.

5.4 Concept Hierarchy Analysis - Computer Network Concept Hierarchy

In this section, we show the concept hierarchy extracted from the computer network book in figure 4 where each rect-

angle represents a subchapter in the book and the concept extracted from this subchapter. Rectangles with thick borders represent subchapters with length less than 100 words. There was no extraction on these subchapters. These subchapters do not introduce any concepts in details and thus are filtered in the preprocessing step as discussed in Section 4.1. In this hierarchy, the subchapters "'Computer Networks and the Internet" and "Delay, loss and throughput" are such subchapters.

As we can see, our extractor captures most of the important concepts in each subchapter and provides a reasonable concept hierarchy for the computer network domain.

6. RELATED WORK

Our work is primarily related to two areas of research: Wikification [3, 5, 7, 10, 19, 23] and knowledge extraction from education resources [1, 13, 14, 29, 30, 32].

Wikification automatically links terms in the plain text to appropriate Wikipedia articles. Bunescu and Pasca [3] first explored Wikipedia as a resource for detecting and disambiguating named entities in open domain text. They trained a disambiguation SVM kernel which compared the lexical context around the ambiguous named entity to the content of the candidate Wikipedia page to perform disambiguation on named entities. Mihalcea and Csomai [19] performed automatic keyword extraction and word sense disambiguation with Wikipedia by training a Naive Bayes classifier and using the hyperlink information in Wikipedia as ground truth. Semantic relatedness between Wikipedia candidates [7, 10, 20, 23] are also considered to obtain a coherent disambiguation on named entities. Essentially, besides the content similarity between the entity and Wikipedia candidates, Wikipedia articles selected for the same article should be semantically close to each other. This work also stressed the semantic relatedness between the Wikipedia candidates and optimized the disambiguation results.

Other related research is knowledge extraction from text, course materials and papers [2, 22]. Our focus is primarily on knowledge extraction for educational purposes. Agrawal et al. [1] proposed a method to identify deficient sections and

	Computer Network				Macroeconomics				Precalculus			
	P@1	P@3	P@5	MAP@10	P@1	P@3	P@5	MAP@10	P@1	P@3	P@5	MAP@10
Baseline Method	0.42	0.19	0.16	0.21	0.4	0.33	0.24	0.23	0.23	0.19	0.15	0.18
TitleMatch Feature	0.3	0.13	0.08	0.08	0.5	0.37	0.24	0.27	0.36	0.13	0.08	0.08
CosineSim Feature	0.74	0.48	0.4	0.35	0.57	0.61	0.46	0.33	0.6	0.51	0.41	0.32
Local Features	0.79	0.52	0.43	0.34	0.8	0.52	0.44	0.32	0.8	0.49	0.4	0.34
Global Features	0.38	0.34	0.3	0.3	0.5	0.35	0.32	0.29	0.43	0.3	0.25	0.25
Local+Global Features	0.84	0.52	0.42	0.37	0.83	0.54	0.42	0.34	0.83	0.46	0.39	0.34

Table 4: Subchapter-level experimental results

	P@1	P@3	P@5	MAP@10
Baseline Method	0.4	0.2	0.16	0.29
TitleMatch Feature	0.28	0.12	0.07	0.05
CosineSim Feature	0.74	0.5	0.43	0.36
Local Features	0.76	0.5	0.39	0.35
Global Features	0.45	0.38	0.33	0.25
Local+Global Features	0.8	0.52	0.42	0.36

(a) Ranking precisions on computer network book

	P@1	P@3	P@5	MAP@10
Baseline Method	0.38	0.31	0.24	0.21
TitleMatch Feature	0.57	0.31	0.17	0.12
CosineSim Feature	0.61	0.58	0.54	0.4
Local Features	0.83	0.57	0.46	0.4
Global Features	0.47	0.42	0.31	0.30
Local+Global Features	0.85	0.58	0.45	0.41

(b) Ranking precisions on macroeconomics book

	P@1	P@3	P@5	MAP@10
Baseline Method	0.29	0.23	0.18	0.17
TitleMatch Feature	0.41	0.15	0.09	0.07
CosineSim Feature	0.64	0.52	0.44	0.31
Local Features	0.76	0.56	0.49	0.34
Global Features	0.47	0.42	37.25	0.27
Local+Global Features	0.82	0.51	0.47	0.34

(c) Ranking precisions on precalculus book

Table 3: Book-level experimental results

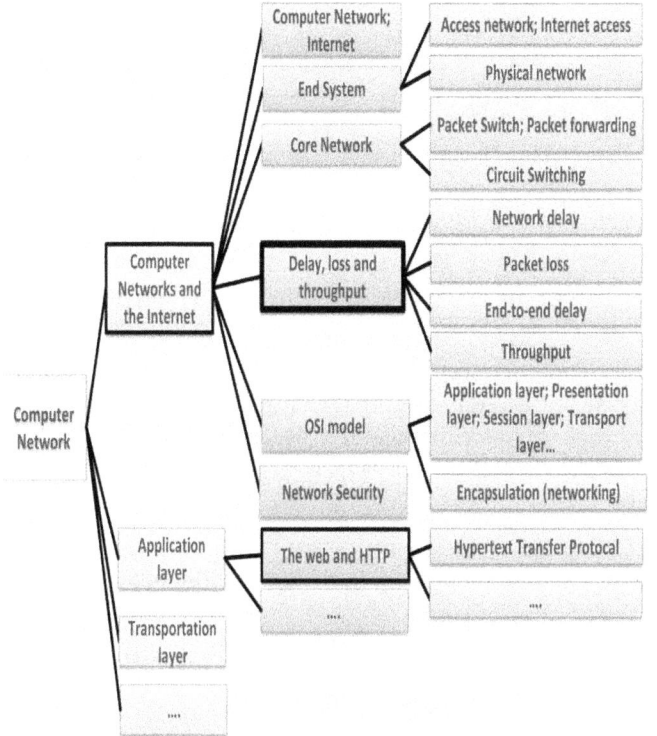

Figure 4: Part of Concept Hierarchy extracted from the computer network book. Rectangles with thick borders represent subchapters with length less than 100 words and are removed in the pre-processing step(See Section 4.1)

enhance these sections using web knowledge. They used concept dispersion and syntactic complexity to identify deficient sections and augmented these sections using Wikipedia. Informativeness was measured based on semantic similarity between a term's context and the its most featured contexts in Wikipedia [29] and was used to automatically create back-of-the-book indexes [31]. Liang et al. [15] proposed an automated book creation framework which incorporated the method proposed in this work. Recently, prerequisite relationships among courses and papers were derived: Yang et al. proposed a learning-to-rank approach to explore prerequisite relationships among courses and constructed a concept graph based on the relationships [32]. Koutrika et al. generated a reading tree for papers by measuring the generality score of a paper and the overlap between two papers [13].

7. CONCLUSION AND FUTURE WORK

We propose a method to extract concept hierarchies from books and formalize the *Concept Hierarchy Extraction from Book (CHEB)* task as an optimization problem with local and global invariants. We consider the local relatedness be-

tween the extracted concepts and a book chapter. Moreover, global features ensure that the extracted concept hierarchy is less redundant, more consistent and follows a consistent learning order. To validate the proposed local and global features, we manually construct concept hierarchies for three well used textbooks. Experimental results show that incorporating the global features can improve the ranking precision. Though the data set used is small, the manually created data set is of high quality and precise enough for us to make an attempt to study the global coherence embedded in the books.

To our knowledge this is the first study that utilizes both a local relatedness and global coherence to extract concept hierarchies from books. Future directions would be to construct concept hierarchies for different domains or from multiple books from the same domain. We will also attempt to infer the prerequisites between concepts in book chapters. Another interesting problem is to use domain specific concept hierarchies to build applications for science education, instruction, and learning.

8. ACKNOWLEDGEMENTS

We gratefully acknowledge partial support from NSF and useful comments from the reviewers.

9. REFERENCES

[1] R. Agrawal, S. Gollapudi, A. Kannan, and K. Kenthapadi. Data mining for improving textbooks. *ACM SIGKDD Explorations Newsletter*, 13(2):7–19, 2012.

[2] H. Alani, S. Kim, D. E. Millard, M. J. Weal, W. Hall, P. H. Lewis, and N. R. Shadbolt. Automatic ontology-based knowledge extraction from web documents. *Intelligent Systems, IEEE*, 18(1):14–21, 2003.

[3] R. C. Bunescu and M. Pasca. Using encyclopedic knowledge for named entity disambiguation. In *EACL*, pages 9–16, 2006.

[4] J. W. Coffey, R. R. Hoffman, A. J. Cañas, and K. M. Ford. A concept map-based knowledge modeling approach to expert knowledge sharing. *IKS*, pages 212–217, 2002.

[5] S. Cucerzan. Large-scale named entity disambiguation based on Wikipedia data. In *EMNLP*, 2007.

[6] S. Downes. E-learning 2.0. elearn magazine, 10.2005. *Online http://elearnmag. org/subpage. cfm*, pages 29–1, 2005.

[7] P. Ferragina and U. Scaiella. Tagme: on-the-fly annotation of short text fragments (by wikipedia entities). pages 1625–1628, 2010.

[8] S. E. Gordon, K. A. Schmierer, and R. T. Gill. Conceptual graph analysis: Knowledge acquisition for instructional system design. *Human Factors: The Journal of the Human Factors and Ergonomics Society*, 35(3):459–481, 1993.

[9] A. C. Graesser and S. P. Franklin. Quest: A cognitive model of question answering. *Discourse processes*, 13(3):279–303, 1990.

[10] X. Han and J. Zhao. Named entity disambiguation by leveraging wikipedia semantic knowledge. In *CIKM*, pages 215–224. ACM, 2009.

[11] G.-J. Hwang, Y.-R. Shi, and H.-C. Chu. A concept map approach to developing collaborative mindtools for context-aware ubiquitous learning. *British Journal of Educational Technology*, 42(5):778–789, 2011.

[12] T. Joachims. Training linear svms in linear time. In *KDD*, pages 217–226. ACM, 2006.

[13] G. Koutrika, L. Liu, and S. Simske. Generating reading orders over document collections. 2015.

[14] M. Larranaga, A. Conde, I. Calvo, J. A. Elorriaga, and A. Arruarte. Automatic generation of the domain module from electronic textbooks: Method and validation. *Knowledge and Data Engineering, IEEE Transactions on*, 26(1):69–82, 2014.

[15] C. Liang, S. Wang, Z. Wu, K. Williams, B. Pursel, B. Brautigam, S. Saul, H. Williams, K. Bowen, and C. Giles. Bbookx: An automatic book creation framework. In *The ACM Symposium on Document Engineering*, 2015.

[16] K. M. Markham, J. J. Mintzes, and M. G. Jones. The concept map as a research and evaluation tool: Further evidence of validity. *Journal of research in science teaching*, 31(1):91–101, 1994.

[17] J. R. McClure, B. Sonak, and H. K. Suen. Concept map assessment of classroom learning: Reliability, validity, and logistical practicality. *Journal of research in science teaching*, 36(4):475–492, 1999.

[18] O. Medelyan, E. Frank, and I. H. Witten. Human-competitive tagging using automatic keyphrase extraction. In *EMNLP*, pages 1318–1327. Association for Computational Linguistics, 2009.

[19] R. Mihalcea and A. Csomai. Wikify!: linking documents to encyclopedic knowledge. In *CIKM*, pages 233–242. ACM, 2007.

[20] D. Milne and I. H. Witten. Learning to link with wikipedia. In *CIKM*, pages 509–518. ACM, 2008.

[21] A. M. Olney. Extraction of concept maps from textbooks for domain modeling. In *Intelligent Tutoring Systems*, pages 390–392. Springer, 2010.

[22] M. Rajman and R. Besançon. Text mining-knowledge extraction from unstructured textual data. In *Advances in Data Science and Classification*, pages 473–480. Springer, 1998.

[23] L. Ratinov, D. Roth, D. Downey, and M. Anderson. Local and global algorithms for disambiguation to wikipedia. pages 1375–1384, 2011.

[24] W.-M. Roth and A. Roychoudhury. The social construction of scientific concepts or the concept map as conscription device and tool for social thinking in high school science. *Science education*, 76(5):531–57, 1992.

[25] S. H. Usman and I. O. Oyefolahan. Encouraging knowledge sharing using web 2.0 technologies in higher education: A survey. *arXiv preprint arXiv:1406.7437*, 2014.

[26] J. D. Wallace and J. J. Mintzes. The concept map as a research tool: Exploring conceptual change in biology. *Journal of research in science teaching*, 27(10):1033–1052, 1990.

[27] K. Williams, J. Wu, and C. L. Giles. Simseerx: a similar document search engine. In *DocEng'14*, pages 143–146. ACM, 2014.

[28] I. Witten and D. Milne. An effective, low-cost measure of semantic relatedness obtained from wikipedia links. In *AAAI'08*, pages 25–30, 2008.

[29] Z. Wu and C. L. Giles. Measuring term informativeness in context. In *HLT-NAACL*, pages 259–269, 2013.

[30] Z. Wu, Z. Li, P. Mitra, and C. L. Giles. Can back-of-the-book indexes be automatically created? In *CIKM*, pages 1745–1750. ACM, 2013.

[31] Z. Wu, P. Mitra, and C. L. Giles. Table of contents recognition and extraction for heterogeneous book documents. In *ICDAR*, pages 1205–1209. IEEE, 2013.

[32] Y. Yang, H. Liu, J. Carbonell, and W. Ma. Concept graph learning from educational data. In *WSDM*, pages 159–168, 2015.

Combining Advanced Information Retrieval and Text-Mining for Digital Humanities

Antoine Widlöcher[1,2,3]
antoine.widlocher@unicaen.fr

Nicolas Bechet[7]
nicolas.bechet@irisa.fr

Jean–Marc Lecarpentier[1,2,3]
lecarpentier@unicaen.fr

Yann Mathet[1,2,3]
yann.mathet@unicaen.fr

Julia Roger[1,4,5,6]
julia.roger@unicaen.fr

[1]Normandie Univ, France
[2]UNICAEN, GREYC, F-14032 Caen, France
[3]CNRS, UMR 6072, F-14032 Caen, France
[4]UNICAEN, Identité et Subjectivité, F-14032 Caen, France
[5]UNICAEN, MRSH, Pôle Document Numérique, F-14032 Caen, France
[6]CNRS, USR 3486, F-14032 Caen, France
[7] Univ. Bretagne-Sud, UMR 6074, IRISA, F-56000 Vannes, France

ABSTRACT

Digital Humanities make more and more structured and richly annotated corpora available. Most of this data rely on well known and established standards, such as TEI, which especially enable scientists to edit and publish their work. However, one of the remaining problems is to give adequate access to this rich data, in order to produce higher-order knowledge.

In this paper, we present an integrated environment combining an advanced search engine and text-mining techniques for hermeneutics in Digital Humanities. Relying on semantic web technologies, the search engine uses full text as well as complex embedding structures and offers a single interface to access rich and heterogeneous data and meta-data. Text-mining possibilities enable scholars to exhibit regularities in corpora. Results obtained on the Cartesian corpus illustrate these principles and tools.

Categories and Subject Descriptors

H.3.1 [**Information Storage and Retrieval**]: Content Analysis and Indexing; H.3.2 [**Information Storage and Retrieval**]: Information Storage; H.3.3 [**Information Storage and Retrieval**]: Information Search and Retrieval; H.5.2 [**Information Interfaces and Presentation**]: User Interfaces; I.2.7 [**Artificial Intelligence**]: Natural Language Processing; I.7.2 [**Document and Text Processing**]: Document Preparation; J.5 [**Computer Applications**]: Arts and Humanities

DocEng'15, September 8-11, 2015, Lausanne, Switzerland.
Copyright is held by the owner/author(s). Publication rights licensed to ACM.
ACM 978-1-4503-3307-8/15/09 ...$15.00.
DOI: http://dx.doi.org/10.1145/2682571.2797067 .

Keywords

Digital Humanities; Information Retrieval; Text Mining

1. INTRODUCTION

Document engineering and more generally computing capabilities have deeply transformed Humanities. Wide access to rare resources, easy reading or visualization of complex or fragile items, collaborative work on shared data as well as extended capabilities in terms of Information Retrieval (IR hereafter) and Data-Mining (DM hereafter) are well-known advantages of so-called Digital Humanities (DH hereafter), which enhance traditional methodologies. As a consequence, more and more structured and richly annotated corpora are available to DH scholars. Most of this precious data relies on well known and established standards, enabling scientists to edit and publish their work.

However, giving adequate access to this rich data remains an open problem. In order to produce higher-order knowledge, researchers in Humanities need tools that fit the specific needs of their research field. In this paper, we direct our attention towards the requirements of a significant number of works in DH concerning IR and DM. This article focuses on the sub-areas of DH where both so-called *close reading* and *distant reading* of mainly textual data are required. Indeed, we more specifically focus on works where it is sometimes necessary to observe phenomena on quite large pieces of corpora, and sometimes necessary to observe these phenomena at a very local level, in context. For research fields such as philology, genetic editing or diplomatic editing, large-scale observation enable scholars to exhibit meaningful regularities, specificities or anomalies. However, close reading is also necessary to observe occurrences of targeted phenomena in context.

Some works in the area of philosophy well illustrate this perspective and these needs concerning textual data. Philosophy turned the corner of DH quite recently, but online editions of authors such as Montaigne[1], Nietzsche[2] or Leibniz[3] are now available and well-known. The Corpus Descartes project[4] takes place in this context. It is a research project which aims at providing an online edition of the works and correspondence of René Descartes, the French philosopher, as well as convenient tools for corpus analysis. It illustrates what may be called an *instrumented corpus* [31].

In this paper, we propose an architecture to fulfill the specific requirements of such projects from a computational point of view. The main requirement is to provide advanced IR and DM possibilities regarding full text as well as complex embedding structures. As an example of the principles and methodology introduced in this paper, we present our experiments on this Cartesian (XML-TEI encoded) corpus, which lead us to define and implement an advanced search engine relying on semantic web standards as well as text-mining tools suitable for hermeneutics in DH[5].

In Section 2, we focus on some of the most important properties of a significative number of DH tasks, properties that require suitable tools, and we illustrate these properties with the particular needs of the Corpus Descartes project. The state of the art (Section 3) then presents available tools enabling scholars to explore available corpora and shows that the access to and the usage of these data remain an open problem. Our system, developed as a response to these constraints within the Corpus Descartes project, is introduced in Sections 4, 5 and 6. Section 4 focuses on the preprocessing of the data concerning the part-of-speech tagging, the validation of the tagged data and the construction of a RDF graph representing all available information for subsequent processes introduced in the two next Sections. Section 5 introduces the Corpus Descartes search engine, which relies on this RDF graph and allows expressive queries on all the annotated structures, in order to *locate occurrences* of terms or of combination (or patterns) of terms. Section 6 focuses on text-mining possibilities to *discover new knowledge* on data, expressed as frequent or emerging patterns of forms, lemmas or morpho-syntactic tags. In order to give a first qualitiative evaluation of the proposed environment, and to illustrate its usefulness, Section 7 finally presents an example of use case answering to the question : how does a scholar test a philosophic hypothesis concerning concepts using the proposed environment?

2. REQUIREMENTS FOR HUMANITIES

In this Section, we focus on specific properties and needs of works related to the Humanities. We illustrate these re-

quirements using the representative needs and data of the Corpus Descartes project.

2.1 Delicate and rich data and metadata

DH mainly work on *sources* encoded in digital corpora. These sources may embed images, audio or video but we consider here textual features only. For an important part of DH studies (to which our work is dedicated), this textual data is *delicate* (resulting from a fine-grained editorial process) and should be as *perfect* as possible.

Textual data irreducible to raw text.

This delicate textual data is irreducible to raw text and involves elements resulting from scrupulous editorial work. In particular, these elements concern important structures of the text (logical, rhetorical...) and additional metadata or annotations resulting from their analysis. Most sources use the well-established XML-TEI standard[6] for the representation of texts and metadata in Digital Form.[7] For example, within the Corpus Descartes project, in addition to the full text of the original edition, we have to deal with logical structures (parts, subparts, pagination in various editions, paragraphs, marginal notes...) as well as historical, philological, philosophical or bibliographical notes, all encoded using TEI. Computational work on this delicate data should not reduce or degrade them by regarding sources as plain text. In particular, all the encoded structural elements should provide relevant contexts for corpus exploration tasks.

Enrichment of data.

In addition to the structures encoded during the editorial process, a large range of enrichments are necessary to support the subsequent exploration of textual data. Part-of-speech (POS hereafter) tagging, lemmatization and stemming are common examples of such useful pre-processing, needed to reduce the diversity of forms or to give a more accurate interpretation of them. Segmentation in sentences, chunking or syntactic structure analysis are also often required, but much more complex Natural Language Processing (NLP) tasks may also be necessary: anaphora resolution, named-entity recognition... The enrichment of data may also concern the addition of domain specific knowledge to the original data. For example, occurring forms may be linked to terminologies or ontologies modeling meanings or relations between concepts. Within the Corpus Descartes project, we only had, for now, to identify sentence boundaries, to tokenize words, to lemmatize and POS-tag them. However, an expressive enough framework is required to enable, in the future, the identification and representation of more complex linguistic structures, especially from a syntactic and an argumentative point of view.

Perfection of data.

Even if particular tasks may tolerate noise, it is however often necessary to ensure the *perfection* of data and metadata, since it is often a prerequisite for the reliability of sub-

---

[1]The MontaigneProject: http://www.lib.uchicago.edu/efts/ARTFL/projects/montaigne/.

[2]http://www.nietzschesource.org. See also [11].

[3]http://www.leibniz-edition.de

[4]The Corpus Descartes project is led by the Identité et Subjectivité research team (University of Caen, France), in scientific collaboration with the Centro di studi su Descartes e il Seicento (University del Salento (Lecce)), the Centre d'études cartésiennes (University of Paris IV), the GREYC research laboratory in computer science (University of Caen) and Noopsis, a private company specialized in Text-Mining and Natural Language Processing Technologies. The corpus is available at: http://www.unicaen.fr/puc/sources/prodescartes/.

[5]The system presented in this paper is available for testing at: https://descartes.greyc.fr.

[6]http://www.tei-c.org/index.xml

[7]For a non exhaustive list of projects using TEI, see for example http://www.tei-c.org/Activities/Projects/. The scientific and editorial benefits of encoding ressources in XML-TEI are not to be proved. From the many bibliographical references dealing with TEI from the earlier 1990's, one can read, for example : [17], [1], [8].

sequent analysis. For example, when looking for occurrences of a philosophical concept in order to analyse its genesis, no silence, no false negative is allowed. Therefore, all resources on which subsequent search or analysis may rely (raw text, lemmas, POS tags...) should then be controlled and, if necessary, corrected after each step of the preparation process. Then, systems using these resources should not compromise or hide their perfection.

2.2 Distant, in context and in situ reading

Need for data visualization.

For a significative number of areas of DH (including for example philology or genetic editing), it is often necessary to observe targeted phenomena *in context* (corresponding to the so-called close reading). For some works related to the concrete form of texts, considering raw text as well as its composition, its editing and its formatting, there is even a need to observe phenomena *in book* or, more generally, *in situ* (a kind of very close reading).

Given richly encoded and annotated sources, it is then necessary to provide rendering and Reading Interfaces (RI hereafter). RI must take full account of the original form of the source and of all the information and knowledge resulting from the editorial process. This paper does not focus on the rendering issue, for which many solutions based on web technologies already exist. For example, Figure 1 illustrates the reading interface of Corpus Descartes, implemented by the Pôle Document Numérique of the Maison de la Recherche en Sciences Humaines (MRSH) and the Direction du Système d'Information (DSI) of the University of Caen.

Figure 1: Reading interface for Corpus Descartes

Need for information retrieval.

Scholars need to find locations in corpora where searched terms, expressions or combination of terms or expressions occur. From this point of view, broad spectrum IR solutions have a limitation concerning the *expressivity of the query*. A typical query sent to a search engine for DH may not only use searched forms (or descriptors), but also constraints on structural contexts where they occur and on annotation or meta-data linked to these forms. For example, we would like to enable a query such as: "I am looking for a sentence containing both 'A' and 'B', sentence occurring in a paragraph, annotated by 'Annotator C', and located in a section whose title contains 'D' and in a text written by 'Author D' between 1643 and 1646."

Another important requirement concerns *the scale of responses*. Even if many search engines return full documents as responses to a query, this is not an adequate granularity for most of corpus studies. Passages are preferred to whole documents since documents may be very large. For example, finding that words 'A' and 'B' appear in a given book would not be considered useful if we do not learn their relative locations at the same time. Searching cooccurrences in the same document, in the same paragraph or in the same sentence are very different tasks and support very different interpretations.

Need for text mining.

Whereas IR *searches for* locations of occurrences of combination of terms explicitly given, it is often needed to *discover* unexpected combinations as revealing significant relations between forms or concepts, specificities of a subcorpus. Such discoveries may for example reveal a topic or a style. Hence, corpus exploration often needs textual DM (including here text-mining, statistical analysis of textual data, lexicometry...). While IR mainly supports the study of previously formulated hypothesis, DM allows the emergence of new hypotheses.

2.3 Integrated environments for DH

RI, IR and DM should not be regarded as totally separate tasks. Research in DH may on the contrary benefit from their cross-fertilization. Figure 2 illustrates this virtuous circle: IR selects subcorpora satisfying explicit constraints (presence of terms or of combination of terms); DM makes it possible to discover regularities, unexpected coocurrences, and so on in these subcorpora; these regularities may be observed in context or *in situ* using IR and RI possibilities.

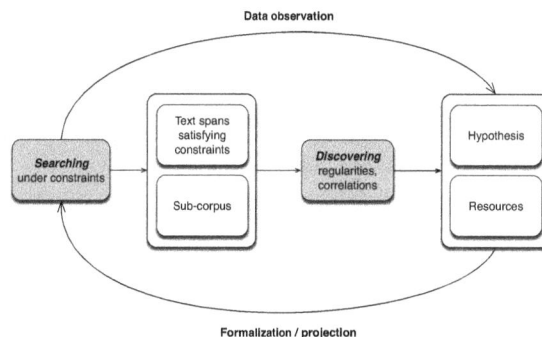

Figure 2: Cross-fertilization of RI, IR and DM

3. STATE OF THE ART

If many corpora in DH already exist, the properties and requirements presented in Section 2 make suitable computational systems necessary to fully exploit them.

Search engines.

For textual corpus studied in Humanities, a search engine is an obvious necessity. Most of the online corpora in DH offer search engines. For example, the Nietzsche Source online edition features an efficient search engine. It enables advanced search of passages containing one or several terms or expressions, also combining constraints on sub-corpora and/or periods. The response to a query gives access to the corresponding passages, making it possible to observe searched elements in context. Similar features are provided by Philologic[8] which is used in some ARTFL Projects[9] such as Perseus[10] or the Montaigne Project. Philologic, which support TEI data, provides very useful options including constraints on distance between searched terms in the same sentence or in the same paragraph, display of found occurrences in concordancers or collocation tables.

Text visualization tools, words in context.

For a long time, scholars have used concordance to observe words in context [14]. A lot of tools rely on this principle, ranging from classical concordancers where keyword occurrences are listed and aligned, surrounded by snippets of context in which they occurs, such as AntConc [5][11], to more sophisticated visualization methods and interactive concordance such as Word Trees [30].

Exploration tools for XML data.

Widely spread encoding methods relying on XML (mostly XML-TEI) make it possible to use low-level tools to manipulate or explore encoded data. Among the vast amount of tools, noteworthy examples are the various hierarchic visualizations featured by BaseX[12] for exploring XML data. Tools such as CorpusReader [19] enable preprocessing and querying by integration of annotation data from different annotation schemes and tag sets. TAPoRware XML Tools[13] enable users to perform text analysis (using for example concordance, cooccurrence or collocation) on XML documents.

Methodologies for text analysis.

Various methodologies may be used to explore textual data. Some of them, such as statistical analysis of textual data and lexicometry [18] are specifically devoted to text analysis and are well-known in DH areas. More general approaches may be used on textual data, such as itemset pattern mining [3] or sequential pattern mining [4]. These approaches come from KDD (Knowledge Discovery in Databases) and DM research fields, which aim at extracting valid, novel, useful and understandable patterns from data [13]. Other methodologies coming from machine learning areas may also be used, especially for classification purposes.

Integrated environments for analysis & visualization.

A wide range of environments, most of them referenced on the gateway provided by TAPoR[14] (Text Analysis Portal for Research), provide implementation (or bridge to available tools) of the above methodologies for text analysis as well as corpus management facilities and data visualization possibilities. TextGrid[15], WordSeer [22][16], or Voyant-

Tools[17] are noteworthy examples of such integrated environments. Other tools or frameworks mainly focus on quantitative analysis of textual data and on what we call here, generally speaking, text-mining. TXM[18] [16], coming from the statistical data analysis and lexicometry tradition [18] and designed to support analysis on TEI data, provides a powerful environment for quantitative analysis with advanced visualization features. The PhiloMine [10][19] extension to PhiloLogic provides support for a variety of machine learning, text mining, and document clustering tasks and a useful bridge to the Weka[20] toolkit.

Online "rich" instrumented editions and corpora.

Another approach is to provide what we call here "rich" editions and corpora. These online environments integrate textual data (corpora or editions) enriched with interactive tools to explore and manipulate them. Examples of such editions are the aforementioned Montaigne and Nietzsche Source projects, as well as the online edition of "la Queste del Saint Graal" [20]. In some way, the Monk project[21] also combines textual data and mining tools. The Corpus Descartes project also offers such tools and illustrates what may be called an instrumented corpus in DH.

An open problem.

Despite the vast amount of related work, giving adequate access to available richly annotated corpora, in order to produce higher-order knowledge, remains an open problem. The following appear to be of particular relevance:

1. For IR and DM, corpora are often seen as raw text, ignoring available TEI structures and specific contexts in which the intended target occurs. Taking domain knowledge, annotations or linguistic information into account, in order to express broader or more accurate queries or data selection is often not possible.

2. If the observation of words *in context* is a well-established tradition, this is less true for observation *in situ*.

3. Even though many available tools make XML structure exploration or text analysis quite easy, most of the time these tools require specific computational or statistical skills, and cannot be used, as such, by all researchers coming from Humanities.

4. DH scholars may suffer from the lack of integration of the broad range of available tools. While working on one dataset, it is necessary to constantly handle data (import, export, convert...) in order to use complementary functionalities implemented in separate tools. We advocate the fact that integrated rich digital editions must provide exploration tools out of the box.

4. DATA PREPROCESSING

This Section introduces the preprocessing steps before IR and DM can take place.

---

[8]https://sites.google.com/site/philologic3/home
[9]http://artfl-project.uchicago.edu
[10]http://perseus.uchicago.edu
[11]http://www.laurenceanthony.net/software/antconc
[12]http://basex.org
[13]http://taporware.ualberta.ca/~taporware/xmlTools/
[14]http://tapor.ca
[15]http://www.textgrid.de
[16]http://wordseer.berkeley.edu

[17]http://voyant-tools.org
[18]http://textometrie.ens-lyon.fr
[19]https://code.google.com/p/philomine
[20]http://www.cs.waikato.ac.nz/ml/weka/
[21]http://monk.library.illinois.edu

4.1 RDF representation of data

Our goal is to give access (for IR or DM) to a wide range of heterogeneous information coming from various sources: a) from TEI documents (structures, texts, notes, etc); b) from additional processes (segmentation in sentences, morpho-syntactical, etc); c) from external resources (terminologies or ontologies). And an important aspect of this work is to be able to query the data through a *unified* interface. These sources may be queried all at once.

Data used in DH often comes with embedded information, usually containing overlapping structures. Techniques to encode these have evolved [27] and data is, nowadays, usually encoded as embedded markup or as a graph structure. Pros and cons of both approaches are well-known [23]. XML related techniques (such as TEI) give a straightforward structure to textual content. However, embedded markup has limitations such as inability to overlap, sequential order of annotations for example. On the other hand, the use of graph structures such as RDF enables a general framework for storing annotations about a document.

In our project, most of the knowledge about documents is embedded in a *tree structure*, encoded as XML-TEI. However, additional annotations in independent layers (linguistic, philological, philosophical...) potentially lead to overlapping structures not easily representable as tree. Furthermore, scientific annotations linking passages, linguistic relations, or relations between concepts are some examples of reticulation leading to cross-linked patterns for which *graph structures* provide a better representation. In order to provide an expressive enough framework, a RDF[22] graph is used as a unified model to represent all the available information. Figure 3 illustrates the preprocessing steps: a first set of information imported from TEI structures, additional annotations produced manually or automatically and external resources are represented in one graph. Subsequent processes for IR and DM use this RDF graph.

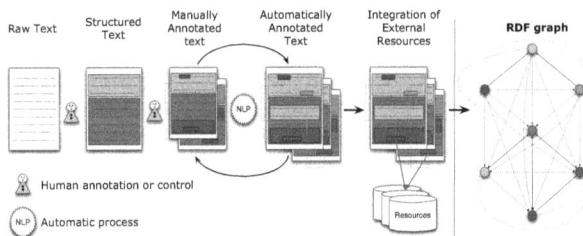

Figure 3: All information represented by a graph

Since everything is turned into a graph, all structures coming from the TEI reference (sections, subsections, paragraphs, notes, page breaks...) become vertices of the graph. In addition, each piece of text or unit (single words, sentences, paragraphs...) also becomes a vertex, and topological relations (imbrication, order...) become edges. Whenever it makes sense, a node has an URI referring, via an XPointer and a string-range, to the exact position of the corresponding element in the source. This preserves a strong link with the original TEI reference, and makes it easy to go from the graph to the exact position of the text in its original context.

Finally, tabular representation is also generated as input for morpho-syntactic tagging and DM tools. For each word,

[22]http://www.w3.org/RDF/

English	Modern French	Classical French
then	ensuite	en suite
when	lorsque	lors que
a hundred times	cent fois	centfois
instead of	au lieu	aulieu
because	parce que	parceque
I have	j'ai	iay

Table 1: Modern French vs. Classical French

each sentence or each paragraph, the URI preserves the mapping to the graph and allows bridges to other tools.

4.2 Part-of-speech tagging & lemmatization

Query expansion, more accurate interpretation of words, or reduction of the diversity of forms often make POS tagging and lemmatizaton necessary. However, some works in DH deal with under-resourced languages. For example, scholars working on Cartesian data have to deal with Classical French[23] and Neo-Latin languages. For such under-resources languages, very few computational tools, especially part-of-speech taggers and lemmatization tools, are available. Furthermore, since it cannot be tolerated to miss any occurrence for any query, control and correction are then necessary steps. Whenever working with such languages, we use a two-steps strategy to build the tagged data: 1) setting the best possible tagger for our data; 2) then check and correct manually the tagged data sets.

Working with Latin and French.

As far as Latin is concerned, a specific set of parameters does fortunately exist for the TreeTagger [26]. However, it was trained on data corresponding to an older Latin and we cannot expect perfect results on the Cartesian corpus. It nonetheless saves time and constitutes a useful first step: experts just have to validate the data and correct errors.

To our knowledge, no tagger is available as far as Classical French is concerned. However, modernized versions of the corpora with respect to the sole orthography aspect are fortunately available. They preserve the original syntax, in that all the words appear in their original order. Therefore, we use Treetagger for Modern French. Once this modernized data is tagged, we project the result on the Classical French version. Unfortunately, this projection is not straightforward since the number of words may vary from Classical to Modern French. It may increase (agglomeration) or decrease (desagglomeration). Table 1 shows examples of both. Additionally, punctuation is often modified from Classical to Modern version, which was another problem.

Data validation.

Thanks to the first step, we get a fairly advanced state of tagging (however not perfect), which avoids an expert to have to fully choose the tags manually. At this stage, an expert has a limited number of corrections to perform. We developed a validating tool to help with the correction task.

Once the RDF graph is produced and the part-of-speech tagging is performed and validated, the data is ready for IR and DM. The next Section explains how these are performed.

[23]Not to be confused with Old French, Classical French is quite similar to Modern French but without orthographical stability.

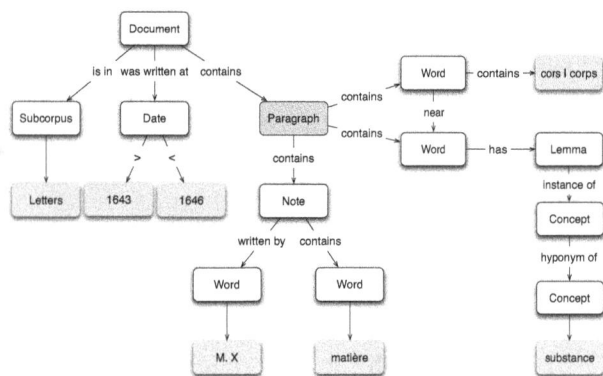

Figure 5: Queries as graphs

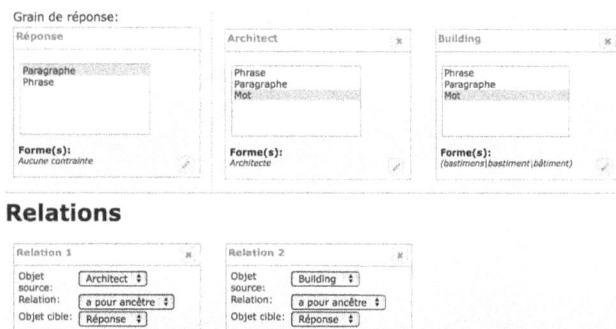

Figure 6: Graphical edition of a SPARQL query

5. SEARCHING OCCURRENCES

The search engine, illustrated in Figure 4, mainly relies on the generated RDF graph encoding all the available information: TEI structures, textual data, position of substructures in structures, position of words in their context and so on. Using only such graphs, it is possible to identify contexts (sections, paragraphs, sentences...) containing terms or combination of terms, as well as the accurate position of these terms in these contexts, all positions refering only to the TEI reference.

A typical response of the search engine is a set of excerpts (emphasizing the constituents of the query) and associated links pointing to the reading interface and providing (via adequate XPointers) information needed 1) to focus on the satisfying text span and 2) to emphasize the constituents of the query *in situ*.

5.1 Queries as graphs, using SPARQL

As illustrated in Figure 5, a complex query may also be represented as a graph. And such a graph may be translated into a SPARQL query[24], which has a very large expressivity. However such a query may be quite complex, because of optimization constraints and because quite confusing information has to be collected, concerning for example position of elements used when returning to te text.

As a consequence, it is necessary to provide convenient graphical user interfaces (GUI) making it possible for a user

---

to formulate his query in a simple manner. A first GUI, illustrated in Figure 6, enables the graphical edition of a SPARQL query. Vertices are represented by boxes : one box for the response context (paragraph, sentence...) and one box for each constituent searched for, i.e. for each searched term. Each box constraints TEI type as well as the textual content of elements, using the power of regular expressions. Edges of the query-graph are also represented by boxes allowing the user to select the type and the targets (vertices) of relations.

5.2 Simplified GUI for the search engine

The GUI presented above, expressive enough to benefit from all information available in the RDF graphs, remains quite complex and confusing for most users, ignoring the very structure of initial TEI data and the resulting RDF graph.

The simplified GUI illustrated in Figure 4 hides these subtle complexities. In the default mode[25], the user only has to select the subcorpora (several parts of the *Discours de la Méthode* in the example), the response context (here, the sentence level), and to specify searched cooccurring terms separated by blanks, using regex expressivity ("vérité" in several forms and "raison").

5.3 Morphological expansion of queries

For DH purposes, as mentioned above, no silence may be tolerated: missing an occurrence would have huge consequences. That is the reason why morpho-syntactical resources have to be validated. This validation however takes a lot of time and should not lock the entire exploration environment. If morphological query expansion was automatically done on the server-side, inaccuracy in the morphological resource could result in false negatives, which, again, are not acceptable. So, in order to give the user a maximum control, we use the following workaround. When formulating his query, the user is proposed several possible expansions for the forms he entered, via a popup relying on morphosyntactic resources. He can easily select some of these forms or manually expand the list if some forms are missing. In such a way, a query is only about *forms* for which perfect recall (no silence at all) can be ensured.

5.4 Implementation of the search engine

Concerning the implementation of this search engine, let us simply mention that it mainly relies on the Java/JEE framework[26] and on JQuery[27] as GUI toolkit on the client-side. It is currently deployed on Glassfish[28]. RDF graphs are deployed in the Sesame triple-store[29]. For better performances, several graphs correspond to different parts of the whole Cartesian corpus, which may be queried in parallel.

6. DISCOVERING NEW KNOWLEDGE

KDD (Knowledge Discovery in Databases) and DM (Data Mining) provide techniques to extract rich and understandable representation of data named *patterns*. Within the

---

[24] http://www.w3.org/TR/sparql11-overview/

[25] Other modes not discussed here rely on slightly different principles.
[26] http://www.oracle.com/technetwork/java/javaee
[27] http://jquery.com
[28] https://glassfish.java.net
[29] http://www.openrdf.org

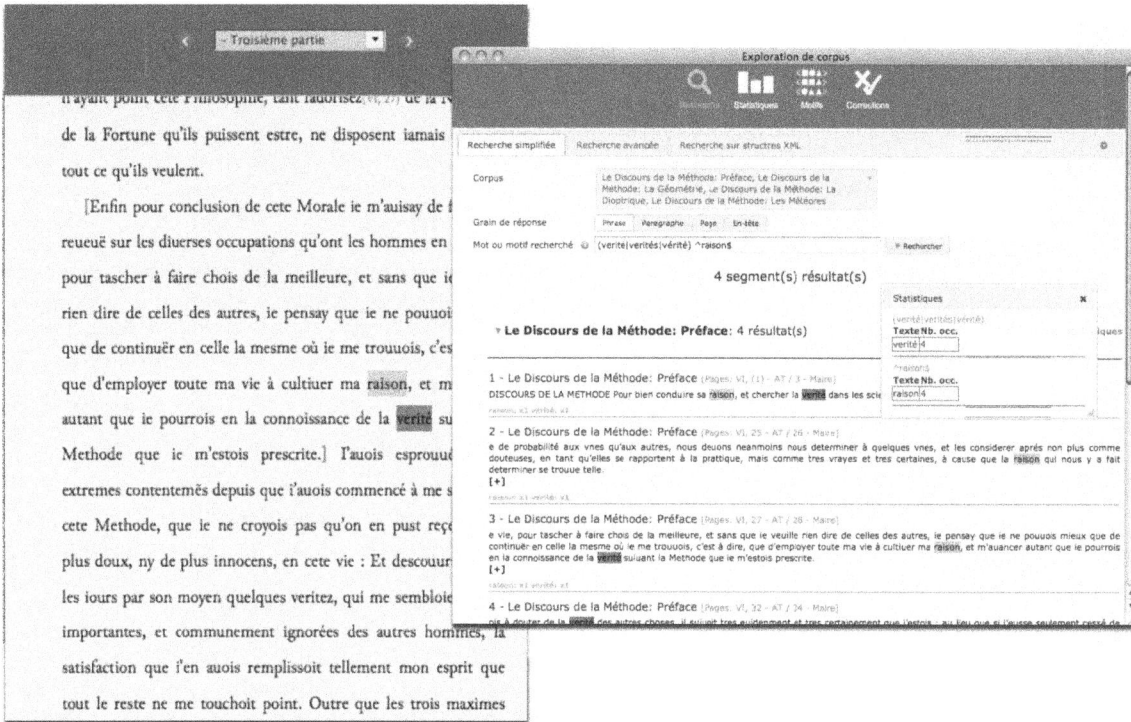

Figure 4: The Corpus Descartes search engine

Corpus Descartes project, we developed tools using pattern mining techniques which enable scholars to 1) discover unexpected cooccurrences from Cartesian data and 2) discover specificities of a corpus by contrast to another. More specifically, we use two kinds of patterns to discover new knowledge: *itemsets* and *sequential patterns*.

id	transaction
1	abc
2	abcd
3	abx
4	bcy

Table 2: Transaction DB

id	Sequence
1	$\langle (a)\ (a\ b\ c)\ (a\ c)\ (d)\rangle$
2	$\langle (a\ d)\ (c)\ (b)\rangle$
3	$\langle (a\ b)\ (d)\ (b)\ (c)\rangle$
4	$\langle (a\ d)\ (b)\ (b)\rangle$

Table 3: Sequential DB

6.1 Background

Itemset Mining.

Itemset mining also called pattern mining was introduced in [3] in order to extract relevant information from a transaction database. Let $\varphi = \{i_1, i_2, \ldots, i_k\}$ be a set of *items*. Each *transaction* in a Transaction Database (TDB) is associated with an *itemset*, also called a *pattern*, which is a subset of φ. We say a transaction *supports* an itemset I' if $I \subseteq I'$. Let τ be a TDB and I an itemset. The number of transactions in τ that support I is called the frequency of I (noted $freq(I)$). The *support* of I in τ is defined as $freq(I)/N$ (noted $sup(I)$), where N is the total number of transactions of τ. I will be a *frequent itemset* in τ if $sup(I) \geq minsup$ with $minsup \in [0,1]$, a user-defined minimal support threshold. I is a *Frequent Closed Itemset* in τ if I is a Frequent Itemset, and if there exists no itemset I' in τ such as $I \subset I'$ and $freq(I) = freq(I')$.

Let Table 2 be an example of transaction database (DB) and $minsup = 1/2$. The itemset $P = abc$ is a frequent itemset because $sup(P) = 1/2 \geq minsup$ (transaction ID 1 and 2). P is also a closed frequent itemset because it does not exist an itemset I such as $P \subset I$ and $sup(P) = sup(I)$. There is an important number of algorithms allowing to extract frequent itemsets or closed frequent itemsets from transaction database such as [15, 2, 6, 29].

Sequential Pattern Mining.

Sequential pattern mining is a data mining technique introduced in [4] to find regularities in a Sequence Database (SDB). Authors introduced the notion of *sequences* which are an ordered list of itemsets, denoted by $s = \langle I_1 \ldots I_m \rangle$. For instance, $\langle (a)\ (a\ b\ c)\ (a\ c)\ (d)\rangle$ is a sequence of four itemsets. A sequence $S_1 = \langle I_1 \ldots I_n \rangle$ is *included* in a sequence $S_2 = \langle I'_1 \ldots I'_m \rangle$ if there exist integers $1 \leq j_1 < \ldots < j_n \leq m$ such that $I_1 \subseteq I'_{j_1}, \ldots, I_n \subseteq I'_{j_n}$. The sequence S_1 is called a *subsequence* of S_2, and we note $S_1 \preceq S_2$. For example, $\langle (a)(a\ c)\rangle$ is included in $\langle (a)(a\ b\ c)(a\ c)(d)\rangle$. Like in itemsets mining, the frequency of a sequential pattern P (noted $freq(P)$) is the number of sequences from a sequential database ς supporting P. Similarly, the *support* of P in ς is defined as $freq(P)/M$ (noted $sup(I)$), where M is the total number of sequences of ς.

A *frequent sequential pattern* is a sequence such that its support is greater or equal to a given support threshold $minsup$ (just like in itemsets mining tasks). A frequent sequential pattern [32] S is *closed* if there is no other fre-

163

quent sequential pattern S' such that $S \preceq S'$ and $sup(S) = sup(S')$.

Table 3 illustrates a SDB of 4 sequences. For example, $sup(\langle(a\ b)(c)\rangle) = 1/2$, since sequences 1 and 3 support $\langle(a\ b)(c)\rangle$ in a total of four sequences. With $minsup = 1/2$, the sequential pattern $\langle(a\ b)\rangle$ is not closed because $sup(\langle(a\ b)\rangle) = sup(\langle(a\ b)(c)\rangle)$ and $\langle(a\ b)\rangle \preceq \langle(a\ b)(c)\rangle$.

There are a lot of algorithms to extract sequential patterns or closed sequential patterns like [28, 32, 33].

Emerging Pattern Mining.

According to [25], emerging patterns (EP) are sets of items whose frequency changes significantly from one dataset to another. They allow to discover specific patterns of datasets, and are also powerful method for constructing accurate classifiers. Introduced by [12], EP's aim is to capture significant changes and differences between datasets. Originally used with itemsets, EP are also used with sequential patterns like in [24]. Let ϕ be a positive number, $D1$ and $D2$ be two transaction databases, I an itemset, and $sup_1(I)$, $sup_2(I)$ it respective support in $D1$ and $D2$. I is said to be a $\phi - emerging pattern$ from $D1$ to $D2$ if $GrowthRate(I) \geq \phi$ is superior to a given threshold called "emergence rate", where $GrowthRate(I)$ is defined as $\frac{sup_1(I)}{sup_2(I)}$.[30]

6.2 Frequency and Cooccurrences Analysis

The first tool we built makes it possible to extract, given few easy-to-understand parameters, all the observed cooccurrences from a subcorpus. If we consider terms as items, and sentences as transactions, we can easily transpose the problem of itemset extraction to the problem of extraction of cooccurrences from a text. The support of an itemset is the number of sentences containing the itemset (*i.e.* the cooccurrences). In order to extract patterns, this tool uses LCM[31] algorithm [29].

More specifically, user has to : 1) Choose a corpus from the available data; 2) Choose the kind of wanted cooccurrences. Users can extract cooccurrences of terms, or cooccurrences of lemmas; 3) Choose between an extraction of *frequent itemsets* (no condensed representation) or *closed itemsets* (using condensed representation); 4) Choose the minimal and the maximal number of cooccurring terms by choosing an interval; 5) Choose the minimal number of sentences supporting the cooccurrences; 6) Define a stop-list if needed, in order to extract only relevant terms.

For example, in Descartes' *Epistola ad Voetium*, some of the cooccurring terms extracted are:

"liber ratio"	In 9 sentences
"thesis liber"	In 5 sentences
"nomen liber"	In 6 sentences
"nomen thesis"	In 6 sentences
"verbum ratio"	In 6 sentences
"verbum thesis"	In 9 sentences
"puto liber"	In 6 sentences

6.3 Specificity Analysis

A second tool uses data mining techniques to provide a specificity analysis. This tool uses multiple techniques (itemset mining, sequential pattern mining and emerging patterns) in order to extract emerging thematic or stylis-

tic knowledge from a corpus compared to another one, by comparing corpora's patterns (or sequential patterns).

For a non-sequential analysis, we can use an itemset mining algorithm (the LCM algorithm) and extract specific emerging cooccurrences (of forms, lemmas, tags or combination of them) which characterize, for example, the topic of a text. In order to extract sequential patterns we make use of the algorithm proposed in [7]. The emerging patterns are extracted using the method proposed by [24].

This specificity analysis tool have the same parameters as the cooccurrences analysis tool introduced above, with an additional parameter indicating the emerging threshold.

Section 7 provides some examples of emerging patterns found in the Cartesian corpus.

7. PHILOSOPHICAL USE-CASE

Importance of in situ *reading.*

Philosophical and editorial assumptions, in direct connection with the Cartesian theory of knowledge, implies the possibility to observe the results of exploration tools *in situ*. Indeed, the linear reading is needed to understand the truths transcribed by Descartes in his books. The printed book, in the case of Descartes, defines materially, by the succession of its pages, the order to be followed to truly learn. For the heuristic of reading to operate, the order of reasons should never be broken. It is necessary to experience the chain without missing any link, within the argumentative discourse structure.[32] Furthermore the prints reviewed and corrected by Descartes himself (who was implied in the publishing of his works) are the authentic sources to which today's reader must refer. For Descartes, the layout of the printed text has an influence on its interpretation.[33] More generally, the theory of "mise en livre", formalized by two distinguished historians of the book Henri-Jean Martin and Roger Chartier [9], applies very well to Descartes' work. The reading interface and the exploration tools proposed in the Corpus Descartes, which enable *in situ* observation of searched or discovered patterns, take these strong contraints into account.

Testing an hypothesis using these tools.

We want to check the precise location of the emergence of a philosophical concept in the Cartesian corpus. This technical concept is that of the doubling of onto-theo-logy, formalized by Jean-Luc Marion [21]. According to him, it appears in *Primae* and *Quartae Responsiones* of the *Meditationes de prima philosophia* (1642). This concept implies the extension of the concept of cause (*causa*) to all the concepts which designate the being (*Deus, cogitatio/idea*).

In order to test this hypothesis, using *Objectiones et Responsiones* of *Meditationes de prima philosophia*, we look for thematic specificities (expressed as patterns of terms co-

---

[30]$GrowthRate(I) = 0$ (resp. ∞) if $sup_1(I) = sup_2(I) = 0$ (resp. $sup_1(I) = 0$ and $sup_2(I) \neq 0$).

[31]We use the following implementation of LCM: http://code.google.com/p/lcmplusplus/

[32]Descartes himself prescribes "Those who visit Tables books that in order to pick out the subjects they want to see, and to exempt the trouble to read the rest, will derive no satisfaction from them, for the explanation of the issues that marked there depends almost always so specifically what precedes them, and often what follows, we do not hear well if it reads attentively throughout the book." *Discours de la méthode*, AT VI, 486 (we translate).

[33]Thus, some "fautes de l'impression" "déguise[nt] le style", and "corrompent le sens", *Letter to Huygens*, 29 juillet 1641, AT III, 771.

Primae Obj. et Resp.	Quartae Obj. et Resp.
idea perfectio : 3.009	**essentia causa : 91.377**
causa res : 4.062	angulus rectum : 3.775
causa artificium : 86.664	res substantia : 4.153
Deus nomen : 9.999	res distinctio : 9.691
existentia conceptus : 14.444	res cognitio : 6.645
causa quæ : 5.416	res Deus : 2.567
causa intellectus : 19.258	**modus causa : 13.291**
intellectus Deus : 11.234	verbum ratio : 4.153
intellectus imperfectio : 24.073	Deus essentia : 2.186
idea res intellectus : 16.507	**ratio causa : 7.120**
idea ens : 4.622	panis vinum : ∞
causa idea : 10.504	**Deus ratio causa : 10.383**
ens intellectus : 18.055	res modus : 2.643
causa idea artificium : 72.220	res corpus : 2.542
causa ratio : 4.333	**ratio effectus : 16.614**
intellectus natura : 9.027	res|reus essentia : 8.307
idea artificium : 36.110	essentia existentia : 2.907
	res meditatio : 2.931
	meditatio corpus : 4.531
	Deus causa : 9.493
	mens corpus : 3.775
	corpus essentia : 49.842
	judicium idea : 24.921
	corpus species : 7.120
	res causa : 27.690
	res author : 8.307
	corpus homo : 2.769
	res Deus causa : 66.456

Table 4: Emerging cooccurrences

occurring in the same sentence) of the targeted subcorpora. A cooccurrence is here considered as a specificity of a subcorpus with respect to another subcorpus if the ratio between the two frequencies is greater than a certain threshold (the rate of emergence). The cooccurrences that are listed in Table 4 are specific to a subcorpus composed of a set of *Objectiones* and associated *Responsiones*) when one compares this set with other sets of *Objectiones* / *Responsiones* present in the *Meditationes de prima philosophia*. The rate of emergence is also given. Greater rates indicate more specific patterns.

These emerging patterns allow to confirm that these subcorpora are a privileged place for mobilization of the concept of *causa* announced in the middle of the *Meditatio* III.[34] The request of *causa*, although situated in *Responsiones*, insofar as it is a requisite of the reason, remains necessary for the performance of Cartesian metaphysics, and what Jean-Luc Marion called the doubling of onto-theo-logy [21, p. 122]. The discovery of the rate of emergence of cooccurrences that describe the submission of the being to the cause (including God) in *Responsiones* I and IV confirms their thematic affiliation with *Meditatio* III which introduced the concept of *causa*.

According to the usages and constraints mentioned above, the cooccurrences can be interpreted *in situ*, within the argumentative structure of *Responsiones* VI edited according to Descartes' typographical recommendations.

8. CONCLUSION

If many projects in Digital Humanities provide richly annotated corpora, the usage of these data to produce higher order knowledges remains an open problem. Mainly because available search engines do not give a full access to all

the encoded information for information retrieval, and because text-mining environments often require computational or statistical skills, which most of researcher of Humanities field do not have.

Within the Corpus Descartes project, we designed an environment for both information retrieval and text-mining intended for Digital Humanities. It relies on a unified representation of all structures, annotations and resources coming from TEI corpora, domain specific knowledge or computational processes, in a graph structure. A search engine enables complex queries on this structure, making it possible to find terms or combination of cooccurring terms in specific context, and to return to the text to see them *in situ*. Users also benefit from query expansion mechanisms, using morpho-syntactic resources for Neo-Latin and Classical French. This exploration environment also features datamining tools, for remarkable cooccurences and contrastive specificity discovery.

Even though the environment was successfully experimented on a specific corpus, it is important to notice that our methodology and the software components may be used for other data. Further work with philosophers will take place to improve our hypotheses and improve the provided tools. Finally, we plan to publish the software as an open-source package for other DH researchers to use.

9. ACKNOWLEDGMENTS

The Corpus Descartes project (2009-2014) was supported by the French Agence Nationale de la Recherche (ANR-09-BLAN-0353-01). The work presented in this paper was also supported by the French Contrat de Projet État-Région (CPER) and the Région Basse-Normandie.

The authors would like to warmly thank Jérôme Chauveau (DSI, University of Caen) and Frédérik Bilhaut (Noopsis, Caen), who strongly contributed to the development of the search engine, and Sylvain Loiseau (University of Paris 13 & SeDyL laboratory), who contributed to the lemmatization and POS-tagging of data in Classical French.

10. REFERENCES

[1] *TEI: Text Encoding Initiative*, volume 24 of *Cahiers Gutemberg*, 1996.

[2] R. C. Agarwal, C. C. Aggarwal, and V. V. V. Prasad. Depth first generation of long patterns. In *Proceedings of the sixth ACM SIGKDD International Conference on Knowledge Discovery and Data Mining*, pages 108–118. ACM Press, 2000.

[3] R. Agrawal, T. Imieliński, and A. Swami. Mining association rules between sets of items in large databases. In *Proceedings of the 1993 ACM SIGMOD International Conference on Management of Data*, SIGMOD '93, pages 207–216, New York, NY, USA, 1993. ACM.

[4] R. Agrawal and R. Srikant. Mining sequential patterns. In *Proceedings of the Eleventh International Conference on Data Engineering*, ICDE '95, pages 3–14, Washington, DC, USA, 1995. IEEE Computer Society.

[5] L. Anthony. Developing AntConc for a new generation of corpus linguists. In *Proceedings of the Corpus Linguistics Conference (CL 2013)*, pages 14–16, Lancaster University, UK, 2013.

[34]When the *ego* (*cogito*) itself goes in search of the basis for its own cogitative existence (respectively AT VII, 108, 18-22; AT VII, 238, 11-18).

[6] R. J. Bayardo, Jr. Efficiently mining long patterns from databases. *SIGMOD Rec.*, 27(2):85–93, 1998.

[7] N. Béchet, P. Cellier, T. Charnois, and B. Crémilleux. Sequence mining under multiple constraints. In *Proceedings of the 30th Annual ACM Symposium on Applied Computing*, SAC'15, pages 908–914. ACM, 2015.

[8] L. Burnard, K. O'Brien O'Keefe, and J. Unsworth, editors. *Electronic Textual Editing*, 2006.

[9] R. Chartier. Du livre au lire. *Sociologie de la communication*, 1(1):271–290, 1997.

[10] C. Cooney, R. Horton, M. Olsen, G. Roe, and R. Voyer. PhiloMine: An Integrated Environment for Humanities Text Mining. In *Proceedings of Digital Humanities 2008 (Posters)*, pages 237–238, Oulu, Finland, 2008.

[11] P. d'Iorio, editor. *HyperNietzsche. Modèle d'un hypertexte savant sur Internet pour la recherche en sciences humaines. Questions philosophiques, problèmes juridiques, outils informatiques.* Presses Universitaires de France, Paris, 2000.

[12] G. Dong and J. Li. Efficient mining of emerging patterns: Discovering trends and differences. In *Proceedings of the Fifth ACM SIGKDD International Conference on Knowledge Discovery and Data Mining*, KDD '99, pages 43–52, New York, NY, USA, 1999. ACM.

[13] U. M. Fayyad, G. Piatetsky-Shapiro, and P. Smyth. Advances in knowledge discovery and data mining. pages 1–34, Menlo Park, CA, USA, 1996. American Association for Artificial Intelligence.

[14] M. Fischer. The KWIC index concept : A retrospective view. *American Documentation*, 17(2):57–70, 1966.

[15] J. Han, J. Pei, and Y. Yin. Mining frequent patterns without candidate generation. *SIGMOD Rec.*, 29(2):1–12, 2000.

[16] S. Heiden. The TXM Platform: Building Open-Source Textual Analysis Software Compatible with the TEI Encoding Scheme. In R. Otoguro, K. Ishikawa, H. Umemoto, K. Yoshimoto, and Y. Harada, editors, *Proceedings of the 24th Pacific Asia Conference on Language, Information and Computation*, pages 389–398, Sendai, Japon, Nov. 2010. Institute for Digital Enhancement of Cognitive Development, Waseda University.

[17] N. Ide and J. Véronis, editors. *Text Encoding Initiative: Background and Context*. Text, Speech and Language Technology. Kluwer, Dordrecht, 1995.

[18] L. Lebart, A. Salem, and L. Berry. *Exploring Textual Data*. Text, speech, and language technology. Kluwer Academic, 1998.

[19] S. Loiseau. CorpusReader : construction et interrogation de corpus multiannotés. *Revue Traitement Automatique des Langues (TAL)*, 49(2):189–215, 2008.

[20] C. Marchello-Nizia and A. Lavrentiev, editors. *Queste del saint Graal*. Published online by la Base de Français Médiéval, Lyon, France, 2013. http://catalog.bfm-corpus.org/qgraal_cm.

[21] J.-L. Marion. Redoubled Onto-theo-logy. In *On Descartes' Metaphysical Prism, Constitution And The Limits Of Onto-Theo-Logy In Cartesian Thought*, pages 118–127. Chicago University Press, Chicago, 1999. Jeffrey L. Kosky (trad.).

[22] A. Muralidharan, M. A. Hearst, and C. Fan. Wordseer: A knowledge synthesis environment for textual data. In *Proceedings of the 22Nd ACM International Conference on Conference on Information & Knowledge Management*, CIKM '13, pages 2533–2536, New York, NY, USA, 2013. ACM.

[23] S. Peroni and F. Vitali. Annotations with earmark for arbitrary, overlapping and out-of order markup. In *Proceedings of the 9th ACM Symposium on Document Engineering*, DocEng '09, pages 171–180, New York, NY, USA, 2009. ACM.

[24] M. Plantevit and B. Crémilleux. Condensed representation of sequential patterns according to frequency-based measures. In N. M. Adams, C. Robardet, A. Siebes, and J.-F. Boulicaut, editors, *IDA*, volume 5772 of *Lecture Notes in Computer Science*, pages 155–166. Springer, 2009.

[25] K. Ramamohanarao and J. Bailey. Discovery of emerging patterns and their use in classification. In T. D. Gedeon and L. C. C. Fung, editors, *Australian Conference on Artificial Intelligence*, volume 2903 of *Lecture Notes in Computer Science*, pages 1–12. Springer, 2003.

[26] H. Schmid. Probabilistic part-of-speech tagging using decision trees. In *Proceedings of International Conference on New Methods in Language Processing*, pages 44–49, Manchester, UK, 1994.

[27] C. Sperberg-McQueen and C. Huitfeldt. Goddag: A data structure for overlapping hierarchies. In P. King and E. Munson, editors, *Digital Documents: Systems and Principles*, volume 2023 of *Lecture Notes in Computer Science*, pages 139–160. Springer Berlin Heidelberg, 2004.

[28] R. Srikant and R. Agrawal. Mining sequential patterns: Generalizations and performance improvements. In *EDBT*, pages 3–17, 1996.

[29] T. Uno, M. Kiyomi, and H. Arimura. Lcm ver.3: Collaboration of array, bitmap and prefix tree for frequent itemset mining. In *Proceedings of the 1st International Workshop on Open Source Data Mining: Frequent Pattern Mining Implementations*, OSDM '05, pages 77–86, New York, NY, USA, 2005. ACM.

[30] M. Wattenberg and A. B. Végas. The Word Tree, an Interactive Visual Concordance. *IEEE Transactions on Visualization and Computer Graphics*, pages 1221–1228, 2008.

[31] C. Welger-Barboza. Les digital humanities aujourd'hui: centres, réseaux, pratiques et enjeux. In P. Mounier and M. Dacos, editors, *Digital Humanities. Les transformations numériques du rapport aux savoirs*, 2009.

[32] X. Yan, J. Han, and R. Afshar. Clospan: Mining closed sequential patterns in large databases. In *SDM*, 2003.

[33] M. J. Zaki. SPADE: An efficient algorithm for mining frequent sequences. *Machine Learning Journal*, 42(1/2):31–60, Jan/Feb 2001. special issue on Unsupervised Learning.

The Delaunay Document Layout Descriptor

Sébastien Eskenazi - Petra Gomez-Krämer - Jean-Marc Ogier
Laboratoire L3i
Avenue Michel Crépeau
17042 La Rochelle Cedex 1 - France
{sebastien.eskenazi; petra.gomez; jean-marc.ogier}@univ-lr.fr

ABSTRACT

Security applications related to document authentication require an exact match between an authentic copy and the original of a document. This implies that the documents analysis algorithms that are used to compare two documents (original and copy) should provide the same output. This kind of algorithm includes the computation of layout descriptors from the segmentation result, as the layout of a document is a part of its semantic content. To this end, this paper presents a new layout descriptor that significantly improves the state of the art. The basic of this descriptor is the use of a Delaunay triangulation of the centroids of the document regions. This triangulation is seen as a graph and the adjacency matrix of the graph forms the descriptor. While most layout descriptors have a stability of 0% with regard to an exact match, our descriptor has a stability of 74% which can be brought up to 100% with the use of an appropriate matching algorithm. It also achieves 100% accuracy and retrieval in a document retrieval scheme on a database of 960 document images. Furthermore, this descriptor is extremely efficient as it performs a search in constant time with respect to the size of the document database and it reduces the size of the index of the database by a factor 400.

Keywords

layout descriptor, Delaunay, stability, hashing, retrieval, classification

1. INTRODUCTION

Many documents need to be secured, ideally by the means of an electronic hash. If two documents have the same hash, then they are authentic copies of each other and if their hashes are different, one of the two documents is fraudulent or at least different from the other one. This concept works well for naturally born digital documents. However, nowadays a document, the so-called hybrid document, is often used in electronic or paper form according to the need.

2015 Association for Computing Machinery. ACM acknowledges that this contribution was authored or co-authored by an employee, contractor or affiliate of a national government. As such, the Government retains a nonexclusive, royalty-free right to publish or reproduce this article, or to allow others to do so, for Government purposes only.

DocEng'15, September 8-11, 2015, Lausanne, Switzerland.
© 2015 ACM. ISBN 978-1-4503-3307-8/15/09 ...$15.00.
DOI: http://dx.doi.org/10.1145/2682571.2797059.

Hence, the hybrid document undergoes a lifecycle of printing and scanning and thus different degraded versions of the document exist as the printing and scanning process introduces specific degradations in the document such as print and scan noise [13]. Thus, the concept of a digital hash can not be applied. For this reason, our work intends to develop an advanced digital hash for the field of securing hybrid documents, the so-called hybrid security. Our idea is to extract the layout, the text and the images from the document to compute a stable hash that will be the same for all the authentic copies of the document.

To our knowledge, the closest work is a hash [18] based on pixelwise signal analysis techniques which is not satisfactory because of its large size. Other hashes such as the 2D-Doc [3] require the emitter of the document to precise the information used for hash computation, e.g. the name and the address of the beneficiary in the context of an invoice, and thus secures only partially the document (the provided information, but for instance not the layout). Thus, an ideal hash computation process is to automatically extract the content of the document (text, layout, graphics) and use it in the hash computation. A smaller hash than [18] will result as the amount of information to be secured is smaller since the image is not processed pixelwise. Anyhow, this hash will still allow to secure the whole information of the document. In consequence, this requires document analysis techniques with an extreme stability especially with regard to print and scan noise. The first step in a document analysis process is often the segmentation of the document. Hence we need to evaluate the stability of a segmentation algorithm.

Before going any further it is important to understand the difference between accuracy and stability. Accuracy requires a groundtruth to evaluate how close a result is to this ground truth. Accuracy can be evaluated with only one result as long as there is also a ground truth. Stability does not require a ground truth. Stability requires at least two results with similar inputs to see how close these results are together compared to how close the inputs were. In our case, similar inputs are photocopies of the same document. A consequence of this is that an algorithm can be very stable and yet not be accurate. For instance an algorithm that always makes the same mistakes, or namely in the case of a layout descriptor always describes only one region, would have an absolute stability and zero accuracy. The contrary is not true. An algorithm with an absolute accuracy will always produce results that are identical to the ground truth and hence identical between each other. A perfect layout descriptor will also be perfectly stable.

Hence we do not need a ground truth to evaluate the stability of a segmentation algorithm but we still need a proper metric or criteria to know when to outputs are similar or not. This also raises the question of defining what are similar outputs of a segmentation algorithm. Our point of view is that two segmentation results are similar if they contain the same layout. This layout is also part of the semantic content of the document that has to be secured.

Since we make a difference between the segmentation and the layout of a document, it is necessary to define it clearly. According to [7], the physical layout of a document refers to the physical location and boundaries of various regions in the document image. The physical layout extraction typically relies on a page segmentation algorithm. The page segmentation computes the boundaries of the various regions in the document image. Then, based on these boundaries, the layout extraction determines the spatial relationships between these regions. We simplify the above definition by only keeping the physical locations of the regions for the layout. We consider that the position of the region boundaries is the page segmentation. The region boundaries of page segmentation vary in case of noise and are thus very unstable. Hence, we consider that the three segmentation results shown in Figure 1 have different segmentation results but identical layouts. This is of course a point of view which may not be shared by everyone but it allows us to achieve the required level of stability.

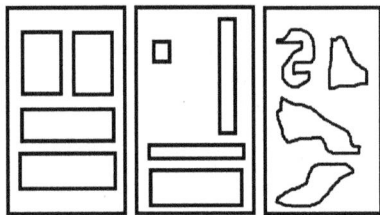

Figure 1: Three layouts that we consider to be identical

Now we need a layout descriptor that is at least as stable as the best segmentation algorithm. We can never measure anything more stable than the descriptor, hence our requirement for stability. The Delaunay Layout Descriptor is made to identify layouts with the highest level of stability.

It has been designed for document authentication. Assuming we have a copy of a layout and the descriptor of the original layout, the authentication process is as follows. First we compute the layout descriptor on the copy. Then we match it with the descriptor of the original layout.

It can also be used for document retrieval based on the document layout with unprecedented results. For a document retrieval scheme, we would have one layout and a database of hashes of layout descriptors. We would retrieve the layout by matching its descriptor with the database.

We will now consider the state of the art under this new perspective in section 2. Then we will present the computation and the matching algorithm for the Delaunay Layout Descriptor (DLD) in sections 3 and 4. Section 5 presents the metrics and the dataset used for the evaluation of the descriptor. Finally, the last three sections 6, 7 and 8 detail our results, discuss the pertinence of our descriptor and conclude.

2. STATE OF THE ART

As far as we know, only few works have been presented on layout descriptors. For instance, the Description and MOdification of Segmentation DMOS with the EPF grammatical language [9] can be used to provide an original layout description. It extracts content from a document by identifying its layout. The DMOS paradigm requires the user to a priori define the layout with EPF and is not based on- or extracted from the content of the document image to be processed. Hence the layout description is not adaptive to the layout of the document at hand.

Álvaro and Zanibbi [1] propose a layout descriptor for handwritten math expressions. They use a polar histogram and a support vector machine to classify the spatial relationship between two elements. There are five classes: horizontal, superscript, subscript, below, and inside (e.g. in a square root).

The other layout descriptors are made for document classification and retrieval. The MPEG-7 standard [14] includes a color layout descriptor. It divides an image into an 8 by 8 grid, takes the mean color value of the grid, converts it into the YCbCr color space and runs a discrete cosine transform on it. Esposito et al. [11] use a set of 7 quantized position and size attributes (e.g. width, height, on top of) whose values can make 171072 combinations. Cesarini et al. [6] modify the X-Y cut algorithm and use the cut sequence to encode the layout. This descriptor is tied to the segmentation algorithm and hence not very useful in a general case. There are also many graph-based layout descriptors [4, 12, 17] using features such as distance, size, position, angles and other metrics.

While the above presented descriptors do not consider robustness to noise, rotation and scale, Gordo and Valveny [12] present one which is meant to be invariant to scale and rotation. Unfortunately, by "invariant" the authors mean reasonably invariant. For instance, if we consider two copies of the same document, a small difference is accepted as long as the descriptors of the copies can be matched. This "weak" invariance is not enough for security applications which require an exact invariance, e.g. the values of the descriptor should remain the same.

There is one last descriptor that is not made for layout analysis but which presents some interesting features: LLAH [19]. Nakai et al. designed it to retrieve text documents in a database with an image captured by a camera. Based on the description of the connected components spatial organization, it describes the local layout around each word in the document. It uses a set of affine invariants computed at the center of each word in the document. The descriptors reflect the spatial relationships between a word and its neighbors making a word neighborhood descriptor. Each word neighborhood descriptor is stored in a database with a hashing technique. This technique allows constant time retrieval which in practice leads to real time retrieval. The matching is made with a voting algorithm counting how many word neighborhoods of the document can be matched in the database. It cannot be used for layout description because it requires more centroids than the number of regions that we would find in a common document. Also it only retrieves one document per query and cannot cluster identical documents.

The main drawback of state-of-the art layout descriptors is the number of thresholds and parameters to adjust. The more thresholds and parameters are used in the computation, the more unstable the descriptor will be. Thus, the ideal stable descriptor neither uses thresholds nor parameters.

3. THE DELAUNAY LAYOUT DESCRIPTOR

Considering our last comment, one should ban the use of "continuous" values such as distances or areas. If a length can vary between 1 and 100, then it has 99 thresholds. An interesting descriptor without any threshold would be a graph joining the centroids of the regions of the layout. One way to compute such a graph is to use the Delaunay triangulation of the centroids. There are three properties of a Delaunay triangulation that influence its practical use and stability.

PROPERTY 1. *Given a set of points, there always exists a Delaunay triangulation except when all the points are aligned.*

This property is of the highest interest as it proves that we will always be able to compute a Delaunay triangulation. Yet, it also highlights one case of instability: aligned points. While this will never occur for the whole page, it can occur locally and create local instabilities.

PROPERTY 2. *The Delaunay triangulation tries to maximize the minimum value of the angles inside each triangle.*

This leads to only few near flat triangles whose degenerated form could lead to an instability.

PROPERTY 3. *When a subset of four or more points can be placed on the same circle, the Delaunay triangulation of the points is not unique.*

This means that in this case, the Delaunay triangulation is not stable.

This is why, our descriptor is based on the Delaunay triangulation of the centroids of the regions of the layout. This triangulation is represented as a graph whose root node is the top left centroid. From there we use a breadth first traversing algorithm to order the graph and to compute its adjacency matrix. The adjacency matrix is the descriptor which we call the Delaunay Layout Descriptor (DLD). It has no parameter and virtually no threshold.

The computation of the Delaunay Layout Descriptor is based on a preliminary step: we extract the centroids of the regions of the layout. Two steps follow: the triangulation of these centroids and the computation of the adjacency matrix of the triangulation which is seen as a graph.

3.1 Delaunay triangulation of the centroids

The algorithm adds three points outside of the document image in order to compute the triangulation. One is far in the top left direction and will be the root of the graph. These points are the furthest points from the center of Figure 2.

The pseudo code of the triangulation algorithm is:

```
Delaunay(vertices set V)
vertex list Tv
triangle list Tt
create 3 outer vertices v1, v2, v3
Tv.add(v1)
Tv.add(v2)
Tv.add(v3)
Tt.add([v1, v2, v3])
```

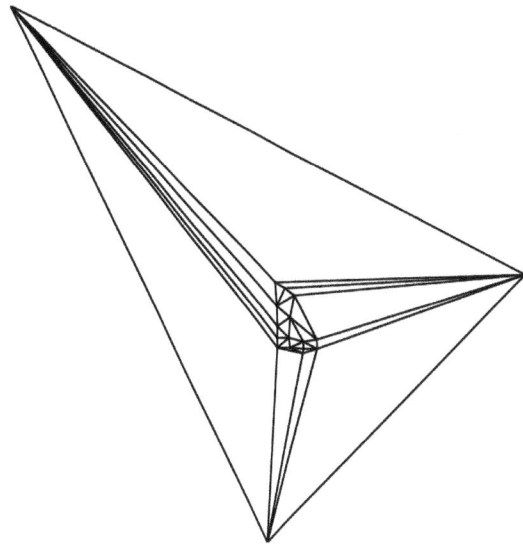

Figure 2: Example of a Delaunay triangulation produced by OpenCV. The vertices in the center are the centroids of the regions of the layout.

```
for all vertices a in V
  Tv.add(a)
  triangle list RemovedTri
  for all triangles t in Tt
    if a is inside the circum circle of t
      Tt.remove(t)
      RemovedTri.add(t)
    end if
  end for
  update(Tv, Tt, RemovedTri)
  delete RemovedTri
end for
```

The update method updates the removed triangles to include the new vertex a (the last vertex in Tv). This is done by adding the vertex a to these triangles. This makes quadrangles that are split along one diagonal to make new triangles that will be added to Tt. The condition to choose along which diagonal to split the quadrangle is detailed in the next section.

3.2 Graph transformation of the Delaunay triangulation

The Delaunay triangulation can easily be seen as a graph but this graph needs to be ordered in a stable manner. To this intend we use a variant of the breadth-first search (BFS) algorithm starting from the top left corner. Our algorithm is described below in pseudo-code.

```
Del2Graph(graph G, start vertex v)
vertex list Vl
Vl.push(v)
mark v as done
for i=0; i<G.nbVertices-1
  vertex list Children
  for all vertices a in G.adjacentVtx(Vl(i))
    if a is not done
      Children.push(a)
      mark a as done
```

```
      end if
   end for
   order(Children)
   for all vertices a in Children
     Vl.push(a)
   end for
   delete Children
end for
return Vl
```

The top left corner is a good starting point because the algorithm always generates it. Our algorithm differs from the BFS in the ordering of the children of a given node. Let us consider the situation of Figure 3 where A is a parent node and B and C are its children. x is the horizontal axis. B and C are ordered by increasing value of the angles $\overrightarrow{Ax}, \overrightarrow{AC}$ and $\overrightarrow{Ax}, \overrightarrow{AC}$ in $[-\pi; \pi]$. Here, both angles are negative and C comes before B.

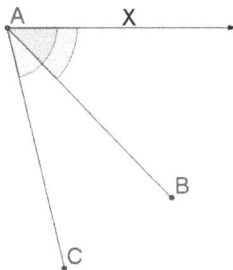

Figure 3: One node with two children

Once the graph is ordered we compute its adjacency matrix. This matrix is the DLD. The DLD can be hashed with any hashing algorithm such as MD5 [20] or SHA-256 [5] in order to reduce its size to 128 or 256 bits respectively. MD5 is more compact than SHA-256 but cannot be used for secure applications. It should only be used in a document classification and retrieval scheme.

4. DLD MATCHING

We have created a descriptor with no threshold or parameter. However this is not sufficient for an absolute stability. We have seen that there are three cases of instability: aligned points, flat triangles and cocyclic points. Flat triangles and aligned points cover the same geometric situation. There is also a fourth one related to the ordering of the graph. Thus, we propose an appropriate matching algorithm absorbing these possible sources of unstability of the descriptor. It creates the possible variations of the descriptor and finds the exact matches with the descriptor(s) that we want to match. The way the matching algorithm handles the flipping of edges inside a quadrangle, the instability due to near aligned points and the instability due to the implicit threshold at $-\pi/\pi$ in the ordering of the graph is explained in the following.

4.1 Edge flipping

The Property 2 can be achieved by appropriately choosing the diagonal to split the quadrangles in the update function of the triangulation algorithm. If we consider the quadrangle ABCD of Figure 4, it can be split along $[AC]$ or along $[BD]$ to make two triangles. To choose which edge must be created, the algorithm computes the sum of the opposing angles: $\widehat{ABC} + \widehat{CDA}$ and $\widehat{BCD} + \widehat{DAB}$. One of them is bigger than $180°$ (this is a trivial mathematical property since their sum is equal to $360°$). To statisfy Property 2, the quadrangle must be split along the segment that joins the opposing angles whose sum is the biggest. Here it is $\widehat{ABC} + \widehat{CDA} = 200°$ and the quadrangle will be split along $[BD]$.

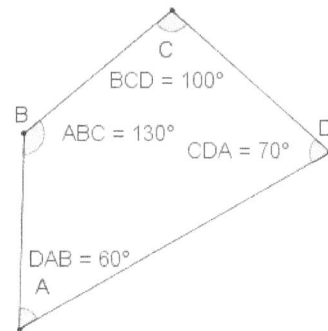

Figure 4: Example of a quadrangle that needs to be triangulated

One immediate source of instability comes when the sums are both equal to $180°$. This means that all four vertices are on the same (circum) circle and there are two possible triangulations of the quadrangle. This explains Property 3. The situation worsens in the digital world due to the discretization of of the coordinates in the integer pixel values. This introduces an error on the angle measurements which needs to be taken into account. There exists an instability area when a couple of opposing angles forming a quadrangle have a sum within $[180° - \epsilon; 180° + \epsilon]$. If this is the case, we will flip $[AD]$ to $[BC]$ and try to match both possibilities of splitting the quadrangle.

The parameter ϵ remains to be found and can be defined by the user. The value of ϵ will be discussed in the next section.

4.2 Aligned points

As stated in Property 1, for any number of aligned points there exists no triangulation. If a subset of our centroids is aligned, this will create a zone of instability as this subset will be difficult to triangulate. Furthermore, we just stated that there is an error margin on angle measurements. This increases the zone of instability due to aligned points.

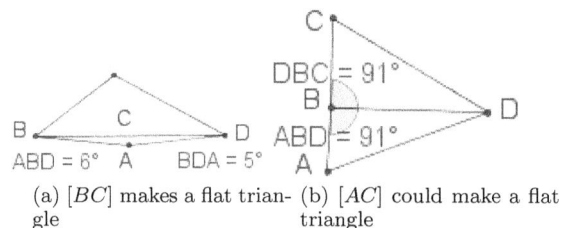

(a) $[BC]$ makes a flat triangle   (b) $[AC]$ could make a flat triangle

Figure 5: Two situations with nearly aligned points

Let us consider the two situations of Figure 5, and the point of view of the edge $[BD]$. Situation 5a occurs when

$\widehat{ABD} + \widehat{ADB} < \epsilon$. In this case, the edge makes a flat triangle with A. This should be triangulated the other way (with $[AC]$ splitting the quadrangle). The situation 5b is a proper triangulation. However, it could very well have been triangulated the other way around with $[AC]$ splitting the quadrangle. This situation occurs when $\pi + \epsilon > \widehat{ABD} + \widehat{DBC} > \pi - \epsilon$.

We perform similar tests on both sides of the edge and with both vertices of the edge. This defines the zone of instability related to the alignment of points. If this situation occurs for an edge, we flip the edge/diagonal inside the quadrangle and try to match both splitting configurations.

To prevent this situation from occuring too often, one should try to segment text columns rather than text paragraphs or text lines. Text lines and paragraphs are usually aligned in the same column.

4.3 Ordering implicit threshold

The algorithm to transform the Delaunay triangulation into a graph contains a step when the children of a node are ordered. This step contains an implicit threshold. With the notations of Figure 3, let us consider that $\widehat{\overrightarrow{Ax}, \overrightarrow{AC}} < -\pi + \delta$. If we make an angle measurment error of $\epsilon > \delta$ then we can have $\widehat{\overrightarrow{Ax}, \overrightarrow{AC}} < -\pi$. This angle will be congrued back inside $[-\pi; \pi]$ to become $\widehat{\overrightarrow{Ax}, \overrightarrow{AC}} + 2\pi < \pi$. This changes the ordering of C from being the first to being the last child.

To deal with this, we define an instability zone equal to $[-\pi; -\pi + \epsilon] \cup [\pi - \epsilon; \pi]$. If one or more children are within this zone of instability, we change the ordering of the children of the current node by performing a circular permutation. We then try to match all the possible orderings of the graph.

4.4 Matching

Now that we have identified all the sources of instability, we can test all their combinations to match the layout L. While there are no parameters to computes the DLD, the matching algorithm has two parameters related to the performance requirements that we have. The first one is ϵ for angle error and the second one is n for the number of simultaneous instabilities.

When combining several instabilities we recompute them. For instance, we apply one instability. Then we recompute the instabilities and only after that do we apply a second instability. This is motivated by the fact that applying one instability in a quadrangle can create new instabilities for the edges of the quadrangle.

The number of instabilities due to the Delaunay triangulation can potentially be rather big. As the combinatorial of their combinations will grow exponentially, we limit the number of simultaneous instabilities to a value n. For instance, if $n = 2$, we will only consider the cases when a maximum of two instabilities occur in the whole layout.

The ordering instabilities are quite rare as we start from the top left corner and they occur for the children on the left of the current node. Hence we will test all the ordering instabilities. The matching procedure becomes:

```
Match(layout L, database S,
  angle ε, nbInstabilities n)
list of indexes Matches
Matches.add(find L in S)
for all  delaunayInstabilities(ε, n)
  modify L
```

```
for all orderingInstabilities(ε)
        modify L
        Matches.add(find L in S)
    end for
end for
return Matches
```

5. EVALUATION

This section presents the metrics and the dataset we used for the evaluation of the Delaunay Layout Descriptor.

5.1 Metrics

We chose to evaluate the Delaunay Layout Descriptor with three criteria. The stability is the prime criteria for security applications. It is usually quantified with the probability of false positives. We studied a second scenario based on document classification and retrieval. This scenario contains two metrics: precision and recall. Finally, we also took into account the computational complexity of the descriptor.

5.1.1 Probability of false positives

The probability of false positives (PFP) is the probability that two identical layouts cannot be matched together. They will be considered different and potentially fraudulent. If this probability is too high, too many documents will have to be manually verified and the system will be too expensive and useless. The PFP of the layout descriptor will also be a lower boundary for the PFP of the segmentation algorithms that we could want to evaluate. The PFP should be as low as possible. It is equal to $1 - stability$.

We consider a set of k copies of the same layout. We want to match one against all. This produces $k - 1$ matches. We consider that a copy of a layout will not occur twice - scanning a document twice never produces exactly the same image. Hence we should not match a layout copy with itself and we subtract one match.

Assuming t matches fail, the probability of false positives is equal to:

$$PFP = \frac{t}{k-1} \qquad (1)$$

We then take the average of the PFPs for all the copies of all the layouts.

5.1.2 Classification and retrieval scheme

In this scenario we compute the descriptors for a database of layout copies to obtain a set of m descriptors. Some layout copies can of course have the same descriptor. Then we match each layout copy with this set of descriptors.

For a given query (layout copy), we are supposed to retrieve k layout copies. Here we include matching the query with itself as this is a classification task. Out of these only $q = k - t$ are retrieved and an extra p wrong results are retrieved.

The precision and recall are given for one query by:

$$Precision = \frac{q}{q+p} \qquad (2)$$

$$Recall = \frac{q}{k-1} = 1 - PFP \times \frac{k-1}{k} \qquad (3)$$

A precision of 1 means that no wrong results are returned and a recall of 1 means that all the right results are returned.

We will also use the classification accuracy which can be computed for the whole dataset (m layouts and m queries):

$$CAccuracy = \frac{1}{m}\sum_{i=1}^{m} q_i \qquad (4)$$

Where q_i is q for the ith query.

5.1.3 Computational complexity

The computational complexity is of interest for both the computation of the descriptor and the matching of the descriptor. They are usually dependent on the number of regions in the layout and the number of documents in the database respectively.

We will also look at the size of the descriptors. This parameter is important as it affects the size of the hash and it also affects the size of the index if we want to index a database.

5.2 Testing dataset

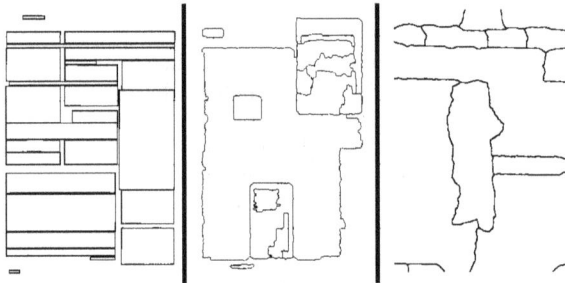

Figure 6: Three layouts produced by PAL, JSEG and Voronoi from left to right.

To test our algorithm we created a database of 15 layouts similar to the ones in Figure 6. These layouts are the results obtained by three segmentation algorithms PAL [8], JSEG [10] and Voronoi [15] on 14 random documents of the PRiMA dataset used for the Page Segmentation Competition of ICDAR 2009 [2]. We chose this dataset and those layouts as they are varied and contain both Manhattan and non Manhattan layouts. Among these 15 layouts two of them are identical but obtained with a different segmentation algorithm: they have the same number of regions with approximately the same size and the same positions. The layouts contain between 6 and 28 regions. For PAL we only used the block information as we have already stated that text line segmentation will create too much instability.

Figure 7 represents the creation process of the dataset. We printed each layout twice on one printer (arrow number 1). Then we photocopied the prints (arrow 2) making 4 pages (2 prints + 2 copies). We photocopied these four pages again (arrow 3) making 8 pages (2 prints, 4 copies, 2 double copies). We then scanned in black and white these pages twice on two scanners (arrows 4 for first scanner and 5 for the second) making 32 layout images. We repeated this process with an other printer making a total of 64 images of the same layout. The total size of the dataset is then $15 \times 64 = 960$ images. The scanners added salt and pepper noise which created many regions made of one or two pixels. Such noise would not be produced by a segmentation algorithm and we removed it by hand from the dataset images.

The dataset contains scale variations as the printers add margins around the layout images and hence change their scale. We also used batch scanners that have introduced a surprisingly significant amount of skew (about $5 - 10°$).

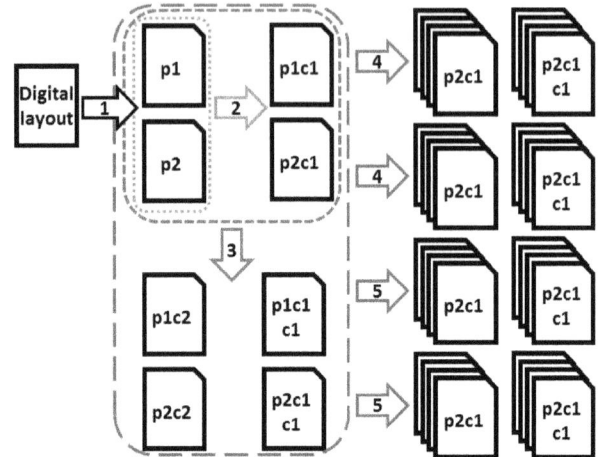

Figure 7: The creation process of our dataset.

This dataset will allow us to test the robustness and stability of our descriptor to real print and scan noise. It is available on `http://shades.univ-lr.fr/datasets/`.

6. RESULTS

We compare the results of our descriptor with two other methods: the one of Gordo and Valveny (G & V) [12] and the one of Nakai et al. (LLAH) [19]. Table 1 summarizes all the results except for precision and recall. The symbol $\downarrow$ indicates that the metrics should be as low as possible to be good and $\uparrow$ means the contrary.

6.1 Probability of false positives

The probability of false positives is the metric representing the stability of the descriptor. The lower it is, the more stable the descriptor is.

6.1.1 Intrinsic PFP

If we try to find an exact match for the descriptors without any matching algorithm we obtain what we call the intrinsic probability of false positives (iPFP).

As there has not been any previous evaluation of the stability of a layout descriptor we implemented the descriptor of Gordo and Valveny [12] and tested it for comparison without any matching algorithm. The descriptor contains four informations:

- The angle between the edge joining the centroid of a region and the centroid of all the regions and the horizontal x axis

- The length of this edge

- The area of the region

- The type of the region (text or non text)

We only used the first three informations and set the fourth one to text all the time as it was not available. This will

172

Table 1: Summary of the results

Metric	DLD	G & V	LLAH
iPFP ↓	0.26	1.00	1.00
PFP ↓	0.00	1.00	1.00
Precision ↑	1.00	0.82	0.93
Recall ↑	1.00	0.82	0.94
Computational cost of descriptor ↓	$\mathcal{O}(n \log \log n)$	$\mathcal{O}(n \log n)$	$\mathcal{O}(n)$
Size of the descriptor ↓	$\mathcal{O}(1)$	$\mathcal{O}(n)$	$\mathcal{O}(n)$
Computational cost of matching ↓	$\mathcal{O}(1)$	$\mathcal{O}(m)$	$\mathcal{O}(1)$
Matching time ↓	0.1-23.9 s	0.06 s	0.07 s
Memory use ↓	284(96) Mo	4.7(3.9) Go	120(32) Go

only increase the stability of the descriptor as there will be one less variable per region.

We also compare our results with LLAH. For this we simply use the usual LLAH descriptor computed for each layout.

Gordo and Valveny's and the LLAH descriptor have an iPFP of 1 while the Delaunay Layout Descriptor has an iPFP of 0.26. The results for these descriptor are expected as they use numeric values. Changing any angle/length/area by one pixel will change the descriptor and make it unstable. This would be the same for any other descriptor based on voting or distance computation.

6.1.2 PFP

The matching algorithm has two parameters: the error on the angle measurement that we accept and the maximum number of instabilities that can occur at the same time. The angle error related to the digitization of the images can be estimated to be below $\epsilon = 5°$. We found experimentally that the angle variation introduced by the use of a second segmentation algorithm for the same layout is $10° \leq \epsilon \leq 15°$. We tested the algorithm with $n = 1$, $n = 2$ and $n = 3$ instabilities. We did not try to have more combinations as the results were already perfect up to the fifth decimal. Figure 8 summarizes the results. The lines are named PFP5° or PFP15° according to the value of ϵ. The adjunction of an s (PFPs) means that each layout is the result of only one segmentation algorithm and we removed the duplicate layout that was the results of a second segmentation algorithm. The vertical scale is logarithmic.

Since the Algorithm of Gordo and Valveny as well as LLAH do not propose any algorithm absorbing their own instabilities, their PFP is equal to their iPFP.

Having two instabilities at the same time is enough to have a PFP below 1%. No more than three simultaneous instabilities ever occurred. This highlights the stability of the algorithm. One can also notice that a 5° angle error is sufficient if we use one segmentation algorithm per layout. Two different layouts can be segmented with different algorithms. This situation is usually the case in a digitization framework. These values are (almost) perfect and do not need to be improved any further. Since there is no point in achieving a PFP lower than the one we achieve we do not find it necessary to compare it with the other algorithms.

6.2 Retrieval

Similarly to what we did for the probability of false positives, we can compute the precision and recall of our system. The precision is always 100%. The recall is shown in Fig-

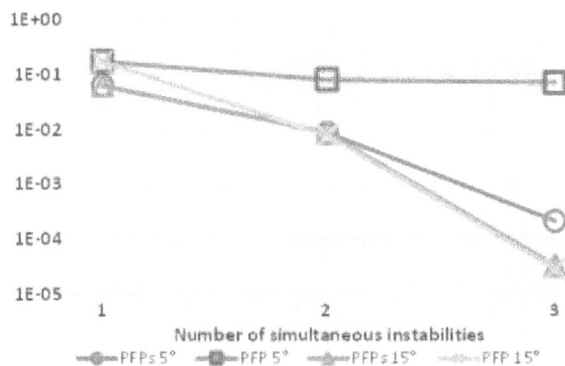

Figure 8: The values of the PFP for different situations and sets of parameters.

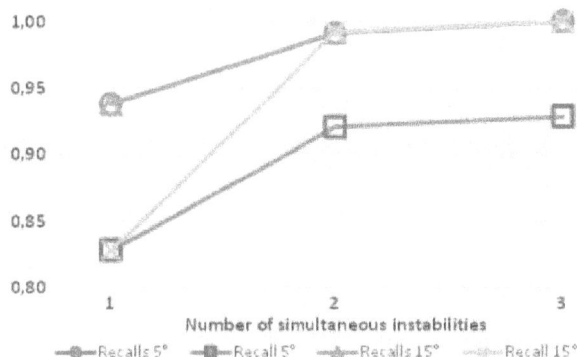

Figure 9: The values of the recall for different situations and sets of parameters.

ure 9 for the same cases as the PFP. Once again these results are nearly perfect and don't need to be improved.

Gordo and Valveny's descriptor achieves a precision and recall of 82% in the case of a single segmentation algorithm and 78% otherwise.

LLAH usually only returns the document with the highest number of votes. In order to obtain a retrieval algorithm, we used the list of votes that were returned for all the documents for one query. The results returned are the ones with more votes than a given threshold. This threshold is the same for all the queries. We chose the threshold that gives the closest values between precision and recall. With this scheme, LLAH reaches a precision of 93% and a recall of 94% if we consider only one segmentation algorithm per

173

layout. It goes down to 90% and 89% respectively in the case of two segmentation algorithms.

6.3 Computational cost

We consider that n is the number of regions in a document and m is the number of layouts in the database.

6.3.1 Descriptor computation

The worst case computational cost of the Delaunay triangulation is $\mathcal{O}(n^2)$ as implemented in OpenCV 2.4.9[1] but it can brought down to $\mathcal{O}(n \log n)$ with the sweep line algorithm [16]. For most cases, it will actually be $\mathcal{O}(n \log \log n)$. The transformation of the Delaunay triangulation into an ordered graph costs $\mathcal{O}(n)$ as each centroid is processed once. The total computational cost of the descriptor is then $\mathcal{O}(n^2)$ in its current implementation and it can be optimized to $\mathcal{O}(n \log n)$ and to $\mathcal{O}(n \log \log n)$ in the general case.

Gordo and Valveny's descriptor can be computed in $\mathcal{O}(n \log n)$ because of the sorting algorithm required to sort the features by ascending order of their first value. LLAH can be computed in $\mathcal{O}(n)$ as each region is only processed once independently from the other regions.

6.3.2 Size of the descriptor

The DLD has a constant size, hence its memory size is $\mathcal{O}(1)$ with respect to n. The other descriptors are computed region wise and hence use a memory size of $\mathcal{O}(n)$.

6.3.3 Matching computation

Regarding the matching of one layout with the database, for the DLD it can be achieved in $\mathcal{O}(1)$ with respect to m. This is due to the use of cryptographic hashing (we are looking for an exact match) and is similar to LLAH. Gordo and Valveny's descriptor requires $\mathcal{O}(m)$ computations as the query needs to be matched on a one by one basis with all the layouts in the database.

6.4 Experimental results

In a practical case, there are two main criteria to compare algorithms: how much time do they take to execute and how much memory do they require. The measurements were made on an Intel Core i7 3740QM with 8 cores at 2.7GHz and 8GB of RAM.

6.4.1 Matching time

Computing the descriptor takes on average 12 ms. Matching a layout with the whole database with an angle error of $5°$ and a maximum of 2 simultaneous errors takes on average 0.1 seconds and 1.5 seconds with 3 simultaneous instabilities. If we use an angle error of $15°$, these values go up to 0.8 and 23.9 seconds respectively. It should be noted that this matching time is independent from the size of the database and could be improved as the computation of the instabilities and of their combinations has not been optimized at all.

Gordo and Valveny's algorithm takes 49 ms to compute a descriptor and 61 ms to match a query. LLAH takes 56 ms to compute a descriptor and 69 ms to match a query.

6.4.2 Memory usage

While the memory usage should be directly related to the size of the descriptor, its practical implementation and implementation constraints can change it significantly. One should keep in mind that two descriptors using respectively n bits and $1000 \times n$ bits scale up with $\mathcal{O}(n)$. Yet one uses a thousand times more memory than the other.

To compute this metric for all descriptors, we assume a database of one million layouts and 20 documents/images per layout. This makes a database of 20 million documents. We also consider that each document contains 12 regions on average and that an integer is stored on 32 bits (or 4 octets) of memory. The values in brackets in Table 1 indicate theoretical values while the other values are obtained experimentally.

The memory space taken by the DLD can be 128 bits for non secure applications and 256 bits for secure applications. Each layout will then require $(128 + 20 \times 32)/8 = 96$ octets. 128 bits for the descriptors and 20×32 bits for the 20 numbers of the associated documents. The whole database will then require 96 Mo. This value does not take into account implementation constraints such as memory alignment and storage structure (unordered_map in our case). We created an index for a virtual database and it uses 284 Mo of memory.

Gordo and Valveny's descriptor contains 4 values per region plus one value to identify the document. Hence the theoretical size of the database would be $(4 \times 12 + 1) \times 4 \times 20\text{E}6 = 3.9Go$. Experimentally we obtained a size of 4.7 Go.

LLAH stores one hash (one integer) per word in the document. In Takeda *et al.*'s paper they consider a normal number of 200 words. Each word is associated to a document which means that there are two integer values per word: the hash and the number of the document. Hence the theoretical size of the index is $2 \times 4 \times 200 \times 20\text{E}6 = 32Go$. This value neglects the possible collisions e.g. the words that have the same hash. For each collision, there is one hash/integer less to store. Experimentally, Takeda et al. obtained a size of 120 Go (in RAM memory). Because of hardware constraints we were not able to reproduce this result but this does not change the evaluation of our algorithm which uses far less memory.

7. DISCUSSION

One could wonder about how much the adjacency matrix of the Delaunay triangulation of the layout is representative of this layout. The performance of the DLD proves this representativeness. The DLD does not use the size of the regions, neither does it use the distance between the centroids of these regions. But, for a mostly convex region, the bigger the region, the further its centroid will be from the other centroids. Hence the area of a region is reflected by the distance between the centroids. The Delaunay triangulation is directly dependent on these distances between the centroids and their relative positions. Hence, the DLD indirectly contains both informations. It is invariant to scale and to a certain extent to rotation. This is expected as rotating a layout too much can change this layout.

---

[1] http://opencv.org/

8. CONCLUSION

In this paper we present a stable document layout descriptor (Delaunay Layout Descriptor) based on a Delaunay triangulation of region centroids. It comes with a matching algorithm to obtain outstanding performances. Currently it is the only available algorithm that can be used in a security application thanks to the possibility of applying a cryptographic hashing to it.

We have shown that it improves the state of the art in every aspect except for the matching time which could be improved. Its stability, precision, and recall reach 100% in our experiments. It also reduces by a factor 400 the memory required to index a document database and can match a document against a database of any size in less than a second up to 28 seconds depending on the required level of performance.

When using the Delaunay Layout Descriptor, one should have in mind one tip to leverage all its power. The segmentation algorithm should not produce too many aligned regions. Hence, it should not segment text lines but rather text paragraphs or even better: text columns. Our test dataset contains layouts with as little as 6 regions and as much as 28 regions which proves that the descriptor should work in most cases. Furthermore, we tested the DLD with several copies of a 7x4 grid layout and it performed perfectly again. This means that while the above advice remains valid, the DLD still performs adequately if it is not respected.

Finally, the Delaunay Layout Descriptor is fast, stable, robust, precise and concise beyond all expectations. From our point of view, it solves the issue of describing a layout. Its implementation could probably be improved as it has not been extensively optimized especially regarding the combination of the instabilities. The next challenge is to have a segmentation algorithm with the same level of performance as our descriptor will not work if the layout is wrong or unstable. We could have attempted to create such a segmentation algorithm before but the analysis of the stability of a segmentation algorithm requires an extremely stable tool to compare the layouts it produces. This is why we created the Delaunay Layout Descriptor before trying to design a stable segmentation algorithm.

Acknowledgment

This work is financed by the ANR (French national research agency) project SHADES referenced under ANR-14-CE28-0022.

9. REFERENCES

[1] F. Álvaro. A shape-based layout descriptor for classifying spatial relationships in handwritten math. In *Proc. of the 2013 symposium on Document engineering*, pages 123–126. ACM, 2013.

[2] A. Antonacopoulos, D. Bridson, C. Papadopoulos, and S. Pletschacher. A realistic dataset for performance evaluation of document layout analysis. In *Proc. of 10th International Conference on Document Analysis and Recognition (ICDAR)*, pages 296–300. IEEE, 2009.

[3] ANTS. Spécifications techniques des Codes à Barres 2D-Doc. Technical report, ANTS, 2013.

[4] A. D. Bagdanov and M. Worring. First order Gaussian graphs for efficient structure classification. *Pattern Recognition*, 36:1311–1324, 2003.

[5] J. Bryson and P. Gallagher. Secure Hash Standard (SHS), 2012.

[6] F. Cesarini, M. Lastri, S. Marinai, and G. Soda. Encoding of modified X-Y trees for document classification. *Proc. of 6th International Conference on Document Analysis and Recognition (ICDAR)*, 2001.

[7] B. B. Chaudhuri. *Digital document processing. major directions and recent advances.* Springer, 2007.

[8] K. Chen, F. Yin, and C.-l. Liu. Hybrid page segmentation with efficient whitespace rectangles extraction and grouping. In *Proc. of 12th International Conference on Document Analysis and Recognition (ICDAR)*, pages 958–962. IEEE, Aug. 2013.

[9] B. Coüasnon. DMOS, a generic document recognition method: application to table structure analysis in a general and in a specific way. In *International Journal on Document Analysis and Recognition (IJDAR)*, volume 8, pages 111–122. Springer-Verlag, 2006.

[10] Y. Deng and B. S. Manjunath. Unsupervised segmentation of color-texture regions in images and video. *Pattern Analysis and Machine Intelligence (PAMI)*, 23(8):800–810, 2001.

[11] F. Esposito, D. Malerba, and G. Semeraro. Multistrategy learning for document recognition. *Applied Artificial Intelligence an International Journal*, 8(1):33–84, 1994.

[12] A. Gordo and E. Valveny. A rotation invariant page layout descriptor for document classification and retrieval. In *Proc. of the 10th International Conference on Document Analysis and Recognition (ICDAR)*, pages 481–485. IEEE, 2009.

[13] T. Kanungo, R. M. Haralick, and I. Phillips. Global and local document degradation models. In *Proc. of 2nd International Conference on Document Analysis and Recognition (ICDAR)*, pages 730–734. IEEE, 1993.

[14] E. Kasutani and A. Yamada. The MPEG-7 color layout descriptor: a compact image feature description for high-speed image/video segment retrieval. In *Proc. of 2001 International Conference on Image Processing (ICIP)*, volume 1. IEEE, 2001.

[15] K. Kise, A. Sato, and M. Iwata. Segmentation of page images using the area voronoi diagram. *Computer Vision and Image Understanding*, 70(3):370–382, June 1998.

[16] G. Leach and G. Leach. Improving worst-case optimal Delaunay triangulation algorithms. In *Proc. of 4th Canadian Conference on Computational Geometry*, pages 340–346, 1992.

[17] J. L. J. Liang, D. Doermann, M. Ma, and J. Guo. Page classification through logical labelling. In *Proc. of 16th International Conference on Pattern Recognition (ICPR)*, volume 3, pages 477–480. IEEE, 2002.

[18] A. Malvido Garcià. Secure Imprint Generated for Paper Documents (SIGNED). Technical Report December 2010, Bit Oceans, 2013.

[19] T. Nakai, K. Kise, and M. Iwamura. Use of affine invariants in locally likely arrangement hashing for camera-based document image retrieval. *Lecture Notes in Computer Science (LNCS)*, 3872:541–552, 2006.

[20] R. Rivest. The MD5 message-digest algorithm. Technical report, Internet activities board, 1992.

An Approach to Convert NCL Applications into Stereoscopic 3D

Roberto Gerson de Albuquerque Azevedo, Guilherme F. Lima, Luiz Fernando Gomes Soares
Department of Informatics
Pontifical Catholic University of Rio de Janeiro (PUC-Rio)
Rio de Janeiro, RJ, Brazil
{razevedo, glima, lfgs}@inf.puc-rio.br

ABSTRACT

This paper presents and discusses the internal operation of NCLSC (NCL Stereo Converter): a tool to convert a 2D interactive multimedia application annotated with depth information to a stereoscopic-multimedia application. *Stereoscopic-multimedia applications* are those that codify both the left-eye and right-eye views, as required by stereoscopic 3D displays. NCLSC takes as input an NCL (Nested Context Language) document and outputs an NCL stereoscopic application codified in side-by-side or top-bottom format (both common input formats for 3DTV sets). NCL is the declarative language adopted in most Latin America countries for terrestrial digital TV middleware systems and the ITU-T H.761 Recommendation for IPTV services. However, the proposed approach is not restricted to NCL and can be used by other languages. The depth annotation allows for positioning each 2D graphical component in a layered (2.5D or 2D+depth) user interface. It is used by NCLSC to compute the screen parallax (offset) between the graphical elements in the left and right views of the resulting stereoscopic application. When the resulting application is presented on stereoscopic 3D displays, such screen parallax induces retinal disparity, which creates the illusion of floating flat-2D graphical elements. NCLSC does not require any additional native middleware support to run in currently available 3D-enabled TV sets. Moreover, NCLSC can adapt, at run-time, the output application to different display sizes, viewer distances, and viewer preferences, which are usually required for a proper balance between artistic effects and user experience.

Categories and Subject Descriptors

I.7.2 [**Document and Text Processing**]: Document Preparation— *Hypertext/hypermedia*; D.3.4 [**Programming Languages**]: Processors—*Preprocessor*.

Keywords

Document Processing; Stereoscopic Multimedia Applications; 3DTV; Ginga; NCL

DocEng '15, September 08-11, 2015, Lausanne, Switzerland
© 2015 ACM. ISBN 978-1-4503-3307-8/15/09... $15.00
DOI: http://dx.doi.org/10.1145/2682571.2797064

1. INTRODUCTION

The human vision system uses oculomotor, monocular, and binocular cues to perceive depth [1]. *Oculomotor* cues are those related to our ability to sense the position of our eyes and the tension of their muscles. *Monocular* cues are those perceived by each eye and are observable in flat two-dimensional (2D) images. They include occlusion, relative sizes, familiar sizes, texture gradients, and shadows. *Binocular cues*, are those that depend on both of our eyes working together. Since our there is a horizontal separation between our two eyes, each one has its own perspective of the world. Therefore, each eye receives slightly different images of the world, and the same point in the world can be projected into slightly different positions in each eye's retina. The distance between corresponding points in the images projected on each eye's retina is known as *retinal disparity*. Based on retinal disparity, the brain can fuse the left and right images received by each eye and infer relative depth information. Retinal disparity is precisely the depth cue that stereoscopic 3D (S3D) displays aim to stimulate in order to produce the illusion of depth [2].

In the beginning of this decade, there was a significant commercial effort in the development of S3D displays, particularly for the entertainment industry. Such interest has resulted in an increased availability, at affordable prices, of high-quality S3D displays [3]. While the hype and marketing efforts of the early 2010s surrounding the S3D display technology has now faded out—it has given space to development of 4K and 8K displays—the availability of high-quality S3D displays allowed designers to start thinking about and exploring new uses for digital stereoscopy beyond its ordinary use in entertainment movies. A notable example is the research initiated in the Human-Computer Interaction (HCI) community on the use of the depth information as an active element in user interfaces [4] [5] [6] [7] [8] [9] [10] [11]. For instance, such studies show that it is possible explore the 3D effect as a mean to spatially structure user interface (UI) elements [12]. In this new context, a tool that allows for the development and deployment of interactive stereoscopic applications can help researchers in prototyping such systems. Consequently, it can also assist in the understanding of how stereoscopy and depth perception can be used to create innovative user interfaces.

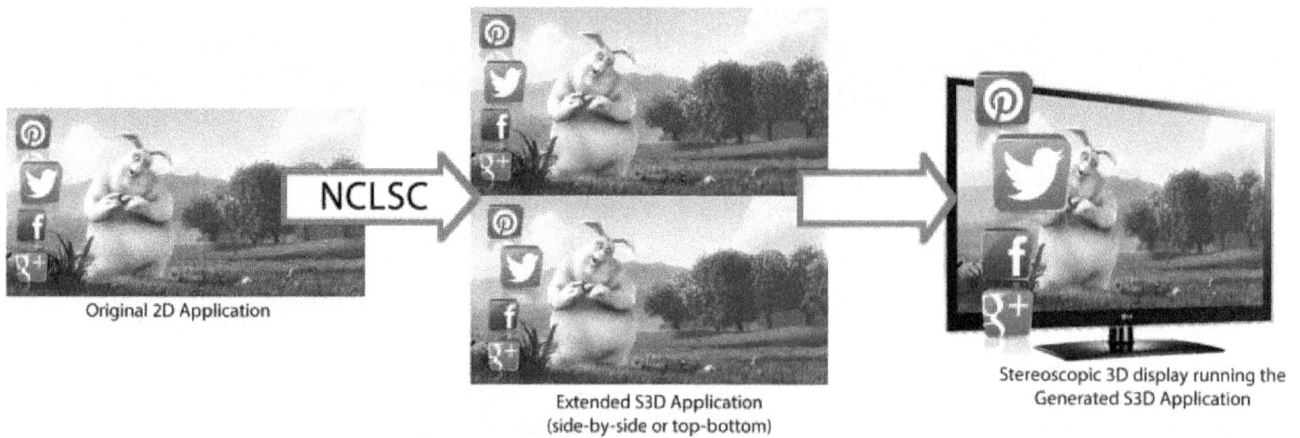

Figure 1. NCLSC approach to support stereoscopy at the application-level.

Motivated by that new context, this paper presents *NCL Stereo Converter* (NCLSC). NCLSC is a tool to convert 2D multimedia applications written in NCL (Nested Context Language [13]) to equivalent stereoscopic-multimedia applications (see Figure 1). *Stereoscopic multimedia applications* (or *stereoscopic applications*) are applications that codify both the left and right-eye views required by S3D displays. NCL is a declarative language for designing interactive multimedia applications. It is the declarative language adopted by most Latin America countries in their terrestrial digital TV middleware systems [14], and by the ITU-T H.761 Recommendation for IPTV services [15]. More precisely, the NCLSC tool takes as input an NCL document with additional depth annotation and produces an equivalent stereoscopic document. For each 2D graphical element (any element with visual presentation) in the input document, NCLSC produces two instances with the same presentation content (one for each view required by S3D displays) but in different positions. The depth annotation in the input document is used to control the screen parallax (offset) between those two instances. When presented on S3D displays, the screen parallax (parallax, from now on) is what produces the retinal disparity depth cue. As a result, the stereoscopic multimedia application allows 2D content to float in and out of the screen. Figure 2 depicts the relationship between the different types of parallaxes (positive, zero, and negative) and the perception of depth in S3D displays.

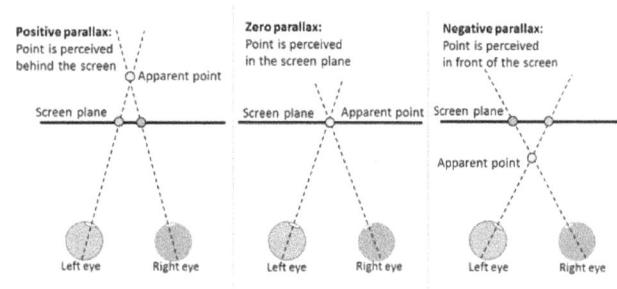

Figure 2. Relationship between positive, zero, and negative parallaxes and depth perception in S3D displays.

Unlike mechanisms for converting 2D-to-S3D video, a built-in feature of most 3DTV sets available today, this paper does not intend to convert mono-media content (the main video in the case) from 2D-to-S3D. Instead, the focus of this paper is to convert 2D interactive multimedia applications to their stereoscopic versions, in which 2D objects may have depth positioning. NCLSC works at the multimedia scene representation level. The 2D graphical

elements that constitute a scene can then float in or out of the screen, resulting in a layered-like (2.5D or 2D+depth) user interface. Automatic 2D-to-S3D conversion mechanisms for video-only are typically based on fallible heuristics to infer the depth information. In contrast, since NCLSC uses depth information supplied by document authors (and that can be customized by end users), it does not suffer from such incorrect depth estimation.

One of the main advantages of the NCLSC approach is that its output applications can run on multimedia language players without any native support to stereoscopy. As long as the hardware supports one of the output format provided by NCLSC, the stereoscopic application produced can simulate actual depth even if the language player does not support stereoscopy. Another interesting characteristic of NCLSC is that it explores as much as possible the declarative constructions of the multimedia language to provide a fine-grained synchronization between the produced left and right views, as discussed in Section 3. Fine-grained synchronization is required to reach an acceptable quality of experience (QoE) [16]. Moreover, NCLSC can adapt, at run-time, the produced application to different display sizes, viewer distances, and viewer preferences. As the author is usually not aware of all variables in the user's execution environment, this is a required feature for a proper balance between artistic effects and user experience.

The remainder of the paper is organized as follows. Section 2 presents the related work and compares them with the NCLSC approach. Section 3 introduces the conversion process employed by NCLSC, its architecture, and implementation. Section 4 presents multimedia applications developed using NCLSC, showing the viability of the proposed approach. Section 5 discusses the relative complexity of the produced stereoscopic applications, the problems that can disturb the end-user QoE, and the limitations of the proposed solution. Finally, Section 6 presents our conclusions and future work.

2. RELATED WORK

Stereoscopy is a key technology to improve 3D-scene immersion in virtual reality (VR) systems [17] [18]. Therefore, most players of declarative 3D-languages for VR applications, such as VRML [19], X3D [20], etc., can render 3D scenes in stereoscopic mode. The use of VR languages, however, are overkill when the aim is to develop simple user interfaces (UIs) in which most objects are two-dimensional but can float in or out of the screen when the application is rendered on a stereoscopic display. VR languages require authors to handle inherently complex 3D concepts, such as camera positioning, lightning, etc., which are are not only a burden for non-expert authors but also more prone to errors than employing straightforward concepts of high-level 2D-only multimedia languages. Examples of those high-level 2D-only language are SMIL [21], HTML [22], and NCL [14]. Moreover, if the aim is to reach users that already have 3DTV-enabled sets or that run on off-the-shelf Web browsers, VR languages cannot be used, since their players are not usually available on such systems.

The alternative of using 2D multimedia languages with depth extensions to program simple stereoscopic UIs is worthy. The extensions allow the association of depth information to flat graphical objects. Systems with such extensions are commonly referred to as 2D+depth or 2.5D systems (see Figure 3). Previous experiments have reported that 2D and 2.5D programming systems are more effective for defining many kinds of user interfaces than complete 3D environments [23] [24] [25].

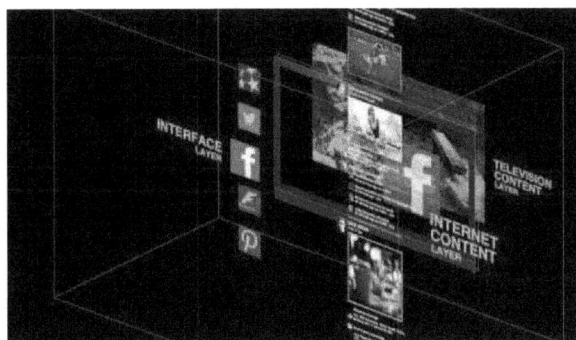

Figure 3. An example of a 2.5D user interface. Source: SeeSpace (http://inair.tv).

Other researchers have also identified the need for stereoscopic extensions in 2D multimedia languages. Jung et al. [26] discuss a system to integrate interactive content into a broadcast 3DTV environment. In their system, the additional 3D content are stereoscopic images (codified in side-by-side) whose presentation is controlled using an XML file. That file describes a set of extra properties for each image, such as timing, translation, and rotation. The approach proposed by Jung et al. is not based on any standard multimedia language, but there are proposals in this direction.

W3C (World-Wide-Web Consortium) is currently adding support to stereoscopic content to the CSS language [27]. The proposal draft introduces new CSS properties that allow authors to define objects as stereo-content, with counterparts for the right-eye defined separately. Similarly, Chen et al. [28] and Zhang et al. [29] propose stereoscopic extensions to the CSS 3D Transforms. Those extensions were implemented in the WebKit HTML rendering engine[1]. For each 3D webpage, Chen et al.'s modified browser creates two slightly different images, representing the left and right-eye views of the page which are then combined to create the illusion of depth. In [30], Liu et al. propose stereoscopic 3D extensions to Scalable Vector Graphics (SVG) [31], which are also implemented over WebKit.

Aiming at supporting multi-view displays, which includes the simpler binocular displays, Le Feuvre [32] and Azevedo et al. [33] [34] propose depth-based extensions to SVG and NCL,

respectively. Both proposals allow for the association of depth maps to graphical objects, which are used to control the depth of each objects' constituent pixel. Le Feuvre implemented his extensions in the GPAC multimedia framework [35]; Azevedo and Soares implement their extensions in the reference implementation of Ginga [14][2].

All proposals mentioned above rely on the platform's native support for parallax or depth-based extensions to work. In contrast, the NCLSC approach computes the parallax among objects at the application level, creating what we call an "equivalent stereoscopic version" of the application. The main advantage of this approach is that it does not require the existence of mechanisms for handling stereoscopy at the language player level. However, using solely NCLSC, one cannot achieve the control level, i.e. per-pixel depth control, of more intrusive methods such as those of Le Freuve and Azevedo et al.

The aforementioned extensions for 2D languages are relatively recent—their introduction was mainly driven by the growing availability of affordable 3D displays. Nonetheless, since the 1990s, there have been webpages that use anaglyph methods[3] to achieve stereoscopic effects. Some of those are written in pure HTML or SVG, whereas others use JavaScript [37] or Adobe Flash[4] to achieve the desired effects. Similar to the NCLSC approach, they produce stereoscopic effects at the application level. However, both views must be explicitly coded by the author, while using NCLSC the views are automatically generated from a single annotated input document.

Among the related work, the proposals of Zhang et al. [38] and Chistyakov et al. [39] are those closest related to NCLSC. Both proposals implement a JavaScript library that generates stereoscopic webpages. Zhang et al. rely on the HTML5 Canvas API [40] to generate the left and right views of the webpage. Chistyakov et al. use the DOM API [41] to duplicate the HTML elements and produces the final stereoscopic application. Similarly, NCLSC also produces a new declarative stereoscopic version of the application. However, using the declarative constructions of NCL, NCLSC can ensure a frame-based synchronization between the two instances (left and right) of dynamic media objects (such as videos and script-base animations). The synchronization problems of left and right view have not been handled or discussed by the approach of Chistyakov et al.. Moreover, NCLSC implements additional features, such as the adaptation of the output application to processing parameters (e.g., display size, viewer distance, and parallax scale factor).

---

[1] Available at: http://www.webkit.org

[2] Available at: http://git.telemidia.puc-rio.br

[3] The anaglyph method [36] is a stereoscopic format in which the left and right-eye images are color-coded and combined into a single image. When the combined image is viewed through glasses (filters) with lenses of the corresponding colors, a 3D image is perceived. Different complementary color combinations have been used over the years, but the most common are red and cyan.

[4] Available at: http://www.adobe.com/products/flash.html

3. NCLSC ARCHITECTURE AND IMPLEMENTATION

The process used by NCLSC to convert a 2D multimedia application into an equivalent S3D (Stereoscopic 3D) application consists of three phases: media cloning, layout adjustment, and behavior cloning. Figure 4 depicts each of these steps.

The *media cloning* phase focuses on what will be presented. In this step, the processor duplicates the objects with graphical content. Each new duplicated object will represent the left and right views of the original object in the resulting stereoscopic application.

The *layout adjustment* phase determines, statically, where and how the duplicated objects produced in the previous phase will be initially presented. In defining their initial presentation position, the processor can introduce parallaxes between the object's position representing the left and right views. Such a parallax is what induces binocular disparity and allows the brain to interpret the 3D depth information during a stereoscopic 3D content presentation.

The *behavior cloning* phase focuses on the dynamic behavior of media objects, i.e., when they appear or disappear and when their spatial properties change during the multimedia presentation. In this phase, the processor must correctly duplicate the behavior of the original application into an equivalent behavior affecting both the left and right views of the resulting application. Moreover, the processor must guarantee that dynamic (run-time) changes on any view are replicated on the counterpart.

As previously shown by subjective experiments (see [16], for example), it is crucial that both the left and right views of the application are always synchronized. Even small synchronization skews between the views can deteriorate the quality of the resulting stereoscopic presentation, annoying users, and eventually making the presentation impractical [16]. An essential requirement for NCLSC is, then, that it must guarantee a fine synchronization between the left and right views of the resulting stereoscopic application. The following three subsections detail the NCLSC phases.

3.1 Media Cloning

In an NCL [13] document, media objects to be presented are defined via <media> elements. In the media cloning phase, the converter identifies and duplicates all <media> elements of the input document that have a graphical representation. Whenever duplicating a <media> element, the converter must also duplicate all its child elements. In order to maintain the resulting document valid, the id attribute of each cloned <media> element is updated to be unique in the document.

In NCL, a <media id="A"> element refers to some content via its *src* attribute, which defines the URI of the object's content. If the URI scheme is equal to "ncl-mirror" and the specific part of the scheme refers to an identifier of another media object, both objects will have the same content; they will present exactly the same frame of the content, independently of their starting time [42]. Since NCL player must guarantee that behavior, NCLSC uses this NCL feature to solve the problem of synchronization skew between the left and right views of the same content. Moreover, since they are different media objects, their properties may have different values, for instance, those that define their position on the screen.

Therefore, to guarantee a frame-based synchronization, for each pair of duplicated elements (left and right instances) one element uses the mirror source mechanism to refer to the other, which keeps the same value defined in the original element in its *src* attribute.

To illustrate the processing done during the media cloning phase, consider the following NCL code chunk:

```
<media id="video"  src="file:///video.mp4">
  <property name="explicitDur" value="50s"/>
  <area id="a1" begin="10s" end="20s"/>
</media>
```

After the media cloning phase, the <media> element is replaced by the following pair of <media> elements:

```
<media id="video-L" src="file:///video.mp4">
  <property name="explicitDur" value="50s"/>
  <area id="a1" begin="10s" end="20s"/>
</media>
<media id="video-R" src="ncl-mirror://video-L">
  <property name="explicitDur" value="50s"/>
  <area id="a1-R" begin="10s" end="20s"/>
</media>
```

Each media object above represents a view—video-L represents left-view, and video-R the right-view—of the original element in the resulting stereoscopic document.

3.2 Layout Adjustment

In the layout adjustment phase, NCLSC replaces the properties of the <media> elements duplicated in the media cloning phase that specify their initial positioning and dimension. In an NCL document, initial placement and dimension of objects are defined either by <region>, <descriptor> or <property> elements. For simplicity, in the remainder of this section, we present the layout adjustment phase assuming only the side-by-side output format. However, the derived equations are easily adaptable to similar formats such as the top-bottom, which is also supported by NCLSC.

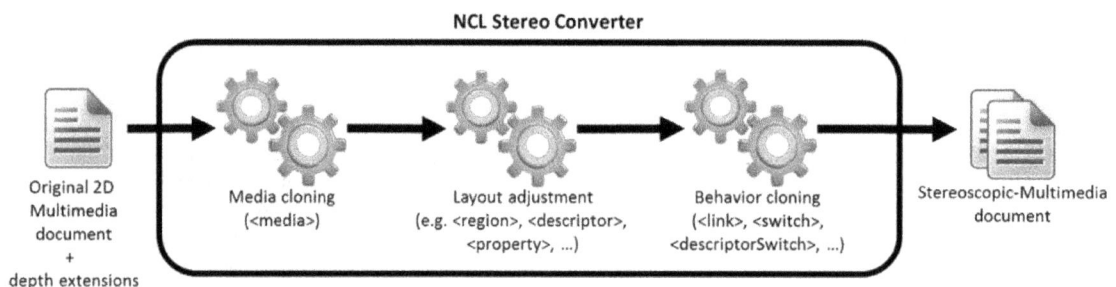

Figure 4. The three phases of NCLSC conversion process.

Assuming a side-by-side output format, for each cloned media object, the converter updates the values of three properties: `left`, `right`, and `width`. The `left` property specifies the distance between the left margin of the screen and the left margin of the object being presented. In NCL, this value can be either absolute (e.g., 10px), or relative (e.g., 10%) to the screen width (see Figure 5). For instance, let $left(x)$ be the `left` property value of a media object x, defined as a percentage (%) of the screen width. Then, the corresponding left and right-view instance values in the resulting document, $left(x_l)$ and $left(x_r)$ are given, respectively, by the following equations:

$$left(x_l) = \frac{left(x)}{2} \quad \text{and} \quad left(x_r) = \frac{left(x)}{2} + 50\% + \delta(x)$$

where $\delta(x)$ is the parallax (also given as a percentage of the screen width) between the left and right-view instances of the resulting elements in the output document. $\delta(x)$ is computed from the depth information of the 2D object, as discussed later, in Section 3.2.1.

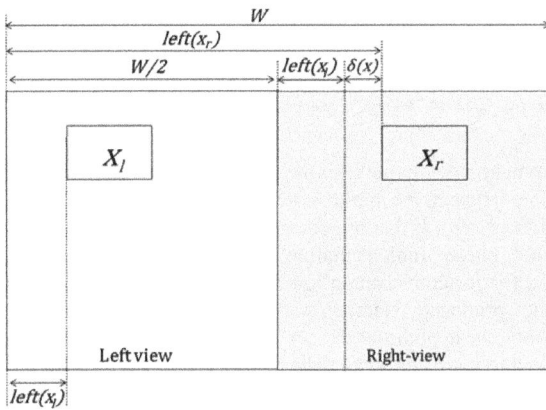

Figure 5. Spatial properties in a stereoscopic application for the side-by-side output format.

The `width` property for left and right view <media> element must be half of the original `width`.

The equations to compute the resulting left and right-view values for the `right` property and for the cases in which the property values are given in pixels are similar. The equations are similar to the ones used by the top-bottom output format, as well. However, in the last case, the three properties that must be updated are `top`, `bottom`, and `height`.

NCL allows for defining spatial and temporal portions of media object's content, called anchors, using <area> elements. Anchors are used to define events, as explained in the next section. If an anchor is defined by spatial coordinates, these coordinates must also be redefined in the left and right view instances. Horizontal and vertical coordinates are defined in a way similar to `left` and `bottom` properties, respectively.

To illustrate the process performed by NCLSC in this phase, consider the <media> element in the code chunk of Section 3.1 with the additional spatial properties and the object's depth parameter defined by NCL <property> elements:

```
<media id="video" src="file:///video.mp4">
  <area id="a1" begin="10s" end="20s"/>
  <property name="explicitDur" value="50s"/>

  <property name="depth" value="1"/>
  <property name="left" value="10%"/>
  <property name="width" value="80%"/>
</media>
```

After the execution of media cloning and layout adjustment phases, NCLSC replaces the following pair of <media> elements replaces for the original <media> element:

```
<media id="video-L" src="file:///video.mp4">
  <area id="a1-L" begin="10s" end="20s"/>
  <property name="explicitDur" value="50s"/>

  <property name="depth" value="1"/>
  <property name="left" value="5%"/>
  <property name="width" value="40%"/>
</media>
```

```
<media id="video-R" src="mirror://video-L">
  <area id="a1-R" begin="10s" end="20s"/>
  <property name="explicitDur" value="50s"/>

  <property name="depth" value="1"/>
  <property name="left" value="57%"/>
  <property name="width" value="40%"/>
</media>
```

The anchor defined by the <area> element is not redefined, except its *id* attribute value, because it is not a spatial anchor. The depth property is still present in the final stereoscopic document because its value can be changed during the document presentation, as discussed in Subsection 3.3. The next subsection discusses how NCLSC calculates the parallax value of a given object.

3.2.1 From depth to screen parallax

The final parallax value $\delta(x)$ for a media object x is obtained from the depth parameter $depth(x)$, as follows:

$$\delta(x) = \begin{cases} -(s \times depth(x) \times max_{\delta+}), & if\ depth \geq 0 \\ -(s \times depth(x) \times max_{\delta-}), & otherwise \end{cases}$$

in which $depth(x)$ is the current value of the x's depth property in the range $[-1.0, 1.0]$; s is a viewer-supplied scale factor in the range $[0,1]$; $max_{\delta+}$ is the maximum positive parallax allowed by the display; and $max_{\delta-}$ is its maximum negative parallax (both $max_{\delta+}$ and $max_{\delta-}$ are given as a percentage of the screen width). The negative sign at the front of the term is required because positive depths (in front of the screen) must produce negative parallaxes, whereas negative depths (inside of the screen) must produce positive parallaxes.

The $max_{\delta+}$ and $max_{\delta-}$ variables denote the maximum positive and negative parallax that still allows for a good QoE using a particular display.

While using a fixed parallax value between the left and right views is sufficient for achieving depth perception on S3D displays, some studies have reported that if the parallax value is kept fixed while the display size and viewer distance vary, there is a significant drop in the observed quality of experience (QoE) of the presentation [43] [44].

The calculation above allows NCLSC to adapt the resulting stereoscopic application to different display geometries, viewer distances, and user preferences. The s scale factor is a user-supplied parameter that allows end users, in line with their preferences, to adjust the final parallax. It can be modified at any time during the application execution. This parameter allows end users to have some degree of control over their depth perception, which contributes to the overall QoE.

If the author needs (or wants) to use a fixed parallax settings he still can do it by hardcoding the `parallax` property (specified as pixels or percentage of the screen). In the previous example, it is sufficient to include a `<property>` element with attribute name equals to "parallax" and its corresponding value. In this case, it is recommended to choose a fixed parallax value that works reasonably well across a large range of display sizes and viewing distances. An example of such rule-of-thumb is the percentage rule [45], commonly used in cinematography, which states that: (i) negative parallax (nearer to the screen) should not exceed 2%–3% of the screen's width; and (ii) positive parallax (farther from the screen) should not exceed 1%–2% of the screen.

3.3 Behavior Cloning

In the behavior cloning phase, NCLSC replicates the behavior of each original media object onto that of its resulting left and right instances.

In NCL, the application behavior is defined by causal relationships (mainly specified by `<link>` elements). NCL is an event-oriented glue language. Occurrences of events trigger actions that cause the occurrences of other events. NCL has three types of events: *presentation* of a set of information units (an anchor) of a media object; *selection* of an anchor being presented; and *attribution* of a value to an object's property. More precisely, the `onBegin`, `onEnd`, `onPause`, `onResume`, or `onAbort` conditions for any event type may cause the `start`, `stop`, `pause`, `resume`, or `abort` actions for other (or the same) events. Link conditions and actions are associated with media objects through `<bind>` elements, defined within a parent `<link>`. As an example, consider the following code block:

```
<link id="orig-link" xconnector="onBeginStop">
  <bind role="onBegin" component="x"/>
  <bind role="stop" component="y"/>
</link>
```

The above link establishes that when the media object x starts its presentation, media object y presentation must be stopped.

NCL behavior is also guided by content and presentation adaptations, represented by `<switch>` and `<descriptorSwitch>` elements, respectively. Because these elements are "syntactic sugars" to more complex structures of `<link>` elements [46], the remaining of this section only details how NCLSC handles the `<link>` conversion.

The `<link>` conversion can be done in at least two ways:

(i) each original `<link>` element generates two links with the same conditions, but with actions targeting the `<media>` elements representing the left views or the right views, respectively; or

(ii) the original link generates only one `<link>` in which each action is duplicated to operate on both views.

In both cases, if any condition of the original link refers to a `<media>` element that has been duplicated in the media cloning

phase, in the produced link (or links) the condition must refer to the new left view instance.

As an example, take the link `orig-link`, depicted in the previous code block, and let's assume that the a media x has been duplicated in the media cloning phase. Thus, if the link update method (i) is applied, the following two links replace the `orig-link` element:

```
<link id="orig-link-L" xconnector="onBeginStop">
  <bind role="onBegin" component="x-L"/>
  <bind role="stop" component="y-L"/>
</link>


<link id="orig-link-R" xconnector="onBeginStop">
  <bind role="onBegin" component="x-L"/>
  <bind role="stop" component="y-R"/>
</link>
```

Alternatively, if the link update method (ii) is applied to `orig-link`, then the following is produced as output:

```
<link id="orig-link" xconnector="onBeginStop">
  <bind role="onBegin" component="x-L"/>
  <bind role="stop" component="y-L"/>
  <bind role="stop" component="y-R"/>
</link>
```

The synchronous hypothesis is an assumption that considers that the time between the application of an action and its effect can be considered zero. If that hypothesis can be assumed with respect to the NCL player implementation the two aforementioned methods (i) and (ii) for converting a link have the same effect on the QoE of the produced stereoscopic application. However, if the synchronous hypothesis cannot be assumed, the first alternative can lead to a greater delay between the action's effects on the two view instances. Although the media cloning phase has guaranteed a synchronized presentation of the two media views when they are on display, it cannot ensure that the two media views start at the same time. Therefore, NCLSC employs the second approach to guarantee that the NCL player will execute both actions (in the right and left-instances) as close as possible to each other.

In addition, if the original `<bind>` element specifies the assignment of a value of a spatial property of the original `<media>` element, such change must be replicated to the left and right view instances. Properties are specified through the `<property>` element, and spatial properties include `left`, `right`, `top`, `bottom`, `width`, `height`, and `depth`. The changes in the values of those properties must be in agreement with equations in Section 3.2. Sometimes, however, the spatial properties values cannot be computed statically. To calculates the values at run-time, NCLSC redirects any attempt to change positioning properties to an NCLua script node. This script computes the final positioning property for the left and right view instances and redirects these changes to the corresponding target view instances.

Figure 6 shows the conversion process for dynamic changes in spatial properties and how the original `<link>` is modified to use the NCLua script as a proxy to update these properties.

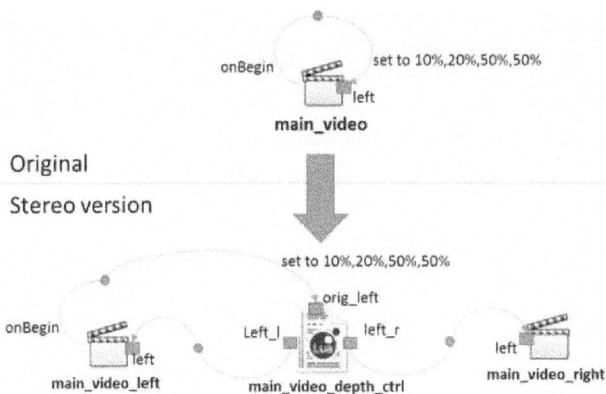

Figure 6. NCLua script controlling positioning property.

4. USING NCLSC

NCLSC is implemented as a Lua script that can be used as both a standalone application or an embedded NCLua media object that can modify the application in which it is inserted. NCLSC is available as free software (GNU Public License v.3) and its source code is available at http://github.com/robertogerson/nclsc.

The standalone version of NCLSC can be used at the server-side or the client-side. For example, in IPTV or hybrid broadcast/broadband DTV systems the conversion process can be performed at the server side before sending the requested application to the client. In this case, when requesting an application, the client must inform the display screen size, the optimal viewer distance, and the scale factor, so that the proper parallax parameter can be calculated.

Applications transmitted by broadcast, however, cannot be converted at the server side, because they target clients with different characteristics and needs. In this case, there are two possibilities. First, NCLSC can be embedded in the language player (or middleware); the language player then is responsible for recognizing the 2D+depth properties of the received application and converting the application to a new its stereoscopic version, if an S3D display is available. Second, the application transmitted by broadcast can be a wrapper application embedding NCLSC, implemented as an NCLua media object, as shown in the following code chunk.

```
<body>
   <port id="entry" component="nclsc"
   <media id="nclsc" src="nclsc.lua">
    <property name="url" value="original-2d.ncl"/>
   </media>
</body>
```

In this case, the original application is passed as a parameter to NCLSC using the <property> element. When the application starts, NCLSC starts (see <port> element), produces the stereoscopic application corresponding to the original application and adds this new application into the wrapper application. Finally, NCLSC starts the new application.

Based on the wrapper approach, several demo applications have been developed. The demo applications explore the depth function as an active element of the user interface. For example, the depth is used as a clue to what is the currently activated element in a menu. Figure 7 depicts some applications running on stereoscopic and binocular auto-stereoscopic 3D displays.

(a)

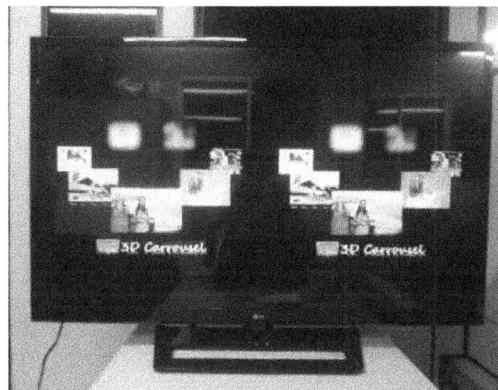

(b)

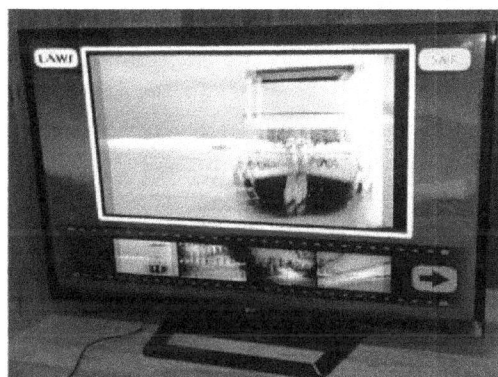

(c)

(d)

Figure 7. Application demos generated with NCLSC running on 3D displays.

Figure 7a shows an application that augments the broadcast video with stereoscopic subtitle and menus. Both, the menu (color buttons at the top of the screen) and the subtitle (at the bottom), are presented outside of the screen. In the figure, the stereoscopic 3D function of the TV is turned off—this is the why both views of the applications are being shown side-by-side. The subtitle is synchronized with the main video whereas the menu allows the user to change the subtitle language and color. The current selected element in the menu is shown with a greater depth.

Figure 7b shows a carousel-like user interface that explores the real depth information. The first item (the one currently on focus) is presented in front of the screen while the depth of the others decrease linearly. When the viewer presses the directional keys, the currently focused item changes and the carousel rotates accordingly, changing the position and depth of all items in the carousel. In Figure 7b, as in Figure 7a, the stereoscopic 3D function of the TV is also turned off.

Figure 7c shows an interactive touristic guide application that presents photos of a city sightseeing. The bottom menu allows the user to navigate between the available pictures. Here the depth information is explored by bringing the currently selected picture to the front of the TV and by showing, at the bottom, which menu element is on focus.

Figure 7d shows the same application as Figure 7c but this time presented on a binocular auto-stereoscopic tablet (with a display size of 10.1"). In this case, the parallax of the elements on the left and right views is adapted to the size of the tablet's display, as discussed in Subsection 3.2.

5. DISCUSSION

At this point, some remarks can be made concerning the space and time complexity of the produced stereoscopic applications, the problems that can disturb the end-user QoE, and the limitations of the proposed solution.

5.1 Space and Time Complexity

The processing overhead of the produced stereoscopic application, in comparison with the original one, heavily depends on how a particular language player is implemented and for what tasks it is optimized. Thus, instead of providing measurements with running applications, which would be specific to a middleware implementation, this section presents the analysis of the complexity of stereoscopic multimedia applications produced by NCLSC.

Consider an original document with N media objects and L links. After the media cloning phase, the produced stereoscopic application has at most two times more media objects than the original one, that is, 2N media objects. This worst-case scenario occurs when every media object has a graphical representation and needs to be duplicated. Moreover, for each duplicated object in this first phase, NCLSC can add one NCLua script object to control the parallax between the left and right view instances at runtime. This processing is also done in the behavior cloning phase. Thus, in the worst case, the total number of media nodes in the output document is 3N.

For each link in the original document that changes a spatial property, the behavior cloning phase outputs tree links. These links are responsible to redirect changes on spatial properties to the associated NCLua script object and then to the left and right view instances (see Figure 6). Therefore, in the worst case, the total number of links in the output document is 3L.

The running time complexity of the resulting application can be estimated from the number of events generated at runtime, where an event is any change in the application state. In the worst case, the number of events generated by the produced stereoscopic application is twice that generated by the original application. That is, in the worst case one may end up running two instances of the same application—each event is duplicated.

5.2 Quality of Experience

Two main parameters affect the QoE of the output applications: the parallax between the left and right view instances of a same media object; and the synchronization skew between the two views. The former is in complete control of the application author, who is tasked with the handling of depth (or the parallax itself) of the media objects. He can manipulate the depth information to preserve or improve the QoE. NCLSC only gives him the tools, as discussed in Section 3.2.1. The end user can also customize his experience by controlling the final parallax through the scale factor.

Keeping the views in sync is more challenging. We must assure that the left and right view instances begin their presentations at the same time and keep their presentation as close as possible of a frame-by-frame synchronization. Frame synchronization is preserved in NCLSC implementation by taking advantage of the "ncl-mirror" scheme of NCL to duplicate objects with the same content (see Section 3.1). If the same starting times for the left and right views will be kept is a question that depends on the particular NCL player implementation. In some implementations, the synchronous hypothesis can be assumed, and this problem may be mitigated. However, in other implementations, the synchronous hypothesis can only be assumed if the start action on the right view immediately follows the start action on the left view. Therefore, the QoE depends on how the NCL player serializes actions that must occur at the same time. In most cases the alternative of duplicating the <bind> elements of a link, during the behavior cloning phase, produces a better QoE than duplicating the link.

5.3 Limitations

As previously mentioned, one of the main advantages of using the NCLSC solution is that it does not need native S3D support from language player. Despite that, some limitations must be mentioned.

An inherent restriction of NCLSC is that each graphical object has only one depth specification for its whole content, which, as previously discussed, results in a layered interface. For instance, it is not possible to rotate the object to create perspective effects. If this feature is required, a possible solution is to employ CSS 3D Transforms, but the mapping of the resulting CSS 3D Transforms into the stereo content still need to be defined.

Moreover, the use of script languages instead of native software support causes some overhead that can influence the performance of the application. During the tests using the Ginga-NCL reference implementation, only minor overhead was identified, but more in-depth research still needs to be performed.

A further limitation of NCLSC's approach concerns the selection of content anchors. NCL applications have no control of the pointer device, which is under complete control of the NCL player implementation. Thus NCLSC is not able to duplicate pointers correctly to the left and right view instances, providing an S3D view. Even if it could be represented in an S3D view, the use of 2D pointers in S3D systems also has other major drawbacks, such as the position of the cursor in depth and handling of occlusions [47]. Whereas this could be a bigger issue in PC environments, we consider it a minor one in interactive TV, since, in this case, the primary interactive device is the remote control, and one navigates using its navigational keys.

6. CONCLUSIONS

This paper discusses an approach to convert a 2D interactive multimedia application annotated with depth information to a stereoscopic-multimedia application, allowing 2D content to float in and out of the screen.

We have focused on the process of converting a flat NCL application into an equivalent S3D application. The proposed approach, however, is not restricted to the context of NCL. In fact, it can be extended to other 2D multimedia languages, such as SMIL, HTML5, and SVG. But when doing so, the fine-grained synchronization between the left and right sides of the application must be carefully handled. For instance, current HTML5 browsers do not guarantee a fine synchronization between two <video> tags and have no support similar to the NCL `ncl-mirror` scheme. Such a feature could be implemented, but it would require some workarounds, for example, by means of the HTML Canvas API.

The abstract process illustrated in Figure 4 can also be used as a guideline to implement a similar feature via imperative languages, such as the script languages, or through XML transformation languages, such as XSLT [48].

As future work, we plan to:
- support media objects with native stereoscopic content (e.g., objects with content captured from stereoscopic cameras). For that, we must define how to crop the different left and right view of the object's content and display them synchronously, using high-level language resources;
- extend NCLSC for multiview 3D displays, which may stress the system;
- integrate depth extensions in high-level authoring tools; and
- use NCLSC in the development of stereoscopic multimedia applications for 3DTV and 3D Cinema, and measure end-user QoE.

7. ACKNOWLEDGMENTS

This work was partially funded by CAPES, CNPq, and FAPERJ. The authors would like to thank these Brazilian Research Agencies for their support.

8. REFERENCES

[1] Goldstein, E.B. 2014. *Sensation and perception.* Wadsworth, Cengage Learning.

[2] Lebreton, P. et al. 2012. Evaluating Depth Perception of 3D Stereoscopic Videos. *IEEE Journal of Selected Topics in Signal Processing.* 6, 6 (Oct. 2012), 710–720.

[3] Dufaux, F. et al. eds. 2013. *Emerging technologies for 3D video: creation, coding, transmission, and rendering.* John Wiley & Sons Inc.

[4] Lin Du et al. 2011. Immersive 3D user interface for 3D TVS. (May 2011), 1–4.

[5] Huhtala, J. et al. 2011. Evaluating depth illusion as method of adding emphasis in autostereoscopic mobile displays. (2011), 357.

[6] Sunnari, M. et al. 2012. Studying user experiences of autostereoscopic 3D menu on touch screen mobile device.

[7] Wu, S.L. 2010. Depth in Dedicated Mobile Device User Interfaces for Auto-Stereoscopic Displays. *Delft University of Technology, Netherlands.* (2010).

[8] Colley, A. et al. 2013. Investigating Mobile Stereoscopic 3D Touchscreen Interaction. *Proceedings of the 25th Australian Computer-Human Interaction Conference: Augmentation, Application, Innovation, Collaboration* (New York, NY, USA, 2013), 105–114.

[9] Ventä-Olkkonen, L. et al. 2013. How to Use 3D in Stereoscopic Mobile User Interfaces–Study of Initial User Perceptions. *Proc. Academic MindTrek. ACM.* (2013).

[10] Woo, S. et al. 2012. Reinforcement of spatial perception for stereoscopic 3d on mobile handsets. *CHI'12 Extended Abstracts on Human Factors in Computing Systems* (2012), 2075–2080.

[11] Broy, N. et al. 2014. FrameBox and MirrorBox: Tools and Guidelines to Support Designers in Prototyping Interfaces for 3D Displays. *Proceedings of the 32Nd Annual ACM Conference on Human Factors in Computing Systems* (New York, NY, USA, 2014), 2037–2046.

[12] Broy, N. et al. 2015. Evaluating Stereoscopic 3D for Automotive User Interfaces in a Real-World Driving Study. (2015), 1717–1722.

[13] Soares, L.F.G. and Lima, G.F. 2013. *NCL Handbook.* Technical Report #18/13. Pontifícia Universidade Católica do Rio de Janeiro.

[14] Soares, L.F.G. et al. 2010. Ginga-NCL: Declarative middleware for multimedia IPTV services. *IEEE Communications Magazine.* 48, 6 (Jun. 2010), 74–81.

[15] ITU-T 2011. Recommendation ITU-T H.761: Nested Context Language (NCL) and Ginga-NCL for IPTV Services. ITU-T.

[16] Goldmann, L. et al. 2010. Temporal synchronization in stereoscopic video: Influence on quality of experience and automatic asynchrony detection. (Sep. 2010), 3241–3244.

[17] Fuchs, P. et al. eds. 2011. *Virtual reality: concepts and technologies.* CRC Press.

[18] Mihelj, M. 2014. *Virtual reality technology and applications.* Springer.

[19] Carey, R. et al. 1997. *ISO/IEC 14772-1: 1997 Virtual Reality Modeling Language (vrml97).*

[20] 2013. *X3D Architecture and base components V3.* ISO/IEC.

[21] Bulterman, D. et al. 2008. *Synchronized Multimedia Integration Language (SMIL 3.0).* W3C.

[22] 2014. *HTML5.* W3C.

[23] Cockburn, A. and McKenzie, B. 2002. Evaluating the effectiveness of spatial memory in 2D and 3D physical and virtual environments. *Proceedings of the SIGCHI Conference on Human Factors in Computing Systems* (2002), 203–210.

[24] Sopin, I. and Hamza-Lup, F.G. 2010. Extending the Web3D: design of conventional GUI libraries in X3D. *Proceedings of the 15th International Conference on Web 3D Technology* (2010), 137.

[25] Herigstad, D.A. 2014. Off-screen media: spatial display and interaction in augmented television. (2014), 155–156.

[26] Jung, K. et al. 2008. 2D/3D Mixed Service in T-DMB System Using Depth Image Based Rendering. *Advanced Communication Technology, 2008. ICACT 2008. 10th International Conference on* (Feb. 2008), 1868–1871.

[27] Hang, S. and Lee, D.-Y. 2012. *Extensions for Stereoscopic 3D support.*

[28] Chen, Q. et al. 2014. The rendering context for stereoscopic 3D web. (Mar. 2014), 90111P.

[29] Zhang, J. et al. 2014. A rendering approach for stereoscopic web pages. (Mar. 2014), 90111O.

[30] Liu, Z. et al. 2014. The design and implementation of stereoscopic 3D scalable vector graphics based on WebKit. *Proc. SPIE* (Mar. 2014), 90111R.

[31] McCormack, C. et al. 2011. *Scalable Vector Graphics (SVG) 1.1 (Second Edition)*. W3C.

[32] Le Feuvre, J. 2010. SVG Extensions for 3D displays Enabling SVG on auto-stereoscopic displays. *8th International Conference on Scalable Vector Graphics* (2010).

[33] Azevedo, R.G. de A. and Soares, L.F.G. 2013. NCL+Depth: Extending NCL for Stereo/Autostereoscopic 3D Displays. *Proceedings of the 19th Brazilian Symposium on Multimedia and the Web* (New York, NY, USA, 2013), 185–192.

[34] Azevedo, R.G. de A. and Soares, L.F.G. 2014. Ginga extensions to support depth-based 3D media. *3DTV-Conference: The True Vision - Capture, Transmission and Display of 3D Video (3DTV-CON), 2014* (Jul. 2014), 1–4.

[35] Le Feuvre, J. et al. 2007. GPAC: open source multimedia framework. (2007), 1009.

[36] Dubois, E. 2001. A projection method to generate anaglyph stereo images. (2001), 1661–1664.

[37] Flanagan, D. 2002. *JavaScript: the definitive guide.* O'Reilly Media, Inc.

[38] Zhang, S. et al. 2012. 3D Webpage Rendering by Canvas. *Advances on Digital Television and Wireless Multimedia Communications.* W. Zhang et al., eds. Springer Berlin Heidelberg. 411–417.

[39] Chistyakov, A. et al. 2013. Bringing the Web Closer: Stereoscopic 3D Web Conversion. *Human Computer Interaction.* Springer. 22–25.

[40] Cabanier, R. et al. 2014. *HTML Canvas 2D Context.* W3C.

[41] Hégaret, P.L. et al. 2004. *Document Object Model (DOM) Level 3 Core Specification.* W3C.

[42] Soares Neto, C. de S. et al. 2010. The Nested Context Language reuse features. *Journal of the Brazilian Computer Society.* 16, 4 (Nov. 2010), 229–245.

[43] Shibata, T. et al. 2011. The zone of comfort: Predicting visual discomfort with stereo displays. *Journal of Vision.* 11, 8 (Jul. 2011), 11–11.

[44] Chen, Y. et al. 2014. Overview of the MVC+D 3D video coding standard. *Journal of Visual Communication and Image Representation.* 25, 4 (May 2014), 679–688.

[45] Mendiburu, B. 2012. *3D TV and 3D cinema tools and processes for creative stereoscopy.* Focal Press/Elsevier.

[46] Lima, G.A.F. and Soares, L.F.G. 2013. Two normal forms for link-connector pairs in NCL 3.0. *Proceedings of the 19th Brazilian symposium on Multimedia and the web* (2013), 201–204.

[47] Schemali, L. and Eisemann, E. 2014. Design and evaluation of mouse cursors in a stereoscopic desktop environment. (Mar. 2014), 67–70.

[48] Kay, M. 2013. *XSL Transformations (XSLT) Version 3.0.* W3C.

AERO: An extensible framework for adaptive web layout synthesis

Rares Vernica
HP Labs
Palo Alto, California, USA
rares.vernica@hp.com

Niranjan Damera Venkata
HP Labs
Chennai, Tamil Nadu, India
niranjan.damera-venkata@hp.com

ABSTRACT

We present AERO, an extensible framework for adaptive web layout synthesis. The goal is to provide an underlying software architecture to allow general adaptive layout behaviors. The framework consists of a 1) a suite of templates specified in HTML/CSS, 2) A hierarchical, highly customizable scoring function specification and 3) An evaluation engine that leverages native browser rendering to rapidly render content and apply the scoring functions. Unlike current responsive layout frameworks for web (e.g., Twitter Bootstrap) that have pre-configured grid layouts that adapt in a manually pre-encoded content-independent manner, AERO allows layout to adapt automatically based on multiple content-dependent criteria like aesthetic quality, cropability of individual images, layout A/B testing results, Ad placement etc.

Categories and Subject Descriptors

I.7.4 [**Computing Methodologies**]: Document and Text Processing—*Electronic Publishing*

General Terms

Algorithms, Design

Keywords

automated publishing; layout; framework; adaptive; extensible

1. INTRODUCTION

Responsive web design (RWD) involves designing layouts that adapt to changing window size and hence to different devices. RWD layouts are very popular in modern web design. The most popular responsive layout framework for the web is Twitter Bootstrap [1]. The web designer is responsible to carefully orchestrate the fate of individual content

blocks as the window size is changed. Bootstrap's grid layout uses a 12 column grid and allows `<div>`s to span an integer number of columns. The column-span and block level re-flow behavior can be controlled by special classes that must be placed by the designer up-front. This is a content-independent process that usually ends up re-flowing blocks to new rows or changing column-span as resizing occurs. Clearly, this process is inflexible in optimizing presentation, especially with content variations, since it is not able to handle complex layout criteria like optimizing content arrangement for aesthetic quality, intelligent image re-cropping, optimizing arrangement for visual attention or maximum click rates etc. Indeed there are three distinct criteria that may be considered: 1) Aesthetic arrangement of content on the page 2) Intrinsic, potentially content-dependent meta-data (block importance, cropability of images, font-size tolerances etc.) 3) External criteria such as Customer Relationship Management (CRM) data on a specific user, A/B visual attention results, revenue potential etc.

Our focus in this paper is to present a web based layout synthesis framework that uses multiple criteria to adapt web layouts. Rather than focusing on individual layout algorithms we focus on the tools required to support flexible specification of layout primitives and layout scoring functions. These components are designed to be extensible to accommodate the various design goals.

The fundamental layout primitive we use is the layout template. We organize templates into a collection/suite of templates describing possible layouts of the various content elements. Web layouts based on a template specification and filling approach were described in [3] and are still actively being worked on by the W3C [4]. Coupling a template with content and a hierarchical scoring function allows us to attach an evaluation (JavaScript) at the DOM-node level that can be content based, filtered up to score the whole template, incorporate external input from databases, etc. Finally the evaluation engine can efficiently evaluate multiple templates from the suite and pick the best one that is customized for the presentation of specific content based on specified criteria. The AERO framework has already been used in production in systems like HP METIS [5].

While this framework shares some similarity to the browser based layout technology described in [6], the key distinction stems from the need for pagination (required for print-layouts). The method in [6] uses specific template level scoring functions (derived from a probabilistic document design model) and computational evaluation of templates instead of actual rendering during the evaluation process. Explicit rendering in the evaluation phase allows the framework in this paper to support general web templates instead of restriction to a class of computationally tractable print templates.

In this paper, we start by taking about content and template representation in Section 2. Next we talk about scoring and layout in Section 3. We conclude the paper in Section 4 with a discussion of our results.

2. REPRESENTATION

The input to our AERO synthesis framework is set of content and a suite of templates. The content is composed of text, images, and other multimedia elements that need to be laid out. The template suite contains a set of templates that can be used for layout. The output of the framework is a document that has the optimal content laid out using the optimal template. The optimization is done using a fully-customizable scoring function.

2.1 Content

The content input type is plain HTML 5 content. Styling and other formatting attributes are not expected in the content. In general, the content is a sequence of headings, paragraphs, figures, etc. The order of the content corresponds to the reading order. We use the HAML[2] format to encode the HTML content and we store it in JSON. At run-time, we use a jQuery HAML plugin to convert the JSON to DOM objects. This format allows for easy generation of content upstream and processing in the layout engine. Furthermore, each piece of content (paragraphs, figures, etc.) contains various annotation attributes which denote what adjustments can be made to the content. For example, the annotations denote various crop transformations that are possible to the figures, optional figures, optional paragraphs, etc. Below is an example of input content:

```
[
  ["%h1", "San Diego"],
  ["%p", "San Diego is the eighth-largest city..."],
  ["%figure",
    ["%img", {"src":"http://...",}],
    ["%figcaption", "Kumeyaay people lived..."]],...
]
```

2.2 Templates

The templates used in the AERO framework are organized in suites. A template suite is composed of individual templates which correspond to a specific presentation. For example, one template suite corresponds to PC presentation while another one corresponds to mobile presentation, one template suite corresponds to reading presentation while another one corresponds to interactive presentation, etc.

Each template suite is placed in one directory and contains a CSS file applicable to all the templates in a suite as well as an index file which lists the templates in the suite. Each template is stored in an individual directory. Each template is represented by three files, a **structure** file, a **style** file, and a **scoring** file.

Template Structure: We use HTML for defining the template structure. The structure of each template is represented by a HTML snippet which is intended to be used in the context of a document. A template can contain one or more *paths* which, in general, correspond to columns. Each path has one or more *flow* boxes in which any type of content can be placed. Finally, the templates also contain *fixed*

boxes in which specific types of *top-level* content needs to be placed. We define top-level content units as the content units which are not contained in any other content unit. Fixed boxed are usually assigned to content which can be presented out of flow, like images. Below is an example of a template structure:

```
<div class='path' id='template1-path1'>
  <div class='flow-wrapper template1-flow1-wrapper'>
    <div class='fig-1-col' id='template1-fig1'>
      <figure class='fixed'></figure>
    </div>
    <div class='flow template1-flow1'></div>
  </div>
</div>
<div class='path' id='template1-path2'>
  <div class='flow-weapper template1-flow2-wrapper'>
    <div class='flow template1-flow2'></div>
  </div>
</div>
```

This template contains two paths. The first path contains one fixed box for a figure and one flow box. The second column contains only one flow box. Each flow box is accompanied by a flow-wrapper box. The wrapper boxes are used for overflow and underflow detection and described in the next section. HTML Classes are used to identify the type of element. Besides the tags for paths and boxes, the HTML template can contain other static tags for template static content like document headers and footers. The fixed boxes play a critical role in deciding whether the template is chosen or not for a particular page. A particular template is only used if content for all the fixed boxes is available.

Template Style: The template style is defined using CSS markup. Besides the template specific CSS, the suite CSS is available to the template as well.

Template Scoring: A scoring function is provided for each template. The scoring function is implemented in JavaScript and can contain any arbitrary code. This is one of the key advantages of the AERO framework. The scoring file is interpreted in the JavaScript interpreter when the template is loaded. The scoring code registers one scoring function for the template to which it belongs. We discuss the scoring model extensively in the next section.

A template of particular importance is the *fallback* template. The fallback template is used for unusual content for which none of the suite templates can be used. Displaying the fallback template is equivalent with displaying an error message. The fallback template displays a partial rendering of the content and allows the page to continue being rendered. Usually, the same fallback template is used across multiple template suites.

3. LAYOUT AND SCORING

For making layout decisions, the AERO framework uses a *layout-and-measure* approach, as opposed to *measure-and-layout* approaches (used in probabilistic document design [6]). That is, various content combinations are rendered in various templates. For each combination, measurements of how well the content fits in the template are made. The measurements are combined into a scoring function. In consequence, multiple content and template combination are assigned a score. The template-content combination with the largest score is used. This layout-and-measure approach leverages the extremely optimized rendering engines present in modern web browsers. Moreover, as web browsers become even more efficient this framework will benefit as well.

3.1 Layout Engine Overview

The AERO layout engine loops over valid content combinations and for each content combination it loops over the templates in a suite. Each viable content-template pair is laid out by modifying the DOM structure and having the web browser render it. Once rendered, the layout is measured and the scoring function is evaluated. The highest scored content-template pair is used in the final layout.

The engine makes sure it uses only valid combinations of content. That is, content is in the pre-specified reading order, all required figures are included, etc. Moreover, the framework allows for pre-specified modifications to the original content, like image cropping. More advanced content modifications could be imagined, like image collage generation or text summarizing. The main flow of the AERO layout algorithm is as follows:

```
1. Load Template Suite, Content, and Images
2. Hyphenate Content; Add IDs to top-level elements
3. Initialize Page

4. WHILE Content combinations exist
   5. FOR EACH Template
      6. Load Template Structure and CSS in DOM
      7. Populate Fixed template boxes
      8. IF Fixed boxes not filled, THEN BREAK
      9. FOR EACH Content element
         10. Insert Content element in Flow box
         11. IF Overflow or Invalid detected,
             move to next Flow box, ELSE BREAK
      12. Compute Score
13. Select Content-Template pair with Best (Max) Score
14. Re-render the Best Content-Template pair
```

3.2 Overflow Detection

In Section 2.2 we described the structure of the AERO templates. We have seen how each flow box is wrapped into an flow-wrapper box. Using this inner-outer box pair we are able to detect box overflows. It works as follows. The outer box has a fixed height given by the template, while the inner box has height set to `auto` and a fixed width given by the template. Below is an example CSS that is used to specify an inner-outer box pair:

```
.template1-flow1-wrapper {
    height: 767px;
}
.template1-flow1 {
    height: auto;
    width: 540px;
}
```

At layout time, multiple content chunks (or parts) can be rendered in one flow box. The chunks include text, images, videos, etc. As content is inserted, the actual height of the flow box increases. After inserting a new chunk of content, we compare the height of the flow box (inner box) with height of the flow-wrapper (outer box). If the height of the inner box exceeds the height of the outer box, an overflow has occurred and the change has to be reverted.

3.3 Scoring

The AERO framework offers great scoring flexibility. As we have seen in the previous section, each template has a JavaScript file associated to it which contains a scoring function. That is, each AERO template defines a scoring function using a predefined prototype. Once defined, the scoring function is registered using a special API call. The same function can be registered for multiple templates. At run-time, when the scoring function is called it receives as argument a pointer to the DOM node on which to compute the score. Below is an example of a scoring function definition and registration for a template called "template1":

```
var getScore = function($page) {
  // ...
};
window.aero.Suite.singleton.register('template1', getScore);
```

Due to its flexibility, the scoring function in AERO can incorporate a multitude of facets. We classify these facets in three categories: aesthetic, intrinsic, and external.

Aesthetic based: The aesthetic-based scoring facets incorporate a multitude of aspects related to the aesthetic characteristics of the template used. They include which exact template was used, some templates could be favored over other templates. They also include metrics related to the allocation of space. That is, how much space is left blank and where it is. Some templates might favor more white space while others might favor filling up the space as much as possible.

Intrinsic based: Many scoring facets can be defined directly from the content. We call these facets intrinsic based. They include any changes made to the figures, such as: including or excluding optional figures or text, figure cropping, or figure sequence. Any such adjustments made to the figures could be penalized more or less by the scoring function. Other facets can be defined based on the content composition, that is, ratio of text to images. For example, in a set of content where the text to images ratio is skewed towards text, the use of optional images can have a significant boost on the score. Finally, if different multi-media elements are used in the content (such as video or audio clips), the scoring function could assign different weights to each.

External based: Besides scoring facets derived directly from the content, additional scoring facets can be derived indirectly from the content with the use of additional information. We call such facets external based. The additional information includes content popularity information such as which images or paragraphs are more popular. In the scoring function, using a popular piece of content could result in a score boost. Various revenue models can be used as a scoring facet as well. These could include an advertising model where customers get charged if a piece of content is present in the final document. In this case, the score gets a boost if the revenue gets a boost. Finally, the resulting document can be part of an A/B testing campaign and as such, the scoring function can incorporate which pieces of content should be used for one group of users vs. another. Since all these additional information is not directly available in the content we discuss ways of addressing this at the end of this section.

Depending on the application in which the final document is used, the scoring function for a template can incorporate a multitude of such facets, resulting in a very powerful scoring capability. Finally, the scoring function also captures exception cases. One such example discussed earlier is overflow. That is, if an overflow occurs, the scoring function activates

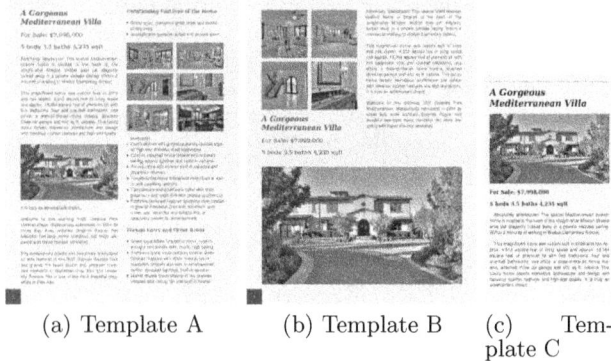

(a) Template A   (b) Template B   (c) Template C

Figure 1: AERO Layout Options.

the overflow bit in the result. When the layout engine reads the active overflow bit, it stops adding content to the current column and either switches to the next column or next template. Besides overflow, the template can define other invalid cases. Such cases can include: heading as the last element on a column, two sequential figures with no text in between, etc. The template scoring function looks for such cases and, if detected, it activates the invalid bit. When the layout engine reads the active invalid bit, it dis-considers the current allocation and continues with other allocations.

3.4 Implementation Considerations

To help template writers specify scoring functions the AERO framework provides an extensive suite of helper functions which can be used in the template scoring function. Such function include: computing white space left on a column, detecting a header as the last element on a column, combining scores for multiple columns, etc.

All the information necessary to compute the external-based scoring facets can be very dynamic and it is not directly available in the content. As a consequence these information needs to be fetched at layout time. We use Ajax based calls to the backed for retrieving any additional pieces of information. The backend uses a fast key-value store for retrieving pre-stored values and a processing backend for computing values on the fly.

To load a template suite CSS, the HTML file using AERO has a preassigned `<link>` tag. The framework dynamically updates the DOM and sets the `href` attribute of the tag to point to the template suite CSS. All the template suites include a special suite signature at the end of the CSS file. This signature sets a predefined style and contains the suite name. Since the actual loading of the CSS file happens asynchronously we keep checking until the predefined style has been defined. This signifies the CSS has been loaded and the processing can continue.

Based on the presentation conditions a particular template suite is selected when the layout engine is started. If the presentation conditions change and the template suite needs to be changed, the layout engine needs to be rerun.

4. RESULTS

To evaluate the results produced by the AERO framework we use a content example from the real estate industry. The content is a fictional real estate property advertisement. It contains headings of different sizes, paragraphs of text, itemized lists, and seven images. We use one template suite designed for use on a PC and another template suite for use on mobile devices. The PC suite has two templates: Template A and Template B. Both templates have two columns. The mobile suite suite has only one template with one column: Template C.

Template A: The first template has one fixed image box on the first column and six fixed image boxes on the second column. The scoring function for the first template uses only aesthetic-based facets. That is, it tries to minimize the white space and fill all the fixed boxes. The scoring function marks as invalid any content adjustments.

Template B: The second template has four fixed image boxes on the first column and an additional fixed image box spanning both columns at the bottom of the page. The scoring function for the second template uses facets from all three categories: aesthetic, intrinsic, and external. The aesthetic based facets of the scoring function are similar to the ones used for the first template. Regarding the intrinsic facets, the scoring function allows for cropping of images and for trimming the content. Finally, the scoring function includes external faces which allow for specific images to boost the score if used.

Template C: The mobile template uses a simple structure with no fixed boxes, only one flow box. The scoring function is similar to the one used in Template A, but allows for trimming the content.

Figure 1 shows the results produced by the AERO framework using the three templates. Notice how for Template A all the content is used, including the seven images. For Template B, since image cropping is allowed, images are cropped to $1:1$ ratio. Moreover, not all the content is included. Only five of the seven images are used and later paragraphs are missing. Finally, the image showing the front view of the property was marked as popular and provided a score boost, hence ended up in the box spanning both columns. Template C shows the responsive capabilities of the framework.

5. REFERENCES

[1] Bootstrap: The world's most popular mobile-first and responsive front-end framework. `http://getbootstrap.com`.

[2] HAML - Beautiful, DRY, well-indented, clear markup: templating haiku. `http://haml.info/`.

[3] C. Acebal, B. Bos, M. Rodríguez, and J. M. Cueva. ALMcss: A Javascript Implementation of the CSS Template Layout Module. In *Proceedings of the 2012 ACM Symposium on Document Engineering*, DocEng '12, pages 23–32, New York, NY, USA, 2012. ACM.

[4] B. Bos and C. Acebal. CSS template layout module. `http://dev.w3.org/csswg/css-template-1/`. W3C Editors Draft: 2014-09-30.

[5] J. Hailpern and et. al. To Print or Not to Print: Hybrid Learning with METIS Learning Platform. In *Proceedings of the 2015 ACM SIGCHI Symposium on Engineering Interactive Computing Systems*, EICS '15. ACM, 2015.

[6] T. Hassan and N. Damera-Venkata. The Browser as a Document Composition Engine. In *Proceedings of the 2015 ACM Symposium on Document Engineering*, DocEng '15. ACM, 2015.

Automatic Text Document Summarization Based on Machine Learning

Gabriel Silva ,
Rafael Ferreira
UFRPE/UFPE, Recife, PE,
Brazil
{gfps, rflm}@cin.ufpe.br

Rafael Lins, Luciano
Cabral, Hilário Oliveira
UFPE, Recife, PE, Brazil
{rdl, htao}@cin.ufpe.br

Steven J. Simske
Hewlett-Packard Labs.
Fort Collins, CO 80528, USA
steven.simske@hp.com

Marcelo Riss
Hewlett-Packard Brazil
Porto Alegre, RS, Brazil
marcelo.riss@hp.com

ABSTRACT

The need for automatic generation of summaries gained importance with the unprecedented volume of information available in the Internet. Automatic systems based on extractive summarization techniques select the most significant sentences of one or more texts to generate a summary. This article makes use of Machine Learning techniques to assess the quality of the twenty most referenced strategies used in extractive summarization, integrating them in a tool. Quantitative and qualitative aspects were considered in such assessment demonstrating the validity of the proposed scheme. The experiments were performed on the CNN-corpus, possibly the largest and most suitable test corpus today for benchmarking extractive summarization.

Categories and Subject Descriptors

I.2.7 [**Natural Language Processing**]: Text analysis.

General Terms

Algorithms, Experimentation

Keywords

Text Summarization; Extractive features; Sentence Scoring Methods

1. INTRODUCTION

Automatic document summarization is a research area that was born in the early 1950's. Recently, with the pervasiveness of the Internet and the fast growing number of text documents the search for efficient automated systems for Text Summarization (TS) has gained importance and may

DocEng'15, September 8-11, 2015, Lausanne, Switzerland.
© 2015 ACM. ISBN 978-1-4503-3307-8/15/09 ...$15.00.
DOI: http://dx.doi.org/10.1145/2682571.2797099.

even be seen as a way to "compress" information [12]. TS platforms may receive one or more documents as input to generate a summary. Such technique is classified as extractive when the summary is formed by sentences of the original document, or abstractive, when summaries modify the original sentences chosen to yield a better quality summary [11]. In general, abstractive summarization may be seen as a step further ahead of extractive summarization and research in that area may be considered in the very beginning. The extractive summarization techniques (RTS) select the sentences with the highest score from the original document based on a set of criteria. The Extractive Summarization methods are better consolidated and may be considered efficient in the automatic generation of summaries [12, 11, 4].

Summaries may also be classified as generic or query dependent or driven. Generic summaries analyze the text as a whole without prioritizing any aspect. On the other hand, query dependant or driven summaries look at the text trying to find sentences that may answer a query from the user. Text summarization may also be seen as a text compression strategy. The vertical compression rate of a summary may be defined as the ratio between the number of sentences in the original document and the number of sentences in the summary. Another possibility is horizontal sentence compression in which each sentence may be summarized by removing non-essential information. In this case the compression rate is measured by the ratio between the number of words in the original document and the number of words in the summary. Both compression rates are important factors that influence the overall quality and purpose of the summary. This paper focuses exclusively in extractive vertical summarization.

Extractive text summarization techniques are split into three categories [4]: word-based, sentence-based, and graph-based scoring methods. In the methods based on word scoring each word receives a score and the weight of each sentence is the sum of all scores of its constituent words. Sentence-based Scoring analyzes the features of the sentence and its relation to the text. Cue-phrases (such as "it is important", "in summary", etc.), resemblance to the title, and sentence position are examples of sentence-based scoring techniques. Finally, in graph-based methods, the score of a sentence reflects some relationship among sentences. When a word or sentence refers to another one, an edge is generated with a weight between them. The sum of the weights of a sentence is its score. This article analyzes 15 sentence scoring methods, and some variation of them, widely used and referenced in the literature applied to document summarization in the last 10 years. The scoring methods comprise the feature vector that will be used to train the classifier and to rank sentences, totaling 20 features. The key point in this paper is to use Machine Learning techniques to analyze such features in a way to point out which of them better contribute to yield good quality summaries.

Quantitative and qualitative strategies are used here as ways of assessing the quality of summaries. The quantitative assessment was performed using ROUGE (Recall-Oriented Understudy for Gisting Evaluation) [9], a measure widely accepted for such a purpose. In addition, another quantitative analysis was performed by three people who analyzed each original text and generated summaries following a methodology that is better described below. The qualitative assessment is made by counting the number of sentences selected by the system that coincides with the sentences selected by all the three human users. The results obtained shows the effectiveness of the proposed method. It selects two times more relevant sentences to compose the summary. Moreover, it achieves results 71% better in evaluation using ROUGE 2 metric.

2. THE CNN CORPUS

The CNN corpus developed by Lins and his colleagues [9] consists of news texts extracted from the CNN website (www.cnn.com). The main advantage of this test corpus rests not only on the high quality of the writing using grammatically correct standard English to report on general interest subjects, but each of the texts of the news article is provided with its highlights, which consists of a 3 to 5 sentences long summary written by the original author(s). The highlights were the basis for the development the gold standard, which was obtained by the injective mapping of each of the sentences in the highlights onto the original sentences of the text. Such mapping process was performed by three different people. The gold standard was formed with most voted mapped sentences chosen. A very high degree of consistency in sentence selection was observed. The CNN-corpus is possibly the largest existing corpus for benchmarking extractive summarization techniques. The current version has 400 documents, written in the English language, totaling 13,228 sentences, of which 1,471 were selected for the gold standards, representing an average compression rate of 90%.

3. THE SYSTEM

The steps for creating the methodology for obtaining the extractive summaries are presented in the following sections.

3.1 Text pre-processing

The news articles obtained from the CNN website must be carefully chosen in order to contain only text, thus news articles with figures, videos, tables and other multi-media elements are discarded. Besides that, the article must be "complete" with the text, highlights, title, author(s), subject area, etc. All such data is inserted in a XML file. The text part of the document in then processed for paragraph segmentation, sentence segmentation, stop word re-

moval and stemming. Each text paragraph is numbered, as well as each of their sentences. Then, sentence segmentation is performed by Stanford CoreNLP[1]. Stop words [5] are removed since they are considered unimportant and can indicate noise. Stop Words are predefined and stored in an array that is used for comparison with the words in the document. Word Stemming [13] converts each word in its root form, removing its prefix and suffix of the specified word is performed. After this stage the text is structured in XML and included in the XML file that corresponds to the news article. As the focus here is in the text part of the document for summarization all other XML-file attributes will no longer be addressed in this paper.

3.2 Feature Extraction

The XML document after preprocessing is represented by the set $D = \{S_1, S_2, ..., S_i\}$, where S_i is a sentence in the document D. The preprocessed sentences are subjected to the feature extraction process so that a feature vector is generated for each sentence, $V_i = \{F_1, F_2, ..., F_i\}$, where V_i is the feature vector of each sentence S_i. As already mentioned extractive summarization use three scoring strategies [4]: (i) *Word*: it assigns scores to the most important words; (ii) *Sentence*: it accounts for features of sentences, such as its position in the document, similarity to the title, etc; (iii) *Graphic*: it uses the relationship between words and sentences.

Table 1 shows the features analyzed in this work and their kind of scoring. They correspond to the most widely acknowledged techniques for extractive summarization reported in the literature.

Table 1: *Number of summaries sentences into gold standard.*

Feature	Name of Extractive Summarization Strategy	Type of Scoring
F01	Aggregate Similarity	Graph
F02	Bushy Path	Graph
F03	Centrality	Sentence
F04	Heterogeneous Graph	Graph
F05	Text Rank	Graph
F06	Cue-Phrase	Sentence
F07	Numerical Data	Sentence
F08	Position Paragraph	Sentence
F09	Position Text	Sentence
F10	Resemblance Title	Sentence
F11	Sentence Length	Sentence
F12	Sentence Position in Paragraph	Sentence
F13	Sentence Position in Text	Sentence
F14	Proper-Noun	Word
F15	Co-Occurrence Bleu	Word
F16	Lexical Similarity	Word
F17	Co-Occurrence N-gram	Word
F18	TF/IDF	Word
F19	Upper Case	Word
F20	Word Frequency	Word

---

[1]http://nlp.stanford.edu/software/corenlp.shtml

3.3 Classification model

The steps for creating the classification model used to select the sentences that will compose the summary are detailed here.

The first step has the purpose of reducing the problems inherent to feature extraction of each sentence. First, the feature vectors that have missing information and outliers (when all features reach the maximum value) are eliminated. Another problem addressed here is basis unbalance, whenever there is a large disparity in the number of data of the training classes, the problem known in the literature as a problem of class imbalance arises. Classification models that are optimized with respect to overall accuracy tend to create trivial models that almost always predict the majority class.

The algorithm chosen to address the problem of balancing was SMOTE [3]. The principle of the algorithm is to create artificial data based on spatial features between examples of the minority class. Specifically, for a subset (whole minority class), consider the k nearest neighbors for each instance belonging to k for some integer value. Depending on the amount of oversampling chosen k nearest neighbors are randomly chosen. Synthetic samples are generated as follows: Calculate the Euclidean distance between the vector of points (samples) in question and its nearest neighbor. Multiply this distance by a random number between zero and one and add the vector points into consideration. This causes the selection of a point along a line between the two points selected. This approach effectively makes the region the minority class becomes harder to become more general [3].

Then, the system perform a feature selection, which is an important tool for reducing the dimensionality of the vectors, as some features contribute to decreasing the efficiency of the classifier. Another contribution of this study is to identify which of the 20 most used features in the last 10 years in the problems of extractive summarization contribute effectively to a good performance of classifiers. The experiment was conducted under the corpus of 400 news CNN-English.

The experiments were performed with selection algorithms of WEKA[2], three were chosen and applied on the balanced basis for defining the best attributes of the vector. Below, the methods of selection of attributes are listed: (i) **CFS Subset Evaluator**: Evaluates the worth of a subset of attributes by considering the individual predictive ability of each feature along with the degree of redundancy between them; (ii) **Information Gain Evaluator**: Evaluates the worth of an attribute by measuring the information gain with respect to the class; (iii) **SVM Attribute**: Evaluates the worth of an attribute by using an SVM classifier. The top five characteristics indicated by the selection methods were chosen. Figure 1 shows the profile of the selected features.

The selected features demonstrate the prevalence of language independent features such as the position of text, TF/IDF and similarity. This allows summarization texts in different languages.

Five classifiers were tested using the WEKA platform: Naive Bayes [8], MLP [7], SVM [7], KNN [1], Ada Boost [6], and Random Forest [2]. The results of the classifiers were compared with seven summarization systems: Open

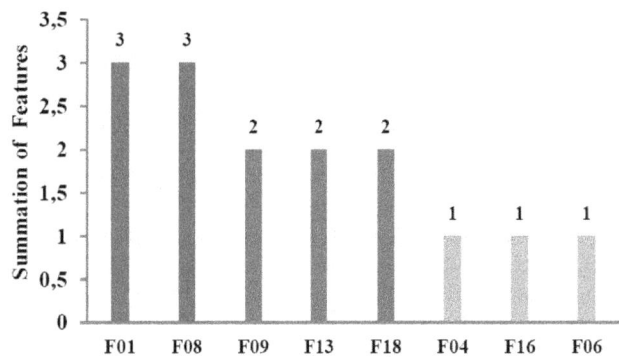

Figure 1: Selected Features

Text Summarizer (OTS), Text Compactor (TC), Free Summarizer (FS), Smmry (SUMM), Web Summarizer (WEB), Intellexer Summarizer (INT)[3], Compendium (COMP) [10].

Figure 2 presents the proposed summarization method, showing the number of correct sentences chosen from the human selected sentences that form the gold standard. This experiment used 400 texts from CNN news.

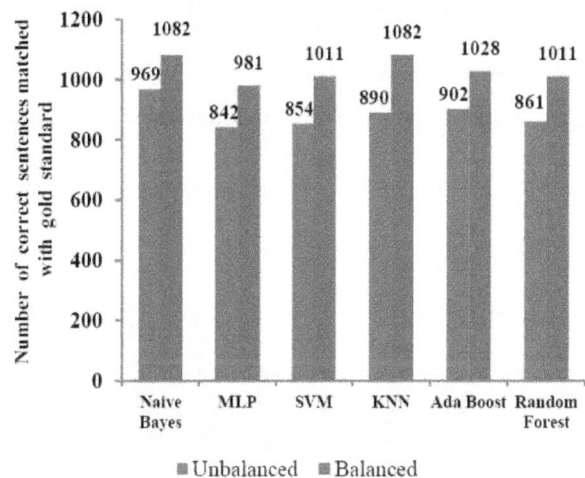

Figure 2: Evaluation of the classifiers for summarization

The classifiers were tested with variations of parameters with and without adjustment and balancing of the base. The technique chosen to validate the models was the Cross-Validation. The tests performed with the unbalanced basis yielded an accuracy of 52% and balanced with the base yielded 70% accuracy. The Naive Bayes classifier achieve the best result in all cases. In qualitative evaluation it reach 969 and 1082 correct sentences selected to the summary on unbalanced and balanced cases respectively. In the first case Naive Bayes outperforms in 7.42% the second place (Ada Boost) and it selects the same number of important sentences of KNN on balanced case.

---

[2]http://www.cs.waikato.ac.nz/ml/weka/

[3]libots.sourceforge.net, www.textcompactor.com, freesummarizer.com, smmry.com, www.websummarizer.com, summarizer.intellexer.com

Figure 3 and 4 presents the comparison of the Naive Bayes classifier results against the seven summarization systems. The superiority of the proposed method was proved on both evaluation. In the qualitative assessment the proposed method reach 1082 correct sentences selected, which means an improvement of more than 100% in relation to Text Compactor the best tool found in the literature. In number it obtained 554 more correct sentences. Using ROUGE the Naive Bayes Classifier achieve a result 61.3% better than Web Summarizer, the second place. The proposed method reach 71% of accuracy while WEB obtained 44%. These results confirms the hypothesis that using machine learning technics improves the text summarization results.

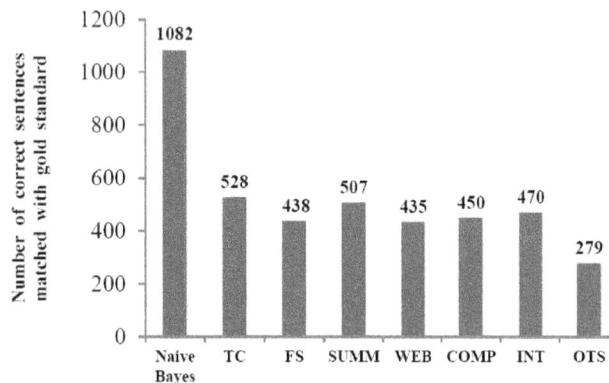

Figure 3: Evaluation of the summarization systems

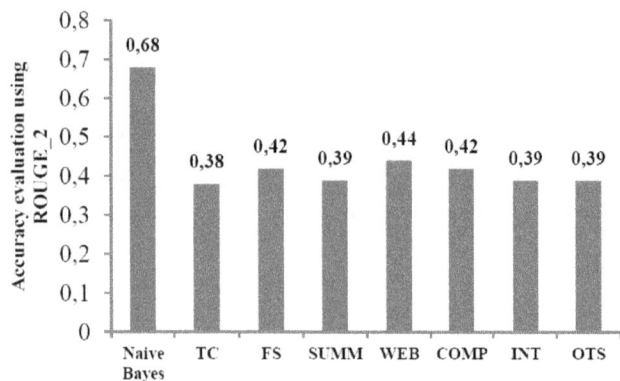

Figure 4: Precision of the Summarization Systems using ROUGE 2

4. CONCLUSIONS AND LINES FOR FURTHER WORKS

Automatic summarization opens a wide number of possibilities such as the efficient classification, retrieval and information based compression of text documents. This paper presents an assessment of the most widely used sentence scoring methods for text summarization. The results demonstrate that a criterions choice of the set of automatic sentence summarization methods provides better quality summaries and also greater processing efficiency. The proposed system selects 554 more relevant sentences to the summaries,

which means an improvement of more than 100%, in relation to the best tool found in literature. It was also evident that the balancing judgment on the basis of examples yields gains in the performance of the sentence selection system. The next step is the validation of the experiments in other summarization test corpora for texts other than news articles. Although the CNN-corpus may possibly be the largest and best test corpus for assessing news articles today, the authors of this paper are promoting an effort to double its size in the near future, allowing even better testing capabilities.

5. ACKNOWLEDGMENTS

The research results reported in this paper have been partly funded by a R&D project between Hewlett-Packard do Brazil and UFPE originated from tax exemption (IPI - Law number 8.248, of 1991 and later updates).

6. REFERENCES

[1] D. W. Aha, D. Kibler, and M. K. Albert. Instance-based learning algorithms. *Mach. Learn.*, 6(1):37–66, Jan. 1991.

[2] L. Breiman. Random forests. *Mach. Learn.*, 45(1):5–32, Oct. 2001.

[3] N. V. Chawla, K. W. Bowyer, L. O. Hall, and W. P. Kegelmeyer. Smote: Synthetic minority over-sampling technique. *J. Artif. Int. Res.*, 16(1):321–357, June 2002.

[4] R. Ferreira, L. de Souza Cabral, R. D. Lins, G. P. e Silva, F. Freitas, G. D. Cavalcanti, R. Lima, S. J. Simske, and L. Favaro. Assessing sentence scoring techniques for extractive text summarization. *Expert Systems with Applications*, 40(14):5755 – 5764, 2013.

[5] W. B. Frakes and R. Baeza-Yates, editors. *Information Retrieval: Data Structures and Algorithms*. Prentice-Hall, Inc., Upper Saddle River, NJ, USA, 1992.

[6] Y. Freund and R. E. Schapire. Experiments with a new boosting algorithm. In *International Conference on Machine Learning*, pages 148–156, 1996.

[7] S. Haykin. *Neural Networks: A Comprehensive Foundation*. Prentice Hall PTR, Upper Saddle River, NJ, USA, 2nd edition, 1998.

[8] G. H. John and P. Langley. Estimating continuous distributions in bayesian classifiers. In *Proceedings of the Eleventh Conference on Uncertainty in Artificial Intelligence*, UAI'95, pages 338–345, San Francisco, CA, USA, 1995. Morgan Kaufmann Publishers Inc.

[9] C.-Y. Lin. Rouge: A package for automatic evaluation of summaries. In M.-F. Moens and S. Szpakowicz, editors, *Text Summarization Branches Out: Proceedings of the ACL-04 Workshop*, pages 74–81, Barcelona, Spain, July 2004. Association for Computational Linguistics.

[10] E. Lloret and M. Palomar. Compendium: a text summarisation tool for generating summaries of multiple purposes, domains, and genres. *Natural Language Engineering*, FirstView:1–40, 2012.

[11] E. Lloret and M. Palomar. Text summarisation in progress: a literature review. *Artif. Intell. Rev.*, 37(1):1–41, Jan. 2012.

[12] A. Patel, T. Siddiqui, and U. S. Tiwary. A language independent approach to multilingual text summarization. In *Large Scale Semantic Access to Content (Text, Image, Video, and Sound)*, RIAO '07, pages 123–132, Paris, France, France, 2007. LE CENTRE DE HAUTES ETUDES INTERNATIONALES D'INFORMATIQUE DOCUMENTAIRE.

[13] C. Silva and B. Ribeiro. The importance of stop word removal on recall values in text categorization. In *IJCNN 2003*, volume 3, n/a, 2003.

Searching Live Meeting Documents
"Show me the Action"

Laurent Denoue
FX Palo Alto Laboratory
3174 Porter Drive
Palo Alto, CA 94304

denoue@fxpal.com

Scott Carter
FX Palo Alto Laboratory
3174 Porter Drive
Palo Alto, CA 94304

carter@fxpal.com

Matthew Cooper
FX Palo Alto Laboratory
3174 Porter Drive
Palo Alto, CA 94304

cooper@fxpal.com

ABSTRACT
Live meeting documents require different techniques for effectively retrieving important pieces of information. During live meetings, people share web sites, edit presentation slides, and share code editors. A simple approach is to index with Optical Character Recognition (OCR) the video frames, or key-frames, being shared and let user retrieve them. Here we show that a more useful approach is to look at what actions users take inside the live document streams. Based on observations of real meetings, we focus on two important signals: text editing and mouse cursor motion. We describe the detection of text and cursor motion, their implementation in our WebRTC (Web Real-Time Communication)-based system, and how users are better able to search live documents during a meeting based on these extracted actions.

Categories and Subject Descriptors
H.3.1 [**Content Analysis and Indexing**]: *Indexing methods.* H.4.3 [**Communications Applications**]: *Computer conferencing, teleconferencing, and videoconferencing.* I.7.5 [**Document Capture**]: *Document analysis, Optical Character Recognition.*

General Terms
Algorithms, Experimentation, Human Factors.

Keywords
Live document search; indexing; real-time search; OCR; screen-sharing; video conferencing.

1. INTRODUCTION
WebRTC browser-based systems are powering a new revolution in video conferencing, and one important aspect concerns screen sharing during these online meetings. Oftentimes, people need to show other peers a deck of slides, web site designs, or discuss implementation details in a code editor.

Screen-sharing videos, either live or recorded, can be considered a new kind of document, respectively "live video documents" or

"video documents". As with other types of documents, users might want to retrieve them, either during a meeting or after it has been recorded. By their nature, these video documents often contain text, and one natural way to retrieve them is by implementing keyword search.

However, the sheer amount of data (potential 30 new "pages" every second) does not make retrieval very manageable, both from the system's or the user's point of view. Fortunately, after observing our own use of video conferencing as well as analyzing one hour of screen sharing between members of another distributed team, we noticed that user's actions inside these documents can provide us with three useful signals, namely mouse cursor motion, text selection and editing. In this paper, we describe how to automatically extract these actions on live video documents, and how we use them to improve retrieval and presentation of search results. Figure 1 shows an example analysis of a 15 seconds video document where a user was discussing a slide; here the user circled around 2 main areas ("documents" and "demonstration"), and selected 2 words in the slide ("live" and "FXPAL").

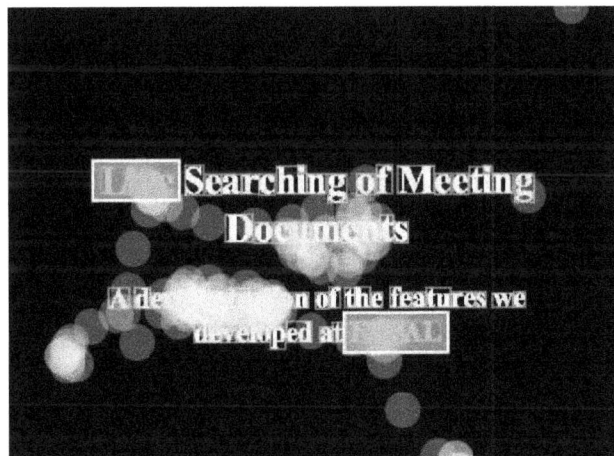

Figure 1. Detecting user actions on live meeting documents: yellow circles indicate detected mouse motion; white bordered rectangles show detected text selections

2. RELATED WORK
The idea of using users' actions to improve document skimming and retrieval was pioneered by [4]. Videos indexing also uses motion found in videos in order to segment them, allowing users to more easily visualize clips and retrieve objects (e.g. show me

videos containing a cat). They focus on videos such as TV footage or casual user-generated videos (e.g. TREC competitions). To our knowledge, no previous work has specifically looked at extracting motion from screen sharing sessions and how to use it for better retrieval and presentation.

On web pages, mouse and keyboard tracking is used to monitor user's actions in order to design better web sites, detect when a search query was useful or not [7], or infer the emotional state of the user [8]. They have not been used to better index the pages being interacted with, and they can readily access mouse and keyboard events by injecting Javascript code inside web pages.

As opposed to instrumenting web pages with Javascript, detecting text and mouse actions in video documents is more challenging. In the next section, we first describe a typical scenario, and then present methods to automatically extract text and mouse actions, how they are used during indexing and presentation.

3. SCENARIO

During a hypothetical meeting, users need to edit a presentation. The keyword "live" appears on many slides. Without looking at what users do during the session, retrieval would produce many slides containing the keyword "live". Traditional document retrieval deals with this problem using the term frequency and inverse term frequency (TF/IDF). But in our meeting case, many key-frames contain "live", resulting in a very low discrimination between all the key-frames, leading to a poor results page.

Instead, if we extract user's actions from the video, one slide clearly stands out because the user was circling her mouse cursor around it. At another time in the meeting, another user was actually editing the keyword "live". With this extra information, a search engine would be able to retrieve these 2 key-frames.

Besides being used to better identify important segments in video documents, these signals can also be used to present the results to users. For example, Figure 1 shows a key-frame with mouse and text selections, giving users a fast overview of what happened when this slide was shared during the meeting. Alternatively, the recovered mouse motion could be animated over the key-frame so as to replicate what happened during the meeting without having to store the actual video sequence.

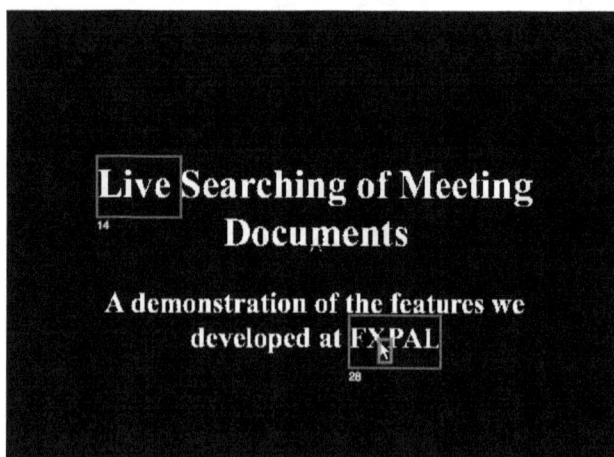

Figure 2. Text selections are shown in green rectangles along with the number of frames when motion rectangles have overlaid more than 3 bounding boxes of characters recognized by the OCR (here 14 and 28 times).

4. IMAGE PROCESSING

The system is implemented using WebRTC to connect participants. When a person shares her screen, the system receives a stream that is rendered by a VIDEO object in HTML5. The VIDEO is drawn periodically into a CANVAS object to process its pixel data. (See [2] for more implementation details)

4.1 Detecting Text Selections

In order to detect mouse cursor motion, a frame rate above 10 frames per second (FPS) is desirable. Below 3 FPS, the methods described below are able to detect text selections but fail to detect mouse motion.

To obtain a good text from the OCR, incoming frames are binarized and the bounding boxes of their connected components are used to form lines. Each line is scaled up to 20 pixels because the OCR engine we use requires text heights of at least 20 pixels.

The method for detecting mouse or text selection is to compute the frame difference between two consecutive frames.

Unlike previous work for indexing lecture videos and slides ([5] and [9], the content of screen-sharing sessions is very dynamic. A simple frame difference with too high a threshold would miss potentially important mouse motion and text edits, such as adding the word 'ok' in a text editor, or highlighting a word on a slide deck.

After experimenting on several video recordings, we found 32 to be a good threshold when computing the binary frame difference of two consecutive gray scale images with pixel values ranging from 0 to 255. We also extract their connected components, to be used to detect motion, in less than 25 milliseconds.

When the user double clicks on a word, the frame difference yields a strong rectangular area. If this area overlaps a word, the system detects a text selection; it also keeps track of the number of times this word was selected, which is used later for retrieval. Figure 2 shows the 2 detected text selections, along with the number of times a selection was detected. (14 and 28 times in this video clip)

4.2 Detecting Mouse Motion

As opposed to text selections, when the user moves her mouse cursor, the old and new positions are clearly seen by the bounding boxes of the connected components, see Figure 3.

Figure 3. Mouse motion is detected by connected components of the difference between 2 frames; it is typical to see the old (blue) and new (red) cursor positions

The new mouse position is selected as the box that is most different from the previously selected mouse position. This algorithm is accurate enough to let the system know what characters have been touched or circled by the mouse cursor, see Figure 4.

Observations of actual screen-sharing sessions revealed that users often move their cursor back and forth over an area to underline a word in a document, or in small circles around a word or paragraph to "highlight" them.

To account for these observations, areas of change are ranked higher if they have a longer time span and cover a shorter area. This measure ranks low when a user moves the cursor quickly to reach a menu across the screen, but high when she moves the cursor around a word in a document during a few seconds.

Unlike the cursor of the person sharing her screen, cursors of the other participants are simply recorded in the browser window through Javascript as they move over the shared view.

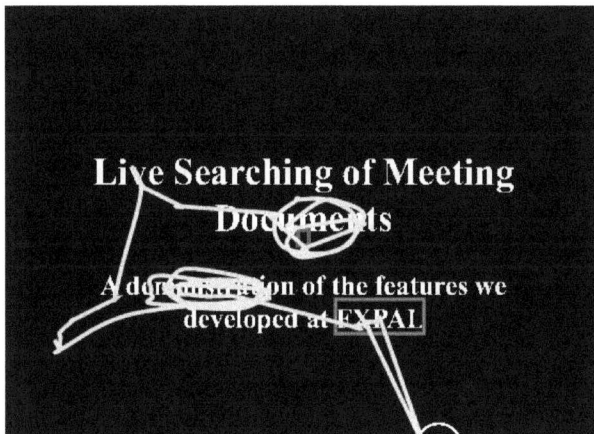

Figure 4. The rendering shows detected mouse motion, interpolated for smooth rendering between 3 points. They show the two areas where the user circled over the words "Documents" and "demonstration"

4.3 Markups

In addition to implementing shared cursors, every participant in our meeting system can markup shared screen content using an "ink" tool. When the user draws over a text area (detected again using the bounding boxes of connected components), the tool draws a straight highlight that follows the text line. Otherwise a freeform ink mark is drawn. Like the mouse and text selections detected from the video stream, these marks are also incorporated into the indexing step described below: they give further evidence that something of interest has happened over this content.

5. INDEXING AND RETRIEVAL

Many strategies could be devised to incorporate the additional signals gathered by the text and mouse detectors. For now, we are most interested in letting users search for previous frames while the meeting is taking place, not after. Our current strategy is to represent the matching frames by little dots in the main timeline, allowing users to get a quick overview of where results are located at previous times, letting them quickly jump to a particular matching key-frame by positioning the timeline at these locations.

5.1 Indexing

OCR text results are added to a normal index of words, including where on the screen they appeared. We normalize their locations by dividing the frames into 32x32 cells, and proceed similarly to normalize the locations of detected text and mouse actions. Each word thus belongs to one or more cells. Along with OCR text data, we also store the text and mouse detector results into cells, where the value of the cell indicates how much text selection or mouse motion happened. It enables users to filter search results more precisely, for example to retrieve only frames where a particular keyword was being selected as opposed to being circled over. Mouse events from remote participants are also incorporated at this stage. Figure 5 illustrates how the word weights are computed according to the amount of text and mouse actions.

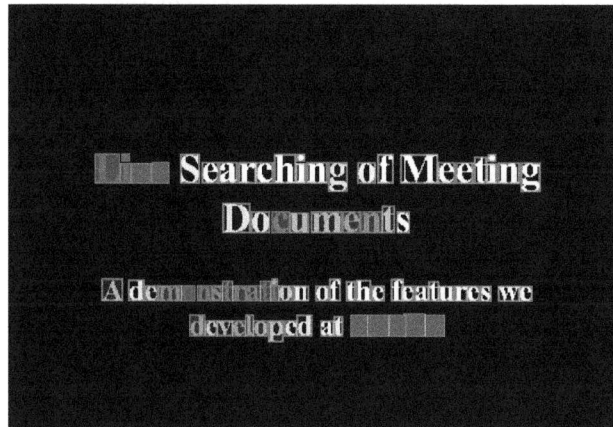

Figure 5. After analysis, the content boxes from the video document receive weights based on detected user actions; here the two text selections that happened during the meeting are clearly seen as dark blue, compared to lighter tint for mouse motion.

5.2 Retrieval and filters

When the user searches for a keyword, frames that contain this keyword are retrieved. An importance is calculated by adding the amount of action linked to the matching keywords. Obviously, the result set is filtered by user preferences (e.g. "show only text selections").

6. USER INTERFACE

Since the main focus in this work is to support search during an ongoing meeting, we chose to use the timeline as the main interface to show results matching the user's query. The timeline shows matching times with white bars, as shown in Figure 6 bottom.

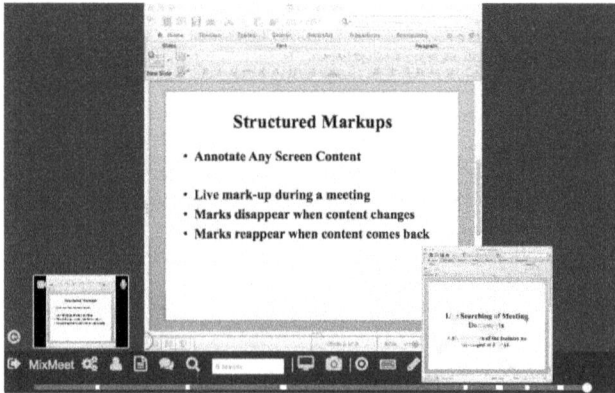

Figure 6. The user searched for "live"; the timeline shows white marks indicating matching frames; the user skims the timeline and sees the matching key-frame (bottom right of screenshot) enhanced with mouse actions

When the user hovers her mouse over the timeline, the system shows a thumbnail of that key-frame, similar to what other video players do. Unlike previous tools, an enhanced key-frame is generated by overlaying text and mouse actions, giving users a better sense of what happened during that time. This visualization was inspired by previous work on enhanced thumbnails for bookmark retrieval [10], where the authors overlaid keywords over web thumbnails and showed an improved retrieval time. Similarly, emphasizing the motion provides users with a quick way to determine if this segment in the meeting is indeed the one they want to review, or if they should keep skimming the timeline for more relevant hits.

7. CONCLUSIONS AND FUTURE WORK

We described how using content analysis helps better retrieve meeting content from screen-sharing sessions. These video documents contain a lot of redundant text; content analysis focused on text and mouse motion detection helps retrieval by identifying the points in time when the keywords were selected or acted on by meeting participants. We also described how to use this motion data to enhance the presentation of matching key-frames.

Future work will include testing the retrieval efficiency against a traditional text retrieval benchmark as well as evaluate the usefulness of these enhanced key-frames. In particular, they might become more useful during post-meeting retrieval tasks: users could be shown animated key-frames instead of statically tinted key-frames in place of static search snippets.

Because content is analyzed in real-time, other interesting services could be added such as on-demand translation for keywords, text selection for copy and paste, and increased awareness of remote participants' cursors by artificially emphasizing their appearance through color, size and ghost trailing.

Speech is yet another important signal we could use for retrieval; some browser vendors such as Google Chrome offer live speech to text for web applications through the Web Speech API; while the quality is not yet good enough for live transcripts, the text will provide enough words for retrieval purposes, especially if combined with words recognized on screen by the OCR engine, as was shown in [1] and [3].

8. ACKNOWLEDGMENTS

We thank Lynn Wilcox and Dick Bulterman for supporting this research.

9. REFERENCES

[1] Cooper, M. (2013, March). Presentation video retrieval using automatically recovered slide and spoken text. In IS&T/SPIE Electronic Imaging (pp. 86670E-86670E). International Society for Optics and Photonics.

[2] Denoue, L., Carter, S., & Cooper, M. (2013, September). Content-based copy and paste from video documents. In Proceedings of the 2013 ACM symposium on Document engineering (pp. 215-218). ACM.

[3] Hauptmann, A. G., Jin, R., & Ng, T. D. (2003, January). Video retrieval using speech and image information. In Electronic Imaging 2003 (pp. 148-159). International Society for Optics and Photonics.

[4] Hill, W. C., Hollan, J. D., Wroblewski, D., & McCandless, T. (1992, June). Edit wear and read wear. In Proceedings of the SIGCHI conference on Human factors in computing systems (pp. 3-9). ACM.

[5] Yang, H., Siebert, M., Luhne, P., Sack, H., & Meinel, C. (2011, November). Lecture video indexing and analysis using video OCR technology. In Signal-Image Technology and Internet-Based Systems (SITIS), 2011 Seventh International Conference on (pp. 54-61). IEEE.

[6] Gutwin, C., Dyck, J., Burkitt, J. 2003. Using Cursor Prediction to Smooth Telepointer Jitter. In *Proceedings of the ACM Conference on Supporting Group Work*.

[7] Huang, J., White, R. W., & Dumais, S. (2011, May). No clicks, no problem: using cursor movements to understand and improve search. In *Proceedings of the SIGCHI Conference on Human Factors in Computing Systems* (pp. 1225-1234). ACM.

[8] Weinmann, M., Schneider, C., & Robra-Bissantz, S. (2011). MOUSEREC—Monitoring Online Users' Emotions by Recording and Evaluating Cursor Movements.

[9] Adcock, J., Cooper, M., Denoue, L., Pirsiavash, H., & Rowe, L. A. (2010, October). Talkminer: a lecture webcast search engine. In *Proceedings of the international conference on Multimedia* (pp. 241-250). ACM.

[10] Woodruff, A., Faulring, A., Rosenholtz, R., Morrsion, J., & Pirolli, P. (2001, March). Using thumbnails to search the Web. In *Proceedings of the SIGCHI conference on Human factors in computing systems* (pp. 198-205). ACM.

Multimedia Document Structure for Distributed Theatre

Jack Jansen
CWI: Centrum Wiskunde &
Informatica
Science park 123
1098 XG Amsterdam, the
Netherlands
+31 20 5924300

Jack.Jansen@cwi.nl

Michael Frantzis
Department of Computing

Goldsmiths

London SE14 6NW, United
Kingdom

m.frantzis@gold.ac.uk

Pablo Cesar
CWI: Centrum Wiskunde &
Informatica
Science park 123
1098 XG Amsterdam, the
Netherlands
+31 20 5924300

P.S.Cesar@cwi.nl

ABSTRACT

This paper explores the suitability of structured (and declarative) multimedia document formats for supporting a novel type of performing arts: distributed theatre. In distributed theatre, the actors are split between two (or more) locations, but together deliver a single performance mediated by the cameras, the internet, and projection technologies. Based on our efforts to make an actual distributed theatre production happen (the Tempest by Miracle Theatre), this paper reflects on our experience. Our findings are divided into two main areas: workflow and document structure. We conclude that novel types of video-mediated applications, like distributed theatre, require new manners of authoring documents. Moreover, specific extensions to existing document formats are needed in order to accommodate the new requirements imposed by such kind of applications.

Categories and Subject Descriptors

D.3.2 [**Language Classifications**]: Specialized application languages; H.4.3 [**Information System Applications**]: Communication Applications - Computer conferencing, teleconferencing, and videoconferencing; I.7.2 [**Document and Text Processing**] Document Preparation - Languages and systems.

General Terms

Design, Experimentation, Human Factors.

Keywords

Video conferencing, Remote audience, Theatre.

1.   INTRODUCTION

In this paper we investigate distributed theatre performances and the technical means to support them. The setting is a theatre play where actors and audience are in multiple locations, and audiovisual streams combined with prerecorded media are used to present a unified experience to the spectators, whether present in

one of the theaters or watching from home. When, where and how media and live streams are played back is an integral part of the performance. This should therefore be under control of the artistic director, and will be different for each location at various times during the performance. In addition, the performers in the different locations should be able to act together in a seamless way, as if they are co-located. The requirements can be viewed as combining distributed multimedia playback and telepresence.

Performance artists have creatively made use of physical and, more recently, digital illusionary tools: "there is nothing in cyberspace and the screened technologies of the virtual that has not been already performed on the stage. The theatre has always been virtual, a space of illusory immediacy." [4]. It is not our intention to survey all the various efforts from artists to exploit technology to enhance performances, since [1] and [5] already provide comprehensive overviews. Nevertheless, there are a number of recent pieces that showcase current directions and challenges. "Skype Duet" [10] is a distributed live performance between New York and Berlin. In "Graphic Ships" [6] musicians and a dancer are distributed across locations. Visuals are created based on the movements of the dancer, captured by motion sensing, and create a graphic score from which the live musicians improvise the musical accompaniment. The audience sees the live movement of the local dancer, the visualisation her movement creates and simultaneous projections of the multi-sited musicians themselves.

All these pieces connect two or more locations with the aim of creating a single performance, similar to our experimental performance. Figure 1 shows a scene from "the Tempest" by Shakespeare, performed by *Miracle Theatre*, as experienced from the two theaters, with Ariel (left) in conversation with Prospero (right). In each location there are multiple HD video cameras to capture the scene from different angles. Head-worn wireless microphones capture the audio from each actor. Multiple HD projection screens are embedded in the set to display video

Figure 1 - One scene from "the Tempest", as seen from the two theatres

Theatre 1   Theatre 2   Home Audience

Figure 2 - Schematic representation of locations, audiences and actors

streams from the remote theatre and prerecorded media. Obviously, audio and video need to have low latency and good synchronization to enable fluent interaction between actors [8]. One of the screens is semi-transparent, and this is used in combination with precise timing of prerecorded media and lighting to make "magic" things happen. In addition, the streams and prerecorded media are used to create a single stream for home viewers. Our solution hinges on the fact that the theatre performances we target are scripted: visual layouts and scene transitions and such can be designed before the actual live show.

Figure 2 gives a schematic representation of the setup, and shows that different camera angles and compositions can be used for the different locations. The choice of what to show where, and how to show it (such as the "giant talking head" seen in theatre 1) is a creative choice, made to fit the current scene artistically.

Our setup is intended to be relatively easy to deploy: off-the-shelf hardware, standard broadband internet connections and affordable in personnel cost. While we primarily address distributed theatre we believe the ideas are extensible into other areas where interactions are (somewhat) scripted, such as distributed lectures and classrooms. Our hypothesis is that we can use existing structured multimedia document formats to assist the creative process of designing the visual layouts as well as enabling a single person to manage all locations during the live performance.

2. PROBLEM STATEMENT

The problem statement can be summarized as "*Enabling a creative director to design scene and media changes for multiple locations, and coordinate these centrally during the performance*". The distributed nature of our setting means that the coordination becomes an enabling feature (in stead of merely a convenience, in a single-location setting). The problem statement leads to two sets of requirements: those motivated by the creative process and those from a purely technical media handling perspective.

It emerged that the scripting requirements, and associated model, for the former were distinctive from existing forms of media handling, in particular because of the needs of distributed theatre. Cinema production has the concept of a shooting script which can offer a useful starting point, even though it does not necessarily contain the information of how scenes will be shot and a strict timeline need not be adhered to (the order and content of a narrative can easily be changed before and after capture). In live television, the narrative of events is fixed and strictly governed by the real time constraints of the live action. The distributed theatre model is in some ways closer to videoconferencing, but distinct from it in the fact that the representation can benefit from the

larger number of cameras and shots available in television production but it still follows the format of a script, a script that forms an inherent part of the creative theatrical artifact. Our solution will have to provide a good balance between things that can be designed in advance and decisions that should be taken live at showtime.

There is also a technical issue that our solution needs to address. Synchronization and timing need to be handled locally for each location, so that we can maintain lip-sync and correctly time playback of prerecorded media and transitions that need to be synchronized with activity on the stage, or lighting changes and such. However, control on a higher level, the representation script, needs to be centralized. The *representation script* and its associated centralized control interface, *Sync Control*, and the corresponding *Sync Editor*, are not discussed in this paper due to lack of space. The video communication platform, and its innovations, developed to address the challenge of supporting complex use cases for multimedia communication between ad hoc groups is described elsewhere [13].

3. DOCUMENT STRUCTURE

Let us examine how we used structured multimedia documents to enable the requirements set out in the previous section. Reactive declarative multimedia documents have been studied extensively within the document engineering community, for various use cases [9, 12]. Our solution is designed around 3 concepts which are visualized in figure 4: *layouts*, *regions* and *streams*. A layout determines what is seen in one location at a certain point in the play, which can range from a single fullscreen live video region to a complex composition of multiple live regions, prerecorded media (audio, video, image, text) with precise cropping, positioning and begin and end timing, transitions between those, etc. Layouts have symbolic names and layouts with the same name are tailored to each playback location. The home video feed from figure 4 shows an example layout showing two cropped video feeds and a static logo image.

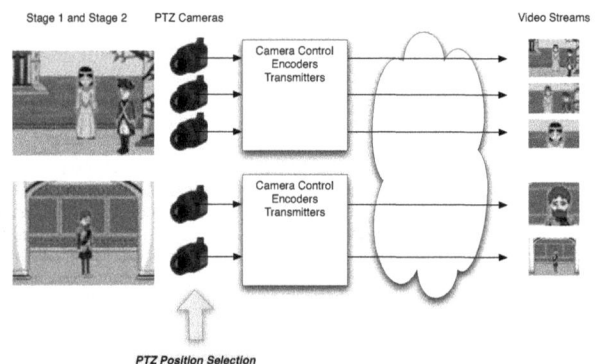

Figure 3 - Video capture

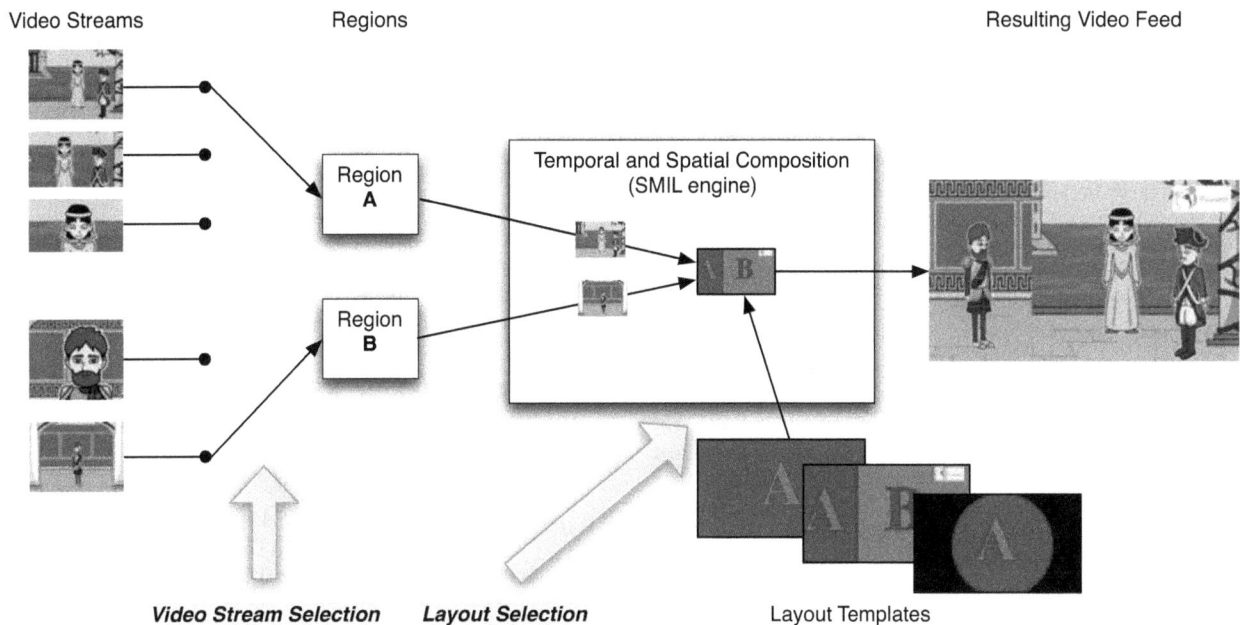

Figure 4 - Video composition (shown for the home audience feed)

Within a layout we can reference regions, which are live stream placeholders and again symbolically named. Regions are long-lived and survive layout switches, so that live streams can continue playing seamlessly during a layout switch. Regions that are not currently visible are on "stand by" so they can start rendering instantaneously when called up during a layout switch or a visual transition within a layout.

Assignment of live video streams to regions is a separate concept from switching layouts, to forestall an explosion of the number of layouts. Also, hard cuts from one camera to another are the most common visual changes. A final concept, *PTZ position*, is used on the video capture side (figure 3). These are per-camera symbolic names such as "*Prospero extreme closeup*" or "*total wide*" and can be called up at will during show time, ideally when the feed from the given camera is not active.

We have implemented streams and regions in a SMIL [3] boilerplate document, and layouts as fragments of SMIL code. These are combined into a single SMIL document per location before document playback.

4. WORKFLOW

The extended document structure, as laid out in Section 3. can support the representation requirements. Nevertheless, there are also a set of requirements for enabling the creation of the documents. Supporting these requirements is extremely important, given that the representation script is an intrinsic part of the theatrical experience. In our specific use cases, creating the multimedia documents is primarily the task of the creative director, who knows what should be shown, and when, and where. There are also technical issues involved, however, such as understanding limitations such bandwidth budgets and the fact that SMIL code needs to be written manually at the moment. This is the domain of the technical director, who closely cooperates with the creative director.

The creative director, while building the representation script, describes the required layouts and PTZ positions to the technical director, who creates the SMIL fragments. These fragments are

then assembled into preview documents, one for each location. These preview documents can be played back with an ordinary SMIL player, and contain all prerecorded media and transitions, but use placeholder videos for the live streams. This allows the creative director to check that the composition and transitions work artistically (and that the technical director has understood his intentions correctly).

During on-location dress rehearsal cameras and screens are placed, and the actual PTZ parameters for each shot are determined and recorded. The layouts are fine-tuned, primarily positioning and sizing of items to cater for the physical location of projection screens and such. At this point the final per-location SMIL documents are created. During show time the creative director (or an operator under his instructions) uses the sync control tool to simply step through the layout and camera switches at the right time, for all locations at once. If the need arises special layouts (opening and closing screens and such) can be called up at the press of a single button.

The workflow is similar to theatre lighting: design and fine-tuning happen before the show, and during the performance these prerecorded settings care called up with the press of a button.

5. IMPLEMENTATION

Our implementation consists of a capture and playback engine in each theatre, a playback engine for the home feeds and a single centralized component for sync control (in addition to centralized components for audio and video routing and such [13]).

At show time, the per-location SMIL documents are played back by engines based on the Ambulant [2] SMIL player, with a control module that allows the SMIL code to be modified in a controlled manner using ActiveMQ messages from the central Sync Control component. The playback engines for the theaters also incorporates additional modules to control PTZ cameras and grab/encode/transmit video. The playback engine that creates the feed for the home viewers has modules to do all rendering offscreen and encode and transmit the rendered video stream.

The documents for all locations are structurally the same but different in details, such as which regions are active in which layout and placement of media. Sync Control is isolated from these differences because it communicates with the engines only using symbolic names for streams, regions, layouts and shots. Hereby Sync Control is solely responsible for the global representation script, while the individual engines are responsible for timing, synchronization and layout. The yellow arrows in figures 3 and 4 show how Sync Control can influence the engines.

Changing a multimedia document during playback can have serious consequences for the timegraph and lead to temporal inconsistencies, as we have investigated in earlier work [7]. The scripted nature of a distributed performance has allowed us to use a solution that is similar to the distributed gaming use case from that paper: the multimedia document itself is static and all dynamic changes are implemented through modification of SMIL State variables. *Streams* are implemented through SMIL `<video>` elements that are active throughout the performance, but their rendering position, size and z-order are modified as they are assigned to a region and set to size (0, 0) when not assigned to a *region*. *Layouts* are SMIL `<par>` nodes with a begin condition depending on a SMIL variable which is set to activate the layout. They contain all the prerecorded media playback and transitions and such, and also update the region positions (and therefore the live stream rendering positions). This method of changing stream assignments and layouts ensures temporal integrity of the presentation.

6. DISCUSSION

From a creative and artistic perspective the solution as implemented was capable of expressing all the requirements and intentions of the director and crew of the theatrical performance. There were no instances of limitations in the amount of expression offered by SMIL and our associated implementation. The orthogonality of streams and layouts enabled seamless continuation of live streams during layout switches.

The original workflow was based on the principle that the creative director would mark up the representation script which would then become the narrative or theatrical source for media control. However, during the course of the rehearsal it became clear that the capacity to preview and edit on the fly was crucial to a successful production. This brings with it the requirements for flexibility in the document structure to support this process. A limitation of the method of using SMIL fragments was that changing something on the fly required "restarting the world". Note that fixing this would not necessarily be at odds with [7] as the changes required in the documents on the fly would primarily be about details in timing and layout.

In addition, there was the difficulty in allowing technically inexperienced users to define new layout types and shot positions without the need to communicate with the technical director. A possible direction of future work could be developing a templating system (for example such as [11]) and/or interface which would offer a generic model which could be then be easily adapted for different productions, and involve built in compatibility with preview tools as well as script editing tools.

From the perspective of workload the workflow (and the document structure to support it) performed fine. There were some issues with fine-tuning layout requiring someone to go from one location to the other to see things with their own eyes, but during show time the representation script execution was handled smoothly by a single person.

7. ACKNOWLEDGEMENTS
Part of this work has been done in the Vconect project, funded by the European Community's Seventh Framework Programme (FP7/2007-2013) under grant agreement no. ICT-2011-287760. We would like to thank our Vconect partners, especially Doug Williams and Rene Kaiser and Miracle Theatre, especially Bill Scott for enabling us to do this work.

8. REFERENCES

[1] J. Birringer. 2008. Thinking Images: Paul Kaiser and Marc Downie in conversation with Johannes Birringer. In *PAJ: A Journal of Performance and Art* (30) 2, 2008, 17-37.

[2] Bulterman D.C.A., et al. 2004. AMBULANT: A Fast, Multi-Platform Open Source SMIL Player. In *Proceedings of ACM International Conference on Multimedia* (New York, USA, 2004).

[3] D. Bulterman and L. Rutledge. 2004. *SMIL 2.0: Interactive Multimedia for Web and Mobile Devices.* Springer-Verlag, Heidelberg, Germany, ISBN: 3-540-20234-X.

[4] M. Causey. 1999. The Screen Test of the Double: The Uncanny Performer in the Space of Technology. *Theatre Journal* (51) 4, 1999, 383-394. DOI=10.1353/tj.1999.0083.

[5] S. Dixon. 2007. *Digital Performance, a history of new media in theatre, dance, performance art, and installation.* Cambridge MA: MIT, 2007. ISBN: 978-0-262-04235-2.

[6] *Graphic Ships.* 2014. Retrieved 27-May-2015 from https://vimeo.com/83458633

[7] Jansen, J., Cesar, P. and Bulterman. D.C.A. 2010. A model for editing operations on active temporal multimedia documents. In *Proceedings of the 10th ACM symposium on Document engineering (DocEng '10).* ACM, New York, NY, USA, 87-96. DOI=10.1145/1860559.1860579.

[8] I. Kegel, et al. 2012. Enabling 'togetherness' in high-quality domestic video. In *Proceedings of the ACM international conference on Multimedia* (MM '12). ACM, New York, NY, USA, 159-168. DOI=10.1145/2393347.2393375

[9] P. King, et al. Behavioral reactivity and real time programming in XML: functional programming meets SMIL animation. In *Proc. ACM DOCENG'2004*, pages 57–66. ACM, 2004.

[10] Skype Duet. 2011. Retrieved 27-May-2015 from http://per-aspera.net/en/skype-duet

[11] Soares, L.F.G., et al. 2012. Architecture for hypermedia dynamic applications with content and behavior constraints. In *Proceedings of the 2012 ACM symposium on Document engineering (DocEng '12).* ACM, New York, NY, USA, 217-226. DOI=10.1145/2361354.2361403

[12] Viel, C.C. et al. Go beyond boundaries of iTV applications. In Proceedings of the 2013 *ACM symposium on Document engineering (DocEng '13).* ACM, New York, NY, USA, 263-272. DOI=10.1145/2494266.2494287

[13] D. Williams, et al. 2015. A Distributed Theatre Experiment with Shakespeare. In *Proceedings of the ACM international conference on Multimedia.*

Change Classification in Graphics-Intensive Digital Documents

Jeremy Svendsen and Alexandra Branzan Albu
University of Victoria
Victoria, Canada
jeremys@ece.uvic.ca, aalbu@uvic.ca

ABSTRACT

This paper proposes an approach for the automatic detection and classification of changes occurring in images of documents with identical content, but generated with different software versions, or under different operating platforms. Our work is performed on a database of digitally-born business documents created using financial reporting tools. The proposed method involves a multi-stage process, where the end goal is to present to a human user the reports which have changed and the changes which were detected. Our main contribution is related to matching and comparing of graphical document elements. This paper focuses on detection of local, translation-based changes. Future work will explore other local changes involving size, color, and rotation.

Keywords

Computer Vision, Document Image Analysis, Electronic Documents, Change Detection

1. INTRODUCTION

Professional digitally-born documents need to be rendered on screen in a consistent way. Ideally, the graphical rendering of identical content in digitally-born documents should be invariant with respect to different operating platforms and to updates of reporting software. In practice, changes in the appearance of documents occur quite frequently. Such changes may have a significant impact on the readability of a document, thus they need to be detected and corrected. The manual detection of such changes is a tedious, resource-consuming and error-prone process and therefore an automatic process is highly desirable. Moreover, it is useful to not only detect changes, but also to characterize and classify them in order to enable the human operator to make informed decisions about whether these changes are acceptable or not.

This paper proposes an approach for the automatic detection and classification of changes occurring in images of

DocEng'15, September 8–11, 2015, Lausanne, Switzerland.
© 2015 ACM. ISBN 978-1-4503-3307-8/15/09 ...$15.00.
DOI: http://dx.doi.org/10.1145/2682571.2797079.

documents with identical content, but generated with different software versions, or under different operating platforms. Our work is performed on a database of digitally-born business documents. Such documents were generated by a business intelligence reporting tool [1]. All documents in our database are graphics-intensive such that they primarily contain tables and charts (i.e. composite document elements), with no text in paragraph form. Therefore, commercial OCR packages are not helpful for identifying changes.

There is a significant amount of related work in document layout analysis, which aims at partitioning the image of a document page in classes such as text, charts, tables etc. Our approach goes a step further by identifying possible differences among the classified objects. If such differences exist, then they are classified and the result of this classification is presented to a human operator for further decision making processes.

The remainder of this paper is structured as follows. Section 2 overviews work related to our proposed approach. Section 3 describes our proposed approach, while section 4 presents experimental results. Conclusions and future work directions are described in section 5.

2. RELATED WORK

Our proposed method performs change detection and classification at the object level. All relevant objects in the images to be compared need to be segmented and classified. We thus survey methods related to document layout segmentation, and of detection of tables, charts, and duplicate documents.

Six popular layout segmentation algorithms are compared by Shafait et al. [8] based on how well they segment textual information. They differentiate between bottom-up and top-down algorithms. Bottom-up algorithms identify small document elements first, then they combine them into larger structures. Top-down methods start by finding large components and then they split them up into smaller parts.

Kboubi et al. [3] propose a fusion of several different commercial OCR software packages for an increased performance of table detection. Mandal et al. [6] detect tables using vertical and horizontal projection profiles. Their approach uses the fact that gaps between two adjacent rows and two adjacent columns appear as zeros in the vertical and horizontal projection profiles respectively.

Chart classification is performed using either machine learning or heuristic (rule-based) algorithms. Zhou and Tan [11, 12] classify charts into different categories using a Hidden Markov Model (HMM) and a neural network. The HMM is combined with a high-level analysis to isolate specific information about each chart class. In a more recent paper, Huang et al. [2] apply a modified version of the Diverse Density algorithm to improve on the HMM and neural network approaches. This new approach is less dependent on low-level features like foreground/background transition.

Chart recognition can also be performed by directly detecting all components of the chart. Liu et al. [4] create an edge map, then convert these edges into a series of lines and arcs using Directed Single-Connected Chains (DSCC).

An application area related to our research is the detection of duplicate documents. Lopresti [5] outlines how two text-intensive documents can be similar or different in terms of layout and textual content and detects duplicates using string matching. While string matching works well for comparing text blocks, it is not applicable to graphic elements which are predominant in business documents.

3. PROPOSED APPROACH

The proposed system is composed of four stages which are shown in figure 1. The first two stages are performed in parallel on the two images to be compared. Since most of the changes of interest are local and affect only certain elements of the image, the first stage segments the page into blocks (see 3.1), while the second stage classifies the segmented blocks (see 3.2). The third stage matches the classified elements and is presented in 3.3. The final stage compares the matched elements and is described in 3.4. If a change is detected, then information gathered during the classification and segmentation stages is used to classify the change (see 3.4). Our original contribution is mostly contained within stages three and four.

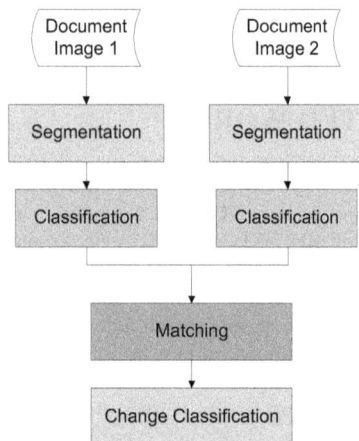

Figure 1: Overview of the proposed approach.

3.1 Segmentation

Our segmentation approach [9] is an extension of the Recursive XY-Cut algorithm by Nagy et al. [7]; in addition to splitting the block in the horizontal and vertical directions, we also oblique cuts. See our previous paper [9] for a complete description of the method. We use a top-down approach which exploits white space to first identify large blocks; these blocks are split recursively into smaller blocks.

In order to preserve the hierarchy, when a block is split, the newly created blocks are considered children of the original block. Cut directions are alternated in the recursive process, so that all connected document regions are properly isolated. Figure 2 shows a situation where multiple iterations are required to segment the image.

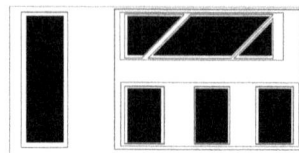

Figure 2: Colour-coded iterative outputs of the segmentation step by oblique cuts. The progression sequence is red, blue, green, brown.

3.2 Classification

The next step is to classify the segmented regions which we refer to as blocks. Every block on the page is classified, including larger ones which may contain children. Seven block classes are considered (solid region, text, table, chart, line, small block, and combined) and the default unknown class. A small block is a block which is not large enough to be classified as anything else. The combined class is attributed when a block contains two or more children which have different classes. For example, if a report contains both a table and a chart, the root block which represents the entire page will be classified as combined. If a block does not fit the pattern for any of the seven defined classes, it is classified as unknown.

Blocks are classified based on what primitives they contain as well as on their size, shape, and orientation. A primitive is defined as a simple visual component of the document image which cannot be broken up into smaller logical subcomponents. In our case, three primitives are used, namely lines, text, and solid regions. The lines and text are self-explanatory terms. A solid region is a connected region filled with a homogeneous color. An example of a solid region would be one bar belonging to a bar chart (see figure 6).

In order to recognize charts and tables, we identify and search for the distinctive patterns which characterize each class. The following subsections describe the detection processes for charts and tables.

3.2.1 Detection of Pie Charts

To detect pie charts, we use their characteristic elliptical shape. Figure 3 shows the flowchart for the proposed algorithm. We start by binarizing the block of interest because we are only interested in the shape of the graphics. Next, morphological closing with a 3x3 structuring element is performed in order to remove connecting lines and text. The Canny edge detector is applied to the closed image. These first three steps are illustrated in figure 4. In addition to computing the edge map, we also find the best fit for an ellipse over the original chart image using the least squares method. Figure 5 shows the best fit ellipse superimposed on the original chart image. The final step is to find the overlap between the found ellipse and the edge image. If the overlap exceeds a given threshold, then a pie chart is detected.

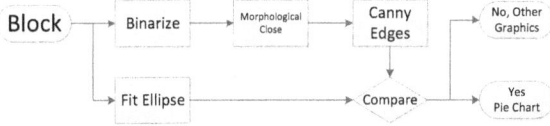

Figure 3: Flowchart for detecting pie charts.

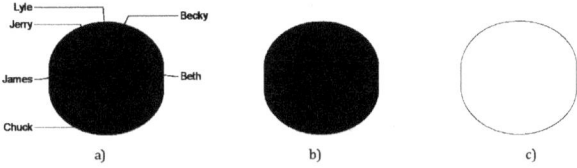

Figure 4: The steps used to find the edge map for the same chart seen in figure 5. a) Binarized version of the pie chart. b) Output of morphological closing. c) Edge map computed using the Canny algorithm on b).

3.2.2 Detection of Bar Charts

To detect bar charts, we search for their horizontal and vertical axis, which are detected using the vertical and horizontal projection profiles. Long straight lines appear as strong local maxima in the projection profile. Axis are detected when local maxima exceed a certain threshold in both the vertical and horizontal projection profiles, in a similar manner to Yokokura and Watanabe [10]. Figure 6 shows a bounding box around the axis detected by the proposed method.

3.2.3 Detection of Tables

Two types of tables are prevalent in business documents, and they are detected using distinct methods. Tables which contain a characteristic grid pattern and line separators are detected using a simple method that detects the gridlines. Tables without gridlines are detected with the method by Mandal et al. [6]. This method uses the horizontal and vertical projection profiles to recognize regions in which text is organized along columns and rows.

3.3 Matching

The output of the segmentation step is a collection of blocks structured in a tree-like hierarchy. The blocks to be matched belong to two different, already segmented images (*reference* and *comparison*), each corresponding to a

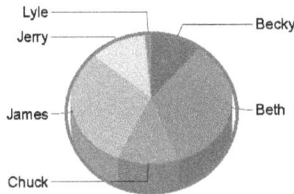

Figure 5: Example of ellipse fitted over a pie chart (best viewed in color)

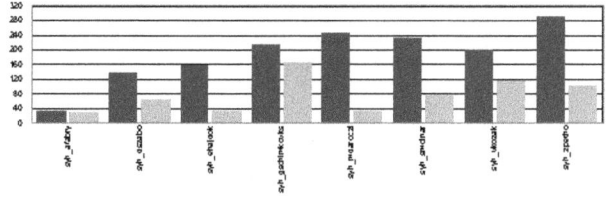

Figure 6: Example of axis detection; the red bounding box follows the horizontal and vertical axis. (best viewed in color)

given page in a document. The two images are supposed to be identical; however, in practice, small differences are often present, thus our goal is to identify and describe those differences on a block-by-block basis.

Each block has several fundamental properties; for matching purposes, we will consider three of them related to the block's size, location, and type (class).

A size-based comparison of the blocks is performed by equation 1, where $A(b_1)$ and $A(b_2)$ are the areas of the blocks b_1 and b_2. This measure is a modified version of the Jaccard index.

$$SR(b_1, b_2) = \frac{A(b_1) \cap A(b_2)}{\max(A(b_1), A(b_2))} \qquad (1)$$

Differences in the spatial location of the blocks are measured by equation 2. Considering the sets of edge pixels corresponding to each block, we define the block displacement BD as the minimum distance between two edge pixels located each in one set.

Any two blocks in partial overlap have a 0-valued block displacement and a perfect score of 1 for the location match score L. For non-overlapping blocks, the location match L uses a predefined constant C_1 (with a default value of 0.2) which controls how much the displacement penalizes the location match score L.

$$L(b_1, b_2) = \left(\frac{1}{1 + C_1(BD(b_1, b_2))} \right) \qquad (2)$$

If two blocks have the same size ($SR(b_1, b_2) = 1$), a pixel-by-pixel comparison is performed to determine if the blocks are perfectly identical. The pixel-by-pixel matching score $E(b_1, b_2)$ is binary, with a value of 1 if the two blocks are identical and 0 otherwise.

The class and sub-class matching scores ($BC(b_1, b_2)$ and $BSC(b_1, b_2)$) are also binary, with a value of 1 if the class or subclass is the same, and 0 otherwise. More information about block classes and subclasses is found in section 3.2.

There are many ways to combine the property-specific matching scores in order to define a global score for the quality of a match. We propose the global matching score defined by equation 3, where C_E, C_{BST}, and C_{BT} are constant parameters. Default values for C_E, C_{BST}, and C_{BT} are of 0.7, 0.2, and 0.1 respectively. The equation and its default parameters were chosen to yield a higher global matching score for two blocks which are pixelwise identical than for two blocks found in identical locations. Note that the default choice of parameters bounds the global matching score between 0 and 1. Here are two simple examples of extreme values for the matching score. A perfect matching score of 1

205

is measured for two blocks which are pixel-by-pixel identical and have the same location on the page. Two blocks with different classes and disjoint have a matching score of 0.

$$M = (C_E \cdot E + C_{BST} \cdot SR \cdot BSC + C_{BT} \cdot SR \cdot BC) \cdot L \quad (3)$$

Given two segmented images (*reference* and *comparison*), the matching process adopts a brute force approach. Every block in the *comparison* image is compared to all blocks in the *reference* image and matched with the block that yields the maximum matching score. *The algorithm stops looking for a match if a perfect matching score of 1 is computed.* A block is left unmatched if all its matching scores fall below 0.1.

3.4 Change detection and classification

A change is detected when two matched blocks are characterized by a matching score that is imperfect (less than 1) and have a matching threshold greater than 0.1. An unmatched block denotes the absence an entire block from the *comparison* image with respect to the *reference* image. This is a special type of change, which we do not discuss further since it occurs very rarely in our database. This paper focuses on detecting and characterizing the most frequent change, which is due to translatory motion. This change is detected by computing the displacement between the centroids of the two matched blocks.

Once all changes detected, the *comparison* documents can be classified according to the change that has occured with respect to their *reference* counterparts, and to the block class. For instance, all documents containing a chart translation may belong to the same class. This change-specific organization allows a user to inspect only documents containing a specific type of error, which is a significant advantage when the database of documents is very large.

4. RESULTS

Our dataset consists of 322 pairs of digitally-born document images (*reference* and *comparison*) created using financial reporting software by SAP [1].

To evaluate the algorithm, an important step is to create the ground truth for translation-based changes to all block types (text, lines, solid regions, and charts). The ground truth was created by visual inspection of the difference image computed using the *comparison and reference* image pairs.

Table 1 shows the results of the experimental evaluation process, in terms of true positives (TP), false positives (FP), false negatives (FN), precision (P) and recall (R).

Table 1: Experimental evaluation

Block Type	TP	FP	FN	P	R
Line	1552	63	1	0.96	1.00
Text	229	174	84	0.57	0.73
Chart	13	2	4	0.87	0.76
Solid Region	18	7	0	0.72	1

One may note that most errors occur in the detection the text blocks. This was due to a very common change, consisting of a shift of the underline under the text block. Our approach erroneously detected this change as a translation of the entire text block, when in fact only the underline shifted.

5. CONCLUSION AND FUTURE WORK

We present a method for comparing business documents which are similar, but contain minor changes which may affect their quality. Our method involves a multi-stage process where the end goal is to present to a human user the reports which have changed and the changes which were detected.

This paper reports on detection of translation-based changes. A straightforward extension is explore other changes involving size, color, and rotation of various types of blocks.

6. ACKNOWLEDGMENTS

The authors thank the SAP Vancouver Academic Research Center (ARC) for their support.

7. REFERENCES

[1] http://www.crystalreports.com/.
[2] W. Huang, S. Zong, and C. L. Tan. Chart image classification using multiple-instance learning. In *WACV '07.*, 2007.
[3] F. Kboubi, A. Chabi, and M. Ahmed. Table recognition evaluation and combination methods. In *DAR*, 2005.
[4] R. Liu, W. Huang, and C. L. Tan. Extraction of vectorized graphical information from scientific chart images. In *ICDAR 2007.*, 2007.
[5] D. P. Lopresti. Models and algorithms for duplicate document detection. In *ICDAR '99*, 1999.
[6] S. Mandal, S. Chowdhury, A. Das, and B. Chanda. A simple and effective table detection system from document images. *IJDAR*, 8, 2006.
[7] G. Nagy, S. Seth, and M. Viswanathan. A prototype document image analysis system for technical journals. *Computer*, 25(7), July 1992.
[8] F. Shafait, D. Keysers, and T. Breuel. Performance comparison of six algorithms for page segmentation. In *DAS VII*. 2006.
[9] J. Svendsen and A. Branzan-Albu. Document segmentation via oblique cuts. *Proc. SPIE*, 8658, 2013.
[10] N. Yokokura and T. Watanabe. Layout-based approach for extracting constructive elements of bar-charts. In *Graphics Recognition Algorithms and Systems*, volume 1389. 1998.
[11] Y. Zhou and C. L. Tan. Chart analysis and recognition in document images. In *DAR*, 2001.
[12] Y. Zhou and C. L. Tan. Learning-based scientific chart recognition. In *GREC*, 2001.

Fine Grained Access of Interactive Personal Health Records

Helen Balinsky
HP Laboratories
Bristol, UK
Helen.Balinsky@hp.com

Nassir Mohammad
HP Laboratories
Bristol, UK
NMohammad@hp.com

ABSTRACT

Electronic Personal Healthcare Records (PHRs) provide the means for individuals to hold, update and share their medical information in a digitally accessible form. However, the sensitive nature of healthcare information and the functional limitations of PHRs has resulted in their acceptance remaining relatively low. This is primarily due to fears of security and privacy in the current central authority based technologies on offer. In order to alleviate these concerns, whilst maintaining security, ease of access and distribution, we propose a PHR format that utilizes and extends a secure composite document format, Publicly Posted Composite Documents [1], originally designed for cross-organizational business workflows. The proposed PHR ensures data is always encrypted whilst traversing non-secure channels, with fine-grained access control built in to enable multiple people to have differential access to the same PHR. End-to-end encryption using Password Key Derivation Functions ensures no central authority is required to have access to plaintext data or decryption keys. This allows safe cooperation with Cloud Service Providers (CSPs) who act as the primary storage and vehicle by which PHRs can be shared. Our PHRs are designed to be partially downloaded and exported on request, and to gather PHR formatted data securely from an ecosystem of healthcare devices.

Categories and Subject Descriptors

I.7.m [**Computing Methodologies**]: Documents and Text Processing - *Miscellaneous*

General Terms

Management, Security and Performance.

Keywords

Publicly Posted Composite Documents; Security; Embedded Access Control; Workflows; Personal Healthcare Records

1. INTRODUCTION

The adoption of electronic Personal Healthcare Records (PHRs) is a natural progression from paper-based records and processes to increase efficiency, lower costs and embolden individuals with easily accessible health information. In an ever inter-connected world of devices and users the integrity and privacy of medical records is

DocEng '15, September 08-11, 2015, Lausanne, Switzerland
© 2015 ACM. ISBN 978-1-4503-3307-8/15/09...$15.00
DOI: http://dx.doi.org/10.1145/2682571.2797098

also of paramount importance. PHRs are needed to empower patients, and to provide them with the ability to check their records for any inconsistencies and medical errors regardless of location [2]. Furthermore, the guaranteed provision of fine grained and continuously changing patient information to different professionals, at different times and locations, while maintaining the high levels of security and privacy required by healthcare regulatory standards pose significant challenges. Despite special financial stimuli for increasing PHR usage, acceptance remains relatively low due to fears of security and privacy of non-medical cloud providers that are not subject to the same stringent laws and regulations as healthcare organizations. Such concerns are valid for personal information, since data leaks or system compromise, could result in substantial harm, embarrassment or cost to an individual.

2. PHR PRIOR ART

While some PHR services concentrate on selective diseases more comprehensive solutions exist that cater for the whole range of personal healthcare. Dossia [3] is an open source PHR service offered by some of the largest employers in the USA. It provides user access to health information regardless of health plan, employer or physician, whilst providing the ability to download full or partial records electronically. Microsoft HealthVault [4] is another popular PHR service, which enables multiple individuals to access, the same PHR (e.g. mother, father and son) and integrates access through popular consumer portals like Windows Live and Facebook. The application also allows individuals to share only a part or the whole PHR with other professionals such as a d octor, pharmacist or hospital administration. World Medical Card [5], and Apple's Health Kit and Health [6] also provide centralization of personal health information and records, with the latter integrating with the iOS app library to create solutions that dynamically utilize this information. Though the PHR services offer increased value to an individual, the current solutions have not dramatically increased their adoption [7]. The holding of clear text data by a provider does not sit well with users concerned about the security and privacy of their data and the potential unauthorized exposition, exploitation or mining for value extraction.

3. PROBLEM STATEMENT

A number of key issues must be addressed by a PHR system to satisfy accessibility, security and privacy concerns:

P1. The PHR needs to be a self-contained tamper proof digital bundle for integrating differently formatted data, e.g. a physician report, immunization status, radiology images, a prescription, or an insurance claim. An individual PHR must not be accidentally disintegrated and lost.

P2. A PHR needs to be persistent and accessible by its owner anytime and from anywhere, available for update by authorized healthcare/insurance providers, and for emergency access by A&E units.

P3. Sensitive healthcare information must always remain in the firm control of the PHR owner, without the need for a trusted third party. The major concern of patients sharing their healthcare information with IT providers is that the latter are not subject to the same stringent regulations as healthcare providers.

P4. Due to the consumer nature of PHRs and the associated usability and costs, we cannot rely on PHR owners using or maintaining access to PKI. Instead, suitable mechanisms for access need to be provided such as PIN/password/passphrase for PHR owners, whilst simultaneously providing PKI-based access to healthcare professionals and insurance providers.

P5. A PHR owner should be able to share only partial versions of his PHR with different professionals, e.g. prescriptions with pharmacists, payments with an insurance company, long-term medical history with diagnosticians.

P6. Often, a PHR needs to be a recognized official record bound to the electronic identity of a patient with authenticatable medical records, e.g. an electronic prescription verifiable by a pharmacist.

P7. With the current integration of portable devices (mobile phones, watches, smart clothing, activity monitors, hospital computers, etc.), PHRs need to be able to distribute themselves across different capability devices for access and generation and seamlessly integrate into an individual's lifestyle and activities.

P8. Patients could benefit from PHRs containing live dynamic objects, which integrate into an individual's life, e.g. flagging dangerous drug-drug interactions or managing appointments and reminders.

4. OUR SOLUTION

Our solution utilizes PPCD [1], which was originally developed for business document workflows. The PPCD format successfully addresses a number of crucial PHR problems (**P1, P3, P5**). It enables combining of differently formatted content-parts into one secure bundle, ensuring confidentiality and authenticity of each content-part. It also provides a secure way to share data between multiple distributed parties without any central authority maintaining access control or gaining access to clear text information.

PPCD-based PHRs, are ideally suited for persistent online storage, where Cloud Service Providers (CSPs) guarantee storage and service availability, without any ability to access PHR content. Furthermore, the PPCD format enables multiple users to differentially access the same document using their private key, thereby enabling partial (purpose-specific) export of data out of the bundle. However, PPCD technology as a PHR format has a number of shortcomings that need to be addressed: P2, P4-P8. In the following sections, we briefly review the structure of PPCD and detail our extensions and protocols to introduce the dedicated healthcare record (PPHR) format that builds on all the key benefits of PPCD technology, whilst allowing us to create dynamic, interactive and fully flexible records.

4.2 PPCD Brief Structure Overview

PPCD is a SQLite–based serialization that can contain multiple documents of different sensitivity and formatting. Content-parts are individually encrypted and signed with read access provided by releasing the corresponding symmetric encryption/decryption key (E) and the right to modify is granted by the signature key (S) paired to verification key V. The subsets of these keys are stored in a keymap unique for each authorized user. Keymaps are, in turn, encrypted by hybrid encryption including the participant's public key and stored in a fast filtration entry-table. Distribution of content-part keys according to access rights granted provides a built-in mechanism for differential and fine-grained access to content-parts by multiple agents accessing the same PPCD. The PPCD handling environment (HE) [8] also provides a user interface for building and viewing information on a range of devices.

4.3 Assembly of Personal Identity Information

A PPHR is often required to be bound to an individual and verifiable by healthcare professionals. This could be accomplished by an official governmental/national record service, where patient's National or Social Security Number together with their biometric data are digitally signed by a recognized authority, e.g. a Government Department of Health. The PPHR-ID is stored as an additional (inseparable) encrypted content-part together with its official signature. Upon arrival at a healthcare point, the PPHR-ID can be verified by healthcare professionals using the authority's public certificate and the biometric information matched to the patient to prevent identity fraud. Any medical record can subsequently be signed together with PPHR-ID.

4.4 PHR Owner Access

PKI or IBE schemes are not ideal for establishing patient access. Fig. 1 illustrates access to a PPCD where a user decrypts row by row the encrypted text field Fig. 1(a) with their private key, until it matches the clear text of Fig 1(b). If matched, the private key is used to decrypt the symmetric keymap decryption key K, Fig 1(c), which is then used to decrypt the corresponding keymap ID, Fig 1(d).

Encrypt$_A$("PPCD")	"PPCD"	Encrypt$_A$(K)	Encrypt$_K$(keymap ID)
(a)	(b)	(c)	(d)

Fig. 1. *Example PPCD entry-table row using PKI*

Encrypt$_A$("PPCD")	"PPCD"	Encrypt$_A$(keymap ID)
(a)	(b)	(c)

Fig. 2. *Example PPHR entry-table row*

However, in the PPHR format, we additionally utilize a Password Key Derivation Function (PKDF) to derive a master secret, from which generate a set of secret keys. The first secret key is used to encrypt the owner's keymap ID. When accessing, the owner decrypts field Fig. 2(a) row by row until the result matches Fig. 2(b) in the same row. This enables the correct recovery of the keymap ID, Fig. 2(c), and the decryption of the owner's keymap. The additional symmetric keys can be distributed by the PHR owner to family members, guardians or caretakers who may need to be given full or partial access. The master secret is also used to derive a pair of signature/verification keys, so that the PPHR and partial versions can be signed by the owner. The owner certificate is not signed by any trusted Certificate Authority (CA), and hence needs to be distributed directly. Note that the PPHR contains both the original PPCD-type and the new entry-tables to provide for both password-based and private key access.

4.5 Export and Synchronization of Partial PPHR

To share PPHRs with healthcare or insurance providers PPHR owners need to export partial PPHR or provide partial access (read, synchronize) to an on-line master copy. Our export protocol between an owner and healthcare provider, H, is as follows:

1. A PPHR owner prepares export of material based on the anticipated task e.g. visit to a family doctor, pharmacy or insurance administrator. If a public key of the party is known then the partial PPHR can be fully formed, otherwise the entry-table is added when the public key is known in future. Existing medical records are exported with read-only access; whilst new empty content-parts (for new contents) are created with read-write access.
2. Upon arrival, the PPHR owner acquires the public key of H, creates the corresponding entry in the entry-table of the partial PPHR, which is either handed over to H or access is provided to it online.
3. Upon receiving the PPHR, H verifies authenticity of the PPHR using the owner's signature certificate, which is also handed over by the owner.
4. H verifies the PPHR-ID using a known signature authority certificate, and confirms biometric details (e.g. photo).
5. H updates empty records, encrypts and digitally signs them using PPHR provided keys. In case of important (accountable) medical records, H signs the record clear text in combination with the PPHR-ID using H's own private signature key, certified by a trusted CA:

   $D = DigitalSignature_{HprivKey}(important_content \,||\, PPHR\text{-}ID)$,
   where || denotes concatenation.

   The corresponding entry in the content-parts table is illustrated in Fig.3. Two extra fields are added, to store: a) H generated signature, *D*, and b) H's signature verification certificate signed by trusted CA. As with other content-parts, every field is encrypted using the encryption key provided by the PPHR for this content-part. The record is then altogether signed by the PPHR signature key provided for this content-part.
6. If the online PPHR version was provided then H directly synchronizes the modified parts to it. Otherwise, the updates are handed over to the owner's device, which automatically synchronizes to the master copy.
7. If at a certain point the owner wants to lock the changes made by H, and revoke read-write access, the owner re-encrypts and signs the modified content-parts using a set of newly generated keys.

Content-part ID	Encrypted Data	D	Certificate of H	PPHR Signature

Fig. 3: *Example of an important content-part medical record, certified together with PPHR-ID by a healthcare professional, whose CA-certified signature verification certificate is also stored.*

4.6 PPHR Connection to Healthcare Devices

PPHRs can interact with a plethora of online devices monitoring health and activity. This ensures PPHRs can integrate into their owner's lifestyle, especially with the rise of Internet of Things (IoT) devices within a person's home and environment. An online device (watch, sensor mat, cardiac monitor, etc.) can be granted access to upload data to dedicated content-parts in the master online version.

PPHR is further extended to create a device profile-table, which is protected exactly as the content-parts table. In the content-parts table, a new column is added to contain references to device profiles. A new device profile is added to this table. Here we describe the protocol:

1. The PPHR owner creates a new entry in the profile-table for the device.
2. The PPHR owner's creates new empty content-parts with read-write access for storing monitored data and adds reference to the device's profile from the profile-table.

3. A tiny partial PPHR is generated to include direct URL location of the online content-part, content-part encryption and signature keys. The partial PPHR is encrypted by hybrid encryption, which includes the device's key read from the device's profile.

4. The partial PPHR is imported to the device.

5. The device generates data, which is periodically encrypted and signed by the corresponding content-part keys and uploaded to the specified online location.

4.7 Interactive Content-Parts

PPHR extends upon the existing technology by enabling healthcare professionals, H, to add Active Objects (AOs) that can be read and enacted by the owner's device to make the PPHR a live record that can interact with an individual's health and lifestyle data. For application convenience a new AO-table table is created, which is protected exactly the same way as the content-parts table. A healthcare provider professional may add AOs into a PPHR by following the same protocol as section 4.5. Here, the healthcare professional receives the PPHR and is able to modify empty AO-parts with granted access in the AO-table to effectively insert new AO.

In the simplest instance AOs are calendar entries (.ics) which may, for example, represent a receptionist providing reminders for the next appointment, a doctor providing a schedule for taking medicine, and a pharmacist providing reminders for collecting repeat prescriptions. In a more elaborate environment, a family doctor could setup allergy AOs that monitors recent data from the plethora of devices in a patient's home to aid diagnosis. In another case, a pharmacist may set an AO that maintains the current list of medicines taken by the patient. As soon as a new medicine is prescribed, the AO automatically checks and alerts the patient of any potential drug-drug interactions. In yet another example, the healthcare data from monitoring devices can be automatically processed by the corresponding AO, which periodically uploads statistics to the master PPHR and to the doctor. If life-threatening deviations are observed the AO may automatically alert the emergency services using the local device services.

5. IMPLEMENTATION

We have implemented our solution on desktop computers and portable mobile devices by extending the PPCD format and the handling environment [8] to suit our PPHR requirements. A rudimentary CSP solution has also been implemented using HP Cloud services as the means to hold and carry PPHRs. This has enabled owners of a PPHR to access continuously their data online and to share partial PPHRs with other parties. We have also embedded partial PPHR into low powered IoT devices, so generated health data can be synchronized into the master PPHR.

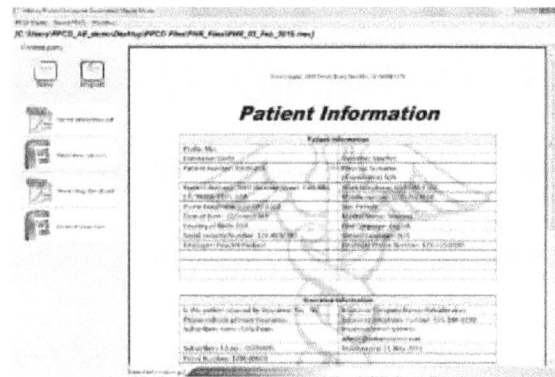

Fig. 4 *Snapshot of PPHR handling environment*

6. CONCLUSION AND NEXT STEPS

In this paper we extend PPCD [1] technology for a novel PPHR format. Fine-grained access to an owner's content-parts is provided so that multiple healthcare professionals can differentially access the same PHR. We utilise CSPs for storing and sharing encrypted and authentic data, so that the owner's PHR is always available online, yet its contents unavailable to a third party host. Due to the consumer nature of PHRs, PKI or IBE based access is replaced by PKDFs where appropriate. Furthermore, PHR owners are able to export partial PHRs in a distribution format upon request to a healthcare professional. Security and privacy concerns are addressed by providing end-to-end encryption, communication and synchronizing protocols, so that healthcare professionals and devices can create, upload and sync PHR formatted data. We also introduce AOs that allow healthcare professionals to add features into the PHR so that actions can be carried out over certain times and events. In future, it would be useful to establish templates for creating a host of common PPHRs. We would also like to restrict access to designated environments, e.g. hospitals, and incorporate audit mechanisms.

7. REFERENCES

[1] Balinsky, H.Y. and Simske, S.J. Differential Access for Publicly-Posted Composite Documents with Multiple Workflow Participants, ACM Symposium on Document Engineering, pp.10, 2010, Manchester, UK

[2] Blue Button, http://www.healthit.gov/patients-families/blue-button/about-blue-button

[3] Dossia, http://www.dossia.com/

[4] Apple Healthcare, https://www.apple.com/uk/ios/whats-new/health/

[5] Microsoft HealthVault, https://www.healthvault.com/gb/en

[6] World Medical Card, http://www.wmc-card.com/

[7] Davies, P. (30 July 2012). "Should patients be able to control their own records" BMJ 345 (e4905).

[8] Balinsky, H and Perez, D., Handling Environment for PPCDs, Data-Driven Process Discovery and Analysis, LNBIP, Volume 203, 2015, pp 48-64.

Does a Split-View Aid Navigation Within Academic Documents?

Juliane Franze
Faculty of IT
Monash University, Australia
&
Fraunhofer ESK
Munich, Germany

Kim Marriott
Faculty of IT
Monash University, Australia

Michael Wybrow
Faculty of IT
Monash University, Australia

{Juliane.Franze, Kim.Marriott, Michael.Wybrow}@monash.edu

ABSTRACT

Paper is still the dominant medium in academic reading. One reason is the ease of navigation within a paper document. We therefore investigate how to provide a more paper-like navigation within an academic document when read digitally. We present the results of a user study in which we compare the standard single-view hyperlink navigation with a split-view navigation. The split-view offers the reader a primary reading view of the document as well as a contextual view next to it. When a hyperlink is activated in the reading view the contextual view shows the referenced element. While we found no difference between user performance, the split-view was preferred by almost all users to the standard single-view navigation model.

Categories and Subject Descriptors

H.5.4 [**Information Interfaces And Presentation**]: Hypertext /Hypermedia—*Navigation*; I.7.1 [**Document And Text Processing**]: Electronic Publishing

Keywords

Technical reading; digital documents; human factors; usability

1. INTRODUCTION

Researchers dedicate increasing amounts of time to searching and reading academic documents such as conference papers and journal articles online [5, 6]. Nonetheless, our recent survey of academics found that about half of the respondents still preferred to read scientific documents on paper [2]. The most common reasons survey respondents gave for choosing paper over digital reading were: ease of annotation, physical comfort and tangibility, portability, ease of navigation and better comprehension. Similar findings are also reported by other research [1, 3, 4, 7, 8].

In this paper we investigate how to better support navigation within academic documents when read in digital form. Navigation within the documented (i.e., intra-document navigation) is of particular importance in academic reading as documents are most often read non-linearly [3] with readers jumping back and forth to find particular information or figures.

Participants in our previous survey [2] indicated that they wanted support for hyperlinked navigation so they could jump to a desired figure, reference or section without manually scrolling or panning to find it. Such navigation is commonly provided in web browsers and PDF viewer software. Users can click on a hyperlink in the text and the document view will jump to show the referenced element and then, when ready, the reader can use the back arrow to return to the previous position, see Figure 1. While this allows jumping to an element it also distracts the flow of reading [5]. On paper a person can use their finger to mark the position but in a digital environment this is not of much help when pages are scrolled. From our experience (received in the survey [2]) we know that it is common for a reader to lay different pages of a document side-by-side on a flat surface. This allows a figure to remain in view while another page referring to it is read.

These observations have motivated us to develop a split-view based hyperlink navigation model in which the reader has both a primary reading view of the document and a contextual view beside it. When a hyperlink is activated in the reading view the referenced element will be shown in the contextual view. There is no need for additional user interaction to return to the original reading position as the reading view remains visible while allowing a side-by-side examination of the two parts of the document. This model is shown in Figure 2. We conjectured that the split-view supports intra-document navigation similar to paper navigation. Users would therefore be likely to prefer it to the traditional single-view hyperlink navigation model.

The main contribution of this paper is to present the results of a user study in which we compared the standard single-view hyperlink navigation with a split-view navigation. Eight participants took part in the study. We evaluated both preferences and task performance. The task was to find semantic errors in the document, similar to those a reviewer might look for. We found that while the participants had similar task performance with both views, they overwhelmingly preferred the split-view to the standard single-view (7 of 8 participants). This provides strong support for using split-view navigation in applications designed for reading scientific papers.

2. RELATED WORK

Prior research has found that paper still provides better support for researchers when reading and working with academic documents. For instance, Sellen and Harper [7] state that paper provides more navigation flexibility, easier rearrangement of docu-

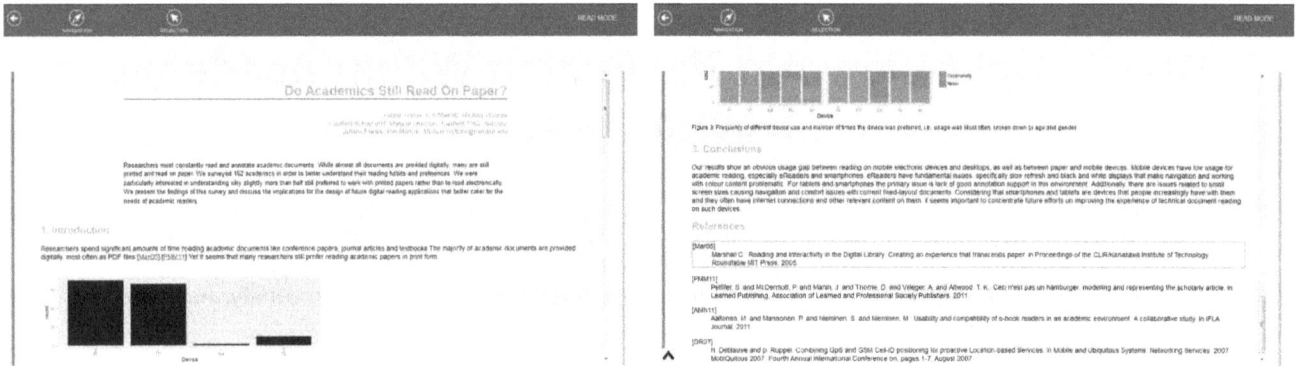

Figure 1: Standard single-view navigation model. The figure on the left shows the beginning of Text A as it appears in the WebView presentation mode of our tool. If the reader clicks on a citation, the document scrolls to the cited reference which is highlighted to make it easy to find (right). Once the reader has finished reading the reference the Back arrow will return them to the original citation.

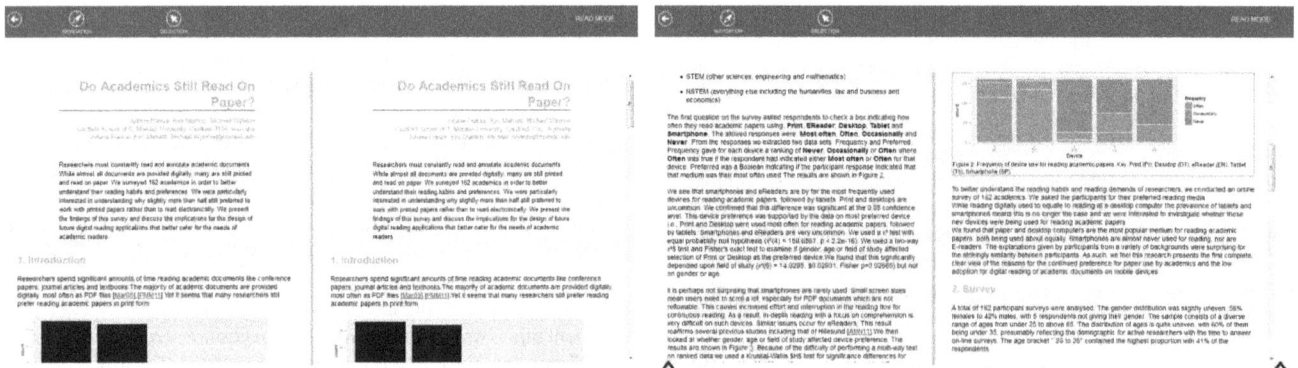

Figure 2: Split-view navigation model. The figure on the left shows the beginning of Text A as it first appears in the SplitView presentation mode of our tool. If the reader clicks on a hyperlink, such as a reference to a figure, the contextual view in the right column scrolls to the hyperlink target, as shown on the right.

ments (for cross-referencing) as well as allowing more flexible annotation. Takano *et al.* [9] recently provided a broad analysis of work-related reading by observing how it is conducted on paper in order to draw conclusions on how to improve digital reading applications. A number of researchers have tried to provide more paper-like behaviour in a digital reading applications while enhancing this with digital features that paper cannot provide.

Pearson *et al.* [6] present a digital version of a reading desk that mimics the key properties of a desk and a book sitting on it. A two page PDF document is displayed on the screen with space on all sides allowing users to place post-its for bookmarks and annotations. The post-its are visible during reading and can be added, modified or removed via mouse-clicks. This feature was well regarded by participants of a small study which found that navigation was easy and all items had good visibility on the screen.

Chen *et al.* [1] presents a prototype reading environment that removes the space limitations of a single digital screen. It uses multiple interconnected electronic devices to allow the reader to 'spread out' papers on different screens and provide an experience comparable to paper. The system is designed to distribute and rearrange the content across the devices allowing users to view information simultaneously on multiple screens.

Like our work, both systems have the similar motivation of providing users additional space and more paper-like features for work-

ing with documents, rather than just displaying a document in a single full screen view. Our research differs in its focus on intra-document navigation and a targeted user study.

3. PRESENTATION TOOL

We have implemented a prototype web-based tool for reading academic documents that provides the two navigation modes required for the study: a standard single-view (called *WebView*) and a two column split-view (called *SplitView*).

The prototype was programmed with web technologies: HTML, LESS, jQuery and AngularJS. The application was designed to support all screens and media types and used a template controller that allows standard LaTeX documents to be displayed after conversion into a JSON (JavaScript Object Notation) format. So far the transformation from LaTeX into JSON is only partly automatated and needs to be enhanced in further versions.

The WebView offers the same features as a browser-based layout of an HTML text document, including intra-document hyperlink navigation, hierarchical navigation and re-flowable layout. The WebView is shown in Figure 1. Whenever the user clicks on a figure reference, section reference or citation the page scrolls to the corresponding item. The Back button allows the reader to return to his/her former position in the text. In addition, the user is provided with adjustable margins (shown by bars on the left and right) so that they can adjust the line length to a comfortable value where they dislike the default. (Respondents to our earlier survey [2] requested this feature).

The SplitView provides the same features as the WebView but with a different layout. The screen is divided into two vertical columns, positioned side by side (see Figure 2). The left column is the primary "reading" view, designed to always stay at the position in the text the reader is currently reading. The right column is intended to show a "contextual" or "reference view." Whenever the user clicks on a figure reference, section reference or citation in either view the contextual view scrolls to the corresponding item. As with the WebView, the reader can adjust the margins and the proportion of the screen given to each column. The default is to give them equal width.

Thus the SplitView allows the reader to read and scroll linearly through the contextual view without losing their current position in the reading view, simultaneously the contextual view provides the hyperlinked information right alongside the corresponding text. This also reduces the need for user interaction since there is no need to scroll back to the last position or use the Back command to navigate back.

This approach offers the opportunity to view a figure shown in an earlier section but referred to in a later section and have this displayed right next to the reference (see Figure 2). Such referencing is common in scientific documents and is why we conjectured that the split-view would support intra-document navigation that was more similar to that provided by paper and that users would prefer it to the traditional single-view hyperlink navigation model.

4. USER STUDY

In order to investigate our statements we conducted an open-ended qualitative user study. The study was designed to answer three questions for digital academic reading:

- Is the split-view based hyperlink navigation model preferred to the traditional single-view hyperlink navigation model?

- Does the split-view based hyperlink navigation model improve performance on tasks which require careful reading of two different parts of the document?

- How could the preferred mode be improved to provide better hyperlink navigation within a document?

4.1 Method

Participants: 8 participants were recruited for the study from a departmental email list. All were postgraduate Information Technology students or academic staff and were aged between 23 and 36. There were five male participants and three female.

Equipment and Materials: We prepared one article for training and two short research articles for the study. The two research articles, "Text A" and "Text B", were each about 1200 words long and had a comparable number of sections, references and figures. They were based on an extended version of [2]. In each of the two articles we introduced four errors:

- One was a mismatch between the number of items in a list of items and the number given in the preceding section. This could be detected by simply reading the main text and so we did not expect a higher detection rate in either navigation mode. In Text A, for instance, the error was in the section

  153 participants gave a field of study. We grouped these into 6 classes:

  - BIOMED (life sciences, health, psychology and psychiatry);
  - ICT (computer science, IT, telecommunications, information systems and knowledge management);
  - STEM (other sciences, engineering and mathematics);
  - NSTEM (everything else including the humanities, law and business and economics)

- Two errors were a mismatch between the data given in a graph and the interpretation in the text. This required comparing the text with the figure, we expected this to be easier in the SplitView. In Text A for instance, the text referred to the following graphic

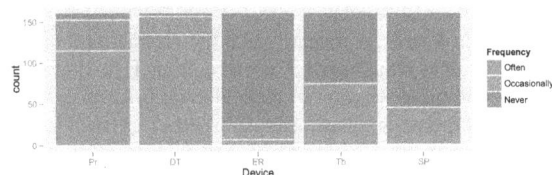

where the caption explained that "Pr" was print, "DT" was desktop/laptop etc and the text stated:

> We see that smartphones and eReaders are by far the most frequently used devices for reading academic papers, followed by tablets. Print and desktops are uncommon. We confirmed that this difference was significant at the 0.05 confidence level.

- One error was a mismatch between the actual author of a cited paper and the author used to refer to it in the text. This required comparing the text with the reference. Again we expected this to be easier in the SplitView.

Procedure: The experiments were performed in a private office using a desktop computer, with a single participant at a time. The experiment was carried out at Monash University in Melbourne. The study took between 30 to 45 minutes, depending on the speed of reading of each participant. It consisted of 4 parts:

- First the participant was asked demographic questions to ascertain their reading habits and prior experience with on-line reading applications.

- The participant was then trained with each of the navigation modes–WebView and SplitView–using a training document that was unrelated to the actual test document. The starting navigation mode was alternated and counterbalanced between participants.

- After training with each navigation mode, the participant was asked to read one of the text documents (randomised and counterbalanced) with this mode and to identify any errors in the document. They were asked to read the document "carefully" and were informed that the document contained a "number of" semantic and contextual errors.

- Finally, the participant was asked about their experience with the two modes. They were asked which was their preferred mode and to identify ways in which they thought it could be improved.

While we were interested in user performance on the task, one of the main reasons for including it was to give the participants a reason to properly use and experience both navigation modes when carefully reading a document.

4.2 Results and Discussion

In the survey we found that participants were not particularly good at identifying errors in the documents but overwhelmingly preferred reading with the SplitView. Participants' error finding success as well as their preferences are given in Table 1.

The overall low rate of spotting errors could be a result of choosing errors that are quite difficult to find. However it can be seen that participants who took more time to read the document carefully were likely to find more errors. The main reason for task difference was therefore simply the amount of time the user spent reading the document. We also see that the navigation mode is not correlated with task performance or with the kind of errors identified.

The data on preference, however, clearly shows a clear bias for the SplitView. This was supported by user comments, for instance:

> When I just read linearly, like the abstract and introduction, I do not need a second column [...]. But once I read the discussion or methodology I like to see the corresponding figures, equations, etc., right next to my reading text.

The single person that preferred the WebView was the only person in the study indicating that he usually read academic documents digitally. The reason given for preferring the WebView was that the text in the SplitView looked significantly more than in the WebView. However we suspect that part of the reason may have been their familiarity with a single-view hyperlink navigation.

Responding to the question of how the navigation modes can be improved, participants suggested providing more interactive exchange between the two columns, having an additional expandable overview column as well as a "SelectView" where the reader could place selected items, like on a clipboard. They also suggested enhance viewing individual items, e.g., making figures rotatable in order to better read their scale description, or providing small hyperlinked overviews for every reference showing where they appear in the text.

5. CONCLUSION

In this paper we introduced a simple split-view based hyperlink navigation model for reading academic documents in which the reader has a primary reading view of the document as well as a contextual view. This was motivated by respondents in a previous survey who identified ease of navigation as a primary reasons for preferring to read paper over digital documents. We felt that a split-view would support similar navigation to paper where different document pages can be laid out side-by-side on a flat surface.

We conducted an open-ended qualitative user study in order to evaluate the split-view based hyperlink navigation model and compare it to a traditional single-view provided by most digital document reading applications.

Referring back to the questions the study was intended to answer, we found that the split-view based hyperlink navigation model was preferred to the traditional single-view hyperlink navigation model. Our study did not, however, find that the split-view based hyperlink navigation model improved performance on tasks which required careful reading of multiple parts of the document.

The study yielded a number of good suggestions on how to further improve a hyperlinked navigation, including a more interactive exchange between items and columns, greater flexibility for column layout, and enhanced viewing options for figures or overviews.

We plan to implement and evaluate these suggestions in a future version of the prototype. We also wish to explore how the tool can be extended to allow users to layout more than one document next to each other in order to compare different academic articles.

	WebView				SplitView				
	E1	E2	E3	E4	E1	E2	E3	E4	Pref
P1	-	-	-	-	-	-	-	Y	Split
P2	-	Y	-	-	-	Y	-	-	Split
P3	-	Y	-	-	-	-	-	-	Web
P4	Y	Y	Y	-	-	Y	-	-	Split
P5	-	Y	-	-	-	Y	-	-	Split
P6	-	-	-	-	-	Y	-	-	Split
P7	Y	Y	-	-	-	Y	-	-	Split
P8	Y	Y	-	-	Y	Y	-	-	Split

Table 1: Results from the user study showing the errors that different participants were able to identify while using the different navigation modes. Error E1 was the incorrect number of list items, E2 and E3 the erroneous interpretation of a figure, and E4 the wrong reference.

6. REFERENCES

[1] N. Chen, F. Guimbretiere, and A. Sellen. Designing a multi-slate reading environment to support active reading activities. *ACM Transactions on Computer-Human Interaction*, 19(3):18:1–18:35, Oct. 2012.

[2] J. Franze, K. Marriott, and M. Wybrow. What academics want when reading digitally. In *Proceedings of the 2014 ACM Symposium on Document Engineering*, pages 199–202. ACM, 2014.

[3] T. Hillesund. Digital reading spaces: How expert readers handle books, the web and electronic paper. *First Monday*, 15(4), 2010.

[4] F. Jabr. The reading brain in the digital age: the science of paper versus screens. *Scientific American*, 11, 2013.

[5] Z. Liu. Reading behavior in the digital environment: Changes in reading behavior over the past ten years. *Journal of Documentation*, 61(6):700–712, 2005.

[6] J. Pearson, G. Buchanan, and H. Thimbleby. The reading desk: Applying physical interactions to digital documents. In *Proceedings of the SIGCHI Conference on Human Factors in Computing Systems*, CHI '11, pages 3199–3202. ACM, 2011.

[7] A. J. Sellen and R. H. Harper. *The Myth of the Paperless Office*. MIT Press, 2003.

[8] H. Shibata, K. Takano, and K. Omura. Impact of the use of a touch-based digital reading device in immersive reading. *SID Symposium Digest of Technical Papers*, 44(1):45–48, 2013.

[9] K. Takano, H. Shibata, J. Ichino, H. Tomonori, and S. Tano. Microscopic analysis of document handling while reading paper documents to improve digital reading device. In *Proceedings of the 26th Australian Computer-Human Interaction Conference on Designing Futures: The Future of Design*, OzCHI '14, pages 559–567. ACM, 2014.

An Approach for Designing Proofreading Views in Publishing Chains

Léonard Dumas
Laboratoire Heudiasyc. UMR
7253 CNRS*
leonard.dumas@hds.utc.fr

Stéphane Crozat
Unité ICS / EA 2223 Costech*
stephane.crozat@utc.fr

Bruno Bachimont
Laboratoire Heudiasyc. UMR
7253 CNRS*
bruno.bachimont@hds.utc.fr

Sylvain Spinelli
Kelis, Thourotte, France
sylvain.spinelli@kelis.fr

*Sorbonne universités
Université de Technologie de Compiègne
CS 60 319 - 60 203 Compiègne Cedex, France

ABSTRACT

Documentary production often involves a revising process in which documents need to be proofread. This important task faces new challenges when dealing with digital documents. Indeed, three features of digital writing are problematic: (1) documents evolve very frequently and cannot be proofread each time as a whole, (2) interactions provided by hypertexts make the task less efficient and (3) document repurposing increases the *views* of content to proofread. As an advanced digital writing technology, XML publishing chains are a relevant framework for studying proofreading of digital documents. This paper argues the need for proofreading views, which enable the comparison of two versions of the document based on a diff algorithm. It also proposes a design approach based on case studies within Scenari publishing chains, involving the annotation of content and the validation of modifications.

Categories and Subject Descriptors

I.7.1 [**Document and Text Processing**]: Document and Text Editing—*Document management, Version control*

Keywords

XML Publishing Chain, Fragmented Document, Proofreading, Diff, Interactivity, Repurposing, Polymorphism.

1. INTRODUCTION

Proofreading is a common task in document revising process. Also known as *critical reading*, it involves a higher cognitive effort than reading for comprehension [17]. We analyze how document proofreading is impacted by digital technology and address this issue within Scenari[1], an open-

---

[1]http://scenari-platform.org

DocEng'15, September 8-11, 2015, Lausanne, Switzerland.
© 2015 ACM. ISBN 978-1-4503-3307-8/15/09 ...$15.00.
DOI: http://dx.doi.org/10.1145/2682571.2797096.

source software suite of XML publishing chains developed by the Kelis company. According to [7], a publishing chain is a documentary production system implementing original digital writing functions, such as polymorphism or transclusion. Polymorphism is the ability to shape a content in a variety of ways, which leads to break the traditional unity of document into: a generative view (XML resource), its published views (e.g. HTML or PDF documents) obtained by transformation and its editing views (WYSIWYM editors) enabling the modification of generative views [1] [16] [18]. Transclusion consists in decomposing a generative view in autonomous fragments linked together, thus allowing content reuse among several documents. Hence, the documentary production is based on a *network of fragments* [2]. Polymorphism and transclusion stimulate *repurposing*, defined as "a documentary process consisting in building a new document with archives" [8].

2. CHALLENGES

Instability. Digital writing allows the progressive refinement of texts, whose former states can be preserved [10]. For instance in Wikimedia projects, about 10 edits are made each second (see Wikipedia statistics[2]). This instability makes the proofreading of entire documents impossible in practice. Change detection algorithms and difference rendering (*diff*) are commonly used to overcome this problem. As an example, Wikipedia's revision history allows to compare two versions of an article with help of a side-by-side diff, which can be used by proofreaders to validate edits or to go back to a former version.

Interactivity. On the interaction level [10], digital documents enable manipulations that delinearize reading, which makes proofreading less efficient. In hypertext documents, interactions are provided through links. Stretch text [15] allows to vary the level of detail in the content. For instance, links in the main text (inline links) can be activated to display additional information, either in a collapsible block ("see also"...), in a tooltip (definitions, bibliography...) or in a modal window (for a larger content). Some hypertexts organize content in a network to provide multi-linear readings. Regarding linear, hierarchically organized documents, hypertexts also allow to dispatch the content on several pages (e.g. one page per section) that the reader can navigate

---

[2]http://en.wikipedia.org/wiki/Wikipedia:Statistics

either in a linear manner (previous/next links) or through outline links.

Repurposing. According to [3], the ability to refer to an authenticated, fixed and consensual version of content is necessary for document objectification, which we assume is even more important when dealing with proofreading. However, objectification is compromised by the separation imposed by repurposing between generative and published views. Indeed, the generative view alone does not allow to put oneself in the position of the reader, while published view are all partial, which in practice leads to a round-trip proofreading between all these views [9]. Thus the gain of repurposing in writing implies a drawback in proofreading, which is subjected to redundancy among multiple views.

In publishing chains, existing views are appropriate for editing and reading, but not for proofreading. Our approach consists in applying polymorphism to obtain proofreading views. In the rest of this paper, we propose design strategies for these views based on two case studies which enable us to think of the variety of cases to consider (which interactions in published views, which repurposing logic...).

3. RELATED WORKS

Versioning tools allowing to manage documents' instability are a largely covered topic. Version control systems such as Subversion [6] allow to save the files' edit history. For instance, two versions having conflicts can be compared and manually or automatically merged. Diff algorithms, which are either line-based (for text files) or tree-based (for XML documents), allow to compute differences between two versions, and return a *delta* indicating edit operations necessary to transform the one version into the other [13] [4]. Edit operations can be used to build a visual representation of differences, for example in a side by side comparison, or by a merge algorithm, as with the three-way merging technique, in which two versions are merged with respect to their common ancestor, as shown by [14].

Interactivity can be handled by adapting content presentation to proofreading. This is near to the issue of comfort reading of web articles for example, which is often disrupted by ads, menus, links, unadapted colors or typography, etc.. Some applications aim at refining content presentation of web articles, especially when they are to be read on small devices (mobiles, e-readers...) or printed out. The selection of content that should be kept is a research topic in document engineering, as shown by [5].

Proofreading views are related to the concept of *reference view*, which is defined as "a view allowing to review all the information provided by the generative view (content, metadata, structure, typing...)" [7]. Proofreading views complete this concept by addressing the readability issue from the proofreading task perspective.

4. CASE STUDIES

We present two proofreading cases occurring in the context of pedagogical publishing chains (Opale[3] [11] and Topoze). The first one deals with pedagogical modules written by students within a data warehouse course at the University of Technology of Compiègne. The second one concerns a database of 1200 quizzes used in placement tests in the context of the Faq2Sciences[4] project led by Unisciel[5]. In both cases, content is annotated, then modified based on these annotations, and finally must be validated in its new version using a diff function. These cycles are multiple (*instability*), content contains glossary stretch text and/or hypertextual quizzes (*interactivity*) and in the pedagogical modules example, content aims simultaneously at at least two versions, short and long (*repurposing*).

Figures 1 represents the tree of fragments for both examples. Figure 2 (Opale) shows the editing view of a fragment. Annotations can be made on various levels of content (a). The diff function allows to render the differences (b1) with one of the older entries in the edit history (b2). Content can be filtered (c) for its repurposing in the short and/or long version, which implies that the same module must be proofread in two different contexts. Already subjected to fragmentation and gathering too much functions when using diff in addition, editing views become overloaded and thus unadapted for proofreading. Figure 3 (Opale) shows the published view of a module. It is divided into several pages that must be navigated either with previous/next links (a) or through the outline (b). Glossary entries are transformed into tooltips displayed when the reader clicks on the term (c). Figure 4 (Topoze) shows quiz groups in the published view of a placement test. In each quiz group, only a *random* subset of all its quizzes is displayed for each reader. Indeed, the test is used for a training purpose, which explains content variability to the detriment of the comprehensiveness needed in proofreading. The view is designed so that the reader first answers the quizzes and then sees the score, as well as the solutions and the explanations. Moreover, the placement test is a multi-linear hypertext organized in steps, for instance quiz group steps, through which the path is personalized according to the reader's scores to quizzes. Thus, published views are not more appropriate for proofreading because of all the required actions they demand in order to proofread the whole content, as well as the possible non-closure of the combination of possibilities.

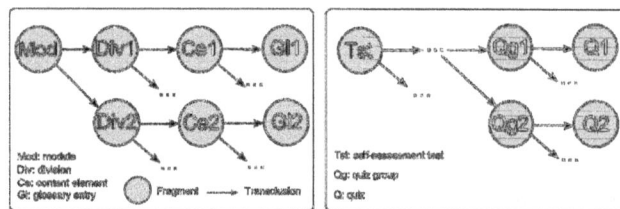

Figure 1: Trees of fragments in Opale (left) and Topoze (right) publishing chains

5. CONTRIBUTION

Our design approach of proofreading views is based on two strategies: **linearization** and **tabulation**. We define linearization as the ability to transform content in order to facilitate linear reading. Linearization depends on the nature of the concerned content, and more especially the reading order(s) it provides. For a tree-structured content, an unique reading order is generally provided with help of an outline. Linearization of such content is feasible by applying a single-page transformation to the generative view. For a

---

[3]http://scenari-platform.org/projects/opale/en/pres

[4]http://faq2sciences.fr/

[5]http://www.unisciel.fr/

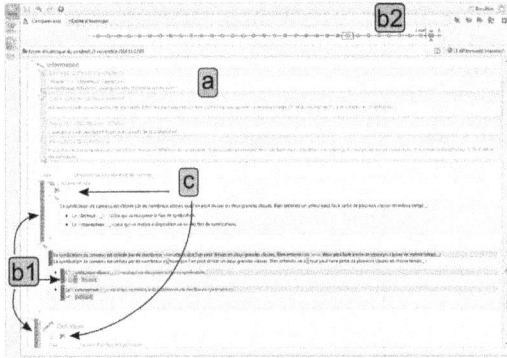

Figure 2: Editing view of a fragment in Scenari (Opale)

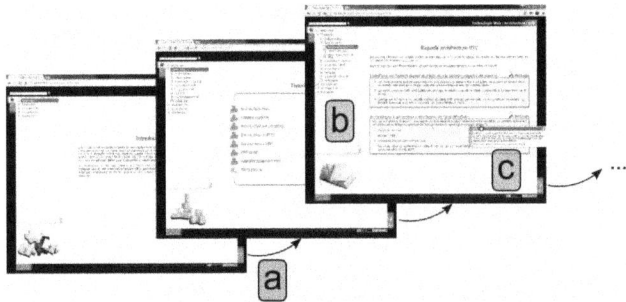

Figure 3: Published view of a pedagogical module (Opale)

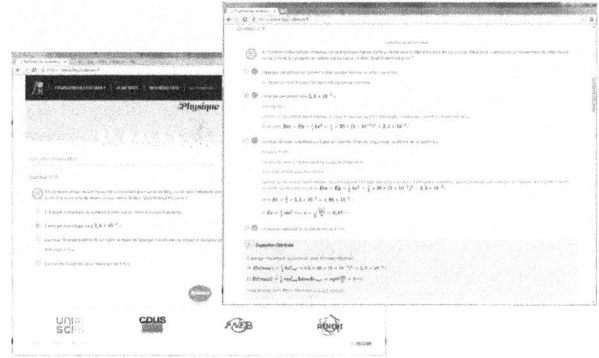

Figure 4: Quiz without (left) and with (right) solution in placement test published view (Topoze)

server side. The differences returned by the algorithm are then analyzed on the client side and appropriately rendered by DOM manipulations. Figure 5 shows the proofreading view designed for the pedagogical modules, which has been tested in three validation cycles. The tree-structured content has been linearized in one single page. Figure 6 shows the proofreading view designed for the quiz database, which has been used for a total of twenty hours of annotation. Quizzes have been proofread group by group. Indeed, each group can be read separately from the rest of the placement test in which it occurs. The linearization of quiz groups consisted in removing quizzes' check boxes/radio buttons and displaying their solutions and explanations in the same unique page. The random selection of quizzes has also been removed in order to proofread all quizzes of a group. Feedback from these experiments stresses the interest of a linearized view for proofreading in comparison with performing the same task in editing or published views.

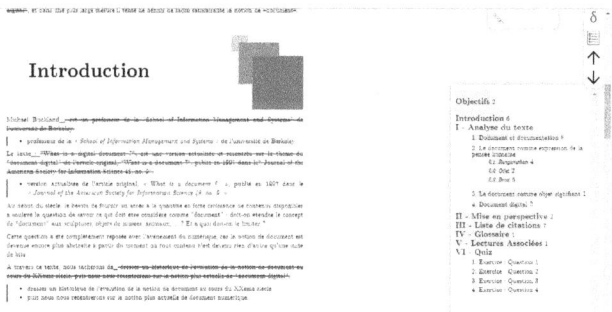

Figure 5: Module proofreading view (Opale)

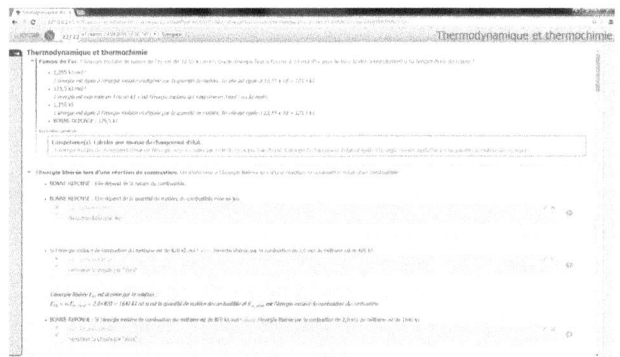

Figure 6: Quiz group proofreading view (Topoze)

graph-structured content, multiple reading orders are possible. Thus, all of these orders have to be linearized separately, which implies a redundant reading for nodes belonging to several paths. Another solution is to identify which nodes may be autonomous and linearizable units of reading (i.e. not requiring previous and following nodes), so that they can be proofread independently of the graph. The connection between nodes can be proofread based on a overview of the graph. For stretch text, linearization consists in finding static alternatives to their respective interactions in web published views. For instance, the additional text may be included inside the content. This solution suits when the stretch text is non-disruptive, i.e. when it does not disrupt the reading linearity between what precedes and what follows. When the stretch text is however disruptive regarding the surrounding content, it is preferable to reflow it in an appendix. For content subjected to repurposing, linearization does not eliminate the redundancy in proofreading. It must then be combined with tabulation, which we define as the ability to factorize content and parallelize multiple repurposing contexts. For instance, tabulation can be applied on generative views that can be published in several adaptations using content filters. The filtering metadata is used not for excluding content, but for splitting the text on several columns.

6. EXPERIMENTS

This section illustrates the application of the design approach to the case studies. The diff function is a prototype we developed for these experiments. It consists of a Javascript module integrated to the proofreading view and allowing the selection of a former version for comparison. We use a diff algorithm developed by Kelis, which is run on the

7. WORK IN PROGRESS

In this section, we present two elements from the approach that we have not implemented. Figure 7 (left) shows a sketch of tabulation in an Opale module, where the long and short versions are displayed side by side. The letters represent blocks that are either common (A, D) or specific to the long (B, E) or short version (C). Rectangle's height represent the content size of each block. Vertical synchronization is applied to (1) common blocks (see D for example) to avoid redundant proofreading, and (2) specific blocks between two pairs of common blocks (see B and C for example) in order to reduce the vertical gaps breaking up the text, even though some of them may remain (between C and D for example). Figure 7 (right) shows a graph overview of a placement test in Topoze, which can help to proofread the multiple paths using an UML activity diagram. Action nodes represent quiz group steps, while decision nodes represent the possible paths to other quiz group steps depending on the score.

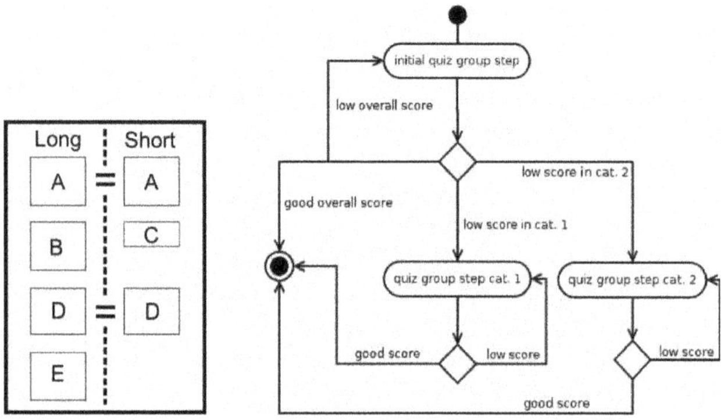

Figure 7: Tabulation sketch for proofreading of short and long versions of a module (left) and activity diagram for proofreading multiple paths in the placement test (right)

8. CONCLUSION

In this paper, we have tackled the issue of proofreading of digital documents by considering three digital writing features that make this task problematic. Based on two case studies in Scenari publishing chains, we proposed and applied an approach for designing proofreading views involving two strategies: linearization and tabulation. We assume that annotation and validation take advantage of linearization, as all differences and comments are displayed in the same page and with less interactivity. Whereas linearity brings back to the stability of the graphical reason [12], it must deal simultaneously with the irreducible complexity of the computational reason [3].

9. ACKNOWLEDGEMENTS

We thank Ludovic Gaillard for giving us the opportunity to undertake the case study within the Faq2Sciences project.

10. REFERENCES

[1] J. André, R. Furuta, and V. Quint. *Structured documents*. Cambridge University Press, 1989.

[2] T. Arribe. *Conception des chaînes éditoriales : documentariser l'activité et structurer le graphe documentaire pour améliorer la maîtrise de la rééditorialisation*. PhD thesis, Université de Technologie de Compiègne, 2014.

[3] B. Bachimont. *Ingénierie des connaissances et des contenus*. Hermès, 2007.

[4] G. Barabucci, U. M. Borghoff, A. Di Iorio, and S. Maier. Proceedings of the international workshop on document changes: Modeling, detection, storage and visualization (dchanges 2013). Published on CEUR-WS: 31-Aug-2013, Florence, Italy, September 10, 2013. http://ceur-ws.org/Vol-1008/.

[5] R. Chamun, D. Pinheiro, D. Jornada, J. B. S. de Oliveira, and I. Manssour. Extracting web content for personalized presentation. In *Proceedings of the 2014 ACM symposium on Document engineering*, pages 157–164. ACM, 2014.

[6] B. Collins-Sussman, B. Fitzpatrick, and M. Pilato. *Version control with Subversion*. O'Reilly Media, Inc., 2004.

[7] S. Crozat. Chaînes éditoriales et rééditorialisation de contenus numériques. In *Séminaire IST Inria : le document numérique à l'heure du web de données*, pages 179–220. ADBS, 2012.

[8] S. Crozat. Structured and fragmented content in collaborative xml publishing chains. In *Proceedings of the 2012 ACM symposium on Document engineering, DocEng '12*, pages 145–148. ACM, 2012.

[9] S. Crozat and B. Bachimont. Réinterroger les structures documentaires: de la numérisation à l'informatisation. *Information-Interaction-Intelligence*, 4(1), 2004.

[10] S. Crozat, B. Bachimont, I. Cailleau, S. Bouchardon, and L. Gaillard. Éléments pour une théorie opérationnelle de l'écriture numérique. *Document numérique*, 14(3):9–33, 2011.

[11] A. Gonzales-Aguilar, M. Ramírez-Posada, and S. Crozat. Scenari-opale: cadena editorial digital para la producción de contenidos e-learning. *El profesional de la información*, 21(4):433–438, 2012.

[12] J. Goody. *La raison graphique : la domestication de la pensée sauvage*. Minuit, Paris, 1979.

[13] J.-W. Hunt and M. D. MacIlroy. An algorithm for differential file comparison. *Bell Laboratories*, 1976.

[14] T. Lindholm. A three-way merge for xml documents. In *Proceedings of the 2004 ACM symposium on Document engineering*, pages pp. 1–10. ACM, 2004.

[15] T. H. Nelson. *Computer Lib: Dream Machines*. Tempus Books of Microsoft Press Redmond, 1987.

[16] R. Power, D. Scott, and R. Evans. What you see is what you meant: direct knowledge editing with natural language feedback. In *ECAI*, pages 677–681, 1998.

[17] J.-Y. Roussey and A. Piolat. Critical reading effort during text revision. *European Journal of Cognitive Psychology*, 20(4):765–792, 2008.

[18] K. Van Deemter and R. Power. Authoring multimedia documents using wysiwym editing. In *Proceedings of the 18th conference on Computational linguistics*, pages 222–228, 2000.

High-Quality Capture of Documents on a Cluttered Tabletop with a 4K Video Camera

Chelhwon Kim
University of California, Santa Cruz
Santa Cruz, CA, USA
chkim@soe.ucsc.edu

Patrick Chiu
FXPAL
Palo Alto, CA, USA
chiu@fxpal.com

Henry Tang
FXPAL
Palo Alto, CA, USA
tang@fxpal.com

ABSTRACT

We present a novel system for detecting and capturing paper documents on a tabletop using a 4K video camera mounted overhead on pan-tilt servos. Our automated system first finds paper documents on a cluttered tabletop based on a text probability map, and then takes a sequence of high-resolution frames of the located document to reconstruct a high quality and fronto-parallel document page image. The quality of the resulting images enables OCR processing on the whole page. We performed a preliminary evaluation on a small set of 10 document pages and our proposed system achieved 98% accuracy with the open source Tesseract OCR engine.

Categories and Subject Descriptors

I.7.5 [**Document and Text Processing**]: Document Capture – *document analysis, Optical character recognition (OCR), scanning.*

Keywords

Document capture; tabletop system; computer vision; reconstruction; image processing; video processing; OCR

1. INTRODUCTION

In multimedia communication and collaboration, people desire to exchange and interact with physical objects such as paper documents as they would with their digital counterparts. Tabletops augmented with video cameras or projectors is a way to bridge the physical and digital worlds. In particular, research systems for working with paper documents have been developed over the years (e.g. [11], [6], [7]). These systems dealt with problems such as user interaction, selection of a small region for capture, and document page tracking. However, the problem of capturing a whole document page located anywhere on a cluttered tabletop has not be adequately addressed. The ability to provide a high-quality image of a page would enable a more seamless transition between the physical and digital worlds.

In the digital world, OCR (Optical Character Recognition) is a powerful tool for analysis and understanding of the document content. Having high-quality images is essential for OCR. This allows one media (text) to be extracted from another (video). With the text extracted via OCR, there are many possible applications including: indexing & search systems, document repositories, and language translation.

One limitation of previous systems is that they used low resolution video cameras. For example, CamWorks [11] and FACT [7] used VGA or HD video cameras (640 x 480 and 960 x 720 respectively), which can capture only small parts of the document page at high resolution. With recent technology like 4K video cameras (4096 x 2160), it is more feasible to tackle the problem since a document page (8.5" x 11") at 300 dpi (a standard resolution for OCR) has similar pixel resolution (3300 x 2250).

Even with sufficient resolution, a captured image may suffer from noise and geometric distortion. We present some methods to improve the image reconstruction. In particular, we developed a multi-frame stop-motion capture technique along with an image fusion process.

To cover the entire tabletop, the camera must be able to point at any part of the surface. We mount the camera overhead on a robot turret which has pan and tilt servos. It is automatically controlled to sweep over the surface for document detection and capture.

For more realistic scenarios, the document pages must be detected on a tabletop that is cluttered with other objects (e.g. coffee mugs, pens, etc.). To deal with this, we use on a text probability map computed from a training set of document images.

In this paper, we propose a system that employs a two-stage approach for detection and high-quality capture of paper documents placed anywhere on a cluttered tabletop. We evaluated our system using an open source OCR Engine (Tesseract [14]) and obtained 98% accuracy.

2. RELATED WORK

CamWorks [11] is a research system that employs a video camera mounted over an author's desk. It supports capturing text segments on the page selected by the user. The user interface shows the video image of a page of the document, where the user can select material to be copied. The small regions selected are captured with a very low-resolution video camera (640x480).

The FACT system [7] used a video camera (960 x 720) to track a pen tip for user interaction with the contents of a document page. It does not capture high quality document images, instead it takes a different approach by linking a paper document in the camera view to an online version of the document. The link is determined by matching feature points on images of the document pages.

A video based document tracking system [6] was developed to track documents on a desktop surface. It is able to identify the document page objects by detecting when the page is brought into the camera's view and placed on the desk. The camera resolution was 1024x768 and OCR was not performed.

DocEng '15, September 08 - 11, 2015, Lausanne, Switzerland

© 2015 ACM. ISBN 978-1-4503-3307-8/15/09 ···$15.00

DOI: *http://dx.doi.org/10.1145/2682571.2797074*

(a)

(b)

Figure 1. System setup: (a) the camera is attached to a robot turret mounted above the table, (b) tabletop with documents and cluttered with other objects.

In summary, none of the existing video camera based tabletop systems can cover an entire table surface and capture a full document page at sufficient quality for OCR.

3. SYSTEM OVERVIEW

We installed a 4K camera (Point Grey Flea 3) mounted on a pan-tilt robot turret (with two Dynamixel servos) above a table to look for documents placed anywhere on the cluttered tabletop. See Figure 1. The camera has resolution 4096 x 2160. The distance of camera from the center of the table is determined so that we have a 300 dpi image with approximately 20 pixels x-height to achieve optimal OCR performance.

Our proposed system has two stages. First, the system scans the tabletop to detect text areas by moving the camera along a predefined path while it stops and captures a part of the tabletop surface at grid positions. Figure 3a shows the captured images. These tabletop images are converted into a text probability map by using a pre-computed text probability histogram and an image-stitching method based on known camera orientations recorded at the positions (Figure 2b). This gives text blobs which indicate the locations of document papers on the tabletop surface.

The second stage is to capture each document page. From the detected text blobs, the system generates scan paths (blue lines in Figure 2b) whereon the camera's viewpoint moves and captures a sequence of frames (Figure 2c). The camera uses a stop-motion technique: it stops moving when it captures a frame. The captured frames are fused together by a conventional image-stitching method (Figure 2d). Finally, the system corrects the perspective distortion in the fused document image by finding a quadrilateral formed by two horizontal lines along the text lines and two vertical lines along the vertical paragraph margins (Figure 2e).

4. TECHNICAL DETAILS

4.1 Document Paper Detection

We use the "Bag of Keypoints" method [2] to detect text regions in the captured image. Instead of building a classifier for {text, non-text}, we compute a histogram of text occurrences based on SIFT keypoint features and use this to compute the probability map of a new image. More precisely, we first extract 128-dimensional SIFT descriptor vectors [8] from the document page images in a training set. Then we cluster these SIFT descriptor vectors into a set of visual words (i.e. clusters) using the hierarchical k-means clustering algorithm [10]. We compute a histogram of occurrences of visual words based on the number of SIFT descriptor vectors assigned to each cluster. The normalized histogram of occurrences of visual words in the training dataset serves as a probability model which provides the probability of text occurrences given the quantized image features in an image. This normalized histogram is pre-computed offline.

For each of the tabletop images (Figure 2a), we compute a text probability map based on the trained probability model and the SIFT feature points extracted from the image. Specifically, we assign a 2D Gaussian kernel density to each feature point location, weighted by the normalized frequency of the visual word corresponding to the feature descriptor. The corresponding visual word is determined by a fast k-Nearest Neighbor search algorithm [10]. Finally, we sum up all the Gaussian kernels to produce the final probability map.

All the computed text probability maps are stitched together by estimating relative shift for each tabletop image to one particular image based on homography induced by the relative camera orientations based on the pan-tilt parameters. The final binary map is computed by thresholding the stitched text probability map and applying a morphological filter (Figure 2b). The text blobs in the binary map are detected by the connected component labeling (red rotated rectangles in Figure 2b). As each text blob indicates the candidate location of a document paper on the tabletop, we define a camera scan path over the document paper by selecting the top and bottom center of the text blob (red circles) and generate a list of camera capture points on a line joining the two points (blue arrows). For each point, we recover the corresponding pan and tilt values (camera orientation) by interpolating (or extrapolating) the known nearby data points that are the locations of the aligned image tiles in the map (green circles in Figure 2b). Finally, a sequence of images captured at the list of points (Figure 2c) is processed to reconstruct a document image.

4.2 Reconstruction

The captured multiple document images are stitched together by the general image-stitching method described in [13]. We first align all images by estimating relative shift for each frame to one particular frame. Since the images contain sufficient textures on text regions we can use point feature based homography. Homography produces the relative shift of pixels with sub-pixel accuracy so the interpolation is necessary when the pixels in each frame are brought to the reference image pixel grid. The aligned pixels at the same grid pixel location of the reference image are combined by a simple arithmetic mean. Finally, a sharpening filter is applied to the combined image to remove blurring.

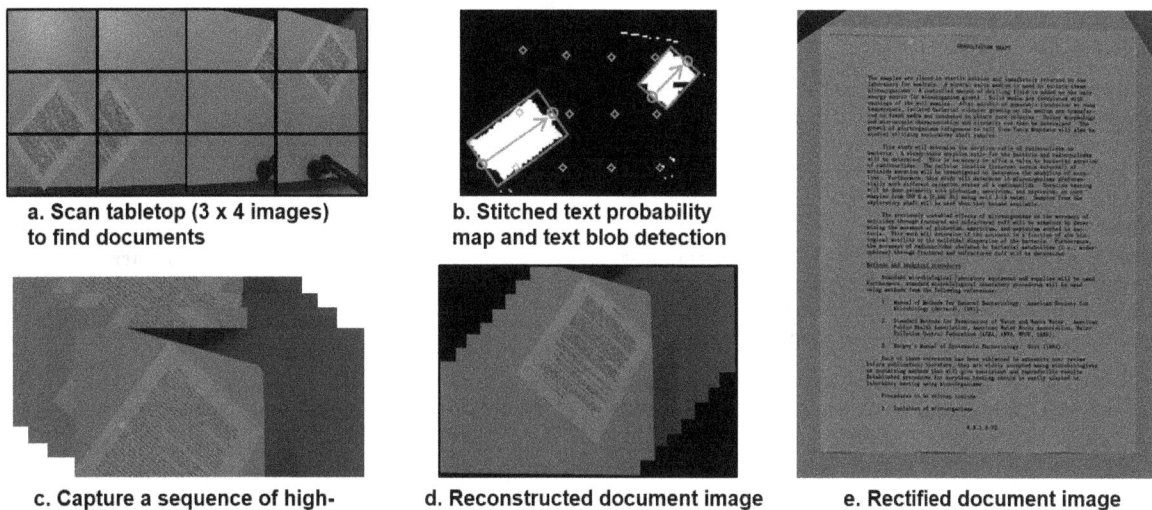

a. Scan tabletop (3 x 4 images) to find documents

b. Stitched text probability map and text blob detection

c. Capture a sequence of high-resolution document images

d. Reconstructed document image

e. Rectified document image

Figure 2. Overview of process.

4.3 Perspective Rectification

The reconstructed image still has perspective distortion so we correct it and recover the fronto-parallel view of the document page. Our correction method finds homography between a source quadrilateral formed by two horizontal lines along the text lines and two vertical lines along the vertical paragraph margins and its corresponding target quadrilateral (upright rectangle) similar to [1] and [3].

We first detect line segments along the text lines by the probabilistic Hough transform algorithm [9] (red line segments in Figure 3a), and the end points of the detected line segments are used to estimate two vertical lines along the vertical paragraph margins using the RANSAC based line-fitting algorithm (See blue and green lines in Figure 3a.). We use these two fitted lines as the left and right sides of the source quadrilateral.

In order to get the top and bottom sides of the source quadrilateral, we find a rotated rectangle around a text blob detected by the same method described in the Section above on document paper detection. (See red rectangle in Figure 3b.) Then the line segments of top and bottom sides of the rotated rectangle are rotated around their midpoint and aligned with the direction from the midpoint to a vanishing point to which the text line segments converge. The vanishing point can be estimated by RANSAC-based method [5]. Finally, the four sides of the source quadrilateral are found with the fitted two vertical lines. (See blue

quadrilateral in Figure 3b).

The target quadrilateral is estimated by using the width/height ratio of a back-projection of the source quadrilateral onto the table surface in space. To do this, we recover 3D coordinates of four vertexes of the source quadrilateral by finding intersecting points between back-projection rays of the vertexes and the table surface provided that the camera intrinsic matrix and the table surface orientation are estimated. After that, the width/height ratio is then a ratio between an average length of top and bottom sides and the one of left and right sides of the back-projected quadrilateral on the plane. The width is fixed to a certain number of pixels and the height is computed using the computed aspect ratio. After the four vertex correspondences of source and target quadrilateral are computed, the homography is obtained using the Direct Linear Transformation algorithm [4].

5. PROTOTYPE IMPLEMENTATION

The hardware and tabletop setup is described above (Section 3). The software is implemented in C++ and uses the OpenCV library [12]. On a desktop computer (Windows 7, Intel Core i7 3.6GHz CPU with 16GB RAM), execution time for the first stage of detecting documents takes 11 seconds on average. For the second stage of capture and reconstruction of a page, it takes 20 seconds for capturing and fusing the 8 images of resolution 4096x2160 and for correcting the perspective distortion in the fused image.

In the training of the text probability histogram (described in Section 4.1), we used scanned document images in the UNLV-ISR OCR dataset [15]. About 800K SIFT features were extracted from about 800 document page images. Figures were manually removed in the document images. To reduce computation time, we down-sampled the image tiles to 20% of the original size. The width of Gaussian kernel and threshold value used in the text probability map computation are empirically determined to smooth and to threshold the text probability values until the map produces at best one text blob per document.

6. EVALUATION

We performed a preliminary evaluation based on OCR on a small set of 10 document pages. Five of them are from the UNLV-ISR OCR dataset in one-column layout, and five are from papers

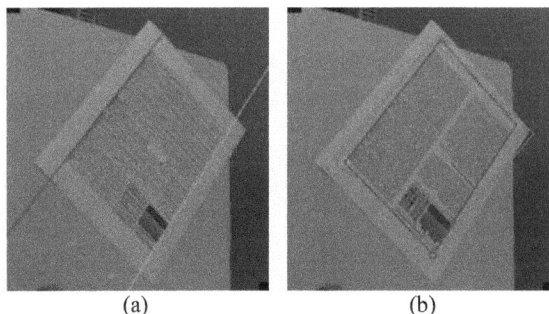

(a)   (b)

Figure 3. Perspective distortion correction: (a) text line segments and two vertical lines, (b) source quadrilateral.

published in IEEE format in two-column layout. These were printed out on paper using a laser printer.

The tabletop was cleared of cluttered objects so that the pages can be placed systematically on the surface. The pages were placed flat on the tabletop surface without rotation. Each of the 10 pages was placed at three different locations {0cm, 68cm, 92cm} from the center of the camera along the diagonal of the tabletop surface. With a typical large desk size of 60"x30", placing an 8.5"x11" piece of paper at a corner corresponds to the 68cm location; this is the location of maximum distortion on the desk surface. To see how the performance drops off at a farther distance, we tested it at the 92cm distance, which would be beyond a typical desk surface.

For the OCR, we use the open-source Tesseract OCR engine [14]. To measure the difference between two text strings, we use edit distance (Levenshtein distance), normalized by dividing by the length of the ground-truth string. Then we take the *OCR score* to be 1.0 minus the normalized edit distance (so that zero distance corresponds to 100% accuracy).

The OCR results are shown in Figure 4. Our system achieved 98% OCR accuracy and showed stable results over the three different locations. As a benchmark, we ran the Tesseract OCR engine on the document images obtained by a generic flatbed scanner, and the result was 99% accuracy. Comparing to the benchmark shows that our system, despite the geometric distortions and uncontrolled lighting conditions, can perform almost as well as a flatbed scanner.

We also evaluated a *single-frame* method without fusion. This only corrects the perspective distortion in a single image frame of document page using the same approach in the proposed system. However, since a single frame can cover only a small field of view of document page depending on its distance from the camera, we generate a virtual single frame with a larger field of view that covers a whole document page. We do this by concatenating two or three frames using the same stitching method as in the reconstruction step (Section 4.2), except that we take only a single pixel from the aligned pixels sitting on the same pixel location in the reference image instead of averaging them. For the sake of fair comparison, we applied the same sharpening filter to the concatenated image. The Single-frame method achieves 98% OCR performance for documents at the center of the table (0cm), but its performance drops down to 90% as the distance of document increases to the farthest location (92cm).

7. CONCLUSION & FUTURE WORK

We presented a novel system for capturing high-quality document page images on a cluttered tabletop. It goes beyond existing systems by providing sufficient resolution and quality for full-page OCR. Our preliminary evaluation shows that it can achieve a high rate of accuracy.

For future work, one direction is to explore continuous capture of the tabletop over a long period of time in a natural setting. This requires better handling of multiple document pages on the tabletop. Occlusion of the document pages by hands or other objects is another problem for further work.

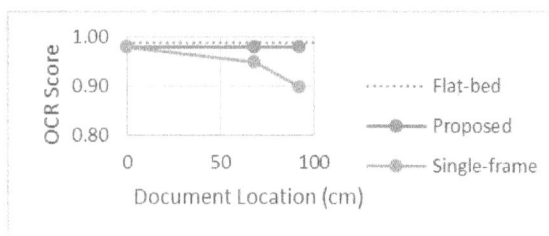

Figure 4. OCR performance.

8. REFERENCES

[1] Clark, P., Mirmhedi, M. Rectifying perspective views of text in 3D scenes using vanishing points, *Pattern Recognition,* 36: 2673–2686 (2003).

[2] Csurka, G., Dance, C.R., Fan, L., Willamowski, J., Bray, C. Visual categorization with bags of keypoints. *Proc. of ECCV Intl. Workshop on Statistical Learning in Computer Vision* (2004).

[3] Dance, C.R. Perspective estimation for document images. *Proceedings SPIE Document Recognition IX (2002).*

[4] Hartley, R., Zisserman, A. *Multiple View Geometry in Computer Vision*. Cambridge University Press (2003).

[5] Hwangbo, M., Kanade, T. Visual-inertial uav attitude estimation using urban 643 scene regularities. *Robotics and Automation (ICRA 2011)*, pp. 2451–2458.

[6] Kim, J., Seitz, S., Agrawala, M. Video-based document tracking: Unifying your physical and electronic desktops. *Proceedings of UIST '04*, pp. 99-107.

[7] Liao, C., Tang, H., Liu, Q., Chiu, P., Chen, F. FACT: fine-grained cross-media interaction with documents via a portable hybrid paper-laptop interface. *Proceedings of ACM Multimedia '10*, pp. 361-370.

[8] Lowe, D.G. Distinctive image features from scale invariant keypoints. *Intl. Journal of Computer Vision*, 60: 91–110 (2004).

[9] Matas, J., Galambos, C., Kittler, J.V. Robust detection of lines using the progressive probabilistic Hough transform. *CVIU* 78 1, pp 119-137 (2000)

[10] Muja, M., Lowe, D.G. Fast approximate nearest neighbors with automatic algorithm configuration. *Intl. Conf. on Computer Vision Theory and Applications (VISAPP 2009).*

[11] Newman, W., Dance, C., Taylor, A., Taylor, S., Taylor, M., Aldhous, T. CamWorks: a video-based tool for efficient capture from paper source documents. *Proc. ICMCS '99*, pp 647–653.

[12] OpenCV. http://opencv.org/

[13] Szeliski, R. Image alignment and stitching: a tutorial. *Found. Trends. Comput. Graph. Vis.* 2, 1 (Jan. 2006), 1-104.

[14] Tesseract. https://code.google.com/p/tesseract-ocr/

[15] UNLV-ISR OCR dataset. https://code.google.com/p/tesseract-ocr/wiki/TestingTesseract

Segmentation of Overlapping Digits through the Emulation of a Hypothetical Ball and Physical Forces

Alberto N. G. Lopes Filho and Carlos A. B. Mello
Centro de Informática, Universidade Federal de Pernambuco
Recife, PE, Brazil
{anglf,cabm}@cin.ufpe.br

ABSTRACT

This paper presents an algorithm for segmenting pairs of overlapping handwritten digits. Digits can be found overlapped in text depending on writing style and organization; digits in close proximity or with elongated strokes may also overlap with their neighbors. Applications such as automated character recognition are directly affected by overlapping characters and their segmentation. The proposed approach is based on the emulation of inertia and a deformable hypothetical ball. The strokes act as a pathway for the ball to run and create the segmentation. The results of the algorithm are subject to a digit recognizer and it is shown that the method performs well and presents lower computational cost when compared to other segmentation approaches.

Categories and Subject Descriptors

I.4.6 [**Image Processing and Computer Vision**]: Segmentation – *pixel classification.*

General Terms

Algorithms, Experimentation

Keywords

Document image processing, overlapping digits, physical forces, deformable ball, segmentation.

1. INTRODUCTION

Segmentation plays an important role in several document image applications [7]. Handwritten text present challenges of high complexity when compared to typewritten text. Due to the nature of handwriting, some problems may arise, caused namely by less organized writing patterns. This may lead to characters written in close proximity, causing their strokes to overlap. Overlapping characters present complex challenges for the segmentation and recognitions phases, since it causes components to be linked together, making the identification of each single component non-trivial. Automatic recognition applications must approach these problems in order to achieve satisfactory recognition rates. A case of overlapping characters is shown in Figure 1a and Figure 1b,

DocEng '15, September 08 - 11, 2015, Lausanne, Switzerland
© 2015 ACM. ISBN 978-1-4503-3307-8/15/09…$15.00
DOI: http://dx.doi.org/10.1145/2682571.2797080

more specifically, these are cases where two digits overlap, leading to a possibly incorrect segmentation and further incorrect recognition.

This paper presents a method for segmenting overlapping digits. More importantly, the focus is on horizontally overlapping pairs of digits (as in a string of digits). In our focus, this overlap creates a linked component consisting of two independent digits that present an elevated degree of complexity for the recognition phase. A similar situation consists of touching characters, as shown in Figure 1c and Figure 1d. This is, however, a different problem and not the focus of this paper (it is suggested the reading of [2]). The presented method relies on emulating inertial force and a deformable ball in order to segment the digits. This method is inspired on a method previously proposed in [6][14] which also tackle the problem of horizontally overlapping digits. These methods, however, rely on the use of thinning algorithms to perform segmentation, increasing its computational cost to $O(n^2)$. Another method that tackles overlapping symbols is shown in [13], which uses over-segmentation to separate overlapped digits. It generates a large number of candidate pairs for segmentation. The pair with the highest confidence score given by a recognizer is chosen as the resulting segmentation. While this method may prove to be efficient, its computational cost is high at $O(2^n)$. Surveys about character segmentation methods can be found in [1][5].

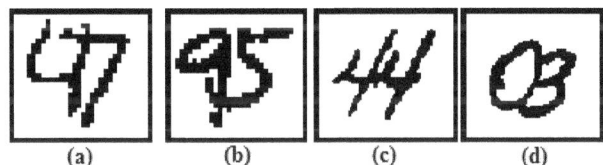

Figure 1. (a-b) Overlapped digits, (c-d) touching digits.

The remainder of this paper is organized as follows: Section 2 presents the proposed algorithm. Section 3 shows the results of the method and analysis, while Section 4 concludes the paper and brings some final remarks regarding future works.

2. PROPOSED METHOD

The method proposed herein is based on the use of a hypothetical ball that will use the strokes of the digits as pathways, or tunnels, which it can use to move through. As shown in [3][4], physical forces such as inertia or centripetal force can be used for character image processing purposes. More exactly, these two previous examples use physical forces for reconstruction of broken handwritten digits. These forces have also been applied to the task in focus, segmentation, as shown in [14], which makes an approach that uses the thinned versions of overlapped digits to apply the forces for segmentation. The proposed method models physical forces to govern how the ball will behave when moving through the pathways. The digits are processed in their original form, where the ball will have a deformable nature in order to fit evenly inside the stroke, avoiding the thinning phase. The proposal can be broken down into three steps: start point determination, segmentation and repositioning of segmented strokes.

2.1 Start point determination

The first step towards segmenting the overlapped digits is determining where the ball will start its traversal. The manner in which the method is developed provided it with a characteristic that makes the segmentation of the strokes not heavily dependent on the location of the start points. This becomes evident when discussing the repositioning phase. Therefore, the determination of start points is set as a simple algorithm, not requiring a method of higher complexity, as shown for example in [12]. The principles of pen-down and pen-up movements are used for this process of setting start points. When the author places the pen on paper, or pen-down, and starts writing, it is natural to assume that the stroke gains in width as the pen stabilizes on the paper. Therefore, the start section of the stroke should possess a smaller width value. Same principle is applied to when the author finishes writing the stroke; the pen-up movement should produce a decrease in stroke width, leading to the end section. The method, therefore, searches for four sections of the overlapped digits that possess the smallest stroke width value. Since the digits in question are horizontally overlapped (one digit on the left and the other on the right), the four start points are set according to their expected location: topmost leftmost, topmost rightmost, bottommost leftmost and bottommost rightmost corners. To set the exact coverage of each of the four areas, the algorithm considers the bounding box that surrounds the overlapped digits. For the topmost leftmost corner, for example, from the bounding box limits, the algorithm searches for strokes from the top limit extending downwards a distance d_height and from the left limit extending right a distance d_width:

$$d\_height = k * \text{height\_of\_bounding\_box} \qquad (1)$$

$$d\_width = k * \text{width\_of\_bounding\_box} \qquad (2)$$

The weight k is set to 0.25 in order to provide a window large enough to detect strokes. This value was obtained through experimentation on the database used in this work. The other three areas are calculated analogously. Figure 2 shows an example of the areas used to search for the start points.

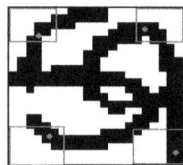

Figure 2. Examples of areas used to find start points.

In case a search does not find any strokes, the area is increased by 10% to further search for a stroke. This start point calculation is intended to generate two points located within each of the overlapped digits. Even if the start points are not located at the exact start and end positions of the stroke, the proposed method is able to overcome this.

2.2 Segmentation

The second step of the algorithm is the ball movement itself, which generates the segmented strokes. Before the ball actually starts to roll down the stroke, its radius must be determined. The initial radius is found using the start point as the center of the ball. Stroke width is calculated for the position of the stroke that corresponds to the start point; it corresponds to the diameter of a ball that would fit evenly in that stroke. Since each start point is not guaranteed to be located exactly at the beginning or ending of a stroke, the segmentation method must perform two ball runs for each start point, in opposite directions of the stroke. The center point of the ball is used as reference. The algorithm makes the ball traverse the stroke by analyzing the unvisited neighbors of its current center position in an 8-pixel neighborhood. A neighbor is considered available if it is an ink pixel and it has not been previously visited. If there is only one available neighbor, the decision is trivial. The algorithm updates the current position of the ball center to that of the unvisited neighbor, the radius for this position is calculated and the stroke points that fall within the coverage of the ball are recorded. The algorithm then proceeds to the next iteration. If the current ball center point contains more than one unvisited neighbor, then a decision must be made as to which will be the next visited point, using inertia.

The use of inertia for the decision depends on a history vector that must be stored by the algorithm. The history vector is created at the beginning of the algorithm and is updated every iteration. This vector contains the last three movements made by the run. Each movement indicates a direction that was taken by the ball. The history vector's size was set at three according to the overall image sizes that are being used. A larger history vector would include movement information that would be located too far away from the current position, providing information that would not be useful. A set of weights is assigned to each movement of the history vector, applying greater importance to the most recent position changes. The values of the weights used for this method are established as 6, 4 and 3. This assures that the last direction taken is the one that receives the greatest importance. It does not, however, take full control of the decision, since, if the second and third to last directions are the same, when combined, they overcome the importance of the last direction taken. The values assigned to the weights were chosen to guarantee the behavior mentioned above. The next visited ball center point is the one that produces the least change in the previously determined direction, reflecting the principle of inertia. Figure 3 illustrates the principle of inertia and how it is used by the algorithm. The center of the ball has arrived at position 4 after already visiting positions '1', '2' and '3'. Position '4', has two unvisited neighbors ('6' and '7'). Ideally, to maintain direction of movement, the next visited position would be '5', which is unavailable. The next visited position that is chosen is position '7', as it causes the least change in direction.

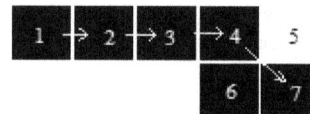

Figure 3. Use of inertia applied to define the next position of the ball's center.

The method takes into account another variable in its calculations, which is the radius that is calculated for each new visited center position. The first constraint is the size that the radius can assume.

The ball is allowed to shrink in size to the smallest limit possible, which would be a radius of '0' (a single pixel). The ball increasing, however, is limited. The radius can only double in size in relation to its original value. This limit is set in order to avoid the ball from increasing to a size that would not correspond to a stroke, which could happen in an overlap area between two strokes. The second constraint brought by the radius influences directly in the ball's movement. A center point may have an available neighbor, but a movement to that neighbor may not be possible if the ball does not fit with its resulting radius in the direction of the movement. An example of this is shown in Figure 4, where the ball is traveling in a horizontal direction and has arrived at ball center position marked as '1'. The next movement of the center would be to position marked as '2', yielding a radius of value '2', for example. This would not be possible for there is no more room for the ball to move to the right with the radius size calculated for position '2'. The next visited position would therefore have to be chosen among positions '4' and '3'.

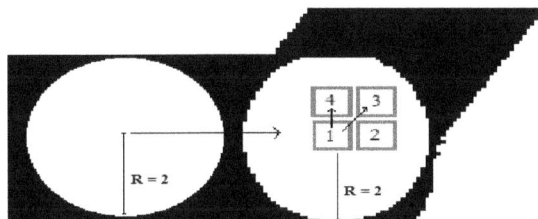

Figure 4. How the radius is used to calculate ball size and restrain movements.

The final step in the segmentation phase is determining when the ball should stop rolling down the stroke. There are three rules that determine when the traversal should stop: if the ball reaches an endpoint, if the ball has no other possible position to visit or if the ball begins to roll down a path that has previously been visited.

2.3 Repositioning of resulting strokes

The final step in the algorithm is to perform repositioning of the segments that were created after the segmentation process. This repositioning is performed to treat small segments that might have been created. Depending on the overlap of the characters, the position of the start points or even how the characters are written themselves, the segmentation phase might create small segments that do not correspond to entire character, but rather to only a small portion. Small segments that should be linked to larger segments are identified as isolated strokes. An isolated stroke may be identified by the following rules: it is small (in our case, for digits, this means that it possesses a total pixel count of less than 40% of the total ink pixels present in the image); its points are not used to form a complete segment; it touches another segment.

Once an isolated segment is identified, it is merged with the complete segment that it touches. If it touches more than one segment, it merges with the segment that has more shared points. Figure 5 exemplifies the repositioning phase.

An important characteristic of our algorithm is its computational cost, $O(n)$, where n equals the length of the digits' corresponding skeleton. Since the ball does not need to have its center point reaching the end of the stroke, the traversal of the ball is analogous to traversing the length of the stroke's skeleton. This cost is lower than the cost of [13], $O(2^n)$, where n is the number of nodes in a graph representing the skeleton of the digits. In this case, the algorithm tags the strokes' points as singular or regular.

Singular points are used as nodes of a graph, where the combination of nodes will produce the segmentation candidates. Through experimentation, it can be concluded that n is in the order of the tens. The cost is also lower than [14], which is $O(n^2)$ due to the thinning, where n equals to the length of the image

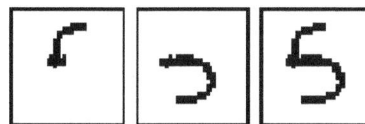

Figure 5. (left - center) Segments created by segmentation. (right) Result of repositioning phase.

3. RESULTS AND ANALYSIS

The method used two distinct image databases, one for its development and the other for testing. The development phase used digits obtained from the NIST SD 19 database [11]. These digits were extracted and then automatically overlapped by creating a random intersection between them. Once the method was developed, testing phase began. For the experiments, two other algorithms are used for comparison: Renaudin *et al.* [13] over-segmentation method and Roe and Mello [14] physical forces coupled with digit thinning method. The test database contains digits extracted from the MNIST database [8], which are also automatically overlapped. The comparative tests were conducted on a set of 57 overlapped digit pairs, yielding a total of 114 standalone segmented digits. This dataset was used for testing as it is the same dataset used in [14], from which we were able to obtain the results generated by the two algorithms used for comparison. Figure 6 shows examples of images present in the test database and their segmentation results by the proposed method. The results of each algorithm were submitted to a handwritten digit recognizer based on MLP structure [9][10]. Roe and Mello method did not reach acceptable recognition values, which can be explained by the output that this algorithm generates: a thinned version of the input. Roe and Mello method did, however, produce satisfactory results from a visual perspective. The rates attained by Renaudin *et al.'s* method and the proposed method can be seen in Table 1.

Figure 6. (left) Original images. (center-right) Correct segmentations by the proposed method.

Table 1. Recognition rates for segmented digits

Algorithms	Rates given by the recognizer	
	Recognition rate	*Error rate*
Proposed method	71.43%	28.57%
Renaudin *et al.*	66.33%	33.67%

As shown in Table 1, the proposed method's outputs of segmented digits achieved a 71.43% recognition rate when

225

submitted to the classifier, surpassing Renaudin's method by 5 percentual points. The superior recognition rate was achieved with lower computational cost as stated before. Despite considering that the task of segmentation is not a trivial one, the error rate warrants an in depth look as to what caused it and what can be done to improve the total success rate of the algorithm. When analyzing the resulting images, some factors were identified as being responsible for major part of the failed outputs of the method. The first factor that is passible of improvement is the determination of the start points for the method. It is our belief, that by improving this phase of the algorithm, the final results will show improvements. Another factor is the repositioning phase, where in some cases, two segments that would need to be merged, were not contemplated and therefore generated an erroneous segmentation. A deeper study into the characteristics of these strokes and to why they were not contemplated by the repositioning phase is needed in order to determine what improvements can be made in this phase. Figure 7 shows an example of failed segmentation by our algorithm. The method fails as the overlap between strokes creates a merge that generates one stroke instead of an intersection.

Figure 7. (left) Original image. (center-right) Incorrect segmentations by the proposed method.

4. CONCLUSIONS

This paper presents an algorithm for segmenting horizontally overlapped pairs of handwritten digits. The segmentation method is based on the use inertial force and a deformable ball. The method does not use any type of recognizer to aid its segmentation and because of this, has the advantage of being font and author independent. Another advantage is its computational cost, which is O(n). The success rate of the method for individual digits was recorded at 71.43%. While segmentation is not trivial, the success rate may be further boosted. Some of the method's features were identified as passible of enhancements, such as the determination of start points and the repositioning phase.

For future works, besides the enhancements previously mentioned, a database of real images of overlapping characters will be created in order to test the algorithm on alphabet characters. Centripetal force will be integrated alongside inertia to determine how the ball will behave. Along with the integration of this force, tests will be conducted to verify its effectiveness.

5. ACKNOWLEDGMENTS

This research is sponsored by FACEPE IBPG-0460-1.03/09.

6. REFERENCES

[1] Casey, R.G and Lecolinet, E. 1996. A Survey of Methods and Strategies in Character Segmentation. In *IEEE Transactions on Pattern Analysis and Machine Intelligence*. 18, 7, (July. 1996) 690-706.

[2] Lacerda, E. B. and Mello, C. A. B. 2013. Segmentation of Connected Handwritten Digits Using Self-Organizing Maps. *Expert Systems with Applications*. 40, 15 (November. 2013) 5867-5877.

[3] Lopes Filho, A.N.G. and Mello, C.A.B. 2012. A novel method for reconstructing degraded digits. In *12th International Conference on Document Analysis and Recognition*. (Seoul, Korea, October 14-17, 2012) 733-738.

[4] Lopes Filho, A.N.G. and Mello, C.A.B. 2013. Degraded Digit Restoration Based on Physical Forces. In *Proceedings of the IEEE International Conference on Systems, Man, and Cybernetics*. (Washington, DC, USA, August 25-28, 2013) 195-199.

[5] Lu, Y. and Shridhar, M. 1996. Character Segmentation in Handwritten Words-An Overview. In *Pattern Recognition*. 29, 1, (January. 1996) 77-96.

[6] Mello, C.A.B., Roe, E. and Lacerda, E.B. 2008. Segmentation of overlapping cursive handwritten digits. In *Proceedings of the 8th ACM Symposium on Document Engineering*. (São Paulo, Brazil, September 16-19, 2008). ACM, New York, NY, 271-274.

[7] Mello, C.A.B. et al. 2012. *Digital Document Analysis and Processing*. 1st Edition, Nova Science Publishers.

[8] MNIST Database of handwritten digits. Link: http://yann.lecun.com/exdb/mnist/. Accessed in May 2015.

[9] Neves, R.F.P., Lopes Filho, A.N.G., Mello, C.A.B. and Zanchettin, C. 2011. A SVM Based Off-Line Handwritten Digit Recognizer. In *IEEE International Conference on Systems, Man, and Cybernetics*. (Anchorage, Alaska, USA, October 9-12, 2011) 510-515.

[10] Neves, R.F.P., Zanchettin, C. and ., Lopes Filho, A.N.G. 2012. An Efficient Way of Combining SVMs for Handwritten Digit Recognition. In *22nd International Conference on Artificial Neural Networks*. (Lausanne, Switzerland, September 11-14, 2012) 229-237.

[11] NIST Special Database 19. URL: http://www.nist.gov/srd/nistsd19.cfm. Accessed in May, 2015.

[12] Plamondon, R. and Privitera, C. M. 1999. The Segmentation of Cursive Handwriting: An Approach Based on Off-Line Recovery of Motor-Temporal Information. In *IEEE Transactions on Image Processing*. 8, 1, (1999) 80-91.

[13] Renaudin, C., Ricquebourg, Y., Camillerapp, J. 2007. A General Method of Segmentation-Recognition Collaboration Applied to Pairs of Touching and Overlapping Symbols. In *Proceedings of the 9th International Conference on Document Analysis and Recognition*. (Curitiba, Brazil, September 23-26, 2007) 659-663.

[14] Roe, E. and Mello, C.A.B. 2009. Simulating inertial and centripetal forces for segmentation of overlapped handwritten digits. In *Proceedings of IEEE International Conference on Systems, Man, and Cybernetics*. (San Antonio, TX, USA, October 11-14, 2009) 143-147.

Document Changes: Modeling, Detection, Storage and Visualization (DChanges 2015)

Gioele Barabucci
Cologne Center for eHumanities
Universität zu Köln
Cologne, Germany
gioele.barabucci@uni-koeln.de

Angelo Di Iorio
Department of Computer Science
Università di Bologna
Bologna, Italy
diiorio@cs.unibo.it

Uwe M. Borghoff
Institute for Software Technology
Universität der Bundeswehr München
Neubiberg, Germany
uwe.borghoff@unibw.de

Sonja Maier
Institute for Software Technology
Universität der Bundeswehr München
Neubiberg, Germany
sonja.maier@unibw.de

Ethan Munson
University of Wisconsin-Milwaukee
Milwaukee, WI, USA
munson@uwm.edu

ABSTRACT

The DChanges series of workshops focuses on changes in all their aspects and applications: algorithms to detect changes, models to describe them and techniques to present them to the final users are only some of the topics we investigate. The workshop is open to researchers and practitioners from industry and academia.

In this edition, we will follow up on the discussion of DChanges 2014 about algorithms and interfaces to better understand and exploit detected changes, and about standards for modeling and transmitting changes.

Particular attention will also be given to the use of these techniques in digital humanities – for instance in the studies of collation, text genetics and plagiarism detection – and for real-time collaborative editing.

Categories and Subject Descriptors

I.7.1 [**Document and Text Processing**]: Document and Text Editing—*Version control; Document management*

Keywords

applications; change analysis and interpretation; change detection; change tracking

1. INTRODUCTION

The goal of the DChanges series of events is to share ideas, common issues and principles about models and algorithms for change tracking and detection, versioning, collaborative editing and related topics.

This is the third edition of the workshop. The previous ones were quite successful and generated lively and fruitful discussions among participants. This edition will follow up on these discussions and will report on recent progress in the area.

In particular, we will focus on the use of diff, change-tracking, and versioning techniques in the field of digital humanities. Real-time collaborative editing, which is steadily gaining importance not only for researchers and scholars, will be a second key topic of the workshop.

We will also focus on how changes are interpreted and visualised. Both of the last two editions, in fact, made evident the need for novel interfaces for dealing with changes: existing ones do not scale very well when dealing with many changes, changes at different levels of abstraction are often not sufficiently taken into account, detection and visualization are often inter-mixed, and versioning techniques are still difficult for non-technical people.

Updated information about DChanges 2015 will constantly be available at `http://diff.cs.unibo.it/dchanges2015/`.

2. PROGRAM

The program pics up the structure of DChanges 2013 [1, 2] and of DChanges 2014 [3, 4]. Such a continuity is a key aspect of our vision, a crucial step towards the creation of a more connected community of researchers.

At the time of preparation of this summary, we have not finalized the program, yet. We plan to have four main sessions: an initial keynote, a first series of presentations on research topics, a second series of presentations on more practical topics, and finally, a round-table discussion.

DocEng'15, September 8–11, 2015, Lausanne, Switzerland.
ACM 978-1-4503-3307-8/15/09.
DOI: http://dx.doi.org/10.1145/2682571.2801032 .

2.1 Research Papers

The main part of the workshop is the session devoted to the presentation and discussion of research papers. We are currently selecting research papers that represent well the topics of DChanges and show where the research is leading.

All presented papers will be included in the proceedings of the workshop, in a volume of the ACM International Conference Proceedings Series (ICPS).

2.2 Application and Demo Notes

The second series of talks will focus on more practical issues: the main topic addressed will be the gap between theory and practice that must be crossed when implementing tools for actual users. People from industry and academia will exchange their views in an open session.

All presented notes will also be included in the proceedings of the workshop.

2.3 Round-Table Discussion

Ample space will be given to open discussions at the end of the workshop. The goal is twofold: fostering research collaboration and eliciting topics and suggestions for the next edition of the workshop. The round-table, in particular, will start with a topic suggested by the organizers, but will be open to the ideas brought by the participants.

A summary of the round-table discussion will be published online at `http://diff.cs.unibo.it/dchanges2015/` soon after the conclusion of the workshop.

3. PEOPLE

The workshop is organised by the same group of people as last year: Gioele Barabucci, Uwe M. Borghoff, Angelo Di Iorio, Sonja Maier and Ethan Munson.

An international program committee helped the organizers getting in touch with the researchers, selecting the best submissions, and improving them.

The organizers thank them all: Serge Autexier (DFKI Bremen), Martin Dias (INRIA Lille Nord Europe Research Center), Boris Konev (University of Liverpool), John Lumley, Pascal Molli (Université de Nantes - LINA), Sebastian Rönnau (Ravensburger Digital GmbH), Yannis Tzitzikas (University of Crete and FORTH-ICS), Fabio Vitali (Università di Bologna), Jean-Yves Vion-Dury (Xerox Research Centre Europe) and Loutfouz Zaman (York University).

4. REFERENCES

[1] BARABUCCI, G., BORGHOFF, U. M., DI IORIO, A., AND MAIER, S., Eds. *DChanges 2013: Proceedings of the International Workshop on Document Changes: Modeling, Detection, Storage and Visualization, Florence, Italy, September 10, 2013* (2013), CEUR Workshop Proceedings, 1008.

[2] BARABUCCI, G., BORGHOFF, U. M., DI IORIO, A., AND MAIER, S. Document changes: modeling; detection; storing and visualization (DChanges). In *ACM Symposium on Document Engineering 2013, DocEng '13, Florence, Italy, September 10–13, 2013* (2013), S. Marinai and K. Marriott, Eds., ACM, pp. 281–282.

[3] BARABUCCI, G., BORGHOFF, U. M., DI IORIO, A., MAIER, S., AND MUNSON, E., Eds. *DChanges 2014: Proceedings of the 2nd International Workshop on Document Changes: Modeling, Detection, Storage and Visualization, Fort Collins, CO, USA, September 16, 2014* (2014), ICPS, ACM.

[4] BARABUCCI, G., BORGHOFF, U. M., DI IORIO, A., MAIER, S., AND MUNSON, E. Document changes: modeling, detection, storage and visualization (DChanges 2014). In *ACM Symposium on Document Engineering 2014, DocEng '14, Fort Collins, CO, USA, September 16–19, 2014* (2014), S. J. Simske and S. Rönnau, Eds., ACM, pp. 207–208.

Document Engineering Issues in Document Analysis

Charles Nicholas
Computer Science and Electrical Engineering
University of Maryland, Baltimore County
Baltimore, MD 21250 USA
nicholas@umbc.edu

Robert Brandon
Computer Science and Electrical Engineering
University of Maryland, Baltimore County
Baltimore, MD 21250 USA
robe1@umbc.edu

ABSTRACT

We present an overview of the field of malware analysis with emphasis on issues related to document engineering. We will introduce the field with a discussion of the types of malware, including executable binaries, polymorphic malware, malicious PDFs, and exploit kits. We will conclude with our view of important research questions in the field.

Categories and Subject Descriptors

K.6.5 [**Management of Computing and Information Systems**]: Security and Protection—*Invasive Software*

Keywords

Document engineering, malware analysis

1. INTRODUCTION

Malware analysis has become an important field within the general area of cybersecurity. Skilled malware analysts are in high demand, and are employed in cybersecurity firms, financial institutions, intelligence and law enforcement agencies, and other large organizations. The field of malware analysis grew out of computer forensics, since forensic examiners were usually called to the scene when a malware problem was found.

For many years, most malware was written for the Windows OS and the x86 architecture. Windows is still an important malware target, since so many PCs run it, but in recent years the amount of malware targeted to mobile devices, especially the Android platform, has grown enormously. Although it focuses on the Windows platform, we have found that Sikorski's "Practical Malware Analysis" [2] is the best single resource for this area.

2. TOOLS AND TECHNIQUES

In the tutorial we will present an overview of the field of malware analysis, with emphasis on topics we suspect are

DocEng'15, September 8-11, 2015, Lausanne, Switzerland.
ACM 978-1-4503-3307-8/15/09.
DOI: http://dx.doi.org/10.1145/2682571.2801033.

of special interest to the Document Engineering community. Teaching materials for Android malware are starting to become available, but for our purposes we will focus on the Windows environment, since that platform is more likely to be more familiar to more people.

Malware on the Windows platform is often, but by no means always, found in executable binaries. Malware can be examined in static form, e.g. by inspection of the PE header and system call import table. Windows provides tools for such activity, and many third party tools do so as well. IDA is a powerful disassembler, which allows the analyst to examine a suspect binary in a variety of forms, including raw assembly code, and call graphs. Basic IDA functionality can be augmented with plug-ins written in C or Python.[1]

Malware can also be studied in dynamic form, that is, by running it and watching what happens. OllyDbg is one of several powerful debuggers available for the Windows platform that has gained a following among malware analysts. [1] Dynamic analysis is usually done from the safe confines of a virtual machine, running under the auspices of VirtualBox, for example. [2]

Some collections of malware specimens are available to researchers, and these will be used as examples as appropriate. Alas, there is no shortage of malware to be studied, since malware production is easily automated. Collecting malware specimens for analysis is an important sub-area, and anti-virus companies for example devote much effort to this.

As time permits, we will discuss recent and ongoing work in malware analysis-in-the-large, which (to us) refers to finding patterns and trends in collections of malware. Malware specimens can be subjected to cluster analysis, based on static and dynamic characteristics. Malware attribution is and will remain a difficult problem, for reasons which we will explain.

3. AUDIENCE PARTICIPATION

Tutorial participants are welcome to bring their own laptops. We recommend installing a virtual machine platform such as Virtual Box, with virtual machines running Windows and Linux. Participants that have IDA Pro (the free version 5.0) and OllyDbg installed, as well as the Windows Sysinternals Suite [3] may be able to run some examples with

---

[1] http://www.ollydbg.de

[2] https://www.virtualbox.org

[3] https://technet.microsoft.com/en-us/sysinternals/default

us. However, participants who choose to leave their laptops at home will be at no disadvantage.

Charles Nicholas is a professor of computer science at UMBC. Robert Brandon is a doctoral student in computer science at UMBC, with many years of practical malware analysis experience.

4. REFERENCES

[1] C. Eagle. *The IDA PRO Book*. no starch press, 2008.
[2] M. Sikorski and A. Honig. *Practical Malware Analysis*. no starch press, 2012.

Developing Web Applications with Document Engineering Technologies and Enjoying It!

Stéphane Sire
Oppidoc
D160 La Chauvière,
85000 La Roche Sur Yon, France
s.sire@oppidoc.fr

ABSTRACT
This tutorial proposes a practical software development method for building web applications using the XQuery and XSLT languages for manipulating semi-structured data. This method captures solutions and practices that we have applied during the last 4 years into many projects. It can be used on any XML database, as it requires only a thin layer to analyze and route incoming HTTP requests to a simple pipeline rendering the page. We will demonstrate it with a real world example developed with eXist-DB and the Oppidum lightweight XQuery framework.

Categories and Subject Descriptors
D.2.11 [**Software Architectures**]: Domain-specific architectures – *languages and systems, markup languages, scripting languages*

Keywords: Web application, XML databases, pipelining languages, XSLT, XQuery, Document engineering

1. INTRODUCTION
Document technologies have been around for a while now with applications ranging from automatic data exchange between heterogeneous applications to document publishing for multiple channels. Those technologies are all based on *open standards*, most of which are edited by the World Wide Web consortium (XML, XPath, XSLT, XQuery to cite the major ones). Together they form *the full XML stack*.

The full XML stack is the native idiom for storing and processing *semi-structured data*, which is at the heart of *document and data-oriented applications*. Such applications range from web-based content management solutions to complex business applications such as cooperative workflows.

The tutorial will show that the full XML stack is a powerfull alternative to develop web applications. To some extent it's the only stack with the Node.js/JSON stack allowing to work end-to-end with the same formalism between data and program (XML+XQuery for the first vs. JSON+Javascript for the second).

The tutorial will present several application examples and their architecture. We will discuss best practices on code and data

Permission to make digital or hard copies of part or all of this work for personal or classroom use is granted without fee provided that copies are not made or distributed for profit or commercial advantage and that copies bear this notice and the full citation on the first page. Copyrights for third-party components of this work must be honored. For all other uses, contact the Owner/Author. Copyright is held by the owner/author(s).

DocEng '15, September 08-11, 2015, Lausanne, Switzerland
ACM 978-1-4503-3307-8/15/09.
http://dx.doi.org/10.1145/2682571.2801034

organization and highlight some programming techniques to augment productivity and code maintainability.

2. APPLICATION ARCHITECTURE
To work with a full XML stack we propose to map the *RESTful architecture* of a web application to an XML document that we call the application mapping. This is similar to the way classical web development frameworks such as Ruby on Rails or Express on Node.js define the URL input space of an application as routes.

2.1 Mapping
The RESTful architecture defines the resources and actions on resources composing the application. The application architecture defines the representations available for each resource and how to bring the result of each action [1]. Since the resources of an application are addressed using hierarchical Uniform Resource Locators (URLs), we found it natural to describe the nested structure of the URL input space using an XML specific language.

For instance table 1 shows an extract of a polling application mapping. It contains a collection of personalized feedback forms reachable through "/forms/7a5f-44c4-868d" like URLs, and a collection of answers reachable through "/answers/7a5f-44c4-868d" like URLs. The anonymous (i.e. w/o name attribute) item element inside the collection element represents the resource associated respectively with a form or its answer.

Table 1. Mapping example

```
<site>
  <collection name="forms">
    <item epilogue="home">
      <model src="modules/poll/run.xql"/>
      <view src="modules/poll/run.xsl"/>
    </item>
  </collection>
  <collection name="answers">
    <item method="POST">
      <model src="modules/poll/read.xql"/>
      <action name="POST">
        <model src="modules/poll/write.xql"/>
      </action>
    </item>
  </collection>
</site>
```

2.2 Pipelines
The database is a natural store for data resources. It is also a runtime engine thanks to the XQuery and XSLT language integration into most native XML databases.

At first glance it is possible to perform every rendering of resources or actions using either an XSLT transformation of an XML document or using an XQuery script doing some processing and returning a representation. However web applications use recurrent patterns, which quickly become cumbersome to replicate into each XSLT or XQuery script. Those patterns include :

- ☐ Access control
- ☐ Page templating (*wireframe design*)
- ☐ Localization of page content

After some experiments, including an XForms system [3], we found that a generic pattern was to render every request by executing a three-tier sandwich of an XQuery script, an XSLT script and a final XQuery script. Each step processes the data it receives from the previous one and combines it with data from the database. The first step takes its input from the HTTP request.

This programming model can be implemented in XML databases as long as they support a way to call an XQuery entry point for every incoming HTTP request, and a way to chain XQuery and/or XSLT scripts from XQuery. Our implementation for eXist-DB resulted into the Oppidum XQuery framework [2].

The figure 1 illustrates the central role played by the mapping to convert incoming URLs into a pipeline specification. Pipelines are defined by annotating the mapping with *model* and *view* elements and with *epilogue* attributes, as illustrated in table 1.

Figure 1. The mapping defines a pipeline for each resource

The table 2 summarizes the role of each step in a pipeline. When applying this method software programming consists of creating the mapping file, and implementing the model, view and epilogue scripts. We found that a single *epilogue.xql* script per application can implement the last step. The Oppidum framework analyzes incoming HTTP requests against the mapping to generate a pipeline and to execute it.

Table 2. The 3 steps pipeline and its usage

Pipeline step	Language	Role
Model	XQuery	☐ read data from DB ☐ write data to DB ☐ generate view model
View	XSLT	☐ turns view model to page fragments
Epilogue	XQuery	☐ copy page fragments to target page template ☐ navigation menu generation ☐ localization

3. CONVENTIONS
As with any other web application framework it is primordial to adopt conventions on code and data file organization.

3.1 Code
XML databases can execute XQuery / XSLT scripts either from the file system or from the database. Following the pipeline model introduced above, we identified two radically different ways to organize code. One is to group together all the models and all the views (e.g. models/[forms.xql, answers.xql] vs. views/[forms.xsl,

forms.xsl]). The other is to make functional grouping (e.g. forms/[model.xql, view.xsl] vs. answers/[model.xql, view.xsl]).

3.2 Data
XML databases are organized into collections in a similar way to hierarchical file systems. Similarly to code files layout we identified good practices to consistently separate application data from application configuration data and to store them in different collections with consistent naming conventions across projects.

4. DESIGN PATTERNS
Two patterns have emerged as cornerstones to augment productivity, reliability and maintainability of code.

4.1 CRUD Controllers
When an application resource support the classical Create, Read, Update, Delete actions it is useful to group its implementation in a single XQuery file named after the resource (e.g. enterprise.xql) or alternatively to group the actions by file in a common place (e.g. persons/[create.xql, update.xql, read.xql, delete.xql]).

4.2 Domain Specific Languages
The separation of the model from the view in the pipeline encourages developers to invent markup languages. This internal markup is only used for communication between a model and a view. For instance it is particularly useful to describe complex view compositions and to factorize the generation of the corresponding HTML components into shared XSLT libraries. This is similar in intent to the HTML 5 web components but server-side. We will show several examples.

Domain specific languages can also be used to describe algorithms with markup languages. For instance we have invented one to describe the computing of user's action lists in a workflow application. This is similar in intent to rule-based programming.

5. PRESENTER INFORMATION
Dr Stéphane Sire has been involved in software design and development during the last 15 years with focus on user interface (UI) design and document engineering. He has developed languages and tools for UI programming and web application development across different research and private sector organizations. He earned a PhD in computer science in 2000 from University of Toulouse 1, France. He founded *Oppidoc* in 2012 to promote web application development using a full XML stack through an open source XQuery framework called *Oppidum*.

6. ACKNOWLEDGMENTS
Our thanks to Christine Vanoirbeek from the Media research lab at EPFL where we start exploring these issues. Parts of this work are supported by the CoachCom2020 coordination and support action (H2020-635518) of the European Commission.

7. REFERENCES
[1] Allamaraju, S. 2010. *RESTful Web Services Cookbook*. O'Reilly Media / Yahoo Press.

[2] Sire, S. and Vanoirbeek, C. 2013. Small Data in the large with Oppidum. *XML London*, June 15-16th, 2013, London. http://xmllondon.com/2013/xmllondon-2013-proceedings.pdf

[3] Tennison, J. 2008. *XRX: Mapping URLs with Orbeon Forms*. O'Reilly News. http://news.oreilly.com/2008/07/xrx-mapping-urls-with-orbeon-f.html

What Is This Thing Called Linked Data?*

Manuel Atencia
Univ. Grenoble Alpes, LIG
CNRS, LIG
Inria
Grenoble, France
manuel.atencia@inria.fr

Jérôme David
Univ. Grenoble Alpes, LIG
CNRS, LIG
Inria
Grenoble, France
jerome.david@inria.fr

Philippe Genoud
Univ. Grenoble Alpes, LIG
CNRS, LIG
Grenoble, France
philippe.genoud@imag.fr

ABSTRACT

The Linked Data initiative has made it possible for the web to evolve from being a global information space in which only documents are linked to one in which both documents and data are linked: a web of documents and data. This tutorial aims to give an overview of the principles, models and technologies underlying Linked Data.

Categories and Subject Descriptors

H.3.5 [**Information Storage and Retrieval**]: Online Information Services—*Data sharing*; H.3.5 [**Information Storage and Retrieval**]: Online Information Services—*Web-based services*

Keywords

Linked Data, Semantic Web, RDF, SPARQL, RDF-S, OWL

1. TOPIC AND GOAL

The Linked Data initiative promotes exposing, sharing and connecting structured data on the Web [2]. Linked Data has brought a large amount of data in the form of RDF triples, nowadays rising up to more than 89 billions of triples distributed over datasets of many different domains, such as media and life sciences, and geography, to name a few.[1] As a result, the Web has gone from being a global information space in which only documents are linked to one in which both documents and data are linked: a web of documents and data. This has attracted many organizational bodies that today publish and consume linked data, ranging from public and private companies (BBC, New York Times) to public institutions (UK government).

The goal of this tutorial is to present an overview of all the principles, models and technologies of Linked Data. We will

---

*This title is inspired from Alan Chalmers' book *What is this thing called science?*

[1]http://stats.lod2.eu/

DocEng'15, September 08-11, 2015, Lausanne, Switzerland.
ACM 978-1-4503-3307-8/15/09.
http://dx.doi.org/10.1145/2682571.2801035.

start by reviewing Tim Berners-Lee's Linked Data principles and motivating Linked Data and its precursor the Semantic Web. We will explain the RDF data model for distributing data on the Web. Then, we will introduce the SPARQL protocol and query language for RDF data. We will finish by briefly introducing semantic modeling with the RDF-S and OWL ontology languages. Below we elaborate a bit more on these topics.

2. CONTENT OF THE TUTORIAL

The tutorial will consist of two sessions, one dedicated to theory, and another one to practice. The theoretical session will mainly cover the topics summarized below.

2.1 Linked Data Principles

Tim Berners-Lee [1] outlined four main principles that are the guidelines for publishing linked data on the web: (1) use URIs to name (identify) things, (2) use HTTP URIs so that people can look up these names, (3) when someone looks up a URI, provide useful information, using open standards such as RDF, SPARQL, etc., and (4) include links to other URIs so that people can discover more things.

2.2 Distributing Data on the Web with RDF

RDF (Resource Description Framework) [4] provides a graph model for publishing and interlinking data on the web. RDF allows to describe web resources by using URIs to identify resources and represent (binary) relations between resources. RDF does not only provide a graph model but it also serves as a foundation for other standards for querying data (like SPARQL) and reasoning over data (RDF-S, OWL).

2.3 Querying Linked Data with SPARQL

SPARQL [5] builds on top of RDF and it provides (1) a query language for accessing RDF graphs; (2) an XML format for representing the results of a query; and (3) a protocol to submit a query to a distant server and receive the results through HTTP. Linked Data applications typically rely on SPARQL for consuming linked open data.

2.4 Semantic Modeling with RDF-S and OWL

Even though Linked Data needs no more than RDF and SPARQL (apart from URI and HTTP) to be deployed, we consider that a tutorial on Linked Data should also briefly introduce RDF-S [3] and OWL [6] ontology languages. These languages allow to specify the semantics of the vocabularies employed to describe data, which ensures the interpretation and use of these data. Furthermore, by specifying a logical semantics, it is possible to do reasoning over data and, for example, detect possible logical inconsistencies in datasets.

2.5 Hands-on Session

A second session of the tutorial will be devoted to practical work, and participants will learn how to use different tools to transform raw data into linked open data and how to query linked data. For this, we will use the OpenRefine tool and Apache Jena ARQ.

3. TUTORIAL PRESENTERS

Dr. Manuel Atencia is an associate professor at Univ. Grenoble Alpes (Grenoble, France) and member of the LIG & Inria - Exmo research team. He received his PhD in Informatics from the Autonomous University of Barcelona (Barcelona, Spain). His research interests are knowledge representation and reasoning, and the Semantic Web; more specifically, the formal study of ontology alignment, and the development of models and algorithms for trust and entity disambiguation in the Semantic Web. His research has been published in the most relevant conferences and top journals of these areas. Manuel Atencia also teaches masters courses in Web and Semantic Web technologies.

Dr. Jérôme David is an associate professor at Univ. Grenoble Alpes and member of the LIG & Inria - Exmo research team. He received his PhD in Informatics from the University of Nantes (Nantes, France). His main research interest is the Semantic Web and, more precisely, ontology matching and data interlinking algorithms. He has designed several tools which manipulate semantic web data such as AROMA, an ontology matching method which is one of the most scalable matching tools which participate in the OAEI evaluation campaigns. He also has developed algorithms for extracting keys and link keys from linked data. Theses works have been published in the most relevant conferences and journals in semantic web and artificial intelligence. Jérôme David also teaches masters courses in programming and Web technologies.

Dr. Philippe Genoud is an associate professor at Univ. Grenoble Alpes. After finishing his PhD in computer graphics at Joseph Fourier University (Grenoble, France) in 1989, he worked during ten years at Inria where he focused on knowledge and representation topics. In 2011 he joined the STeamer team of LIG working on representation of spatio-temporal information. His current fields of research are the Semantic Web and Linked Data. Philippe Genoud teaches computer science in masters at Univ. Grenoble Alpes, more specifically, courses in object-oriented programming, Web applications and Semantic Web.

4. REFERENCES

[1] T. Berners-Lee. Linked data - design issues. Retrieved july 23, <http://www.w3.org/designissues/linkeddata.html>. 2006.

[2] C. Bizer, T. Heath, and T. Berners-Lee. Linked Data - The story so far. *International Journal on Semantic Web and Information Systems*, 5(3):1–22, 2009.

[3] D. Brickley and R. V. Guha. RDF vocabulary description language 1.0: RDF Schema. W3C Recommendation 10 February 2004. <http://www.w3.org/tr/rdf-schema/>. 2004.

[4] R. Cyganiak, D. Wood, and M. Lanthaler. RDF 1.1 Concepts and Abstract Syntax. W3C Recommendation 25 February 2014. <http://www.w3.org/tr/rdf11-concepts/>. 2004.

[5] S. Harris and A. Seaborne. SPARQL 1.1 Query Language. W3C Proposed Recommendation 8 November 2012. <http://www.w3.org/tr/sparql11-query/>. 2012.

[6] P. Hitzler, M. Krötzsch, B. Parsia, P. F. Patel-Schneider, and S. Rudolph. OWL 2 Web Ontology Language Primer (Second Edition). W3C Recommendation 11 December 2012. <http://www.w3.org/tr/owl2-primer/>. 2012.

Author Index

Aizawa, Akiko 13

Albert, Andrew 97

Atencia, Manuel 233

Azevedo, Roberto
  Gerson de Albuquerque 177

Bachimont, Bruno 215

Balinsky, Helen 207

Banerjee, Siddhartha 51, 117

Barabucci, Gioele 227

Batista, Jamilson 65

Bechet, Nicolas 157

Borghoff, Uwe M. 227

Böschen, Falk 35

Bowen, Kyle 121, 147

Braga, Christiano 133

Brandon, Robert 229

Branzan Albu, Alexandra 203

Brautigam, Benjamin 121, 147

Cabral, Luciano 69, 191

Carter, Scott 195

Cesar, Pablo 199

Chiu, Patrick 219

Concolato, Cyril 85

Cooper, Matthew 195

Crozat, Stéphane 215

Cutter, Michael P. 75

Damera Venkata, Niranjan 3

David, Jérôme 39, 233

Denoue, Laurent 195

Di Iorio, Angelo 107, 227

Diem, Markus 93

dos Santos, Joel A. F. 133

Doyle, Michael 97

Drzadzewski, Grzegorz 61

Dueire Lins, Rafael 65

Dufourd, Jean-Claude 85

Dumas, Léonard 215

Eskenazi, Sébastien 167

Euzenat, Jérôme 39

Ferreira, Rafael 65, 69, 191

Ferreira, Rodolfo 65

Ferreira de Oliveira,
  Maria Cristina 97

Fiel, Stefan 93

Frantzis, Michael 199

Franze, Juliane 211

Freitas, Fred 69

Genoud, Philippe 233

Giannella, Raffaele 107

Giles, C. Lee 121, 147

Giles, Clyde Lee 47

Gomez-Krämer, Petra 167

Goncu, Cagatay 89

Hassan, Tamir 3, 17

Hersch, Roger David 21

Hollaus, Fabian 93

Hunter, Andrew 17

Islam, Aminul 43, 97

Jansen, Jack 199

Kaplan, Frédéric 73

Kido, Yusuke 13

Kim, Chelhwon 219

Kleber, Florian 93

Kou, Xinxin 43

Layaïda, Nabil 133

Lecarpentier, Jean-Marc 157

Leijen, Daan 129

Lesnikova, Tatiana 39

Liang, Chen 121, 147

Lima, Guilherme F. 177

Lins, Rafael Dueire 69

Lins, Rafael 191

Lopes Filho, Alberto N. G. 223

Maier, Sonja 227

Manduchi, Roberto 75

Marriott, Kim 89, 125, 211

Mathet, Yann 157

Mei, Jie 43

Mello, Carlos A. B. 223

Milios, Evangelos E. 43, 97

Minghim, Rosane 97

Mitra, Prasenjit 47, 51, 117

Mohammad, Abidalrahman 97

Mohammad, Nassir 207

Moh'd, Abidalrahman 43

Muchaluat-Saade, Débora C. 133

Munson, Ethan 227

Nicholas, Charles 229

Ogier, Jean-Marc 167

Oliveira, Hilário 191

Paik, Hye-Young 25

Paoli, Jean 1

Peroni, Silvio 107

Poggi, Francesco 107

Pursel, Bart 121, 147

Rastan, Roya 25

Rau-Chaplin, Andrew 43

Ray Choudhury, Sagnik 47

Riss, Marcelo 65, 69, 191

Roger, Julia 157

Roisin, Cécile 133

Sablatnig, Robert 93

Sarkis, Mira 85

Saul, Sherwyn 121, 147

Scherp, Ansgar 35

Shepherd, John 25

Shi, Mingzheng 125

Silva, Gabriel 65, 191

Simske, Steven J. 65, 69, 191

Sire, Stéphane 231

Soares, Luiz Fernando Gomes ... 177

Soto, Axel J. 97

Spinelli, Sylvain 215

Sugiyama, Kazunari 51

Suzuki, Nobutaka 143

Svendsen, Jeremy 203

Tang, Henry 219

Tomaz, Hilário 65

Tompa, Frank Wm. 61

Topic, Goran 13

Venkata, Niranjan Damera 187

Vernica, Rares 187

Vitali, Fabio 107

Walger, Thomas 21

Wang, Shuting 121

Wang, Shuting 147

Widlocher, Antoine 157

Williams, Hannah 121, 147

Williams, Kyle 121, 147

Wu, Yang 143

Wu, Zhaohui 121, 147

Wybrow, Michael 125, 211

Yao, Zhimin 43

Yokono, Hikaru 13

www.ingramcontent.com/pod-product-compliance
Lightning Source LLC
Chambersburg PA
CBHW061405210326
41598CB00035B/6108